SAN FRANCISCO

The Bay and Its Cities

SAN FRANCISCO

THE BAY AND ITS CITIES

NEW REVISED EDITION

GLADYS HANSEN, *Editor*

*Originally Compiled by the Federal Writers' Project of
the Works Progress Administration
for Northern California*

AMERICAN GUIDE SERIES

ILLUSTRATED

HASTINGS HOUSE · *Publishers* · New York

Library of Congress Cataloging in Publication Data
Main entry under title:
San Francisco, the bay and its cities.
(American guide series)
"Originally compiled by workers of the Writer's Program of the
Work Projects Administration in Northern California."
Bibliography: p.
1. San Francisco—Description—Guide-books. 2. San Francisco Bay
region. I. Writer's Program. California. San Francisco, the bay and its
cities. II. Title. III. Series.
F869.S3W95   1973   917.94'6   72–5854
ISBN 0–8038–6692–5

A Note About the New Edition

SAN FRANCISCO, THE BAY AND ITS CITIES, was originally planned and carried out by the Northern California Writers' Project of the Works Progress Administration. It was first published in 1940 as a volume in the distinguished AMERICAN GUIDE SERIES, and was sponsored at that time by the California State Department of Education. A second revised edition was published in 1947.

Enactment of the WPA was emergency legislation intended to overcome some of the distressing effects of the great depression of the 1930's. One of its laudable provisions recognized the importance of writers in the American culture and provided useful employment for many of them in the preparation of these guides. Henry G. Alsberg became director of the Federal Writers' Project and outlined many of the patterns followed by the Series; Walter McElroy was California State Supervisor and editor of the original edition as well as the revised edition of 1947. Many of the leading writers of California took part in the preparation of these books, and the comprehensiveness of their analysis and the depth of their historical research are displayed in these pages.

The present edition has retained the fine essays that open this volume, with such emendations as time has made necessary; the rest has been updated to reflect the current scene. The Guide profits by the inclusion of new illustrations and the final figures of the 1970 Census, which, by comparison with those of 1960, show the extraordinary migration of people to the Pacific Coast, which has helped give California first place in population among the states.

Contents

I. Gateway to the West

II. "The City"

III. Around the World in San Francisco

IV. Around the Bay

V. Appendices

Illustrations

Reproduced from photographs in the Special Collections Department of the San Francisco Public Library, Civic Center, San Francisco, by courtesy of the Library.

Maps

PART I

Gateway to the West

The Bay and the Land

". . . an immense arm of the sea, or an estuary, which pene-trated into the land as far as the eye could reach . . ."
—PADRE JUAN CRESPI

WHEN the first settlers, led by Lieutenant Jose Joaquin Moraga, arrived June 27, 1776, on the site of San Francisco, the American people were yet to declare themselves a Nation—though within seven days they would do so, 3,000 miles away on the Atlantic seaboard. Seven decades would pass before the heirs of '76 would raise their flag on this site. Two years more, and the name of San Francisco would go round the world.

It "never was a village"—this had been its proud boast. Where barren sand dunes, marshes, and brackish lagoons had surrounded an abandoned mission and a decaying fort with rusty cannon, San Francisco sprang into life overnight—a lusty, brawling he-man town of tents and deserted ships. Business, mushroomlike, flourished in mud-deep streets. Almost before it had achieved a corporate identity, San Francisco was a metropolis—to be named in the same breath with Boston or Buenos Aires, Stockholm or Shanghai.

When the other cities of the Coast were still hamlets in forest clearings or desert cow-towns, San Francisco was "The City." It is "The City" still. Massed on the tip of its Peninsula, its skyscrapers tower skyward from the peaks of the highest hills: great shafts of concrete banked in swirling billows of white mist when the fogs move in from the sea—glittering with pinpoints of reflected light from their countless windows when the sun shines from a clear blue sky. Crowding on each other, the hills rear their endless terraces of buildings, descending to the water's edge like steps, cleft by streets that strike up the steepest slopes and plunge down the deepest valleys with reckless fidelity to their straight and narrow paths.

Around the curving Peninsula's tip jut widespread fingers that are piers harboring their great ships. Soaring to heights greater than the hilltop skyscrapers, the girders of the bridge towers lift their slim steel spans high above the smokestacks of passing ships. Over their suspended roadbeds traffic streams across the racing tides of the Golden Gate to the bluffs and thicket-choked gullies of the Marin shore and across the Bay's wide sweep of gray-green water to the mainland. There, on the eastern shores of the Bay, rising like the tiers of a vast amphitheater to wooded crests, spread mile after mile of buildings—homes and schools, business blocks and factories. And on every side the age-old hills—vivid with the green of fresh-growing grass after winter rains, sere and brown in summer—encircle the blue water: wilderness neighbor to the city.

THE OPENING OF THE GATE

If some titanic convulsion of the earth were to drain San Francisco Bay of all its waters, it would look merely like one of those shallow, hill-rimmed valleys which stretch away from its upper and lower reaches. Through a gap in the chain of hills along its eastern edge, a great river would pour into its upper end and, winding southward, flood out to sea through a deep gorge hollowed in the coastal range. Within the recent geologic past the Bay was just such a valley, the Golden Gate such a river canyon. But as time went on, the valley sank until ocean waters came flooding through the Gate to submerge all but the peaks of its hills. Last of all in the long series of the earth's transformations from which emerged that part of the planet known as California was the Bay's creation. But the geologic upheavals destined to open the Golden Gate had begun long before.

West of today's Pacific shore, perhaps 500 million years ago, rose a land mass extending into what is now the Pacific Ocean. Where the Sierra Nevada now rises is thought to have been a low land mass, lapped on the Nevada side by an inland sea. As the eons passed, this great basin sea advanced westward into California, retreated and advanced again, until by 200 million years ago it may have reached as far as the site of Monterey—well over toward that westward-lying coast along the ocean.

Eventually the ocean itself found its way into the watery area that later was to become California. The western land mass probably was cut off from the mainland, forming an elongated island of which the present Farallon Islands were a part. Eastward lay a submerged trough, and into this trough sediment was continually draining from the island's slopes. To the incredible depth of over three miles the sediment was laid down in the water, slowly solidifying. From this trough was later elevated the San Francisco Peninsula, its foundations partly composed of the thick deposits which drained from the westward island.

And then began that long series of geologic events which finally resulted in the emergence of the coastline of California. Between 120 and 150 million years ago the ridges of both the Coast Range and the Sierra Nevada were pushed up. Unlike the Sierra Nevada, which was to maintain its general structure despite erosion, the Coast Range rose from the inland sea only to sink again. At least three times the ocean engulfed the region between the Sierra Nevada and the westward island and advanced to the foothills of the Sierra Nevada.

At a point about 36 million years ago, the picture of California begins to emerge in clearer detail. On the eastern border is the wall of the Sierra, following about the same direction as in the twentieth century, but lower, less rugged, its slopes covered with luxuriant vegetation. Still under water, the center of the State is a great inland sound, extending far enough westward to submerge the site of San Francisco. A long island stretches northwest from the present vicinity of Salinas. Islands are scattered in the sound.

For many million years the geography of this California changed little; but great activity was brewing in the earth. Far offshore the bottom of the sea was sinking. As it sank, the land along the coast was thrust upwards, buckling under the pressure. All of California was rising, but the extra thrust upon its western edge caused a slip along which occurred a sidewise movement of at least 700 feet and possibly as much as 20 miles. Along this same fault, extending from Point Arena south to the Mojave Desert, there was to be a shift of about eight feet in the year A.D. 1906, which would cause a great disturbance in the city of San Francisco. (Because the rock mass is broken along the fault, any abnormal strain within the earth is apt to be taken up there; such movements occur frequently, but rarely displace the surface more than two-tenths of an inch.) The same thrusts that were to cause the San Francisco Peninsula's earthquake fault also helped to lift it above the sea. There was pronounced folding of the Coast Range at this time, not only on the Peninsula, but along the line of the Berkeley Hills.

About one million years ago the Great Valley was becoming filled with sediment. Brackish water still covered part of the valley; it drained, not through the Golden Gate, which did not yet exist, but through various other outlets; one at the Russian River and another at Monterey Bay. The San Francisco-Marin area probably was separated from the mainland by marshes, so shallow that they could be crossed by the primitive elephant (whose fossils have been found near Menlo Park). The last great uplift raised the Sierra Nevada Range to a height of 4,000 feet above its present elevation; the Coast Range shared in this uplift.

Most recent of California's important geological events have been those which formed San Francisco Bay and the Golden Gate. As the marshes along the coast and farther inland dried, continued folding in the Coast Range blocked off the drainage of the Great Valley through the Russian River and Monterey Bay, forcing the rivers to find another outlet. They converged in a new course through a canyon north of the Berkeley Hills at what is now Carquinez Strait, thence down through a valley, and finally through the mountains that extended up the San Francisco Peninsula and northward into Marin County.

However solid the earth may have seemed beneath the feet of the first human inhabitants when they came (probably between 30 and 40 centuries ago) to hunt game and pick wild fruit in the coastal valley behind the river's mouth, it was sinking imperceptibly. The sea cliffs to the west were tilting upward on their outer side; but every year the floor of the coastal valley was a little lower. As fast as the sea cliffs rose, the river scoured deeper its channel through them, thus gradually carving down the sides of the Golden Gate. Then finally came a time when the floor of the coastal valley sank beneath sea level. The ocean flooded through the mouth of the river over 400 square miles of the Indians' hunting ground. The land would go on sinking until the very shell mounds which the first settlers left behind them on dry land were lapped by the tides; and yet as it sank, the rivers would lay down their rich silt, torn from mountain sides and lowlands of the Central Valley basin, over the bottom of the Bay. So was made, for how long no one can tell, the harbor known today as San Francisco Bay.

EARTH AND WATER

Midway in the great chain of mountain ridges that stretches along the continent's edge down the southeast-tending California coast is a narrow gap. Between its steep headlands the long Pacific rollers, breaking in spray against the cliffs to north and south, pour in swift tides. As the headlands recede on either side, an expanse of water opens out, stretching eastward to low, gently sloping hills. To the north, wooded peaks rise steeply above bluffs close at hand; to the northeast, barren capes guard a distant strait. Southward a sheet of water extends farther than a man can see, between marsh-edged flat lands. Here, where ocean tides roll in over a valley long sunk below sea level, salt water mingles with fresh, is muddied with the yellow silt of rivers, pouring into the Bay's upper reaches. At either end, sloping valleys walled like the Bay between ranges of hills that parallel each other, east and west, spill their creeks into it. Among the encircling hills, sloughs and canyons twist to the water's edge.

So well hidden from the sea beyond its narrow gateway by mountainous coastal walls that exploring navigators passed it by for more than two centuries, San Francisco Bay is one of the world's largest landlocked harbors. Measured along a straight line from the mouth of Sonoma Creek in the north to the mouth of Coyote Creek in the south, it is approximately 60 miles long and measures 14 miles at its greatest width. Its outlet to the sea, the Golden Gate, is three miles long and, at its widest point, a mile wide. In all, the Bay covers an area of a little more than 400 square miles. Although more than 75 per cent of its area is less than 18 feet deep, it reaches a depth of from 100 to 140 feet in its central part and of 381 feet in the main channel of the Golden Gate. North of its narrowest point, the strait between Points San Pedro and San Pablo—where it is known as San Pablo Bay—the water is shallower.

Into San Pablo Bay empties the drainage of the valleys to the north and the hinterland to the east. Petaluma, Sonoma, and Napa Creeks pour in from the north. Through narrow Carquinez Strait, six miles long, joining San Pablo Bay with shallow Suisun Bay to the east, pour the combined waters of California's two great rivers, the Sacramento and the San Joaquin, which drain the Central Valley and the Sierra Nevada's western slopes. The gorge cut by the silt-laden river waters, winding out to sea through the succession of bays and straits, can be traced by the yellow stream that crosses the Bay's blue ripples. The river's ancient delta, built up through the ages before the ocean broke through the Golden Gate, has been traced as far out to sea as the Farallon Islands, 32 miles off Point Bonita.

The peaks of low hills once rising from the drowned valley's floor are islands now. Opposite the Golden Gate, rocky Alcatraz (130 alt.) rises abruptly from the swift tides. Northward, divided by narrow straits from the coves and inlets of the Marin shore, rise green-clad Angel (782 alt.) and Belvedere (350 alt.). A little to the southeast the rugged hump of Yerba Buena (339 alt.) appears almost midway across the Bay.

From opposite sides of the Golden Gate the sheer bluffs at land's end of the San Francisco and Marin Peninsulas face each other. The narrow hilly strip of the San Francisco Peninsula stretches 30 miles southward from the Golden Gate between Bay and ocean, tapering in width from 7 miles at its tip to approximately 21 where it merges with the mainland. On the Bay side it is bordered with mud flats and salt marshes; on the ocean, with rugged cliffs and sandy beaches. The tip of the Peninsula, walled off from the south by the steep narrow ridge of San Bruno Mountain (1,315 alt.), is a rough square with jagged outlines, scored haphazardly by rocky hills and winding valleys, once a rolling waste of sand dunes and marsh-girt lagoons. In the center of this area rises a dominant crescent-shaped range, culminating in Twin Peaks (910 alt.), Mount Davidson (938 alt.), and Mount Sutro (918 alt.). Southward spreads a zone of billowing hills, merging into San Bruno Mountain. Beyond troughlike Merced Valley, cutting from Bay to ocean parallel with San Bruno Mountain, the Peninsula is scored with parallel ridges running north and south—among them, Buriburi Ridge (700 alt.), the Sawyer Ridge (about 1,220 alt.), and Montara Mountain (1,944 alt.). Between the Buriburi and Sawyer

Ridges lies a 15-mile-long segment of the San Andreas Rift Valley, following the course of the San Andreas earthquake fault. Farther south the Santa Cruz Mountains, of which these Peninsula ridges are the northern offshoots, lift their wooded slopes to greater heights. Some 80 miles from the tip of the San Francisco Peninsula they taper off into low hills where Monterey Bay cuts its crescent line into the coast.

The Golden Gate is but a narrow break in the great mountain chain of the Coast Range, which continues northwest up the Marin Peninsula under the name of the Bolinas Ridge. An irregularly shaped, deeply and intricately dissected mountain mass, the Marin Peninsula is criss-crossed by ridges radiating from its highest point, at the southern end of the Bolinas Ridge—Mount Tamalpais (2,608 alt.). The deep canyons that scar the flanks of the ridges widen into gently sloping valleys merging with salt marshes on the Bay side; on the ocean side they twist tortuously to the sea, where the hillsides end abruptly in sheer cliffs. Paralleling the Bolinas Ridge on the west is the long narrow valley which follows the course of the San Andreas fault. Its northern reaches are filled with the waters of marsh-bordered Tomales Bay, extending southeastward like a thin finger, laid along a line as straight as if it had been sheared off with a knife. To the west, hilly, triangular Point Reyes Peninsula juts into the ocean like a plowshare, sheltering behind its long promontory curving Drake's Bay with its white-faced cliffs like the chalk cliffs at Dover. East of the Marin Peninsula's hilly mass the flat reaches of Sonoma and Napa Valleys merge into tule marshes at the Bay's edge, divided from each other by the gentle slopes of the mountains.

Along the Bay's eastern shore, beyond the narrow coastal plain, stretches the serrated skyline of the Berkeley Hills, culminating in Bald Peak (1,930 alt.) ; and behind, across a line of narrow, shallow valleys, rise the rugged crests of a parallel ridge culminating in Rocky Ridge (2,000 alt.). To the east, broad flat Ygnacio Valley extends north to the shores of Suisun Bay and south into the narrow, level San Ramon Valley. From the valley's edge steep slopes rise in long sweeping lines to the summit of Mount Diablo (3,849 alt.). To the south, San Ramon Valley meets narrow, 40-mile-long Livermore Valley. Beyond, the ridges of the Mount Diablo Range extend to meet the Mount Hamilton Range, paralleling the Peninsula ridges and the Santa Cruz Mountains across the Bay.

South of the Bay's southern tip, the fertile plains of the Santa Clara Valley extend for 70 miles between the walls of the Mount Hamilton (4,029 alt.) Range and the Santa Cruz Mountains, 15 miles apart—a long, narrow extension of that same valley whose upper reaches, now submerged, are the Bay itself. From the marshes of the Bay's southern end, the valley floor slopes upward gradually toward the south, where offshoots of the two mountain ranges curve inward and enclose it.

THE CLIMATE

The Bay of San Francisco and its shores share with the rest of the Coast the moderate climate which it owes chiefly to the prevailing winds off the Pacific. Because of the break in the coast line the region has a climate even milder than enjoyed elsewhere along the Coast, because it receives more than its share of ocean-cooled air currents, sucked in by forced draft through the Golden Gate. Their deflection in various directions by the hills gives contingent sections widely differing weather.

At the tip of the San Francisco Peninsula, the mean annual temperature is 56.4° F.; the mean temperature of the coldest month, January, is 50° F. and of the warmest month, September, 61.5° F. But just northward across the Gate, mean temperatures are approximately five degrees lower in winter and five degrees higher in summer. Cold months are likewise colder and warm ones warmer on the eastern side of the Bay and down the Peninsula. The average annual rainfall at Kentfield in Marin County, less than 15 miles north of the Gate, is more than twice that of San Francisco—45.33 inches as against 21.85 inches. South of the city, rainfall decreases progressively, reaching an average of 15 inches at San Jose.

Although the tip of the San Francisco Peninsula enjoys sunshine for an average of 66 per cent of all the daylight hours in the year, it has acquired a more celebrated reputation for its fogs. They are of two principal varieties. Tule fog, a winter phenomenon, consists of low-hanging clouds of condensed vapor which drift about the Bay in serpentine fashion, sometimes blanketing completely one section of city or Bay while another is bright with sunlight. Most prevalent is the white fog which forms off the headlands on either side of the Golden Gate and drifts inland as the temperature rises inland in the warm valley section of the State. This fog forms in huge blankets, averaging about 1,700 feet thick, sometimes shrouding the entire tip of the Peninsula and spreading across the Bay to its eastern shore.

The Bay region, like most of the California coast, knows two seasons —the wet and the dry—and throughout much of the area the difference in average temperatures between them is seldom more than ten degrees. Even this slight difference is usually nullified by cooling breezes off the ocean which take the sting out of summer heat. At the tip of the San Francisco Peninsula early autumn is actually warmer than summer— for summer is the season of fogs. Only the rains, which come between October and May, call more than momentary attention to the change in seasons.

The temperature, rainfall, and even the winds follow predictable cycles, permitting residents to fall into a pattern of adaptations, less pronounced than those required by four seasons, but quite as regular. The weather's summer schedule is particularly dependable. A San Franciscan knows, almost to a certainty, that he will waken on a July morning in a world of light, bright fog and little wind. By noon the sun will be shining, and still will shine at midafternoon, though presently it will be hidden by the billows of white vapor that tumble over the hills and through the Gate. Within an hour a stiff salt breeze will be driving this fog, like a band of frantic wraiths, through hills and valleys; but the wind will be dying and the fog dispersing by half past seven. With the lengthening of night will come a softness, lightness, and clarity in the air which makes sleep seem a dullard's habit.

WILD LIFE

Simple and clear was the pattern of vegetation around San Francisco Bay before the coming of the white man. Along the coast, in the region of greatest winter rain and heaviest summer fog, were the redwood forests, extending almost without interruption from southern Oregon to San Francisco Bay and continuing south in canyons and other fog traps to the coast below Carmel. The grass and oak savannah extended eastward to the Sacramento Valley and along the floors of the principal inter-mountain valleys of the Coast Range. A thicket of low-growing chaparral clothed the interior ranges and the dry southern slopes. Fringing the Bay were marshes choked with tule rushes.

Conspicuous changes have taken place in the outlines of the three major types of vegetation. Much of the forest has been replaced by grass, brush, or crops; the early grassland area is occupied by cultivated land. However, the region is fortunate to possess many game preserves, water districts, and other sections where natural conditions still prevail and many more that have restored. The residents have made progress in the restriction of destructive lumbering, bad range management, poor fire control, and unregulated killing of game and fish.

Typical virgin areas of forest are preserved in Muir Woods National Monument and Santa Cruz Redwood Park. Here are trees, many from 1,000 to 2,000 years old, rising 300 feet or more with diameters of 12 to 16 feet. Their clean, gently tapering shafts, clothed with thick, purplish, massively fluted bark, rise uninterrupted by branches for approximately a third of their height. The foliage is delicate and feathery, but dense enough to keep perpetual twilight on the forest floor. Scattered among the great columns are smaller trees: broad-leaf maple, madrone, golden chinquapin, and California laurel. In separate stands, usually along the ridges at the inner margin of the fog belt, is found the somber, massive Douglas fir. Forming close thickets are huckleberries, azaleas, rhododendrons, California buckthorn (the dried bark of which is medicinal cascara sagrada), salal, wild currants and gooseberries, salmon- and thimble-berries, and elder. And in the damper shade, watered by the fog which the trees precipitate, Woodwardia and sword ferns give cover to mosses, dogtooth violets, true violets, wild ginger, redwood sorrel, trillium, fritillaria, clintonia, and the pungent yerba buena which gave San Francisco its first Spanish name.

The redwood forest and its associated meadows and streams are particularly rich in animal life; raccoons, skunks, wild cats, woodrats, and weasels are fairly common. As is natural in so deep a forest, birds are not conspicuous. Those most often seen are the varied and hermit thrushes, quail, flycatchers, California tanagers, robins, various sparrows and warblers.

The chaparral formation in California is remarkable, both for its high degree of development and for its numerous methods of adjustment to the long dry summers, wet winters, periodic fires, and intense sunshine. Its root systems are often extensive; its leaves protect themselves from excessive evaporation by turning their broad surfaces away from the sun, by growing in small, needle-like shapes, and by resorting to other devices such as thick skins, coatings of fuzz, exudations of resin, and restriction in the number of "pores." Many typical shrubs have the ability to sprout after fires from the root's crown. Others seed profusely and grow vigorously in burnt-over soil. The most widespread members of the chaparral are the various species of ceanothus, used by the Indians for soap; manzanita, with white bell-like blossoms, red or chocolate bark, neat oval leaves; California buckeye, which blooms in heavy clusters and bears fig-shaped fruits; chamise (*adenostoma*); chaparral pea; many dwarf oaks; and yerba santa, with pale lavender flowers and leaves spotted with resin.

The chaparral was the home of the extinct California grizzly and the now rarely seen California condor. Typical of both chaparral and grasslands are the brush rabbit, coyote, gray fox, various rats and mice, pocket gophers, and moles. Some of the more distinctive birds are the California jay, stellar jay, California thrasher, Anna hummingbird, house finch, mourning dove, and valley quail. Hawks, owls, and buzzards are very common.

Formerly the savannah was covered with a thick sod of perennial grasses; today it is dominated by the aggressive annual wild oat, a Spanish importation. However, the spring still brings a flourishing abundance of California poppies, lupines, nemophilas, cream cups, brodiaea, owl's clover, Indian paintbrushes, irises, shooting stars, and many composites.

One of the region's most interesting natural environments is the marshy border of the sloughs and estuaries where willows and cotton-woods grow. Wading birds are numerous; also the great blue heron, night heron, bittern, egret, and snowy egret. The estuaries, filled with tule rushes, are favorite nesting places for pelicans, coots and ducks, wrens, red-winged blackbirds, and many warblers.

Along the seacoast too, there is a distinct community of wild life. Gulls, terns, cormorants, and brown and white pelicans congregate in numbers. Hair seals and sea lions are still abundant, though the fur seal has disappeared.

Offshore, all along the Pacific Coast of North America, grow great beds of brown kelp, plants which in some cases are as large as redwood trees. This dense marine thicket provides shelter for a host of small fish, many of them valuable for food. Perch and rock and tom cod are typical species. Other ocean fishes found fresh in San Francisco markets are sea bass, various flatfish, halibut, and salmon. Crab, abalone, clams, shrimp, and oysters (both native and planted) are the principal shellfish. Bay and river fishes include shad, steelhead, striped bass, and several species of native and imported trout.

In the middle of the twentieth century the San Francisco Bay communities are as close as any urban area in the United States to primitive landscapes. At distances but little farther than city limits are forests, thickets of chaparral, and tule marshes, so wild that any explorer but the more experienced woodsman might easily imagine himself the region's first inhabitant.

Even though the half-way mark of the twentieth century has been reached and passed, San Francisco Bay communities are still as close as any urban area in the United States to primitive landscapes. At distances within easy reach of the automobile are forests, thickets of chaparral, and tule marshes, so wild that any explorer but the more experienced woodsman might easily imagine himself the region's first inhabitant.

A Frontier to Conquer

"The hills were wardens of the far-sought gold
And streams were glad in valleys unprofaned . . ."
—GEORGE STERLING, *The Homing of Drake*

FROM the chalk-white bluffs of the bay sheltered by Point Reyes, the coast-dwelling natives saw with amazement an immense object borne on billowing wings loom out of the mist at sea on June 17 (Julian Calendar), 1579. The man whom they sent the next day to reconnoiter paddled back excitedly to tell of living beings, white of skin and bearded, aboard this apparition. Concluding that these visitors were no less than spirits returned from the dead, the Indians timorously kept their distance, prepared to make—if necessary—proper obeisance. For three days longer the spirits remained in their abode, which rested on the water, its wings folded. On the third day it moved in toward the shore, and the spirits landed.

So came the first white men to set foot in the region of San Francisco Bay—men of Francis Drake's company in the *Golden Hinde*. They had left England a year and a half earlier in company with four other ships, bound round the world in the service of Queen Elizabeth to plunder the ships and cities of her enemy, Philip II of Spain. Now only the flagship remained.

After two days ashore, they were visited by the awed inhabitants of the country, who brought gifts of feathers and tobacco. "This country our Generall named *Albion*," the chaplain wrote, both because "of the white bancks and cliffes" and in order that "it might haue some affinity, euen in name also, with our own country . . ." And before Drake's five weeks' stay had ended, he recorded further, "our Generall caused to be set vp a monument of our being there, as also of her maiesties and successors right and title to that kingdom; namely, a plate of brasse, fast nailed to a great and firme post; whereon is engrauen her graces name, and the day and yeare of our arriuall there, and of the free giuing vp of the prouince and kingdom, both by the king and people, into her maiesties hands . . ." Thus having established his Queen's title to a new kingdom on the other side of the world, Francis Drake lifted anchor on July 23 and sailed away. The Indians were grief-stricken. As night fell, they lighted beacon fires on the hills.

NATIVES OF THE COUNTRY

In the Indians' geography the only land that lay beyond the smooth disc of the Pacific Ocean was the island where dwelled their dead. The Bay itself was to them no "harbor," for their small tule rafts never carried cargoes out the Golden Gate. Even the pass through the Coast Range at Carquinez Strait, to which stagecoach and railroad, as surely as the rivers, finally were to gravitate, had no great importance to a fleet brown foot that daily climbed the mountain barrier for rabbits. In all those ways that the contours of the region were to influence the welfare of white inhabitants, the Indians were affected little. But for other reasons the Bay environment impressed its pattern upon them.

It was the Bay that set the sleepy rhythm of the Indians' days. It determined, first, the location of their villages. A few groups lived on the ocean front and a few more on the banks of streams among the wooded hills, but most of them settled at the mouths of estuaries, on the Bay beaches. There the struggle for existence almost was reduced to reaching out a hand for supplies that the waters laid upon their door-steps: for mussels, soft-shell clams, and seaweed, and the driftwood used to cook them. The marine vertebrates swam so close to shore that the Indians could run into the waters and catch them—a feat noted by Drake.

In developing their handicrafts, the Indians were influenced by the abundance of tule grass in the marshes. They made no pottery, but from woody stems and fibers they constructed water-tight baskets, often decorated with shell beads, which they used as cooking utensils. Their houses were circular structures of poles usually tied together at the top and thatched with brush or tule matting. Rushes were used, too, for the short flaps worn as skirts by the women, though occasionally these garments were made of deerskin or of bark fiber. The men generally went entirely naked, except in the early morning when they sometimes plastered themselves with a coating of thick mud for warmth.

On the basis of their crafts, mythology, or language, the California Indians can be classified in large groups, but such inter-relationships were involuntary. The intense particularism of local communities gave rise to marked variations, even between closely related groups. In small villages, usually comprising about 15 families each, lived the Indians of the Bay region. Each village claimed a well-defined territory with seasonal campsites reserved for its own use. If a deer hunt or a sum-mer wandering took its inhabitants as far as 50 miles, the racial brothers they encountered might be wholly alien to them and their dialects in-comprehensible. However, although they recognized no allegiance beyond that which they paid to their village chief, the peoples of the Bay region were all of one linguistic family, the Penutian. The greater part of the Bay area was occupied by the Costanoan, whose territory included the San Francisco Peninsula, the coast country as far south as Point Sur, and the eastern shores of the Bay as far inland as the Mount Diablo Range. North of the Bay, as far east as the Sonoma Valley and as far north as the Russian River, lived the Coast Miwok. Eastward, beyond the Sonoma Valley, the Wintun held the shores of San Pablo and Suisun Bays.

Among all the peoples of the earth, no others are known who kept so long unchanged their ways of living and thinking. During the last 30 to 40 centuries when western civilization was making its cyclical and labored rise, time stood still for the Bay Indians. Early white visitors remarked that these natives were squalid and listless. However, most such observers had seen them after the mission system had begun forcing upon them an alien civilization. In 1579 Drake's men had noted that the Miwok Indians handled their bows and arrows "very skilfully," that their spokesman was "using sich violent Gestures, and so strong a Voice, and speaking so fast that he was quite out of Breath," and that these Indians "run very swiftly, and long, and seldom go any other Pace. . . ." It was after 40 years of mission rule, in 1816, that the Frenchman Louis Choris described the apathy of the San Francisco Costanoan: "I have never seen one laugh. I have never seen one look one in the face."

Apathetic though they may have seemed to white men who could not understand their failure to take up arms in their own defense, still they were not lacking in sensitivity, for they gave lyrical expression to their feeling for the environment in their mythology and songs. In the beginning, the Costanoan told each other, waters covered all of the earth except the summit of Mount Diablo. There lived a coyote, a humming bird, and an eagle, and as the waters receded these three, but chiefly Coyote, created the world. Their myths about Coyote's subsequent adventures are a mixture of ribald humor and idealism. The Indians worshipped the sun with offerings, and held sacred the towering redwood trees. To the Coast Miwok, Mount Tamalpais, whose long eastward slope resembles the figure of a sleeping woman, was the human bride of the sun god, who fell from his arms as he was trying to carry her to his celestial world. When summer fog wrapped the figure, the Indians told each other that this was her fleecy blanket, made by the god from his tears.

Even critical white observers found the Costanoan songs peculiarly pleasing. In some of them the singers tried to express the sensibilities of small woodland animals—of the wood-rat, for instance:

> "I dream of you,
> I dream of you jumping.
> Rabbit, jack-rabbit and quail . . ."

Apparently they were aware that their Bay and its peninsulas were the dramatic western boundary of a great land, for another of their songs began:

"Dancing on the brink of the world . . ."

Such imagery suggests that the native singers were not wholly apathetic and morose. When the white man came, to prove that their coast was not the world's brink and to put an end forever to the dancing, apathy may not have been the only reason they did not laugh.

THE WHITE MEN CAME

Grim, medieval Carlos V of Spain—uncertain of his geography, but with his black eyes fixed on galleons bearing spices and treasure across the vast Pacific—had ordered Hernando Cortez, in the course of the expedition on which he set forth in 1532, to "seek a natural port well north of New Spain" where "my navigators may find refuge, refit and rest." From such a safe harbor, far up the unexplored California coast, His Most Catholic Majesty had hoped that "they may then continue the voyage from Manila to Acapulco with a greater degree of safety from the enemies of my country."

Spanish navigators required 227 years to carry out this royal decree; and even then, it was not his Majesty's sailors but rather his soldiers, led by Don Gaspar de Portola, who early in November of 1769 first discovered the great landlocked anchorage now known as San Francisco Bay. Not even Portola, to whom the glory has gone, was the first actually to see that body of inland water large enough to contain "all the ships of Spain." From the summit of the Montara Ridge Don Gaspar himself saw no more than the Gulf of the Farallones and, purple in the distance, the long headland which the navigator Sebastian Vizcaino, in 1603, had named Punta de los Reyes (Sp., King's Point). It fell to soldiers of his expedition whose names with one exception are unknown to look first on San Francisco Bay.

Finding on the jagged shoreline no resemblance to the huge and sheltered bay described by Vizcaino in 1603, Portola's party had followed the shore of Monterey Bay without recognizing it to the mouth of the San Lorenzo River, present site of Santa Cruz. Pushing on through redwood trees, over ridges, arroyos, and creeks, they trudged past Half Moon Bay. Rising before them in the October rain they saw the rocky barrier of Montara Ridge, and at its base made their camp. The next day being clear, they surveyed from the summit of Point San Pedro the far-off purple cape of Point Reyes.

Gazing at the distant headland christened in honor of the Three Wise Men of the East who had brought gold and frankincense and myrrh to the infant Jesus, Don Gaspar decided it might be worthwhile to search the intervening coastline for that Puerto de San Francisco which shipwrecked Cermeno had happened upon in 1595. Portola therefore put one of his scouts, Sergeant Jose Francisco Ortega, in charge of a party of ten, presumably to explore the region as far north as Point Reyes.

Sergeant Ortega's little band of soldiers never reached their rather ambiguous goal. Precisely what they did, where they went, and what they saw are mysteries which still tantalize the imagination of historians. Some authorities have advanced the theory that Ortega's progress northward was halted by the Golden Gate, for which reason he must have been the first to look into San Francisco Bay from the vicinity of Point Lobos. However probable, the theory is pure conjecture based mainly on the fact that the exploring party, in the three days it was given to accomplish its purpose, had sufficient time to traverse the Peninsula to its end. The diary kept by Padre Juan Crespi, chronicler of Portola's expedition, gives scant information on this vexing possibility. And his diary, overburdened as it is by the padre's preoccupation with the needs of Pqrtola's men suffering from scurvy and diarrhea, is the only reliable record of these events.

The San Francisco Peninsula's abundance of roots, acorns, grasshoppers, sparrows, and squirrels may have been responsible for the tameness of the aborigines, but it hardly served to supply the lack of red meat and green vegetables which had brought Portola's men to the point of starvation. It was therefore mainly a desperate abdominal urge which drove them on to some rather extensive exploration of the area around San Francisco Bay—exploration which would later result in the establishment of the northernmost outpost of Spanish civilization in the New World.

According to Padre Crespi's diary, which is corroborated by Miguel Costanso, Portola's engineer, the second exploring party was allotted four days for their itinerary and "their ration of flour to keep off hunger for that time." They started on the afternoon of November 7. On the night of November 10, wrote Crespi, "the explorers returned, very sad, and no longer believing in the report of the heathen, which they confessed they had not understood. They said that all the territory which they had examined to the northeast and north was impassable because of the scarcity of pasture and especially because of the ferocity and illtemper of the heathen, who received them angrily and tried to stop their passage. They said also that they had seen another estuary of equal magnitude and extent with the one which we had in sight and with which it is communicated, but that in order to go around it one would have to travel many leagues; and that they saw no signs that might indicate the proximity of the port where it terminates, and that the mountains were rough and difficult."

So well does Crespi's description apply to the *contra costa* (Sp., opposite shore), it is fairly obvious that this exploring party discovered San Pablo Bay, probably from the rugged shoreline of Pinole Point, at that time inhabited by the Wintun Indians, who later proved a menace to Spanish settlers north of San Francisco Bay. Their failure to report having seen the Golden Gate indicates that they may have travelled inland, possibly up the Moraga Valley. Certain it is that famished as they were, and presumably mounted on mules equally famished, they took the easiest route they could find.

Discouraged by their inability to reach the entrance of what they still believed was the port of Monterey, in the vicinity of Point Reyes, Portola's expedition began the long trek homeward to San Diego. The whole course of their explorations had been determined by their first view of the Gulf of the Farallones, which tallied with Cabrera Bueno's description of the old Port of San Francisco, derived originally from reports of Spanish galleons dropping anchor there for wood and water some 200 years before. Even if they had been able to see the Golden Gate from Point San Pedro, however, it is doubtful that they would have followed a different course, so convinced were they that Point Reyes was the headland of a great arm of the sea extending inland east of the rocky peninsula shaped like a plowshare which lies between Bolinas Lagoon and Tomales Bay.

Padre Junipero Serra, father superior of the Franciscan missionaries in California—lean, ascetic, sometimes merciless, but a more efficient administrator than most secular representatives of Spain in the New World—came north by ship the following year (1770) to establish a mission on Monterey Bay, discovered finally at the cost of a second expedition. Even before the founding of this future capital of Alta California, Serra had insisted that surely one of the projected missions in the territory should be dedicated to the patron saint of his order. To this the Visitador-General, Don Jose de Galvez, had answered dryly: "Let him find the port bearing his name and he will have his mission there." Now that Portola had been led by Divine Grace to St. Francis' port, it became an obvious duty to establish a mission there without delay.

Hence, in the spring of 1772, Portola's young lieutenant, Pedro Fages, and Padre Crespi led a party of 12 soldiers from Mission San Carlos Borromeo (now Carmel Mission) to select a suitable site for the new mission near the entrance to what was now called the Port of Our Father St. Francis. The Fages expedition proceeded up the Salinas and Santa Clara Valleys, and northward around the eastern shore of San Francisco Bay. From the present site of Oakland, which they passed on March 27, they must have had a fair view of the Golden Gate. Next day, from the hills below which Berkeley now stands, they saw through the Golden Gate the peaks of the southeast Farallon Islands rising on the horizon. Though Costanso later claimed that Portola's men were the first to see the famous strait, the honor doubtless belongs to the Fages party.

From the Richmond Hills the explorers travelled northward to the south shore of San Pablo Bay a few miles east of San Pablo Point and then eastward past Carquinez Strait to the present site of Martinez. They skirted Suisun Bay and followed the south bank of the San Joaquin River almost to where Antioch now stands. Finding the San Joaquin too wide to cross, the Fages party decided to return to Monterey. On their homeward journey they passed through the Pacheco Valley, west of Mount Diablo through the San Ramon Valley, and down through Alameda Canyon to the site of the future Mission San Jose. From their camp near the present village of Milpitas they continued down the old trail to Monterey which, beaten by the pack trains of the explorers who came after them, was to extend the great Camino Real (Sp., King's Highway) from Mexico to the northernmost limits of the Spanish Empire.

The new Spanish viceroy at Mexico City, farsighted Antonio Bucareli, was determined, at the risk of losing one of his clumsy little ships on the dangerous California coast, to settle for once and for all the question of San Francisco Bay. He therefore sent Lieutenant Juan Manuel de Ayala on the *San Carlos* with instructions to make a further survey of the Gulf of the Farallones. As darkness fell on August 5, 1775, the *San Carlos,* having sent a launch ahead to find anchorage, sailed cautiously through the Golden Gate and anchored for the night. On August 7 it moved to a new anchorage on the north side of Raccoon Strait and a week later to another in Hospital Cove off Angel Island.

The hardy band of settlers whom Juan Bautista de Anza led through incredible hardships all the way overland from Tubac in Sonora province had arrived on the present site of San Francisco with a platoon of soldiers and two priests by the time the *San Carlos* sailed a second time through the Golden Gate. With the assistance of the ship's carpenters and crew, Lieutenant Jose Joaquin Moraga's soldiers were able, on September 17, 1776, to raise the standard of Carlos III of Spain over the quarters of the *comandante* (commander) in the Presidio. The occasion was celebrated with a high mass, the firing of cannon, and the chanting of a fervent *Te Deum*.

The opening and dedication of the new Mission San Francisco de Asis (later known as Mission Dolores) on the grass-clad slope near a small lake, dolefully named by the padres Laguna de los Dolores (Lake of Sorrows), was delayed until October 8, 1776 because of the absence of Moraga on an exploring expedition.   Moraga's expedition observed the feast-day of Saint Francis by proving conclusively that the Golden Gate was the only entrance to San Francisco Bay. Father Serra stated on his arrival at the new mission "Now Our Father St. Francis, the cross-bearer in the procession of missions, has come to the final point of the mainland of California; for in order to go farther on, ships will be necessary."

Unfortunately, St. Francis' new mission lacked adjacent arable land. Anza's poverty-stricken settlers, and the few who came after them, soon found the fertile Santa Clara Valley to the south more suitable for them than the wind-swept, flea-infested sandy wastes of the area dedicated to their patron saint.   Therefore, on January 12, 1777, the new Mission Santa Clara was founded down the peninsula.   And three miles south of it arose the first purely civil settlement in California—the *pueblo* (town) of San Jose.

Before the close of the century two more Franciscan missions had been established in the Bay area: Mission Santa Cruz, on August 28, 1791, and Mission San Jose de Guadalupe, on June 11, 1797.   The lands which reminded Anza's settlers of the fertile valleys of Valencia soon brought prosperity to these adobe outposts of Catholicism; their baptismal fonts grew muddy with the dirt of Indians saved from the wrath of God.   Only by slow degrees, however, did the reluctant aborigines desert their mud huts and childlike savage habits for the adobe barracks, the lengthy prayers and hard work of the missions. Though the padres occasionally lost patience and punished petty crimes with rawhide when sweet words were of no avail, they did not generally ill treat their converts.   On the whole the condition of the Indians was improved by their strange new masters in cassocks with shaved heads whose God hung nailed upon a cross.   Of course, they learned to speak Spanish and did the manual labor of plowing and harvesting; they excelled in handicraft and later as herders of cattle and sheep.   By 1800 intermarriage had produced many *mestizos* (half-breeds) among the 30,000 Indians converted by the Bay region missions.   Within the following decade, however, the neophytes were decimated by measles and smallpox epidemics.

Alarmed by the catastrophic mortality, which was threatening the mission with extinction, the fathers transferred a number of neophytes to the more salubrious climate of the north Bay region.   The experiment proved successful; the health of these invalids was greatly improved.   On December 14, 1817, the *asistencia* (chapel) of San Rafael was founded at the present site of the town of San Rafael.   Young Padre Jose Altimira planned a more radical solution to the problem, namely, complete abandonment of Mission Dolores and transference of its neophytes along with those at San Rafael to a new mission at Sonoma. Accordingly Mission San Francisco Solano was founded in 1823—without, however, the authorization of church dignitaries, who objected. A compromise was reached, permitting the new mission and Mission Dolores and San Rafael as well to remain. It was to be the last mission founded in Alta California.

Even after the outbreak of the Napoleonic wars, when trade with foreigners was declared illegal, *alcaldes* (mayors) and *comandantes* averted their eyes from the illicit traffic with American whalers and traders who brought oil, tea, textiles, silk, and household utensils in exchange for hides and agricultural products piled up in the storehouse of the missions. Rezanov's unromantic followers who settled around Fort Ross on Bodega Bay, and whom Governor Pablo de Sola distrusted, were being welcomed to Yerba Buena Cove with urbane politeness in 1821—while the viceregal regime in Mexico City was being overthrown. The interregnum of General Agustin Iturbide's regency, immediately succeeded by the short-lived Empire of Mexico, passed almost unobserved by the Emperor's subjects in Alta California; and news of the institution of a republican regime, which reached the territory in January, 1822, was received without much enthusiasm. At Mission Dolores, Father Esténaga delivered a sermon praising the constitution of the new Republic of Mexico and said a mass for its future greatness. The Presidio guns were fired, a few cheers went up; and when the echoes of the celebration had died away across the great Bay, the straggling settlement relaxed into its accustomed *siesta*.

YANKEE INVASION

The Bay region, despite a half century of misrule that combined paternalism with neglect, had attained economic independence when on Jan. 4, 1823, the Mexican Republic issued a colonization degree for Alta California. The decade that would elapse before the secularization of the missions was to witness the heyday of Hispano-Mexican colonization on the Pacific Coast.

Mission San Jose in 1825 owned 62,000 head of cattle, as many sheep, and other livestock; in 1828 Mission Santa Clara had, besides other livestock, 14,500 head of cattle and 15,500 sheep. Mission Dolores' economic importance was, however, eclipsed by the cove of Yerba Buena to which the Bay area missions and ranchos brought their produce in oxcarts for trade with foreign ships. Besides their great herds, which furnished the hides and tallow sought by European and American traders, the missions owned vast fields planted in wheat and maize and other crops primarily for domestic consumption. Cloth, a coarse kind of serge, was woven from wool; and the *aguardiente* (brandy) distilled from the vineyards of Mission San Jose was the delight of foreign visitors. The missions, designed originally to form the nuclei of *pueblos* and intended to relinquish control of their Indian convert-citizens to the civil authority, had become so wealthy by 1830 that they were reluctant to fulfill a destiny which would deprive them of their power.

This system of monastic feudalism was likewise perpetuated by the vast ranchos, ranging from one-half to more than sixteen square leagues (a league being equal to about 4,438 acres), granted by Spanish governors to soldiers of the Portola and Fages expeditions. During the years of Mexican rule grants were also made to Americans and other foreigners who showed a disposition to settle the country in a neighborly manner. Rancho San Antonio, the 48,000-acre domain within whose former boundaries now stand the cities of Alameda, Albany, Berkeley, Emeryville, Oakland, Piedmont, and San Leandro, and Las Pulgas (the fleas), the 35,240-acre rancho granted in 1824 on which stand almost as many Peninsula towns, were typical of these feudal estates. Here, in their adobe ranch houses, the lordly dons entertained friends and relatives with lavish hospitality. They were grateful for the luxuries brought to Yerba Buena Cove by foreign traders whose followers would one day dispossess them.

When the missions were secularized about 1834, the great landowners came into possession of most of the mission lands—and of their Indian charges as well. The plan had been that the mission communities should be organized as towns, enough land set aside for the support of the clergy, and the surplus divided among the Indians. But to the administrators appointed by the government, rather than to the Indians, went the greater part of the flocks and herds and grain fields. Relieved from the discipline of the monks, the freed neophytes were the easy prey of gamblers and thieves. Without any direction, spiritual or economic, they became scattered on the great ranches whose owners under Mexican grants were getting control of the best of the lands in the coast valleys. All the while tuberculosis and smallpox and a declining birth rate were steadily reducing their numbers. The state of affairs at the Mission Dolores was typical. The *pueblo* did not develop into a prosperous town. Padre Rafael de Jesus Moreno pointed out that the commissioner was acting for his own advantage rather than for the good of the Indians. Likewise there were charges and countercharges at Santa Clara, San Jose and the other missions around the Bay. All of them fell into neglect and decay. There were only 50 Indians at San Francisco when the French explorer and scientist, Duflot de Mofras, was there in 1841.

International rivalries meanwhile were shaping the future of Alta California and the Bay area. Fort Ross, less than 100 miles north of the Bay, was developing into something more formidable than an outpost of Russian hunters of seal and sea otter who chased their prey from the Farallon Islands right into San Francisco Bay. Representatives of Britain's Hudson's Bay Trading Company, who came to make surveys of the Bay region and to twit the *comandante* of Yerba Buena's presidio on the sad state of his defenses, had a knowing political gleam in their eyes.

Least suspect of all were the Americans. Unlike some other foreigners settling in the Bay region, they assumed no official character which could be construed as representing aggressive designs on the part of the United States. The majority of Yankee immigrants, in fact, adopted unhesitatingly the religion and customs of the Mexicans; they renounced their American citizenship and married into leading Mexican families. Not for some years after the first trappers had begun to cross the Sierra were the Yankees regarded by Mexican authorities with suspicion such as the Russian incursion into the Bay area had received since 1812.

Secure behind their stockades and twelve brass cannons at Fort Ross, the Russians ignored repeated orders to leave the country. As early as 1817 Governor Pablo Vicente de Sola had reported to his superiors in Mexico City that he could not drive them out with the forces at his command, whose weapons were effective only against Indians armed with bows and arrows. Now that Mexico was an independent nation she no longer had protection from the Spanish navy, and no supply ships had arrived at Yerba Buena since 1811. Captain William Shaler, describing San Francisco Bay in 1805, found the entrance defended only "by a battery on which are mounted brass 8-pounders, which afford only the show of defense; and the place could make no resistance against the smallest military force . . ." The Castillo de San Joaquin, here described, was not improved by subsequent decades of neglect.

Whether or not the provincial authorities recognized the fact, from 1823 onward the American government had entered into the long-range struggle of world powers for control of Alta California. Concern over Russian inroads into the Bay region prompted Andrew Jackson's administration to undertake negotiations with the Mexican government for acquisition of Alta California. What "Old Hickory" had his eye on was that portion of Mexican territory north of the 37th parallel, including San Francisco Bay, which had been described to him as "a most desirable place of resort for our numerous whaling vessels . . . in the Pacific, far superior to any to which they now have access." The $3,500,000 which Jackson offered Mexico's President Santa Anna was, however, refused; and the American government's subsequent attempts to bring the Mexicans to terms met with no better success.

American citizens meanwhile were far from idle. From frontier settlements in Missouri, Kentucky and Tennessee, trappers and fur traders in coonskin caps and greasy buckskin had been threading their way across the plains and mountains of the West. First of these restless Yankees to reach Alta California by an overland route was Jedediah Smith. In the fall of 1826 this "Pathfinder of the Sierras" had opened the way for American settlement of the Sacramento and San Joaquin Valleys. That his presence in the Bay region was unwelcome is apparent from the fact that, on his arrival at Mission San Jose, Padre Narciso Duran locked him in an outhouse; and upon his release Governor Jose Maria de Echeandia gave him two months to get his fur traders out of the country.

The feudal *rancheros* had no great interest in encouraging trade and industry, but under Governor Jose Figueroa's liberal regime San Francisco Bay was declared a port of entry and, in 1835, the *pueblo* of Yerba Buena was laid out on the cove. Appointment of a harbormaster and lifting of restrictions on trade with foreign shipping opened for the Bay area a decade of friendly relations between Mexicans and Yankee settlers which might eventually have resulted in peaceful annexation of California by the United States. The appointment of Thomas O. Larkin as United States Consul to Alta California in 1843 was made, apparently, to encourage the *Californios* to sever their ties with Mexico and seek protection under the American flag.

The loss of Texas to Sam Houston's rebellious settlers in 1836 left the regime in Mexico City in too perilous a state to cope with the political intrigue among its representatives in Alta California; and some of these began to depend upon certain foreign elements in the province to maintain their despotic rule against rival officials and a citizenry from which arose the rumblings of revolt. Their most powerful aide in the vicinity of the Bay area was Johann Augustus Sutter, Swiss immigrant and adventurer extraordinary, who had established a settlement in the Sacramento Valley. At Sutter's Fort were welcomed the American immigrant trains whose oxcarts came straggling down through passes in the high Sierra after 1841.

In 1841, when the Russians decided to withdraw from Fort Ross, Sutter had acquired all their territory around Bodega Bay. In return for assisting General Mariano Guadalupe Vallejo, *comandante* of Sonoma, to disperse the roving brigands which General Manuel Micheltorena brought with him from Mexico when he came to displace Governor Juan Bautista Alvarado at Monterey in 1842, the redoubtable Sutter was left unmolested to play off one rival official against another. Even when this "Lord of the Marches" threatened to "proclaim California a Republic independent of Mexico" if he were not given leave to do as he pleased, Vallejo dared not break off friendly relations with him. He wrote unhappily at the time, when American immigration was filling the Bay area with Yankee settlers, that "the only certainty is that Californians will die," and again, "I dare not assure myself that

California will be saved." He drew what consolation he could from the fact that Sutter had prevented further encroachment of the British Hudson's Bay Company and kept his political rival, Juan Bautista Alvarado, at a safe distance; but he saw the Americans taking over the country.

When the first overland party from Missouri arrived at the ranch of Dr. John Marsh near Mount Diablo in November 1841, they were permitted to settle unmolested. Governor Micheltorena had orders to put a stop to all immigration; but his disreputable army had made him unpopular and he was dependent on American support to put down the conspiracies of rival officials who openly defied his authority. Furthermore, the crafty Alvarado had left the treasury of the province empty; and the secularization of the missions in 1834 had already destroyed the source of funds by which presidio garrisons had been maintained. To aggravate this precarious situation even more, the American and British consuls in Monterey were keeping their respective governments informed of the events leading to a crisis in which intervention of some sort would decide the future of the territory.

Such was the state of affairs in California and the Bay region when, in December 1845, Captain John Charles Frémont entered the province. As United States topographical engineer in command of two previous expeditions sent to survey California's natural resources, Frémont was received on January 27, 1846 in Monterey without serious misgivings by Mexican authorities, who gave him permission to obtain supplies pending his promised departure into Oregon. Little more than a month later, however, Frémont's followers joined him near San Jose, marched across the Santa Clara Valley and through the Santa Cruz Mountains, and camped near Monterey.

Promptly ordered to leave the country, Frémont made a show of resistance, swearing that "if we are hemmed in and assaulted we will die, every man of us under the flag of our country." Being neither hemmed in nor assaulted, Frémont's party withdrew up the Sacramento Valley to Sutter's Fort and proceeded north toward Oregon. His martial depredations caused Larkin to petition Consul John Parrott at Mazatlan to send a warship to Monterey.

Whether acting on secret orders received from the United States State Department or on his own initiative, Frémont suddenly retraced his steps and set up headquarters at Marysville Buttes in the Sierra foothills. From here a party of about a dozen Yankee hunters and trappers —in command of Ezekiel Merritt, a settler from Rancho Barranca Colorado (Red Bluff)—was ordered by Frémont to seize 170 horses being taken from Sonoma to Santa Clara by a party of Castro's men. The captured animals having been delivered to Frémont's new camp on the Bear River, Merritt's party of 20 marauders crossed the hills into Napa Valley.

At daybreak on June 14, General Mariano G. Vallejo in his house at Sonoma was roused without warning by this little band of men and called upon to surrender. Somewhat puzzled, but courteous as always, he invited them in. On being informed that they were acting under Frémont's orders, he proceeded to wine and dine his callers to the point of stupor while terms of surrender were being discussed. At length the captors were able to agree on a declaration to which three of them put their names—Ezekial Merritt, Robert Semple, and William Fallon. They presented it to Vallejo: "We, the undersigned having resolved to establish a government upon republican principles, in connection with others of our fellow-citizens, and having taken up arms to support it, we have taken three Mexican officers as prisoners: Gen. M. G. Vallejo, Lieut. Col. Victor Prudon and Capt. Salvador Vallejo." But dissension then broke the ranks of the insurrectionists, frightened by the magnitude of their exploit. William B. Ide, a Yankee settler with the gift of oratory, saved the day. Cried he: "I will lay my bones here before I will take upon myself the ignominy of commencing an honorable work and then flee like cowards, like thieves, when no enemy is in sight. In vain will you say you had honorable motives. Who will believe it? Flee this day, and the longest life cannot wear off your disgrace! . . . We are robbers, or we must be conquerors!"

Taking possession of the *pueblo* without opposition, the rebels impatiently hauled down the Mexican flag. It occurred to them that a new flag was needed to replace it. On a piece of homespun to which was attached a strip of red flannel they painted a red star and the crude figure of a grizzly bear. "My countrymen," orated Lieutenant Henry L. Ford as the new standard was hoisted up the flagpole, "we have taken upon ourselves a damned big contract." But the insurgents' chosen leader, William B. Ide, who promptly dubbed himself "Commander-in-chief" and later "President of the California Republic," was undaunted. He invited "all peaceable and good citizens of California . . . to repair to my camp at Sonoma, without delay, to assist us in establishing and perpetuating a Republican government, which shall secure to all civil and religious liberty, which shall detect and punish crime; which shall encourage industry, virtue and literature; which shall leave unshackled, by fetters of commerce, agriculture and mechanism."

Though Frémont would admit no direct responsibility for the "Bear Flag" rebellion, he ordered the arrest of Jacob Leese, Vallejo's brother-in-law, because he was a "bad man"; and according to Leese's account, he also threatened to hang Sutter for demanding that consideration be shown a man of Vallejo's pro-American sympathies. It was generally assumed, by both Yankee settlers and *Californios* in the Bay region, that Frémont was in command of a movement to seize the territory.

General Castro, learning of the affair at Sonoma, sent a force of

50 or 60 men under Joaquin de la Torre to attack the "Bears." Marching northward from San Rafael, De la Torre's contingent was joined by Juan Padilla's roving bandits. On the morning of June 24, 1846, the *Californios* were attacked at the Olompali Rancho near Petaluma by 17 or 18 men under Lieutenant Henry L. Ford. After a charge in which one of De la Torre's men was killed and several wounded by Ford's riflemen, the *Californios* retired and the Americans returned to Sonoma.

Until this first battle of the war Frémont had taken no open part in the events which his presence doubtless had precipitated. Now, however, as he says in his *Memoirs,* "I have decided that it was for me to govern events rather than to be governed by them. I represent the Army and the Flag of the United States." Furthermore he realized that "at last the time had come when England must not get a foothold; *that we must be first.* I was to *act,* discreetly but positively." And act he did, though neither he nor his Mexican opponents were as yet aware that their respective countries were already at war below the Rio Grande.

Arriving at Sonoma on June 25, Frémont assumed command of the Bears and with a combined force of 130 men marched to meet De la Torre's detachment at San Rafael. Here occurred an incident which ever since has blemished Frémont's reputation. This was the murder of three innocent *Californios*—the twin sons of Yerba Buena's first *alcalde,* Francisco de Haro, and old Don Jose Berryesa, father of the *alcalde* of Sonoma who was then among Frémont's prisoners at Sutter's Fort. On being informed by Kit Carson that these three were about to land from a boat at Point San Pedro, Frémont is reported to have said: "I have no room for prisoners." Kit Carson, G. P. Swift, and one of Frémont's trappers shot down the three unarmed men.

Outnumbered and badly armed, De la Torre's forces fled across the Bay to join Jose Castro's at Santa Clara. Following Frémont's raid on the old Castillo de San Joaquin, Dr. Robert Semple, participant in the Bear Flag affair at Sonoma, led ten men on a foray into Yerba Buena which captured Robert Ridley, ex-factor of the local Hudson's Bay Company post.

After thus putting down all military resistance of the *Californios* in the Bay region Frémont returned to Sonoma to declare the independence of California and place the country under martial law for the duration of the conflict. While continuing "in pursuit of Castro" in the valley of the Sacramento (actually Castro already had begun his retreat southward from Santa Clara), Frémont received news that the United States naval commander on the Pacific Coast, Commodore John D. Sloat, had raised the American flag at Monterey and had ordered the U.S.S. *Portsmouth* to do likewise at Yerba Buena. Thenceforth the Bay region heard only distant rumblings as the Yankee invasion progressed southward with mild skirmishes in the Salinas Valley, to end at last in a decisive victory for the Americans at the San Gabriel stream (Montebello), January 8–9, 1847.

The Treaty of Guadalupe Hidalgo, February 2, 1848, gave California to the United States. The Bay region's Bear Flag war was only an incident in the hasty transfer of a vast territory from one nation to another. But it marked the beginning of a new era, and the end of an old one. And Jose Castro himself, *comandante-general* of the forces of the north in the struggle of the *Californios* against the Yankee invaders, foresaw in some degree what that new era would be like when he told an assembly at Monterey: "These Americans are so contriving that some day they will build ladders to touch the sky, and once in the heavens they will change the whole face of the universe and even the color of the stars."

Emporium of a New World

". . . San Francisco . . . the sole emporium of a new world,
the awakened Pacific . . ."

—RICHARD HENRY DANA

HARDLY had the dead hand of Mexican rule been lifted from the Bay region when the Gold Rush struck it like a hurricane. The thousands who flocked to the shores of San Francisco Bay in 1848 at first asked little. But when the excitement died down the little gold frontier town had become a city, and its people demanded much: wharves, and dry paved streets; homes and stores, with firm foundations on which to build them; and a transportation system that would encompass not only the land about the Bay, but the Bay itself. Almost overnight the fleet of steamers and sailing ships which glutted with the manufactured products of Eastern merchants the wharves of San Francisco, Stockton, and Sacramento established the Bay's maritime supremacy on the Pacific Coast.

Mining camps developed into towns and cities amid the rich agricultural lands of the Sacramento and San Joaquin valleys; and around the old *pueblos* of San Jose and Santa Clara the vast ranchos of the Mexicans and Spaniards became orchards, fields, and vineyards. From these, and from the soil of Sonoma County, from Napa Valley and from the counties of the *contra costa,* would come the "green gold" which a vast system of canneries and packing houses now prepares for distribution all over the world. To supply this populous hinterland with commodities, and to bring down to the harbors of the Bay its tons of exports, a network of railroads and highways, bridges and improved inland waterways had to be established. Throughout almost a century Bay region industrialists, farmers, and shippers have had to struggle with problems of engineering to overcome deficiencies in an area otherwise ideally suited to the building of prosperous communities and metropolitan centers.

For all its magnificence and its utility, San Francisco Bay was, until completion of its two great bridges, an obstacle to transportation which prevented development of large sections of Marin County; and it isolated the industrial centers of the East Bay from financial and distribution facilities of San Francisco. Phenomenally rapid as its progress had been, the new unity created by the bridges assured a future of much more intense and orderly development for all communities of the Bay region.

Today, the San Francisco Bay region is the market place and work-shop for a population of over 4,500,000 people—a great harbor ringed with industry, sheltering vessels from all ports of the globe, terminus for transcontinental railroads and a multitude of airlines, and in spite of the postwar rise of the Port of Los Angeles the Bay is still the Pacific Coast leader in the handling of general cargo, the 42 terminals of the Port of San Francisco alone handling such diverse products as cotton, grain, bananas, copra, paper, and industrial machinery of any and all kinds. Since World War II, the Bay's cargo trade has shifted from coastal and intercoastal shipping to one dominated by foreign trade; in 1960 the Bay handled nearly 30 per cent of the coast's foreign trade, by dollar volume.

WORLD PORT

John Masefield's "dirty British coaster with salt-caked smokestacks" is but one of the myriad craft, from nations all over the world, which have come and gone through the Golden Gate since Lieutenant Manuel de Ayala's little *San Carlos* first dropped anchor in San Francisco Bay in 1775. Across the racing tides of that narrow channel have swept the white sails of the clipper ships that brought the Argonauts; through it have steamed sidewheelers and modern freighters, sleek liners and palatial yachts, naval armadas and army transports, fishing boats and nuclear-powered aircraft carriers; and over it have passed the silver wings of the great China Clippers, supersonic fighters, and the immense jetliners of today.

The pioneer Pacific Mail Steamship Company's 1,000-ton side-wheeler, *California,* already had sailed from New York for the Pacific Coast by way of Cape Horn, with no passengers, when the news of the discovery of gold in California reached the East. When the *California* anchored at Panama on January 30, 1849, she found hundreds of frenzied gold-hunters who had made their way across the Isthmus awaiting her. On February 28, topheavy with several times her capacity of 100 passengers, she steamed through the Golden Gate—the first vessel to round Cape Horn under her own steam and sail into the Bay of San Francisco. Pacific Mail promptly hurried completion of two sister ships; but these were not enough. Its fleet rapidly grew to 29 steamships destined to carry 175,000 people to San Francisco within a decade.

During the height of the Gold Rush, however, demand so far out-distanced supply in the maritime industry that chaos reigned, retarding for several years development of regular and systematic commercial facilities. The rapid increase in population—from about 860 to almost 42,000 by the end of 1852 in San Francisco alone—brought a wide and insistent demand for manufactured goods, tools, machinery and food products which undeveloped local industry could not supply. Eastern shippers, without accurate knowledge of local requirements, sent tons of merchandise for which San Francisco could find no use. The market was glutted; prices crashed; goods of every description were left to rot in the holds of ships, on the wharves, and in the city streets. Fully as demoralizing to maritime commerce was the wholesale desertion of ship's crews, who joined the wild rush to the mines. San Francisco Bay in the early fifties presented a sight seldom seen in the history of the world: a veritable forest of masts rising from hundreds of abandoned ships.

With the gradual stabilization of trading conditions, however, maritime commerce was revived until the rapid increase in shipping made necessary the immediate building of extensive piers and docking facilities. Prior to the Gold Rush all cargoes had been lightered ashore in small boats, usually to the rocky promontory of Clark's Point at the foot of Telegraph Hill. When in the winter of 1848 the revenue steamer *James K. Polk* was run aground at the present intersection of Vallejo and Battery Streets—at that time part of the water front—the narrow gangplank laid from deck to shore was considered a distinct advance in harbor facilities. The brig *Belfast* was the first vessel to unload at a pier: she docked in 1848 at the newly completed Broadway Wharf—a board structure ten feet wide. Others were soon built. By October 1850, 6,000 feet of wharfage had been constructed at a cost of $1,000,-000. As the tidal flats were filled in, the piers were extended: Commercial Wharf, at first extending only 30 feet into waters only two feet deep, became Long Wharf as it was lengthened to 400 feet to provide docking facilities for deep water shipping.

During the boom years of the 1850's competition between Eastern shippers became so sharp that a type of sailing vessel faster than the old schooners and barques constructed on the lines of whaling ships had to be built. Between 1850 and 1854, 160 fast clipper ships were launched on the Eastern seaboard to supply the demand for speed and more speed to the Pacific Coast.

"On to the mines" was the order of the day for both passengers and cargoes landed on San Francisco's water front. The fastest way to the mines was by water—through San Pablo Bay, Carquinez Strait, and Suisun Bay, and up the San Joaquin River to Stockton, or up the Sacramento to the town named for it. The first steamboat in the Bay, the 37-foot sidewheeler *Sitka,* imported in sections from the Russian settlement at Sitka, Alaska, and reassembled, had already attempted the trip to Sacramento, requiring six days and seven hours. Vessels better equipped for the journey were soon imported. Meanwhile, lighter craft were pressed into traveling service. Since 1835, when William A.

Richardson had begun operating two 30-ton schooners with Indian crews to transport the produce of missions and ranches from San Francisco and San Jose to trading vessels anchored in the Bay, a variety of small vessels had plied the waters inside the Golden Gate. In 1850 Captain Thomas Gray's propeller steamer *Kangaroo* began the first regular run, twice weekly, between San Francisco and San Antonio Landing (now Oakland) in the East Bay. On September 2, 1863, the San Francisco and Oakland Railroad Company, first in the Bay region, began running the *Contra Costa* six times daily from its Oakland wharf to Broadway Wharf in San Francisco; and the following year, the San Francisco and Alameda Railroad Company inaugurated train-ferry service from Alameda Wharf with the *Sophie McLane*. At the Alameda Wharf, on September 6, 1869, the steamer *Alameda* took on the first boatload of passengers arriving on the Pacific Coast by transcontinental railroad.

After the opening of ferry slips at the two-mile Oakland Long Wharf in 1871 and at a new San Fransisco passenger station at the foot of Market Street four years later, the ferry fleet grew rapidly in size. In 1879 the world's largest ferry, the *Solano,* began transporting whole railroad trains across Suisun Bay from Benicia to Port Costa. The ferry system was extended until by 1930 the 43 boats operating between San Francisco and Oakland, Alameda, Berkeley, Sausalito, and Vallejo comprised the largest transportation enterprise of its kind; in that year they carried more than 40,000,000 passengers.

The lifting of the Mexican regime's restrictive measures against foreign trading brought the Pacific whalers to San Francisco. As early as 1800, whaling vessels had begun to anchor in sheltered Richardson's Bay, then known as Whaler's Bay, off the site of Sausalito, where they took on wood and water. The first captain of the port, shrewd William A. Richardson, had collected fees for piloting the whalers to their anchorage. But Mexican regulations and tariffs forced the whaling industry to base its operations in the Sandwich Islands. After American occupation, San Francisco merchants, foreseeing profits to be gained from yearly outfitting of the whalers and their crews, made hardy efforts to center the industry here. They succeeded to such an extent that by 1865 a total of 34 whalers, with a combined tonnage of 11,000 tons, anchored in the Bay.

As late as 1888, San Francisco was still Pacific Coast whaling headquarters. But the whaling fleet dwindled rapidly after 1900—as tugboats for pursuit ("killer" ships) and steam-driven processing plants (factory ships) supplanted sailing vessels—until in 1938 the California Whaling Company, sole survivor in the industry, called in for the last time its remaining ships.

Within two decades after the building of its first wharf, the tip of the San Francisco Peninsula was saw-toothed with piers. The water front had been pushed into the Bay as the shallow waters of Yerba Buena Cove were filled in. In 1873, two years after control of the San Francisco water front had been acquired by the State, the construction of a great sea wall was begun by the State Board of Harbor Commissioners; and in 1878, the 200-foot wide Embarcadero was laid out. San Francisco's great era of maritime commerce was entering into the full stride of its phenomenal development.

While shovels and picks and gold pans rusted in thousands of back yards, the State turned from gold mining to agriculture and manufacturing. Sacramento and Stockton, great mining centers during the Gold Rush, became agricultural capitals of northern California. The two great rivers sweeping inland to these cities became arteries of commerce. Barges and river boats stopped at numberless docks and landings to pick up the diversified products of the rich land that swept for miles on either side of the broad rivers. And the products of the great agricultural hinterland, flowing into San Francisco Bay, contributed heavily to its export trade. From 1860 to 1875 exports from San Francisco grew in value from $8,532,439 to $33,554,081. By 1889 the figure had increased to $47,274,090 and imports had grown correspondingly in value.

The era of the clipper ships, which had abandoned the San Francisco run and entered the China trade, had given way to a new phase of shipping which called for the transport of heavy industrial products and for the expansion of foreign trade. Successors to the clipper ships were square-rigged sailing vessels, sturdily built, with spacious holds, for carrying heavy cargoes of freight, fish, and agricultural products. Only when displaced by the fast freight steamers of the late nineteenth century did the square-riggers pass from the shipping lanes and from San Francisco Bay. The ships of the Alaska Packers' fleet, last of these great windjammers, were dismantled early in the 1930's. Meanwhile the first of the roving cargo carriers known as "tramp steamers" had passed through the Golden Gate in 1874. By the end of the following year more than 30 of these vessels had arrived. Their number increased rapidly until the rise late in the century of the great modern steamship lines, which absorbed the independent shippers who had dominated the pioneer era. By the middle 1870's the growth of logging camps and sawmills in the timber regions of the State had also created a demand for large fleets of freighters.

Regular monthly service for freight and passengers was established between San Francisco and the Orient in 1867 by the Pacific Mail Steamship Company, which had for several years prior been transporting thousands of Chinese coolies to supply the demand for cheap labor during the building of the Central Pacific Railroad. By 1878 the Pacific Mail had established regular sailings to Honolulu, carrying merchandise which was exchanged for raw sugar, pineapples, coffee, and hides. Five years later the Oceanic Steamship Company entered this lucrative field of trade, and in 1885 extended its service to the ports of Australia and New Zealand. Within the following decade the names of William Matson and Robert Dollar were becoming known in maritime circles. As sea-borne commerce expanded during the last two decades of the nineteenth century, other lines developed. Among these pioneers of American shipping on the Pacific Coast were the American-Hawaiian, United Fruit, and Panama-Pacific Lines. The Kosmos Line, later absorbed by the Hamburg-American Steamship Company, inaugurated the first monthly sailings to Hamburg and other European ports in 1899. By 1916 the American-Hawaiian Steamship Company's fleet of 26 steamers with a capacity of 296,000 tons was said to be the largest tonnage under single ownership operating under the flag of the United States.

When the Panama Canal was opened in July 1914, the maritime commerce of San Francisco Bay entered its modern epoch of expansion. Along San Francisco's Embarcadero, until the outbreak of the war at the end of 1939, were represented more than 175 steamship companies whose vessels, both of domestic and foreign registry, called at nearly every port of the seven seas. Of these, at least half were engaged in coastwise, intercoastal, or transatlantic trade service (via Panama Canal); the others trade with Mexico and Latin America, Hawaii, Australia and the Orient, the African coasts, or offered round-the-world passenger service. From Puget Sound to Madagascar are known the spread-eagle insignia of American President Lines ships (which superseded the huge dollar sign of the Dollar Steamship Company), the blue-and-white smokestacks of California and Hawaiian, and the Matson Line's substantial "M." No less familiar to San Franciscans and other Bay region residents are neat Dutch liners and freighters bound for Rotterdam or Antwerp out of Batavia in the East Indies, for which San Francisco was a regular port-of-call. Ships of Japan, the Bay region's most valuable customer, ships of France, British ships of the P & O Orient line, ships of the Republic of the Philippines, ships from Scandinavian countries and the Netherlands can regularly be seen alongside piers of San Francisco's waterfront, or in other harbors scattered around the Bay.

Among San Francisco's variegated imports have been copra, sugar, coffee, radio and television parts, paper, rubber goods, and textiles. Chief exports are industrial machines; petroleum products; chemicals; lumber; barley; canned and cured fish; and raw cotton. Of the 87,000,000 tons of inbound and outbound cargo cleared by Pacific

Coast ports in 1940, San Francisco Bay handled 23,000,000 tons or 26 per cent. Ranking fourth among the Nation's ports in peacetime commerce, it cleared more military cargo than any other following Pearl Harbor. At the height of the Nation's war shipbuilding program, San Francisco was foremost. As the war ended the San Francisco Port of Embarkation, designated by its Commanding General "the most important port in the world," was operating at new highs.

The Port of San Francisco is much more than the 18 miles of berthing space which flank San Francisco's Ferry Building on either side. Actually it consists of the series of bays extending northeast from the Golden Gate to the confluence of the Sacramento and San Joaquin Rivers and southward almost to San Jose. Harbor facilities are supplied by the half-dozen cities and industrial centers scattered along 100 miles of shoreline enclosing 450 square miles of water. These ports within a port are as interdependent as are the economies of the different cities and towns of the Bay region.

Thus a vessel in from the Hawaiian Islands may discharge pineapple at San Francisco and raw sugar at Crockett before proceeding to the Port of Oakland to take on a cargo of canned and dried fruits for the Orient, or a coastwise vessel up from Nicaragua or Honduras with a hold full of green coffee will unload at San Francisco before crossing to Oakland for automobiles for South or Central America. A tanker coming in through the Gate may steam directly to the Standard Oil docks at Richmond, or the Shell pier at Martinez; or it may make for the Selby Smelting Company's wharf at Selby.

An air view of San Francisco Bay's littoral—its miles of public and private wharfage; its manifold industrial plants crowding the water's edge; its deep-water anchorage for warships; its airports and islands and dockyards—will alone reveal the stupendous picture of this port. And in October 1936 travelers to and from San Francisco Bay were provided with such a view when Pan-American Airways launched the first transpacific commercial passenger flight to Manila. To the historic roll call of ships that have sailed through the Golden Gate have been added the names of those that have flown over it—the China Clippers, the DC-3s, the DC-8s, the Electrajets, and the Boeing 727s.

SMOKESTACKS AROUND THE BAY

Less than a century spans the interval between the primitive looms and forges, kilns and winepresses of the missions around the Bay and the giant factories, shipbuilding yards, and refineries with their soaring smokestacks that congregate about the water's edge today. Where cattle grazed the lonely hills—almost within the memory of living men—furnishing hides for the illicit trade with Yankee sea captains, now rise Contra Costa's sugar and oil refineries, steel mills, explosive and chemical plants. Where whaling boats embarked from San Antonio Landing to carry wild fowl, bear, and deer across the Bay to market, now spreads the East Bay's crowded belt of canneries and factories. And where whalers and hide traders once tied up on the other side of the water, San Francisco's printing and coffee roasting plants, meat-packing and canning establishments crowd to the shore.

The infant city by the Golden Gate grew rich overnight as industries sprang up to supply and outfit the Gold Rush population. Within little more than a decade after Stephen Smith had established his steam-powered grist- and sawmill—California's first—at Bodega in 1843, San Francisco had built stagecoach and wagon factories, flour mills, and breweries. Boot and shoe factories and plants for the grading and manufacture of wool endeavored to fill the need for clothing and blankets. As was natural in a city which was in the habit of burning down two or three times a year, lumber mills flourished. To supply the miners' demands for picks and shovels and pans, the Donahue Brothers established their foundry (later the Union Iron Works) as early as 1849. Since metal was scarce, San Francisco's pioneer machine shops and iron moulders were soon hammering iron wagon wheel rims and harness chains into miners' tools.

After the overland railroad began providing transportation to and from the East for both freight and passengers in 1869, San Francisco's industries expanded rapidly. The development of quartz mining and the growth of large-scale agriculture spurred the manufacture of mining and milling equipment. Other leading industries during this era, in order of importance, were breweries and malt houses, sash and blind mills, boot and shoe factories, tin-ware manufacturing, flour milling, and wool grading and manufacture. Of lesser importance were the tanneries, coffee and spice processors (now one of the city's leading industries), rolling mills, box factories, soap works, cracker factories, and packing plants. Over all, annual industrial output for the two decades of 1870-90 rose from $22,000,000 to $120,000,000.

The rapidly expanding mining industry had created a tremendous demand for special mining machinery. By 1860 San Francisco had 14 foundries and machine shops employing 222 men and turning out nearly $1,218,500 worth of products annually. With the development of quartz mining and the growth of mining in Nevada, it became the un-disputed Western capital for mining machinery. But mine machinery did not long remain the sole concern of local industry and soon, with typical audacity, the comparatively inexperienced machine shops of San Francisco blithely were turning out such complex pieces of workmanship as railway locomotives, flour mills, steamships and lesser objects of everyday utility. By the end of the nineteenth century, San Francisco's machine shops constituted an industry of international stature, supplying flour-milling machinery and equipment for the entire Pacific area, including such widely separated places as South and Central America, Japan, China, Mexico, New Zealand, Siberia, and Australia.

When the miners turned away from the creeks and climbed the hills to follow the quartz ledges, they needed explosives. It was in San Francisco in 1867 that Julius Bandmann took over exclusive rights to manufacture dynamite under the Nobel patents. At his plant in Rock Canyon he put together and discharged three pounds of dynamite—the first, so far as can be determined, ever to be manufactured in the United States. In 1888 he moved his plant to Contra Costa County, where it became the Giant Corporation, a subsidiary of the Atlas Corporation. As the West began tearing down whole mountains to dam rivers and blasting highways along granite cliffs, other explosive manufacturing plants were opened—the Hercules at Pinole and the Trojan at Oakland.

In 1865 Thomas Selby, a San Francisco hardware merchant, built a tall tower at First and Howard Streets for the purpose of dropping lead shot. But the lead ore, mined in California and Nevada, had first to make the long trip to Europe for smelting. Selby began to smelt the ore himself in a small plant in North Beach. The business grew and he moved, first to Black Point, then to Contra Costa County. In 1905 the Selby plant was taken over by the American Smelting Company. Its tall chimney can be seen for miles around. Some of the ore from the famous mines of California and Nevada has been treated there—antimony, lead, silver, and gold, including all of the latter two metals needed by the United States Mint in San Francisco.

Another industry which had gained an early foothold in San Francisco was sugar refining. The story of how a German immigrant boy, Claus Spreckels, graduated from his small San Francisco grocery business to become a millionaire sugar tycoon is typical of the swashbuckling manner in which many robust San Francisco pioneers acquired fortune and fame. Captain Cook, discovering the Sandwich Islands—later the Hawaiian Islands—in 1788, commented on the size and fine quality of the sugar cane he found growing there. Until Spreckels became interested, all the cane from the Islands passed through San Francisco on its way to the East to be refined. Acquiring an early interest in Hawaiian plantation lands when he won part of the island of Mauai in a poker game with Kalakaua, the island king, Spreckels built a refinery here in 1863. Dissatisfied with results, he sold out and went to Germany, France, Austria, and Belgium to study the latest methods of refining. Returning to San Francisco, he built a second refinery. In 1882 he moved his plant to the water front at the foot of Twenty-third Street, where ships from the Islands could unload the cane directly into the refinery. There he installed improved methods of refining, and the plant, later enlarged and reorganized, remained the leading such concern in the Bay region for many years.

The California and Hawaiian Sugar Refinery at Crockett in Contra Costa County, a comparatively late comer, has developed into a giant corporation that grows, mills, refines, and distributes—as sugar and sugar products—nearly 80 per cent of all the cane that comes from the Hawaiian Islands.

Men who had come to dig gold in California had remained to farm. Soon California's fertile inland acres were sprouting the "green gold" for which the State was to become world famous. Even before the great wheat farms of the 1870's and 1880's had been supplanted by fruit and vegetable ranches, a few men had foreseen that this "green gold" might be shipped to the whole world if only it could be preserved against perishability, and packaged.

In 1854 Daniel R. Provost, member of an Eastern fruit preserving firm, had stepped ashore in San Francisco to represent his company here. He rented a small building on Washington Street, where he repacked Eastern jellies in small glass containers. Two years later he enlarged the business and began to make preserves and jellies from California fruits. This was the first time native fruit had been preserved commercially on the Pacific Coast.

Francis Cutting came three years later. He went into the fruit and vegetable-preserving business on Sacramento Street, where his unusual window displays attracted hungry customers. He added tomatoes to his line of products and in 1860 received a shipment of Mason jars which were well received in San Francisco. People began to refer to San Francisco as a fruit-packing center.

In 1862 Cutting received from Baltimore his first shipment of tin plate, at a cost of $16 a box. That year he shipped California canned fruit to the Fifth Avenue Hotel in New York City, to the Continental Hotel in Philadelphia and to the Parker House in Boston. He canned 5,400 cases of California fruit in 1862. California's giant canning industry was born. In 1899 eleven pioneer companies merged to become the California Fruit Canners Association. The industry expanded rapidly.

San Francisco developed a luxury line of fruits and vegetables put up in glass containers and the Illinois Glass Company arrived in Oakland to provide the jars. Typical of the canning industry today is the California Packing Corporation—Calpak—the world's largest canner of fruits and vegetables, with headquarters in San Francisco. Calpak owns and cultivates more than 100,000 acres in nine states, and its Del Monte label is known all over the world. Food processing is today the region's largest single manufacturing industry.

Despite the fact that no oil is produced within 300 miles of the Bay, the center of its oil industry, Contra Costa County, has developed, in the brief interval since a China-bound steamer sailed west with a cargo of oil in 1894, into the clearing house for one-eighth of the entire world's supply of gasoline and petroleum products. All the way from the San Joaquin Valley's southern end, where oil was discovered late in the nineteenth century, pipes were laid to connect with Bay shore refineries. Standard Oil was the first of the large companies to build one; its Richmond plant was opened soon after the first ferry connection was made with San Francisco. It put out one of the early wharves at Point Orient, linking the East Bay directly with the Far East by means of its tankers. Today five of the world's largest refineries overlook the water from San Pablo Bay's southern shore.

Oil, canning, meat packing—these are the Bay region's biggest industries. For the most part, their operations are centered across the Bay from San Francisco. Long the West's chief industrial center, the city itself had passed its zenith as a manufacturing center by the turn of the century. In its place, the East Bay came forward as factories found industrial sites cheaper and rail connections more convenient on the mainland. The city of San Francisco itself assumed its present role of financial and marketing center for an industrial area embracing the whole Bay region—that of front office for the plants across the water. Although outranked in dollar value by both wholesale and retail trade, its manufacturing concerns nevertheless provide employment for more than 55,000 people, more than that provided by government, services, and retailing. Today, as she has been throughout her history, San Francisco is the largest banking center west of Chicago. In 1967 her three largest banks showed total deposits of more than $23,000,000,000, ten billion dollars more than that shown by the largest banks of any other Pacific Coast city. The Bank of America, headquartered in San Francisco, is the largest bank in the world.

Along the shores of Alameda and Contra Costa Counties stretches an industrial belt of bewildering complexity. Alameda County alone contains the plants, warehouses, and subsidiaries of no less than 43 of the country's 87 billion-dollar manufacturing corporations, with products ranging from light bulbs to sea-going freighters, from cookies and crackers to preserved dog food. Three of the major automobile corporations long ago chose the East Bay as a prime location for assembly plants —General Motors, Ford, and Chrysler—but it is the home, too, for more esoteric vehicle manufacturing. Trucks of the Peterbilt Motors Company in Newark can be found on any highway in the United States, and the equipment produced by the Caterpillar Tractor Company of San

Leandro can be found carving out roads and building dams from the Andes to the Far East. In 1921 the Atlas Imperial Diesel Engine Company of Oakland built the first solid-injection marine Diesel engine to be manufactured with commercial success in America, and today the Union Diesel Engine Company, which has been building gas engines since 1885, remains one of the country's leading producers. Both the United States Steel Corporation and the Kaiser Steel Corporation maintain East Bay plants, and perhaps nothing more thoroughly typifies the region's emergence as an industrial and commercial center than the Kaiser Corporation's selection of Oakland for its world headquarters building in 1963.

Postwar development gave rise to industries previously seen in only Buck Rogers comic strips. Rarefied electronics manufacturing is one of the prime employers in San Mateo and Santa Clara counties, and the aerospace industry—electrical machinery, ordnance, instruments—employs more than 70,000 people in the entire Bay Area. Equally symptomatic of postwar development are the atomic research laboratories of the Sandia Corporation at Livermore and the Lawrence Radiation Laboratory of the University of California at Berkeley—as well as the linear accelerator operating near Stanford. And for all this San Francisco remains the financial hub.

ENGINEERING ENTERPRISE

The discovery of gold brought thousands clamoring to the muddy shores of the shallow indentation known as Yerba Buena Cove, which extended in an arc from the foot of Telegraph Hill to the present Montgomery Street and around to the foot of Rincon Hill. One of the first acts of the newcomers as a corporate body was to begin grading away the sand hills along Market Street and dumping them into the mud flats of the cove. The project was many years in completion. Before it was finished, about 1873, they had already begun building a sea wall several blocks east of the shoreline so that ships could unload directly upon the wharves without the aid of a lighter.

The construction of the sea wall, a stupendous project for its time, took many decades to complete. A trench 60 feet wide was dredged along the line of the proposed water front, and tons of rock blasted from Telegraph Hill were dumped into it from lighters and scows. The rocks were allowed to seek bed-rock of their own free weight; when settling ceased, a layer of concrete two feet thick and ten feet wide was laid on top of the resulting embankment.

While this work was going on, the reclamation of the mud-flats and shallows of the original cove was progressing. Some of the city's lesser hills were dumped bodily into the area between the old water front and the new sea wall until the business and financial district of lower Market Street—everything east of Montgomery Street—arose from the sea.

Agitation for rail connections to link the Bay with the outside world had begun as early as 1849. By 1851, $100,000 worth of stock had been sold for a projected line between San Francisco and San Jose. Three successive companies achieved little; but the fourth not only reached Menlo Park, but extended its line down the Peninsula to San Jose and was completed January 16, 1864. September of 1863 had seen completion of the San Francisco and Oakland Railroad Company's line from downtown Oakland to the Oakland ferry wharf.

Meanwhile, San Francisco's "Big Four" were pushing their Central Pacific rails over the mountains to join the Union Pacific in Utah. The first transcontinental railroad, completed in May 1869, extended only as far west as Sacramento. But the "Big Four," determined that San Francisco should be the focal point of a country-wide network of railroad lines, systematically acquired control over every means of entry to the Bay region from all directions. Having bought a short railroad between Sacramento and San Jose, they built a branch to Oakland, purchased the two local roads connecting Oakland and Alameda with the East Bay water front; and taking over another line between Sacramento and Vallejo, they extended it to Benicia, where they inaugurated ferry service to carry their trains across Suisun Bay, installing the world's largest ferryboat for the purpose. Finally they bought the San Francisco and San Jose Line. The Bay was encompassed by the tracks of the "Big Four."

"The railroad has furnished the backing for a great city," reported the San Francisco *Bulletin*, "and the need now is for a thousand miles of local railroads in California." The four went about answering the need. They completed a line southward to Los Angeles through the San Joaquin Valley on September 5, 1876. Their monopoly of rail transportation was unchallenged until completion in 1898 of a competing line financed by popular subscription, which was sold in the same year to the Atchison, Topeka, and Santa Fe Railroad Company. The "Big Four," meanwhile, were gradually extending the original San Francisco and San Jose line until in 1901 it stretched all the way down the coast to Los Angeles. On August 22, 1910 the Western Pacific line from Oakland through Niles Canyon, Stockton, Sacramento, and the Feather River Canyon to Salt Lake City was opened to traffic. By joint agreement in 1904 the Southern Pacific and the Santa Fe began consolidating a group of short lines in the northern coast counties—including the San Francisco and North Pacific from Tiburon to Sherwood and the North Shore from Sausalito to Cazadero—into one line extending from the tip of the Marin Peninsula northward to Trinidad, near Humboldt Bay, finally opened November 17, 1914.

Meanwhile a growing San Francisco had spread beyond the limits set for it in the imagination of its first settlers. Tycoons of mine, ship, and railroad began to build grotesque, grey wooden mansions, tired-looking beneath their burdens of architectural bric-a-brac, on the city's highest elevations. They then were confronted with a new, and purely local, problem of transportation—that of devising a vehicle capable of surmounting hills too steep for horses. The result was the invention, by local manufacturer Andrew S. Hallidie, of the cable car. The inaugural trip of the first car, over the newly laid line on Clay Street between Kearny and Jones Streets, was a civic event. On the morning of August 2, 1873, the unfinished car was sent down the hill and back. That afternoon a public trial trip was made: many people climbed into and upon the car, which was intended to hold only 14, but in spite of the overload, it literally made the grade. Thirty days afterward the line was put into regular operation. The principle of cable traction was not new. The crowning engineering achievement lay in adapting it to street transportation—in solving the problem of how to make a moving cable follow the contour of the street and how to devise a grip which could not tear the cable apart by too sudden a jerk. The cars promised in their day to become the prevailing type of public conveyance in all of America's larger cities. They still survive in the city of their birth, an antique touch in a streamlined world.

Before introduction of the cable car, horse cars and omnibuses had been the prevailing means of street transportation. The first such line, starting in 1852, had been the Yellow Line, a half-hourly omnibus service which carried 18 passengers at a fare of 50¢ apiece from Clay and Kearny Streets out the Mission Street plank toll road to Mission Dolores. In 1862 the first street railroad on the Pacific Coast had begun providing service from North Beach to South Park. A steam railway began operation on Market Street in 1863, but sand and rain repeatedly filled the cuts, and omnibuses constantly obstructed the tracks and in 1867 horse cars were substituted. Even after cable car tracks were installed on Market Steet (hence the name South of the Slot for the district south of Market) a horse car line paralleled them until 1906. An electric line was in operation on Eddy Street as early as 1900. In 1902 began the unification of all the city's lines, except the California Street cable, into one system, which became the Market Street Railway Company. The opening of the Municipal Railway—first city-owned street railway system in the United States and second in the world—in 1912 began an era of competition which lasted until 1944, when the two systems were merged into a single municipally owned and operated network.

On September 22, 1853, the consciously progressive city by the Golden Gate had made another—and very different—stride toward conquering the distances that lay between the communities of men.   On that date was opened for use the first electric telegraph on the Pacific slope, connecting the San Francisco Merchants' Exchange with six-mile-distant Point Lobos.   It was built to announce the arrival of vessels at the Gate (previously signalled to the town by the arms of the giant semaphore atop Telegraph Hill).   Two days later, James Gamble started out from San Francisco with a party of six men to put up wire for the California State Telegraph Company, which had obtained a franchise from the Legislature for a telegraph from San Francisco to Marysville by way of San Jose, Stockton, and Sacramento.   On September 25th the wire was in place.   On October 24, 1861, the first direct messages between New York and San Francisco passed over the wires of the first transcontinental telegraph line.

One year after Alexander Graham Bell had invented the telephone, in 1876, Frederick Marriott, Sr., publisher of the San Francisco *News-Letter,* had a wire installed between his office and his home.   In February 1878 the American Speaking Telephone Company began regular service with 18 subscribers.   Soon afterwards the National Bell Telephone Company offered competition.   The early switchboard consisted of two boards affixed to the wall, each with a row of brass clips into which holes were drilled to receive the plugs making the connections. In the National Bell Telephone Company's office, bells above these boards notified the operator of a call.   Since the bells sounded exactly alike, however, a string had to be attached to each bell tapper and a cork to each string; the antics of the cork called the attention of the operator to the line that demanded attention.

On January 25, 1915, the first transcontinental telephone line was opened.   Dr. Alexander Graham Bell in New York spoke to his former employee, Thomas Watson, in San Francisco, repeating his sentence of an even more memorable occasion: "Mr. Watson, come here, I want you!" The occasion marked the culmination of the city's sixtyfive-year history of demanding—and getting—direct communication with the centers of the East.

A still greater stride in communication was made on December 13, 1902, when the shore end of the first transpacific cable was laid in San Francisco by the Commercial Pacific Cable Company (organized in 1883 by Comstock king John W. Mackay).

A more homely problem—a vexatious one for San Francisco since 1849—was that of its water supply.   In early years water had been brought from Marin County on rafts and retailed at a dollar a bucket. Throughout the latter half of the nineteenth century, local sources of supply were exploited by private companies.   When these failed to keep pace with the requirements of the rapidly growing metropolis, the City and County of San Francisco began in 1914, after a long and bitter struggle with monopolistic interests, the construction of the Hetch-Hetchy system.

Heart of the system is O'Shaughnessy Dam, towering 430 feet high across the granite-walled course of the Tuolomne River, high in the Sierra Nevada in Yosemite National Park. The mountain waters impounded are piped to San Francisco by gravity through tunnels and steel pipes over 163 miles of mountains and valleys. Besides the main dam and reservoir at Hetch-Hetchy, the system includes a number of subsidiary storage reservoirs and power stations with a combined capacity of more than 150,000 horsepower. The dam was completed in 1923, the aqueduct in 1934.

The East Bay, too, had been faced with a similar situation regarding its water. From several wells in the vicinity and the surface run-off of San Pablo and San Leandro Creeks the region long had drawn a water supply whose quality was impaired by the inflow of salt water from the Bay and whose quantity was estimated at about one-sixth of that soon to be required. In the same year the O'Shaughnessy Dam was completed to impound waters for thirsty San Franciscans, the East Bay Municipal Utility District was organized. Eight years later it had completed the 358-foot-high Pardee Dam on the Mokelumne River in the Sierra foothills, a 98-mile aqueduct, two subsidiary aqueducts, and auxiliary storage reservoirs.

Long before the waters of the Sierra Nevada were generating power to light the homes of the Bay region—on the evening of July 4, 1876—Reverend Father Joseph M. Neri presented electricity to San Franciscans, operating on the roof of St. Ignatius College three large French arc searchlights with an old generator that had seen service during the siege of Paris in 1871. This was an occasion surpassing even the lighting of the city's first gas lamps on February 11, 1854—illumination provided by gas manufactured from Australian coal by the San Francisco Gas Company (first of its kind on the Pacific Coast).

George H. Roe, a local money broker whose interest in electricity had been aroused when he found himself owner of a dynamo taken as security for a loan, organized in 1879 the California Electric Light Company and erected a generating station on a small lot near the corner of Fourth and Market Streets. Early consumers paid $10 a week for 2,000 candlepower of light—which was turned off promptly at midnight. By 1900 a number of other companies had been organized. Through a merger of two of the largest, in 1905, was incorporated the Pacific Gas and Electric Company, which now operates two steam-electric generating stations in San Francisco and six across the Bay. One of the latter, near Pittsburg, generates over 600,000 kws. of power, quite enough to supply two cities the size of San Francisco. By 1958 the company—already one of the largest public utility companies in the world—had thirteen steam-generating plants and 62 hydroelectric plants scattered from the Kern River in the south to the Pitt River in the north, with a total installed capacity exceeding three-and-one-half million horse-power. And to meet the growing needs of the 89,000 square miles it serves today, the company is exploring the use of atomic energy for additional generating plants.

In the meantime, San Francisco's hills again had proven to be—and this time literally—stumbling blocks to the city's progress; for, as they halted further expansion, the town became cramped for space. Answer to the new problem was the construction of a series of five railway tunnels known as the Bay Shore Cutoff; completed in 1907, they brought the Peninsula towns within commuting distance of "the city" and opened up a large new residential area. In 1914 the city's North Beach section was made more easily accessible by a tunnel driven through Nob Hill on Stockton Street. Two years later the completion of the 2¼-mile Twin Peaks Tunnel provided a short-cut to the district west of Twin Peaks, doubled the city's potential residential area, and brought a rich financial return to property owners, business men, and real estate promoters. Another tunnel was bored to carry streetcars under Buena Vista Heights.

By the third decade of the twentieth century the fast-growing East Bay communities were confronted, as San Francisco had been, by the need of making similar improvements on nature. In 1928 a $4,496,000 automobile and pedestrian tube was laid beneath the Oakland Estuary to connect Oakland with the island city, Alameda. The Posey Tube (named for its designer and engineer) is unusual in that it is constructed of twelve prefabricated tubular sections, 37 feet in outer diameter, which were "corked," towed across the Bay, and sunk into a great trench dredged on the bottom of the estuary. The center one of the tube's three horizontal sections accommodates traffic; the lowest is a fresh air duct; the uppermost, an outlet for foul air.

More than 1,000 men toiled three years to build the impressive Broadway Tunnel connecting East Bay cities with Contra Costa County, which cost $4,500,000 before its completion in 1937. This twin-bore automobile tunnel was expanded recently to accommodate traffic on the newly-constructed freeway system linking the many suburban communities east of the Berkeley Hills to one another and to the vast complex of the metropolitan Bay Area—a project not yet complete but already one of the most ambitious in urban America.

But when engineers had created a city where mud flats had been, had surmounted the hills of that city and the hills and valleys of the region beyond, had learned to talk over miles of wires and harnessed mountain streams to provide drinking water and electricity for a people, they had still to span the great body of water on whose shores the people lived. Not until 1927 was the Bay first bridged when the narrowest width at its extreme southern end was crossed by the Dumbarton Drawbridge, connecting San Mateo and Alameda Counties.

Carquinez Strait, the narrow entrance from San Pablo Bay to Suisun Bay, was next to be spanned. Carquinez Bridge is a tribute to the imagination and determination of two business men—Avon Hanford and Oscar Klatt. In 1923 their company secured a toll bridge franchise and—despite the admonitions of engineer and layman that the water was too deep and swift to permit a bridge at the site—construction was begun. In 1927 the $8,000,000 structure was opened to traffic. The great double pier rests on sandstone and blue clay at a depth of 135 feet below mean water level, over which the steel construction towers, for four-fifths of a mile, 314 feet above the strait.

March 3, 1929, saw completion of what was then the longest highway bridge in the world—the twelve-mile San Mateo Toll Bridge, crossing seven miles of water a few miles north of the Dumbarton Bridge. A new, freeway-speed enlargement of the bridge was opened for traffic in 1968, significantly expanding its capacity and sharply reducing travel time between the shores of the southern Bay.

The San Francisco-Oakland Bay Bridge was opened in November, 1936. It has six lanes for westbound traffic on its upper deck and six lanes for eastbound traffic on its lower deck. Its length, including all approaches, is more than eight miles. Clearance above water at the central pier is 216 feet, sufficient to clear the mast of the largest ships. The west crossing—between San Francisco and Yerba Buena Island—consisting of two suspension bridges anchored in the center to a concrete pier, is unique in bridge construction; it is so built that the roadway forms a single smooth arc. Connecting the east and west crossings is the largest diameter tunnel in the world, blasted through Yerba Buena Island's 140 acres of rock. It is 76 feet wide and 58 feet high; through it an upright four-story building could be towed. Three pioneer tunnels were bored through the rock and then broken out until they became one horseshoe-shaped excavation. A viaduct 540 feet long was constructed 20 feet from the floor of the tunnel to carry the wide roadbed of the bridge's upper deck. The extraordinary depth of the bedrock to which concrete supports for the towers had to be sunk through water and clay presented bridge builders with an exceptional problem. To solve the problem, engineers devised a new system of lowering the domed caissons, controlled by compressed air. In the case of the east tower pier of the east crossing, bedrock lay at such a depth that it could not be reached. The foundations were laid at a depth greater than any ever before attained in bridge building.

In 1965 the State Department of Public Works engaged in reconstruction that further increased the usefulness of the bridge.

Six months after the opening of the San Francisco-Oakland Bay Bridge, San Francisco was linked to the northern Bay shore by the world's longest single span, the Golden Gate Bridge. It measures 4,200 feet between the two towers and 8,940 feet in all. Its towers rise 746 feet above high tide; its center span, 220 feet above high water. The tops of the towers rise above the waters of the Golden Gate to the height of a 65-story building. Most spectacular feat in the bridge's construction was the building of the south tower's foundation. Because of the swift tidal flow at this point, spanning the Golden Gate had long been considered impossible. Working on barges tossed continually by swells as high as 15 feet, seasick workmen built from bedrock a huge concrete fender completely enclosing the site. Inside this fender, which later became part of the structure, caissons were sunk.

When the two towers were finished, workmen clambering along catwalks strung between them spun the giant cables from tower to tower. Into the spinning of each of the cables (which measure $36\frac{1}{2}$ inches in diameter) went 27,572 strands of wire no thicker than a lead pencil. To support them, each tower has to carry a vertical load of 210,000,000 pounds from each cable and each shore anchorage block to withstand a pull of 63,000,000 pounds. From these cables the bridge was suspended by traveler derricks invented to perform jobs of this kind.

At about the time the two bridges were being woven into the Bay region's design of living, Treasure Island was rising from the rocky shoals just north of Yerba Buena Island. An outline of the island-to-be was drawn in tons of quarried rock. Inside it were dumped 20,000,000 cubic feet of sand and mud dredged from the bottom of the Bay. When the job was completed a 400-acre island was ready for the $50,000,000 Golden Gate International Exposition of 1939. Shortly after the Exposition closed, the island was taken over by the United States Navy as a training and embarkation center, which function it serves today.

Postwar development saw the rise of the metropolitan Bay Area's expansive freeway system which today laces all of the region's counties in a high-speed network of communication. Nor have only functional needs been considered—Oakland's graceful MacArthur Freeway was recently declared the most beautiful freeway in the United States. An even more dramatic chapter in the history of Bay Area engineering has been the development of Bay Area Rapid Transit (BART), a billion-dollar, 75-mile public transport system planned to link all the major cities of San Francisco, Alameda, and Contra Costa counties. A 3.3-mile twin bore tunnel through the Berkeley Hills and a four-mile tube beneath the Bay are of themselves astounding engineering feats.

A new era in transportation opened when airplanes took over the passenger business of the railroads and motor trucks preempted their freight. A great international port developed at San Francisco, handling more than 700,000 pasengers a year. Commuter flights connected the Oakland and San Mateo-Sunnyvale airports with San Francisco and helicopters served intermediate needs. The multiplication of executive planes added substantially to the extent of air fields, and warehouses went up to store cargo. New technical devices were applied. Air communication and transportation were ready for the 21st century.

Civic Center and Public Buildings

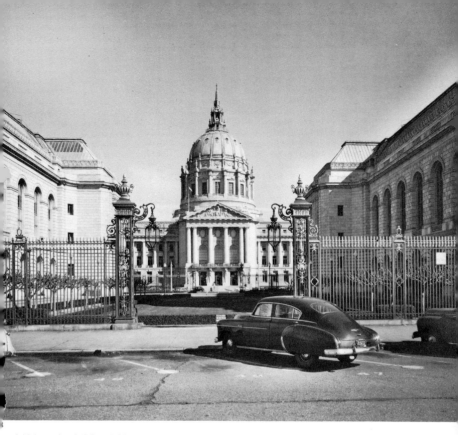

SAN FRANCISCO CITY HALL, FLANKED BY THE OPERA HOUSE
AND THE VETERANS BUILDING

SEAL OF THE CITY AND COUNTY OF SAN FRANCISCO

PRESIDENT EISENHOWER AT THE TENTH ANNIVERSARY
OF THE UNITED NATIONS' CHARTER, JUNE 30, 1955

SECRETARY OF STATE DEAN ACHESON SIGNING THE
JAPANESE PEACE TREATY, JUNE 8, 1951

STANDING ARE SEN. JOHN SPARKMAN, REP. JAMES P. RICHARDS,
SEN. ALEXANDER WILEY, AMBASSADOR AT LARGE JOHN FOSTER
DULLES, SEN. BOURKE B. HICKENLOOPER AND SEN.
H. ALEXANDER SMITH

CIVIC CENTER FROM THE AIR, LOOKING WEST

GRAND STAIRCASE, SAN FRANCISCO CITY HALL

UNITED STATES POST OFFICE, MISSION AND FIFTH STREETS

PACIFIC COAST STOCK EXCHANGE, PINE AND SANSOME STS.

Golden Era

"Mind before mines ought to be the motto . . . of every educated Californian."

—Reverend H. W. Bellows

TO THINK of its power and influence," marveled Horace Greeley at San Francisco's pioneer literary journal, the *Golden Era,* "when the population is so sparse and the mail facilities so poor." The *Era's* youthful founders, Rollin M. Dagget, who was only nineteen years old when he arrived on the Coast, and J. MacDonough Foard, who was only twenty-one, had followed Greeley's own advice: "Go West, young man!" The phenomenal success of their attempt to spread enlightenment on such matters as education, literature, and the fine arts through the *Era's* columns, beginning in 1852 when the infant city could not yet supply itself with even the common necessities of life, was indicative of that hunger for all the arts and refinements of civilization which inspired the Argonauts almost as much, it would seem, as the quest for gold. "To encourage virtue and literature" had been one of the announced objectives of the founders of the Bear Flag Republic in 1846. Certain it is that "virtue and literature"—and art, and learning, and architecture—have received rare encouragement in the cities around San Francisco Bay. Even the earliest saloons insisted on hanging paintings on their walls and providing *musicales* for their patrons! The Gold Rush may have swept San Francisco's first public schoolmaster, Thomas Douglas, off to the mines six weeks after he called his first class to order, but countless others who took his place would demonstrate a steadier adherence to the motto the Reverend Bellows framed for "every educated Californian."

CENTERS OF LEARNING

To trace the pioneer impetus in the educational field is like watching the man in the old story who brought water on mule-back from the ocean to the Colorado River. One disbelieves, and yet one sees the thing happening: individual after individual carrying obstacles before him that look insurmountable, impelled by nothing but his own belief and courage. There is Colonel Thomas J. Nevins, who first revealed to the Common Council of San Francisco that children were among the products of the gold-bearing State. The council, in those days when only the color of gold could put a man in action, was inclined to distrust Colonel Nevins' report until he thrust under their noses a census of his own taking, and illustrated it by samples of both sexes. The result was an ordinance for the establishing of the free common school system. That was in 1851. Nevins had earlier, of his own accord, set up a school in Happy Valley, south of Market Street, and could be seen each day following an express wagon along San Francisco streets, gathering up children and expressing them to the Happy Valley schoolhouse. And even earlier yet, Yale graduate Thomas Douglas had opened on April 3, 1848 California's first public school in a small shack on Portsmouth Square, beginning with six pupils, whom he taught until the Gold Rush, following shortly afterward, bore him off to the mines.

There is John G. Pelton, who came around Cape Horn from Andover, Massachusetts, determined to lay the foundations of a public school system in the illiterate West. Pelton even brought a school bell with him, which was tied to the mast and rang the watches on the tedious voyage from the Atlantic to the Pacific. He arrived with $1.50 in his pockets, not enough to remove books, globes, maps, and bell from the sandy beach where they had been landed. Some unnamed visionary rescued him and his wife. As soon as a boarding house opened by Mrs. Pelton was under way, he started a free school in the basement of the Baptist Church.

Writes John Swett, who became principal of one of the schools established after the ordinance of 1851: "This school [the Rincon School] was . . . in a small rented house planted in the middle of a sandbank on the corner of First and Folsom Streets. . . . There was neither a blackboard nor map. . . . The only apparatus consisted of a wooden water pail and a battered tin dipper, from which the children drank water brought from a well not far distant, the owner of which allowed the boys to draw one bucket of water a day." An early teacher is pictured scooping the drifted sand from under the pot outside his tent door, proceeding to boil his potatoes and brew his kettle of tea for a solitary supper after his day's work.

Ambitious in the face of difficulties is a list of geography questions propounded by an early school board president who prided himself on being able to teach more in one day than any teacher in San Francisco. The questions were (1) name all the rivers of the globe; (2) name all the bays, gulfs, seas, lakes and other bodies of water on the globe; (3) name all the countries of the world; (4) name all the cities of the world. It is told that when a young man from Texas had worried through the questions in arithmetic and had come to these on geography, he examined them carefully, then walked up to the chairman's table and handed them to him, saying, "If the Board wants me to prepare a primary geography, they must pay me for it."

The first kindergarten was opened in September 1863, by "Professor" Charles and Madame Weil, at 41 South Park Street. Schools sprang up quickly in imitation of the first successful private children's school, and by the end of the century there were easily a hundred of them in the city. Child education, however, did not receive mature attention until the advent of Miss Emma Marwedel in 1878. Miss Marwedel was one of the earliest child educators in the East to teach story-telling and drawing to children, and she left a highly successful school in the Nation's capital to organize a kindergarten in Los Angeles. During this period of teaching and training she instructed Kate Douglas Wiggin in kindergarten work.

Later Miss Marwedel and Mrs. Wiggin were associated in conducting San Francisco's famous Silver Street Kindergarten, parent institution of all Pacific Coast kindergartens. It was located in the notorious Tar Flat district around Second and Harrison Streets where ". . . life is sodden and aimless . . . children are often born of drunken mothers, and show deformities and mental deficiencies and inherited diseases . . . kindergarten teachers in their visiting sometimes find mothers helpless with drink . . ."

Fighting against such conditions, Miss Marwedel and Mrs. Wiggin taught the ever-increasing classes games, music, and the elements of cultural education, and with the help of other assistants made their school one of the most active educational forces in the history of Western child training. When Mrs. Wiggin later gained international fame by writing such books as *Rebecca of Sunnybrook Farm* and *Mrs. Wiggs of the Cabbage Patch,* she continued the crusade for child education. In San Francisco during her last few hours of intolerable illness, Miss Marwedel said to followers: "Have faith in the kindergarten . . . I believe in its power to reform the world."

Jean Parker, who believed the education of a child should include more than arithmetic, history, grammar, and other basic studies, first introduced useful and practical accomplishments—such as domestic science classes, school luncheons, girls' and boys' clubs, manual arts, and physical culture—to California juvenile education. San Francisco's 130 city-operated public schools, using teaching methods developed by this revolutionary, must stand as living memorials to the woman about whom was said: "She knew the new education before it poured in a beneficent flood over the land, and she created while others evolved laboratory schemes of advancement . . ."

The rise of colleges and universities followed the same impulse which broke through the apathy of a raw and materialistic civilization to establish the common schools. On the eastern side of the Bay, at a time when Oakland was a cluster of houses and Berkeley but an expanse of neighboring fields, when the first transcontinental railroad had not reached California, and Tiburcio Vasquez was harassing honest men in the San Joaquin Valley, the University of California was opened in 1868.

Leland Stanford came to California in 1852, penniless, to sell salt pork and miners' sieves in a store at Michigan Bluff. After a while he was able to bring his wife out from the East, and for a time they made their own furniture from drygoods boxes—but only for a time. On a November morning in 1885, Senator and Mrs. Stanford gathered a group of men in their Nob Hill home in San Francisco and presented to them the founding grant of Stanford University. Without ostentation and seemingly the least impressed of all present, the Senator deeded over to this board of trustees 83,200 acres of the richest farmlands in California, and declared his intention of bequeathing to the institution the bulk of his estate, then estimated at $30,000,000. The world gasped. Never before had an educational institution come into existence on foundations so munificent. But that was the least cause for astonishment. There was not even a flag stop where the doors of the university were to open, nothing but unbroken stretches of grain. Furthermore, the university at Berkeley had not yet reached the 400 mark in its graduating classes, and, as the *New York Mail and Express* remarked, the need for another university at such close quarters was about as urgent as for "an asylum of decayed sea captains in Switzerland."

Nevertheless, the very daring of the enterprise, and the beauty and fitness of the Romanesque buildings as they arose, arcade on arcade, against the low tawny hills, together with the word broadcast by Dr. David Starr Jordan, "The winds of freedom blow!", drew a student body of 465 in the first year. Among that first generation were Herbert Hoover, Ray Lyman Wilbur, Vernon Kellogg, Holbrook Blinn, Will and Wallace Irwin, and Charles K. Field. It was Senator Stanford's idea that the university he had founded should be a place for specialization, with the primary emphasis on usefulness. In terms of this ideal the growth of the university has been molded, with the gradual elimination of work of general and elementary nature and the expansion of research and graduate studies. On the other hand, Mrs. Stanford's insistence was on the spirit of democracy, an objective aided by the fact that both students and faculty were necessarily resident on the campus, from the very earliest days when the great iron triangle sounded for communal "Grub!" As a consequence, it has become a Stanford claim that no student can consider his college career a success if, when he graduates, he is not known by his first name to at least three professors.

But pioneer education was not reserved for men only. On an acreage in the foothills of Alameda County, ideals of manners and "ladyhood" were taught young women who had no designation to set beside their names but some vague territorial address such as "Nevada." In a society founded by adventurers, this was indeed stemming the stream.

Dr. Cyrus Taggart Mills had reached California in the 1860's, then a man of middle age, his only fortune a small one acquired by missionary toil and close saving. Purchasing the ground where Mills College now stands, he transported to it Benicia Seminary, and under mansard roof and cupola "beautifully frescoed" within with well-meaning cherubs, garlands of roses, and be-ribboned musical instruments, Dr. Mills and his wife taught the daughters of miners "to spell correctly, to read naturally, to write legibly, and to converse intelligently."

Numerous other educational institutions arose during the 20 years after Mrs. Olive Mann Isbell taught her youngsters in a stable where she saw her wedding handkerchief used as a flag of truce to the Mexicans. In 1854 the Sisters of St. Dominic opened St. Catherine's Academy at Benicia; today as the Dominican College of San Rafael, it is particularly noted for its school of music. The University of San Francisco had its beginning one year later as St. Ignatius College, built on land described as "the sand dunes near the little town of San Francisco"—the present site of the Emporium. In 1863 Archbishop Alemany founded St. Mary's College, since transferred from San Francisco to Oakland and more recently to Moraga.

It is primarily in scientific discovery that the pioneer spirit now evinces itself, and it is in science that California scholars have made their greatest mark. In the Radiation Laboratory of the University of California stands a gigantic contrivance that looks like a Brobdingnagian cheese, but has been compared more appropriately to a huge machine gun. This cyclotron Dr. E. O. Lawrence directs against atoms—objects so small that the entire population of the world would require 10,000 years to count the number of them in a drop of water. Before Dr. Lawrence's experiments the only bullets powerful enough, and at the same time tiny enough, to crack through the nucleus of the atom were the natural emanations of radium, an extremely expensive commodity and one available in very small quantity. By means of the cyclotron the nuclei of a special type of hydrogen atom may be utilized for the same purpose. These nuclei, fired at the rate of a hundred thousand billion a second against whatever element is exposed to the machine, satisfy both the necessity for tremendous force and the necessity for infinitesimal smallness.

The reason for this vindictive effort to break up the innocent atom lies in the tremendous energies released by the cracking open of the atomic nuclei, energies which are the most tantalizing forces known to man. Already the atoms of all the available (some 30 different) elements have been blasted by the stream of so-called "deuterons" emitted by the machine. The rearrangement in pattern and size of the atomic nuclei of these elements has resulted in the realization of the old dream of the alchemists—the transmutation of one element into another, of platinum into iridium and gold, of bismuth into polonium and lead. It has resulted also in the creation of substances never yet found in nature, substances whose common characteristic is the fact that they are all radio-active. Several of these new forms show promise in the treatment of certain radio sensitive diseases. Even more sensational is the liberation of the "neutron ray," a ray similar to X-ray but far more effective in the treatment of tumorous and cancerous tissue, and now regarded as one of the most promising developments in the scientific fight against cancer.

Dr. Ernest Linwood Walker, quiet and sincere student, professor of tropical medicine in the University of California Medical School, some years ago swept aside the veil of superstition and fear which for thousands of years had blinded men to the real nature of leprosy. He was able to identify the bacterium cultivable from leprosy as a soil-growing organism, and he suggests, as an alternative hypothesis to contagion, the entrance of this soil bacterium into the human body through soil-contaminated wounds as the primary mode of infection in leprosy. Wild rats are subject to a leprosy-like disease, from which the same soil organism can be cultivated and for which a similar mode of infection is suggested. No longer were bells to be rung as the leper approached, and the dreadful cry, "Unclean!" go from mouth to mouth.

A housewife who opens a can of peaches is protected by a long series of intensive researches carried on in the university laboratories. Dr. Carl Meyer and his assistants, after working on the subject of botulism (food poisoning), were able to reduce poisoning from commercially packed foods to the extent that now there is actually more danger from foods preserved in the home.

In the Engineering Materials Laboratory, preparatory to the building of Hoover Dam, concrete was accorded unusual attention. It was tested by delicate instruments, in turn lovingly coddled and lovingly smashed and given ideal conditions and the worst conditions—in order that one of the engineering projects of the modern world might guard the waters of the Colorado River. Within adiabatic calorimeters—cork-lined rooms with doors like those of the refrigerator of a butcher shop —samples of various types of concrete were housed in cylindrical compartments; electrical resistance thermometers were imbedded in the concrete. The concrete was tested under various stages of dampness, with and without loads; its strength was measured in a universal testing machine of 4,000,000-pound capacity. Its durability was gauged under artificial weather conditions duplicating those to which the dam would be subjected. This testing laboratory has been concerned in an advisory capacity with engineering projects including the Colorado River Aqueduct into Los Angeles, the San Francisco-Oakland Bay Bridge, the

Golden Gate Bridge, Pine Canyon Dam, and Oakland's Broadway Tunnel.

At Stanford University aeronautical, astronautical, and nuclear research has been carried on since World War II, and today it is the home of the Stanford Linear Accelerator Center, a two-mile-long, $114,000,-000 installation capable of producing a beam with energy of from 10 to 20 billion electron volts. The Stanford Medical Center became in 1968 one of the world's foremost institutions for the practice of heart transplant surgery.

In the same way that research is integrated with the commercial life of the State, so also is it integrated with the life of California farmers, returning to them millions of dollars, saved through improved agricultural methods. In more than one curious instance, experiments carried on for the benefit of agriculture have had their effects in a totally different field of industry. When Charles B. Lipman and Dr. Aaron Gordon began their extensive research and experimentation into the problem of treating pear-blight by injecting a poisonous solution in the trunks of the trees, it was hoped the solution would act on the bacteria causing the blight. Unfortunately it was not successful with pear trees, but it was remarkably successful with telephone poles. The problem now became a totally different one, that of protecting piles and timbers, used in marine construction and by power companies, from the depredations of various types of borers. The process, which is like embalming, consists in injection of the poisonous solution into the circulatory system of the living tree or cut pole. Practical tests on telephone poles and piles before they are cut have shown it to be a cheap and efficient method of protecting them from marauding organisms, fungi, and molds.

These are a few of the values immediately accessible and easily visualized by the layman who is interested in "results" from the State's educational system. Yet even in the liberal arts department, there is the eternal individual with warmly giving hands and heart fixed on the future. Josiah Royce, one of the truly great "great men" who have come from the University of California, speaks of climbing around under the eaves of Bacon Hall, where the books belonging to the old College of California were stored. There, where deep dust stood on ancient theological and scientific treatises, he gathered, according to his own statement, the most profound intellectual impressions of his life.

The immense collections of the present University Library came into being, step by step, with the gifts of individuals who had felt a similar debt to "book-learning." One of the most delightful of these collections is lodged in the Morrison Library, on the ground floor of the building. The story of its foundation parallels Walter Scott's preface to *Quentin Durward*. Just as Sir Walter was introduced by the fantastic Marquis de Hautlieu, with many apologies for tattered tapestry and tenant owls, to the turret room of a ruined castle where were deposited "the precious relics of a most splendid library," so, demurring in housewifely fashion for the untidiness of the attic, the widow of Alexander F. Morrison led her guests, one evening after dinner, to a garret lit up like an Aladdin's cave with the splendor of 15,000 books which she wished to give to the university as a memorial to her husband. These books, so vital a part of her own life, were not to be swallowed in the catacombs of the stacks, but were to form a room of their own where students, sans notebooks, might genuinely recreate themselves intellectually.

The Bancroft Library is, of course, one of the most important of the individual collections, and becomes each year increasingly the center of research for students of the history of the Pacific Slope and Hispanic America. Scholars in constantly larger numbers come from the East and abroad to consult these rich manuscripts and printed materials. Similarly unique in its own field is the Hoover Library on War, Revolution, and Peace, at Stanford, containing documents relating to the World War—government reports, unofficial publications, periodicals, books, pamphlets, and manuscripts, some of so confidential a nature that they will not be available for use for 40 years.

It has been said that the degree of civilization attained by any nation may be estimated from the provision it makes for study of the stars. Certainly, paradoxical as it may seem, no one has ever asked that Lick Observatory show its credentials in the shape of "practical" benefits. The discovery of a fifth moon in Jupiter or a shadowy duplicate streak across Mars has satisfied the public mind as much as an honest piece of cement or the last meal of a mealy-bug issuing from the university laboratories. This tolerance for sidereal phenomena is, as a matter of fact, a good deal more respectable than the tolerance which James Lick himself felt for starry matters. It is said of him that he "had never looked through anything larger than a ship's spy-glass," and when he was consulted at his Alviso flour mill in 1887 on the subject of a university foundation for scientific studies, he "listened patiently, but it made no more impression on him than on the fruit trees" he was walking under. Yet he founded—for what reason no one can surmise—the observatory on Mount Hamilton, one of the nine branches of the University of California. There, in the base of the pier on which the observatory rests, rests also the body of James Lick.

And there, through telescopes a good deal larger than a ship's spy-glass, have been discovered the several satellites of Jupiter additional to the four discovered by Galileo in 1610. There have occurred the first great successes in photographing comets and the Milky Way, teaching more about the structure, formation, and dissolution of the comet's tail than had been learned in all previous time. There the sulky steps of the young blue stars have been measured, the staid stride of the middle-aged yellow stars, and the fine gallop of the old red stars.   There the advance through space of our own solar system has been set at 12.2 miles per second in the direction of the constellation of Hercules.   Whether this would have meant much or little to James Lick, no one can say, for he "wot not of it" under his fruit trees at Alviso.

Notoriously unexciting as is the history of education, the hardihood of those first California educators—considered now from a safe distance in time—seems no less awe-inspiring than the hardihood of their contemporaries who forged across the Sierra Nevada, seeking gold.   For the apathy they faced and overcame was no less cold and cruel than the Sierra.   Nevertheless they opened school in stable and tent.   And it is still their day—the day of the pioneer—in the halls now decently clad with stucco and adorned with drinking fountains, while the chimes of Berkeley's Campanile proclaim the international frontiers of education, ringing out, slowly and liquidly, a tune from Heine or an old English carol or "The Goden Bear."

ARGONAUTS OF LETTERS

In 1864 an earthquake damaged San Francisco but left Oakland unharmed.   Discussion ensued as to the reason for Oakland's invulnerability.   Bret Harte, citing "Schwappelfurt, the celebrated German geologist," endeavored to explain the singular fact by suggesting that there are some things the earth cannot swallow.   Whether Harte's affection for Oakland was paralleled by a similar affection for San Francisco is a question; he was given a job in the mint so that he could write stories, but as soon as he had written the stories he left and went to wear his green gloves in Boston and to part his Dundreary whiskers in London.

Bret Harte is not the only writer who, wearing the local label, conducted himself with an astonishing resistance toward this geographical section.   Harte left it bodily.   Mark Twain, Joaquin Miller, and others found the city's frank money grubbing and social vulgarity unbearable.   Boston and New York, London and Paris seemed to offer a more soothing atmosphere for artistic nerves jangled by such excesses of gross materialism.   And yet Harte endowed California with its earliest literary prestige.   He discovered and romanticized the Argonauts, at a time when it could be said of the urban intellectuals of whom he was one, that, like the Hangtown girls,

> "They're dreadful shy of forty-niners,
> Turn their noses up at miners."

And there is ironic justice in the fact that once he had created the Argonaut of California fiction, he tucked up his mustachios and departed.

It is the California setting, particularly the setting of San Francisco
—its place on the sea, facing the Orient, with its back to the mines—
which alone has inspired in its writers a continuity of tradition. The
region gave elbow room for the unpredictable expansion of certain individual writers, elbow room they would not have had elsewhere. The
effect has been what some critics call the "virility" of Californian literature. This is the one tradition to which it is possible to point—the
defining effect of the region on its writers.

San Francisco's literary beginnings were its pioneer journals—the
first of which, the *Golden Era,* was founded in 1852 by J. MacDonough
Foard and Rollin M. Daggett. In March 1857 the *Golden Era*
printed a slight, sentimental poem, "The Valentine," signed "Bret."
Its author followed with more verses and sketches. Another contributor
was Samuel Langhorne Clemens, a young Missourian, signing himself
Mark Twain. The two men met soon after May 1864, while Clemens
was employed on the *Call,* which shared a building with the local
United States Mint. Later Harte became temporary editor of the
Californian, and engaged Clemens to write regularly for the publication.
Harte laid the foundation for Western romance, and Twain crystallized
Western humor.

Harte played the more irrational, the more unpredictable part, and
in this way the more truly "Californian" part; for scarcely a year before
the appearance of *The Luck of Roaring Camp,* he was writing editorials
(as editor of *The Overland Monthly*) on the unromantic ugliness of
such place names as Poker Flat and Red Dog Gulch, advising young
writers to steer away from the appellation "honest miner," since "the
less said about the motives of some of our pioneers the better; very
many were more concerned in getting away from where they were, than
in going to any particular place." And in his editorial in the second
number of *The Overland Monthly* he prophesied that it would be 300
years before the red shirts of the pioneers would become romantic and
their high boots heroic. One of the worst of prophets, he had just
finished writing the story that would do more than anything else to
make the red shirts romantic and the high boots heroic. It was contained in the same issue.

The Luck of Roaring Camp had more than its author's own resistance to his environment to overcome. The resistance of proofreader
and printer was so strenuous that it was almost still-born—and American local-color with it. Cherokee Sal's profession shocked the young
lady who read proof. A reference to obstetrics threw her into hysterics.
And finally Kentuck's exclamation over the baby—"The d——d little
cuss!"—brought her hurriedly to the printer, who shared her appalled
conviction that the story should never see the light. Dictatorial interference alone saved it for the August number of the *Overland.* What

happened then was a publishing miracle, which brought offers from the *Atlantic Monthly,* a letter from Charles Dickens, and an announcement from Henry Adams that there was just one hopeful thing in a hopeless world—Bret Harte.

Harte is usually associated with the Argonauts of '49 and '50, whereas he is a writer of the later fifties and the sixties, writing of "the disused ditches, the scarred flats, the discarded levels, ruined flumes, and roofless cabins." His Yuba Bill he very probably rode beside, on some dusty stagecoach, but as he himself says in *A Lonely Ride:* "The road from Wingdam to Slumgullion (that is, in the heart of the mining country) knew no other banditti than the regularly licensed hotel-keepers." Harte's Indians were the Indians whose carcasses he saw floated by the raft-load down to Uniontown after a cutthroat revel of some upstanding citizens inspired by whisky and manifest destiny. His "heathen Chinee," who "for ways that are dark and for tricks that are vain" was so very peculiar, was one of the unfortunates who were being attacked with all the violence of anti-oriental chauvinism.

California "romance" and California "savagery" of the sort that appeared in Harte's writing give striking point to the story told by Mark Twain of how Harte drew the railroad tracks under the grizzly bear for the *Overland's* title-page. A grizzly, the old grizzly that had been the State's totem ever since the Bear Flag days, had been selected as emblem for the *Overland Monthly.* The grizzly was drawn, engraved and printed, but he seemed a very lonely bear. "As a bear, he was a success—he was a good bear—" says Mark. "But then, he was an objectless bear—a bear that *meant* nothing in particular . . . simply stood there snarling over his shoulder at nothing . . . But presently Harte took a pencil and drew these two simple lines under his feet and behold he was a magnificent success! the ancient symbol of California savagery snarling at the approaching type of high and progressive Civilization, the first Overland locomotive!" This, however, was not the only significance of the symbol, as Harte would prove by his almost immediate departure down those tracks for an Eldorado that lay in the opposite direction, the direction of the East and Europe. He left California's "savagery" to John Muir, in whose gentle hands the mining camps were erased from the mountains; and California's "high and progressive Civilization" to Henry George, whose *Progress and Poverty* was to issue from San Francisco.

The unshorn gentry of the mining towns had at first provoked satire among San Francisco wits, and then, by Harte's unpredicted gesture, romance. But satire remained a strong undercurrent. Twain's description of the celebrated jumping frog of Calaveras County might be a typically monstrous understatement for the "honest miner" himself: "You never see a frog so modest and straightfor'ard as he was, for all he was so gifted. And when it come to fair and square jumping on a dead level, he could get over more ground at one straddle than any animal of his breed you ever see." Twain, who had adopted his pseudonym in 1863, mounted as a humorist on the back of this frog, for he wrote the sketch and won his first fame all in one leap. He remained in California from May 1864 until December 1866, and worked on the San Francisco *Morning Call* for a few months. Of the writers with whom he had contact, most were humorists: it was the typical humor of the Comstock Lode era that crystallized in his style at this time— coupling the tall tale of the barroom with excessive understatement. By the time he left California, his popularity in the East had become enormous. And like Harte, he sought those greener pastures.

Besides Harte and Mark Twain, the *Golden Era,* the *Californian,* and the *Overland* had other contributors whose fame spread beyond the local boundaries. Prentice Mulford's rollicking satire of frontier heroics found great favor. Charles Warren Stoddard, the poet, a close friend of Harte, later became the celebrated author of *South Sea Idyls* and *The Lepers of Molokai.* Ina Coolbrith, who contributed poems to the *Californian* under Harte's editorship, was many years afterward named the "poet laureate" of California. *Songs from the Golden Gate* contains many of her finest lyrics. Another distinguished contributor was Edward Rowland Sill, author of *The Hermitage* and other volumes of verse.

Joaquin (Cincinnatus Heine) Miller, "the Poet of the Sierras," was deeply impressed by the city's literary atmosphere when he first came to San Francisco as a young man. "I have seen the world well since," he said many years later, discussing the *Golden Era,* "yet those carpeted parlors, with Joe Lawrence and his brilliant satellites, outshine all things else, as I turn to look back." His name, Joaquin—replacing the ridiculous Cincinnatus Heine—was derived from Joaquin Murrieta, the Mexican outlaw in California. Miller's fame, however, originated not in San Francisco but in London, where he became a nine days' wonder as a fiery poet and a convincing representative of the "Wild West," with his high top boots, red flannel shirt, a sombrero, and his long hair falling, Indian-fashion, upon his shoulders. In his grandiloquent poetry he celebrated the deeds of pioneers, Indians, and bandits amid the natural marvels of the West. Except for "Columbus," which is still in the school boy's repertoire, he is remembered today for his attitudes rather than for his verse. In his hilltop eyrie, "The Hights" (*sic*), overlooking Oakland, he settled down, after his wanderings abroad, to practice his odd histrionics until his death in 1913.

Ambrose Bierce was another who found elbowroom for the development of an even more intense individuality, but the stamp of the region upon him was of a different sort. For a quarter of a century he was a

literary figure, *the* local literary figure, and the years which he dominated stretched into an era vastly different from the era of the Argonauts
as the "unutterably gorgeous" society of the 1860's gave way to the
sand-lot crusades of "the terrible seventies." This was the era of novels
such as *On the Verge,* abounding in voluptuous ladies at the pianoforte,
and in French quotations; of the poets such as Richard Realf, whose
record for bigamy won as much sympathy as his record for bad verse;
of essays on Petrarch and of editions of Heredia. It was the era of the
false front, and it showed even worse propensities in the eighties—Greek
porticos flanked by bay windows, Corinthian columns leading up flights
of wooden steps, conical towers, and Queen Anne flourishes. From
Nob Hill to Barbary Coast, barbarism and greed destroyed the possibility of good work in the arts.

This was Ambrose Bierce's domain. He declared himself in 1877
with the first issue of the *Argonaut:* "It is my intention," he said, "to
purify journalism in this town by instructing such writers as it is worth
while to instruct, and assassinating those that it is not." His column,
appearing consecutively from 1868 to 1900, was a vivid experience in
the lives of innumerable Westerners. He had deliberately set himself
the task of direct attack on individuals. It was his moral function, and
possibly the only function open to him in his time and in San Francisco.
His style he had acquired in the beaver-hat age, an age of gesture and
flourish; and he patched it together with ideas of "elegance" gained in
London, and delivered his opinions with a bludgeon-like ponderosity
suitable for denting the pates of a hoodlum citizenry. He himself
summed up his literary proclivities in a fable: "A rattlesnake came
home to its brood to die—I have been bitten by the editor of a partisan
journal, it said."

Irony indeed—and poetic justice, perhaps—in the career of this
Titan who had San Francisco for his malfeasant Olympus, is the very
name of the column which carried his "homicidal paragraphs": *Prattle.*
Another irony is his mysterious end in Mexico, trailed by apocryphal
tales of an old man shot by a firing squad. Still another is the end met
by those disciples who called him "Master"—Herman Scheffauer, who
took his own life in a Berlin hotel, and George Sterling, who committed suicide in San Francisco's Bohemian Club. But these futilities
cannot be laid at Bierce's door, by calling him, as some critics have done,
a "death man." The style of the time, in a community of contradictions, was morbid. Bierce's own style, if it is measured in terms of the
resistance he put up to those contradictions, was one of tremendous
vitality.

To combat those same contradictions required even more vitality of
Bierce's successors. From an Oakland cannery, where ten hours a day
of taut nerves prevented a moment's attention to the frequent victims

who had their fingers snapped off by the machinery, Jack London was graduated to become "the prince of the oyster pirates." He has indicated the reason for his choice of a profession: "Every raid . . . was a felony. The penalty was state imprisonment, the stripes and the lockstep. And what of that? The men in stripes worked a shorter day than I at my machine." With Whiskey Bob, Joe Goose, Nicky the Greek, Soup and Stew Kennedy, Clam Bart, Irish and Oyster Kelly, Patsy Haggerty, Harmonica Joe, Hell and Blazes, and young Scratch Nelson of the monumental shoulders, he discovered the social conditions which fecundated his talent. Having nearly forfeited his life to a Chinese shrimp poacher who marooned him on an island off the Marin shore—a story he tells in *Tales of the Fish Patrol*—he learned enough wit to leave oyster pirating and seek the primitive salt in a three-topmast schooner bound for a larger universe.

The Sea-Wolf, The Call of the Wild—these titles indicate not only London's place in space, on a bay crowded with ships that offered adventure far from "the man-city and its snarling roar"; they indicate also his place in time, when the romantic gesturer had to turn from Oscar Wilde's hothouse, and go hunting with "huskies" on the last big hunt before the world closed up its frontiers. Lonodon came back from the South Seas and wrote of nut-brown queens, who sat on swan-skins and greeted a chance traveler thus: "Stranger, I reckon you're sure the first white man that ever set foot in this valley. Set down an' talk a spell, and then we'll have a bite to eat. Which way might you be comin'?" And of primitive Teutons in the clothes of James Ward of Ward, Knowles and Company, who dictated to their stenographers by day and chased coyotes on the hills of Mill Valley by night.

But California's most spectacular and widely read California author was much more than a romantic gesturer. London's social philosophy was direct and radical. And the themes he dealt with were those of elemental physical conflict. In the handling of swift action he has scarcely been surpassed. Superlatively strong men stalk through his books, which were based directly on his own experiences. *Martin Eden* and *John Barleycorn* are semi-fictionized accounts of his own life, alternating between infantile romanticism and profound disillusionment. Mostly self-educated, he wrote, in 16 years, 43 volumes, besides acting as war correspondent and cruising in his yacht, the *Snark*. He died at his ranch in Glen Ellen, California, in 1916, of uremia.

He had long been a victim of ill health, disappointments at the hands of his friends, overwork in order to maintain a large establishment, and that battle against drink described in *John Barleycorn*. As a voice of his time and region, a spinner of yarns, a furious prophet, London gained an audience as large as that of any author of his time.

In this period, Frank Norris comes closest to the accent of greatness. And misses it. While London wrote of James Ward, who puzzled philologists at the University of California by his chants in primitive Germanic, Norris wrote of McTeague of McTeague's Dental Parlors, whose ambition was to have projecting from the corner window over Polk Street "a huge gilded tooth, a molar with enormous prongs, something gorgeous and attractive." While London wrote of Klondike huskies, Norris wrote of B Street Station:

"Near the station a bit of fence painted with a cigar advertisement reeled over into the mud, while under its lee lay an abandoned gravel wagon with dished wheels . . . Across the flats, at the fringe of the town, were the dump heaps, the figures of a few Chinese ragpickers moving over them . . . Across the railroad tracks, to seaward, one saw the long stretch of black mud bank left bare by the tide, which was far out, nearly half a mile. Clouds of seagulls were forever rising and settling upon this mud bank; a wrecked and abandoned wharf crawled over it on tottering legs; close in an old sailboat lay canted on her bilge . . ."

In the dynamic fictions of Frank Norris and Jack London an awareness of social forces is more evident than in any earlier Western writing. Norris, who came to California from Chicago at fourteen years of age, laid his early novels, *Blix, Vandover and the Brute,* and *McTeague,* in San Francisco. The essence of the city's life—at North Beach, Telegraph Hill, Nob Hill, Russian Hill, the Polk Street district—is reflected, although not without certain youthful exaggeration, in their pages. Norris determined to explore, on a large scale, the economic mainsprings of society. *The Octopus* and *The Pit* were the two first volumes of an intended trilogy, "The Epic of Wheat." In *The Octopus* is depicted the stranglehold of a railroad on California wheat growers and the entire State. *The Pit* is placed in Chicago, the world's wheat market. The third volume, *The Wolf,* to have been an account of the consumers of wheat the world over, was never written. In the midst of his ambitious plans, Norris died at the age of 32. Although marred by melodramatic excesses, a confusing tinge of mysticism, and an apparent lack of clear understanding of the issues involved, his novels, in their search for truth, in their tone, stand as distinguished landmarks at the threshold of the era of realism in American letters.

The society which London attacked with merciless fury and Norris probed with surgical ruthlessness was gently scolded in *The Lark,* edited by Gelett Burgess in the nineties, which for the whole of its two years sustained a wondrous buoyancy. It was read throughout the country, though Burgess often mocked the staid with such ditties as:

"I love to go to Lectures,
And make the Audience Stare,
By walking 'round upon their heads,
And spoiling People's hair!"

Conventional readers tolerated his nonsense because Burgess always kept it "clean" and because it was young as they never had been young; its more sophisticated comments escaped them, being whispered, as Albert Parry says, "in exquisite innuendo." Its chief contributors were Ernest Peixotto, Bruce Porter, Florence Lundborg, Carolyn Wells, Yone Noguchi—besides Burgess, whose "Purple Cow" classic first appeared in its pages. The New York *Times* nicknamed the group *Les Jeunes.* It was abandoned while still thriving and making money because, as Burgess wrote to Carolyn Wells, "I wanted it to die young and in its full freshness." Its whole staff, except Noguchi, moved to New York. But Burgess remembered San Francisco, for in *The Heart Line* he satirized both practitioners and victims of palmistry and astrology, cults which have always thrived in a city where so many have lived dangerously.

After the turn of the century an increasing number of young San Franciscans hoping for a career in literature yearned toward the cultural centers in the East and Europe; but many still received their impetus from the local scene. "The Man With the Hoe," published in a San Francisco newspaper, made famous overnight the young San Jose poet, Edwin Markham. The coterie of writers who frequently met at Papa Coppa's restaurant during the years just preceding the earthquake and fire of 1906 included Jack London, Wallace and Will Irwin, the short-story writer James Hopper, the imperious and aging Ambrose Bierce and his two brilliant pupils, poets Herman Scheffauer and George Sterling. Having learned from Bierce nothing of that writer's Swiftian vigor but only his magniloquence, Sterling was invoking in such volumes as *The Testimony of the Suns* a Platonic idea of California scenery, largely in the colors of purple and crystal. The Irwins each celebrated the Chinatown of the pre-fire era—Will in *Pictures of Old Chinatown* and Wallace in *Chinatown Ballads;* after the fire, Will wrote a requiem for "The City That Was," while Wallace, who had gained his early fame with such verses as *Love Sonnets of a Hoodlum,* turned to novel writing.

Charles Caldwell Dobie, 26 at the time of the fire—when he helped his mother transport the family treasures beyond the reach of the flames —was later to describe the more picturesque aspects of the city as it had been in *San Francisco: A Pageant, San Francisco Tales,* and *San Francisco's Chinatown.* Another of those for whom the "days of old, days of gold" have provided a rich vein to tap for literary purposes is Stewart Edward White, author of *The Gray Dawn* and *The Forty-Niners.*

Even before the turn of the century Gertrude Atherton's literary explorations had been leading her back to California's Spanish beginnings. She wrote of Magdalena Yorba, half-Spanish and born tongue-tied, and of her father, Don Roberto, a bank president, who practiced "hip-hip-hooray!" in his study and hanged himself with the American flag. From the Spanish period, which she celebrated in *The Dooms-woman, The Californians, The Splendid Idle Forties,* and *Rezanov,* she went on to the American era in *Ancestors* and *Patience Sparhawk,* and then, having covered California, shifted to Montana, Greece and Africa. *Rezanov,* love story of the visiting Russian officer and the San Francisco Presidio *comandante's* daughter, probably has remained her most popular novel. In *Adventures of a Novelist* (1932) she looks back on the five decades of her literary career.

Charles Norris, like his brother Frank, wrote "to make people think." Characteristic of his novels—conceived on a less ample scale than those of his brother—are *Brass,* an attempt to present different phases of "what we understand by marriage"; *Pig-Iron,* concerned with the materialistic influence on American life; and *Bricks Without Straw,* dealing with the ever recurring battle of ideals between parents and children. His wife, Kathleen Norris, who in her early youth was a San Francisco newspaper woman and a contributor to local periodicals, completed the noted family; her first publication was the novel, *Mother* (1911), and until her death in 1966 she produced nearly sixty novels, all observing the proprieties of middle-class family life.

Even Gertrude Stein, when she turned to description of the local scene in *The Making of Americans,* wrote of a vanished yesterday—of her girlhood in an old-fashioned house with verandas amid the tangled rambler roses and eucalyptus trees of suburban Oakland. But the postwar writers have now been succeeded by post-post-war writers who have put nostalgia behind them. William Saroyan might have been born anywhere—anywhere that there was a colony of Armenians—but he happens to have been born in the San Joaquin Valley, and the majority of his earlier stories reflect his goings to and fro about the rich valley earth and that much of the cosmos located between Carl Street, San Francisco, and the Civic Center.

John Steinbeck gathered California local color during most of his career—although straying from it in such books as *The Winter of Our Discontent* (1961) and *Travels with Charley* (1962)—and his sensitive, often lyrical renderings of the landscape and people of the Salinas Valley and Monterey ensured his place in the history of American letters. His best-known novel, *The Grapes of Wrath* (1939), will probably stand as one of the most moving and powerful books of twentieth-century American literature and it was this, most likely, that brought him the Nobel Prize for Literature in 1962. Steinbeck lived in the East until his death December 20, 1968. His ashes were returned to Salinas, California for interment in the family plot.

In the following twenty years, California did not produce a novelist whose work could match the impact of Saroyan and Steinbeck, although some novelists managed to illuminate the California scene, and especially that of the Bay Area. Niven Busch's *California Street* (1957) was more successful than his later *The San Franciscans* (1961). Far more compellingly, Stanford's Wallace Stegner has taken on the tensions and confusions of twentieth-century American life in two novels whose setting is the suburban communities south of San Francisco: *A Shooting Star* (1964) and *All the Little Live Things* (1967).

While Jack Kerouac's novel *On the Road* (1958) is held by some to be the archetypical work of the so-called beat generation of the 1950's, that period can be described more accurately as a generation of poets. San Francisco was an absolute welter of poets in these years—including Allen Ginsberg, Kenneth Rexroth, Kenneth Patchen, Robert Duncan, William Everson, and Lawrence Ferlinghetti—and their work has had measurable influence on American letters. Less can be said of the generation that has replaced them, for the hip generation is a generation of non-writers. Children of the full-flowering electronic age, they have found their life-styles in social and political activism and their poetry in music—and there are those who say that the "San Francisco sound" is the sound of a new American literature.

ART AND ARTISTS

Of all Apollo's embattled stepchildren who have attempted to create works of artistic value amid the Bay region's turbulent economic development, few have achieved so much as its painters and sculptors. Enormous is the variety of their work—much of it derivative and mediocre, some of it distinguished by originality. If theirs is not yet a tradition of masterpieces, they nevertheless have put behind them almost a century of aesthetic ferment, of tireless experimentation.

San Franciscans, whatever their qualifications for aesthetic judgment, have always been outspoken critics of their city's art and artists. Before a monument may be erected or a mural finished, citizens from the mayor downwards must have their say. An opinion delivered by members of the Art Commission—the city's final arbiter of art works and public buildings—condemned the proposed erection of Beniamino Bufano's gigantic statue of St. Francis on Twin Peaks. "It looks like a holdup," they said of the design for this 156-foot figure of stainless steel with arms upraised in supplication; and local factions were aroused anew by a syndicated columnist's nation-wide crusade against what he termed "God-awful statuary" as represented by Bufano's unorthodox model. This controversy had been preceded by the public turmoil attending the painting of murals in the Coit Tower, which was marked by political tail-twisting such as Diego Rivera practiced on his patrons in his Rockefeller Center murals in New York. To bring this hectic tradition up to date, Hilaire Hiler threatened to leave uncompleted his murals in the lobby of Aquatic Park unless plans were abandoned to install furniture not in keeping with his decorative motif. The files of the *Alta California,* the *Wasp,* the *Overland Monthly,* and the *News-Letter* offer plentiful testimony, in saltier epithets of earlier decades, that such controversies are by no means confined to the present generation.

The plastic arts have been a product and a reflection of the cultural growth of the Bay region, and of San Francisco in particular. As the rough-and-ready decades of the Gold Rush passed, a kind of poker-faced conservatism settled on the metropolis dominated by the bonanza millionaires. Its culture froze in the urbane, ornamental, shock-proof mold of the 1880's and remained always slightly out-of-date until rejuvenated after the calamity of 1906. Its painters, depending wholly on the patronage of a *nouveau riche* society, offered productions acceptable to a clientele whose tastes were dictated by extravagant notions that had nothing to do with art. In their imitation villas and chateaux the families of the bonanza elite wanted interior decoration that would be "elegant" and dazzling and grand, something flamboyant enough to impart an overwhelming impression of social prestige. Whenever these "cultural accoutrements" could not be produced locally in sufficient quantity, all Europe was ransacked for an astonishing assortment of paintings, sculpture, stained glass, tapestries, furniture, and bric-a-brac. The result, as that gaudy generation's sophisticated and refined descendants laughingly acknowledge, was hideous and absurd.

If, as John P. Young's history of San Francisco points out, most of the city's literati in the 1860's ignored the local scene, "no such accusation can be brought against the painters of the period, for their subjects were almost wholly Californian." Pioneer of this California School was the artist of whom the *Alta California's* discerning critic observed: "Few men dare paint flesh, against a pink cushion, Nahl has dared, and won (!)" This was with reference to Charles Christian Nahl's (1818–75) three separate renderings of *The Rape of the Sabine Women.* Painted in the pseudo-classical manner of the Düsseldorf School, this romantic work was long considered his masterpiece. Unfortunately for his reputation, many of his more relevant and minutely authentic studies of Gold Rush scenes have either been scattered among private collections or lost. Though the M. H. de Young Memorial Museum contains some of his paintings, his most representative works, including *The Fandango* and *Sunday at the Mines,* are in the E. B. Crocker Art Gal-

lery at Sacramento.   Descendant of a long line of German artists, Nahl
was indebted to his ancestry for what talent he had.   In subject matter
and technique he was influenced by the classic revival and by his early
studies under Horace Vernet in Paris.

Expert draughtsman that he was, Nahl revealed in his canvases a
love of detail for its own sake which make them primarily exercises in
careful documentation: genre paintings in which the sitter for a portrait,
accompanied by his favorite domestic animals, appears against a bucolic
background of his own countryside.   His restless energy and versatility
enabled him to make hundreds of drawings for engravers, supplying
popular demands for illustrations depicting Gold Rush scenes.   His
designs for the 18 woodcuts in Alonzo Delano's *The Idle and Industrious Miner, a Tale of California Life* are a marvel of draughtmanship
which enliven with droll humor that collection of melodramatic verses.
"It was inevitable," says Eugen Neuhaus in his appraisal of Nahl, "that
a man of his innate endowments and extraordinary powers of observation should be inspired to depict in his own medium . . . the early
California glorified by Bret Harte . . . ; and it is from these pictorial
records that we today get by far the best idea of those stirring times.
. . . The Nahl who will live in the annals of art is not the painter of
remote, academic historical scenes; it is the artist of the life in the California mines, as lived by an adventurous, polyglot society of Americans,
Indians, Mexicans, and Europeans, of which he himself was a part."

Painting in California would have remained a purely provincial art
had not the literature of the Gold Rush with its wondrous accounts of
the natural scenery of the West publicized for the Atlantic seaboard and
for Europe the Sierra Nevada's fabulous grandeur.   To the "increasing
astonishment and reverential awe and rapture" of millions of Americans,
the "California School" arose to rival those landscape painters who were
glorifying the Hudson River Valley.   Prodigious as these Hudson River
wonders appeared, they presumably could be put to shame by more
gigantic representations of the "magnificent scenery of that marvellous
region, where the roar of the cataract and the roll of the thunder
reverberate like the tread of the countless millions who evermore march
to the westward."

If today the vast landscapes painted by Albert Bierstadt (1830-
1902) seem impressive only in size, they nevertheless furnish a com-
mentary on the popular taste which once acclaimed them as masterpieces.
Their depiction of cyclopean gorges and mountain peaks—with every
detail, down to the minutest leaf and pebble, described with an exacti-
tude approaching photography—have also a certain expansive ˙gusto
which must have appealed to a public thrilled by the first full flowering
of its national spirit.   Bierstadt, born in Düsseldorf and brought to
America as a child, came West with General Lander's expedition of

1858. His *Rocky Mountains,* a huge canvas of ponderous detail and uncertain perspective, "threw the people into an ecstasy of delight" and he "bounded at one step to celebrity." S. G. W. Benjamin, whose *Art in America* confutes some of the prevailing artistic credos of his generation, remarks that since Bierstadt was "naturally an artist of great ability and large resources," he "might easily have maintained a reputation as such if he had not grafted on the sensationalism of Düsseldorf a greater ambition for notoriety and money than for success in pure art."

Bierstadt's contemporary, who succeeded him as "artist in waiting to the Yosemite Valley," was Thomas Hill (1829-1908). Beginning his career as a coach painter, Hill depicted panoramic views of entire mountain ranges which constituted the *reductio ad absurdum* of the California School's approach to landscape painting. His celebrity, like Bierstadt's, was spectacular; but today the works of these two boosters of Western natural scenery are looked upon as curiosities of a fabulous epoch.

The reputation of Thomas Moran (1837-1926) has suffered less from the refinement of popular taste than either of these flamboyant representatives of the California School. Having studied abroad, he enriched his canvases with the influence of Turner. If in his own time his works received less vociferous acclaim than inferior productions, his solid talent is today being appreciated. With William Keith's, the landscapes of Moran represent the best accomplishments—almost the sum and substance—of the California School.

Like Bierstadt, Hill, and Moran, Toby Edward Rosenthal (1848-1916) achieved celebrity abroad. Born in New Haven, Connecticut, he studied in San Francisco with the Mexican painter, Fortunato Arriola, in Munich at the Royal Academy, and with Raupp and Piloty. After gaining local fame, he maintained a studio in Munich, where he turned out excellent examples of the solid craftsmanship, the minuteness of literal detail, the sentiment and the "homely philosophy" of the Munich school of genre painters. His method of painting was laborious, scholarly; he spent three years in literary research, travel, and sketching to produce a single canvas, *The Trial of Constance de Beverley* (illustrating Scott's *Marmion*), now in the possession of Stanford University. "I have spared," he wrote in 1882 while at work on it, "no labor, time, nor money in my endeavour to make *Marmion* my greatest work," and the remark reveals his attitude toward painting; to him it was related to archeology, literature, philosophy. Only incidentally, however, can Rosenthal be considered a Bay region painter. His *The Cardinal's Portrait* and the *Seine Madonna,* both at the California Palace of the Legion of Honor, keep his curious local reputation alive.

It was only natural, once the novelty of wealth had begun to wear off and a new generation had been born to inherit it, that the patrons of art should take their cultural ambitions less casually. It was inevitable, too, that artists of the Bay area should forsake the old methods and adopt the technique of the Barbizon School—exemplified by such painters as Corot and Millet, who strove to render nature in her aspects of light and air rather than in pictorial detail. Yet of the San Francisco painters who came under the influence of the forerunners of Impressionism, only one seems to have gained a lasting distinction.

William Keith (1838-1911), born in Scotland, came to California in 1859. Eschewing the colossal marvels so loved by Bierstadt and Hill, he translated the more benign aspects of the lower altitudes into turgid. dreamy landscapes, painted with the molasses-like *impasto* that was a fault common to the Düsseldorf School, resulting from the use of bitumen. He was content to paint brooding and tranquil landscapes— the interplay of light and shade in groves of live oaks, forest glades, hillsides, and brooks. His style relates him somewhat to the Barbizon school; his lyric tranquillity, to George Inness, who was his intimate friend. His ambition, like Vincent Van Gogh's, was to achieve with paint the effect of music. Often he succeeded. Unfortunately, his use of bitumen to achieve subtlety of tone has caused many of the paintings to fade into indistinctness. Keith was the only California painter to whom a whole room was devoted in the United States section of the Panama-Pacific International Exposition's Fine Arts Galleries, yet until recently he has remained almost unknown outside the State. At the Keith Memorial Gallery in St. Mary's College at Moraga and at the Bohemian Club in San Francisco are many of his paintings.

The influence of Keith was strong on the minor painters who banded together in the Bohemian Club after its foundation in 1872. Little of the California sunlight is reflected in Arthur Mathews' somber work, but his murals in the Mechanics'-Mercantile Library, in the Lane Medical Library, and in the Masonic Temple illustrate an architect's sense of values. Typical of Gottardo Piazzoni's conventionalized California seacoast and hill country landscapes are his Public Library murals, subdued in tone. A sincere and accomplished landscapist, Xavier Martinez settled in Piedmont to paint the quiet beauties of the East Bay hill country in a number of canvases owned by the Oakland Art Gallery. Other Bohemians were Bruce Porter, architect and mural painter; Charles Dickman and Henry Joseph Breuer, landscapists.

Twenty-three local artists organized in 1871 the San Francisco Art Association and the following year opened headquarters in a loft-like gallery over a market, where as a visitor to their spring exhibitions put it, "Art was pervaded with the aroma of fish and the sound of the butcher's cleaver was heard." With a collection of casts of classic statuary—the gift of the Republic of France to this gallant undertaking of culture in the Far West—the association opened its school in 1874 with Virgil Williams as master. From such humble beginnings the association was elevated when Edward F. Searles, who had married Mark Hopkins' widow, presented it in 1893 with the Nob Hill castle of the railroad tycoon. The house was described by Amelia Ransome Neville as "a mess of anachronisms. One entered portals of a feudal castle to pass into the court of a doge's palace, all carved Italian walnut with a gallery around the second story where murals of Venetian scenes were set between the arches. These were the work of Jules Tavernier, French artist, who stopped in California after a trip to the South Seas, where he painted long before Gaugin." In gratitude, the association named its school the Mark Hopkins Institute of Art.

The first California sculptor whose name reached beyond the State was Douglas Tilden (1860-1935) who, himself deaf from the age of five, studied in Paris with the deaf-mute sculptor Paul Chopin. At intersections along San Francisco's Market Street, the heroic-style commemorative monuments for which he was famous overlook the passing traffic—the *Mechanics' Monument* with its three brawny artisans straining to force a huge mechanical punch through a plate of metal, the *Native Sons' Monument* with its bronze miner waving a flag, the *Spanish War Monument* with its young soldier marching beside an equestrian Victory. Public parks and squares are plentifully adorned with the sculpture of such pupils of Tilden's as Robert Ingersoll Aitken (1878—), sculptor of the *Victory Monument* in Union Square and the *William McKinley Monument* in Golden Gate Park, and M. Earl Cummings (1876-1936), sculptor of the *Hall McAllister Monument* beside the City Hall and the *Robert Burns Monument* in Golden Gate Park.

To the rest of the country until recent years, however, Tilden's self-taught younger contemporary, Arthur Putnam (1873-1930), was almost the personification of California sculpture. From youthful experience in riding, driving cattle, working in the forest, and laboring in a South San Francisco slaughterhouse, Putnam gained a remarkable knowledge of animal life, tamed and untamed. Masterful in composition, his bronze lions, leopards, and pumas show close observation, a thorough knowledge of animal anatomy, and a sensitive feeling for rhythm and movement. His figures of children, rabbits, and fish equal in charm his savage subjects. Among his best known works are *The Snarling Jaguar* in New York's Metropolitan Museum and *The Death* in the Boston Museum. The California Palace of the Legion of Honor has a collection of his works.

At the Panama-Pacific International Exposition in 1915 (where Putnam was represented only by an ornate mermaid fountain modelled from his designs—described by Sheldon Cheney as "typical of the fine strength of his work, and at the same time appealing by the grace of its sinuous lines") one of his students, Ralph Stackpole, was exhibiting a variety of sculpture, including *The Man with a Pick,* which was "justly admired as a sincere portrayal of a simple laboring type," and an unnamed kneeling figure by the Palace of Fine Arts lagoon, "one of the most appealing bits of all the Exposition sculpture, well expressing devotion and reverence." Another young San Francisco sculptor represented was Haig Patigian, whose bas-relief friezes and four nude male figures —*Steam Power, Invention, Electricity,* and *Imagination*—for the Palace of Machinery served "to carry out the sense of immensity and strength that characterizes the entire building," although "lacking the refinement that would make them interesting as something besides vigorous types."

The wealth of sculpture and painting displayed at the 1915 exposition was to "focus the artistic expression" of San Francisco Bay region artists as the art of the Columbian Exposition at Chicago had done for the artists of the Nation. The "far-reaching effect" of the Panama-Pacific Exposition, wrote Cheney, was to show "the immense value of coordination of all the arts . . . The great thing here is the complete harmony of purpose, of design, and of color, in the combined work of architects, sculptors, painters, and landscape gardeners." It had the farther-reaching effect, perhaps, of educating public taste to the point where for the first time local artists could begin to expect informed criticism of their work.

Judging "the first definite exposition of the new point of view crystallized by the influence of the Panama-Pacific International Exposition," a critic of the San Francisco Art Association's Forty-second Annual Exhibition was pleased to note that at last "the noble lines of the California hills are being painted without pseudo-idealistic, romantic preconceptions." Comparing the canvases on view at the latter exhibition with "previous Western 'animals',," a critic in *The International Studio* found "almost no vestige of the 'brown sauce' school of yesterday" and little which was "reminiscent of Keith, Whistler, and the Barbizon School—three influences which, but a very short time ago, dominated the California annual exhibitions."

In the exposition's Palace of Fine Arts, the French section had exhibited "a number of examples of the new and ultra-new schools, from Monet and Degas to Redon and Puy." During the quarter-century interval before San Francisco staged its next exposition, local artists began to modify their styles under influences even more revolutionary— Cézanne, Van Gogh, Picasso, Rousseau, di Chirico, Dali, and the other godfathers of modern art. Among others, Lucien Labaudt and Jane Berlandina were successful in grafting the best traditions of French art upon the local heritage. Some of the influences were first-hand ones. Henri Matisse, for example, spent some time in San Francisco painting the Steinhart Aquarium's tropical fish. Foujita came to teach some of modern Japanese art's pellucid quality to a group which was naturally receptive to an oriental treatment of local materials. When the Mexican muralist, Diego Rivera, came to paint frescoes for the San Francisco Stock Exchange and the California School of Fine Arts, his influence on many of the local painters—Victor Arnautoff, Ralph Stackpole, and Bernard Zakheim, among others—was tremendous. The visit of German exile Hans Hoffman, the Munich abstractionist, to teach summer classes at the University of California greatly inspired a group of the younger East Bay artists, including Vaclav Vytlacil, Beckford Young, Edgar Dorsey Taylor, and Florence Swift.

Even the California School of Fine Arts (as the Mark Hopkins Institute of Art had been renamed upon its removal to new quarters on Russian Hill in 1926), which had hitherto exhibited an academic bias, responded suddenly to the new influences. Feeling that the kind of painting they had learned abroad from followers of impressionism or pointillism offered no further promise of development, many of the painters associated with the school became devotees of Cézanne. Two of these, Lee Randolph and Spencer Macky, studied briefly in Paris in 1926 under André Lhote, teacher and exponent of Cézanne's methods. The courses given here by Arnold Blanch and Maurice Sterne furthered the spread of modern influences. In later years the school, then directed by Douglas MacAgy, kept well abreast of contemporary developments. Members of its faculty in the 1940's were such distinguished local artists as Ansel Adams, Dorr Bothwell, William Gaw, James McCray, David Park, and Clay Spohn. To the school also come noted New York artists as sessional instructors. Industrial designer Walter Landor, ceramist Carlton Ball, and jewelry designer Franz Bergmann conducted notable classes in their respective fields.

Aside from a series of exhibitions held at the Palace of Fine Arts following the 1915 exposition, no public galleries presented really comprehensive collections of foreign masterpieces until 1930. Lloyd Le Page Rollins, appointed director of San Francisco's California Palace of the Legion of Honor, then made it his policy to secure traveling exhibits of international importance; his policies were continued by Dr. Walter Heil. The huge annual exhibitions of contemporary American work which the Palace of the Legion of Honor inaugurated in 1946 promised to give an important impetus to local painting. During recent years the M. H. de Young Memorial Museum also has presented frequent showings of important contemporary painting, both American and foreign. In 1935 the San Francisco Art Museum in the Civic Center was opened under the competent, dynamic leadership of Dr. Grace McCann Morley. It has since become a center of education and appreciation of modern art. The response of the public has been remarkable.

During the 1930 depression the earliest large Government-supported mural job, the decoration of Coit Tower, undertaken by the Civil

Works Administration in 1933, was a cooperative endeavor involving a number of San Francisco's best-known artists, including Ralph Stackpole, Bernard Zakheim, Lucien Labaudt, Victor Arnautoff, Otis Oldfield, Rinaldo Cuneo, John Langley Howard, William Hesthal, Jane Berlandina, Ray Boynton, and Maxine Albro. The murals, showing particularly the influence of Diego Rivera, are distinguished by skilled craftsmanship. Many of these artists came together soon afterward in the WPA Art Project, whose decoration of the Aquatic Park Casino was one of the stellar achievements of the WPA program nationally; their work is to be seen in public buildings throughout the Bay Area. And again at the close of the same decade, the Golden Gate International Exposition employed many of the best local talents in a large-scale endeavor —painting, modeling, decorating—while at the same time it made available for study the most comprehensive world-wide collection of art yet seen here.

On the eve of World War II, San Francisco artists united, putting to use their rich experience in collaboration to stage a huge open-air art show which attracted 30,000 visitors. After the interruption of the war years they formed in 1946 a widely representative Committee for Municipal Art to create public support for an annual open-air exhibit to be financed by Art Commission appropriations.

In San Francisco as elsewhere, the mid-1940's found artists responsive to a variety of influences. No longer dominant was the social-scene school of the pre-war years, following the lead of the Mexican muralists —as perhaps most clearly represented by the large murals of Bernard Zakheim in the Jewish Community Center and the University of California Medical School, crudely drawn, beautifully designed, at once complex and brutal. The distinctively Californian work of the watercolorists with its nervous brushwork and vivid palette—in which Dong Kingman and George Post were outstanding exponents—still held, of course, a commanding place in the local scene. But San Francisco painters were more and more following such international trends as surrealism—reflected by Dorr Bothwell, Leah Rinne Hamilton, Clay Spohn, and others; expressionism—as seen in such work as Karl Baumann's and Theodore Polos'; abstraction—of which Claire Falkenstein, George Harris, and Charles Howard were distinguished exponents. More and more the work of artists who had previously worked in a realistic direction, such as Emmy Lou Packard and Hamilton Wolf, was showing the deeper apprehension of reality sought in abstract experiment; and the work of some of the youngest artists, such as Robert McChesney and Byron Randall, likewise was demonstrating the trend toward imaginative transcendence of the literal.

Of Matthew Barnes, a San Francisco painter whose long career made him a contender for national recognition, William Saroyan once wrote: "As he sees it, the world is a place where all who live are no more than visitors . . . A lonely place. Earth and sea and sky, mountain and plain and tree. Sun and Moon. And then the places of men: road and gate and house . . . City and streets and the immortal visitor of the earth: yourself."

The plastic arts in particular underwent a renascence in the Bay Area, constituting a "school" in at least the geographical sense. Ralph Stackpole was the leader, with his adaptation of the earthy simplicity of Mayan art to themes that were modern but nearly always elemental. His granite proletarian figures beside the entrance of the San Francisco Stock Exchange are representative of his work. This building, constructed in 1929, features interior bas-reliefs by other notable sculptors of the period—Ruth Cravath, Adeline Kent, and Robert Howard—while the Maritime Museum's facade (1939) shows the simple, decorative art of Sargent Johnson, and its interior boasts two animal sculptures by Beniamino Bufano. Bufano, of course, has long since become one of San Francisco's more pungent legends, and is one of her few workers in the plastic arts whose reputation has transcended regional appreciation. His massive, stylized human and animal figures are scattered throughout the Bay Area; many of them, suitably, can be found in parks and children's playgrounds, for Bufano's work has a special appeal for children—and Bufano himself has long maintained that children are the only critics to which he cares to pay heed. His most famous works are the statues of Sun Yat Sen in St. Mary's Square (1937) and the renowned St. Francis of Assisi currently on display in front of the Longshoremen's Memorial Building on the waterfront.

Unlike literature, the plastic and graphic arts have not suffered from the generation gap; the present generation still expresses itself in art, as any one of several annual arts festivals—from Berkeley to Santa Rosa—will indicate, and does so with a high degree of skill and imagination. San Francisco herself remains in the mainstream of the art world, and while she has yet to effectively challenge the continuing eminence of New York (or the renascence going on in Los Angeles), the work of her artists continues to find its way into American life. New, and sometimes startling, approaches to the cinematic arts attempted by San Francisco's "underground" film makers have had considerable influence. Even more significant has been the "psychedelic" poster art of such painters as Wes Wilson, whose broadly stylized convolutions have been systematically mimicked in everything from television commercials to billboard advertising. Art is alive and well in North Beach, in the Haight-Ashbury, in Berkeley, and the artists of the Bay Area will find their niche in the future.

Calendar of Events

The events listed below, with few exceptions, are held annually in San Francisco.

JANUARY

San Francisco Sports & Boat Show, Cow Palace. Golden Gate Kennel Club All Breed Dog Show, Cow Palace.

FEBRUARY

Chinese New Year Celebration, Chinatown.

MARCH

Mobile Home & Travel Show, Cow Palace. St. Patrick's Day Parade. Junior Grand National Livestock Exposition & Horseshow, Cow Palace. Macy's Flower Show, Macy's, Stockton & O'Farrell Sts. Antiques Show & Sale, Brooks Hall.

APRIL

Easter Sunrise Services, Mt. Davidson. Spring Comes to Maiden Lane, late March, early April (Thursday, Friday, Saturday). Cherry Trees in Bloom, Japanese Tea Garden, Golden Gate Park, first week in April. International Sport Cycle Exposition, Brooks Hall. Nihonmachi Cherry Blossom Festival, Japantown and Japanese Trade Center, late March, early April. Boy Scouts of America "Scout-O-Rama," Cow Palace, alternate years in Oakland, held at Oakland Coliseum. Rhododendrons in Bloom, Golden Gate Park & Union Square, late April-early May.

MAY

Latin American Fiesta, Mission District, early May.

JUNE

Upper Grant Avenue Street Fair, Grant Ave. from Vallejo to Filbert St.

JULY

Fourth of July Celebration and Fire-works Display, Candlestick Park.

AUGUST

Ice Follies, Winterland. San Francisco Flower Show, Hall of Flowers, Golden Gate Park. Ringling Bros. and Barnum & Bailey Circus, Cow Palace.

SEPTEMBER

San Francisco Municipal Outdoor Art Festival, Civic Center Plaza.

OCTOBER

British Week. International Ski and Winter Sports Show, Cow Palace. Blessing of the Fishing Fleet, Church of SS. Peter and Paul and Fisherman's Wharf. Columbus Day Celebration, North Beach, Aquatic Park. Grand National Livestock Exposition, Horse Show & Rodeo, Cow Palace.

NOVEMBER

Antique Show & Sale, Brooks Hall. San Francisco International Film Festival, Palace of Fine Arts Theater, late October, early November. Import Car Show, Brooks Hall.

SPORTS

San Francisco Giants Baseball, Candlestick Park, April thru September. San Francisco Warriors Basketball, Civic Auditorium and Cow Palace, October-March. San Francisco 49ers Football, Candlestick Park, September-December. Wrestling, Cow Palace, once a month (Saturday). Master Mariners Regatta, San Francisco Bay, mid-May (Sunday).

PART II
"The City"

General Information

Air Services: San Francisco International Airport, 12 *m.* south of Post Office on US 101 in San Mateo County. San Francisco-Oakland Helicopter Airlines, between San Francisco Airport and Berkeley, Marin County, Palo Alto, San Francisco Heliport (Ferry Bldg.) and San Jose-Sunnyvale. Airport Bus Service, 375 O'Farrell.

Buses: Continental Trailways, 44 4th St. Greyhound Bus Lines, 7th near Market. Airport bus, 375 O'Farrell. *Interurbans:* A C Transit to East Bay, from 1st and Mission Sts. Northgate Transit to North Peninsula from bus stop near 275 Winston Dr. *Sightseeing Tours,* Gray Line, 420 Taylor.

Fares. Streetcars and Buses: Municipal Railway, 25¢, express, 30¢; Cablecars, 30¢; free transfers. Sunday and holidays tour ticket, 50¢. *Jitneys:* From Embarcadero, via Mission to County line, 30¢; to 22nd St., 20¢.

Railroads: Santa Fe, 425 Mission. Southern Pacific, 3rd and Townsend.

Bay Cruises: Gold Coast Cruises, Pier 45. Red & White Fleet, Pier 43½.

Bridges: San Francisco Oakland Bay Bridge; toll 50¢. Golden Gate Bridge; toll 50¢, pedestrians, 10¢.

Piers: Embarcadero, foot of Market Street.

Traffic Regulations: Speed limit 25 mph, except on freeways, then 55-65 mph as posted. Street parking prohibited during certain hours as indicated by signs or painted curbs. Wheels must be blocked against curb when parking on a grade.

Information Service: Better Business Bureau, 414 Mason; Calif. State Auto Assn. (A.A.A.), 150 Van Ness; Calif. State Chamber of Commerce, 275 Bush; Calif. State Dept. of Motor Vehicles, 1377 Fell; Chinese Chamber of Commerce, 730 Sacramento; Down Town Assn., 582 Market; International Hospitality Center of the Bay Area, 55 Grant Ave.; Japanese Chamber of Commerce of Northern Calif., World Trade Center; National Auto Club, 65 Battery; Redwood Empire Assn., 476 Post; San Francisco Bay Area Council, World Trade Center; San Francisco Chamber of Commerce, 420 Montgomery; San Francisco Convention & Visitors Bureau, Fox Plaza; San Francisco Hotel Assn., Inc., 370 Geary; San Francisco Public Library, Civic Center; Travelers Aid Society of San Francisco, 38 Mason; U.S. Forest Service, 630 Sansome; Visitors Information Center, 476 Post.

Motion Picture Theaters, 1st run: Alexandria, 5400 Geary; Alhambra, Polk & Green; Bridge, 3010 Geary; Cinema 21, 2141 Chestnut; Coronet, 3575 Geary; Fox Warfield, 982 Market; Golden Gate, Golden Gate Ave. at Taylor; Larkin, 816 Larkin; Metro, Union at Webster; Metro II, 2240 Union; Music Hall, 931 Larkin; Northpoint, 2290 Powell; Presidio, 2340 Chestnut; St. Francis, 965 Market; Stage Door, 420 Mason; Vogue, Sacramento & Presidio Ave.

Television Stations, 7. Radio, A.M., 12; F.M., 15.

Legitimate Theaters: Curran, 445 Geary; Geary, 415 Geary; Opera House, Van Ness & Grove.

Little Theaters: Committee, 836 Montgomery; Encore, 422 Mason; Little Fox, 533 Pacific; Playhouse Repertory, 422 Mason; Surf-Interplayers, 747 Beach.

Night Clubs: Basin Street West, 401 Broadway; Bocce Ball Club, 638 Broadway; Earthquake McGoon's, 630 Clay; Finocchio's, 506 Broadway; Playboy Club, 736 Montgomery; Red Garter, 670 Broadway; Sinaloa, 1416 Powell.

Hotels: Canterbury, 750 Sutter; Clift, Geary & Taylor; Del Webb's Townehouse Motor Hotel, Market at 8th; Fairmont, Calif. & Mason; Hilton, Mason & O'Farrell; Holiday Inn Hotel, Kearny & Washington; Huntington, 1075 Calif.; Jack Tar, Van Ness & Geary; Mark Hopkins, Calif. & Mason; Miyako, Post & Laguna; San Franciscan, 1231 Market; Sheraton-Palace, Market & New Montgomery; Sir Francis Drake, Powell & Sutter; St. Francis, Powell & Geary.

Motels: Cable Motel, 1450 Lombard; Continental Lodge, 2550 Van Ness; Holiday Inn, Civic Center, 50-8th Street; Holiday Inn, Fisherman's Wharf, 1300 Columbus; Holiday Lodge, Van Ness at Washington; Red Coach Motor Lodge, Polk & Eddy; Villa Roma, 1212 Columbus; Travelodge at the Wharf, 250 Beach.

Y.M.C.A.'s and Y.W.C.A.'s: Y.M.C.A. Assoc. Hq, 220 Golden Gate; Y.M.C.A. Hotel, 351 Turk; Buchanan Branch, 1530 Buchanan; Chinese Branch, 855 Sacramento; Embarcadero, Army & Navy, 166 The Embarcadero; Golden West, 333 Eucalyptus Dr.; Mission, 4080 Mission; Park Presidio, 360-18th Ave. Y.W.C.A. Hotel, 620 Sutter; Clay Street Center, 965 Clay; Western Addition Center, 1830 Sutter; Residence Club, 940 Powell.

Garages: Downtown. Civic Center Plaza Garage, Civic Center Plaza; Downtown Center Garage, Mason & O'Farrell; Fifth & Mission Parking, 833 Mission; Japanese Trade Center Garage, 1660 Geary; Nob Hill Center Garage, 1045 California; Olympic Garage, 665 Sutter; St. Mary's Square Garage, 433 Kearny; Union Square Garage, Geary, Post, Powell & Stockton.

Senior Centers: Downtown Senior Center, 445 O'Farrell; Golden Gate Park Senior Center, 37th Ave. & Fulton; Portola Senior Center, Felton & Holyoke; San Francisco Senior Center, Aquatic Park, Foot of Polk Street; Yerba Buena Senior Center, 1111 Buchanan.

RESTAURANTS

Downtown: Adolph's, 641 Vallejo; Alexis, 1001 California; Amelio's, 1630 Powell; Bardelli's, 243 O'Farrell; Ben Johnson, The Cannery; The Battery, 325 Sacramento; Bernstein's Fish Grotto, 123 Powell; Chez Leon, 124 Ellis; Chez-Marguerite, 2330 Taylor; The Coachman, 1057 Powell; David's, 480 Geary; Des Alpes, 732 Broadway; Domino Club, 25 Trinity; Doro's, 714 Montgomery; Ernie's, 847 Montgomery; Fleur de Lys, 777 Sutter; Grison's, Van Ness & Pacific; India House, 629 Washington; Red Knight, 624 Sacramento; La Bourgogne, 320 Mason; Laffite's, 2301 Powell; Le Boeuf, 545 Washington; Leopard, 140 Front; L'Etoile, 1075 California; Le Trianon, 242 O'Farrell; L'Orangerie, 419 O'Farrell; Omar Khayyam's, 196 O'Farrell; Owl 'N' Turtle, 615 Washington; Paoli's, 565 Commercial; Rathskeller, 600 Turk; Restaurant de France, 780 Broadway; Shadows, 1349 Montgomery; Trader Vic's, 20 Cosmo Place.

Historic San Francisco: Blue Fox, 659 Merchant; Jack's, 615 Sacramento; Garden Court, Sheraton Palace Hotel, Market & New Montgomery; Ritz Old Poodle Dog Restaurant, 65 Post; Schroeder's Cafe, 240 Front; Tadich Grill, 240 California.

Chinatown: Empress of China, 838 Grant Ave.; Far East, 631 Grant Ave.; Four Seas, 731 Grant Ave.; Golden Pavilion, Sacramento & Grant Ave.; Imperial Palace, 919 Grant Ave.; Kan's, 708 Grant Ave.; Louie's, 1014 Grant Ave.; Nam Yuen, 740 Washington; Sai-Yan, 641 Jackson; Sam Wo, 813 Washington; Tao Tao, 675 Jackson.

Italian: Alfred's, 886 Broadway; Caesar's, 2299 Powell; Del Vecchio's, 391 Broadway; Fior D Italia 621 Union; La Strada, 443 Broadway; Lupo's, 1042 Kearny; New Joe's, 540 Broadway; Oreste's, 118 Jones; Orsi, 375 Bush; Polo's, 34 Mason; Rocca's, 555 Golden Gate Ave.; Sorrento, 341 Columbus; Vanessi's, 498 Broadway; Veneto, Mason & Bay.

Fisherman's Wharf: Alioto's #8; Alioto's Pacific Fair Restaurant; Borruso's Lighthouse Seafood Grotto; Castagnola's; DiMaggio's; Exposition Fish Grotto #1; Fishermen's Grotto #9; Franciscan; Lighthouse Seafood Grotto; Meigg's Wharf, 99 Jefferson; Sabella's; Scoma's, Pier 47; Tarantino's Tokyo Sukiyaki, 225 Jefferson.

Western Addition: Bengal Lancer, 2032 Union; Blue Boar Inn, 1713 Lombard; Cafe El Portal, Fulton & 8th Ave.; Captain's Galley, 2241 Chestnut; Car Barn, 1725 Filbert; The Cooperage, 1980 Union; El Sombrero, 5800 Geary Blvd.; Hippo Hamburgers, Van Ness & Pacific; Luchina Russian Restaurant, 1829 Clement; Monroe's, 1968 Lombard; O Sole Mio, 2031 Chestnut; Old Colony, 2239 Clement; Original Joe's #2, 2001 Chestnut; Pine Tree, 3601 California; Place Pigalle, 3721 Buchanan; Suehiro, 1737 Post; Tia Margarita, 300-19th Ave.

ART MUSEUMS

California Palace of the Legion of Honor, Lincoln Park. Hours: 10 a.m. to 5 p.m. daily.

M. H. De Young Memorial Museum, Golden Gate Park. Hours: 10 a.m. to 5 p.m. daily.

San Francisco Museum of Art, War Memorial Veterans Building, Van Ness & McAllister. Hours: Tuesday-Friday 10 a.m. to 10 p.m., Saturday 10 a.m. to 5 p.m., Sunday 1 to 5 p.m., closed Monday & holidays.

International Child Art Center, Ghirardelli Square, 900 North Point. Hours: Tuesday-Friday 11 a.m. to 5 p.m., Saturday, Sunday 12 noon to 6 p.m.

Baseball: Candlestick Park, home of the Giants.

Basketball: Y.M.C.A., 220 Golden Gate Ave. Civic Auditorium & Cow Palace, San Francisco Warriors.

Billiards: (Only downtown parlors listed): Cochran's, 1028 Market; Country Club Billiards, 1849 Van Ness; Downtown Bowl Billiard Salon, Jones & Eddy; Palace Billiards, 949 Market.

Bowling: Bagdad Bowling, 1900 Noriega; Broadway Van Ness Bowl, 1463 Broadway; Downtown Bowl, Jones & Eddy; L & L Castle Lanes, 1750 Geneva; Lincoln Bowl, 319-6th Ave.; Marina Bowl, 1725 Filbert; Mission Bowl, 3140 Mission; Park Bowl, 1855 Haight; Sports Center Bowl, 3333 Mission.

Cricket: Julius Kahn Playground.

Cycling: (Bicycle renting establishments) Fischer Bicycle Shop, 640 Stanyan; Kezar Cyclery, 854 Stanyan; Lincoln Cyclery, 4621 Lincoln Way; Stanyan Street Cyclery, 672 Stanyan.

Fishing: Lake Merced, Skyline Blvd. and Harding Road; Municipal Pier at Aquatic Park, N. end of Van Ness Ave.; water front piers, along Embarcadero.

Football: Kezar Stadium; Candlestick Park.

Golf: Harding Park Golf Course, Harding Road & Skyline Blvd., 18 holes; Fleming Golf Course, located inside Harding Park, 9 holes; Sharp Park Golf Course, Highway #1, Pacifica, 18 holes; Lincoln Park Golf Course, 34th Ave. & Clement St., 18 holes; McLaren Park Golf Course, 2100 Sunnydale Ave., 9 holes; Golden Gate Park Golf Course, 47th Ave. & Lincoln Way, 9 holes. Free putting greens at Funston & Stern Grove. Driving cage at Funston.

Private Golf Courses: Olympic Club Golf Course, Skyline Blvd.; Presidio Golf Club, in the Presidio (U.S. Military Reservation); San Francisco Golf Club, Junipero Serra Blvd. & Brotherhood Way.

Handball: Y.M.C.A., 220 Golden Gate Ave.; Golden Gate Park— four courts, two indoor and two outdoor, located near Big Rec Playfield, 7th Ave. and Lincoln Way.

Ice Hockey: Cow Palace.

Ice Skating: Legg School of Ice Skating, 45-11th Street; San Francisco Ice Arena, 1557-48th Ave.

Riding: Golden Gate Park Riding Academy.

Rifle Range: Sharp Park, Highway #1, South Pacifica.

Roller Skating: Skateland at the Beach Roller Rink, Balboa & Great Highway.

Sailing: Lake Merced Sport Center—adjacent to Harding Park Golf Course on Skyline Blvd.

Skeet & Trap Shooting: Lake Merced Field, Skyline Blvd.

Softball: Rolph, Funston & Hayward Playgrounds.

Swimming Pools: (Municipal) Balboa Pool, San Jose Ave. & Havelock; Coffman Pool, Visitacion Ave. & Hahn; Fleishhacker Pool, Sloat Blvd. & Great Highway; Garfield Pool, 26th Street & Harrison; Hamilton Pool, Geary Blvd. & Steiner; King Pool, 3rd Street & Carroll Ave.; Larsen Pool, 19th Ave. & Wawona; Mission Pool, 19th Street & Linda; North Beach Pool, Lombard & Mason; Rossi Pool, Arguello Blvd. & Anza. (Private) Y.M.C.A., 220 Golden Gate Ave.; Y.W.C.A., 620 Sutter Street.

Park & Recreation Centers: Alamo Square, Hayes & Steiner; Alta Plaza, Scott & Washington; Aptos, Aptos & Ocean Ave.; Argonne, 18th Ave. bet. Geary & Anza; Balboa (Clubhouse), Ocean & Circular Ave.; Bayview, Third & Armstrong Streets; Bernal Heights, Moultrie St. & Jarboe Ave.; Big Rec, 7th Ave. & Lincoln Way; Cabrillo, 38th Ave. near Cabrillo; Cayuga, Cayuga & Naglee; Chalmers, Alice, Brunswick & Whittier; Chinese Playground, Sacramento & Waverly; Chinese Center, Mason & Washington; Cow Hollow, Baker bet. Filbert & Greenwich; Crocker-Amazon, Geneva Ave. & Moscow; Douglass, 26th St. & Douglass; Duboce, Duboce Ave. & Scott; DuPont Tennis Courts, 30th Ave. bet. Clement & Calif.; Eureka Valley, Collingwood Street near 18th St.; Excelsior, Russia & Madrid; Folsom, 21st St. & Folsom; Fulton, 27th Ave. & Fulton; Funston, Chestnut & Buchanan; Garfield, 26th & Harrison; Gilman & Griffith; Glen Park, Chenery & Elk; Grattan, Stanyan & Alma; Hamilton Center, Geary & Steiner; Hayes Valley, Hayes & Buchanan; Hayward Boys, 1001 Turk; Hayward Girls, Laguna bet. Golden Gate & Turk; Herz, Francis J., Visitacion & Hahn; Hunters Point Gym, #1 Kiska Road; Hunters Point Recreation

Center, 195 Kiska Road; Hunters Point Milton Meyer, 195 Kiska Road; Jackson, 17th St. & Carolina; Junior Museum, J. D. Randall, 16th St. & Museum Way; Junipero Serra, 300 Stonecrest Drive; Kahn, Julius, Spruce at Pacific; Kimbell, Raymond S., Geary & Steiner; Lafayette, Washington & Laguna; Larsen Park, 19th Ave. & Vicente; Laurel Hill, Euclid & Collins; Lee, Joseph, Oakdale Ave. & Mendell; McCoppin, 24th Ave. & Taraval; Merced Heights, Byxbee & Shields; Midtown Terrace, Clarendon Drive & Olympia Way; Miraloma, Omar & Sequoia Ways; Mission Dolores, 19th St. & Dolores; Mission, 19th St. & Linda; Mountain Lake, 12th Ave. & Lake; Murphy, J. P., 1960-9th Ave.; Noe Valley Courts, 24th St. & Douglass; North Beach, Lombard & Mason; Ocean View, Capitol Ave. & Montana; Parkside Square, 26th Ave. & Vicente; Peixotto, Sidney, 15th St. bet. Beaver & Roosevelt Way; Portola, Felton & Holyoke; Potrero Hill, 22nd St. & Arkansas; Presidio Heights, Clay near Walnut; Richmond, 18th Ave. bet. Lake & Calif.; Rochambeau, 24th Ave. bet. Lake & Calif.; Rolph, James Jr., Potrero Ave. & Army; Rossi, Angelo J., Arguello Blvd. & Edward; St. Mary's, Murray St. & Justin Drive; Silver Terrace, Thornton Ave. & Bayshore Blvd.; South Sunset, 40th Ave. bet. Wawona & Vicente; Stern Grove, 19th Ave. & Sloat; Storyland (Parties) Great Highway & Sloat Blvd.; Sunnyside, Forrester & Melrose; Sunset Recreation Center, 28th Ave. & Lawton; Sunset Heights, 12th Ave. & Pacheco; Sutter, Louis, University & Wayland; Upper Noe, Day & Sanchez; Visitacion Valley, Cora St. & Leland Ave.; Wawona Bowling Greens, 19th Ave. & Wawona; West Portal, Ulloa St. & Lennox Way; West Sunset (Bleachers), 41st Ave. & Quintara; Wills, Helen, Broadway & Larkin; Yerba Buena Center, 1111 Buchanan; Silver Tree Day Camp, Glen Canyon; Pine Lake Day Camp, West End of Sigmund Stern Grove.

CHURCHES

Only representative churches of denominations are listed below.

Advent Christian: Parkside Community Church, Ulloa & 24th Ave.

African Methodist Episcopal: Bethel AME, 970 Laguna.

African Methodist Episcopal Zion: First AME Zion Church, 2159 Golden Gate Ave.

Apostolic: The Apostolic Faith Church, 1227 Sutter.

Armenian: St. Gregory Armenian Apostolic Church, 51 Commonwealth.

Assemblies of God: Glad Tidings Temple, 1475 Ellis.

Baptist: First Baptist Church, Market & Octavia.

Christian: Forest Hill Christian Church, 250 Laguna Honda Blvd.

Christian Methodist Episcopal: Missionary Temple Christian, 1455 Golden Gate Ave.

Christian Science: 1st Church, California & Franklin.

Church of Jesus Christ of Latter-day Saints: 3715-26th Street.

Congregational: First Congregational, Post & Mason.

Episcopal: Grace Cathedral, California & Taylor.

Jehovah's Witnesses: North Beach Congregation, 1414 Hyde.

Jewish: Congregation Emanu-El, Arguello & Lake.

Lutheran: St. Paulus, Eddy & Gough.

Moslem Mosque: Islamic Center of S.F., Inc., 400 Crescent Ave.

Nazarene: Church of the Nazarene First, 300 Ulloa.

New Testament: Church of San Francisco, 1760 Washington.

Open Bible: Open Bible Church, 2135 Market.

Orthodox Eastern: Russian Holy Virgin Cathedral, 6210 Geary.

Pentecostal: Bethel Temple, 1325 Valencia.

Presbyterian: Calvary Presbyterian Church, Jackson & Fillmore.

Roman Catholic: St. Mary's Cathedral. Geary & Gough.

Satanic: Church of Satan, 6114 California.

Scientology: Church of Scientology, 414 Mason.

Seventh Day Adventist: Seventh Day Adventist Central Church, 1844 Broderick.

United Methodist: Glide Memorial, 330 Ellis.

Vendanta: Vendanta Society of Northern Calif., New Temple, 2323 Vallejo.

Yoga: International Society of Krishna Consciousness, Inc., 518 Frederick.

San Franciscans: A Portrait

"Nowhere in America is there less in evidence the cold theological eye, the cautious hand withheld, the lifted eyebrow, the distrust of playfulness . . ."
—GEORGE WEST

TO SHARE with San Franciscans their feeling for the city's elusive identity—that prevailing atmosphere which is to San Francisco what dynamic tempo is to New York, what Old World charm is to New Orleans—a visitor does best to wander about its streets. The city has a look of incredible venerability. What remains of the old San Francisco—the roaring boom town of the Argonauts, the Barbary Coast, and the bonanza days—consists mainly of a handful of once proud business buildings, crumbling and obscure, that somehow belie their conversion to modern usage by their appearance of having withstood the passage of an era of violence and romance. Elsewhere, in those parts of the city which survived the calamity of 1906, row on row of Eastlake wooden houses—with their bay windows, corner turrets, and fantastic scrollwork—are reminders of a fabulous past. But although San Francisco is more profoundly steeped in a tempestuous history than any other American city of its age of development, few landmarks of that history remain; the city, for the most part, is the city that rose from the debris of earthquake and fire. Even the rebuilt sections have a look of weathered age. Nor do those sprawling residential districts—real estate developments of more recent years—long escape the mellow tarnish of wind and weather. The very streets, cutting over hill and down valley with resolute forthrightness, are memorials to the men of the Gold Rush, whose roughshod surveys determined the city's main features, imposing on traffic a series of permanent inconveniences which are nevertheless excused for the dramatic vistas they provide. And the old-fashioned cable cars that lurch and sway with clanging bell up and down their precipitous slopes have long since brought to street transportation a spirit of almost festive novelty which it enjoys probably nowhere else.

A tradition which has behind it the most hectic and glamorous epoch of American pioneering is still the factor which determines much of the city's enigmatic charm and governs many of those political, economic, and cultural phenomena by which San Franciscans continue to astonish the world. Every principle of American democracy has been tested here, and what has emerged is a kind of collective wisdom by

which public affairs may be administered with a minimum of interference with personal liberty.   The average San Franciscan still adheres
to the pioneer concept of government: the less of it the better.   His
Argonaut forbears tried to do without it altogether, but found themselves at the mercy of social evils which nothing short of a harsh popular
tribunal could eradicate.   Their subsequent experience with municipal
administrations, reformist and otherwise, led them finally to devise a
city charter of such elaborate checks and balances that corruption on
a grand scale was forestalled.   By resounding majorities bond issues of
a dubious nature are voted down, but not appropriations for education,
for parks and playgrounds—or for expositions and bridges.

What is supremely important to San Franciscans is that they be let
alone to think and act as they please.   Here the accent has always been
on living, and however much the city has changed in other ways, it
neared the end of its first century as an American metropolis with no
let-up in that vigorous search for experience by which San Franciscans
have been enriching their lives since 1848. The difference nowadays
lies in a certain refinement of critical faculties which is having its effect
on all phases of the city's social life.   The crowds who attend concerts
and art exhibits, movies and cabarets, theatrical performances and the
opera constitute audiences whose verdict is something to be respected.
What San Franciscans like they applaud with a sensitive and overwhelming enthusiasm; what they believe will not please them they
simply avoid. The cuisine of their hotels and restaurants is still renowned
the world over; and the typical San Franciscan is something of an epi-
cure. The thousand-and-one treasures of the city's shops find a sophisticated response among San Franciscans to whom luxuries are, and
always have been, aids to graceful living rather than the accoutrements
of fashion. All sorts of exotic importations, brought in by the city's
various ethnic groups, contribute to the fun of being a San Franciscan.
This universal delight in just being alive here, which has amazed so
many outsiders, has its source very largely in a certain playfulness of
spirit—a natural gusto—by which rich and poor alike are able to draw
from some simple experience (a ride on a cable car or a dinner at
Paoli's) a sense of *joie de vivre*.

The Genteel Tradition was never able to take root here. The
virile ethics of the Argonauts forbade it. San Franciscans have always
shown an almost universal disregard for the haughtier privileges of great
wealth. Nob Hill was not a social success: the city's sense of humor,
its love of gaiety, its unfailing urbanity have excluded aristocratic exclu-
siveness. Its absentee aristocracy (descendants of the bonanza millionaires who have retired to estates down the Peninsula or in the
Marin hills) continue to make "The City" the hub of their social
whirl; but San Francisco itself has no recognizable "four hundred."

The city has not a single public place where formal attire is obligatory; almost the only social requirements are that one hold one's liquor well and behave like a gentleman—or a lady. The predominance of highly skilled workers, professional people, and technicians in its population— inevitable in a city which is much more a commercial than an industrial center—determines the social standard, outweighing even the labor movement's more highly publicized influence. But the middle-class influence is modified, not only by labor's strength, but also by the effects of the city's polyglot mixture of nationalities—its vast number of people who have come from every country under the sun, and while becoming citizens in all respects, have retained nonetheless the customs of their homelands.

The best way to insult a San Franciscan is to slap him on the back. Whatever violates his natural urbanity receives a chilly response. Like his Argonaut predecessors he continues to form friendships and choose business associates in the "partner" tradition of the Gold Rush. This delicate social process, which has repelled countless newcomers, has resulted in a population for whom individuality is the keynote; and those of a more gregarious nature quickly retire to places where their back-slapping propensities will be appreciated. Despite this unkind form of social selectivity, San Francisco has been constantly acquiring new citizens from every state of the Union and from abroad—and more than ever during the feverish years of World War II when it was thronged with newcomers arriving to work in its great war industries or passing through on their way to the war fronts. Those who remain partake inevitably of the city's social tradition; and so profoundly will it affect them that, though they may journey to the ends of the earth, this place will always be home to them. The citizen of San Francisco is a citizen of the world.

The City's Growth

*"The Yankees are a wonderful people, wonderful. Wherever
they go they make improvements. If they were to emigrate in
large numbers to hell itself, they would somehow manage to
change the climate."*
—General Mariano G. Vallejo (to President Lincoln).

AT THE crossroads of the great migrations of antiquity arose such
cities as that magical pandemonium the Argonauts inhabited:
Nineveh, Babylon, and Jericho. Although the sin and splendor
of the bonanza epoch have long since given way to the iron age of
corporate industrialism, the successors of the Argonauts have striven
mightily to retain their heritage of hilarious action. Somehow it is all
here, chastened and dispersed, but no less explosive than in the era
before "The Fire": the vigorous delight in living, the susceptibility to
tremendous projects, the vengeful spirit of the Vigilantes, the profound
sophistication and the capacity for Homeric laughter.

THE VILLAGE OF YERBA BUENA (1835–1848)

Dusty, fleabitten little Yerba Buena was in 1835 an insignificant
outpost long frequented by roving seafarers, Russians, and a few nondescript traders who smelled of hides and tallow. But for four redwood
posts covered with a ship's foresail which De Haro's harbormaster,
William Antonio Richardson, erected on "La Calle" in 1835, San Francisco's original site was little more than a waste of sand and chaparral
sloping down to a beach and a small lagoon. *El Parage de Yerba
Buena* (The Little Valley of the Good Herb) it had been named long
before, because of the aromatic vine (*Micromeria Chamissonis*) found
in the underbrush there.

Richardson, young master mariner who had deserted the British
whaler *Orion* in 1822, was appointed Captain of the Port of San Francisco by Governor Pablo Vicente de Sola in 1835 when the Bay was
declared a port of entry. Stocking his huge tent with wheat, hides,
and vegetables, trader Richardson soon supplemented his official duties
by raising two sunken schooners which he put into service transporting
rancho products from one end of the Bay to the other at somewhat
exorbitant rates.

Democratic self-government, of the bureaucratic sort decreed by the
Mexican Republic, came to Yerba Buena before the town itself arrived.
Citizens of the *partido* (civil district) of San Francisco, on Governor

Jose Figueroa's orders, assembled in the Presidio on December 7, 1834 to choose electors for the *ayuntamiento* (district council). On the following Sunday Don Francisco de Haro was elected to the *ayuntamiento* as *alcalde* for the projected *pueblo* of Yerba Buena. As a gesture toward establishing the town, Don Francisco marked out on the ground, from the site of Yerba Buena to the Presidio, *La Calle de la Fundacion* (Foundation Street) and retired thereafter to Mission Dolores to look after private matters.

Richardson, on July 1, 1836, suddenly acquired a neighbor as resourceful as himself—one equipped to do business in really sumptuous style. Jacob Primer Leese, Ohio-born partner in a Monterey mercantile firm, sailed into the cove aboard the barque *Don Quixote* with a $12,000 cargo of merchandise, a six-piece orchestra, and enough lumber to erect a mansion. By July 4, on a lot adjoining Richardson's property, the amazing Mr. Leese had thrown up a frame house 60 feet long, and 25 feet wide. Borrowing two six-pounders from the Presidio and decking his domestic barn with bunting from ships in the cove, Leese summoned all leading Mexican families north of the Bay to an Independence Day celebration—which lasted two days and a night.

Among the guests at Leese's patriotic housewarming had been Captain Jean Jacques Vioget, of the Peruvian brig *Delmira,* who was also a surveyor and a lively man with a fiddle. In the autumn of 1839 this versatile Swiss was commissioned by *Alcalde* de Haro to make the first survey of Yerba Buena. By 1840 on the west side of Montgomery Street, between Clay and Sacramento Streets, next door to the new Hudson's Bay Company's post and saloon he was serving ship's captains, supercargoes, merchants, and clerks in a tavern.

Thirty families, in 1841, comprised the village population. The most impressive house was that of Nathan Spear, who was running the Bay area's only flour mill. Jacob Leese had now transferred his business to Sonoma. Richardson was living across the Bay on his huge Rancho Saucelito, where he continued to collect customs and pocket the funds, claiming that his salary as harbor master was not paid and that he had no other source of income.

Governor Juan B. Alvarado's decrees, restricting trade with foreigners after 1841, drove the American whalers from San Francisco Bay to a new headquarters in the Sandwich Islands; and by 1844, outrivaled by the port of Honolulu, Yerba Buena had fallen back into obscurity. Though that same year saw the election of its first American-born *alcalde,* William Sturges Hinckley, the village continued to languish.

The mock-heroics of "Pathfinder" John Charles Frémont's raid on the Castillo de San Joaquin were Yerba Buena's first warning of impending change. Slipping over from Sausalito on July 1, 1846, the Yankee adventurer spiked the dismantled guns of the old fort. ("So far as can be known," says Hubert Howe Bancroft, "not one of the ten cannons offered the slightest resistance.") Thereafter, for a week, the habitues of Vioget's hangout gave themselves up to warlike gossip, forgetting to play billiards.

Suddenly, on July 9, the U.S.S. *Portsmouth* quietly dropped anchor in Yerba Buena's cove. The villagers—unaware of Commodore Sloat's flotilla off Monterey—were disturbed at breakfast by a roll of drums and a flurry of fifes. When they rushed to the Plaza, Captain John B. Montgomery's 70 sailors and marines were running up the Stars and Stripes on Mexico's flagpole atop the adobe Custom House. Down in the cove the *Portsmouth's* 21-gun salute rumbled into history across San Francisco Bay.

Captain Montgomery on August 26 appointed Lieutenant Washington Allen Bartlett first *alcalde* of Yerba Buena under the American flag. On September 15 Bartlett was confirmed in office by popular vote, with the same powers enjoyed by his Mexican predecessors. His first important decree ordered revision of Vioget's survey, which had served to locate building lots since 1839. Jasper O'Farrell, civil engineer employed for the job, discovered in 1847 that the Swiss tavern-keeper's streets intersected at two and a half degrees from a right angle. His prompt correction of this error, known as "O'Farrell's Swing," left building frontage and vacant lots projecting somewhat beyond the theoretically proper lines of nonexistent curbstones.

On the last day of July 1846, Samuel Brannan, the bombastic Mormon Elder, sailed in through the Golden Gate aboard the *Brooklyn* with his well-armed flock of Latter-day Saints, a hold crammed with farmer's tools, two flour mills, and a printing press. The Mormons provided all that was necessary to pull Yerba Buena out of its rut once more. Within a year· that place which had baffled the urbane and mystical Spaniards for three-quarters of a century would appear on the map of Alta California. Two years later the name of San Francisco would be blazoned in gold on the map of the world.

CAPITAL OF THE GOLD COAST (1848–1856)

"To this Gate I gave the name of 'Chrysopylae' or Golden Gate for the same reason that the harbor of Byzantium was called 'Chrysoceras,' or Golden Horn." Thus Frémont, after gazing at the Bay's entrance from a Contra Costa peak, adorned his report to the United States Congress with an erudite flourish. Little did he suspect how literal was to be the name he had given to that famous strait.

When Brannan's Mormon battalion landed at Yerba Buena in the summer of 1846, the village had 50 or 60 inhabitants. Sam's passengers and crew swelled its population by nearly six-fold. The Plaza, newly named Portsmouth Square, already had its fringe of gambling houses, a hotel and a saloon, and its nucleus of rough characters.

Brannan's bull-throated oratory and domineering personality enabled him to assume leadership of the town's affairs. Within a year he had performed the first marriage and preached the first sermon under American rule, seen to the holding of the first jury trial, established the first newspaper, and sunk all his money in Yerba Buena real estate. In his *California Star,* on January 30, 1847, appeared *Alcalde* Bartlett's ordinance which cut the ground from under the scheme of Thomas Larkin and General Vallejo to adopt the name "San Francisco" for a rival townsite on Carquinez Strait. "It is Hereby Ordained," said the ordinance's clinching paragraph, "that the name of San Francisco shall hereafter be used in all official communications and public documents, or records appertaining to the town [of Yerba Buena]."

Whatever Sam Brannan's original intentions—ostensibly he had brought his cargo of Saints around Cape Horn to establish for Brigham Young a Mormon commonwealth in California—he soon fell somewhat from grace with his followers—and with *Alcalde* Bartlett. The fiery Elder was too deeply involved financially, however, to move on to greener pastures; and though his paper's editor had been rolled down Portsmouth Square in a barrel for lukewarm local patriotism, Sam supported a campaign for public education which resulted in establishment of San Francisco's first school—a frame house on Portsmouth Square which also served successively as town-hall, church, and jail. His own contribution to the spirit of progress was a special edition of the *Star* of which 2,000 copies, carried by horse-borne courier, boosted California all the way to the Mississippi Valley.

The arrival, in the spring of 1847, of Colonel J. D. Stevenson's disbanded regiment of New York volunteers in the Mexican War—"Bowery Boys" schooled in the spread-eagle Americanism of New York's Tammany Hall—so inspired Sam Brannan with faith in California's future that he decided to strike out eastward, meet Brigham Young's stranded pilgrims, and lead them into the Promised Land. This the patriarchal Brigham had already found in Salt Lake Valley, however, and Sam had to retrace his steps to California. Angry and disgusted, he forgot about San Francisco and decided, in the autumn of 1847, to set up a store at Sutter's Fort and help the lord of New Helvetia build a sawmill on the south fork of the American River near the present site of Coloma. When gold was discovered in Sutter's millrace on January 24, 1848, Elder Sam Brannan re-assumed his authority over Mormon miners in the vicinity and began collecting "the Lord's tithes" from them. To the apostle sent to him to claim this illicit revenue Sam retorted: "You go back and tell Brigham that I'll give up the Lord's money when he gives me a receipt signed by the Lord, and no sooner!"

Meanwhile, in San Francisco, Brannan's own newspaper was ridiculing persistent rumors of rich gold strikes in the Sierra foothills. Suddenly the *Star's* owner himself rushed into town with a whisky flask full of the yellow flakes and confounded loiterers in Portsmouth Square with yells of "Gold! Gold! Gold from the American River!" Of the town's 900 inhabitants, only seven were left behind when the renegade Mormon with the bland face and side-whiskers led the first rush to the diggings.

Two hundred and fifty thousand dollars in gold dust came down the Sacramento during June and July of 1848. When news of this reached Mexican and South American ports via vessels from Honolulu, fortune-hunters in thousands swarmed aboard ships bound up the Coast. By New Year's Day, 1849, 6,000 miners were at the diggings. San Francisco was a cantonment of tents with a population of 2,000 excited transients.

On February 28, 1849, the *California,* first steamship to sail through the Golden Gate, arrived with her hold packed with gold-seekers from New Orleans taken on at Panama and her hurricane deck swarming with Peruvians, Chileños and Mexicans. Greeted by San Franciscans with wild cheering and by five American warships in the Bay with broadside salutes, the Pacific Mail steamer was promptly deserted both by passengers and crew in their headlong flight to the mines.

Already embroiled in the slavery issue, the Federal government virtually left California to its own devices for the next four years. The ambiguous powers of San Francisco's *ayuntamiento* were openly flouted by the inrush of fortune-hunters. Many of the town's merchants, who had been quietly getting rich, soon found themselves at the mercy of a lawless mob. Sam Brannan took the chaotic situation in his stride: he returned promptly and did a thriving business selling tacks, canvas, and redwood scantlings to the tent-dwellers who spread out over the sand-hills "like the camp of an army."

The remnants of Colonel Stevenson's regiment soon abandoned the hard toil of the placers and returned to the city, there to style themselves Regulators and enter the employ of shipowners as a police force to track down runaway sailors. In outlandish uniforms, with fiddle, fife, and drum, they soon earned the name "Hounds" for their penchant for "hounding" Mexicans, Peruvians, and others of darker skin to whom they denied all rights in this land "preserved by nature for Americans only, who possess noble hearts." On the night of July 15, 1849, these hoodlums raided the Chilean quarter; in that scene of pillage and general mayhem, one woman was murdered and a Hound stabbed with a bowie knife.

Alcalde T. M. Leavenworth, having neither the legal power nor the courage to make an arrest, let the incident pass; but the town's leading merchants had had enough of lawlessness. Led by Sam Brannan, who stood hurling invective at the Hounds from the rooftop of the *alcalde's* office in Portsmouth Square, San Francisco's first forces of law and order were mobilized. Leavenworth himself was compelled to give them some kind of legal sanction. By sunset 19 of the Hounds had been run down. Next day a grand jury indicted all 19 for conspiracy "to commit riot, rape, and murder." None of these proceedings, of course, had any legal status in California. The verdict was banishment from the territory, but although the Hounds disbanded—and the law-and-order men also—the convicted men could not be deported; and San Francisco's underworld continued to wage a stealthy warfare against the whole community.

W. T. "War-Is-Hell" Sherman presents in his *Memoirs* a graphic picture of the riotous Gold Rush metropolis during the wet winter of 1849 and the spring of 1850: "Montgomery Street had been filled up with brush and clay and I always dreaded to ride on horseback along it. . . . The rider was likely to be thrown and drowned in the mud." Kearny Street was impassable, "not even jackassable," except where it was paved for 25 yards with sacks of flour and bran, tobacco, stoves, and a piano. Drunks, known to stumble into the mire, would suffocate before rescue could arrive.

Portsmouth Square, ringed round on three sides by saloons and gambling dens, was a bedlam that roared night and day. Except for the city's merchants and a few other stationary inhabitants, the population was forever shuttling back and forth between the city and the gold camps. In the period from Christmas Eve, 1849, to June 22, 1851, San Francisco's ramshackle architecture was leveled by six successive fires. Not until after the fifth of these conflagrations did responsible citizens manage to lay charges of incendiarism against the Hounds' successors, the Sydney Ducks.

On June 9, 1851, the first Vigilance Committee was organized in the office of Sam Brannan, who became its president. Two days later, for the theft of a small safe, John Jenkins swung in the moonlight from a gable of the old Customhouse on Portsmouth Square. By July 1 the Vigilantes were so well organized that the city's homicide rate—which nevertheless was to include 1,000 murders between 1849 and 1856—declined temporarily. Among the reputable element, however, duels were common occurrences. Streets and gambling resorts were almost daily the scenes of casual gunfire.

On assuming office in 1850 Mayor John W. Geary had warned the City Council that ". . . we are without a dollar in the public treasury, and it is to be feared the city is greatly in debt. . . . In short, you are without a single requisite . . . for the protection of property, or for the maintenance of order." The warning had little effect. When the public debt had risen to $840,000, it was repudiated. Municipal officials, honest and otherwise, continued to be at the mercy of the Barbary Coast machine which put them in office. Sam Brannan could drum up a lynching as well as any rabble-rouser, but he was no match for those Tammany politicians whose wardheelers stuffed ballot boxes, paid out patronage and bribes, and terrorized voters at the polls. The influx of ticket-of-leave men—ex-convicts from Australia locally known as Sydney Ducks—had brought on a crime wave of alarming violence.

The rich yield of the placers began to run out in 1854. San Francisco went as wild in financial panic as it had been amid the inflation after 1849. One of the victims of the depression, James King of William, vented his chagrin over bad luck on the city's corrupt politicians through editorials in a newspaper he established for the purpose. For his scalping pen, the editor of the *Evening Bulletin* was shot down one day on Montgomery Street by city supervisor James P. Casey.

Already incensed by the failure of a jury to convict the slayer of U. S. Marshal William H. Richardson—one Charles Cora, a gambler, who had resented Richardson's public snubbing of his bagnio-keeping mistress—those San Franciscans grown weary of lawless ways quietly formed the second Vigilance Committee. Under the leadership of merchant William T. Coleman it went about its business with less fanfare, but more efficiency, than the Committee of 1851. Upon the day of James King of William's funeral, the bodies of Cora and Casey dangled from second-story windows of a building on Sacramento Street, later known as Fort Gunnybags.

Since California's admission to the Union in 1850 the new State had made some progress toward stable government. However, the militia recruited in San Francisco on orders from the governor to take over the extra-legal power of the Vigilance Committee was defied with armed resistance. By 1856 the Vigilantes had enrolled most of W. T. Sherman's militiamen within their ranks. At the height of its power the Committee numbered 9,000 men: a military body composed of infantry, artillery, and cavalry detachments. After an altercation with one of its officers a State Supreme Court judge, David S. Terry, was held in Fort Gunnybags, pending recovery of the victim of his bowie knife. During the life of the committee, there had been four executions, and some 30 undesirables had been banished from the State.

On August 18, 1856, the Vigilance Committee disbanded voluntarily. Respect for law and order, which a corrupt government had failed to inspire, was thus established by a popular instrument without legal authority. From the work of this "lawless" body sprang the People's Party which swept the municipal election of 1857 into the hands of men for whom honesty, aside from being the best policy, was a proviso of health and longevity.

BONANZA (1856–1875)

San Francisco's population of 50,000—at no time during the 1850's did it exceed this figure—had been perched on the bandwagon of the Gold Rush for five miraculous years. The roulette wheel was the symbol of its whole economy. When the stream of yellow metal ceased to pour down upon the town, however, the stakes of gamblers and speculators alike vanished into thin air. The crash dealt the relatively small, highly organized community a stunning blow. Inbound shipping decreased by half from 1853 to 1857; liabilities of bankrupt firms totaled more than $8,000,000. Nearly half the city's population was unemployed.

In February and March of 1855 Stockton and Los Angeles papers printed a number of sensational letters giving details of a purported rich strike on the Kern River. Thousands of people abandoned rich claims and steady employment in the rush to the new El Dorado. Additional thousands were preparing to follow when letters from the area brought the discouraging news that there was not work for more than 100 men. The unemployment burden was considerably lightened in 1858, however, when towards the end of summer, 18,000 men joined in a wild exodus to British Columbia's newly discovered Frazier River mines. With recovery came increased commercial activity; and demands from growing agricultural districts for articles of domestic and foreign manufacture laid the foundation of San Francisco's industrial prosperity. More than $4,000,000 a month in gold, besides, was being shipped out through the Golden Gate before the beginning of 1859.

The national controversy over slavery was rapidly dividing Californians into Secessionists and patriots loyal to the Union. As the "irreconcilable conflict" approached a crisis, it became apparent that the State might join the Southern cause. Among San Franciscans this political cleavage was the occasion for personal feuds in which damaging accusations and unprintable remarks led logically to "shooting it out." Consequently when California's champion against slavery in the United States Senate, David C. Broderick, cast aspersions upon Secessionist Judge David S. Terry, chief justice of the State Supreme Court, the latter promptly challenged the somber-faced Senator to a duel. Broderick was killed; 30,000 San Franciscans attended his funeral; Terry was ostracized, and the Senator's martyrdom crystallized Union sentiment among the city's predominantly Yankee population.

Abraham Lincoln's election to the Presidency was acclaimed by San Francisco's Union sympathizers with wild demonstrations in the streets.

Huge mass meetings were addressed by Senator Edward Baker and Unitarian minister Thomas Starr King, both of whom toured the State for the Union cause. Brigadier-General Albert Sidney Johnston, in command of the Presidio and the Department of the Pacific, was displaced by General E. V. Sumner following charges that Johnston was in league with Senator William M. Gwin to turn over California's armed forces to the Confederacy. Sumner's arrest of Gwin left the State's Secessionists without leadership, and their conspiracy collapsed.

With California won for the North, San Francisco proceeded to develop its commerce and industry, in virtual isolation from the War between the States. Its most substantial contribution to the Union cause was the $566,790.66 in gold sent to the United States Sanitary Commission for aid to the sick and wounded among the Northern troops.

The slump in gold production after 1860 found compensation in the growth of new industries and increasing trade. The Nation's treaty with the Hawaiian Islands, permitting free entry of raw sugar, resulted in the establishment of San Francisco's first refinery. The development of transportation brought increasing prosperity to sawmills, foundries, and other enterprises spreading rapidly over the Bay area. On October 24, 1861, San Francisco and New York were connected by telegraph. That same year a young engineer, Theodore Dehone Judah, finally convinced a small group of businessmen that a railroad could be built across the Sierra Nevada.

The possibility of transporting the fabulous silver deposits of Nevada's Comstock Lode to San Francisco by rail inspired even the least imaginative of the city's entrepreneurs. Charles Crocker, Mark Hopkins, Leland Stanford, and Collis P. Huntington—Sacramento merchants with a bare $50,000 among them—saw in Judah's plan their chance to corner for themselves the wealth of California's growing commerce. Prototypes of San Francisco's later financial giants, the predestined "Big Four" organized the Central Pacific Company of California on June 27, 1861. President Lincoln's signing of the Pacific Railroad Bill a year later was the signal for the eight-year race between the Central and the Union Pacific to join the rails of the Nation's first transcontinental railroad.

The completion of this epical undertaking in 1869, though it meant the end of San Francisco's splendid isolation from the national economy, was no occasion for jubilation. The "terrible seventies" were immediately ahead. A goodly portion of the 65,000-odd Chinese coolies whom Crocker and his associates had imported to build the Central Pacific's roadbed came drifting back into the city to compete with jobless whites. Gold production in the State's placer mines, over $44,000,-000 annually until 1860, had shrunk by 1870 to $15,000,000; and unemployment once more became a source of unrest that flared up with increasing violence. The titanic struggle between the Bank of California and its rivals in Virginia City was a speculator's nightmare in which the brokerage firms of Leidesdorff Street were mobbed by suckers rich and poor who sank savings and borrowed funds in "California" and "Consolidated Virginia." Not until the crash of the Bank of California in August, 1875, did the gambling frenzy reminiscent of the Gold Rush fitfully subside. When by 1877 the nightmare was over at last, carefree San Francisco's "Golden Age" was irretrievably gone.

With the advent of hard times the labor unions, into which practically every trade in the city had been organized during the decade after 1865, carried their powerful economic struggles into the political field. The rising Workingmen's Party began holding great mass meetings where an Irish drayman, Dennis Kearney, delivered inflammatory harangues which soon made him the leader of a widespread movement to exclude the Chinese from industries employing white labor. By 1879, however, the Workingmen's Party was coming under the control of cooler heads; and its delegates to the Constitutional Convention of that year brought to Sacramento a program of constructive proposals, several of which were adopted.

For his outspoken charges against local political conditions and for his advocacy of the workingmen's cause, Isaac S. Kalloch, a Baptist minister of considerable oratorical ability, became a candidate for mayor of San Francisco that same year. His bitterest opponents were the De Young brothers, owners and editors of the *San Francisco Chronicle,* who waged a highly personal war of words with Kalloch until the latter's blistering *riposte finale* caused Charles de Young to blaze away at him with a pistol. Not fatally wounded, Kalloch was enthusiastically elected; but the feud went on until, on the evening of April 23, 1880, Kalloch's son forestalled further damage to his father's battered reputation by fatally shooting De Young. With public sentiment in his favor, young Kalloch was acquitted.

BIG CITY (1875-1906)

The city's configuration, minus only its outlying residential districts, is already apparent in Currier and Ives' *The City of San Francisco—1878* (a bird's-eye view). The gospel of bigness which William C. Ralston "the Magnificent" had preached by lavish example had caught the city's imagination. An unkempt metropolis whose nocturnal thoroughfares were still murky with gaslight, a patchwork of paved and cobbled streets with plank sidewalks, San Francisco, by 1885, had ended the first decade of its expansive modern phase. The decade preceding the panic of 1893 was one of general prosperity in which "The Railroad" was able to gain control of the city through the machinations of

Chris Buckley, blind political boss in its pay, while depositors of savings banks viewed their accounts with satisfaction.

San Francisco's population was nearly 300,000 when, in 1893, a Nation-wide depression caused the closing of 18 local banks. Hundreds of the city's unemployed, forming a local contingent of "Coxey's Army," set out for Washington to demand Federal aid. The following year the Mid-winter Fair, designed to facilitate business revival, was partially successful. But the Southern Pacific's monopoly of transportation still prevented any substantial recovery.

When the Bank of California's old enemy, Adolph Sutro, was elected mayor of San Francisco in 1894, the long-drawn-out struggle to break the power of "The Railroad" began. The public still believed, however, that the prosperity of the community depended on the success of the "Corporation"—and that the Corporation depended for success on special privilege—and Sutro's battle against the Southern Pacific was doomed to be a solitary and thankless feud. His successor in office, James D. Phelan, was somewhat more successful. Despite opposition from the railroad's political machine, Phelan in May 1898 obtained ratification of a new charter which was considered a model for progressive municipal government. In an attempt to beautify the city, numerous parks and public playgrounds were established, and so popular had the "city beautiful" movement become by 1899 that $18,000,000 had been voted for public improvements. In his third and last term as mayor, however, Phelan lost his popularity by attempting to break a city-wide strike of teamsters.

Out of this prolonged and violent teamsters' strike of 1901 arose the Union Labor Party. In the election of 1902 its candidate for mayor, Eugene E. Schmitz of the Musicians' Union, was elected by a sizeable majority. Though Schmitz himself seems to have had honorable intentions, he soon came under the dominance of Abraham Ruef, shrewdest of the city's long succession of political bosses. It became common knowledge within the next four years that the entire structure of municipal government was worm-eaten with graft.

For 50 years San Francisco's tenderloin had been a haven for criminals and prostitutes of every sort; and it had its own crude laws, its definite social gradations. Here, in an area roughly bounded by Clay Street, Grant Avenue, Broadway, and the water front, was that infamous quarter named by seafarers for those pirate-infested shores of North Africa: the Barbary Coast. On November 28, 1869, the *San Francisco Call* had deplored the fact that the region abounded in "scenes of wretchedness and pollution unparalleled on this side of the great mountains"; but since its denizens preyed chiefly upon each other and on such victims as were foolish enough to venture among them, the municipal authorities let them go to the devil in their own way. Leaders of the Barbary Coast's gang of hoodlums—criminal descendants of the Hounds and the Sydney Ducks of Gold Rush times—forced profits from the myriad resorts of vice, and in their turn paid protection money to the political machine which was exacting tribute from respectable San Franciscans in other ways.

San Francisco in 1906 had attained the stature of undisputed metropolis of the Pacific Coast. With a population between 400,000 and 450,000, with its great hotels and churches and commercial establishments, its numerous fine schools, libraries, and hospitals, the city by the Golden Gate was a recognized world center of trade and finance and a gay capital of international society on a par with London, New York, and Paris.

At 5 o'clock on the morning of April 18, 1906, the majority of the city's population was peacefully asleep. "Families of artisans and mechanics living in homes and lodging houses south of Market Street were be-stirring themselves. Oil stoves were lighted and smoke was lazily curling out of kitchen chimneys . . . when at 13 minutes past the hour, the deeps of the earth, far down under the foundations of the city, began to rumble and vibrate." Instantly the whole community was awake, transfixed and speechless with alarm. "The earth tremors increased in violence . . . there was a sickening sensation as if everything were toppling. Plaster poured from ceilings . . . heavy furniture moved about banged upon the floor; and then the brick walls gave way . . . Tall structures, ribbed and rocked with steel, swayed like trees in a windstorm, but stood triumphant at the end with scarce a brick or stone displaced."

Such, in Charles Keeler's description, was the first impact of the earthquake. It lasted only 48 seconds. Few persons, outside the downtown business district, had any idea of the extent of the calamity which had befallen the city. Certainly no one dreamed that this was to be but the prelude to its destruction. The crowds of bewildered citizens who rushed out into the streets in their night-clothing, seeing no more than some fallen masonry and sniffing the pall of dust, straggled back to their rooms to wash their faces and get decently dressed.

Well-constructed buildings were hardly damaged at all. The most appalling ruin was that of the great City Hall, on which $7,000,000 of public funds had been squandered. But San Francisco was 90 per cent frame, a larger portion of wooden buildings than any city in the United States. Old lodging houses of the laboring poor, in the congested area south of Market Street, bore the full brunt of the shock; and as these toppled over upon countless screaming victims, fires from overturned stoves within the wreckage blazed up in a score of widely separated places. No alarms were struck owing to complete breakdown of the fire alarm system, and as fire engines went clanging through the streets, a huge cloud of smoke rose over all the southern section of the city.

Crowds of anxious spectators and the horde of refugees from the burning district were amazed at the sight of artillery troops and caissons from the Presidio rumbling down Montgomery Street. The sound of muffled explosions, coming from the edge of the approaching wall of flame, confirmed the rumor that water mains had been disrupted by the earthquake, and that dynamite was being used in a desperate attempt to save the city. As the day advanced the fire swept along the water front, leaped across Market Street. By nightfall Chinatown and all the business district was ablaze. The South of Market area was a charred and smouldering ruin. Endless streams of refugees fled to the hilltops or westward to Golden Gate Park.

By nightfall of the second day, with the raging inferno moving steadily westward as if to engulf the entire city, a last stand was made by the army of fire fighters at Van Ness Ave. With charges of dynamite they blasted to heaps of rubbish the long line of mansions forming that wide thoroughfare's eastern facade. The heartbreaking destruction, at last, turned the tide. Not until Saturday morning, April 21, however, did the fire finally burn itself out among the scattered houses of North Beach. The center of the city—an area of 521 blocks containing a total of 28,188 buildings great and small—had been demolished in 72 hours. Property losses amounted to between $350 and $500 million. Three hundred and fifteen bodies were recovered from the debris and ashes; 352 persons remained unaccounted for. In the Presidio, in Golden Gate Park, and in parks and lots outside the burned area more than 250,000 homeless citizens were encamped; and 100,000 more had fled to safety across the Bay or down the San Francisco Peninsula.

RISING PHOENIX (1906-1940)

To all intents and purposes, though never by actual proclamation of the mayor, the city was under martial law from the morning of the earthquake until about the middle of May. Besides Federal troops and a naval patrol, State militia and the local police force, a citizen's committee appointed by Mayor Schmitz patrolled the city; and on his authority these various law-enforcing bodies were instructed to "shoot to KILL any and all persons found engaged in looting or in the Commission of Any Other Crime." That remarkable propensity for bringing order out of the howling chaos—or, as Josiah Royce puts it, that American genius for self-government—was never better demonstrated than during the weeks of feverish reconstruction which followed the calamity. Despite the enormity of the disaster, it had the salutary effect of reducing all classes and condition of men to the common denominator of the breadline, wherein the goodnatured camaraderie of the early days of '49 was suddenly restored.

For two months following the earthquake and fire the hitherto diverse and antagonistic social elements worked together in jovial accord, and San Francisco was the best-behaved city in America. Night and day the labor of clearing away the rubbish, of laying new foundations, went on at a lively pace. With the opening of a thousand makeshift saloons, however, the city fell from grace; within three months 83 criminal offenses were committed and some 6,000 pistol permits were issued for defense of persons and property.

The ashes of San Francisco were hardly cool when the drive to "clean up the city" that was interrupted by the disaster was resumed. Public-spirited citizens led by ex-Mayor James Phelan and Rudolph Spreckels led the attack against "the System" of Abe Ruef, the municipal government, and the Southern Pacific Company's subsidiary, the United Railways. The graft investigation opened with charges that city officials had granted the United Railways a monopoly of streetcar franchises in exchange for bribes, thus preventing the $11,000,000 municipal railway organized by Spreckels and Phelan from operating traction lines in competition with the private company.

Assisted by Fremont Older, crusading editor of the *Bulletin*, and attorney Francis J. Heney, prosecutor of Oregon's infamous land frauds, the graft investigators established not only the bribe-taking of city supervisors in the matter of railway franchises but also brought to light the complicity of these officials in aiding private corporations to gain control of municipal public utilities. Testimony of the 18 supervisors, who were promised immunity for confessions when faced with proof of their guilt, convicted Abe Ruef and put Mayor Schmitz behind bars.

Despite all this name-calling and legal violence the work of rebuilding the city went steadily on. The $225 to $250 million paid to holders of insurance policies furnished a substantial impetus to rehabilitation. Within the year following the disaster construction amounting to more than $80,000,000 was undertaken. By 1909 construction figures had reached $150,000,000; and the devastated area was almost completely rebuilt by the end of the year.

Reformist Mayor Edward Robeson Taylor, who had succeeded the unlucky Schmitz, was displaced in the election of 1909 by the Union Labor Party's candidate, P. H. McCarthy. Despite apparent collapse of the campaign against the "Interests," the sentiment for reform had permeated the whole State; and the election of Hiram Johnson to the governorship saw the appointment of a Railroad Commission that smashed the power of the Southern Pacific's machine which had dominated California for almost half a century. Following the election of James Rolph, Jr., in 1911, the Union Labor Party went into a decline. It is, however, still the political arm of the American Federation of Labor and endorses candidates but does not run its own slate.

Consistently returned to office for the next 20 years, "Sunny Jim" Rolph was a prince of glad-handers in high-heeled polished boots, ten-gallon hats, and Palm Beach suits who brought to San Francisco a bizarre policy of goodwill that was the outward symbol of confidence and prosperity. His prolonged administration saw the extension of streets into residential districts beyond the hills, electrification of street railways and extended municipal ownership of public utilities; the successful Panama-Pacific International Exposition; the hysteria preceding American entrance into World War I and the speculative boom of the early '20's; the eclipse of social conviviality in the morbid Prohibition days of bad gin, sex, and jazz.

When the State's Red Light Abatement Act and the revoking of dance-hall licenses finally brought to an end in 1917 the long career of the Barbary Coast, old-timers watched its passing with aching hearts. Pride in the splendor of the rising city, however, turned the eyes of San Franciscans to the future as great hotels, lofty apartment houses, and skyscrapers brought to the truncated skyline the aspect of a massive American metropolis. Thrilling tribute to a three-quarter century of progress was the city's Diamond Jubilee of 1925, when the Nation's naval forces—forming a procession 25 miles in length—steamed in through the Golden Gate.

The Nation-wide financial crisis of 1929 did not immediately check San Francisco's business boom, and public improvements continued. In 1930 its population passed the 634,000 mark. The great Hetch-Hetchy dam in the high Sierras was nearing completion, and pending availability of its resources of light and power the city augmented its public utilities by purchasing the Spring Valley Water Company. Municipal government cast off its outmoded legal garment and clothed itself in the shining armor of a new charter. Even the onslaught of the depression which struck the city in 1932, while it brought on a decline in shipping and industry and threw some 70,000 workers out of employment, delayed only for another year the initial construction of the San Francisco-Oakland Bay Bridge. The city's sound financial and business structure enabled it to emerge with losses less serious than those of any other major American city.

The Golden Gate International Exposition of 1939-40, planned as a "Pageant of the Pacific" to celebrate the completion of the two great bridges across the Bay and the Golden Gate, was attended by more than 17,000,000 visitors; it gave to the Bay area the impetus needed to raise San Francisco business to pre-depression levels. More incalculable were the cultural influences derived from this "World's Fair of the West", which pointed toward an era of increasing relations with the nations of the Pacific.

It was not long after the gates had closed for the last time on San Francisco's celebration of international good will, however, that the city found itself facing, from across the Pacific, the threat of attack by enemy planes and ships. Within the first month of World War II San Franciscans learned what war might mean when air raid warning sirens signalled blackouts. The city mobilized for civilian defense. It became a great fort, its harbor blocked by a submarine net, its girdling hills bristling with guns. It became too the greatest shipbuilding center and the chief port of embarkation on the Coast, building a vast fleet of vessels at shipyards around the Bay and loading them with men and weapons to send to the fighting fronts. Population swelled to the bursting point as people flocked from the whole country for jobs in war industries. War workers, merchant marine men, soldiers and sailors thronged its streets. San Francisco went in for all-out war.

The stream of troops and munitions was still pouring westward from the Golden Gate when in February 1945, San Franciscans were electrified by the announcement from the leaders of the "Big Three," meeting in far-off Yalta in the Crimea: "We have agreed that a conference of the United Nations should be called to meet at San Francisco, in the United States, on April 25, 1945 . . ." The city offered its best for the accommodation of the conference: its War Memorial Opera House and Veterans' Building in the Civic Center (*see page 168*) for their deliberations and its biggest hotels to house the delegates and their staffs. For two months, while the United Nations framed their charter for an organization on which the world's hopes for peace would depend, San Franciscans watched delightedly the comings and goings of their international visitors.

The visitors had been gone less than a month when the news of Japan's surrender sent the whole city into one of the Nation's most rip-roaring victory celebrations. Peace found San Francisco tired but happy, looking forward to its hundredth birthday as an American city in the confidence that its second century might bring to realization that era of expanding opportunity which it had prophesied in its "Pageant of the Pacific" on the eve of war.

San Franciscans at Work

"No occupation was considered at all derogatory . . . Every kind of business, custom, and employment, was solicited . . . the field was open, and every one was striving for what seemed to be within the reach of all—a foremost rank in his own sphere."
—J. D. BORTHWICK (1857)

WHEN the first streaks of dawn scatter the night, San Francisco awakes, not to the march of early morning factory workers, but to the whir of limousines speeding brokers to the Stock Exchange. For in San Francisco, because of the difference between Pacific and Atlantic time, they must be at work by six of a summer morning to be on the floor of the Exchange when Wall Street begins trading. In winter, when daylight saving has been discontinued in the

But the stockbrokers are not the earliest risers. At 2 a.m. heavy trucks roll off the freeways with their cargoes of fruits and vegetables and unload at the new Produce Market at Islais Creek, located there since September 27, 1963. And in North Beach the crab fishermen are hurrying to the wharf, anxious to push their small boats through the Gate on an acquiescent tide.

in North Beach the crab fishermen are hurrying to the wharf, anxious

When the siren at the Ferry Building sounds eight o'clock the water front comes suddenly to life. Longshoremen surge through steel-jawed pier doors, teamsters and trucks at their heels. As loading and discharging of cargo proceeds in the nearby warehouses some eight to ten thousand warehousemen sort, check, and pile the thousands of tons of merchandise for storage, transshipment, or distribution. Here, on or near the water front, congregate the crews of the many vessels from tugboats to passenger liners—sailors and marine engineers, radio telegraphers and bargemen, firemen, oilers, and watertenders. Masters, mates and pilots, cooks and stewards join the groups clambering aboard the ships at dock.

The Port's economic impact on the area is not limited to cargo-handling and ship servicing activities, but extends to the city's manufacturing, commercial and financial sectors. Shipborne passengers spend an estimated $1,250,000 annually, while the port operations and Fisherman's

San Francisco in By-gone Days

SAN FRANCISCO POST OFFICE, 1849–1850
AS IMAGINED BY ANDRE CASTAIGNE FOR THE
CENTURY MAGAZINE IN 1891

SHIPS IN THE BAY DURING THE GOLD RUSH
THEIR CREWS WERE OFF TO THE MINES. A SKETCH PUBLISHED
IN THE NEW YORK TRIBUNE, AUGUST 28, 1849

THE MISSION OF SAN FRANCISCO, MISSION DOLORES
(From an Old Print)

FROM TELEGRAPH HILL TOWARD THE GOLDEN GATE IN THE 1880's

A VIEW OF THE WATERFRONT, 1867

GEARY STREET CABLE CARS, 1890's

CABLE CARS ASCENDING GREENWICH STREET, 1884

THE OLD HALL OF JUSTICE BEFORE CONSTRUCTION OF
PORTSMOUTH PLAZA GARAGE, 1962

THE HALL OF JUSTICE AFTER THE FIRE OF 1906

CITY HALL AND ST. IGNATIUS SCHOOL AFTER THE FIRE, 1906

TEMPLE EMANUEL AFTER THE FIRE, 1906

RUINS OF TWO CHURCHES ON CALIFORNIA STREET AFTER THE FIRE, 1906

THE OBSERVATORY, PLEASURE RESORT, 1883. BURNED JULY 25, 1903

PROLONGED USEFULNESS: OLD FIRE HOUSE NOW A MODERN
DWELLING, WASHINGTON AND BAKER STREETS

Wharf are valuable tourist attractions. In all, it is estimated that 65,000 jobs and $450,000,000 in income may be attributed in some way to the activity of the port.

As the men and women who haunt the silent office buildings at night climb aboard outbound streetcars at dawn and stare sleepily out of windows, yawning, anxious only to get home, the trickle of white-collar workers which will soon become a river of humanity is already flowing from the opposite direction. Soon the cars are packed with office workers, doctors, lawyers, stenographers, and salespeople, who populate the downtown area and line lunch counters behind steam-covered windows, seeking the morning cup of coffee. Down the California Street hill come the bulging cable cars to disgorge their human cargoes into the financial district—cars locally dubbed "Stenographers' Specials," loaded with the female office workers whom eastern columnists have called "the most beautiful working-girls in the world." Warehousemen, factory workers, printers mingle with the white-collar workers, clutching transfers, smoking, hurrying to the job. The stream of humanity moving east is joined by another, the commuters coming from the Bay Bridge train terminal, overcoated, packing rumpled newspapers, books, and purses. From the ferries and bridges—from Marin County, Oakland, Berkeley, Alameda, and Peninsula towns—they come. As they pour into the doorways of department stores, shops, and office buildings, there comes to the observer the significance of statistics which say that in San Francisco the ratio of white-collar workers to manual workers is more than that of any other American city.

Meanwhile along the southern shore of the city proceeds the inpouring of the stockyard and industrial workers, the men who sweat in the freight sheds, the sugar refinery in Butchertown, and the fish reduction plant; who toil in the railway repair shops, the shipyards and drydocks, the foundries, the steel and wire and pipe industries, the drab cement and gravel plants.

Among the City's total of more than 387,000 workers in 1969, the greatest concentration occurred in wholesale trade with 79,234 workers; manufacturing employed 57,665 workers; and retail sale 22,100. Of the remaining workers we note a distribution of 54,777 in transportation, utilities, and communications; 63,630 in finance, insurance and real estate; and 85,858 in the service industries. Wages in 1969 amounted to more than $3,000,000,000.

As the morning wears on, the newsboys shout raucously. The owners of flower stands pack bright, dripping carnations and gardenias in colorful rows along the sidewalks. Suddenly the newsboys are silent, waiting later editions and blacker headlines. The buildings spew forth their crowds to seek hurried lunches in drug store, cafeteria, and restaurant.

Women shoppers throng Market Street after lunch, peering into store windows. Uniformed ushers and doormen stand idly by box offices, awaiting matinee crowds. Finally, the sun ducks behind the office buildings, and the homeward rush begins.

As day merges into night, neon lights flash on. Cocktail lounges begin to fill; darkness brings a dinner rush. Musicians and entertainers, waitresses and night cooks scurry through alley entrances to the centers of the city's night life. Taxis move from hotel to night club, from restaurant to bar. Life becomes a rising tide, hidden behind frosted glass, pulsing to the blare of nickel phonographs or the fevered tunes of swing bands.

And then at two a. m. the lights go out; stools and tables are stacked; doors are closed. Musicians and dancers, kitchen help and customers, going home through dark and empty streets, hear the swish of street-cleaning trucks. The flare of an electric welder busy at a street intersection flashes through the night. Soon come the white milk trucks converging to their distribution points, and the mountainous garbage vans clattering from restaurant back doors loaded for suburban pig farms. Already stirring are the produce workers and fishermen whose work is about to begin.

So the day ends and begins again, and time has drawn another 24-hour circle around the city and its workers.

WALL STREET OF THE WEST

San Francisco's Montgomery Street, Wall Street of the West, runs north from Market Street between tall, austere office buildings, a canyon of high finance. What men say in offices, staid restaurants, and soft-lighted bars along Montgomery Street is passed on by the ticker tapes of the Nation, is translated into the languages and dialects of Mexico, South America, Australia, the Orient. Great farms, staggering lumber resources, Hawaiian sugar and Guatemalan coffee plantations, broad oil fields with their forests of derricks, Alaskan fish canneries and some of the largest fruit canneries in the world, shipping lines that encircle the globe, mines and power plants—the life blood of all these is regulated in Montgomery Street's board rooms and brokerage firms.

Up the street toward the Plaza in May, 1848, out of breath and dusty after his trip from the diggings, hurried Sam Brannan. Within five years he would become California's first millionaire—and Montgomery Street would be lined with bankers' offices. As gold dust began coming down the Sacramento, some means for handling it had to be found. The first requisites were scales and a safe, to weigh and store the precious metal; and so storekeepers were the first bankers. Soon merchants, assayers, and express companies were buying up gold dust in exchange for drafts on Eastern banks. And before the end of the year, Stephen A. Wright had opened his Miners' Bank with an advertised capital of $200,000 and was collecting interest of from 8 to 15 per cent a month on real estate loans. He was soon competing with others: Henry M. Naglee; Lucas Turner and Company, represented by William Tecumseh Sherman—and even the Rothschilds.

Rich in gold, San Francisco nonetheless found itself poor in money. A pinch of gold dust substituted for a dollar; a "bit piece" of dollar-length gold wire (divided into eight parts), for smaller coins—"two bits," "four bits," "six bits." The coins of every nation were pressed into service, at a rate of exchange based on their size. English shillings, French francs, and Mexican double-reals were as acceptable as American quarters. Peruvian doubloons, Spanish pesetas, Austrian zwanzigers, Dutch florins, Indian rupees changed hands regularly. Even the price of gold fluctuated from $8 to $16 an ounce until 1851, when it was stabilized at $16. In the absence of a mint, assay offices began to coin 5-, 10-, 20-, and 25-dollar slugs; at one time 14 such private mints were operating. Their coins varied widely in value, ranging from the Pacific Company's $10 gold pieces, worth $7.86, to Kohler and Company's, worth $10.10. Not until 1854, when the United States Mint was opened, were standards for coinage fixed.

The methods of Joseph C. Palmer of Palmer, Cook and Company, express agents who became bankers in 1851, reflected the spirit of the times. It is said a depositor once wanted to withdraw $28,000 from his account with the firm. Palmer's consent was necessary. The depositor found him in a lumber yard a mile from the bank. Neither pencil nor paper nor pen was available. Palmer picked up a shingle and on it, with a piece of red chalk, wrote a check for $28,000 which was readily accepted at the bank.

The express companies did a land-office business shipping gold to the east, receiving deposits, selling drafts and making loans. Outstanding among them was Wells Fargo, a name still familiar throughout the West. As early as 1852 this firm was selling exchange on 53 different cities in the country. In many California mining or ghost mining towns Wells Fargo scales on which millions of dollars in gold dust have been weighed are still on exhibit. The company became a bank in 1866, operating its banking activities in conjunction with its express business until 1878, when the two branches were separated.

The Gold Rush boom had so far overreached itself by 1854 that a crisis in mercantile affairs developed which steadily grew worse until the "Black Friday" of February 23, 1855, began a financial panic which forced 20 of the 42 banking firms to shut their doors forever. Real estate values slumped. Bankruptcies increased from 77 in 1854 to 197 in 1855. "Honest" Harry Meiggs, city alderman, fled to Chile, leaving behind $800,000 worth of bad debts, impartially distributed among the financial houses of the city, which were secured only by forged city warrants. Palmer, Cook and Company failed with a loss of $3,500,000.

When in 1859 the flow of colossal riches from the silver deposits of Nevada mines began, however, a new era commenced which established San Francisco finally as financial center of the West. When the Federal government and all of the Eastern banks left the gold standard in 1862, William C. Ralston convinced San Francisco's business men that California must stay on gold. He pointed out that the Union would need gold, which they could ship to the East and exchange for greenbacks. As greenback values dropped—before the war was ended a gold dollar was worth two greenbacks—the merchants and investors profited handsomely.

As mining activities went on booming, San Francisco became again the turbulent city of the Gold Rush, but no longer was it necessary for a man to dig in the earth to make his poke. Fortunes were made daily —and lost as easily—in mining stocks. In 1862 forty men united to organize the San Francisco Stock and Exchange Board.

In the second year of the war, when President Lincoln signed the Pacific Railroad Bill, the "Big Four" began laying the tracks of the Central Pacific eastward.

The Comstock Lode was pouring wealth into San Francisco, and William C. Ralston had a finger in the most important of the mines. On July 5, 1864, his Bank of California opened with D. O. Mills as president. For more than ten years it was to be the power back of the greatest undertakings in the West. Bank money developed the Comstock Lode—and the Lode repaid more than abundantly. When the "Big Four" were blocked in their efforts to put the railroad through, Ralston loaned them bank money on their personal notes, and assumed personal responsibility for their debts.

The collapse of the short boom in real estate prices which followed the driving of the last spike in the transcontinental railroad in May, 1869, left Ralston holding much property in the Montgomery Street extension south of Market. When it began to appear that the Comstock Lode, in which millions of the Bank of California's deposits had been sunk, was worn out, rumors started that threatened to cause a run on the bank. In September, 1869, the night before the run was expected, Ralston managed a stunt which has never been duplicated. During the night, Ashbury Harpending and a man named Dore, exchanged five tons of gold with the United States Sub-Treasury for coined money. These men carried this load by hand throughout the night. In the morning, when the run began, Ralston was able to put on the tables, in sight of the depositors, an inexhaustible supply of coined money. The panic stopped almost as soon as it had started.

During 1865 and 1866, the mines seemed to have played out as one by one they reached the end of visible ore. Adolph Sutro, a German-Jewish emigrant, conceived the idea of building a tunnel under the Comstock Lode to drain flooded shafts and to reach ore that was too deep for the mining methods of that time. Ralston at first was impressed, but the "Ring" was afraid of anyone's else cutting in on the rich profits of the mines. Ultimately Sutro had to fight the whole Bank of California ring to put the Sutro Tunnel through. His epic nine-year struggle against the Bank was the beginning of the fall of Ralston's empire.

By 1870, according to popular opinion, the Comstock had reached bottom rock, and there seemed little chance of further veins being discovered. But several astute miners were quietly buying up the stock of several of the mines. John Jones and Alvinza Hayward got the Crown Point Mine away from the "Ring." In 1872 two young mining men, John W. Mackay and James G. Fair, who had worked in the Comstock mines, formed an association with James G. Flood and William S. O'Brien, San Francisco saloon keepers who for years had dabbled in mining stocks. For less than $100,000, the quartet quietly obtained control of the California and the Consolidated Virginia, two mines which had yet shown little promise. The discovery of a few veins started the stock market booming. By 1872, stocks which had been listed at $10 a share were bringing hundreds. Consolidated Virginia jumped from $160 to $710. San Francisco went stock-gambling mad. Nowhere could one hear anything but names of mines and stocks—Kentuck, Yellow Jacket, Crown Point, Consolidated Virginia, Ophir, Gould and Curry, Savage. Again the feeling that the riches under the Lode were inexhaustible swept San Francisco.

Then, like a flaming comet over the horizon of Montgomery Street, blazed the news that the "Nevada Four's" two mines, known as the Big Bonanza, covered the richest vein of ore in the Comstock Lode. Mackay, Fair, Flood, and O'Brien had already taken the precaution of buying up all available stock before releasing the news. Holding unlimited funds, they settled down to relentless warfare with Ralston and the Bank of California. The objective was control of the incredibly rich Comstock mines. The physical properties lay elsewhere but the blows were struck on the exchanges of San Francisco's Wall Street of the West.

As the struggle proceeded, San Francisco was swept by an unprecedented frenzy of speculation. Gambling tables in the city were practically deserted. On the street curbs in the financial district women brokers, dubbed "mudhens," hawked stock of all descriptions. Women wearing diamonds and expensive clothes joined the morning crowds flocking to the exchanges.

The downfall of Ralston in 1875 brought financial San Francisco down with him. Resolved to break the Bank of California, the Nevada Four planned to open a rival bank. Ralston meanwhile was seeking control of the Ophir mine, valued fictitiously at $31,000,000, in the belief that it covered part of the Big Bonanza. James Keene, presiding member of the Stock Exchange, quietly bought large blocks of Ophir stock for him. "Lucky" Baldwin, hearing the stock was in great demand, secured many shares which he sold, netting himself a nice profit of millions. Ralston alone was overloaded with Ophir stock when it was disclosed that the mine was an empty hole. William Sharon, Ralston's right hand man, had known—and quietly unloaded his shares in the mine, neglecting to tell Ralston. In February, 1875 a rumor swept the city that the Big Bonanza had given out, and the stock market crashed. The drop in market values shook the Bank of California. It began to be rumored that the bank was unsound, and that Ralston was to blame because of his speculations. The new Bank of Nevada withdrew cash deposits from the leading banks of San Francisco, in order to open its own doors with a $5,000,000 reserve in actual coin. The withdrawals sent most of the banks to the edge of insolvency. Ralston began to sell his holdings wherever possible in order to raise money. On August 26, 1875, after weeks of crashing values in mine shares and an exhausting run, the Bank of California closed its doors.

The next day Ralston, as was his habit, went swimming. His drowned body was found in the Bay off North Beach.

The failure of the Bank of California for a time stopped all trading on the Exchange. The bank was reorganized by D. O. Mills and William Sharon, who had profited heavily by sale of Ophir stock. But when it reopened, it found the Bank of Nevada, opened a few days later by the Nevada Four, already dominant in San Francisco.

Montgomery Street's era of crusading capitalists had come to an end. In the period that followed, high finance pursued a steadier course. In 1875 the San Francisco Clearing House, first in the State, was organized; before the year had passed it was fifth in importance in the United States. The year 1877 saw the establishment of a State Board of Bank Commissioners, despite terrific opposition. In 1882 the present Pacific Coast Stock Exchange was established. The year following, Charles Crocker organized the banking firm of Crocker-Woolworth and Company, which today is the Crocker National Bank. The 1884 depression in the Eastern States was scarcely felt in San Francisco, but closer financial ties brought the effects of the 1893 panic to Montgomery Street within a few months of the time it was felt in New York.

The fire of 1906 was the occasion for the rise of another spectacular figure. Since 1904, A. P. Giannini, a commission merchant who had retired with a comfortable income at the age of thirty-two, had been trying out his banking theories in the Bank of Italy (now the Bank of America), which he and his step-father had founded. Giannini was able to turn the disaster of 1906 to his advantage when he managed to remove the assets and records from his bank before the advancing fire reached them. They were hauled to his San Mateo home in wagons from his step-father's commission warehouse and camouflaged with a heap of fruits and vegetables. The Bank of Italy was the first in the city to be re-opened.

In 1909, Giannini launched a drive to create a State-wide system of branch banks on the theory that branch banking was the best safeguard against failure of banks in single-crop or single-industry regions because they served to spread the risk. His streamlined advertising campaign with full-page advertisements in the newspapers was unprecedented in banking history. He added bank after bank to his chain.

When the Federal Reserve System was established by Congress on December 23, 1913, San Francisco was selected as center for the Twelfth Federal Reserve District, comprising an area including California, Oregon, Washington, Utah, Idaho, Nevada, and most of Arizona. By 1970 the Twelfth District had assets of $10,375,000,000 with 403 banks and 4,550 branches in its territory.

Of the vast financial network comprising present-day San Francisco's citadels of business, the Wells Fargo Bank and Union Trust Company—Wells Fargo merged with the Nevada National Bank in 1905 and with the Union Trust Company in 1924—and the Hibernia Savings and Loan Society alone have had uninterrupted existence since the feverish days in which they were founded. But San Francisco remains the financial capital of the West. Two San Francisco banks have failed since 1920. One, a branch of the Bank of Canton, collapsed during a monetary crisis in the Chinese Revolution of 1926. The other, which opened on June 1, 1962 with the largest capitalization in California history, $4,500,000, was the San Francisco National Bank. It was declared insolvent January 23, 1965. The Bank's Directors were held liable for $20,000,000. Following the stock market crash of 1929, the leading bankers of San Francisco met and pledged a revolving fund of $100,000,000 to protect the city's banks against failure, with the result that not one cent was lost to depositors. Constantly seeking new outlets for investment the city's financial institutions have increasingly assumed closer control of industry and agriculture, of shipping and transportation.

LABOR'S THOUSANDS

San Francisco workers are proud of their unions and jealous of union welfare. Employers estimate that half the population of San Francisco consists of union members and their families. All major West Coast union organizations maintain offices or headquarters in the city. There are an extensive inter-union sports movement and a junior union movement for the children of union men. During the 1930's and early 1940's annual grand balls were sponsored by various unions and attended by thousands of working people and their families. The labor press, steeped in tradition, has a large following of readers. Both the AFL and CIO utilized radio broadcasts to spread their messages in the days when they were separate organizations; more recently AFL-CIO have profited greatly by their cooperation.

During the latter 1930's industry-wide agreements arrived at by bargaining over the round table became fairly common in the Bay area, particularly in the water-front industry, where both labor and employers are strongly organized. Sometimes these conferences were as dramatic in their own way as the strikes or lockouts which they supplanted. Union men and employers, at the appointed hour, crowded into the room, which more often than not would be located in one the city's most modern office buildings. Opponents might exchange guarded jokes. Briefcases were tossed on a table liberally supplied with ash trays. Debate was conducted with an alertness that demanded frequent nervous lighting of cigar or cigarette. The press was often admitted. If an agreement was reached, its terms became big news, splashed at once across the front pages of the city's newspapers. When there was a deadlock, newspaper editors offered their own alternatives in front-page editorials. Citizens wrote letters to their favorite papers suggesting solutions which were printed in the public forum columns. Columnists and radio commentators discussed the issues. Heated debates broke out on early morning streetcars.

The experience of peaceful solution of industrial disputes in these pre-war years undoubtedly was of great aid in maintaining San Francisco's record of almost uninterrupted war production from Pearl Harbor to V-J Day. Not only were strikes and lockouts avoided; labor-management cooperation was a positive force in increasing productivity.

The city's union consciousness had its beginning in the days of the Gold Rush. "There are evidences of such early trade union activity in San Francisco," writes Lucille Eaves, "that one is tempted to believe that the craftsmen met each other on the way to California and agreed to unite." At least one instance proves the point: in 1864, when the

Employers' Association of San Francisco, attempting to smash a strike of iron molders, wired East for strikebreakers, the unions dispatched representatives to Panama who met the men hired to take their jobs; when the ship docked in San Francisco all walked ashore as union brothers. Among the men who came to San Francisco were many from countries of Europe where the struggle for unions already had been in progress for many long years.

To combat an exorbitant cost of living, the unorganized carpenters and joiners struck in 1849, demanding a wage increase, which they won. Before a year had passed the San Francisco Typographical Society had been organized as the first bona fide trade union on the coast. Teamsters, musicians, riggers and stevedores, and building trades workers soon followed suit. These early unions, organized on the basis of immediate demands, appeared and disappeared in bewildering variety until the campaigns for the eight-hour day and against the competition of cheap Chinese labor supplied rallying points around which all could unite with some degree of permanence.

The Chinese were regarded by many employers as a source of cheap labor and were employed here in many trades at a wage lower than the Occidentals. The thousands of laborers who helped build the first railroad across the American continent were paid as little as $30 a month. When the railroad was completed, they flocked to San Francisco. In 1872 it was estimated they comprised nearly half of all the factory workers in the city. During this period there was an intensification of the labor-capital struggle. Labor unions were fighting for the 8-hour day and better working conditions. White employers had no qualms about using Chinese labor as a threat to counter white labors demands. Thus Chinese labor became aligned with the employers as labor's enemy. To combat the competition of Chinese labor they joined in an anti-Chinese campaign that sometimes found outlet in violence. It led finally to adoption of the Chinese Exclusion Act by Congress in 1882. Although anti-Chinese sentiment was widespread for many years after, the admission of Chinese to membership in a number of unions during recent years has marked its passing. A strike here of Chinese girls, members of the International Ladies Garment Workers Union, gained nation-wide notice in 1937 when the attractive and dainty women pickets were pictured in the press of the country.

Out of the turbulence of the anti-Chinese movement arose Dennis Kearney, one-time vigilante and opportunist extraordinary. For a time his violent talks, made on the sand lots in what is now the Civic Center, captured the imagination of thousands. Opposed to him was a sincere young Irishman, a Fenian exile, named Frank Roney. The group around Roney succeeded in discrediting Kearney, who retired to private trade to be heard from no more. But Roney continued an active member of the trade union movement for many years. He organized the Seamen's Protective Association and became its president.

Largely because of Roney's work the Trades Assembly, a city-wide group, succeeded in doubling its membership. His plan of organizing unions into trade councils was later to be adopted on a national scale by the AFL. When the Trades Assembly sent delegates to a convention of the Federated Trades and Labor Union of the United States (which later became the American Federation of Labor), held in 1881, San Francisco labor for the first time became affiliated with an organization national in scope.

Always the lot of American seamen had been a hard one, and San Francisco was known as one of the world's toughest ports. It was common for a seaman ashore after a long trip, his wages in his pocket, to buy a drink at one of the many saloons—and wake up next morning aboard a vessel bound for Shanghai. The practice of kidnapping was so common that the term "shanghai" was applied to it. Against such abuses the Seamen's Protective Association fought.

A fight against wage cuts in 1885 resulted in formation of the Coast Seamen's Union. From this organization came the ascetic Norwegian, Andrew Furuseth. Emotional, sharp-featured, and extremely energetic, Furuseth, who later was known simply as "Old Andy," spent most of his life with the seamen. He was credited with knowing more about sea law than any other man alive. In his later years he helped unite American seamen into the International Seamen's Union, comprising sailors, firemen, and cooks and stewards. Aided by Senator Robert M. LaFollette in 1915, he succeeded in securing passage of the Seamen's Act, a Magna Carta of liberation for these men.

The Employers' and Manufacturers' Association of San Francisco, newly organized, opposed unionization in a campaign that took real effect as the depression of 1893 reached its depths. As union membership dropped to a mere 4,500, at least 35,000 jobless workers tramped the streets of the city in search of food and work. In 1894 the American Railway Unions struck against the Pullman Company in Chicago. Trains stopped and trans-Bay ferry service was paralyzed for ten days. Federal troops marched into San Francisco. In Oakland citizens raided roundhouses to extinguish fires in the locomotives. At this time, too, the Bay area contingent of the famous Coxey's Army was organized. Under the command of "General" Charles T. Kelley the unemployed army, credited with superior discipline, sought refuge for a few days in Oakland, then started on the long box-car ride across the continent.

Meanwhile the men on the water front had organized the City Front Federation. Several times before similar federations had been organized, notably the Wharf and Wave Federation in 1888 and the City Front Labor Council in 1891. But the City Front Federation was the strongest yet to be formed; it was, in fact, one of the best-organized groups of its kind in the country at that time. As the depression gradually became history, other union groups began to show signs of life. Particularly in the building trades did the organizing campaign show results. In December, 1900, the Central Labor Council called a convention of California unions at which a State Federation of Labor was formed. At the same time a State Building Trades Council was set up with P. H. McCarthy as president, an office he held continuously until 1922. Employers, too, were organizing. They built a new association, raised a huge war chest, and instituted a boycott against recalcitrants who recognized union groups. The new association operated secretly.

In 1901 trouble developed between the teamsters and the Draymen's Association that rapidly developed into a lockout. When the City Front Federation came to the aid of the teamsters, Bay area traffic was tied up. After a deadlock lasting two months, Governor Henry T. Gage came to San Francisco and arranged a meeting between employers and workers. A compromise was effected within an hour, the terms of which never were made public. The teamsters became a powerful segment of organized labor. Under the leadership of a broad-shouldered Irishman, Michael Casey, they branched out into fields hitherto untouched by unions. But the City Front Federation, wracked by internal dissension, declined in importance. Sailors, however, emerged in possession of a new agreement with shipowners.

The labor unions, angered by what they considered unnecessary police violence during the teamster struggle, formed the Union Labor Party. Aided by Father Yorke, Catholic priest and intimate friend of Jack London, the new party succeeded in gaining the election of Eugene Schmitz, a member of the Musicians' Union, as mayor. Three labor men were elected to the Board of Supervisors. But Schmitz became the puppet of Abe Ruef, shrewd political boss, and graft, corruption and bribery flourished. Ruef, Schmitz, and the supervisors were indicted by the grand jury in a reform wave that followed the 1906 earthquake. Ruef went to prison, but his henchmen and backers went free. Patrick Calhoun, head of the street railway corporation, which had been implicated in the bribery exposures, engineered a strike of the streetcar workers. Andrew Furuseth, Mike Casey, and Fremont Older attempted to halt the strike but were unsuccessful. When Calhoun imported strikebreakers who terrorized the carmen, it appeared he had saved the city, an impression he deliberately had set out to create. The carmen's union was demoralized.

Meanwhile P. H. McCarthy of the building trades unions had forged to the front. In 1909 he was elected mayor. Under his leadership the Building Trades Council built its own mills and enforced a boycott against mills outside the city, mills with wage rates lower than those of San Francisco.

When the longshoremen struck in 1916 for higher wages, the employers and the Chamber of Commerce organized the Law and Order Committee and issued a lengthy manifesto calling for unity of San Francisco's citizens. The Law and Order Committee succeeded in getting the city to pass an anti-picketing ordinance. Meanwhile, the war in Europe had begun to affect this country, which at the same time was engaged in a punitive expedition against Mexico. The atmosphere was tense. As anti-German sentiment grew, people were seeing spies behind every telephone. The city planned to hold a parade in favor of preparedness.

The parade, held July 22, 1916, had hardly gotten under way when a bomb exploded at Steuart and Market Streets, killing ten persons and injuring many more. Newspapers demanded the arrest of those guilty of the outrage. Among those arrested were Thomas J. Mooney and Warren K. Billings, both of whom were convicted.

Labor in California and throughout the United States was convinced that the two men were innocent. When repeated protests of world-wide scope caused President Woodrow Wilson to request Governor William D. Stevens to exercise leniency, Mooney's death sentence was commuted to one of life imprisonment. Later investigations disclosed irregularity in the conduct of the trial, in the handling and testimony of witnesses, and in the treatment of the jury. Judge Griffin, in whose court the trial had been held, declared in 1929: "The Mooney case is one of the dirtiest jobs ever put over and I resent the fact that my court was used for such a contemptible piece of work." As time wore on Mooney—and Billings —became, for labor, symbols of injustice, until Governor Culbert Olson, fulfilling a campaign promise, was able to pardon Mooney and aid in securing the release of Billings.

In 1921 San Francisco employers again drew closer together, forming the Industrial Association. The building trades unions lost ground when faced with the strong opposition of the new employer group. Metal trades workers and seamen lost strikes in 1921; carpenters, in 1926. Longshoremen, since 1919, had been obligated to become members of the Longshoremen's Association of San Francisco, an organization they considered to be under employer domination. They called it the "Blue Book Union," deriving the name from the color of the membership books. The Industrial Association maintained an employment office, a hotel for non-union workers, and a training school for non-union plasterers, bricklayers, plumbers, and carpenters. The only labor organizations that did not suffer from the general intertia that swept the city's trade union movement during this period were the Railway Brotherhoods. A Brotherhood bank was established in San

Francisco which merged with a non-labor bank after the collapse of the national Brotherhood's banking system.

The depression beginning in 1929 further weakened the organized labor movement until union sentiment began to revive with the passage of the National Recovery Act. The men on the water front were among the first to take advantage of Section 7-a of the act, dealing with labor organization. The longshoremen secured a charter under the International Longshoremen's Association of the AFL and, spurred by the pungent criticism and organizational appeals of an anonymously sponsored mimeograph bulletin, fully 90 per cent of the dock workers joined the ILA. Harry Bridges, wiry Australian longshoreman, came to the front as a leader and spokesman for the new group. A coastwise longshoremen's convention was held in 1934 and demands were made upon the shipowners. Subsequently a strike vote was taken.

On the morning of May 9 longshoremen in San Francisco and other Coast ports walked off the docks in what was to be one of the most dramatic struggles in the history of West Coast labor. On May 13 the teamsters, despite opposition of their leadership, voted unanimously against hauling cargo to or from the docks. On May 15 the seamen joined the strike, presenting their own demands to the employers; licensed officers followed suit. The newspapers reported that on May 15, for the first time in the history of Pacific Coast ports, not a freighter left port. Events were rapidly approaching a climax when the Industrial Association announced to the public that the port would be opened on July 5.

As the morning of July 5 dawned, strikers and police massed in great numbers at the pier from which cargo was to be hauled by non-union truck drivers. The pickets who attempted to approach the pier were forced back repeatedly by police. At Rincon Hill south of Market Street a pitched battle occurred between police and strikers. Two strikers were killed during the day and many were taken to the hospital suffering from wounds and tear gas. A few hours later the National Guard moved into the city and took over the water front.

July 5, now memorialized by the water-front unions each year under the name of "Bloody Thursday," crystallized sentiment for a city-wide general strike in sympathy with the maritime unions. Union after union voted to go out. On July 17, first day of the general strike, it was estimated that 127,000 San Francisco workers had left their jobs. A peculiar silence descended upon the city. Market Street, usually one of the busiest streets in the Nation, appeared deserted.

The general strike was ended July 20 at the instance of the Central Labor Council and thousands returned to their jobs. The water-front unions remained on strike for several days until their demands were given over to mediation. Eventually they gained greatly improved working conditions and, what was most important from their point of view, union hiring halls. A second maritime strike which tied up shipping along the entire coast in 1936 was ended in the first week of the new year with further improved working conditions.

The organization of the Congress of Industrial Organizations in 1935 found San Francisco sentiment divided. The longshoremen and their affiliates voted to join the new group, of which Harry Bridges was later made West Coast Director. The seamen were split; some preferred to remain with the AFL, some for a while maintained an independent status, and some joined the CIO. The effects of the split were felt in the bitter partisanship which appeared in the Maritime Federation of the Pacific, organized following the 1934 strike. During the latter 1930's and the early 1940's, CIO unions made organizational gains, enrolling thousands of members in such basic industries as transportation, utilities, meat packing, rubber, auto and steel. By 1945 they could gather 30,000 marchers into their Labor Day parade.

During the 1938 gubernatorial campaign in California organized labor united in San Francisco, pointing the way for the rest of the State in supporting candidates and issues favorable to the unions. Culbert Olson, the union-backed candidate, won the election. A State antipicketing measure was voted down by a large majority. John F. Shelley, president of the AFL Central Labor Council, who was elected State senator from San Francisco, perhaps described the position of organized labor in the Bay area when he said: "When San Francisco labor is faced with a concrete issue, it will unite."

In 1939 the major employers of the city organized an Employers' Council for the purpose of dealing unitedly with the unions. When Almon E. Roth, chosen to head the group, took over his duties, he told the newspapers that "San Francisco actually has had fewer strikes and labor disturbances in recent years than most American cities of comparable size."

In September, 1948, more than 120 ships were tied up by a nine-week waterfront strike. The longest strike in American shipping history began July 1, 1971. Twenty-four ports were closed and 15,000 longshoremen were idle for 135 days. Work was resumed February 21, 1972, when Harry Bridges, president of the International Longshoremen's & Warehousemen's Union accepted the Pay Board's wage increase from the current $38.52 to $45.00 and on July 1, 1972 to $48.60. The strike was halted temporarily from October 6, 1971, to January 17, 1971, by a Taft-Hartley injunction.

Social Heritage

"San Francisco knows how."
—President William Howard Taft

OF ALL the arts San Franciscans have practiced, the one they have most nearly perfected is the art of living, but hedonism is only one of the elements of which San Francisco's civilized social tradition is compounded. Omar Khayyam's "Take the Cash and let the Credit go" has been as freely accepted for a motto, perhaps, as his "jug of wine" and "loaf of bread"—and more freely than the spiritual precepts of the city's official patron, the gentle St. Francis.

Yet all through this materialism runs a fugitive thread of humanitarian tenderness; a reverence for culture, often uncritical; a fundamental urbanity. Every viewpoint has had its say in the city's long succession of journals and newspapers. Enriched also by this democratic quality is the whole history of the city's devotion to the theater, to musical performances and art exhibits, to restaurants and cabarets and bars. Where so much of living has vitalized a popular culture, the social heritage is bound to have a special richness.

HIGH LIFE AND LOW LIFE

A "sort of world's show of humanity"—such was that San Francisco which so impressed the visiting Britisher, J. D. Borthwick, in 1851, with its "immense amount of vitality compressed into a small compass." Around the same table in the gambling saloons he found "well-dressed, respectable-looking men, and, alongside of them, rough miners fresh from the diggings, with well-filled buckskin purses, dirty old flannel shirts, and shapeless hats; jolly tars half-seas over . . . Mexicans wrapped up in their blankets smoking cigaritas . . . Frenchmen in their blouses smoking black pipes; and little urchins, or little scamps rather, ten or twelve years of age, smoking cigars as big as themselves . . ." Along the streets, old miners were to be seen loafing about "in all the glory of mining costume . . . Troops of newly arrived Frenchmen marched along . . . their persons hung around with tin cups, frying-pans, coffee-pots, and other culinary utensils . . . Crowds of Chinamen were also to be seen, bound for the diggings, under gigantic basket-hats . . ."

After the first rush to the mines, most of this mob of immigrants returned to San Francisco to stay. Careless of the professions to which they had been trained, doctors and dentists became draymen, barbers, or shoeblacks. Lawyers and brokers turned waiters or auctioneers or butchers; merchants became laborers and laborers, merchants. Any and all of them kept lodginghouses and gambling saloons, speculated in real estate and merchandise—always ready to embark on some new enterprise.

Not without reason did the Argonauts boast that no coward ever started for California and no weakling ever got there. The Gold Rush was composed almost entirely of young men, many in their 'teens, with a lust for adventure as strong as their lust for fortune. In this adventurers' paradise, ladies of joy reveled in a degree of latitude rarely heard of in American history. While cribs and brothels catered to the unfastidious, more sumptuous parlors enticed the discriminating. When "the Countess," San Francisco's leading courtesan of 1849, opened her establishment, she sent cards of invitation to the town's leading citizens, not excluding the clergy. Full dress was the rule at this fasionable rendezvous, and six ounces of gold dust, or $96, was the price of an evening's entertainment.

Any talents used to entertain the public were handsomely appreciated. Dr. D. G. Robinson, part-owner of the Dramatic Museum, was elected alderman in 1851 to reward him for the pleasure he had given by renditions of his "Random Rhymes." No one chought it strange in 1849 when the Commissioner of Deeds, Stephen C. Massett, resigned from his job to compose songs and to give recitations and imitations. A strolling piper with "cymbal, triangle, accordion and bass-drum" gathered a "harvest," and "Dancing Billy" earned enough to buy drinks all around each time he stopped, and was able to pay his musician $50 an hour. The musicians "blew and scraped, thrummed and drummed, jingled and banged throughout the live-long day and night."

In every saloon were tables for monte and other card games, or for rondo and roulette and chuck-a-luck. Gambling facilities were the main source of revenue in all hotels. Merchants had to bid against their operators for places to do business; the resorts spilled over onto the wharves. Most of the gold which miners brought to town made its final disappearance over the tables, for the men had a superstition that it was bad luck not to be flat broke when they started back to the mines.

In 1853, the editors of the *Christian Advocate* made a survey of the town and "found, by actual count, the whole number of places where liquor is sold in this city to be five hundred and thirty-seven." Of these, 125 places did not even "keep an onion to modify the traffic." Forty-eight were "dance-houses and such like, where Chinese, Mexicans, Chilean, and other foreign women are assembled." Contemporary writers describe the saloons as "glittering like fairy palaces." The outlying taverns were spoken of with no less warmth: "A jolly place to lounge in easy, ricketty, old China cane chairs and on bulgy old sofas" was MacClaren's, on the lane to the Mission. Little inns with similar charm were strung along all the rural roads.

On Sunday, the Spanish village at the Mission was aglitter with the silver trappings of hitched horses, whose owners, having ridden out from the commercial settlement, were spending the day in the Spanish taverns. The Russ Gardens, along the Mission Road, were taken over on holidays and Sundays by national groups who "leaped, balanced and twirled, danced, sang, smoked and made merry."

Though the 1850's saw no abatement in gambling, drinking, and carousing, the more discriminating element of the population was gradually withdrawing from the more popular saloons and restaurants. New hotels and cafes were being established to meet their demands. The Parker House with its elegant appointments, its apple toddy, and its painting of *Eugenia and Her Maids of Honor,* vied for popularity with the Pisco Punch and the *Samson and Delilah* of the Bank Exchange. Around these, the Tehama, and the St. Francis gathered those who were groping toward refinement and that privacy which their lack of homes denied them. Private gambling dens were set up and a process of social selection began.

Steve Whipple's gambling house on Commercial Street was transformed, in 1850, into the first gentlemen's club, its clientèle girded in swallowtails and flashing diamond cuff links. Such devices for "drawing the line" were not without painful consequences to that spirit of camaraderie which the average forty-niner had naively come to expect of his fellow men. An anecdote of this period tells of a miner, wearing the rough clothes of the "diggings," who wandered inside and was politely informed by a waiter that he had strayed into a private club.

"A private club, eh?" retorted the miner. "Well, this used to be Steve Whipple's place and I see the same old crowd around!"

Nevertheless, San Francisco's leading citizens were determined to create some kind of orderly and civilized social pattern; and this tremendous task was finally solved by elevating the saloon, the cafe, and the theatre to places of social distinction. Even before 1851 there had been attempts to stage decorous balls and parties where "fancy dress" was required, but even the most successful of these affairs could not attract more than 25 ladies. A record was set in June, 1851, by the attendance of 30 fair maidens at the first of a series of *soirées* given at the St. Francis; and when 60 ladies showed up at the July *soirée,* the newspapers commended the St. Francis for the "social service" it had rendered.

But this hotel (which also first introduced bed sheets to the city) was to be the scene of an even greater triumph. This was a grand ball organized by the Monumental Six, the city's first company of volunteer firemen, at which no less than 500 ladies were present. It was said that California was ransacked for this array of femininity, and that some of them were brought by pony express from as far east as St. Joseph, Missouri. The press declared that at last "the elements were resolving themselves into social order."

Since the brilliance of this affair was not immediately repeated, the process of social cohesion threatened to give way once more to the rough-shod individualism of the forty-niners. Even the respectable women of San Francisco complained of the high cost of party dresses and avoided going out into the muddy and rat-infested streets. The men started attending the theater, but it offered little attraction. The rainy season set in and brought monotony to the city which, until then, had never known a dull moment.

In this social emergency, some enterprising individuals hit upon the idea of presenting a series of "promenade concerts." "A large crowd was present on the first evening, but . . . there were no ladies present to join in the ball at the close of the concert; and such a scene as was presented when the dancing commenced beggars description. . . . The music commenced; it was a polka; but no one liked to venture. At last two individuals, evidently determined to start the thing, ladies or no ladies, grappled each other in the usual way . . . and commenced stumping it through the crowd and around the hall . . . As dance after dance was announced more and more joined in, until . . . the whole floor [was] covered with *cotillions* composed entirely of men, with hats on, balancing to each other, chassezing, everyone heartily enjoying the exhilarating dance . . ." Whether or not the affair was a "failure," as McCabe's *Journal* called it, the promenade concerts were abandoned.

What civic-minded San Franciscans could never quite accomplish in the battle for social cohesion was brought about by natural and dire necessity. As a result of the conflagrations that had almost destroyed the city on six successive occasions, there had sprung up a number of companies of volunteer firemen, to which it was generally considered an honor to belong. A parade of San Francisco's firemen was the occasion for the whole State to go on a Roman holiday. Preceded by blaring bands and the gleaming engines decked with flags, the parades stretched a mile in length. Each fireman marched proudly to the martial music, attired magnificently in his red shirt and white muffler, his shiny black helmet, and his trousers upheld by a broad black belt. Each firehouse, on parade days, was thrown open to the public. The city's leading breweries gave kegs of beer, and other firms donated crackers, cheese, and sandwiches.

The engine houses themselves were furnished as lavishly as the hotels and restaurants of the later fifties. Howard Engine, to which Sam Brannan gave allegiance, was one of the most splendid of them all and was especially noted for the brilliance of its social functions. The Monumental Six and the High Toned Twelve might boast more elegant houses, but the "Social Three," as Howard Engine was popularly known, had the only glee club and the first piano. Long afterwards San Franciscans recalled with pride that magnificent dinner the "Social Three" once gave for the visiting firemen from Sacramento. The menu on that occasion, still preserved in the M. H. de Young Museum, was "of cream satin, a foot and a half long and a foot wide, highly embossed, and elaborately decorated in red, pink, and blue, the work of the finest ornamental printers in the city."

So rapidly did the city grow that by 1856 all its aspects of intolerable crudity had disappeared. Plank sidewalks brought a measure of safety to pedestrians, and substantial new buildings were going up in every street. The custom of promenading took hold on everyone; and Montgomery Street became for the next 30 years an avenue filled with the endless pageantry that was old San Francisco.

It was a gay and motley crowd that paraded there every day of the week in the 1850's and 1860's—a crowd utterly democratic and unconventional. From the fashionable quarter at California and Stockton streets came the wives and daughters of San Francisco's wealthy set. "Tall, finely proportioned women with bold, flashing eyes and dazzling white skin" came from the half-world of Pike Street (now Waverly Place). Lola Montez was known to pass along this street, her bold admirers kept at a distance by the riding-whip she carried. Men were still in the majority; bankers, judges, lawyers, merchants, stock brokers, gamblers—all wearing silk hats, Prince Albert coats, ruffled shirts, fancy waistcoats, and trousers fitted below the knee to display the highly polished boot.

Mingling with this passing show were strange public characters whom everyone accepted as part of the parade. "George Washington" Coombs, who imagined himself to be the father of his country, paraded the streets in coat, waistcoat, and breeches of black velvet, low shoes with heavy black buckles, black silk stockings, and a cocked hat. The tall disdainful figure of The Great Unknown, clad in the height of fashion and impenetrable mystery, was the cynosure for all eyes, but never was he known to stop or talk to anyone in the years he followed this solitary course. The street beggars, Old Misery (also known as the Gutter Snipe) and Old Rosey each morning appeared, gathering odds and ends from refuse cans—Old Rosey always wearing a flower, usually a rose, in his dirty coat lapel. There were also the two remarkable mongrels, Bummer and Lazarus, whose relationship transcended ordinary animal affection; together they trotted the same course as the paraders.

Also allowed a certain patronage was Oofty Goofty, the Wild Man of Borneo in a sideshow, who walked the sidewalks of the Barbary Coast, in a garb of fur and feathers, and emitted weird animal cries. Later he launched into new fields, allowing anyone to kick him for 10¢, hit him with a cane or billiard cue for 25¢, with a baseball bat for 50¢. When the great pugilist John L. Sullivan tried his luck with the bat, Oofty Goofty was sent to the hospital with a fractured spine. After his recuperation, he engaged in freak shows as the companion and lover of Big Bertha.

The era was a heyday of street preachers: evenings and Sunday mornings would find Old Orthodox and Hallelujah Cox delivering orations to accumulating multitudes. Stalking them would be Old Crisis, a vitriolic freethinker of the times, who would mount the rostrum when they had vacated. The itinerant patent-medicine distributors also did a thriving business. Of these, the King of Pain, attired in scarlet underwear, a heavy velour robe, and a stovepipe hat decorated with ostrich feathers, rode in a black coach drawn by six white horses. Found daily on the sidewalks around the financial district was a greasy figure, old and lonely, displaying a large banner reading, Money King, You Can Borrow Money Cheap; the King of Pain charged his borrowers exorbitant rates of interest.

Last, but by no means least, came the Emperor Norton attired in his blue Army uniform with its brass buttons and gold braid and his plumed beaver hat. Everybody knew and liked this mildly insane little Englishman, who, after heavy financial reverses had wrecked his mind, styled himself Norton I, Emperor of North America and Protector of Mexico. For two decades, traveling from one part of the city to another, he saw to it that policemen were on duty, that sidewalks were unobstructed, that various city ordinances were enforced. He visited and inspected all buildings in process of construction. The newspapers solemnly published the proclamations of this kindly old man, and his correspondence with European statesman. When in need of funds, he issued 50¢ bonds, supplied by an obliging printer, which were honored by banks, restaurants, and stores. His funeral, in 1880, was one of the most impressive of the times, with more than 30,000 attending the ceremony in the old Masonic Cemetery. When, only a few years ago, his remains were removed to Woodlawn Cemetery, down the Peninsula, an infantry detachment fired a military salute, and "taps" were blown over his grave.

The "golden sixties" saw the flowering of a Western culture, wherein the uncouth, violent San Francisco of Gold Rush days evolved to the tune of Strauss waltzes and polite salutations from carriage windows; and the grand social events of the Civil War period brought to the Oriental Hotel, the Lick House, and the St. Francis a social pageantry, splendid and refined. The tobacco-spitting, gun-toting forty-niner was being taken in hand by such arbiters of propriety as Mrs. Hall McAllister and Mrs. John Parrott. *Nouveau riche* citizens of Northern sympathies were succumbing to the gracious mode of living taught by the Secessionists. The aristocratic Southern set, which insisted on a certain formality, could, however, always forgive those who violated its discipline with charm and wit and good taste. Gradually the fashionable parade of carriages outshone the promenade of Montgomery Street; and the exodus toward Market Street began, which was to erase the most distinguished feature of San Francisco as the city of the Argonauts. But it was in the large ball rooms of private homes that the magnificence of San Francisco's social life was shown to best advantage. Here, seemingly oblivious of the civil strife, San Franciscans gave full rein to their natural gaiety.

The completion of the transcontinental railroad put an end to the splendid isolation in which San Franciscans had reveled for two decades. Soon the fantastic wooden castles of the Big Four were to rise on the summit of Nob Hill, to announce to an astonished citizenry that San Francisco was at last an American city. "California has annexed the United States" was the prevailing opinion, but it was only the final and defiant expression of the pioneer spirit that refused to admit its heyday was over. With money running plentifully, society in the seventies and eighties was tempted to relax, to catch what lavish silver-toned enjoyment emerged from its pompous realm.

Marking the first official get-together of writers, artists, and dilettantes, the Bohemian Club was founded in 1872, with quarters on Pine Street above the California Market. Under the guidance of art-loving Raphael Weill, the club opened its portals to Sarah Bernhardt and Coquelin the Elder and, later, entertained with elegant breakfasts, luncheons, and dinners in the Red Room of its building at Post and Taylor streets. Other notables sampling the Bohemian Club's correct and charming hospitality, which was acknowledged to speak for all San Francisco, were Nellie Melba, Ellen Terry, Rudyard Kipling, Henry Irving, Helena Modjeska, and Ignace Paderewski.

During this era and the Gay Nineties San Francisco was to achieve its reputation as "the wickedest city in the world." The pot-bellied little champagne salesman, Ned Greenway, led society through the artful steps of the cotillion. Sprightly Lillie Hitchcock, as honorary member of the San Francisco Fire Department, aroused disapproving thrills among smart matrons by wearing the resplendent badge presented her by the Knickerbocker 5. Returning from entertainment furnished in the rose-tinged Poodle Dog at Bush and Dupont Streets or from Delmonico's, railroad builders and Comstock financiers chatted of rare vintages.

Along the Barbary Coast, the underworld whirled in fantastic steps to the rhythmic tunes of banging pianos, banjos, tom-toms, and blaring brass horns. It was the era of checkered suits, derby hats, and bright turtleneck sweaters. The police patrolled the district in pairs. Assisted by honky-tonk pianos grinding out "Franky and Johnny," gamblers fleeced their victims with inscrutable calm. From Barbary Coast dives to the Hotel St. Francis came the banjo, with Herman Heller as orchestra leader, soon to be followed by Art Hickman's introduction of the saxophone, which would bring jazz to the modern era.

It was into this phantasmagoric atmosphere that Arnold Genthe brought Anna Pavlova on a slumming tour. At the Olympia, a glittering dance hall, she watched the rhythmic sway of the dancers. Fascinated, soon she and her partner were on the floor. No one noticed them, no one knew who they were. Feeling the barbaric swing of the music, they soon were lost in the oblivion of the time-beats of the orchestra. One couple after another noticed them and stepped off the floor to watch. Soon they were the only dancers left on the floor, the other dancers forming a circle around the room, astonished, spellbound. The music stopped, Pavlova and her partner were finished, there was a moment of silence. Then came a thunderous burst of applause, a stamping of feet, a hurling of caps. The air was filled with yells of "More!" Pavlova was in tears.

San Francisco "remembered" the sinking of the battleship *Maine* with characteristic gusto in 1898. While transports clogged the Bay, the boys in blue camped in the Presidio hills and daily marched down Market Street to the troopships to the tune of "There'll Be a Hot Time in the Old Town Tonight" and other popular ballards of the day. The Spanish War to San Franciscans was almost one continuous fiesta. Too late for the war, the battleship *Oregon* steamed into the Bay to celebrate the victory. Public subscription erected a monument in Union Square to Admiral George Dewey who captured Manila.

Soon the "ridiculous" horseless carriage was snorting along the roads in Golden Gate Park; later it ventured timorously downtown to frighten the bearded or bustled citizens, who viewed the "newfangled contraption" only to maintain that horse and cable cars "were fast enough."

Near the corner of Powell and Market streets, in 1914, stood some of the most famous of the cabarets and taverns in the West. On Powell Street were the Odeon, the Portola Louvre, and the Techau Tavern. Around the corner was the Indoor Yacht Club. On Mason Street flourished the Black Cat, the Pousse Café, and Marquard's, and within walking distance were famous bars, such as the Waldorf and the

Orpheum, and innumerable foreign restaurants. While the graft investigation scandals of 1906 had forced the toning down of the city's night life, it was not until the war years and the advent of Prohibition that the death knell of San Francisco's gaiety was sounded.

Most of the cabarets closed, never again to reopen. San Franciscans disdained grape juice and patronized the bootlegger; they escaped, however, the curse of the gangster, who in most cities crept in with temperance. The Odeon became a cafeteria, as did the Portola Louvre. The Techau Tavern became a candy store; Marquard's became a coffee shop. Over Old San Francisco, twilight had fallen, from which it never would emerge. San Francisco would be the same city when the era of sobriety came at last to its end, but, like wine in a bottle once opened, then corked and laid away, its flavor would be gone.

BEFORE THE FOOTLIGHTS

Through the ingenuous emotions of a child of the eighties, a famous San Franciscan has tried to lay a finger on the special and intrinsic values that have caused San Francisco to be considered a great theater city: "Actors in those days liked to go out to the Coast, and as it was expensive to get back and not expensive to stay there they stayed . . . Uncle Tom's Cabin . . . was very nearly my first play . . . Then I enormously remember Booth playing *Hamlet* but there again the only thing I noticed . . . is his lying at the Queen's feet during the play . . . although I knew there was a play going on there, that is the little play. It was in this way that I first felt two things going on at one time."

The theater-goer here probing back into her childhood was a longtime resident of San Francisco—Gertrude Stein—later associated with the stage herself as the author of *Four Saints in Five Acts*. And the conclusion she draws may be extended to all the theater-goers and actors of San Francisco, who have never lost the feeling of two things going on at one time: that active co-operation of audience and actor.

The Americans who came with their banjos ringing to the tune of "O Susanna!" were not content for long with wandering minstrelsy. By the middle of 1849, they had lined their pockets with gold, were dressed up, and wanted some place to go. In an abandoned schoolhouse, from which the teacher and trustees had departed for the mines, on June 22, 1849, Stephen C. Massett, "a stout red-faced little Englishman," adventurer and entertainer who also called himself "Jeems Pipes of Pipesville," gave a one-man performance of songs and impersonations, for which the miners were happy to pay him more than $500. Following Massett came the first professional company—"h"-dropping Australians—who presented on January 16, 1850, Sheridan Knowles' touching drama, *The Wife*. The excellence of this performance may be judged from the leading lady's speech, quoted from another play, *The Bandit Chief:* " 'is 'eart is as 'ard as a stone—and I'd rayther take a basilisk and wrap 'is cold fangs around me, than surrender meself to the cold himbraces of a 'eartless villain!" The theater was filled with curious, excitable miners, who paid as high as $5 for admission. Yet the miners soon learned to order such hams out of town at the pistol point.

The circus had already come to town, even preceding the Australians. Wandering by way of Callao and Lima, the enterprising Joseph A. Rowe brought his troop to a lot on Kearny Street, opening October 29, 1849. Here materialized a curious phenomenon, the alternation of circus performances with the tragedies of Shakespeare. Rowe on February 4, 1850, put on *Othello*—the first of a long series of Shakespearean performances.

The early 1850's were noted for a series of off-stage tragedies that periodically snuffed out the stage performances. Six disastrous fires brought theater buildings down with the rest of the city. In the period from 1850 to 1860, there were three Jenny Linds, two Americans, two Metropolitans, two Adelphis, to say nothing of structures not rebuilt—the Dramatic Museum, the National, the Theatre of Arts, the Lyceum, and countless others. But with pioneer courage the city rebuilt.

And struggling through these fires to make theater history in San Francisco were Tom Maguire and Dr. David G. "Yankee" Robinson— utterly unlike except for their power as impresarios. With Dr. Robinson came the first crude stagecraft and the first real satires on the local scene. On July 4, 1850, he opened his Dramatic Museum on California Street, with a localized adaptation of *Seeing the Elephant,* a popular circus deception. He started the first dramatic school in San Francisco. An actor himself and a kind of playsmith, he was the life-blood of his theater. One of his plays, *The Reformed Drunkard,* has had many revivals under the title *Ten Nights in a Barroom.*

Beginning as an illiterate cab driver, gambler, and saloon keeper, Tom Maguire came to be one of the country's great impresarios. This man, like the city itself, was fiery, good-natured, both acquisitive and generous; ignorant, uncouth, eager for novelty and yet animated by a childlike passion to be a patron of "culture." Sleight-of-hand artists, opera singers, sensational melodramas, jugglers, minstrels, Shakespeare, leg-shows: all these succeeded each other swiftly at Maguire's Opera House during its eighteen years of existence. The only man comparable to him in his time was P. T. Barnum.

The roaring fifties saw a cavalcade of exits and entrances on the San Francisco stage: James Stark, that ambitious young tragedian; Mrs. Sarah Kirby Stark, his wife, and a noted actress-manager; the prolific and talented Chapman family, headed by William, Caroline and George; the perennial Mrs. Judah as Juliet's nurse; and the unsurpassed family of Booth, magniloquent Junius Brutus and the adolescent Edwin. The "Sensation Era" of the 1860's brought Lola Montez, Adah Isaacs Menken, and Lotta Crabtree, those glamor girls of the Gold Coast. And late in the 1860's came Emily Melville, of musical comedy fame, whose subdued style of the French school usurped the place of the "sensation" manner.

It was the "Sensation Era" which saw the rise of the melodeons or variety houses, whose insouciance and camaraderie of atmosphere were to be found nowhere else but in San Francisco. They reflected the life of the city as the more respectable, more resplendent theaters did not. The girls who so cavorted might be found variously at the Bella Union, Gilbert's, and the other melodeons, in such extravaganzas as *The British Blondes, The Black Crook, The Black Rook, or The Black Rook with a Crook.*

The "big time" theaters of the city came and went, and the "inquitous" Bella Union outlived them all, impudently mocking the pretensions of the great. There were other melodeons: the Alhambra (later the Bush Street Theatre); Gilbert's Melodeon (later the Olympic); the Temple of Music (later the Standard); Buckley's Adelphi; the Pacific Melodeon and hosts of others of less importance. But of all these the Bella Union was the prototype. In the burlesques was the healthy spirit of satire; the minstrels alone had the temerity to deflate the balloon pretensions of the tycoon age. Many of the performers are still remembered: Lotta Crabtree, Joe Murphy "The Great," Joseph and Jeff de Angelis, Eddie Foy, Ned Harrigan, Eliza Biscaccianti, Ned Buckley, James Herne, and the incomparable Harry Courtaine. A periodic drunkard, irresponsible, incurable, the despair of managers and the delight of audiences, Courtaine always returned and was always forgiven because there was no performer like him in the city.

The curtain went up on a new era, when William C. Ralston opened his new California Theater in 1869. In the audience were Bret Harte, Leland Stanford, James Fair, James Flood, John Mackay, and Emperor Norton. The name of the play was *Money*. A *Bulletin* reporter said rapturously of the drop curtain: ". . . the lookers-on were held breathless . . . with a thrill of surprised delight . . ." No less thrilling had been the scene outside the building, where *grandes dames* in full silk gowns had been met by the host, Lawrence Barrett. Presently they heard from his lips the dedicatory poem—a rapturous incoherency from the pen of Bret Harte.

The building of the California Theater was the signal for Tom Maguire's decline. The actors for whom Ralston built this sumptuous house, John McCullough and Lawrence Barrett, had both, ironically enough, been brought to San Francisco by Maguire. When his Opera House, on Washington Street, now "out of the way," was destroyed in 1873, along with its rival Metropolitan, Maguire took over two theaters in the Bush Street district. But the old magic touch was gone. Ralston's entry into the theatrical world was the sign for other wealthy men to follow. In 1876 E. J. "Lucky" Baldwin built the Baldwin Academy of Music. Maguire, finding it harder to raise capital than in the old reckless days, became manager of Baldwin's Academy; but, in 1882, he threw up the sponge and departed for the East, never to return. With him departed an era.

Later houses were chiefly notable for their actor-managers, the excellent stock companies which played there, and the world-famous actors who appeared: Edwin Booth, Lawrence Barrett, Adelaide Neilson, Helena Modjeska, John Drew, Maurice Barrymore, and a host of others. San Francisco was, and long remained, the only city in the United States, outside of New York, where a high-salaried player could be assured a long and lucrative stay.

Probably the most dramatic incident in the history of the San Francisco theater attended the production of *The Passion Play* at the Grand Opera House in 1879. Written by Salmi Morse, a Jew, it was announced for March 8 and 9, with James O'Neill, a Catholic, as the Christus. A storm of protest followed—mostly from clergymen—and the Board of Supervisors threatened to prohibit the performance. They were forestalled by the production of the play on March 3. Riots broke out which threatened the safety of any recognizable Jew appearing on the streets. The production of the play continued, however, with interruptions, until April 21, when Morse withdrew it "in deference to public opinion." The storm so affected him that a few months later he took his own life in New York.

The end of the century saw David Belasco, a humble prompter at the Baldwin Theatre, laying the foundation for his career. It saw little Maude Adams, aged nine, in *Fairfax;* Lillian Russell, a youthful unknown, in *Sparks* at the Standard; and Maurice Barrymore's talented daughter, Ethel, with a company including John Drew. Adelina Patti came to count out her $5,000 in cash every night before going on the stage, and Sarah Bernhardt, cooing, cursing, and dying in 130 roles; Anna Held augmented her theatrical prestige with publicity about beauty baths in milk; and Edith Crane, who appeared as Trilby, had full-sized photographs of her number 3 shoes published in the San Francisco papers. And that same Mauve Decade saw Henry Irving and Ellen Terry; a very risqué play at the Baldwin entitled *Lady Windermere's Fan;* and Blanche Bates in *The Darling of the Gods.* Marie Dressler came to dance the buck and wing, and Harry Houdini to make his mystifying escapes.

All but one of the city's theaters, both elegant and rowdy, were eliminated at a single stroke by the fire of 1906. By that time the early millionaire angels were dying and leaving their money to more sedate institutions such as art galleries, so the local drama began its struggle back with less assistance than it had enjoyed before. The possibility of its recovering an important place in the life of San Franciscans was doomed by the advent of moving pictures. Since then there have been many nights when no curtain rose anywhere in a once-great theatrical town.

The revival of theatrical activity in the amateur and little theater movement of the 1930's was brief but lively in San Francisco, ending with the demise of most groups at the onset of World War II. The Federal Theater Project had staged a successful career in this period, playing to large audiences in the old Alcazar Theater such hits as *Run Little Chillun, The Swing Mikado,* and its "Living Newspaper" plays. It was closed by Congress in 1939, and the war years that followed brought to a halt also the productions not only of most amateur groups but also of the city's distinctive foreign language theaters: Andre Ferrier's Gaieté Francaise or Théatre d'Art, the only permanent French theater in America, and Chinatown's two theaters, the Great China and the Mandarin, dating back to the 1850's, in which travelling companies from China had performed.

The one non-commercial theater group which survived the war as a producing organization was the democratically organized Theater Arts Colony, founded in 1939 under Arthur B. Gleditzsch's direction, offering performances at intervals in its own playhouse and operating a theater and radio school. When peace came it was hoping to build a theater truly representative of San Francisco's cultural background.

In most of San Francisco's schools and recreation centers, however, amateur casts are unceasingly busy learning lines, making costumes, and staging performances. Hundreds of young San Franciscans gained an exceptional appreciation for the drama because Maxwell Anderson, hoarding a trunkful of unproduced plays, put them through their Shakespeare at Polytechnic High. Many worked with Dan Totheroh in the Mountain Play on Mount Tamalpais. Babies made their first acquaintance with the theater in fairy stories staged by The Children's Theater Association.

For San Franciscans the theater has never been a shrine for the cult of indifferentism. Many were the nights when Lola Montez heard cries of "Bravo"; and many were the nights when she was pelted with vegetables. The spontaneity of theater audiences continues to draw comment from both sides of the footlights. John Hobart of the San Francisco *Chronicle* has stated succinctly San Francisco's distinction as a theater city: "New York audiences are quick, but easily bored;

in Chicago, they are over-boisterous; in Boston, they are over-refined; in Los Angeles, they are merely inattentive. But in San Francisco the *rapport* between the people out front and the players behind the footlights is ideal, for there is stimulation both ways, and a kind of electricity results."

MUSIC MAKERS

In one of San Francisco's gambling saloons, the El Dorado, a female violinist, "tasking her talent and strength of muscle," alternated musical offerings with exhibitions of gymnastic skill. At the Bella Union five Mexicans strummed the melodies of Spain. At the Aguila de Ora a group of well-trained Negroes gave the city's first performance of spirituals. Meanwhile, from lesser bars and shanties issued a cacophony of singing, stomping, and melodeon-playing.

This was the town with hundreds of suicides a year, the town that stopped a theatrical performance to listen to an infant crying in the audience. It was the town of Australia's exiled convicts, of professors turned bootblacks, of a peanut vendor wearing a jurists's robes. Men outnumbered women twelve to one, had built a hundred honky-tonks but only one school. Here was humanity suspended in an emotional vacuum—or what would have been a vacuum but for the lady gymnast tripping from trapeze to violin and the Negroes harmoniously invoking glory. The demand for music was furious—and furiously it was supplied. Eveunutally normal living conditions were established; but the stimulus of music had been accepted as a permanent necessity.

The Gold Rush ballads had a tranquil prelude in the Gregorian chant taught by the Franciscan friars to the mission Indians. An observer, visiting one of the missions in later years, spoke of these choirs: "The Indians troop together, their bright dresses contrasting with their dark and melancholy faces . . . They pronounce the Latin so correctly that I could follow the music as they sang . . ." The friars next taught the Indians to play the violin, 'cello, flute, guitar, cymbal, and triangle, and their neophytes surprised them by producing a lyrical rhythm unlike either the religious or secular.

Meanwhile, the Spaniards on their ranchos accompanied the day's activities with singing. In the midst of weaving, cooking, planting, and riding, the *rancheros* found time to celebrate at seed time as well as at harvest; they danced at all three meals. But the Spaniards' lively airs were destined to be silenced by lusty throats crying for gold.

As early as 1849, the city's cafes began to cater to their patrons' diverse musical tastes. At the El Dorado, an orchestra "played without cessation music ranging from Mendelssohn and Strauss to the latest dance trot"; and Charley Schultz, who enticed customers into the Bella Union with his violin and singing, brought to San Francisco the Hawaiian tune, "Aloha," to which he sang, "You Never Miss Your Sainted Mother 'Till She's Dead and Gone to Heaven."

More to the miners' liking were songs that celebrated their own exploits, like "The Days of Old, the Days of Gold, and the Days of '49," first sung by Charles Penzel (known on the stage as Charles Rhodes), who came with the Argonauts. Another favorite was "A Ripping Trip," sung to the tune of "Pop Goes the Weasel":

> "You go aboard a leaky boat
> And sail for San Francisco.
> You've got to pump to keep her afloat,
> You've got that by jingo.
> The engine soon begins to squeak,
> But nary a thing to oil her;
> Impossible to stop the leak,
> Rip goes the boiler."

Other concerns of the miners were chronicled with "The Happy Miner," "The Lousy Miner," "Prospecting Dream," "The Railroad Cars Are Coming," "What the Engines Said," "What Was Your Name in the States?" These ballads were supplemented by songs brought from foreign homelands.

But many citizens soon demanded more cultivated fare. San Francisco's first concert was performed at the California Exchange on Monday afternoon, December 22, 1850—an exquisite execution of the classics on a trombone by Signor Lobero. Shortly after this the Louisiana Saloon gave a concert. But the attempt to uplift was only half successful; later the *Alta California* felt it necessary to admonish the audience: "We would respectfully advise gentlemen, if they must expectorate tobacco juice in church or at the theatre that they . . . eject it upon their own boots and pantaloons . . ." The Arcade Saloon announced a series of "Promenade Concerts a la Julien." The Bella Union countered with the following invitation: "Grand vocal Concert with Accompaniment—to the lovers of Music of Both Sexes—"

The Germans of San Francisco contributed their substantial talents to the city's musical development. *Turnverein* organizations became the center and stimulus of choral societies; by 1853, four German singing societies were in full swing and had held their first May Day festival.

Miska Hauser, Hungarian violinist, originated the first chamber music group. His own words, appearing in his collected letters, tell the story: "The Quartett which I organized so laboriously gave me for a long time more pleasure than all the gold in California . . . the Quartett in its perfection as Beethoven saw it, this mental Quadrologue of equally attuned souls. . . . My viola player died of indigestion—and for some time I will miss the purest of all Musical pleasures. . . . Too bad that the other three were not solely satisfied with the harmonies of the Beethoven Quartett. They want a more harmonic attribute of $15 each for two hours. . . ."

Mr. Hauser may have had some difficulty in sustaining enthusiasm among his attuned souls, but, in the fifties and sixties, opera burst the town wide open. Eliza Biscaccianti, Catherine Hayes, and Madam Anna Bishop gave the city its first reputation as an opera-loving community. When Biscaccianti opened her first opera season on March 22, 1852, at the American Theatre, there were more calls for conveyances than the city could provide. According to the *Alta California* of March 24: ". . . the evening marked an era in the musical, social and fashionable progress of the city." Despite such appreciation, Mme. Biscaccianti returned to San Francisco six years later to find that her place had been taken by Kate Hayes, press-agented as the "Swan of Erin."

San Francisco lionized these singers in a manner befitting the legendary heroines whose lives they portrayed. When Madam Biscaccianti sang Rossini's *Stabat Mater,* "Fire companies came out in full uniform to honor her and on one occasion their enthusiasm was so great they unhitched the horses from her carriage and pulled her to her hotel." To Miss Hayes also the volunteer firemen gave undeniable proof of their delight.

How the firemen found time from drilling, fighting fires, and attending luminaries to make music of their own is a record of ingenuity. Several companies, however, gave band concerts both in and outside the city. Many other amateur groups often augmented professional offerings. Instrumental ensembles and singing societies were formed by immigrants from France, Great Britain, Switzerland, and a little later by Italians, Finns, and other Scandinavians. Professional musicians, amateurs, and audiences were *en rapport* during the invigorating epoch of the Gold Rush. Thus, by 1860, a rich musical tradition was well on its way to becoming permanent.

The development of symphony music was given its initial impulse by Rudolph Herold, pianist and conductor, who came to California in 1852 as accompanist to Catherine Hayes. The first of Herold's concerts of notable magnitude occurred in 1865, when he conducted an orchestra of 60 pieces at a benefit concert for the widows and children of two musicians. In 1874 he began his annual series of symphony concerts with an orchestra of 50 pieces, continued, with no financial succor to speak of, until 1880. After Herold's retirement, symphony concerts were given more or less regularly under such conductors as Louis Homeier, Gustav Hinrichs, and Fritz Scheel. Scheel, who later founded the Philadelphia Orchestra, was a musician of genius, esteemed by such renowned contemporaries as Brahms, Tchaikovski, and Von Bülow.

The Heart of San Francisco

THE RIBS OF ENTERPRISE: THE ALCOA BUILDING

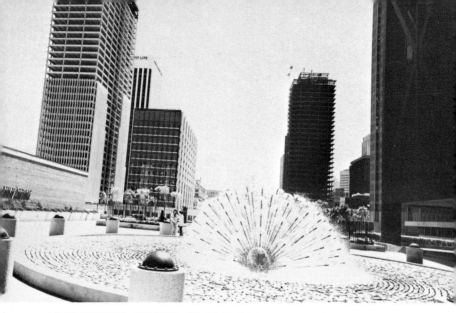

NEW TOWERS ON THE SKYLINE: LOOKING SOUTH FROM
THE ALCOA TERRACE

WESTERN FURNITURE EXCHANGE AND MERCHANDISE MART,
TENTH AND MARKET STS.

IN THE HOTEL DISTRICT; THE NEW HILTON

THE CENTER OF FINANCIAL POWER

MARKET AND BUSH STS. AND ENVIRONS

DETAIL OF FOREGOING VIEW: ZELLERBACH PLAZA,
STANDARD OIL AND WELLS FARGO BUILDINGS

BUILDING THE BAY AREA RAPID TRANSIT STATION
AT MARKET AND FOURTH STS., FEBRUARY, 1969

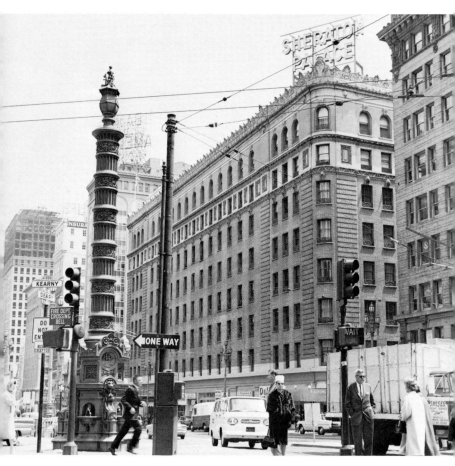

LOTTA CRABTREE FOUNTAIN IN MARKET STREET
AND SHERATON-PALACE HOTEL

No American theater did so much to popularize opera as the Tivoli, best remembered of all San Francisco's theaters, which Joe Kreling opened as a beer garden in 1875, with a ten-piece orchestra and Tyrolean singers. Rebuilt in 1879, it became the Tivoli Opera House. Its career began happily with Gilbert and Sullivan's *Pinafore,* which ran for 84 nights. For 26 years thereafter it gave 12 months of opera each year, never closing its doors, except when it was being rebuilt in 1904: a record in the history of the American theater. For eight months of the year light opera—Gilbert and Sullivan, Offenbach, Van Suppé, Lecoq—was performed, and for four months, grand opera, principally French and Italian, occasionally Wagner. From the Tivoli chorus rose Alice Nielson, the celebrated prima donna.

William H. Leahy, familiarly known as "Doc," who became manager of the Tivoli in 1893, was a keen judge of musical talent. His greatest "find" was Luisa Tetrazzini, whom he discovered while visiting Mexico City, where she was a member of a stranded opera company. In 1905 Tetrazzini made her San Francisco debut at the Tivoli as Gilda in *Rigoletto* and became forthwith the best-beloved singer in the city. When San Francisco was rebuilt after the earthquake and fire of 1906 (as was the Tivoli), Tetrazzini returned to sing in the street, in front of the *Chronicle* office at Lotta's fountain, on Christmas Eve, 1910. Jamming the streets in five directions was the densest crowd ever seen in the city. She also sang at the fourth Tivoli, opened in 1913. But the heyday of the famous theater was over; and on November 23, 1913, it gave its last operatic performance with Leoncavallo conducting his own *I Pagliacci.*

How permanent was the city's musical tradition was proved some 75 years later, when the citizens of San Francisco made their symphony orchestra the first and only one in the nation to be assisted regularly with public money. Since its debut concert in 1911, the San Francisco Symphony has enjoyed more than local respect, under the successive direction of Henry Hadley, Alfred Hertz, Basil Cameron, Issay Dobrowen, Pierre Monteux, Enrique Jorda, Josef Krips and Seiji Ozawa. During the 1934-35 season, conditions became so acute that of the playing personnel only the director, concert-master, and solo 'cellist remained. The situation was remedied by taxpayers who gave a half-cent of every dollar that found its way into the municipal coffers.

Pierre Monteux, conductor (1935-1951), an ex-associate of the Metropolitan Opera and a former conductor of the Boston Symphony and several European organizations, did much to reaffirm the orchestra's position. Beginning in 1937, the season—curtailed during the depression—was increased to 12 concert pairs, carrying over 18 weeks. The San Francisco Symphony was the first major orchestra to admit women to the playing personnel. It has also taken an interest in such youthful to the playing personnel. It has also taken an interest in such youthful prodigies as Leon Fleischer, Grisha Goluboff, Yehudi Menuhin, and Ruth Slenczynski. The orchestra continued to develop during the difficult World War II years to become one of the Nation's major groups. It inaugurated summer concerts in 1945 and the year after, following a season of 63 performances in 20 weeks, made the first North American tour by a Western orchestra. Under Monteux's direction it was presenting at each concert a work new to local audiences and during each season, at least three new works by local composers.

The San Francisco Opera Association owes its existence largely to the energetic Gaetano Merola, who came to California with an organization headed by Fortune Gallo, one of the many traveling companies that visited San Francisco following the twilight of the Tivoli. The present San Francisco Opera Company made its inaugural bow before the public in September, 1923, in the cavernous Civic Auditorium, originally built for convention purposes. In 1932, after 20 years of personal and political wrangling, the War Memorial Opera House— first municipal opera house in the United States—was completed.

By 1970 The San Francisco Opera Co. was staging 12 operas per season, including new productions of the classics, and original works such as *The Visitation, Jenufa,* and Britten's *A Midsummer Nights Dream.*

During World War II a new group rose to prominence when the San Francisco Russian Opera and Ballet Association began presenting beautifully mounted productions of such works as Borodin's *Prince Igor,* Rimsky-Korsakoff's *The Snow Maiden,* and Tschaikowsky's *The Sleeping Beauty.* Growing out of the WPA Music Project's successful revival of *opera bouffe,* Erich Weiler's Comedy Opera in English Company has presented such works as Pergolese's *Maid as Mistress,* Mozart's *The Impresario,* and Offenbach's *Orpheus in the Underworld,* catching their spirit of hilarious pasquinade in librettos pointed up with colloquialisms.

The "quadrologue of equally attuned souls" that Miska Hauser had tried vainly to keep together came to life in the San Francisco String Quartet, a lineal descendant of the earlier Persinger, Hecht, and Abas ensembles, which played for many years in and near San Francisco. The San Francisco String Quartet held the leading position among the city's chamber music artists since 1934. The Budapest, London, and Coolidge Quartets once presented regular annual seasons for many years. Under the auspices of the Music Lovers Society, chamber music of all kinds is given performance.

The impact of the modern environment on the sensibilities of the artist has seldom been better expressed than by San Francisco's Henry Cowell. Though most audiences have been staggered, technically trained composers recognize the theoretical value of Cowell's contribution to modern music. In the Marin hills overlooking the city, Ernest Bloch composed his rhapsody *America,* while serving as director of the San Francisco Conservatory of Music. A teaching position at Mills College brought one of the greatest of modern composers, Darius Milhaud, to the Bay Area, which became his home for many years. Among younger local composers whose works have been played by the San Francisco Symphony Orchestra are Charles Jones and Halsey Stevens. Ray Green and Lew Harrison, local exponents of the modern experimental school, have written instrumental music and brilliant compositions for dance groups. John St. Edmunds, composer of nearly 400 songs somewhat more traditional in technique, received in 1927 the Columbia University Bearns Prize.

To many, the Barbary Coast's unbroken hum of melodeon, piano, Mexican orchestra, and singer was only San Francisco's brawling night voice. But one man caught in these sounds the musical implications of a future rhythm. This man was Ferdinand Rudolph van Grofe—Ferde Grofe—incomparable arranger of jazz, composer of *Grand Canyon Suite* and other notable interpretations of the American scene. As an extra piano player on call at the Old Hippodrome and Thalia, Barbary Coast resorts, he recorded in his mind a medley of folk songs, Negro dance tunes, and sailor's chanties. "The new music in the air along Pacific Street . . . did something to me!"

When Grofe left the Barbary Coast to play the piano with Art Hickman's band at the St. Francis Hotel, the two arranged music that was different and sparkling. Other orchestra leaders who played in San Francisco—Paul Whiteman, Rudy Seiger, and Paul Ash—became conspicuous exponents of this new music. Recent band leaders who have taken off from San Francisco on their musical flights include Paul Pendarvis, Dick Aurandt, Frank Castle, Carl Ravazza, and Ran Wilde.

Home music makers in San Francisco often aspire to the highest professional standards. Amateur groups frequently meet to forget the tensions of the day in the sanity of Brahms or Bach, or in the work of local composers. Both the playing and the composing are marked with a strong beat of self-reliance, in whose echo can be heard the promise of San Francisco's musical future.

SAN FRANCISCO GOES TO CHURCH

For 60 years before the founding of Yerba Buena, the *padres* of Mission Dolores heard their Indian converts recite the *Doctrina Chris-*

tiana, watched their Mexican parishioners lumbering over the sand hills in oxcarts to celebrate saints' feast days. And hardly had the first Argonauts pitched their tents around Portsmouth Square before a Protestant clergyman rose to deliver the doctrine of Methodism. Today nearly 500 churches, representing more than 60 denominations, exert a vast influence over the lives of thousands of San Franciscans. Many were founded amid the turbulence of the Gold Rush, others in the era of industrial expansion. Some have accepted high responsibilities in the city's struggles for public order. Issues of the Civil War, of State and municipal politics were declared from their pulpits.

Sam Brannan's Latter-Day Saints assembled in harbor master William A. Richardson's "Casa Grande" in 1847, but internal dissension— and the Gold Rush—soon caused them to lose their influence. Throughout the winter of 1848 Elihu Anthony, a layman, preached to packed audiences in the Public Institute. His rival, who drew a like number of listeners to this town meeting-house in the Plaza, was the Reverend Timothy Dwight Hunt, a Congregationalist missionary who followed his Argonaut flock from the Sandwich Islands. On his arrival in San Francisco, an enthusiastic citizenry elected him chaplain of the city for one year at a salary of $2,500.

Gold-mad San Francisco offered opportunities for conversion only to such heroic missionaries as that Reverend William "California" Taylor, who conducted open-air meetings on Portsmouth Square in 1849 and became the most renowned of the city's host of street preachers. This resourceful Methodist's approach to the adamantine hearts of his listeners he described later in his memoirs: "Now should a poor preacher presume to go into their midst, and interfere with their business, by thrilling every house with the songs of Zion and the peals of Gospel truth, he would be likely to wake up the lion in his lair. . . . I selected for my pulpit a carpenter's work-bench, which stood in front of one of the largest gambling houses in the city. I got Mrs. Taylor and another lady or two comfortably seated, in the care of a good brother, and taking the stand, I sung on a high key, 'Hear the royal proclamation, the glad tidings of salvation', . . ." The good Reverend Taylor's summons brought people tumbling out of saloons and dancehalls "as though they had heard the cry 'Fire!' 'Fire!' 'Fire!' " Many remained to listen with respect.

In 1854, the Reverend William Anderson Scott, D.D., LL.D., preached his first sermon in San Francisco to a crowd in a dancehall. Neighboring resorts closed during the services, while bartenders, card-dealers, and female entertainers flocked to hear this scholarly Presbyterian from one of New Orleans' largest churches. Subsequent meetings resulted in the construction in 1854 of a church on Bush Street, in a district then notorious for its dancehalls, gambling saloons, and dens of vice. In 1869 this neighborhood became so boisterous that the congregation had to seek a new home. But the Reverend Dr. Scott was no longer on hand to lead them. At the outbreak of the Civil War, he had preached the right of secession to an outraged membership, while a mob of Northerners stormed the front door of his church. Spirited out a rear exit by a loyal female supporter, he was whisked away in a carriage to a ship that took him to safety in New York.

Among claimants to the honor of having erected the city's first Protestant church, Baptists point with pride to that makeshift affair of lumber and sailcloth into which the Reverend Osgood C. Wheeler led his little flock in March, 1849. The Baptist pastor closed his sermon in the spring of that year with a prediction of the city's great commercial future, urging his listeners to build an organization able to cope with so portentous a destiny. The Baptists were to prove equal to their obligations when the Reverend Isaac S. Kalloch headed the reform movement that elected him mayor in 1879.

Meanwhile the six loyal followers of the Reverend Albert Williams, a Presbyterian clergyman, had met in a tent and laid plans for establishing a church of their own. When the prefabricated place of worship arrived from the East and was dedicated, thirty-two ladies attended the proceedings, much to the amazement of the male population.

Just as the Gold Rush offered opportunities for every profession, it welcomed every creed. In such an atmosphere the timid religionist was as lost as the timid gambler, but for the resourceful there was a place. When the luckless miner or workman had nowhere else to turn, he could find a champion of his rights in the pastor of some friendly church. Even the last hours of the Vigilantes' victims were cheered by spiritual consolation.

Of the Protestant sects which have accepted leadership in public affairs, none has had so decisive an influence on San Francisco and the State as the Unitarians. This denomination, during the critical period of the Civil War, had as its Abolitionist representative in California the fiery young evangelist, Thomas Starr King. He was only 35 when, in 1860, he took over the pastorate of San Francisco's Unitarian Church. David Broderick, leading opponent of the State's powerful secessionist minority, had been killed the previous year; and Colonel E. D. Baker, having been elected United States Senator from Oregon, had left California with a ringing appeal for the election of Lincoln. Thus the task of holding the State in the Union column fell on the frail shoulders of the young preacher from Boston, whose personal charm and spellbinding oratory were instrumental in saving California with the election of Leland Stanford as governor in 1861. King's death four years later was due to his strenuous efforts collecting funds for the United States Sanitary Commission, the Red Cross of the Northern armies.

While Lincoln hesitated to proclaim the issue of freedom for the slaves, Thomas Starr King appealed with Abolitionist fervor: "O that the President would soon speak that electric sentence,—inspiration to the loyal North, doom to the traitorous aristocracy whose cup of guilt is full!" That King's idealism went beyond the issues of his day is revealed in his lectures in defense of both the Chinese in California and those white laborers whose hand was raised against them.

The Nation observed King's passing with the firing of minute guns in the Bay; flags hung at half mast on foreign vessels in the Bay, on consulates and all public buildings in San Francisco. In 1927 the California Legislature bracketed his name with Junipero Serra's, and, with the $10,000 appropriated for the purpose in 1913, erected companion statues of these two official California heroes in Statuary Hall, Washington, D. C.

The Episcopal Church can lay claim to the most romantic origin of all local religious institutions. Its *Book of Common Prayer* was used for the first time on American soil by the *Golden Hinde's* chaplain Francis Fletcher, in the service held on the shore of Drake's Bay on June 17, 1579 (old style). Two hundred and seventy years later, in 1849, the Reverend Flavel Scott Mines from Virginia established Trinity Church; and in the same year Grace Church was founded. When Bishop Kip, in 1863, placed his Episcopal Chair in the latter, he thereby made it the first Episcopal cathedral in the United States. Perhaps no other religious leader in the city's history has occupied quite such social prominence as was accorded Bishop Kip. To a gay generation he represented a serenity of faith and a Christian liberalism in which the innocent frivolities of social life might be reconciled with religion. His successor, Bishop Nichols, lived to see the realization of his dream of a cathedral which, when finally completed, would be worthy of his church's ancient tradition. After the 1906 fire, which destroyed the original Grace Cathedral, wealthy families donated sites of their charred mansions on Nob Hill to the Episcopal diocese; and in 1910 the cornerstone of the present majestic Grace Cathedral was laid.

To Gold Rush San Francisco also came leaders of the Roman Catholic faith; and the establishment of American rule offered an opportunity for the Catholic diocese in Oregon to found a pastorate of the Jesuit Order in San Francisco. That the prospects for this venture were more of a challenge than an invitation is clear from the record kept by a colleague of that Father Langlois who, in 1849, arrived to plant his faith "on the longed-for shores of what goes under the name of San Francisco but which whether it should be called the mad-house or Babylon I am at a loss to determine . . ." So hopeless appeared all but a handful of French-Canadians among the Argonauts that the good

Father resolved to depend on these few strayed parishioners to form the nucleus of his congregation.

With the establishment of Bishop Joseph Sadoc Alemany's diocese at Monterey, however, and the early arrival in San Francisco of Father Maginnis to aid in the work, Father Langlois was able to say Mass and baptize the first convert in a new parish chapel. Soon after the arrival from Ireland, in 1853 and 1854, of several Sisters of Mercy, the city's first parochial school had enrolled 300 pupils. Once St. Patrick's Church was established, the firm foundation was laid for the progress of Catholicism in San Francisco. On Christmas Day, 1854, St. Mary's Church was dedicated as the cathedral seat of newly consecrated Archbishop Alemany, whose spiritual domain included California and Nevada.

Despite its history of missionary achievements antedating the signing of the Declaration of Independence, the Catholic Church in San Francisco had to start from scratch, after the 80 years of comparative prosperity in which Mission Dolores had shared. Though title to the land and buildings of Mission Dolores was not restored to the Church until 1860, it was occupied almost continuously by Franciscan or Picpus Fathers between the date of its secularization (1833) and the advent of American rule. The St. Thomas Aquinas Diocesan Seminary, operated at Mission Dolores between 1853 and 1866, was a pioneer in the revival of education; but its efforts to teach white children resemble the arduous pedagogy of the colonial period. Thus matters stood until, in 1855, the Jesuits began the establishment of the College of St. Ignatius, from which the present University of San Francisco has grown. However great the debt owed by Catholicism to the missions and to Junipero Serra, the church in San Francisco has derived its present prosperity from the Gold Rush and bonanza wealth in which it shared.

Two of the city's Hebrew congregations first assembled near Portsmouth Square in 1849. Temple Emanu-El, founded by German Jews, and Temple Sherith Israel, whose original congregation was composed mainly of English and Polish elements, constitute today San Francisco's chief citadels of reformist Judaism. These congregations provide magnificent and modern cultural centers for the city's liberal Jewry. Rabbi Nieto, leader of Sherith Israel congregation for 32 years, played a prominent part in the restoration of the city after 1906. His advocacy of welfare facilities in connection with synagogues resulted in the establishment of Temple Centers throughout the nation. Today in San Francisco the Jews share with the Catholics, in institutions for public welfare which they have separately established, a major responsibility for the city's orphans and aged and destitute; most of the city's hospitals owe their origin and maintenance to Catholic or Hebrew congregations.

Especially characteristic of San Francisco is a host of lesser sects.

From few city directories could be compiled such a list of denominations and churches as this: Seventh Day Adventists (both Greek and Chinese), Mexican Baptists, Buddhists (American and Japanese), Molokans (Russian Christians), Armenian Congregationalists, the Christian Spiritualist Church, the Father Divine Peace Mission, the Glad Tidings Temple, the Golden Rule Spiritualist Church, Jehovah's Witnesses (Negro), the Rosicrucian Brotherhood, the Society of Progressive Spiritualists, the Spanish Pentecostal Church, the Theosophists' United Lodge, the Tin How Temple (Chinese), and the Vedanta Society.

From San Francisco's diverse population, tens of thousands each Easter morning make the difficult pilgrimage up the city's highest hill, Mount Davidson, to worship at the foot of the great cross on the peak. And, here, all forget their differences of creed in a common reverence to that religious spirit which has remained a social force since the city's earliest days.

GENTLEMEN OF THE PRESS

"Some contend," said Yerba Buena's first newspaper in 1847, "that there are really no laws in force here, but the divine law and the law of nature; while others are of the opinion that there are laws in force here if they could only be found." This polite apology for a state of anarchy may have caused some speculation among readers of Sam Brannan's *California Star,* but it foretold nothing of the militant and decisive role journalism was to play for half a century in the public affairs of San Francisco.

More indicative of this role was California's pioneer newspaper, the *Californian,* established in Monterey in 1846 and removed to Yerba Buena a year later. Its editor and publisher, when it became the *Star's* competitor, was that formidable Robert Semple who had helped lead the Bear Flag revolt and published manifestoes of the American occupation. Hardly, however, had Brannan's little sheet begun to ridicule the *Californian's* mild reports of "Gold Mine Found" and "Doc" Semple's patriotic oratory, when news from Sutter's mill race caused both papers to suspend publication. Their publishers and printers joined the stampede to the diggings.

Late in 1848, Edward C. Kemble acquired the *Star,* of which he had been editor when its weekly circulation "outside town and other parts of the globe" was a hundred copies; and, soon after, he bought the defunct *Californian* and combined the two papers under the name *Star and Californian.* With two new associates, printers from New York, Kemble issued in January, 1849, the *Alta California,* which became San Francisco's leading source of news for the next 30 years. Not until

1891 did it finally pass from the scene, having published, in its time, the letters written from Europe by Mark Twain in the 1860's that were compiled in *Innocents Abroad*. Among its managing editors was Frank Soulé, co-author of the *Annals of San Francisco*.

The growth of rival journals, which by 1850 forced the *Alta* to become the first daily, continued throughout the decade with a luxuriance propagated by political factionalism and homesickness among the immigrant population. Not to be outdone, the *Daily Journal of Commerce* was issuing daily editions within 24 hours after its elder rival began doing so. Before the end of 1850, daily editions of *The Herald*, the *Public Balance*, the *Evening Picayune*, the *California Courier*, and the *California Illustrated Times* had appeared.

Despite the high mortality of the press of the Gold Rush era, Kemble in 1858 listed 132 periodicals as having appeared in San Francisco since 1850. Only dailies to survive the decade, however, were the *Alta* and *The Herald*.

That the majority of these organs were rather journals of opinion than newspapers is not surprising. Crime, gold strikes, and other sensational matters were so much the subjects of common knowledge that the press had to search far and wide for news of interest to its readers. The huge influx of immigrants from Eastern communities compelled numerous San Francisco papers to employ correspondents on the Atlantic seaboard, who dispatched bulletins by the steamers that brought also large batches of Eastern newspapers. The Overland Stage, reducing communication between St. Louis and San Francisco to 21 days after 1858, somewhat improved news-gathering facilities; and when a telegraph line was strung in 1861, news of national significance was available. The quality of printing, with the introduction of the Hoe cylindrical press in the 1850's, likewise was improved; and by 1860 a grade of paper better than foolscap was obtainable.

Editorials and classified advertising, however, continued to be the main features of weeklies and dailies alike. Though articles were rarely signed, the style of each editor was instantly recognizable to readers who, according to John P. Young's *History of Journalism in San Francisco*, "looked not so much for intelligence as to see who was being lambasted." This highly personal tone was employed also by editors of less slanderous journals, such as the columnist of the *Golden Era* who addressed his correspondents by their initials and gave fatherly advice. Perhaps this friendly policy had something to do with making the *Golden Era* the city's leading weekly for 30 years after its establishment in 1852.

In the San Francisco of the Gold Rush era, newspaper editors had to be printers, writers of verse, and hurlers of insults; they had to take sides in political controversies, during which their opponents might at any moment attack them in a fist fight or challenge them to a duel. Catherine Coffin Phillips, in her history of Portsmouth Square, states that above one editor's desk was hung this laconic placard: "Subscriptions Received From 9 to 4; Challenges From 11 to 12 only."

Bitterness over the slavery issue was the cause of frequent brawls and armed encounters. Duels were of such common occurrence that newspapers mentioned them only in passing, unless they involved prominent persons. A. C. Russell, an editor on the staff of the *Alta California,* having escaped harm in a duel with pistols, was subsequently stabbed in an "affair of honor" fought with bowie knives. The *Alta's* managing editor, Edward Gilbert, was killed in 1852 by a henchman of Governor John Bigler, who defended his boss against an item intended to make him appear ridiculous. In that same year, the *Alta's* support of David Broderick, campaigning for election to the State Senate on an anti-slavery platform, caused the wounding of another of its editors by an editor of the pro-slavery *Times and Transcript.* An editor of *The Herald,* a daily fighting corruption in municipal politics, was shot in the leg by a city supervisor. James King of William (a distinction invented to avoid confusion with other James Kings), who founded the *Evening Bulletin* in 1855, did not survive his first encounter with a spokesman for the embattled politicians. His death, from a wound inflicted by the supervisor who was editor of the *Sunday Times,* was, however, the signal for mobilization of the Vigilance Committee of 1856. The office of the *Morning Herald,* the *Alta's* most potent rival, was stormed by a mob, who burned its editions in the streets for opposing the committee's work.

The close of the Civil War saw the establishment of the only two daily newspapers that survived long after 1865: the *San Francisco Examiner* and the *San Francisco Chronicle.* The *Dramatic Chronicle,* edited by two brothers in their teens, was so well received after "scooping" the news of Lincoln's death that Charles and M. H. de Young, in 1868, were able to transform it into the daily *Morning Chronicle.* For the next 15 years, under the management of the belligerent Charles, the *Chronicle* entertained its readers with scandal and political onslaughts, while its editor defended himself in duels and libel suits. Following a bitter campaign against the Workingman's Party and its candidate for mayor in 1879, Charles de Young was killed; and for the next 45 years the *Chronicle* was under the direction of his younger brother. Throughout his long career, M. H. de Young, through his managing editor, John P. Young, made his paper a force for political conservatism and social order. Follower of an anti-slavery tradition, the *Chronicle* remained staunchly Republican, its viewpoint attracting to its staff such writers as Will and Wallace Irwin and Franklin K. Lane, who was Secretary of the Interior under President Wilson. Not until the 1930's, however, did it suddenly recapture, under the management of young Paul Smith, the sophisticated quality of its earliest editions.

Leading rival of the *Chronicle* for morning circulation, William Randolph Hearst's *Examiner* was founded on the ruins of the pro-slavery *Democratic Press,* which a mob, provoked by news of President Lincoln's assassination, had wrecked beyond repair. Despite popular indignation, the staff of the *Democratic Press* was carried over intact to the *Daily Examiner.* From its appearance on June 12, 1865, until a wealthy miner named George Hearst bought it in 1880, the *Examiner* defended the interests of Southern Democrats who remained entrenched in California politics. With its transfer to young William Randolph Hearst in 1887, however, began that sensational career which made the *Examiner's* owner a storm center of American journalism for 50 years.

With bonanza millions at his disposal, and a genius for showman-ship, Hearst gathered together a staff that included some of the best newspaper talent that money could buy. S. S. (Sam) Chamberlain, protégé of James Gordon Bennett and founder of the first American newspaper in Paris, became managing editor. The daring resourceful-ness of the *Examiner's* reporters delighted its readers and filled its rivals, especially the *Chronicle,* with alarm. Unheard-of was its print-ing of two full pages of cablegrams from Vienna, relating the mysterious death of Crown Prince Rudolph of Austria and the Baroness Marie Vetsera. *Examiner* correspondents dispatched news from the ends of the earth. Announced with glaring headlines and illustrated with photographs, this dramatization of the news caught the imagination of the public. To the reporting of local news the *Examiner* brought innovations no less startling. One of its editorial writers, the cynical Arthur McEwen, once remarked that reporters risked their necks for the sake of a story to make the public exclaim: "Gee whiz!"

Jack London was on the *Examiner's* brilliant staff in the closing decades of the last century. The modern comic strip was born as cartoonists James Swinnerton, Bud Fisher, Rube Goldberg, R. Dirks, and Homer Davenport labored side by side creating the "Katzenjammer Kids," "Little Jimmy," and "Mutt and Jeff" (created by Fisher from habitués of the old Tanforan Race Track). Ambrose Bierce's "Prattle" made him the most feared of the *Examiner's* columnists. One of his malevolent verses, predicting the assassination of President William McKinley, was interpreted afterwards as an incitation to the act. This gave the popularity of the Hearst papers a setback, but Hearst was already on the way toward establishing his powerful chain. Though the *Examiner* remains one of the leading newspapers on the Coast, it has long since dropped its original pro-labor policy. Vanished also from its offices is that droll atmosphere wherein Hearst himself "would

sometimes preface his remarks to his editors by dancing a jig . . ."
And not since H. D. ("Petey") Bigelow wangled an interview out of
three train robbers in a mountain hideout has the *Examiner* found a
sensation to equal either that story or its author.

Of the city's two former afternoon dailies, the *Call-Bulletin* had
the longer history. Its ancestor, James King of William's militant
Bulletin, fought corruption in politics and finance for half a century.
It was saved from oblivion in 1859, three years after its first editor's
untimely death, by a publisher from New Orleans, G. K. Fitch, who
later sold half his interest to Loring Pickering. Soon afterwards, the
partners acquired the *Morning Call,* a cooperative paper issued by a
group of printers claiming to be "men without frills." Fitch became
editor of the *Bulletin;* Pickering, of the *Call.* Though both papers were
published under the same roof and ownership, their policies were deliberately antithetical. At a time when violent taking of sides was
evidence of red blood, Pickering's *Call* dared to be nonpartisan. Not
less outrageous than its objective reporting was its society page, on
which the doings of the Colonel's lady and Mrs. O'Grady were
chronicled side by side. For 30 years Fitch kept the *Bulletin* alive with
caustic editorials and reportage in the crusading spirit of its founder.
He fought waste in municipal administration and gambling on the stock
exchange, assailed big corporations, and attacked political corruption in
both Democratic and Republican parties.

When, in 1897, the *Bulletin* became the property of R. A. Crothers,
it engaged as managing editor a hard-working journalist from Wis-
consin, whose name was to be associated with San Francisco for the next
two decades. Fremont Older had come West with an ambition to "be
like Horace Greeley," and while he introduced in the *Bulletin* all the
sensational tricks of yellow journalism, he was genuinely motivated
by hatred of injustice and ardor for decency in public affairs. Banner
headlines, cartoons of politicians in striped uniforms, and editorials
solidly documented and barbed with irony revealed the corruption of
the Ruef-Schmitz machine. Triumph of the graft prosecutions made
Older so popular that he was able to name the reform candidate who
was elected mayor. The *Bulletin's* subsequent aid to Hiram Johnson
enabled him to break the railroad monopoly and win the gubernatorial
race of 1910. Older's discovery of perjured evidence in the Thomas
Mooney case, which led him to denounce the prosecution, failed to meet
with such popular acclaim, however. Rather than agree to the milder
policy advised by Crothers, Older resigned from the *Bulletin* in 1918.
Until its merger with the ? *'letin* in 1929, he was managing editor of
the *Call and Post* and thereafter, until his de .. in 1935, of the combined *Call-Bulletin,* which became another link in the Hearst chain.
The merger of the two papers brought an end to the *Post,* which since

1871 had been first the mouthpiece of Henry George of Single Tax fame and then spokesman for the United Railways.

In 1940, celebrating its 85th anniversary, the *Call-Bulletin* moved into new quarters on Howard Street. E. D. Coblentz, a native San Franciscan, returned from New York to act as publisher, relinquishing that post to Randolph Hearst in 1950.

The San Francisco *News* was founded on March 21, 1903, as the 18th link in the Scripps-Howard chain. It adhered to Scripps' declared intention "to put into the homes of workers who had little time to read, honest, fearless thought impartially incorruptible by social, political, or financial influences." Issued originally as the *Daily News* from a mouldy little office "south of the Slot," its penny editions were eagerly bought by workingmen. As late as 1919, a strike of railroad yardmen, though outlawed by union leaders, was headlined with the caption: "Starvation Pay Is Cause of Strike Men Say." A boxed resumé enlarged upon this theme.

In 1923, the *News* acquired a new managing editor, W. N. Burkhart, and in 1930 moved to a plant on Mission Street. Its pro-labor policy became less uncompromising, and it "saw both sides" of the struggle over municipal ownership of public utilities. Thus it was able to cross the social equator of Market Street without losing its circulation in "the Mission."

The *News* merged with the *Call-Bulletin* on August 10, 1959, and six years later on September 13, 1965, the *News-Call Bulletin* and the *Examiner* combined into San Francisco's only afternoon daily.

PART III
Around the World in San Francisco

TOUR KEY MAP
VICINITY OF SAN FRANCISCO

SCALE IN MILES

Civic Center

"Above all the dome, seen so often like that of St. Paul's but dimly through the fog."

—MAURICE BARING

SAN FRANCISCO'S Civic Center constitutes a Beaux Arts monument to the city's cultural tradition, its achievements in democratic government, and its proud position among the commercial centers of the Nation. Dominated by the massive, symmetrical pile of the City Hall—whose dome, surmounted by a gilded lantern, soars high above the city—the block wide plaza, with its fountains flanked by olive trees and topped by a colorful Pavilion of American flags, has been for the last quarter-century the focal point for most public demonstrations. The Civic Center has been the scene of welcome for so many celebrities and so many parades that henceforth—as Charles Caldwell Dobie has suggested—it is likely to become the most popular and historic of the city's landmarks.

The present group of eight buildings, built of California granite in variations of the massive style of the French Renaissance, is an example of city planning to contradict the city's once-famous reputation for letting things run wild. One by one these substantial structures have risen on those blocks within the apex of that angle formed by the convergence of Market Street and Van Ness Avenue which was cleared of debris and ashes after 1906. The $8,000,000 bond issue voted in 1912 laid the foundation for the project. As further funds become available and a need for new units arises, other structures will be added. Perhaps in time the dream of the Civic Center's original designer, D. H. Burnham, will be realized by the extension of its monumental plan to include the entire city.

Municipal government in San Francisco was not always so well-housed or so well-ordered. For more than a half-century after 1776 the seat of local government was a tiny dirt-floored two-room hut, home of the military *comandante* at the Presidio. Here in 1834 met the voters of the district of San Francisco to decide on eleven electors—who later chose the first *ayuntamiento* (town council), consisting of an *alcalde,* two *regidores,* and a *syndico.* These officials entered upon their duties on January 1, 1835. In 1839 the council was abolished. When the State came under American rule in 1846 Lieutenant Washington A. Bartlett of the United States Navy was appointed *alcalde.* Publicly charged in 1847 with misappropriating town funds (amounting to

$750), he was acquitted but nevertheless was withdrawn to the Navy. At a meeting of the common council of six members elected a few months later—which first convened in September 1847—the *alcalde* was permitted to preside over, but not participate in, the discussion. The governmental situation was so confused that the editor of the *California Star* complained plaintively, "we have alcaldes all over . . . who claim jurisdiction over all matters for difference between citizens."

There were to be many complaints, more vociferous, before the government of the growing town became orderly and predictable. At one time no less than three councils each claimed sole right to govern. In 1847 an ordinance provided that two constables should "strictly enforce the law" and "receive for the service of any unit or other process, one dollar, to be paid out of the fines imposed upon cases." In 1848 an ordinance was passed ordering the seizure of all money found on gambling tables, the money to go into the town coffers, but in that same year the lure of gold drained the town of so many inhabitants that at one time not a single officer with civil authority remained. Only 158 people were on hand to cast votes at the election held in October to reestablish some kind of civic administration. Too impatient to wait for the reestablishment of State government, the people met at a public mass meeting in February 1849, organized the Legislative Assembly, and proceeded merrily to make their own laws. The Assembly met 35 times before it was dissolved on June 4 by decree of the military governor of the State, General Bennet Riley. At an election held on August 1, 1,516 votes were cast, all for John W. Geary for *alcalde.* Later that month the *ayuntamiento* purchased the first public building under the American regime—the brig *Euphemia,* which it converted into a jail.

Anticipating by more than four months California's admission to the Union, the city was incorporated April 15, 1850. Under the charter adopted by the already functioning State legislature, a mayor, recorder, and council of aldermen were elected on May 1. The police department was enlarged—but "not to exceed 75 men"—and a fire department headed by a chief engineer was established.

At its first meeting on May 9 the council members promptly rifled the treasury by voting to pay the mayor, recorder, marshal, and city attorney annual salaries of $10,000 and other officials including themselves, $4,000 to $6,000. Later in the year, anticipating the celebration of the admission of the State into the Union, they each awarded themselves a handsome gold medal to cost $150, the expense to be borne by the city. Unfortunately the medals were not completed in time for the celebration; when they did arrive, the town fell into such an uproar that the councilmen prudently paid for the medals out of their own pockets and promptly melted them into "honest bullion." Despite this, sacrifice, the city was $1,000,000 in debt before the end of the year.

The adoption of a new charter by the Legislature in 1851 did little to halt the extravagance of the officials or the depredations of the increasing criminal element. But the Consolidation Act passed by the State Legislature in the same year, which authorized merger of the City and County of San Francisco, creating a Board of Supervisors to replace the double board of aldermen provided for by the charter of 1851, served to establish a more stable civic government. It was to be San Francisco's organic law for 44 years. When the heat of the vigilante movement had subsided, a reform movement headed by the People's Party gained power and held it long enough to put comparatively capable men into office.

When the old city hall burned down, the idea of transforming the Plaza into a reputable center of municipal government moved the council, in 1852, to purchase the Jenny Lind Theater, at Washington and Kearny Streets, for a new seat. So exorbitant was the $200,000 paid for the theater, however, that a storm of public criticism broke out. But the building had to serve. In 1865 the Board of Supervisors refused to pay the city's gas bill. The company promptly removed its lanterns from the street posts and turned off the gas at the city hall. That evening the city fathers, each carrying a flickering candle, stumbled upstairs to discuss the lighting situation.

Finally, in 1870, construction was begun on a new city hall "away out on Larkin Street" at a site then known as Yerba Buena Park (now the site of the Public Library). Originally a tangle of chaparral, this tract had become in 1850 Yerba Buena Cemetery. Economy was the watchword. The city fathers planned construction on the installment basis, paying each installment out of an annual special tax levy. But the piecemeal method of construction boosted costs to more than $7,000,-000, far beyond original estimates, and delayed completion for many years. As the city grew it became apparent that the Consolidation Act no longer sufficed to serve its needs. Twice James Phelan, who headed the reform movement that swept him into the mayor's chair in 1897, attempted, with the aid of a Committee of One Hundred, to secure adoption of a new charter, but without success. But in 1900 the electorate accepted at last a freeholders' charter which loosened the State Legislature's grip on municipal affairs, outlined a definite policy of municipal ownership of public utilities, and substituted civil service for the spoils system in civic administration.

But the new charter was not enough to protect the city government from the Ruef-Schmitz ring, into whose hands it fell in 1902. When the old city hall came tumbling down in less than 60 seconds at the first shock of the earthquake on April 18, 1906, municipal wrath gave impetus to the already gathering movement for cleaning house. In 1908 a supervisors' committee solemnly reported that "so far the most rigid inspection of the standing and fallen walls . . . have (*sic*) failed to disclose any large voids or enclosed boxes, barrels or wheelbarrows that have been told in many an old tale as evidence of lax supervision and contractors' deceits." But many San Franciscans went on believing "many an old tale." And when they decided to build a new city hall, they were determined that its occupants should be more worthy of the public trust and more responsible for the public welfare.

The urgency of rebuilding the ruined city defeated the city planning efforts of Daniel H. Burnham, whose vision of a system of great boulevards encircling and radiating from the intersection of Market Street and Van Ness Avenue (and the extension of the Golden Gate Park panhandle) was not to be realized, but when the city began, in 1912, to plan for the Panama-Pacific Exposition, a part of the scheme was revived in modified form. A permanent staff of architects for the Civic Center (John Galen Howard, Frederick H. Meyer, and John Reid, Jr.) was appointed and a bond issue of $8,800,000 voted for purchase of land and construction of buildings.

Under the municipal ownership provisions of the new charter, Mayor Phelan's dream of "a clean and beautiful City" began to be realized. San Francisco became the first large municipality in the Nation to establish a city-owned street railway system, which opened December 28, 1912. Under the supervision of veteran City Engineer Michael Maurice O'Shaughnessy, construction was begun at Hetch Hetchy of the great dam which bears his name and of the 168-mile aqueduct which brings Tuolumne River water to the city. The work continued over the next two decades until 1934. In 1913, under O'Shaughnessy's direction, the first comprehensive system of boulevards was formulated. In 1927 the San Francisco Municipal Airport was opened. By 1970, the city-owned utilities system was valued at approximately $532,016,434.

Meanwhile the park system was increased to a total of 54 parks, plazas, and squares covering a ninth of the city's area. Since the establishment in 1907 of a Playground Commission (since 1949 the Recreation and Park Commission) the parks have increased to 120, where in a course of a year over 8,000,000 people have participated in the recreational activities offered. The San Francisco Unified School District in its 120th fiscal year, was operating 96 grammar, 17 junior high and 11 high schools, and a junior college, enrolling approximately 18,000 day and evening students. The library system operated a total of 27 branch libraries circulating 3,233,782 volumes annually. The M. D. de Young Memorial Museum and the California Palace of the Legion of Honor, a city-subsidized symphony orchestra and city-owned opera house, San Francisco Yacht Harbor, Aquatic Park with its bathing beach and Maritime Museum, and the municipal Fleishhacker Zoo—all added to San

Francisco's attractions. However, the city can no longer pride itself on its decreasing crime rate as it did between 1938 and 1940 when it was the only large city in the United States to register a decrease. Today its steadily increasing crime rate and the fact that San Francisco serves as a haven for the "anti-Establishmentarian" has provided many new problems for city administrators and police force.

Just as the city had outgrown the Consolidation Act of 1856, drawn up for a city of 40,000, so it outgrew the freeholders' charter of 1900, drawn up for a city of 325,000. Beginning as a comparatively short document, the old charter had grown by process of amendment to 304 pages of articles, chapters, and subdivisions. In 1930 the voters elected a board of 15 freeholders to frame a new charter. Having studied the various forms of municipal government, the freeholders formulated a "strong mayor" plan which was adopted in March 1931 and put into operation in January 1932, under the administration of Angelo J. Rossi. Under the new charter the mayor—wrote Chief Administrative Officer Alfred J. Cleary—is made "a strong and responsible executive, with the power of appointment of the principal officials and members of boards." Officials whose duties are primarily governmental (policy-making) were continued in elective positions; those whose duties are primarily ministerial (carrying out policies), in appointive positions. To the Chief Administrative Officer was entrusted responsibility for supervision of departments headed by the latter and for long-range planning; to the Controller, responsibility for financial planning, management, and control. Under the new charter's provisions, the city's business must be conducted on a cash basis and its budget balanced annually. An eleven-member Board of Supervisors was retained as the legislative branch of government and relieved of administrative duties.

POINTS OF INTEREST

Dominating the Civic Center, the CITY HALL, Van Ness Ave., Polk, McAllister, and Grove Sts., lifts its gold-embellished dome 307 feet 6 inches above ground level—11 feet 7 inches higher than the National Capitol in Washington, D. C., as Mayor James Rolph used to boast. It was Rolph who broke ground for the new structure with a silver spade April 5, 1913. Second unit of the Civic Center to be completed, the City Hall was dedicated December 28, 1915, having cost $3,500,-000. In the great rotunda under the dome, Rolph welcomed the world, receiving a long procession of celebrated visitors: the King and Queen of Belgium, Queen Marie of Rumania, Eamon de Valera, William

Howard Taft and Woodrow Wilson. Here San Francisco made merry all night long to celebrate the Armistice in 1918. Here the funeral of President Warren G. Harding took place in 1923, and here, in 1934, Rolph himself lay in state.

Of gray California granite with blue and gold burnished ironwork, the building conforms to the French Renaissance style of the Louis XIV period, its east and west facades consisting each of a central pediment supported by Doric pillars and flanked on either side by Doric colonnades. Rising four stories high and covering two city blocks, it was

SAN FRANCISCO'S CIVIC CENTER
SCALE IN FEET
0 500 1000

designed by architects John Bakewell, Jr. and Arthur Brown, Jr. as a hollow rectangle, 408 by 285 feet, enclosing a square centerpiece covered by the dome.

On the Polk Street pediment, the symbolic statuary represents San Francisco standing between the riches of California and Commerce and Navigation; on the Van Ness Avenue pediment, Wisdom between the Arts, Learning, and Truth and Industry and Labor. The interior, with its marble tile flooring, is lavishly finished in California marble, Indiana sandstone, and Eastern oak. Grouped around the great central court are the offices of the Registrar, Tax Collector, and Assessor. From the center of the lobby a wide marble staircase leads to the second-floor gallery, off which are the Mayor's office and the chamber of the Board of Supervisors. Similar galleries overlook the court from the third and fourth floors. The vast dome, 112 feet in diameter, weighs approximately 90,000 tons and will withstand a wind load of 30 lbs. per square foot.

Near the Polk Street entrance is a bronze statue of Abraham Lincoln (Haig Patigian, sculptor), seated in meditative pose, one hand resting on his knee. Facing the street named for him is a bronze statue of Hall McAllister (Earl Cummings, sculptor), a distinguished pioneer attorney.

The CIVIC CENTER PLAZA, Grove, Polk, McAllister, and Larkin Sts. The plaza covers a 1,461 car garage and a convention area, Brooks Hall, 280 feet by 360 feet, built at a cost of $4,500,000 and named for Thomas A. Brooks, former city administrator.

CAPTAIN JUAN B. de ANZA STATUE. The 13-foot, copper statue (Julian Martinez, sculptor) was a friendship gift to the City of San Francisco from the State of Sonora, Mexico. It was placed in the Civic Center Plaza September 6, 1967.

The CIVIC AUDITORIUM, Grove St. between Polk and Larkin Sts., was presented to the city by the 1915 Panama-Pacific International Exposition. Events as diverse as political rallies, automobile shows, balls, prize-fights, —bicycle races, and circuses, have been held there. Designed by Arthur Brown, Jr., the structure is four stories high with a facade of California granite ornamented in carved stone and a roof topped by a great octagonal dome. Permanent seating in the auditorium is for 4,416 with portable seating for 4,000. An 11,000-lb. chandelier hangs over the main floor.

The city's public health supervision centers in the four story HEALTH CENTER BUILDING (*open weekdays 8-5*), corner Grove and Polk Sts., erected in 1931-32. It houses various clinics, the Central Emergency Hospital, and Mental Health offices.

Twin structures—the OPERA HOUSE, northwest corner Van Ness Ave. and Grove St., and the VETERAN'S BUILDING (Arthur Brown, Jr., architect), form the War Memorial of San Francisco, erected in 1932 as a tribute to the city's war dead. The buildings are similar in external appearance, patterned in classic style to conform with other Civic Center structures. Against the rusticated terra cotta of their facades, rising from granite bases and steps and surmounted by mansard roofs, are free-standing granite columns.

The Opera House opened on October 15, 1932, with Claudia Munzio singing Tosca. The auditorium, seating 3,250 persons, is richly decorated. The floor of the orchestra pit can be raised and lowered. The stage is 131 ft. wide, 83 ft. deep, and 120 ft. from floor to roof. At the 30-foot-long switchboard, all the lighting combinations required for an entire performance can be set in advance and released in proper order by the throwing of a single switch.

Beyond massive gilt-trimmed iron fences stretch the green lawns of Memorial Court, separating the Opera House and the Veterans' Building. Severely formal, it was designed by Thomas Church with planting in long flat masses.

The four-story Veterans' Building, southwest corner Van Ness Ave. and McAllister St., houses the veterans' organizations on the first two floors. From the vestibule on the main floor of the building, a long columned Trophy Gallery with cast stone walls, vaulted ceiling, and marble floor leads to the Souvenir Gallery. Here the coffered ceiling and stone walls give quiet sanctuary to a display of military medals and souvenirs. In the auditorium, seating 1,100 persons, arched panels between the pilasters of the side walls contain eight murals by Frank Brangwyn depicting earth, fire, air, and water. The third and fourth floors are occupied by the SAN FRANCISCO MUSEUM OF ART, the nation's second museum (after the Museum of Modern Art in New York) devoted to contemporary art. The central feature of the museum is a seventy foot octagonal Statuary Court around which the fourteen picture galleries are grouped (*open Tue-Fri., 10-10; Sat. 10-5; Sun. 1-5*).

The block long (372 ft.), five-story granite STATE BUILDING, McAllister, Polk & Larkin Sts., in the Italian Renaissance style (Bliss & Faville, architects), was built in 1926 at a cost of $1,800,000.

The STATE BUILDING ANNEX is connected with the old State Building and has its main entrance on Golden Gate Ave. Construction of this $6,617,300 seven-story reinforced concrete building began in September, 1957. It is 379 ft. by 118 feet with a garage for 36 cars.

STATE COMPENSATION INSURANCE FUND BUILDING designed by the State Department of Architecture is located at the southwest corner of Golden Gate Ave. and Polk.

PIONEER HALL, 456 McAllister St., houses the Society of California Pioneers museum and library (*open Mon.-Fri. 9-4*). Membership in this society is extended to the male descendants of the men who arrived in California before January 1, 1850.

The SAN FRANCISCO PUBLIC LIBRARY (*open Mon.-Fri. 9 a.m.-9 p.m.; Sat. 9 a.m.-6p.m.*) occupies the block bounded by Larkin, Fulton, McAllister and Hyde Sts. The building is a three-story granite structure in the Italian Renaissance style, an imposing monument to learning but inefficient and not easily adaptable to modern techniques of librarianship. The Main Library building is supplemented by 26 branches located throughout the city, a business library downtown, and a bookmobile and mediamobile.

San Francisco's first public library was a reading room opened in 1878. The founding Board of Trustees boasted among its 11 members Andrew S. Hallidie, inventor of the cable car, and economist Henry George. With an appropriation of $24,000 from the Board of Supervisors, the trustees bought 6,000 books, installed them in a rented hall, and invited the public to come and read, but not to borrow, them. When books were first circulated in 1881, about 10,500 persons held library cards. The number of patrons had tripled and the book collection had grown to 140,000 volumes by 1906, when earthquake and fire totally destroyed the wing of City Hall which had housed the library since 1888. About 25,000 volumes were returned after the disaster from homes and branches, and the library continued operations in temporary quarters.

The present building was an elegant addition to the Civic Center when it was dedicated February 15, 1917. It was designed by architect George W. Kelham, who selected the Italian Renaissance style as "seeming best to represent the scholarly atmosphere which a library should attempt to convey." Of the $1,152,000 expended for construction and equipment, $375,000 was contributed by Andrew Carnegie, who contributed a like amount for the construction of branch libraries.

The building exterior is granite; across its facade are carved the words "May this structure, throned on imperishable books, be maintained and cherished from generation to generation for the improvement and delight of mankind." Over the entrance are Leo Lentelli's statues symbolizing Art, Literature, Philosophy, Science and Law. Inside, the entrance hall, grand staircase, and reference and catalog room are designed in a combination of real Travertine marble, brought from Italy, and a nearly indistinguishable imitation Travertine made locally. The murals overlooking the staircase are by Gottardo Piazzoni, the five panels on the north wall representing a California seascape, those on the south wall a California landscape. Murals by Frank Vincent DuMond depict *Pioneers Leaving the East,* in the History and Social Science Department, and *Pioneers Arriving in the West,* in the Literature, Philosophy and Religion Department.

In 1970 the Library's collection included 1,313,000 volumes, more than 724,000 of them housed in the Main Library building. Book purchases total more than 100,000 volumes annually. The collection also encompasses newspapers from San Francisco, California, and major cities throughout the world and nearly 6,000 different periodicals. Circulation in 1969-70 exceeded 3,130,000.

The Main Library collection is organized according to subject departments. Many literary treasures are housed in the Special Collections Department on the third floor, notable among them the Robert Grabhorn collection on the History of Printing and the Development of the Book—1600 items including samples of the work of every major printer, typographer and bookmaker since Gutenberg. The Nat Schmulowitz Collection of Wit and Humor, from which a display is drawn annually, includes 16,000 volumes of humorous literature of every description. The department also holds strong collections of local history and Californiana and first editions and manuscripts by San Francisco writers including longshoreman-philosopher Eric Hoffer, Ambrose Bierce, Bret Harte, Robinson Jeffers, Jack London, and Mark Twain.

A major service to patrons is the telephone reference facility headquartered in the Catalog and General Reference Department on the second floor. Librarian specialists answer hundreds of quick reference questions daily by telephone and refer in-depth questions to the proper subject department.

Also located in the Main Library is the communications center for the Bay Area Reference Center (BARC), nerve center of a network of northern California libraries linked by teletype and facsimile transmission equipment never before put to use in public library service. From here hard to locate information is dispatched to suburban and rural libraries with limited research facilities.

The Art and Music Department on the first floor, in addition to its book collection, has both instrumental and vocal music scores—some of them unobtainable elsewhere—and a circulating collection of framed art prints.

The Library also maintains collections of juvenile literature, books in foreign languages, government documents, and phonograph records both spoken and musical. Its schedule of programs, free and open to the public, includes lecture and film programs and special events each month in the Main Library and the branches.

CITY PLANNING COMMISSION, 100 Larkin St., located in quarters built as a Hospitality House for World War II servicemen and dedicated August 9, 1941.

MARSHALL SQUARE, Grove, Larkin, Hyde and Fulton Sts., is named for the discoverer of gold in California. The last of the coffins was removed from the sandy graves of the old Yerba Buena cemetery here in 1870. During the following decade the "sand lots" were the meeting place for gatherings addressed by fakirs, phrenologists, and socialists. Unemployed workmen applauded the harangues of an Irish drayman with shouts of "The Chinese must go—Dennis Kearney tells us so!"

The PIONEER MONUMENT, Grove, Hyde, and Market Sts., keeps alive the memory of James Lick, who came to San Francisco in 1847 and died a multimillionaire in 1876. He left the city a bequest of $3,000,000, of which his will earmarked $100,000 for "statuary emblematic of the significant epochs in the history of California . . ." The Pioneer Monument (Frank Happersberger, sculptor), whose cornerstone was laid September 10, 1894, is a great central pediment upholding a bronze figure symbolizing California, with her spear and shield and bear, from whose base project four piers, each supporting subsidiary statuary: Early Days, Plenty, In '49, and Commerce. The central pedestal is ornamented with four bronze bas-reliefs—depicting immigrants scaling the Sierra, traders bargaining with the Indians, cowboys lassoing a steer, and California under the rule of the Mexicans and the Americans. Five relief portraits, of James Lick, John Charles Fremont, Francis Drake, Junipero Serra, and Johann August Sutter also appear on the pedestal.

The grayish-white granite walls of the massive five-story, block-square FEDERAL BUILDING, Hyde, Fulton, McAllister and Leavenworth Sts., was completed in 1936 at a cost of $3,000,000 (Arthur Brown, Jr., architect).

The new $45,000,000, 21-story, FEDERAL OFFICE BUILDING occupies only two-thirds of its block square site, Golden Gate Ave., Larkin, Polk and Turk Sts., the remainder of the block facing on Golden Gate Ave. is a decorative open air plaza complete with fountains. This is the largest Federal Building west of the Mississippi, housing more than 5,000 employees.

Situated just outside the orbit of the Civic Center, the weathered four-story UNITED STATES COURTHOUSE AND POSTOFFICE BUILDING (*open 6 a.m.-12 p.m.*), northeast corner Seventh and Mission Sts., glittered in new white granite grandeur late in 1905. The building on its foundation of piling withstood the earthquake and fire of the following year, but the sidewalk and street—built over the bed of a former stream—sank several feet, and the building now obviously stands higher than the original sidewalk level. Having withstood the flames, it was easily refurbished. The building, designed in Italian Renaissance style by James Knox Taylor, cost $2,500,000, to which $450,000 was added for improvements after 1906. In 1933 a $750,000 annex was added. After Congress had appropriated the original funds, the price of steel dropped sharply below original estimates and in the absence of any law providing for its return to the Treasury, the surplus was spent in lavish interior decorations. Not only were Carrara, Pavonezza, Sienna, and Numidian marble imported but skilled Italian artisans were imported with them to install the verd antique trimmings of the corridors, the elaborate mosaics of the columns and vaulted ceilings. The court chambers were panelled in California curly redwood, Mexican prima vera mahogany, antique oak, and East Indian mahogany, and immense ornate fireplaces, never to be used, were installed.

San Francisco's central Postoffice, with its financial and executive offices, occupies the first floor. On the second floor are the offices of the Railway and Air Mail Services; district chief clerks of the third and fourth postoffice districts and superintendent of the eighth division; and Postoffice Inspector in Charge, whose department includes Arizona, California, and Nevada; Hawaii, Guam, and Samoa.

The United States Circuit Court of Appeals, on the third floor, has the widest territorial jurisdiction of any circuit court in the Nation, hearing cases from Arizona, California, Idaho, Montana, Oregon, and Washington, from Alaska and Hawaii, and from the United States extra-territorial court in Shanghai. Here also are the chambers of the United States District Courts and the offices of divisions of the Department of Justice, of the Mineral Production and Economics Division of the Bureau of Mines, and of the Naturalization Service.

A far cry from these splendid marble corridors was the city's first postoffice, the frame building housing C. L. Ross and Company's New York Store at Washington and Montgomery Streets, where in April, 1849 postmaster John White Geary removed a pane of glass from the front window and began dealing out the 5,000 letters he had brought with him on the *Oregon*. Following the arrival of the fortnightly mail steamer from Panama, wrote the British traveler, J. D. Borthwick, in 1851; "A dense crowd of people collected, almost blocking up the two streets which gave access to the postoffice . . . Smoking and chewing tobacco were great aids in passing the time, and many came provided with books and newspapers . . . A man's place in the line . . . like any other piece of property . . . was bought and sold . . . $10 or $15 were frequently paid for a good position . . . There was one window devoted exclusively to the use of foreigners . . . and here a polyglot individual . . . answered the demands of all European nations, and held communication with Chinamen, Sandwich Islanders, and all the stray specimens of humanity from unknown parts of the earth."

Steamer Day, the beginning and middle of each month, which brought not only the mail but also the Eastern papers—only source of news of the outside world—became a San Francisco institution. For a week the population prepared its letters and its gold dust—of which millions of dollars' worth were shipped East—for the fortnightly out-going steamer. Even after 1858, when the Overland Stage Line to St. Louis began carrying eight mails each month and the Pony Express to St. Joseph two a week, the custom continued, and business men paid their accounts on Steamer Day. Not until the 1880's did the custom end.

Metropolitan Scene

"There are just three big cities in the United States that are 'story cities'—New York, of course, New Orleans, and best of the lot San Francisco."

—FRANK NORRIS

TIMES SQUARE and Piccadilly Circus recall the metropolitan character of New York and London. San Francisco has several landmarks by which the world may identify it, namely the Golden Gate Bridge and the cable cars. Portsmouth Plaza, the Palace Hotel, and the Ferry Building, which served successively as symbols of civic vanity, no longer resound with much more public clamor than many another plaza, hostelry, or terminal. Formerly Market Street accented for the casual observer San Francisco's metropolitan character, but today it can also be demonstrated by the financial district.

Southwestward from the Ferry Building to Twin Peaks Tunnel, Market Street's wide, unswerving diagonal bisects the city. To Market Street, as to Rome, lead all downtown streets, converging from north, southeast, and west at wedge-shaped intersections where traffic tangles bewilderingly. Northward, where slopes rise steeply to hilltops, are shops, clubs, theaters, office buildings, luxury hotels, and apartment houses— the center of San Francisco's commercial activities and vortex of its social whirl. Southward—in what is still "South of the Slot" to old-timers —abruptly begin the row upon row of pawn shops, fly-specked restaurants, and shabby lodging houses that stretch over level ground to the warehouses, factories, and railroad yards along the Bay's edge.

Jasper O'Farrell's survey, a century ago, laid the foundation for Market Street's development. Long before the forty-niners paved it with planks, the tallow and hides of Peninsula ranchos rolled down its rutted trail in Mexican oxcarts to Yerba Buena Cove. Hundred-*vara* lots along the street's southern side were considered ideal business locations; and the width of the thoroughfare determined its future. Steamcars, in the 1860's, brought along it passengers to be deposited in frock coats and crinolines to parade Market Street. Before the disaster of 1906, cable cars went careening up the street, like diminutive galleons riding on waves of basalt pavement whose sand foundation sank unevenly beneath the traffic.

Market Street epitomizes Western spaciousness. At its upper end soar the crests of Twin Peaks, green with grass in spring. Flooded with sunlight on clear days, it contrasts sharply with the dingy canyons of neighboring streets devised for shopping and finance. After dark, gleaming with neon fluorescence of lighted signboards, it is a broad white way. Thanks to the fire of 1906, which piled the thoroughfare high with debris of baroque monstrosities, its contours are obstructed by few grotesque domes and fantastic facades, once the pride of the bonanza generation.

With the proliferation of the automobile, public transit began to diminish in number of fares and services and by 1934 vehicular congestion became common. A subway system was proposed, but was defeated in a 1938 bond election. Major new buildings began to shift away from Market Street and up Montgomery towards Nob Hill. Thus, the great volume of people that were supporting Market Street activity diminished and the street began its physical decline. World War II temporarily reversed this trend, but soon afterward, the previous decline continued. The impact of the Golden Gateway project, improved freeway access, increased parking convenience and the prospect of a rapid transit system started revitalization of real estate activity. The Zellerbach and Standard Oil buildings and the Rockefeller West Complex, all with their adjacent plazas, have begun to appear, and others, like the Citizens Federal Savings Building, have been remodeled. Market Street is being reconstructed to better accommodate the pedestrian by means of the narrowed roadway, the widened sidewalks, the double rows of sycamores, the new brick pavement, and the promised removal of streetcars (but not buses), from the surface. Five subway stations, the Embarcadero, Montgomery, Powell, Civic Center and Van Ness Ave. will help to change Market Street from the clogged artery of vehicular traffic to a quieter, more pedestrian-oriented, shopping and strolling street.

Lower Market has been completely altered in the past decade, save for the Southern Pacific and P.G.E. buildings. Gone are the low-rise buildings serving needs related to the port. With the phasing out of maritime activities, including the ferries, the street has been redeveloped with high-rise office and hotel towers. Where it skirts the Civic Center on its southwestward route, the solid phalanx of office buildings, theaters and stores begins to show gaps, thinning into strings of paint stores, second-hand book shops, and parking lots, until the black mouth of Twin Peaks Tunnel swallows the streetcar tracks. That Market Street along whose broad sidewalks moves the informal pageant of San Franciscans on parade comprises nine blocks between Hyde Street on the west and Montgomery Street on the east.

The windswept corner at Powell and Market begins a gay, devil-may-care street that has for better than half a century fascinated and delighted both native and visitor. Unlike the tiny slow cable cars that clang up and down the Powell Street hill to be reversed on the turntable at Market Street, life always has run fast and a little loose along this narrow urban canyon. On the east corner of Powell and Market stood the Baldwin Theater, housed within a hideously ornate hotel of the period. Around the corner on Eddy Street was the Tivoli Theater, where patrons sat at tables and ate and sipped refreshments while watching the performance. Although the fire of 1906 razed the entire area, Powell Street and environs maintained their reputation by immediately rebuilding. The district became known as the "Uptown Tenderloin." Until the Eighteenth Amendment relegated pleasure spots to back rooms, it was replete with lively restaurants, saloons, and cabarets—whose names make older residents yearn for the "good old days." Techau Tavern stood on the site of the present bank at the southwest corner of Powell and Eddy; the Portola Louvre, across the street. Around the corner at 35 Ellis Street was the Heidelberg Inn, and at 168 O'Farrell Street, the famous old Tait-Zinkand cabaret, across from the Orpheum Theater where vaudeville was born. Mason Street, one block west of Powell, was the White Way, sparkling with the lights of saloons and cabarets.

Powell Street, now relieved of suggested rowdiness by smart hotels, shops, and bars, has outlived its past. The hilarious uptown tenderloin which rivalled the Barbary Coast has receded to streets immediately west. This newer, downtown tenderloin is a district of subdued gaiety that awakens at nightfall—a region of apartment houses and hotels, corner groceries and restaurants, small night clubs and bars, gambling lofts, bookmakers' hideouts, and other fleshpots of the unparticular. Techau's, the dine-and-dance place renowned for "an appearance of Saturnalia," became the name of an ultra-modern cocktail bar at another Powell Street address. The old Portola Louvre at Powell and Market—described as "that which takes the rest out of restaurant and puts the din in dinner"—is now a quiet cafeteria more modestly named.

Between Geary and Post Streets, where Powell Street begins its climb up Nob Hill—that climb which leads it up, up, and up to where stood gaudy mansions of the bonanza "nabobs"—the solemn gray-green stone facade of the St. Francis Hotel faces eastward over the sloping green turf and hedge-bordered promenades of Union Square, which stretch above a super-modern underground garage providing accommodations for parking cars. Here the benches are packed the day long with successful, and not so successful, men and women feeding panhandling pigeons. Here too are held the kickoff ceremonies for civic campaigns, windups of political campaigns, and concerts by visiting musical groups. Along the sidewalks on one side, drivers of long limousines lounge in their cars, waiting for sightseeing customers.

Union Square is the heart of that area of shops and hotels which represents to an international clientele and to San Franciscans the city's traditional demand for quality. Here department stores have for so many decades been custodians of public taste—their founders being patrons of the arts and *bons vivants*—that their very buildings are considered public institutions. Along Grant Avenue, Geary, Stockton, Post, and O'Farrell Streets, the gleaming windows of perfume and jewelry shops, travel bureaus, art goods and book stores, apparel and furniture shops entice throngs of shoppers. Near these stores flower-vendors have the sidewalk stands so dear to San Franciscans. Along Sutter Street are offered rugs from India and Afghanistan, books, art objects from Europe and the Orient, household fixtures and antiques. Here San Franciscans pay gas bills and see dentists, and here are the commercial art galleries.

Kearny Street is the shopping district's eastern boundary. Looking down upon Lotta's Fountain is the remodeled Home Mutual Savings & Loan Association building, formerly the red-brick de Young Building, built in 1890 as the city's first skyscraper. Cape Horn the city's rounders dubbed this breezy crossing, back in the era of free lunches and beer for the common run and champagne for the elite. Here lounged young wastrels whose delight it was to observe the skirts of passing damsels wafted knee-high by sudden gusts.

"All bluffs are called on Kearny Street," wrote Gelett Burgess. Running north from Market Street to the Barbary Coast, it was an avenue of honky-tonks and saloons frequented by racetrack tipsters and other shady professionals. On election nights it was the scene of torchlight parades and brass bands. Of early theaters, the Bush, the Standard, and the California were situated near Bush and Kearny Streets. Among the restaurants that gave San Francisco a name were the Maison Dorée on Kearny between Bush and Sutter Streets, the Maison Rich, a block west at Grant Avenue and Geary Streets, the Poodle Dog at Grant Avenue and Bush Street, and Tortoni's, two blocks west at O'Farrell and Stockton Streets. All served French dinners that were gastronomical delights to a city that always has known how to eat. Another famous restaurant was Marchand's, at Grant Avenue and a little two-block alley called Maiden Lane. Now chaste and renovated, Maiden Lane has been renamed a half-dozen times, but the original name sticks, inducing a wry smile from old-timers.

The inglorious past is slipping fast from Kearny Street. Streamlined clothing establishments for men, smart shops, and cocktail bars are marching northward. A few blocks north is an area known as Manilatown, a low rent haven for elderly Filipino citizens.

Not even the most farseeing mind could have imagined, in San Francisco's toddling days, the narrow canyon between skyscrapers that is present-day Montgomery Street. Being then the waterfront, it was the city's doorstep to the world. The doorstep was gradually moved eastward as filled-in land pushed back the Bay waters, but San Francisco went on doing business in the original location. Into Montgomery—and later Kearny Street, one block west—were compressed most of what the city possessed—banks, customhouse, post office, business houses, newspaper offices, dance and gambling halls, theaters, livery stables, saloons, and restaurants. The streets were ungraded. Kearny was paved with sticks and stones, bits of tin, and old hatch coverings from ships that had tramped the world. The going was difficult, if not downright dangerous, for both pedestrian and rider. In 1849 the site of the Palace Hotel, across from the southern end of Montgomery Street, was Happy Valley —host to a tent settlement of poor immigrants. Market Street was a dream in the brain of young Jasper O'Farrell, who was to engineer San Francisco's street design.

Montgomery Street has thrown off its old boisterous and willful ways. Neat and austere between sheer walls of stone, glass, and terra cotta, it is visible evidence of San Francisco's financial hegemony over the far West. But the past that dies hard in San Francisco still lingers on. Old-fashioned and with clanging bell, the cable cars still lurched in the 1940's over California Street's intersection with Montgomery, past modern business buildings. All day the street's great office structures are beehives, humming with business; its sidewalks are populated with businessmen carrying briefcases, and lined with parked shiny automobiles. But at dark, when the skyscrapers are deserted but for their watchmen and scrubwomen, the deep canyons are black and silent, and the clank of cables, pulling their freight uphill toward the lighted hotels and apartment houses atop Nob Hill, echoes in the stillness.

POINTS OF INTEREST

Looming over the business district at the edge of the Civic Center is the 28-story ONE HUNDRED McALLISTER BUILDING, 100 McAllister St. Built by the city's Methodist churches, it was opened in the late 1920's as the William Taylor Church and Hotel, commemorating a street preacher of the 1850's. Later it became the Hotel Empire and during World War II was acquired by the Federal Government to house Bureau of Internal Revenue and Army Ordnance Procurement offices. Today the building is occupied by the U.S. Army Engineers.

Founded a decade after '49 by John Sullivan, the HIBERNIA SAVINGS AND LOAN SOCIETY (*open 10-3*), corner of McAllister and Jones Sts., has survived decades of prosperity and panic to become one of San Francisco's oldest banks. Its classic, one-story building (Albert Pissis, architect)—whose granite facades were gleaming white when finished in 1892 but have been weathered to a dull gray—survived even the fire of 1906. It is topped by a gilded dome surmounting the Corinthian colonnade which rises at the head of the curved granite steps of the corner entrance. Inside, marble pilasters spring from a floor inlaid with mosaic to represent a mariner's compass card.

In February, 1963, the razing of the Fox Theater began and by May 2, 1966, the $25,000,000 FOX PLAZA BUILDING (Victor Gruen & Assoc., architects) was completed. The 29-story building, bounded by Market, Polk, and Hayes Sts. is a pleasant blending of offices, apartments and shops. Garage space (500 stalls) for both commercial and residential tenants is provided in the two-level basement.

The austere OLD MINT BUILDING, corner of Fifth and Mission Sts., has housed temporary offices of various departments of the Federal Government in its latter days. Its basement walls of Rocklin granite and upper facades of mottled British Columbia bluestone, its pyramidal flight of granite steps climbing to a portico of Doric columns are blackened with grime. Built in 1870-73 to supplant the first branch mint, established in 1854 on Commercial Street, the $2,000,000 structure (A. B. Mullett, architect) was itself supplanted in 1937 by a still newer mint. In 1906, while flames gnawed at its barred and iron-shuttered windows, mint employees aided by soldiers fought a seven-hour battle with a one-inch fire hose and saved $200,000,000. One-third of the Nation's entire gold reserve was housed here in 1934.

"Industrial Gothic" is the three-story CHRONICLE BUILDING, corner of Fifth and Mission Sts., with tall arched windows and high corner clock tower. A morning paper with a 1970 circulation of approximately 476,731 daily.

The narrowest building in San Francisco, the eleven story 130 BUSH BUILDING, is a mere 20 ft. wide. Once called the Liberty Mutual Building it was erected in 1910.

THE EMPORIUM, 835 Market St., (*open 9:30-5:30*) has a massive, gray sandstone facade with three arched entrances opening onto

---

LOCATION OF BUILDINGS ON MAP OF
DOWNTOWN SAN FRANCISCO

1, 2. To Ferry Building and Embarcadero. 3. To San Francisco-Oakland Bay Bridge. 4. San Francisco Terminal. 5. Donahue Monument. 6. Wells Fargo Collection. 7. Lotta's Fountain. 8. Sheraton-Palace Hotel. 9. Telephone Building. 10. Pacific Coast Stock Exchange. 11. Russ Building. 12. St. Patrick's Church. 13. Cable Car Turntable. 14. Native Sons Monument. 15. Union Square. 16. St. Francis Hotel. 17. 415 Sutter Building. 18. Native Sons Building. 19. The Olympic Club. 20. The Bohemian Club. 21. Mark Hopkins Hotel. 22. Fairmont Hotel. 23. Pacific Union Club. 24. Grace Cathedral. 25. Kong Chow Temple. 26. Sun Sung Theater. 27. Chinese Hospital. 28. Bank of Canton. 29. Tin How Temple. 30. Old St. Mary's Church. 31. St. Mary's Square. 32. Portsmouth Square. 33. Montgomery Block. 34. Golden Era Building. 35. Hotaling Building. 36. Stevenson and Booth Houses. 37. Pioneer Park, Coit Tower. 38. SS. Peter and Paul Church. 39. San Francisco Art Institute. 40. Fisherman's Wharf.

a quarter-block-long arcade. It is ornamented with columns in half-relief rising from the fourth-story to the balustrade at the roof edge. Inside, an immense glass-domed rotunda, 110 ft. in diameter and 100 ft. high, ringed by a pillared gallery, rises through four stories to the roof garden. Its present building, replacing one built in 1896 and destroyed by the 1906 fire, stands on the site of St. Ignatius College, now the University of San Francisco.

Traffic waits goodnaturedly at the CABLE CAR TURNTABLE, Market, Powell, and Eddy Sts., where a southbound car comes to a halt every few minutes, while conductor and grip man dismount and push the car around until it faces north.

Traces of discoloration in the sandstone near the entrances of the FLOOD BUILDING, corner of Market and Powell Sts., recall the earthquake and fire of 1906, which broke windows and blackened the walls of the structure a year after its completion. Named for bonanza king James C. Flood, the building stands on the site of the Baldwin Hotel and Theater, built by his contemporary, E. J. (Lucky) Baldwin in 1876-77 and destroyed by fire in 1898. Of gray sandstone, the 12-story structure is wedge-shaped to fit the site, its two facades converging in a rounded corner ornamented with columns in half-relief.

A grassy haven in the midst of the downtown bustle, UNION SQUARE, Powell, Geary, Post and Stockton Sts., spreads 2.6 acres of green lawns around the 97-foot-high granite shaft of the NAVAL MONUMENT (Robert Ingersoll Aitken, sculptor), whose bronze female Victory, armed with wreath and trident, commemorates "the Victory of the American Navy under Commodore George Dewey at Manila Bay, May First, MDCCCXCVIII." President William McKinley broke ground for the monument in 1901 and President Theodore Roosevelt dedicated it in 1903. Union Square was presented to the city in 1850 by Mayor John White Geary. Mass meetings held here on the eve of the Civil War by Northerners demonstrating their loyalty to the Union gave the square its name. During World War II, the square's greenery was dug up and its monument removed while an immense underground garage for automobile parking was constructed here; following completion of the garage, the restored top layer of earth was planted with lawns and shrubbery again and the monument put back.

The ST. FRANCIS HOTEL, Powell, Geary, and Post Sts., is the 14 story, block-long, steel-and-concrete successor to the hotel opened here in 1904 and razed in 1906. The building (Bliss and Faville, architects), is an adaption of the Italian Renaissance style to the modern skyscraper. Its main facade, weathered a somber gray, has three wings, the central one flanked above the second story by deep open courts separating it from the others. The spacious lobby with vaulted ceiling and Corinthian columns is one of the city's most popular meeting places. It is "under the clock" in the lobby that San Franciscans traditionally meet their friends downtown. The famed Mural Room (named for Albert Herter's seven murals, The Gifts of the Old World to the New), closed in November of 1970; the area is now used as part of the lobby and carriage entrance for the new 32-story St. Francis Tower.

The GEARY THEATER, 415 Geary St., (Bliss and Faville, architects), is one of San Francisco's two legitimate theaters, in which touring companies present plays, light operas, and musical comedies.

The neighboring CURRAN THEATER, 445 Geary St., also a legitimate theater, contains murals on the side walls of its orchestra section painted by local artist Arthur F. Mathews.

The modern 17-story white-brick and stone CLIFT HOTEL, 495 Geary St., was opened in 1915 by attorney Frederick Clift. Three new stories and an additional wing were added in 1926.

The 1,200 room SAN FRANCISCO HILTON, an 18-story hotel of 1,200 rooms was opened May 21, 1964. It cost $29,000,000. The site covers 77,000 sq. ft., all of the block of Taylor, Mason, Ellis & O'Farrell Sts., except for the corner occupied by the Airport Terminal building. It is built with reinforced concrete construction considered fireproof, earthquake-proof and sound retardant. Motor arriving guests can register and drive via a unique interior ramp to their rooms on seven floors. On the 16th floor is an open-sky, landscaped courtyard, heated deck and pool. Groundbreaking ceremonies for the Hilton's 43-story $12,700,000 tower were held February 13, 1969. They provided for an observation and cocktail lounge on the 42nd floor.

"Weaving spiders come not here" admonishes the inscription over the Taylor Street entrance of the five-story red brick Italian Renaissance home of the BOHEMIAN CLUB (*private*), corner of Post and Taylor Sts., erected in 1934. Across J. J. Mora's bronze bas-relief on the Post Street facade troop a procession of Bret Harte's characters. The club grew in 1872 from informal Sunday breakfasts at the home of James Bowman, editorial writer on the *Chronicle*. Artist friends sketched so freely on Mrs. Bowman's tablecloths her husband decided that San Francisco intellectuals needed an official club.

For the first few years, quarters were shared with another club, The Jolly Corks. The atmosphere was casual, the furnishings meager. Members who complained of the lack of tables and chairs were reminded that "when a man gets tired of holding his drink all he has to do is to swallow it." The club's monthly High Jinks—their name derived supposedly from Sir Walter Scott's *Guy Mannering*—were debates followed by suppers. The more or less serious High Jinks (later burlesqued by Low Jinks) were sometimes exciting occasions. The story persists that one speaker opened his manuscript to show a wicked-looking revolver, which he placed on the table in front of him, saying: "This is to shoot the first

Bohemian galoot who stirs from his seat before I end this paper." In 1877 the Bohemians moved into quarters of their own on Pine Street. Among the honorary members elected to the club have been Mark Twain, Bret Harte, and Oliver Wendell Holmes.

The Bohemian Club now has a world-wide membership. Once a year they come together for a midsummer frolic in the club's Bohemian Grove, where an original play has been produced since 1880, when the first Midsummer Jinks—an open-air picnic accompanied by speeches and celebrations—was held.

The winged "O" of the OLYMPIC CLUB (*private*), 524 Post St., oldest amateur athletic organization in the United States, has been worn by many star athletes, including "Gentleman Jim" Corbett, the San Francisco bank clerk who became world's heavyweight champion after practice as the club's boxing instructor, and Sid Cavill, one of a famous family of Australian swimmers, who introduced the Australian crawl to America as the club's swimming instructor. Nucleus of the Olympic Club, formed May 6, 1860, was the group which Charles and Arthur Nahl invited to use the gymnastic apparatus they had assembled in their Taylor Street backyard. The organization now has 7,000 members. The five-story brick clubhouse is equipped with a gymnasium, a solarium, squash and handball courts, an indoor track, a billiard room, a marble plunge piped with ocean water, dining halls, a library, and a lounge.

The Corinthian-pillared FIRST CONGREGATIONAL Church, corner of Mason and Post Sts., was founded in 1849 in the schoolhouse on the Plaza, led by a missionary from Hawaii, the Reverend T. Dwight Hunt. Having outgrown the frame structure built at Jackson and Virginia Streets in 1850, the congregation spent $57,000 raised largely by pew rentals on a structure at Dupont (Grant Avenue) and California Streets. In 1872 it moved into a tall-spired red brick Gothic Church on the present site, and in 1915 into the present building; here it was joined in 1937 by the Temple Methodist Chuch, which gave up its William Taylor Church.

The eight-story red brick and buff tile NATIVE SONS OF THE GOLDEN WEST BUILDING 414 Mason St., houses an organization founded in 1875. J. J. Mora's terra cotta bas-reliefs between the upper windows depict epochs in pioneer history. Above the entrance are bas-relief portraits of Junipero Serra, John Charles Frémont, and John D. Sloat. Around the balcony of the auditorium, which seats 1,250, are intaglios portraying California writers.

The (eight-floor) FRENCH LIBRARY (*open 10-6, Sat. 10-2*), conducted by L'Alliance Française, the largest French library in the United States, contains 18,000 volumes. It was founded in 1874 as the Bibliothèque de la Ligue National Française, under the patronage of Raphael

Weill, through the efforts of a society of French residents formed after 1871 to protest appropriation of Alsace and Lorraine by Germany.

Against the dark panelling of the JOHN HOWELL BOOK SHOP (*open 9:30-5:30*), 434 Post St., gleam the rich colors of the rare volumes and the fine prints and paintings which line the walls. One of the world's great antiquarian book stores, it is presided over by Warren R. Howell, who travels extensively to find rare books in all fields. In these sanctums discerning collectors may choose from one of the largest selected stocks of rare books in the country, including first editions of English and American literature, rare Bibles, Western Americana, voyages and travels, and the history of science and medicine. Art connoisseurs will enjoy the extensive collections of city views and western scenes, Audubon and Currier & Ives prints, as well as original paintings by the foremost artists of the old west. Founded in 1912, the store has been in this location since 1924.

Situated on property at Post, Sutter & Stockton Sts., is the new 37-story UNION SQUARE HYATT HOUSE HOTEL (John Graham, architect). Complying with Union Square height restrictions the building facing on Post Street is 80 ft. high with the main 724-room hotel tower rising from Sutter Street.

The vertical lines of the 22-story SIR FRANCIS DRAKE HOTEL, 450 Powell St., culminate in a six-story, set-back tower overlooking city and Bay. The structure (Weeks and Day, architects) was completed in 1928. Four great panels by local muralist S. W. Bergman, depicting the visit of Sir Francis Drake to the Marin shores, decorate the English Renaissance lobby. Newest features of the hotel are the 21st-story Starlite Roof and the Plate of Brasse restaurant, which depicts the splendor of Elizabethan England.

Looming above the business district the 450 SUTTER BUILDING, 450 Sutter St., rises—a massive shaft with rounded corners, faced in fawn-colored stone—25 stories above the street. A striking adaptation of Mayan motifs to functional design, the structure (Timothy L. Pflueger, architect), cost $4,000,000 to build. Its wide entrance, topped by a four-story grilled window in a tree-like Mayan design, is in nice proportion to the facade's severe lines. Large windows, flush with the exterior, flood the offices with light—especially the corner suites, which have six bay windows. The building provides its tenants with a solarium, a doctors' lounge, and a 1,000-car garage.

December, 1914 saw completion of the $656,000 STOCKTON STREET TUNNEL (Michael O'Shaughnessy, engineer), boring 911 feet through Nob Hill from Bush almost to Sacramento Street to connect downtown San Francisco with Chinatown and North Beach. The tunnel is 36 feet wide and 19 feet high.

NOTRE DAME DES VICTOIRES (Our Lady of Victories), 566 Bush St., serves San Francisco's French colony. The church, completed in 1913, is of Byzantine and French Renaissance architecture, constructed of brick with groined twin towers and high arched stained-glass windows.

Since 23-year-old Leander S. Sherman in 1870 bought the shop where he had been employed to repair music boxes, SHERMAN, CLAY AND COMPANY, corner of Kearny and Sutter Sts., has ministered to the city's musical wants.

The historic and famous corner of Montgomery, Market, and Post Sts., is the site of the $21,000,000 CROCKER PLAZA BUILDING completed in 1968. The dark emerald pearl granite was quarried in Norway, processed in Italy, and cut and fitted in South San Francisco. The structure is 38 stories, 533 ft. tall, resting on 650 reinforced concrete piles driven 56 feet below the sidewalk level. Entrance to the lower plaza and the combined BART and municipal transit station can be made via escalators from the 30,000 square-ft. plaza paved in charcoal black granite.

Around the show windows of the florists' shop of PODESTA & BALDOCCHI (*open weekdays 8-5:30*), 224 Grant Ave., passersby cluster to admire flaunting sprays of rare orchids, exquisite lilies, or rich-textured camellias, arranged with spectacular artistry among many kinds of blossoms. In the early spring, the shop is embowered in pink and white flowering branches of fruit trees; at other seasons, in great masses of trailing greenery.

One of the Nation's oldest jewelry establishments, SHREVE & COMPANY (*open 9-5*), corner of Grant Ave. and Post St., have been dealing in precious stones and rare objects of gold and silver since 1852. It is the only large downtown store still operating whose advertisement appeared in the San Francisco City Directory of 1856—when its address was No. 139 Montgomery St.

SUTTER-STOCKTON GARAGE, Sutter & Stockton Sts., is a municipally-owned garage built in 1960 (John Lord King, architect). The checkerboard screen hides the spiral access ramp at its east end. Shops and a bank are on its street level.

To collectors the world over, the name of S. G. GUMP & COMPANY (*open 9:30-5:30*), 250 Post St., means jade, but the firm's agents have scoured the world for more than jade. Show rooms are styled to conform with the rare objects they contain. Since Solomon and Gustave Gump founded the firm in 1865, it has grown into an institution whose buyers gather items for collectors throughout the Nation.

In the store's show rooms are displayed modern china, pottery, glass, linens, silverware, and jewelry; silks, brocades, and velvets; Siamese and

Cambodian sculpture; porcelain and cloisonné, rich-textured tapestries, bronze temple bells, hardwood screens ornamented with jade, and rugs from Chinese palaces acquired after the overthrow of the Manchu government. In the Jade Room all of the eight colors and 45 shades of the stone are represented, including the rarest, that most nearly resembling emerald; pink, so rare that only small pieces have been found; and spinach green, a dark tone flecked with black, used for large decorative pieces. The collection of tomb jade, recovered from mounds in which mandarins were interred, includes pieces 2,000 years old. The Jade Room also contains figurines carved of ivory, crystal, rose quartz, white and pink coral, rhinoceros horn, and semiprecious stones.

Fluctuat nec Mergitur (It floats and never sinks), Paris' own municipal motto, has been the slogan of the CITY OF PARIS (*open 9:30-5:30*), corner Stockton and Geary Sts., since the spring of 1850, when Felix Verdier hung up his motto. It was appropriate, for the contents of La Ville de Paris had been afloat ever since Verdier had left France in a ship whose cargo he bought with profits from his silk-stocking factory at Nimes. A republican, he had preferred exile to the new emperor. Destroyed several times by fire, the store moved each time to larger quarters. When Felix was succeeded, at his death in the late 1860's, by his son Gaston, it was moved into its own building at Geary Street and Grant Avenue. It came to its present location in 1896.

Twenty-four-year-old Paul Verdier had scarcely taken over in 1906 when the building was destroyed. First store in town to reopen, it resumed business in a mansion on Van Ness Avenue. The present six-story building—with its glass dome rising above balconies, its Louis XVI window frames of white enamel and carved, gilded wood—was opened in the spring of 1909. At the peak of the dome appear the original crest of Paris, a ship in full sail, and the motto.

The CROWN ZELLERBACH BUILDING is the first major example of modern glass curtain wall office building construction in San Francisco. It is located on a 1⅓ acre, wedge-shaped site, bordered by Market, Bush, Battery and Sansome Sts. The building rises 320 ft. (20 stories) and has a glass, aluminum, and mosaic tile exterior (Hertzka & Knowles & Skidmore, Owings & Merrill, assoc. architects). The structure covers only one-third of its site, the balance of the triangular block includes American Trust Company's distinctive bank pavilion, and more than an acre of pebbled walkways and gardens.

The free standing INTERNATIONAL BUILDING, California St. at Kearny, adjoins a city park in the heart of San Francisco's financial district. Completed in 1961 (Anshen & Allen, architects), the 22-story structure contains 285,000 gross square feet. A landscaped terrace extends completely around the building, and on the western side widens to 75 feet to provide an attractive area overlooking St. Mary's Square.

The west terrace flies the colorful flags of many nations. The entrance lobby is connected directly with the St. Mary's garage, which shelters 1,000 motor cars.

Young Adolph Roos, who founded the clothing firm of Roos Brothers (now Roos-Atkins), southeast corner 4th & Market, arrived in San Francisco from France in time for the stampede to the Virginia City (Nevada) mines, where he made his stake by out-fitting miners. Returning to San Francisco, he sent for his younger brother Achille; together they opened the first Roos Brothers store on Leidesdorff Street in 1865. From 1908 to 1969 the firm occupied a five story building at Market & Stockton Sts. Remodeled (1936-38) at a cost of $1,000,000 (J. S. Fairweather, building architect; Albert R. Williams, interior architect). On August 4, 1958 Roos Bros. and Robert S. Atkins merged. The new redbrick ROOS-ATKINS BUILDING was completed in March 1960.

The western headquarters of the JOHN HANCOCK MUTUAL LIFE INSURANCE COMPANY is located at Battery & California Sts. Skidmore, Owings & Merrill were the architects of this fifteen story, dark polished granite building, completed in 1959. The building is distinguished for its use of ground level arches surmounted by a square tower-like structure.

The SECURITY PACIFIC NATIONAL BANK BUILDING (*open Mon.-Fri., 10-3*), corner of Market St., Grant Ave., and O'Farrell St., was erected in 1910. The pediment above the Ionic-pillared portico is adorned with Haig Patigian's bas-reliefs of the head of Liberty between flying eagles, based on Augustus St. Gauden's design for $20 gold pieces. Corinthian columns, Travernelle marble pilasters, and Caen stone walls lend richness to the 65-foot-high banking room.

The BANCROFT BUILDING, 731 Market St., is named for the Bancroft brothers—historian Hubert Howe and publisher Albert L.—who conducted in its five-story predecessor (second brick building erected on Market Street) a book-selling and publishing firm. In partnership with George L. Kenny, Hubert Howe Bancroft previously had gone into the book-selling business in quarters on Montgomery Street. Joining the firm, his brother Albert planned the new Market Street office building, opened in 1870. In 1875 the firm announced: "Bancroft's Historical Library is the basis of important scientific and descriptive works of a local nature, and maps or books of reference relating to the Pacific Coast." In the same year appeared the first of Hubert Howe Bancroft's histories, Volume I of his *Native Races of the Pacific Coast of North America*. In the fifth-floor publishing department, Bancroft went ahead with his prodigious labors of compiling in detail the history of all Western America. In 1884 he published the first of his seven volumes on the history of California—carrying a list of quoted authorities 66 pages long. Before his death in 1918, he had accumulated a library of 500 or more rare manuscripts and 60,000 volumes, now housed in the Bancroft Library at the University of California.

The 22-story steel-and-concrete CENTRAL TOWER, corner of Market and Third Sts., defies detection as the old Claus Spreckels Building. It was remodeled along functional lines in 1938. The simply decorated entrance relieves the severity of the unornamented vertical shaft with its six-story tower. In the lobby, the walls are vitriolite brick. In 1895 Claus Spreckels bought the site and erected a 19-story building in which the *Call* was published for a time. During the Spanish-American War, a cannon thundered news of American victories from the roof. Only bright spot in a darkened and devastated area, during the days after April 18, 1906, was the light kept burning in the partly destroyed cupola. In its report the Geological Survey said "the general behavior of this structure demonstrates that high buildings subject to earthquake can be erected with safety even on sand foundations."

The 12-story HEARST BUILDING, southeast corner Market and Third Sts., of white terra cotta with polychrome ornamentation, formerly housed the *San Francisco Examiner,* first paper developed by William Randolph Hearst. On this site stood the Nucleus Hotel, first brick building on Market Street, which surprised everyone by surviving the earthquake of 1868 almost unscathed.

Beloved to old-timers is LOTTA'S FOUNTAIN, corner Market, Geary, and Kearny Sts., the cast-iron shaft presented to the city in 1875 by the actress Lotta Crabtree, who won the adoration of San Francisco in the era of easy money that followed the years of gold. The 24-foot fountain within its granite base, has conventional lion heads, and brass medallions depicting California scenes. In 1853 when Lola Montez visited Rabbit Creek, a small gold camp near Grass Valley, she taught singing and dancing to the eight-year-old daughter of one of the prospectors. Not long afterward her pupil made a sensational first appearance in a Sierra mining town: gold as well as applause was showered upon the young Lotta by generous Argonauts. Her subsequent debut in San Francisco was no less encouraging. At the age of 17 she appeared on the New York stage, and at 44 she retired. Fortunate real estate investments augmented her fortune, which at her death (1924) exceeded $4,000,000. After her retirement her fountain was neglected, and its site, a busy downtown intersection, became known as Newspaper Square from the large number of newsboys who congregated there. In 1910, however, another—and perhaps a greater—singer brought Lotta's Fountain once more into prominence. At midnight on Christmas Eve, hushed thousands massed as Louisa Tetrazzini sang *The Last Rose of Summer* beside the fountain. In remembrance of the event, a bas-relief portrait of the singer by Haig Patigian was added to the monument.

The city's first skyscraper, the red-brick DE YOUNG BUILD-

ING, northeast corner Market, Geary and Kearny Sts., was built by Michael de Young in 1890 (Burnham & Root, architects). Many believed the structure would not survive an earthquake—but the disaster of 1906 proved them wrong. In 1959 the building was purchased by the Home Mutual Savings & Loan Association and completely remodeled at a cost of about $1,000,000. Kurt W. Meyer was the architect.

The FLOWER STANDS that enliven the streets of the shopping district owe their beginning to Michael de Young who allowed the vendors, most of whom were boys of Italian, Belgian, Irish, or Armenian descent, to sell their flowers in front of the de Young Building, protecting them from the policemen. The curbside stands were first licensed in 1904. All attempts to suppress them have been halted by storms of protest from press and public. Their wares change with the seasons—from January, when the first frilled golden-yellow daffodils and great armfuls of feathery acacia with its fluffy tassels make their appearance, to December, when hosts of flaming crimson poinsettias and great bunches of scarlet toyon berries herald the advent of the holidays.

The original PALACE HOTEL, Market and New Montgomery Sts., was (according to Oscar Lewis and Carroll Hall) "at least four times too large for its period and place, but the town had never had a sense of proportion and no one was disturbed." Least disturbed was its builder, William C. Ralston. This "world's grandest hotel" would cover 2½ acres; it would soar to the impressive height of seven stories and contain 800 rooms; its marble-paved, glass-roofed Grand Court would face Montgomery Street through an arched driveway; artesian wells drilled on the spot would supply its storage reservoirs with 760,000 gallons of water; its rooms would contain "noiseless" water closets and gadgets designed to make life at the Palace effortless and luxurious.

Ralston, desirous of developing local industries, financed many factories to supply the hotel's needs until his cautious associate, Senator William Sharon, finally asked: "If you are going to buy a foundry for a nail, a ranch for a plank, and a manufactory to build furniture, where is this going to end?" Ralston continued to pour millions into the structure— and died before its completion, owing the Bank of California $4,000,000. Sharon, who had wondered "where it was going to end," found himself in possession of the hotel.

Through the doors of the Palace, opened in October 1875, passed "the great, the near-great, and the merely flamboyant . . . bonanza kings and royalty alike . . . Grant, Sheridan, and Sherman were feasted in the banquet halls; and the Friday night Cotillion Club danced . . . in the ballroom . . ." Here the graceful manners of Oscar Wilde charmed a local "lady reporter," and James J. Jeffries gave a champagne party for a sweater-clad coterie. Brazil's emperor, Dom Pedro II, said in 1876: "Nothing makes me ashamed of Brazil so much as the Palace Hotel." King David Kalahaua of Hawaii died there January 20, 1891.

The climax came on the early morning of April 18, 1906, when the hotel's guests were shaken violently from slumber and sent into debris-strewn streets. Among the most alarmed was Enrico Caruso; the great tenor joined fellow members of the Metropolitan Opera Company carrying a portrait of Theodore Roosevelt and wearing a towel about his famous throat. Although it suffered only minor interior damage by the 'quake, the Palace succumbed, its elaborate fire-fighting system proving useless against the fire.

Rebuilt in 1909 on the same site, the present eight-story tan-brick and terra cotta structure is in the Beaux Arts tradition. The eighth floor is surmounted by a frieze. Reminders of the past are a porte cochere on the site of the carriage entrance to the Grand Court, facing (across the lobby) the present glass-roofed Garden Court; the Happy Valley cocktail lounge with its Sotomayor murals of Lotta Crabtree and "Emperor" Norton; and the Pied Piper Buffet (*for men*) with its mahogany fixtures and Maxfield Parrish painting, modeled by Maude Adams. No less illustrious than the guests of the old Palace have been the patrons of the new. In 1923 President Warren G. Harding, died in the presidential suite. Today it's the SHERATON PALACE.

The gray stone walls, sometimes floodlighted in gleaming yellow splendor by night, of the monolithic PACIFIC TELEPHONE & TELEGRAPH BUILDING, 140 New Montgomery St., enclose the head offices of a telephone network embracing all the far West. Largest building on the Pacific Coast devoted to one firm's exclusive use at the time of its completion in 1925, it was built at a cost of $3,000,000 (J. R. Miller, T. L. Pflueger, and A. A. Cantin, architects). From each of the four facades of its four-story tower, two huge stone eagles survey the city from their 26-story perches. The terra cotta facade, with its lofty piers and mullions tapering upward in Gothic effect, cloaks but does not hide the structural lines. The building's 210,000 square feet of floor space provide working room for 2,000 employees. In the spring of 1946 the Pacific Telephone and Telegraph Company inaugurated a new era in communication facilities when it offered motorists radio-telephone service between their automobiles and homes or offices.

A monument to San Francisco's early-day regard for learning is the nine-story MECHANICS INSTITUTE BUILDING, 57 Post St., erected in 1910 (Albert Pissis, architect), which houses the Mechanics-Mercantile Library (*open weekdays 9 a.m.-10 p.m., Sun. 1-5*). On December 11, 1854, a group of citizens met in the tax collector's office to found a Mechanics' Institute for the advancement of the mechanic arts and sciences; and on March 6, 1855, they adopted a constitution providing for "the establishment of a library, reading room, the collection of a cabinet, scientific apparatus, works of art, and for other literary and scientific purposes." With four books presented by one S. Bugbee—*The Bible,* the *Constitution of the United States,* an *Encyclopaedia of Architecture,* and *Curtis on Conveyancing*—the library began its activities in June, 1855.

Progress of the association began with the inauguration of annual Mechanics' and Manufacturers' Fairs, September 7, 1857, in a pavilion on Montgomery Street between Post and Sutter Streets. As the fairs became civic events of prime importance, one sprawling wooden pavilion after another was built to house them—six in all, of which the third and fourth occupied Union Square; the fifth, Eighth Street between Mission and Market Streets; and the sixth, the site of the Civic Auditorium. The last of the fairs was held in 1899.

In 1866 the Institute built its first structure on the present site. By 1872 it had collected a library of 17,239 volumes. In January, 1906 it merged with the Mercantile Library Association, organized in 1852 by a group of merchants. The merger of the two associations, whose combined library numbered 200,000 volumes, had scarcely been effected, however, when the fire of 1906 destroyed books, equipment, and building. Hard hit, the Institute nevertheless had acquired a new library of 40,000 volumes by 1912, when it realized from the sale of its pavilion lot to the city the sum of $700,000. Its present collection of about 155,000 volumes is especially notable in the fields of science and technology. The Mechanics' Institute also provides for its members a chess and checker room and a lecture series.

The 13-story CROCKER FIRST NATIONAL BANK, corner of Post and Montgomery Sts., stands on the site of the old Masonic Temple. Oldest national bank in California, it is a merger of the First National Bank, opened in 1871 with James D. Phelan as president, and the Crocker National Bank, organized in 1883 by Charles Crocker, one of the "Big Four." The two banks were consolidated in 1926. Of Italian Renaissance style, its entrance is distinguished by a rotunda supported on granite pillars (Willis Polk and Company, architects).

The new $20,000,000 WELLS FARGO BANK BUILDING, John Graham, architect, Sutter and Montgomery Sts. was completed in 1966. The black marble, columned, 43 story (561 ft.) building owned by the Dillingham Corporation rests on 438 concrete piles driven into bedrock. An underground tunnel connects with the Market & Montgomery BART Station.

The neo-Gothic, gable-roofed 111 SUTTER BUILDING, northwest corner of Montgomery and Sutter Sts., since 1927 has reared its buff-colored terra cotta facades 22 stories above a site which was worth $300 when James Lick bought it and $175,000 when he died. The marble-inlaid lobby and corridors of the interior (Schultze and Weaver, architects)—the pillars adorned with green and white Verde Antique from Greece, the lobby floor with Hungarian red, the corridor floors with Italian Botticino, Tennessee pink, and Belgian black marbles—rival the luxurious interior of the Lick House, which Lick built here in 1862. The latter hostelry boasted $1,000 gas chandeliers, mirrored walls, and mosaic floors of rare imported woods. Trained as a cabinet-maker, the eccentric millionaire finished with his own hands the woodwork of the luxurious banquet hall.

Because of well-balanced construction, the 16-story ALEXANDER BUILDING, southwest corner of Montgomery and Bush Sts., a simple shaft faced in buff-colored brick and terra cotta whose vertical lines give it a towering grace, is considered ideal for studies of earthquake stresses on skyscrapers. Seismographs installed at top, center, and bottom of the structure by the U.S. Geodetic Survey furnish research data for the University of California and Stanford University. The building was erected in 1921 (Lewis Hobart, architect).

The Monument to 1929—thus have financial circles, since the stock market crash, referred to the three-story granite SAN FRANCISCO CURB EXCHANGE BUILDING, 350 Bush St. (J. R. Miller and T. L. Pflueger, architects). Scene of the frenzied speculation of the 1920's, it housed the San Francisco Mining Exchange until 1928, when it was taken over by the newly organized San Francisco Curb Exchange. Remodeled in 1938, when the Curb Exchange was absorbed by the San Francisco Stock Exchange, it now houses the Western Title Insurance Co.

"An example to all Western architects of a model office building," wrote Ernest Peixotto in 1893 of the MILLS BUILDING, 220 Montgomery St., built in 1891 for banker Darius Ogden Mills (Burnham and Root, architects). "It is an architectural composition, and not mere walls pierced by window openings . . . It consists of a two-story basement of Inyo marble, carrying a buff brick super-structure of seven stories, crowned by a two-story attic. The angle piers . . . are massive and sufficient; between them piers spring from the third story, crowned in the eighth by arches . . . The effect of height is strengthened by the strongly marked lines of the piers . . . The focus for ornament is the Montgomery Street entrance, which rises to an arch . . . as large and ample as it should be . . ." So sound was the building's construction that it survived the fire of 1906 with little damage to its exterior. Adhering to the original design, Willis Polk supervised its restoration in 1908 and the erection of additions in 1914 and 1918. When the adjoining 22-story MILLS TOWER (entrance at 220 Bush St.)—to which all but the second of the older building's ten floors have direct access—was erected in 1931, architect Lewis Hobart also followed Burnham's design. The same buff-colored pressed brick especially manufactured for the original building was used on its facade. The buildings contain 1,300 offices and 350,000 feet of floor space.

On the site of the Mills Building in the 1860's stood Platt's Hall, a great square auditorium where people flocked for lectures, concerts, and political conventions. On its stage, Thomas Starr King lifted Bret Harte from obscurity by reading his poem, "The Reveille." Among the attractions which drew crowds were Henry Ward Beecher and General Tom Thumb and his wife.

The block-long RUSS BUILDING, 235 Montgomery St., stands on the ground where Christian Russ, in 1847, established a residence for his family of twelve. Here in 1861 the owner of Russ' Gardens built the Russ House, a hotel long favored by farmers, miners and merchants. Still owned by his heirs, its site, nine decades after Russ acquired it at auction for $37.50, was assessed at $675,000. Construction of today's $5,500,000 skyscraper, begun in July, 1926, was completed in September, 1927. Modernized Gothic, the massive, sandy-hued edifice rises 31 stories, its three wings deployed in the shape of an "E" (George W. Kelham, architect). Its 1,370 offices, comprising 335,245 square feet of floor space, house 3,500 persons, and a 400-car garage.

Pine, Kearny, and California are the streets surrounding the 52-story (757 ft.) BANK OF AMERICA WORLD HEADQUARTERS BUILDING (Wurster Bernardi & Emmons, Skidmore, Owings & Merrill, architects). Originally known as the Bank of Italy, it was founded by A. P. Giannini, former commission merchant, and his stepfather in 1904. First of the city's banks to be reopened after the fire and earthquake of 1906, it grew rapidly in resources when Giannini three years later launched a State-wide system of branch banks. The Bank of America is now the largest commercial bank in the world. For many years it has reported deposits of more than one billion dollars. On January 1, 1970 it had $22,171,413,000. The next six billion-dollar banks were in New York, N.Y. Other billion-dollar banks in San Francisco are the Wells Fargo, Crocker-Citizens, and Bank of California.

The UNITED CALIFORNIA BANK BUILDING, northwest corner of Montgomery and California Sts., marks the site of the PARROTT GRANITE BLOCK BUILDING. The latter, San Francisco's first stone structure, was built in 1852 by Chinese masons of granite blocks quarried in China. When the Chinese struck for higher pay they won their demands because no other available workers could read the markings on the blocks. The old building survived earthquake and fire but was torn down in 1926 when the present building was erected.

Ten lofty granite Tuscan columns flanked by massive pylons dominate the temple-like Pine Street facade of the STOCK EXCHANGE BUILDING (*open Mon.-Fri. 7-2:30*), corner of Pine and Sansome Sts.

(public entrance 155 Sansome St.). The pylons, carved by Ralph Stackpole, symbolizing Mother Earth's fruitfulness and Man's inventive genius, stand on either side of the steps. Above the Pine Street wing, which houses the Trading Room (*members only*), rises the 12-story gray granite tower of the administration wing. Above its doorway, carved in high relief, is Stackpole's *The Progress of Man,* and on the lintel, a sculptured eagle with outstretched wings. The walls of the public lobby are inlaid with dusky red Levanto marble and the ceiling with gold leaf in a geometric star design. A marble stairway ascends to the visitors' gallery overlooking the Trading Room.

Above the high windows of east and west walls of the Trading Room are Robert Boardman Howard's two groups of three sculptured panels—one portraying development of electric power; the other, development of gas power. Along north and south walls extend the quotation boards, their markers' galleries equipped with ticker receiving instruments and headset telephones. Beneath, an annunciator signal system summons members to their booths along the sides of the room. At the center of the brown rubber-tiled trading floor is stationed the telegraph ticker transmitting station, which sends reports of every transaction to brokers' offices along the Pacific Coast. Around it are stationed four oak-panelled hollow enclosures for nine trading posts, each equipped with electrically synchronized stamping devices that indicate the time of every order to a tenth of a minute.

The Lunch Club quarters (*not open to the public*) on the tenth and eleventh floors are decorated with frescoes by Diego Rivera depicting California history.

In the basement of a building a block northward, the Stock and Bond Exchange was organized September 18, 1882, by 19 pioneer brokers. It succeeded several earlier exchanges, of which the first, the San Francisco Stock and Exchange Board, had been established in 1862. Since 1882 the present exchange, due to influences beyond its control, has stopped functioning as the pulse of business life on the Pacific Coast on only three occasions: April 18, 1906, because of the earthquake and fire; July 31, 1914, because of World War I; and March 2-14, 1933, because of the National bank holiday. Its memberships, which sold for $50 in 1882 and rose to an all-time high of $250,000 in 1929, today sell for varying sums.

The BANK OF CALIFORNIA (*open Mon.-Fri. 10-3*), corner of Sansome and California Sts., was erected in 1908 (Bliss and Faville, architects). The gray granite building has tall and finely proportioned Corinthian colonnades. The immense banking room, 112 feet long and 54 feet high, faced in Tennessee marble, resembles a Roman basilica. In the rear on either side of a large clock are carved marble lions (Arthur Putnam, sculptor). Less subdued in its magnificence was the palatial edifice erected on this site to house the bank in 1867, three years after its establishment with Darius Ogden Mills as president and William C. Ralston as cashier. To clear the site they moved the Tehama House—which humorist "John Phoenix" celebrated in *A Legend of the Tehama House*—a popular hostelry among Mexican *rancheros* and military and naval officers. Ralston built a handsome two-story structure with tall arched windows surmounted by medallions and framed in marble columns, a cornice crowned with a stone balustrade supporting fretted vases, doors and balcony railings of bronze, and burnished copper roof. For a decade the bank was the financial colossus of all the territory west of the Rocky Mountains. It reached into Nevada, during the Comstock Lode boom, to establish four branch banks. When the collapse of the silver boom brought it crashing from financial dominance in 1875, the whole State was shaken. But the reorganized bank survived and grew, taking over in 1905 the London and San Francisco Bank, Ltd., with branches in Oregon and Washington, and today has deposits of more than one billion dollars.

A glass case in the main office contains the scales on which Darius Ogden Mills weighed some $50,000,000 of miners' gold in the tent which he set up at Columbia in 1849, before coming to San Francisco to become president of Ralston's bank.

Venerable home of a parent organization of the San Francisco Chamber of Commerce was the 15-story MERCHANTS EXCHANGE BUILDING, corner of California and Sansome Sts. Here until 1911 the city's moguls of industry and agriculture congregated to regulate and put through huge deals in hay, grain, and shipping. In bonanza days Robert Louis Stevenson used to haunt the Exchange's central board room, where he found material—in such men as John D. Spreckels—for heroes of *The Wreckers*.

Since 1851 the main-floor MARINE EXCHANGE (*always open*) has operated continuously except during 1906 and though much of its romantic element was lost with the passing of sailing ships, its function remains virtually the same. Outgrowth of the old Merchants' Exchange and Reading Room established in 1849 by Messrs. Sweeny and Baugh, who operated the signal station on Telegraph Hill, the Exchange is connected with lookout stations which report every movement of local shipping. It receives and compiles complete information from every Pacific Coast vessel from start to finish of every voyage. Files on the Exchange's mezzanine floor record launchings, cargoes, crews, disasters, sales, weather reports—all marine information required by shippers, ship owners, ship chandlers, warehousemen, exporters, and importers. Before the advent of the telephone a messenger boy on horseback rushed news of incoming ships from the Exchange to the city's major hotels.

At one end of the Exchange, beneath an arch set at right angles to the south wall, hangs the original Vigilance Committee bell which hung on top of Fort Gunnybags in 1856. The bell, which once tolled the death knell of Cora and Casey, now clangs to announce to the Exchange some mishap to a ship whose home port is San Francisco.

Though grain, shipping, insurance, and similar firms still occupy this building, which survived the fire of 1906, its chief interest lies in such features as evoke its past. Something of its lusty social tradition survives in the Commercial Club occupying three top stories and in the Merchants' Exchange Club in the basement. Reminiscent of other days are Nils Hagerup's paintings on walls of the main lobby depicting Amundsen's explorations in the *Gjoa* and W. A. Coulter's ships in port and at sea. The latter's huge painting of the San Francisco fire hangs, draped with red velvet, in the billiard room of the Merchants' Exchange Club.

From ground above the hulls of long-buried sailing ships, the FEDERAL RESERVE BANK (*open Mon.-Fri. 8:30-4:30*), northeast corner of Sansome and Sacramento Sts., rears its eight white granite Ionic columns, rising up three of its seven stories to a classic pediment (George W. Kelham, architect). When steam shovels excavated the basement vaults in 1922, they exposed the oaken skeleton of the city's first prison, the brig *Euphemia,* moored at Long Wharf in the 1850's. The Sansome Street entrance leads into a Travertine marble lobby with murals by Jules Guerin. From the Battery Street side, ramps descend to the vaults, where trucks discharge treasure for deposit behind 36-ton doors, under the hawk-eyed gaze of guards.

By day, bathed in sunlight, the 30-story SHELL BUILDING, northwest corner of Battery and Bush Sts., San Francisco headquarters of the Shell Oil Company empire, is a buff, tapering shaft; by night, floodlight-swept, a tower looming in amber radiance. Its Bush Street entrance is enriched with a filigree design in marble and bronze. Erected in 1929 (George W. Kelham, architect), it broke Pacific Coast records for rapid construction, rising three stories each week.

With heroic vigor, the bronze figures of the DONAHUE MONUMENT, Battery, Bush, and Market Sts. (Douglas Tilden, sculptor) —five brawny, half-naked workmen, struggling to force by lever a mechanical punch through plate metal—are poised on their granite base, in a triangular pedestrian island. Executed in 1894, the monument is James Mervyn Donahue's memorial to his father, Peter Donahue, founder of San Francisco's first iron foundry, first street railway, and first gas company. A bronze plaque etched with a map in the pavement at its base marks the shoreline as it was before Yerba Buena Cove was filled in, when Market Street from this point northeast was a 1,000-foot wharf.

On what was the shifting sand of a Yerba Buena beach lot towers the 22-story, gray granite STANDARD OIL BUILDING, southwest corner of Sansome and Bush Sts., erected in 1921 (George W. Kelham, architect). Its cornice-overhung facade, the upper stories adorned with Doric columns, is a modern adaptation of the Florentine style. The two-story vaulted entrance leads into an ornate lobby of bronze and marble.

To trace the origins of the present CROCKER NATIONAL BANK (*open Mon.-Fri. 10-3*), 1 Sansome St., is to follow the ramifications of international finance. One of its parent institutions, the Anglo Californian Bank, Ltd., organized in London in 1873, took over the San Francisco branch of J. and W. Seligman & Company of New York, London, Paris, and Frankfurt. Three years later, Lazard Freres, silk importers and exchange dealers of New York, London, and Paris, opened a San Francisco Branch, out of which grew, in 1884, the London, Paris, and American Bank, Ltd., of Great Britain. The two were consolidated in 1909 under the latter name and a new bank, the Anglo-Californian Trust Company, emerged, to handle the older bank's savings business. The Fleishhacker brothers, Herbert and Mortimer, gained financial prominence as presidents of the two institutions. By 1920 the Anglo-Californian Trust Company had absorbed four San Francisco banks, and by 1928 it had opened eight local branches. From the merger of the two Fleishhacker banks in 1932 came the Anglo California National Bank of San Francisco, which soon reached into the rest of the State, which in turn merged with the Crocker First National Bank in 1956 to form Crocker-Anglo National Bank. On November 1, 1963 Crocker-Anglo National Bank and Citizens National Bank of Los Angeles merged to become Crocker Citizens National Bank. The bank changed its name to Crocker National as of July 1, 1971.

Of the thousands of commuters who once poured daily through the Ferry Building, for six decades San Francisco's chief gateway from the east, most now enter the city through the BRIDGE TERMINAL BUILDING, Mission, First, and Fremont Sts. The low-spreading three-story steel-and-concrete structure, completed in 1939 at a cost of $2,300,000, is the terminal for A C Transit buses carrying passengers over the San Francisco-Oakland Bay Bridge to the East Bay.

The terminal was originally built to handle electric trains. The last train departed the San Francisco Terminal at 1st & Mission at 3 a.m. on Sunday, April 20, 1958. The first replacement bus followed it on the A line 30 minutes later.

The TISHMAN REALTY CORPORATION BUILDING, (John Carl Warnecke, architect) was planned for a site at Market, First, Stevenson and Eckert Streets, becoming the largest and highest structure (40 stories) on Market Street. It is expected that a portion of Eckert Street will be vacated by the city so that a plaza between the Tishman and Standard Oil Buildings can be developed.

On wooden piles driven into the mud of what was Yerba Buena Cove rest the 17 steel-and-concrete stories of the PACIFIC GAS AND

ELECTRIC BUILDING, 245 Market St., headquarters of the Nation's third largest utilities system, which originated with Peter Donahue's gas company (1852) and the California Electric Light Company (1879), both Pacific Coast pioneers. Designed by John M. Bakewell, the building was opened in March, 1925. Over the three-story arched entrance is Edgar Walter's bas-relief symbolizing the application of electric power to man's needs. The granite keystones of the first-story arches, carved by the same sculptor, represent the rugged mountain country whose rushing torrents have been tapped for hydroelectric power.

The new 34-story, PACIFIC GAS & ELECTRIC COMPANY TOWER, is bounded by Beale, Mission & Main Streets. It is linked to the old office complex by a landscaped plaza and a three-story low rise structure (Hertzka & Knowles, architects). The new buildings have a glass and granite facing in order to blend their modern lines with the traditional lines of the earlier building.

Memorial to the company's founder, Swedish sea captain William Matson, is the Viking vessel in bas-relief above the main entrance of the 16-story Matson Navigation Company Building, now called the PACIFIC NATIONAL LIFE BUILDING, 215 Market St. Into Hilo, Hawaii, in 1882, Matson sailed his 200-ton schooner, the *Emma Claudine*. His line grew from one vessel to a great fleet of freighters transporting the sugar and the pineapple of the Islands to the Pacific Coast. When financial ties linked the Matson line with the Big Five who controlled Hawaiian sugar, the company achieved a monopoly of Hawaiian shipping. In 1925 its general manager, Matson's son-in-law, William P. Roth, built the $7,500,000 luxury liner, *Malolo,* to carry tourists to the Islands; began construction there of a luxury hotel, the Royal Hawaiian; and inaugurated a nation-wide advertising campaign to popularize the Paradise of the Pacific. Having bought out two competing lines, he constructed three more liners—the *Lurline* for the Hawaiian service and the *Mariposa* and *Monterey* for service to Australia and New Zealand.

The ten-story SOUTHERN PACIFIC BUILDING, 65 Market St., constructed in 1916, is headquarters for the railroad system inaugurated by the Big Four's Central Pacific in 1869. The building's 506,000 tons of steel and concrete (Bliss and Faville, architects) rest on 60 miles of cedar piling. It stands on the site of the Preparedness Day parade bombing, where ten persons were killed July 22, 1916, in an explosion which led to the conviction and imprisonment of Thomas Mooney and Warren K. Billings.

Landmarks of the Old Town

*"Cities, like men, have their birth, growth and maturer years.
Some are born Titans, and from the beginning promise to be
mighty in their deeds, however wilful and destructive."*
The Annals of San Francisco (1852)

THE MARVEL is not that so little but that so much of the city's
venerable and homely architecture has escaped time's vicissitudes
— of which not the least was the fire of 1906. Recalling the great
fire of 1851—in which the El Dorado gambling saloon was saved by the
citizenry's desperate stand—one may suppose that the area around Portsmouth Square was spared, less by a shift of wind, than by San Franciscans stubbornly defending the cradle of their traditions. Unlike the carefully preserved Vieux Carré of New Orleans, however, it survives, not
through care, but through sheer neglect.

On the muddy shores of a little cove at the southeastern base of a
rocky hill (Telegraph Hill), San Francisco was born. A short distance
inland, Francisco de Haro marked out his Calle de la Fundacion, skirting
the shore on its way north-northwest over the hill toward the Presidio
along the present Grant Avenue. Just north of Washington and Montgomery streets was an inlet from which the shoreline ran diagonally
southeast to Rincon Hill, western terminus of the San Francisco-Oakland
Bay Bridge. From the rocky headland north of the inlet, first called
Punta del Embarcadero and later Clark's Point, now the intersection of
Battery Street and Broadway, William S. Clark built the first pile wharf
in 1847. The line of anchorage was the present Battery Street, where the
Russians loaded grain and meat for their Alaskan colonies, where the
frigate *Artemisia*—first French ship to enter the Bay—anchored in 1827,
and the *San Luis*—first American warship to enter the harbor—in 1841.
When the warship *Portsmouth* dropped anchor July 8, 1846, Captain
John B. Montgomery disembarked at what is now the southeast corner
of Montgomery and Clay streets (*see plaque on Bank of America Building, 552 Montgomery St.*). The Plaza, later Portsmouth Square, was
only 500 feet west of the water's edge.

West of the Plaza, facing the Calle de la Fundacion between the two
cross streets, now Clay and Washington streets, which ran eastward to
the line of Montgomery Street along the water's edge, "the first tene-
ment," reports *The Annals of San Francisco,* had been "constructed in
the year 1835 by Captain W. R. Richardson, and up to the year 1846,

there might not be more than twenty or thirty houses of all descriptions in the place." Richardson's dwelling (*see plaque between 823 and 827 Grant Avenue*) was "a large tent, supported on four redwood posts and covered with a ship's foresail." Near by on July 4, 1836, Jacob Primer Leese completed Yerba Buena's first permanent dwelling—"a rather grand structure, being made of frame sixty feet long and twenty-five feet broad." The first building was erected at the Presidio in 1776, and the first white child was born at the site of Mission Dolores August 10, 1776. Not to be outdone by Leese, Richardson erected his adobe, Casa Grande.

Soon after United States conquest, Americans had built a sprawling town on the cove; by 1847 there were "22 shanties, 31 frame houses, and 26 adobe dwellings." City Engineer Jasper O'Farrell laid out the streets in checkerboard fashion, swinging De Haro's Calle de la Fundacion into line with the north-and-south streets, and extending the town's limits far beyond the district surveyed by Jean Vioget in 1839 (bounded by Montgomery, Dupont, Pacific, and Sacramento Streets)—westward to Leavenworth Street, north to Francisco, south to Post, and southeast beyond Market Street. The year 1848 marked the first building boom. According to *The Annals of San Francisco,* "A vacant lot . . . was offered the day prior to the opening of the [Broadway] wharf for $5,000, but there were no buyers. The next day the same lot sold readily at $10,000." Long before lots could be surveyed, the area was "overspread with a multitude of canvas, blanket and bough covered tents,—the bay was alive with shipping . . ."

The community soon pushed eastward beyond the shore line, supporting itself with piles above the water and over rubble dumped into the tidal flats. Most of Commercial Street was then Long Wharf, built 2,000 feet into the Bay from Leidesdorff Street in 1850. A narrow plank walk, connecting Long Wharf with the Sacramento Street pier, was the beginning of Sansome Street. Into abandoned ships, dragged inland and secured from the tides, moved merchants and lodgers. Of these vessels, perhaps the most famous was the windjammer *Niantic*—one of the first to sail through the Golden Gate after 1849—abandoned by crew and passengers bound for the "diggin's." Doors were cut, the hold was partitioned into warehouses, and offices were built on deck. When the superstructure was destroyed by fire in 1851, the Niantic Hotel, replaced in 1872 by the Niantic Block was erected on the site (*see plaque at nw. corner Clay and Sansome Sts.*). Among other vessels claimed were the *General Harrison,* at the northwest corner of Clay and Battery streets, and the *Apollo,* at the northwest corner of Sacramento and Battery streets.

On Christmas Eve, 1849, fire destroyed the ramshackle city. By May 4, 1851, it had been burned five times. So reluctant were men to invest in San Francisco building enterprises that the East Bay enjoyed a tremendous growth. To restore local confidence, bankers and realtors combined to erect fire- and earthquake-proof buildings. First was the Parrott Block, built of granite blocks imported—cut and dressed—from China, on the present site of the Financial Center building at the northwest corner of Montgomery and California streets. Along Montgomery and adjoining streets arose a series of office buildings—solid, dignified, well-proportioned —few of which still remain.

The life of the town for more than three decades revolved around San Francisco's first "Civic Center," Portsmouth Square—the Plaza of Mexican days. At its northwest corner stood Yerba Buena's government building, the adobe Customhouse, where Captain John B. Montgomery quartered his troops in 1846. Authorized by the Mexican Government in 1844, the four-room, attic-crowned structure with veranda on three sides, was not finished at the time. Soon afterwards occupied by the *alcalde* and the tax collector, it became the seat of city government. From the beams of the south veranda, in 1851, the first Vigilance Committee hanged the thief, John Jenkins. At the behest of the newcomers from the *Portsmouth,* Captain John Vioget, the town's first surveyor, changed the name of his Vioget House, the town's first hotel, to Portsmouth House. In the bar and billiard saloon of the wooden building, at the southeastern corner of Clay and Kearny streets, hung Vioget's original map. Across the street on the southwest corner was the long, one-story adobe store and home of William Alexander Leidesdorff, the pioneer business man from the Danish West Indies, of mixed Negro and Danish blood, who was the American Vice-Consul under Mexican rule. At the first United States election held here on September 15, 1846, Lieutenant Washington A. Bartlett was chosen *alcalde*. Leidesdorff's house was transformed in November by John H. Brown into a hotel, later known as the City Hotel. On the west side of the square was built in 1847 the first public schoolhouse, which soon served also as jail, courthouse, church, and town hall, grandiloquently called the "Public Institute."

Around Portsmouth Square clustered in the early 1850's the noisy saloons, theaters, and gambling houses of the city's first bawdy amusement zone. Not only the first public schoolhouse and the first hotel, but also the first theater faced the plaza: Washington Hall, on Washington Street along the north side, where the city's first play was presented in January, 1850. In the same block were built the Monumental Engine House No. 6, and the Bella Union Melodeon. The famous Maguire's Opera House (*see Social Heritage: Before the Footlights*) rose on the east side of the square. To the east, on the site of the present Hall of Justice, were the rowdy Eldorado gambling house and the Parker House, which became the Jenny Lind Theater in 1850 and the first permanent City Hall two years later.

Today the cradle of old San Francisco is a half-mile inland. Its ageing landmarks, hemmed in by Chinatown and North Beach on the north and west, by the financial and commission districts on the south and east, are all but overlooked. Persistent indeed must be the observer who can discover the few remaining landmarks of the Buena village of Yerba.

Montgomery Street, the water front of '49, commercial artery of the roaring boom town, relaxed into a bohemian quarter long before 1906; artists' studios still occupy buildings which housed journalists and bankers, gamblers and merchants and bartenders, miners and sailors and stagecoach drivers. Realtors, printers, lawyers, and pawnbrokers occupy outmoded structures wherein their forebears speculated on fabulous "deals" in a boom era. Here, Chinese, Filipinos, Italians, Frenchmen, all sorts of Americans, still congregate and engage in business. But sailors from the seven seas gather no more on the slope of Portsmouth Square.

Something of the relative simplicity of the Argonauts—not the gaudy pretentiousness of their bonanza successors—survives in those old buildings with square cornices and simple facades, whose cornerstones were laid upon redwood piling and filled-in land during 1849 and the early 1850's. A few bronze plaques here and there are all that identify San Francisco's memorable landmarks of the Gold Rush era. A few names of defunct firms, in obscure letters across weatherbeaten facades, tell legends which only those knowing the city's lore may fully comprehend. A few steep and narrow streets, a quiet plaza, an odor of decay, and a few scattered relics are all that remain of that once crowded area.

POINTS OF INTEREST

Upon the green, sloping lawns of PORTSMOUTH PLAZA, Kearny, Clay, and Washington Sts., Candelario Miramontes, who resided at the Presidio, raised potatoes in the early 1830's. When the plot became a plaza is not known. Until 1854, when it was graded and paved, it had been graced only with a speakers' platform and a cowpen. Most of the stirring events from the 1840's to the 1860's took place here—processions, flag raisings, lynchings, May Day fetes. When news of the death of Henry Clay was received, all the buildings surrounding the plaza were draped in black. To hear Colonel E. D. Baker's funeral oration here for Senator David Broderick (fatally wounded in a duel September 13, 1859, by Judge David S. Terry) 30,000 people gathered. From 1850 to 1870 the square was headquarters for public hacks and the omnibus which ran from North Beach to South Park. In 1873 crowds gathered to gape at Andrew Hallidie's pioneer cable car climbing the hill on its first trip from the terminus at Clay and Kearny streets. Before 1880 the square ceased to be the center of civic gravity, as the business district moved south and west. Into abandoned buildings moved the Chinese on the west and north, the habitues of the Barbary Coast to the northeast, the residents of the

Latin Quarter on the east. Here terrified Chinese ran about beating gongs to scare off the fire demons during the earthquake and conflagration of 1906; here came exhausted fire fighters to rest among milling refugees; here shallow graves held the dead; and thousands camped during reconstruction. The Board of Supervisors, in December, 1927, restored the square's Spanish designation of "plaza."

Under the boughs of three slender poplars stands the ROBERT LOUIS STEVENSON MONUMENT, the first shrine ever erected to the memory of the man who sought the sunshine here in 1879. A simple granite shaft surmounted by a bronze galleon in full sail, the *Hispaniola of Treasure Island* (Bruce Porter, architect; George Piper, sculptor), the monument is inscribed with an excerpt from Stevenson's "Christmas Sermon." Around it are clumps of purple Scotch heather.

Near the square's northwest corner, the MONTGOMERY FLAG POLE marks the site on which Captain John B. Montgomery first raised the United States flag, July 9, 1846. Erected in 1924 by the Daughters of the American Revolution, it has at its base a plaque inscribed in commemoration of the event.

On January 13, 1971, the new HOLIDAY INN HOTEL was opened on the historic site where the HALL OF JUSTICE, the CITY HALL, and the HALL OF RECORDS had once stood. The new hotel is a spire-like structure of 27 stories and 575 rooms (Clement Chen & Associate, architect). It is supported by a vertical truss arrangement and two giant steel girders and cost $15 million. The history of the site, Kearny and Washington Sts., facing Portsmouth Plaza, goes back more than a century. Here rose the famous Eldorado gambling house, and here, too, was Dennison's Exchange Saloon, where the first official Democratic Party meeting was held October 25, 1849, and where the first of the city's fires broke out two months later. Destroyed in this fire, the Parker House next door, built by Robert A. Parker and John H. Brown, was rebuilt, only to be twice burned again. Destroyed a third time in 1851, the year after Thomas Maguire had converted it into the Jenny Lind Theater, it was reconstructed. When a fifth fire reduced it to ashes in the same year, it was replaced by the third Jenny Lind Theater, built of stone. This the city purchased in 1852 for a City Hall, to which it annexed the four-story building on the site of the Eldorado for a Hall of Records. Razed in 1895, the two buildings were replaced by the first Hall of Justice, which in turn was replaced after 1906 by a somber graystone structure (Newton J. Tharp, architect), which lasted until demolished in April, 1968, for the new hotel.

The building at 498 Jackson St. is associated with the early operations of William Tecumseh Sherman, who built a three-story brick structure to house the banking firm of Lucas Turner & Co. in 1854. It went through the earthquake and fire of 1906 unmarked but was later remodeled and had the top floor removed. The exterior of the first floor on the Montgomery Street side was constructed of white granite blocks while the Jackson Street side is of red brick, as is the second floor. The Montgomery Street facade is a typical Italianate design employing a central entrance surmounted by a closed pediment and flanked on both sides by six windows with flattened arches and modified keystones separated by pilasters. The arched windows are repeated on the second floor in a smaller version set in rectangular brick frames in relief. The Jackson Street side of the building restates the arched windows and pilasters in brick, however every other window is filled in with brick.

William T. Sherman paid $32,000 for the lot and $50,000 for the building. As manager of the new institution, he was overprudent. He refused to allow the occasional overdrafts his depositors demanded and declined to grant credit except on the soundest securities. Finally in 1857 the bank closed. The building presently houses Lenore Linens.

The massive first-story walls of the UNITED STATES SUB-TREASURY BUILDING, 608 Commercial St., erected in 1875-77 on the site of the first UNITED STATES BRANCH MINT, have resisted earthquake, fire, and dynamite. Of the original structure's three stories of red brick, erected over the mint's steel-lined vaults, only the first remains, now roofed over, its square red-brick columns crowned by weathered gray curlicues. The basement houses still the old vaults with their steel-lined walls and intricate locks.

Here, in what was the young city's financial district, the United States Government in 1852 purchased the property of Curtiss, Ferry and Ward, Assayers, for $335,000, and reconstructed the building as a fireproof, three-story brick structure. On April 3, 1854 San Francisco's first mint was opened, equipped to issue $100,000 worth of currency daily. By 1887 San Franciso had coined $242,000,000—almost half as much money as the Philadelphia mint had issued since 1793. As early as 1859, the first mint proved to be far too small; and, finally, the old building was razed, following completion of a second mint, in 1874.

In 1877 the new United States Subtreasury was opened on the site of the first mint. In April, 1906, the structure was dynamited in an effort to halt the flames. Unshaken by the blast, the 30-inch-thick first-story walls also withstood the fire, as did the basement vaults, which held $13 million in gold. When the Subtreasury moved to a new building on the site of the San Francisco Stock Exchange, the old building was taken over by private interests.

At the heart of the old financial center stands the B. DAVIDSON BUILDING, northwest corner of Montgomery & Commercial Sts., whose first story was built soon after the fire of May 4, 1851, for merchant William D. M. Howard. A few years later, two more stories were added. Since 1963 it has housed the BANK OF CANTON.

In excavating a sewer along the Commercial Street side in 1854, workmen uncovered a coffin with a glass window, through which could be discerned a man's features. A coroner's examination disclosed that the man was Hudson's Bay Company's agent, William Glenn Rae, son-in-law of Chief Factor John McLoughlin. Arriving at Yerba Buena in August, 1841, Rae opened his post in the store room with $10,000 worth of goods. To rebels against Governor Manuel Micheltorena in 1844, he

furnished $15,00 worth of stores and munitions. Worried over collapse of the revolt and fearing punishment, Rae took to drinking heavily. On January 19, 1845 he shot himself. He was buried in the garden outside his house.

When the Americans took California in 1846, the Hudson's Bay Company sold its property to the merchants and realtors, Mellus, Howard and Company. Seeing a prosperous future for San Francisco, the Rothschilds of London authorized Benjamin Davidson to open an agency for their banking firm. Of the five banking firms which, according to

◄◄►

The City's Sights

◄◄►

PEACE PAGODA, 110-FT. TALL, ATOP JAPANESE CULTURAL
AND TRADE CENTER

MISSION SAN FRANCISCO DE ASSIS (MISSION DOLORES)

TEMPLE EMANU-EL, AIGUELLO AND LAKE STS.

GHIRARDELLI SQUARE COMPLEX, WITH FOUNTAIN
APARTMENTS AT REAR LEFT

ST. MARY'S CATHEDRAL, GEARY AND GOUGH STS.

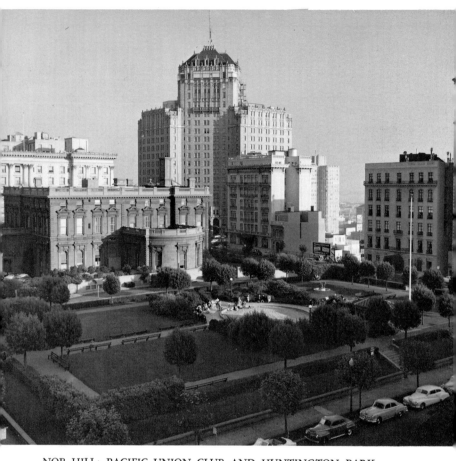

NOB HILL: PACIFIC UNION CLUB AND HUNTINGTON PARK

NOB HILL: THE FAIRMONT AND MARK HOPKINS HOTEL

THE FLOOD BUILDING, MARKET AND POWELL STS., ERECTED 1918

the *Annals of San Francisco,* were operating in the city at the end of 1849, three were situated on Leese's old 100-vara frontage—Davidson; Thomas Wells & Company; and James King of William. Early in 1850, when Long Wharf opened into Montgomery Street, the Hudson's Bay Company's old post was the United States Hotel.

When all of the old building but Leese's original adobe kitchen was destroyed by fire in 1851, William Howard had the room roofed with Australian bricks by Chinese laborers. Soon Howard erected a new brick structure, into which moved the Rothschilds' agent. The iron vaults, where pioneer bankers stored their treasure, remain in the basement, so stoutly constructed that they long defied attempts to open them.

The building known as 415 JACKSON STREET is said to have been built in 1853 and later occupied by the chocolate firm of Domingo Ghirardelli & Co. It is a two-story brick building with cast-iron pilasters on the ground story facade. This story is divided into six bays and the second story reflects this division with its six arched windows. As Ghirardelli branched into other commodities, spices, mustard, coffee, bromo (powdered chocolate), the firm outgrew its Jackson Street location and moved to the Pioneer Woolen Mills in 1897. The building now accommodates interior decorator shops.

The old MONTGOMERY BLOCK, Montgomery, Merchant and Washington Sts. was built in 1853 by Henry W. Halleck, later General-in-Chief of the Union Army under President Lincoln. The block was actually four connected buildings around a courtyard, linked together. When dedicated as the Washington Block on December 23, 1853, it was the largest building on the Pacific Coast. It was popularly called the Montgomery Block, and its builders officially changed the name the following year. Within the year it was San Francisco's legal center, housing the city's first law library. Most of the Adams Express Company's gold bullion was placed in the basement vaults. The second floor housed a huge billiard parlor. Here were the offices of the Pacific and Atlantic Railroad, of the United States Engineers Corps, of the *Alta California* and the *Daily Herald.* For 30 years, the block housed the portion of Adolph Sutro's library, now in the Univ. of San Francisco Library, that escaped the 1906 fire.

As James King of William lay dying in one of the rooms in 1856, prominent citizens organized the Vigilance Committee that hanged his assassin, James P. Casey. King was shot in front of the Bank Exchange Saloon on the ground floor, where brokers did business until establishment of a stock exchange in 1862.

On that April morning in 1906, when flames were bearing down upon the block, soldiers stood powder kegs against the walls, ready to blast a fire-break. Oliver Perry Stidger, agent for the building, begged them to wait, appealing to their civic pride in an impassioned speech. Soon the danger had passed. Since this was the only downtown office building undamaged by the fire, it again became a center of business activity.

In the 1890's artists set up their studios in the Montgomery Block. With them came Frank Norris, Kathleen and Charles Norris, George Sterling, and Charles Caldwell Dobie. Known affectionately as the Monkey Block, it was torn down in 1958. Today it is the site of the Transamerica Pyramid.

The SHIP BUILDING, 716-18-20 Montgomery St., supposedly owes its origin to the gold-seeking master and crew of the *Georgean,* who deserted her in the spring of '49. The schooner lay abandoned in the mud near Sansome Street, her cargo of Kentucky "Twist" (chewing tobacco) and New Orleans cotton molding and unsold, until a speculator claimed salvage rights and beached her on the present site.

Little remains of the original facade, which was covered during remodeling in 1954 and 1959.

The SOLARI BUILDING WEST, 472 Jackson Street, is a two-story, red brick structure with exposed anchor bolts built in 1850-52. It was originally occupied by the French wine and liquor firm of C. Lagauterie & Company, followed by a succession of liquor dealers until 1865 when the French Consulate moved in. The building now houses offices and shops.

A plaque at the GENELLA BUILDING, 728 Montgomery Street, states that the first Masonic Lodge meeting in San Francisco was held on this site in 1849. The three-story brick building was erected in 1853-1854 by Joseph Genella for his china and glassware business as well as his residence. Here in the 1850's Bret Harte wrote *The Luck of Roaring Camp.* As early as 1854, the upper floor was used as a meeting hall for the Odd Fellows. Remodelling has made the building considerably more ornate than the original.

Named for the first of San Francisco's literary periodicals, the two story GOLDEN ERA BUILDING, 730-32 Montgomery St., housed on its second floor for more than two years the weekly established in December, 1852, by youthful J. Macdonough Foard and Rollin M. Daggett. Its circulation among a Gold Rush populace, starved for reading matter, grew enormously. A "weekly family paper," it was devoted to "literature, agriculture, the mining interest, local and foreign news, commerce, education, morals, and amusements." On March 1, 1857, appeared a poem by an unknown author, "The Valentine," first preserved published work of Bret Harte. Among other contributors were Ina Coolbrith, Thomas Starr King, Joaquin Miller, Mark Twain, and Charles Warren Stoddard. It survived nearly four decades. Beneath the Era's original offices, on the ground floor, was Vernon's Hall, rented to fraternal societies and theatrical troupes. In a later era, the building housed a Chinese broom factory.

Sources indicate that this building was constructed in 1852 on the foundations of an 1849 structure destroyed in the fires of 1851. However, cast-iron pilasters in the rear on Hotaling Place bear the date 1857 while those on the Montgomery Street facade are dated 1892. The former could be the date of construction although it would seem likely that cast-iron facades were added at these times.

470 Jackson Street, a three-story, red-brick structure, now called SOLARI BUILDING EAST, was built circa 1852 by Nicholas Larco, a prominent merchant and leader of the Italian colony in San Francisco, who dealt in groceries and liquors as well as being a commission merchant, and occupied the building until 1877. The building at various times housed the consulates of three nations; Chile, Spain and France.

The northwest corner of Jackson & Sansome Sts. is the site of the three-story brick GROGAN & LENT BUILDING, erected in 1858. Severely damaged in the 1906 earthquake it was the first brick building restored after the fire, whether partially or wholly rebuilt is not known.

The two-story unadorned brick building at 530 Washington St., now called the EOI BUILDING, for the firm Executive Office Interiors, was constructed circa 1860 by Ephriam Willard Burr, mayor of San Francisco 1856-69. From 1874 to 1900 Isadore Landsberger and Arpad Harazsthy here promoted a new product, California champagne. The successor firm, known as Arpad Harazsthy & Co. and including Henry Epstein, continued for twenty years. Cellars were used for storage of wines and barrels. Originally built with three stories, the top floor was removed after the 1906 earthquake and fire.

The site of the notorious BARBARY COAST is a block of Pacific St. running east from the Seven Points where Pacific, Columbus Ave. and Kearny St. intersect. Now there are concrete arches at each end labelled International Settlement, which Pierino Gavello, restaurateur and capitalist, developed in 1939, streamlined with the stucco facades and gleaming windows. Where gambling halls, saloons, and brothels once stood, a Chinese restaurant, a Latin American cafe, night clubs and cocktail bars appeared.

The last resort of the old Coast to survive in operation—the former Parente's saloon at 592 Pacific St.—was serving Pisco punches to customers who came to marvel at its famous collection of prizefight pictures up until World War II. But it did not survive unaltered the ensuing transformation of the International Settlement into San Francisco's most hectic concentration spot for night life.

"Give it a *wide berth,* as you value your life," warned the *New Overland Tourist* of Barbary Coast in 1878, describing "the precise locality, so that our readers may *keep away.*" Since the 1860's it had worn the name Barbary Coast, derived probably from sailors' memories of the dives of North Africa. But even in the early 1850's, when the neighborhood was Sydney Town, inhabited by Australian outlaws known as Sydney Ducks, the "upper part of Pacific Street, after dark"—reported the San Francisco *Herald*—"was crowded by thieves, gamblers, low women, drunken sailors and similar characters . . ." The block bounded by Kearny, Montgomery, and Broadway was known as Devil's Acre, and its Kearny Street side as Battle Row. The district contributed a new word, "hoodlum," applying it to the young ruffians who roamed the Coast armed with bludgeons, knives, or iron knuckles. It is thought that the word comes from "huddle 'em!" the cry of the boys as they advanced on a victim. So too the expression "to shanghai" originated here.

The employment of women in the Coast's resorts was forbidden by law as early as 1869, but the Coast paid no heed. Among the most renowned of the Coast's attractions in the 1870's were the Little Lost Chicken, a diminutive girl who concluded her songs by bursting into tears (and picked the pockets of her admirers) ; the Waddling Duck, an immensely fat woman; Lady Jane Grey, who decked herself in a cardboard coronet, convinced she was of noble birth; the Dancing Heifer and the Galloping Cow, whose sister act made the boards of the stage creak.

Wiped out in 1906, the Barbary Coast was revived for another decade of gaudy life. "The quarter did what every courtesan does who finds her charms and her following on the wane," wrote Charles Caldwell Dobie. "It decided to capitalize its previous reputation, buy a new false front and an extra pot of rouge. The result was a tough quarter maintained largely for the purpose of shocking tourists from the Chautauqua circuit." Almost every dance hall put on a good show for the benefit of gaping visitors in "slummers' galleries." "Take me to see the Barbary Coast," said John Masefield—and he was taken, as was nearly every other visiting celebrity, including Sarah Bernhardt and Anna Pavlova.

"The most famous, as well as the most infamous" of the resorts, reminisced photographer Arnold Genthe, "was the Olympia, a vast 'palace' of gilt and tinsel with a great circular space in the center and around it a raised platform with booths for spectators . . . Below us on the floor . . . a medley of degenerate humanity whirled around us in weird dance steps." Of the same description was the Midway (downstairs at 587 Pacific Street)—a training ground for vaudeville acts—its walls decorated with large murals by an unknown Italian artist.

The Barbary Coast's assets as a tourist attraction did not out-weigh its liabilities as a crime center. The Police Commission's revocation of dance-hall licenses in 1913 was a hard blow, but the Coast recovered, and two years later the licenses had to be revoked again. The Thalia went on operating as a dancing academy. Once more liquor permits were cancelled. As late as 1921, Police Chief Daniel J. O'Brien thought it necessary to forbid slumming parties in the area—but the Barbary Coast was dead.

In 1951 the Barbary Coast area, now called Jackson Square, experienced a rebirth. Home furnishings wholesalers have converted this section into one of the most ingratiating districts of the city with the "entrance" to the Square, the Jackson-Montgomery corner, which was the site of the city's first bridge built in 1844 over a backwater, the Laguna Salada, as a short cut to the nearby waterfront.

Once noted for its paintings and well-stocked library, the iron-shuttered HOTALING BUILDING, se. corner Jackson St. and Hotaling Pl., along with the neighboring building across Hotaling Pl. from it, was headquarters for the Hotaling distillery, which acquired early fame as purveyor of whiskey to the Barbary Coast. The two buildings housed offices, warehouses and stables. Surviving the 1906 fire almost unscathed, to stand dominating a razed business district, they inspired Charley Field's contemporaneously famous jingle:

> "If, as they say, God spanked the town
> For being over-friskey—
> Why did he burn all the churches down
> And spare Hotaling's whiskey?"

Long since devoted to other uses than whiskey distilling, the buildings remained the property of the Hotaling family until 1945.

Narrow Hotaling Place, running south to Washington Street, was known as Jones' Alley between 1847 and 1910. Loaded drays rumbled over the planked street to the Broadway wharf; Wells Fargo & Company bore their heavily guarded cargoes to sailing ships, and under the dim gaslights silk-hatted dandies waited in hansom cabs for the beauties from the Melodeon, now the Belli Bldg.

The streamlined 15-story UNITED STATES APPRAISERS BUILDING, Sansome, Jackson, and Washington Sts., in 1945 replaced a brick and wrought-iron structure which was one of the Army Engineer Corps' achievements at the time of its erection, 1874-81. The new building, like the old, incorporates advanced features of modern engineering. Designed to be earthquake-resistant, it rests on a single huge six-foot-thick concrete slab supported by wood piles. Steel-framed, with reinforced concrete floor spans, it is faced with terra cotta of a light granite color. The base is of polished Victorville granite; the entrance is framed in polished black granite with bronze doors; and the lobby is lined with Montana Travertine.

Built to house a number of Federal Government agencies—including the Coast Guard, Bureau of Customs Appraiser and Customs Laboratory, and Immigration and Naturalization Service—the building has been designed for maximum usefulness. Among its facilities are hotel and detention quarters for the Immigration Service, a specially designed layout for appraisal of import goods, a five-range shooting gallery, space for seismograph apparatus, and many research laboratories.

On this site, until after 1850, the tides lapped at the narrow row of piles marking the line of present Sansome Street. "Upon the head of these piles," recalled Barry and Patten, "was nailed a narrow plank walk . . . without rail or protection of any kind . . . pedestrians passed and repassed in the dark, foggy nights, singing and rollicking, as unconcernedly as if their path was broad Market Street . . ."

On piles projecting eastward from what is now the corner of Sansome and Washington streets stood the wooden shanty where in August, 1850, Pedar Sather and Edward W. Church—joined nine months later by Francis M. Drexel of Philadelphia—opened a bank. When fire destroyed the structure, their safe fell into the water; it was fished up, however, and installed in a new building at the end of Long Wharf. The only bank in the city founded as early as 1850 to see the twentieth century, it was reorganized in 1897 as the San Francisco National Bank and finally absorbed by the Bank of California in 1920.

Into the blue mud of the old cove bottom, Army engineers in 1874 began driving 80-foot piles, over which they laid a seven-foot thickness of rip-rapped concrete. On this foundation they erected the three-foot-thick walls of the Appraisers Building. The roof, fabricated of wrought iron in the manner of a truss bridge, rested on the outside walls, supporting a heavy slate covering. The 90 offices had hardwood doors and bronze hardware.

Having survived the 1906 earthquake, the building was threatened by the fire but saved by the Navy. From two tugs anchored below Washington Street, sea water was pumped through fire lines to save the old structure. In 1909, mud began to ooze from beneath its foundations into a sewer excavation along Sansome Street; the southwest corner sank 11 inches, but the structure remained intact.

The UNITED STATES CUSTOMHOUSE (*open 9-5*), Battery, Washington, and Jackson Sts., has occupied this site for more than 100 years; but the block-long, five-story edifice of Raymond granite, its interior resplendent with marble and oak, erected (1906-11) at a cost of $1,600,000, is a far cry from the three-story customhouse and post office, built of cement-plastered brick in 1854, which stood here until 1903. The town's first customhouse on the Plaza was abandoned in 1849; it survived —its porch railings carved by the jackknives of Yankee newcomers—until 1851, outlasting the second, William Heath Davis' four-story structure with its white-painted balconies, to which the collector of the port had removed his offices.

From the ruins of this second customhouse, nearly $1,000,000 in specie was rescued from a large safe, which had preserved it from the flames. The removal of the treasure by the collector of the customs, T. Butler King, "created some little excitement and much laughter," as the *Annals of San Francisco* reported. "Some thirty gigantic, thick-bearded fellows, who were armed with carbines, revolvers and sabres, surrounded the cars containing the specie, while the Honorable T. Butler King stood aloft on a pile of ruins with a huge 'Colt' in one hand and a bludgeon in the other . . . The extraordinary procession proceeded slowly . . . Mr. King marching, like a proud drum-major, at the head . . . peals of laughter and cries of ironical applause accompanied the brave defenders of 'Uncle Sam's' interests to the end of their perilous march. . . ."

The BELLI BUILDING, 720 Montgomery St., formerly Langerman's Bldg., is said to have been built in 1849 or 1850. It was destroyed by fire in 1851 and rebuilt, using the old walls and foundations. The building has been used as a tobacco warehouse, theater—Lotta Crabtree performed here—offices for commission merchants and an auctioneer, Turkish baths, and later a paper warehouse and garment factory. In 1959 Melvin Belli acquired the property for his law offices and made decorative alterations. Plaster covering the old red brick was removed, a cast-iron frame running around the top and sides of windows was exposed, and a wrought iron gate from New Orleans was added. There is an open courtyard between this building and the adjacent one. Shutters on the building are now wooden, replacing the original iron ones, and gas lamps are on the sidewalk and at the doorway.

Chinatown

*"Wherever, in any channel of the Seven Seas, two world-wan-
derers met and talked about the City of Many Adventures, Chinatown ran like a thread through their reminiscences."*
WILL IRWIN

A QUARTER of old Canton, transplanted and transformed, neither
quite oriental nor wholly occidental, San Francisco's Chinatown
yields to the ways of the West while continuing to preserve some
of the heritage of an ancient civilization. Grant Avenue, its main thoroughfare, leads northward from Bush Street through a veritable city-
within-a-city, alien in appearance to all the rest of San Francisco.

Chinatown used to enjoy a measure of civil autonomy unique among
San Francisco's foreign sections. Though police protection, public education and public health are directed by municipal authorities, local affairs
used to be controlled largely by the powerful Chinese Six Companies.
Today, the Chinese have broken out of their isolation and take an active
role in civil affairs.

Along Grant Avenue bright display windows, neon signs, and glazed
tile form a foreground wholly modern for merchandise which conforms
to the age-old pattern of China's craftsmen. The street's smart cocktail
lounges defy ancestral gods by adding American swing to the inducements
of oriental atmosphere and native waitresses in brocaded gowns; its
fashionable cafes, while they serve genuine native goods, advertise more
familiar dishes. Beneath the pagoda-like cornices, electric chop suey signs
perpetuate the popular notion that this dish, imported from the Atlantic
seaboard, is something more exotic than its name, the Chinese word for
hash, indicates. Side by side curio shops offering inexpensive articles of
oriental design are bazaars, wherein the discerning may buy objects
genuine and costly. Within the last two decades however, many sources
of supply have been cut off by the U.S. embargo on goods from Mainland China.

Grant Avenue commercial area is only the bland and somewhat cynical face the settlement turns to the world. More Chinese are the avenue's
northern reaches and the streets that run crosswise from Nob Hill to
Chinatown's eastern boundary, Kearny Street. Along these congested
sidewalks, among cheap shops and restaurants, are the market places
whose distinctive sounds give Chinatown its atmosphere of the Far East.
A curious bazaar of foodstuffs are the poultry markets, where the dis-

plays of dried and pickled fish, and other edibles of all colors and shapes catch the eye. Salted ducks from Hong Kong, glazed with a salty wax—many of them flattened as if starched and ironed—hang in golden rows in grocery stores; and beside them are whole hogs—steaming hot from the barbecue pits—from which portions are cut and sent to Chinatown's dinner tables. Prepared Chinese foods also tempt customers from hot pans, ready for mother to bring home for the family meal. Octopi, shark, and other unusual sea foods are displayed in the many fish markets. Bakery windows are crowded with cakes of almost limitless variety, of which even the most common are decorative and of evasive flavor. The vegetables of Chinatown are a marvel to the stranger: slender string beans, 12 to 14 inches long; snow peas with sweet, tender, edible pods; and many Chinese greens. Bitter melons to be added to beef, fuzzy squashes, winter melons as large as watermelons, bamboo shoots, bean sprouts, and lotus roots are exhibited in bins and crates.

The artistry of the oriental cook is nowhere in the Western world better demonstrated than in San Francisco's Chinatown. In the numerous and inexpensive little Chinese restaurants that crowd the slopes of Jackson, Clay, and Washington streets above and below Grant Avenue, the occidental dines with relish on the meats and vegetables he has looked upon with disfavor in the markets around the corner.

Many of San Francisco's Chinese population, about 70,000, live away from Chinatown, but one will find them flocking to Chinatown during the weekend to shop. Amid the modern throng appear a few of those who still conform to the Chinese style of dress, slim Chinese ladies in the Manchu derived cheang-saam. However, it would be rare to find any men dressed in the native costume.

Young Chinatown has adopted the dress, the slang, and the commercial methods of its American compatriots. Grant Avenue is its creation, with its curious mixture of East and West. Even the few little wall-shops left, where generations of dreamy-eyed old men sitting in the sun have reluctantly bestirred themselves to sell occasional bags of candied melon, ginger, or lichee nuts, are being taken over by alert youngsters, who have stocked these narrow tables and outdoor shelves with souvenirs for the tourist.

The children of Chinatown, most modern element of all, are benefiting most by the inroads of the West. Education is one of the colony's primary interests. The three or four grade schools in the vicinity of Chinatown are filled with bright-eyed Chinese youngsters. The children, expert negotiators of traffic, scamper in small bands from sidewalk to sidewalk on shopping tours for their parents. Many of the older boys spend their evenings at the Chinese Y.M.C.A., and Cameron House; and many of the girls at the Y.W.C.A. Fong-Fong's on Grant Avenue, a soda fountain, lunchroom, and bakery, used to be a widely patronized "Joe College" hangout. Today there are many other competitors.

Old Chinatown watches with silent disapproval the departure of its youth and its children from the ancient customs, brought here from Canton and preserved inviolate for three-quarters of a century.

Though practically every religion has built churches and gained adherents here, the native Chinese temples, or joss houses, which used to be centers of Chinatown's spiritual life, have languished for lack of worshippers. The word joss is a corruption of Dios, Portuguese word for God, which the Cantonese learned from early Portuguese traders at Macao. Many of the furnishings have a history intimately associated with the Chinese immigration during the Gold Rush, to this land they called Gum Sahn (Golden Hills).

Barometers of public sentiment in Chinatown are the sidewalk bulletins before the shops of its two daily newspapers. If the oblong strips of Chinese characters denote light news of local interest, a lively chattering ensues; but let the bulletins be of more serious import, concerned perhaps with events in their embattled homeland, and silence settles over the groups of 50 or more, as each man reads and goes his way without a word of comment.

The one festival in which all Chinatown is united annually is the Chinese New Year, celebrated—according to the lunar calendar and the ancient philosophy of Tung-Fang-So—on the first day of the new moon after the sun enters the sign of Aquarius, between January 20 and February 20. One way to insure prosperity throughout the year is to celebrate Chinese New Year with a banquet. No hastily prepared and hastily consumed feast will do. Hours must be spent in its preparation. Time stands still while one delicious dish follows another in endless profusion. Each diner enjoys a little from each dish, but no one overeats, for the Chinese are gourmets, never gluttons, and the company of friends is the keenest relish of the feast. Children wake up to New Year's Day to be greeted with red envelopes stuffed with new bills to wish them good fortune. The most important thing on this day is to speak only good things, because being the first day of a new year, everything one says or does is symbolic of the entire 364 days to come.

Modern Chinese still honor the age-old custom of naming the years for animals. Twelve animals comprise the symbolic cycle of their lunar calendar. They are shown here, with the cycle of years of the lunar calendar, and the corresponding Western calendar year.

Western Calendar	Symbolic Animals	Lunar Calendar
1971	Boar	4669
1972	Rat	4670
1973	Ox	4671
1974	Tiger	4672

1975	Hare	4673
1976	Dragon	4674
1977	Serpent	4675
1978	Horse	4676
1979	Ram	4677
1980	Monkey	4678
1981	Rooster	4679
1982	Dog	4680

Among the many New Year's festivities are the Miss Chinatown, U.S.A. contest sponsored by the Chinese Chamber of Commerce, and the annual Dragon parade, which brings hundreds of thousands of people into the Chinatown area to view the colorful event.

Chinatown today is the Chinatown that was rebuilt after 1906; the dim, narrow alleys so famed in melodrama are as safe now as brightly lighted Grant Avenue. But Chinatown now occupies more than the cramped space in which the Chinese of Gold Rush days settled, and has expanded beyond the traditional boundaries. The American brig *Eagle,* in the spring of 1848 brought San Francisco's first three Chinese immigrants, two men and a woman. Clipper ships in the China trade during the following decade brought 25,000 peasants from Kwangtung Province. Eager to escape the hard times succeeding the disastrous Triad uprisings and lured by prospects of sudden wealth, they arrived to do the menial work of the Gold Rush. Though many went to the mines, the majority settled in San Francisco. Despite the racial hostility they faced, they early became sellers of wares imported from China, peddlers of fresh vegetables, fishermen, servants, gamblers, and real estate owners.

As the Yankee first settlers, following the expanding water front in the 1850's, moved down the slope toward Montgomery Street, the Chinese inherited their abandoned locations adjoining Portsmouth Square. Because of their value as laborers in the boom years when white labor was at a premium, they were allowed to entrench themselves in what was known to be an ideal residential district sheltered from wind and fog. The growing commercial district below Kearny Street formed the colony's eastern barrier; to the north Pacific Street's course between the Presidio and the water front was a natural boundary; south of California Street, almost in the shadow of Old St. Mary's Church, was a white *demi-monde* dominated by French prostitutes; along the higher slope of what is now Nob Hill, Stockton Street's respectable residential quarter forbade encroachment farther west. Destroyed by the successive conflagrations of the 1850's and 1860's, Chinatown rose repeatedly on old foundations that no sufficient majority of San Franciscans cared to reclaim.

Old Chinatown had neither the native architecture nor the glitter of lights characteristic of its streets today. Dim lanterns, hung on the iron balconies of tenements, furnished by night the only illumination, until gaslights brought their flickering radiance. Overcrowding compelled the Chinese to enlarge their quarters with cellars which were to add many a legend to the colony's ill repute. Even before its traffic in vice and its tong wars reached the alarming proportions of the 1870's, 1880's, and 1890's, Chinatown was a stage set for criminal drama—a place of eerie shadows and flitting figures, of blind alleys and obscure passageways, of quiet stabbings and casual gunfire.

Subjected to increasing racial discrimination, the Chinese inherited the full measure of stigma that had been visited only incidentally upon the Hounds and Sydney Coves. When, after the building of the Central Pacific Railroad, thousands were discharged by the Big Four to swell the already unwelcome horde of competitors with white labor, "Crocker's pets" became the objects of abuse throughout California. Denis Kearney's sand-lot Workingmen's Party drove the hapless orientals from factories, burned their laundries, and threatened their white employers with violence.

The resulting Chinese Exclusion Act of 1882 made no provision, however, for deportation of Chinese lawfully within the country; and San Francisco's Little China remained to outlive half a century of agitation against it. But the exclusion of orientals from their former respectable pursuits made them more than ever the prey of criminal elements. From the bonanza days until 1906, the district was synonymous with the Barbary Coast. The two decades between 1906 and 1927 (when the last tong war occurred) were required to eliminate its opium dens, its vice and gambling rackets, and its menace to public health.

The municipal czardoms of "Blind Chris" Buckley and Abe Ruef subjected Chinatown to domination by their oriental henchman, Fong Ching—better known as Little Pete—and his blackmailing society, Gi Sin Seer. Little Pete operated in a Chinatown where rival tongs fought over the profits of a vice traffic as old as the colony itself. In its most flourishing days, hundreds of slave girls with bound feet were crowded into brothels along Grant Avenue—then the notorious Dupont Street—and adjacent alleys.

For his bribing activities in the case of Lee Chuck, one of his hatchetmen whose ready six-shooter sent a rival sprawling in Spofford Alley, Little Pete served five years in San Quentin Penitentiary. Once back in his old haunts, he began extending his activities beyond the confines of Chinatown. His gang cleaned up $100,000 in a racetrack swindle, which made enemies who swore to get him the instant he should appear without his usual bodyguard of white men. Their chance came on January 23, 1897. Impatient to learn the latest racetrack results,

Little Pete entered a Waverley Place barber shop without his body-guard and paused to have his forehead shaved, his queue plaited, and his ears cleaned of wax. Then "two figures as swift and black as crows dart from nowhere into the doorway. There is a crackle of sound like the sputtering of a string of firecrackers ushering in the New Year: Little Pete falls forward in a crimson pool . . ."

In true gangster tradition, Little Pete's cohorts attempted to give him a magnificent funeral. After two hours of intricate last rites, performed by four priests from his favorite joss house, his casket was placed in a resplendent hearse drawn by six black-draped white horses. Hired mourners preceded the hearse, burning joss sticks and wildly beating the air with uplifted arms. From a carriage, four Chinese busily tossed out bits of paper punched with square holes—to confuse the devils seeking to make off with the spirit of the departed. The fantastic cortege, led by a popular orchestra playing the funeral march from *Saul,* proceeded through streets lined with spectators to the Chinese Cemetery down the Peninsula. Here a mob of onlookers—not hood-lums, but respectable San Franciscans indignant over losing bets on race horses doped by Pete's henchmen—greeted priests and mourners with hoots and clods of earth. The Chinese were compelled to haul the coffin back to the city where, at the old Chinese cemetery Little Pete's remains were interred pending arrangements for shipment to China. The wagon-loads of roast pig, duck, cakes, tea, and gin left beside the grave were guzzled by the crowd of white onlookers.

The Chinatown of Little Pete and his rival tongs was the Chinatown that shared with the Barbary Coast a worldwide notoriety. But always there was the sober, industrious Chinatown of respectable merchants and hard-working coolies; of ancient native customs and religion; and of tra-ditional family life. Quietly this larger element was accumulating wealth, gradually co-operating with the Protestant and Catholic missions, and—after 1906—with the city's police. When it became necessary to erect the new Chinatown upon the charred foundations of the old, Chinese capital and enterprise accomplished the task promptly and with good taste. The colony's southern boundary was extended to Bush Street, claiming the block now occupied by St. Mary's Square.

The last half century has seen various improvements on the district's sudden reconstruction after 1906. But not until recent years was its past —assiduously kept alive by pulp magazines and newspaper supplements— lived down. Naive visitors still expect to be shown opium dens and under-ground passages. The new Chinatown, alert and progressive, is without nostalgia for its long era of dirt and crime. The largest Chinese settle-ment outside Asia, it prefers its modern role as meeting place of East and West.

POINTS OF INTEREST

Site of the KONG CHOW TEMPLE, 520 Pine St., a famous landmark for many years, demolished in 1969. It had been built after the fire of 1906 and was known for its elaborate hangings of silk brocade, wood carvings, and brightly painted passages.

ST. MARY'S SQUARE is a grass-covered plot at Pine, Anne, and California Sts., opposite Old St. Mary's Church. It is a favorite romping place for Chinese children. The Square, once called St. Mary's Alley, has a seamy past, but today has a highly useful function as the roof for St. Mary's Square Garage, opened May 12, 1964, which has 250,000 sq. ft. underground. The Square became a municipal park after the fire of 1906, which wiped out an assortment of shooting galleries and bawdy houses.

From the high western slope of the square at Statue of SUN YAT-SEN faces the East toward China. The 12-foot figure, with head and hands of rose-red granite, wearing a long robe of bright stainless steel, was created by sculptor Beniamino Bufano under the sponsorship of the WPA's Northern California Art Project (formerly the Federal Art Project). Dr. Sun Yat-sen (1866-1925), organizer of the Kuomintang—whose local branch supplied materials for the memorial—visited San Francisco on several occasions. In 1937, Lin Sen, who was then China's president, wrote the words that appear on the steel disc in the granite base of the monument: "Father of the Chinese Republic and First President . . . Champion of Democracy . . . Proponent of Peace and Friendship Among Nations . . ."

N. from Pine St. on Anne St. to California St.; W. on California.

The construction of OLD ST. MARY'S CHURCH, ne. corner Grant Ave. and California St., was inaugurated in 1853 by Archbishop Joseph Sadoc Alemany, and at midnight Mass on Christmas Day, 1854, the edifice was dedicated as the cathedral seat for the Roman Catholic diocese of the Pacific Coast. Until completion of St. Mary's Cathedral in 1894, Old St. Mary's remained the most powerful stronghold of Catholicism in California and Nevada. This stately old structure has been the parish church of the Paulist Fathers for more than 75 years.

Old St. Mary's stands on land donated by pioneer banker John Sullivan, whose wife, Catherine Farrell Sullivan, lies buried in the crypt of the church. Architects Crane and England are thought to have modeled the purely Gothic structure after a church in the Spanish birthplace of Archbishop Alemany. Its red brick and ironwork was shipped around the Horn; granite brought from China was hoisted into place with improvised wooden derricks by Chinese workmen. The two large clocks in the 90-foot-high square Gothic tower were long the community timepieces of early San Franciscans. Beneath the frontal dial still appear the gold letters on black bronze, whose warning was intended to put the fear of God into the roisterers of Dupont Street: "Son Observe the Time and Fly from Evil." As early as 1855, an angry correspondent to the *Alta California* made irreverent protest against the booming bell of Old St. Mary's: "Those who want their sins washed off by those daily ablutions may as well be aroused by their own consciences, without annoying the whole neighborhood."

Completely gutted by the fire of 1906, the interior of the church was rebuilt on its original plan. In January, 1929, the basement was remodeled to form a modern auditorium, Paulist Hall; two months later a five-story structure adjoining St. Mary's on the north was razed and the church building extended to its present length of 153 feet. This latter wing, which maintains the architectural features of the original (Edward A. Eames, architect), houses the PAULIST CIRCULATING LIBRARY (*open weekdays 11-6, Sun. 10:30-1:30*).

N. from California St. on Grant Ave. to Sacramento St.; E. on Sacramento.

The NOM KUE SCHOOL (*open 4-6 p.m.*), 765 Sacramento St., for children between the ages of 6 and 15, supplements the public school curriculum, offering a purely cultural program designed to foster Chinese traditions and customs in American-born Chinese. No commercial subject is taught; emphasis is placed on Chinese language, calligraphy, literature, history, and philosophy, particularly that of Confucius.

Built in 1925 by people from the Namhoi District, the school building follows the official courthouse design of China. A pair of sacred lions guard the set-back upper story. High, narrow windows in many small panels give myriad light reflections to the interior, whose simple teakwood furnishings are relieved by the lavish use of decorative colors; vivid green, yellow, red, and turquoise. The upper floor houses the headquarters of the Fook Yin Tong, a benevolent society formed by people of the Namhoi District.

More than its name implies, is the CHINESE CHAMBER OF COMMERCE, 730 Sacramento St., the only organization of its kind when established in the 1880's. In addition to fostering Chinese business and commerce, the organization aids in solving the housing problem of Chinese in San Francisco; enlightens its countrymen on legal matters; and aids in the liquidation of bankruptcies of Chinese merchants by negotiation rather than by court procedure (*open Mon.-Fri. 10-5; Sat.10-12*).

The Chamber of Commerce has assumed commercial arbitration over matters once handled by the Chinese Six Companies, settling disputes among merchants, and members of their families, and—rarely—among trade organizations (such as the Jewelry Guild or Laundry Workers Association). Since establishment of a similar chamber in New York in 1910, this bureau no longer serves Chinese throughout the United States. Today the Chinese Chamber of Commerce is chiefly known as the organizer of the Chinatown New Year Festival and Beauty Pageant.

Outwardly occidental are the businesslike offices of the KUOMIN-TANG HEADQUARTERS IN AMERICA, 827 Sacramento St., from which are supervised the activities of the 3 regional and 50 branch offices of the Chinese Nationalist Party in the United States (*open 10-12, 2-4*). The San Francisco headquarters was the second established outside China (the first was in Honolulu). The Western Regional Office of the Kuomintang, with jurisdiction over branches in California, Nevada, and Utah, also is located in San Francisco (846 Stockton St.).

The party publishes the Chinese-language newspaper, *Young China* (*51 Hangah*), founded by Dr. Sun Yat-sen.

The irregular series of rectangular terraces forming the CHINESE CHILDREN'S PLAYGROUND (*open weekdays 10-10; play apparatus*), Sacramento St. between Waverly Pl. and Stockton St., are walled by the dark brick of surrounding buildings. During the Sino-Japanese War the playground was the scene of anti-Japanese rallies. The upturned cornices of the small pagoda-like stucco clubhouse are brightly painted.

N. from Sacramento St. on Stockton St.

The CHINESE CONSOLIDATED BENEVOLENT ASSOCIATION, 843 Stockton St., also called the Chung Wah Wui Goon, is best known as the Chinese Six Companies—despite the fact that it long has represented seven companies (*open to visitors 1-5*). These seven associations, each representing a region of Kwangtung Province in old China, are the Kong Chow, Ning Yung, Sam Yup, Sue Hing, Yan Wo, Yeung Wo, and the Hop Wo. (The Chinese system of organization follows three lines: family, of which there are about 26; geographical, hence the seven associations listed above; and fraternal, the tongs, of which there are about a dozen.

With nominal nation-wide jurisdiction, the Six Companies functions as a board of arbitration, settling disputes among organizations and individuals. Chinatown's civic activities, such as the annual United Crusade drive and Rice Bowl parties, are under its management. It assists in maintaining the Chinese Hospital and Chinese schools. A particularly important function is its supervision of the removal of the bones of Chinese dead from American cemeteries to China for reburial or repository in shrines.

Today the Six Companies is not as influential as it used to be. It is a non-profit organization supported by donations from the district associations, and the income from its properties. From among its officers (presidents of the seven associations named above) the presidency is rotated every two months. The brief presidential term is supposedly designed to prevent the acquisition of undue power or influence by any one officer.

The organization occupies a three-story stuccoed building roofed with red tile. White marble steps lead to a first-floor veranda guarded by giant Chinese lanterns. Contrasting with the facade of sky-blue tile are green and gold trimmed balconies opening onto the second and third floors. The interior is sumptuously furnished in the Chinese motif, from the large main-floor meeting hall to the rooms and offices of the upper floors. The upper floors are also used by the Chinese School.

A pioneer of Protestant faith in Chinatown is the CHINESE PRESBYTERIAN CHURCH, 925 Stockton St., founded in 1853. The present building was erected after the 1906 fire upon the ruins of the original structure. The simple, uncarpeted interior resembles that of a country church, with its rough, beamed ceilings, its long pews, and the rows of chairs behind the pulpit; yet its atmosphere is that of the Orient. Three red velvet panels behind the rostrum carry inscriptions, in gold Chinese characters, of the Ten Commandments, the Lord's Prayer, and the Beatitudes.

The Chinese Presbyterian Mission in 1854, published San Francisco's first Chinese and English newspaper, probably the first in the United States, *The Oriental,* which is said to have done much to counteract the local hostility between Chinese and the white race during its two-year existence. A file of the paper is preserved in the San Francisco Theological Seminary at San Anselmo. The church conducts day and evening classes in English for Chinese of all ages.

W. from Stockton St. on Washington St. to Wetmore St.; S. from Washington on Wetmore.

The CHINESE (PRESBYTERIAN) MISSION HOME used to be located at 144 Wetmore St., occupying a small double flat, home of a staff of Chinese girls, and far removed from the busy mission that moved to larger quarters four times after its establishment in 1874. In 1894 a building was erected at 920 Sacramento Street to house the crowded home, later called Cameron House. The following year its management was assumed by Donaldina Cameron, who became Lo Mo (The Mother) to the scores of Chinese girls she rescued from slave operators. Long before her retirement at the age of 70, Miss Cameron had achieved an international reputation. The mission moved to its present quarters in 1939, and is today the center of many activities for the young.

Retrace on Wetmore St. to Washington St.; retrace on Washington to Trenton St.; N. on Trenton.

The CHINESE HOSPITAL, se. corner Trenton and Jackson Sts., was dedicated in 1925. Built for the residents of Chinatown through public subscription, it occupies a four-story, many windowed gray concrete building, decorated by ornamental iron grill work and topped by a large sunroom. Chinatown continues to support its little 58-bed hospital, aided only by the United Crusade. The institution consists, in addition to its general medical department and surgery, of emergency and maternity wards; an eye, ear, nose and throat department; and a clinic with in- and out-patient departments. It is staffed by both Chinese and white employees and officials.

Retrace on Trenton St. to Washington St.; E. on Washington.

What is now OLD CHINATOWN LANE, extending a half-block northward from its entrance near 868 Washington Street—a narrow paved thoroughfare of bazaars and shops characteristic of Chinatown —was once the "Street of the Gamblers," a crowded little lane notorious for its gaming rooms and brothels. Later, it became Cameron Alley (honoring Donaldina Cameron) and kept this name until 1939, when, oddly enough, its dingy tenements were modernized to resemble the untouched Chinatown of a generation ago.

In the CHINGWAH LEE ART STUDIO, reached by a narrow stairway at the far end of the lane, is the largest private collection of Chinese art in California. On exhibit are early tomb wares, Sung stone ware, porcelain of the Ming and Manchu periods, carved jade and ivory, and bronzes and sculptures of the pre-Christian era. Many of the objects are so rare that their like cannot be found in any museum.

The proprietor of the studio, Chingwah Lee, used to divide his time between San Francisco, where he was an appraiser for Chinese merchants and art collectors, and Hollywood, where he used to act in motion pictures. Among the films in which he has appeared are The Good Earth, Thirty Seconds Over Tokyo, and Little Jim. Besides his activities as an appraiser and an actor, his career has included playwriting, lecturing on Chinese art, and writing monographs on Chinese ceramics. He edits and publishes the *Chinese Digest,* only magazine on Chinese culture published in English, and serves as general secretary of the China Cultural Society of America.

S. from Washington St. on Waverly Pl.

The main floor of the four-story, yellow-brick building housing the TIN HOW TEMPLE (*suggested visiting hours 6-10 p.m.*), 125 Waverly Pl., is occupied by the Sue Hing Benevolent Association, by whom the temple is maintained. Maroon-colored balconies run the length of the three upper floors. A wrought-iron gate on the top floor guards the temple of T'ien Hou, Queen of the Heavens and Goddess of the Seven Seas.

It is believed by many Chinese that one of the present altars was brought to San Francisco in 1848, by one of the few Chinese who arrived that year, transferred from a sailing vessel to a house at First and Brannan Streets, and later moved to Waverly Place. When a larger temple erected in 1875 was ravaged by the flames of 1906, the altar and the goddess T'ien Hou were removed temporarily to Oakland. The following year, workmen excavating for the basement of the present building discovered the great temple bell, and it too was reinstalled.

The main altar of the temple presents an intricate carving representing the life story of Confucius. To the left of T'ien Hou sits Moi Dii, god of military affairs, and Ni-Lung, one of the goddesses of motherhood. In front of T'ien Hou are three massive bronze urns containing prayer sticks and a tiny altar light, which is never permitted to burn out. Along the walls are 16 ceremonial wands, resembling ancient Chinese battle-axes, used in early times as implements of warfare against evil spirits. With the altar, set in the center of the sanctuary, are two urns inlaid with Cantonese enamel and precious stones; their designs depict scenes from the life and work of Confucius, whose teachings are especially revered, although Buddhism and Taoism are also represented.

Retrace on Waverly Pl.; E. on Washington St.

The BANK OF CANTON, 743 Washington St., occupies a pagoda-like, one-story building that it acquired in 1961 from the Chinese Telephone Exchange, a commercial institution that used to generate great interest among tourists. Operators in the exchange were required to memorize the numbers of many subscribers, who continued to make calls by name instead of number. Dial phones brought about its closing on January 22, 1949.

PING YUEN (TRANQUIL GARDENS) HOUSING PROJECT, is located on the south side of Pacific between Columbus and Powell. Completed in 1950 and dedicated by Mayor Elmer Robinson October 21, 1951, the project consists of three six-story buildings containing 232 apartments (John Bolles, architect). At the entrance to the project are eight ceramic Chinese guardian dogs created by Mary Erckenbrack. In 1961 Ping Yuen North was completed with 194 apartments.

The GREAT CHINA THEATER, 636 Jackson St., and the MANDARIN THEATER, 1021 Grant Ave., used to be the only theaters in Chinatown. Nightly each would present performances of Cantonese opera. Since World War II these theaters have been showing motion pictures made in Hollywood, Hong Kong, and Taiwan, with Chinese pictures predominating. The Mandarin Theater has changed its name to SUN SING THEATER, while the Great China has been sold to the Shaw Brothers film interests of Hong Kong.

Today there are six theaters in the Chinatown area showing Chinese language pictures. On special occasions troupes organized by opera singers from Hong Kong, give performances in one or another of the theaters.

The CHINATOWN GATEWAY, at Grant Ave. and Bush St., was designed by architect Clayton Lee and dedicated October 18, 1970.

Latin Quarter:
Telegraph Hill and North Beach

"The city is full of bold hills, rising steeply from the deep water. The air is keen and dry and bright like the air of Greece and the waters not less blue . . . recalling the cities of the Mediterranean . . ."

— JAMES, VISCOUNT BRYCE

BETWEEN the two steep hills that loom abruptly from the Peninsula's northeastern bulge—on the east, Telegraph Hill; on the west, Russian Hill—ringed with their tiers of buildings, a narrow valley runs northwestward from the fringes of the financial district to the water front of North Beach. Along its bottom cuts the diagonal of Columbus Avenue, which begins among the clustering shops, cafes, and night clubs at the southern base of Telegraph Hill and ends at the northern base of Russian Hill where Ghirardelli Square, the Cannery, and Aquatic Park are located. Up from this traffic-crowded artery, where stucco-fronted commercial buildings with their awnings and signboards string in long rows, climb endless blocks of weathered frame flats, staggered—step-like—one above another. Here and there a round-bellied window, a red-tiled roof, a patch of green garden breaks the monotony of their ranks. In the salt-fresh, sun-baked air of a clear day, each building stands out sharply, tarnished with a mellow patina of sun, fog, and soot. Seen in such weather, under a hot blue sky, the district is reminiscent of some Mediterranean seaside village spilling to the water from steep heights. And seen when the billowing mists of a smoky twilight stream down the slopes, it has the look of a sprawling hillside town of northern Italy.

Whether imagined or actual, such resemblances could not have failed to suggest themselves to San Franciscans who know that this is San Francisco's Little Italy. It could only have been an imagined resemblance that prompted Ernest Peixotto's often-quoted remark: "If you want to behold a bit of the Bay of Naples, go some misty morning to Fisherman's Wharf." To Robert Louis Stevenson the district was "Little Italy . . . a favorite haunt of mine." In his time, too, it was called Little Mexico (a part of it still is Mexican). And it might once have been named Little Ireland, for as Wallace Irwin wrote of "Telygraft Hill":

"The Irish they live on the top av it,
    And th' Dagoes they live on th' base av it,
    And th' goats and th' chicks and th' brickbats and shticks
    Is joombled all over th' face av it . . ."

Through the years, the face of hill and beach have changed almost beyond recognition, but since the town's beginnings the steep slopes of these northeastern limits have been peopled with a many-tongued foreign colony.   And like Latin Quarters everywhere, the district came in the end to be the traditional haunt of bohemia.

The visitor who boards a bus for North Beach will no more find an ocean beach at the end of the line than will the pedestrian who toils up Telegraph Hill find a telegraph station at the end of his climb. The beach along which bathhouses clustered—in the days when the famous wharf built by "Honest Harry" Meiggs in 1853 still extended into the Bay from the foot of Powell Street—was buried more than half a century ago when tons of earth were dumped into the water, out as far as the sea wall extending along the present water front, finished in 1881.   And long since vanished is that telegraph station on the summit of the hill which was a city landmark for decades after it was connected by wire in 1853 with a lookout station at Point Lobos.   The station replaced the still older semaphore of which Bret Harte wrote in "The Man at the Semaphore": ". . . on the extremest point of the sandy peninsula, where the bay of San Francisco debouches into the Pacific, there stood a semaphore telegraph . . . it signified to another semaphore farther inland the 'rigs' of incoming vessels, by certain uncouth signs, which were passed on to Telegraph Hill, San Fraincisco, where they reappeared on a third semaphore . . . and on certain days of the month every eye was turned to welcome those gaunt arms widely extended at right angles which meant 'side-wheel steamer' (the only steamer which carried the mails) and 'letters from home.'"

The road to the Presidio, which wound over Telegraph Hill's western shoulders and past North Beach, was a track through unsettled wilds until the later 1850's.   For years the only house between Yerba Buena and the Presidio was the hospitable adobe which Juana Briones built in 1836 near the hill's western base, at what is now the intersection of Powell and Filbert Streets.   In the shelter of that Loma Alta (high hill) of the Spanish discoverers, the buxom dark-featured widow of Apolinario Miranda supplied milk and green vegetables to visiting ship's crews, administered to the sick, and sheltered an occasional refugee from the wretchedness of life before the mast.   The travelers of the 1850's found the "old Presidio road . . . neither safe nor pleasant," recalled pioneers T. A. Barry and B. A. Patten.   "The hard adobe soil in summer was like stone, and in the rainy season gummy, sticky and disagreeable.   The steep, shelving, uneven way [made] the carriage perpetually seem as if it were just toppling over. . . . Like all primitive roads, it wound up over the highest, most toilsome way, past cattle-pens, corrals, brick-yards and butcher's shambles, the ground all the way looking as baked and hard as slag or adamant, with no sign of vegetation . . ."

Around Telegraph Hill's southern slopes—no more than a stone's throw from the town's first landing place at Clarke's Point—congregated in 1849 exiles from Australia's penal colonies in a district of grog shops, brothels, and gambling dives known as Sydney Town. Along the hill's western base spread the shacks and tents of Little Chile, settled by Chilenos and Peruvians. At weekly intervals, usually on Sundays, the organized hoodlums who called themselves "Hounds"—many of their number recruited from Sydney Town—used to raid the Chileno quarter, pillaging the houses, robbing and beating the inhabitants, attacking the women. The depredations were only halted by the Vigilance Committee of 1851.

For decades the North Point Docks under the brow of Telegraph Hill, built in 1853 from the foot of Sansome Street, were the landing place for immigrants from France and Italy. From the beginning they settled around the slopes of the hill. The section became a polyglot community, where Irish, Germans, French, Italians, and Latin Americans mingled easily. Although the first Italians had arrived as early as the 1830's, they began to overwhelm the other nationalities with their numbers only toward the end of the nineteenth century. By the thousands they came—laborers, artisans, mechanics, farmers, shopkeepers. As soon as they were well established, they lent passage money to countrymen in the homeland. The majority settled in the North Beach-Telegraph Hill section because it reminded them of their native land, because rents and land were cheap there, and because it was near the Bay where many of them earned their living by fishing. The Irish, the Germans, and the French moved to other parts of the city. When the fire of 1906 began to creep up the slopes of the hill, it was the Italians who saved it. From their cellars they rolled out barrels of red wine and, forming a bucket brigade, protected their houses against the flames with blankets soaked in the wine. The district was formerly theirs, today the area is a potpourri of French, Indian, Japanese, Italian, Greek, Mexican, German and Chinese restaurants and night spots. It is a mosaic of sidewalk cafes, sophisticated cabarets, off-beat bistros, and celebrated jazz cellars.

Little Italy is no longer so little, for the Italians, 80,000 strong, are San Francisco's largest and most powerful national minority. And North Beach is home not only for the Italians who live there but also for those who have moved to other parts of the city or the Bay region. On Sundays and feast days they come back to North Beach to visit relatives and revive old friendships. They fill the bay-windowed flats, lounge in the doorways, and gather in groups for sidewalk discussion. They crowd the lawns and benches in Washington Square. In their eyes is little regret for the vanishing past; in their rich laughter only a hearty appreciation for the present. What if the old stores are beginning to disappear—the dingy shelves and counters stacked with dried mushrooms, anchovies, and the Italian cheeses: Parmesan, Roma, Gorgonzola—the dusty rafters festooned with yards of rich moldy sausages and bunches of aromatic dried herbs: rosemary, thyme, sage and sweet marjoram—the boxes of creamy smooth chocolates from Turin and Perugia? Are not the great new markets, dazzling with refrigerated show cases, filled with the same good things to eat?

In the spring the markets, both old and modern, proclaim the virtues of *capretti,* fresh suckling kid. Occasionally the young goats' heads, replete with tiny horns, are displayed in the windows. Beside them lie huge Easter eggs with *Buona Pasqua* written on them in sparkling sugar. The pre-Lenten season is also the occasion for elaborate displays in shops devoted to imported gravure prints of a religious nature and Carrara marble images of the Virgin.

Formerly this season was marked by the rivalry between the Garibaldi and Bercigliari Guards. Sponsored by competing undertaking establishments, these two drill companies contested at Easter parades and pre-Lenten carnival balls for the choice of a queen and for trophies. Today the Italian Family Club and other social organizations hold pre-Lenten balls, but the maskers are missing, being confined to Italian celebrations of such Anglo-Saxon festivities as Hallowe'en and New Year's Eve.

Keen rivalry still exists, however, among the colony's residents in the choice of a queen for the annual fete on Columbus Day. Elected usually by votes secured through purchases at various North Beach stores, she reigns briefly each October 12. A special mass at the Church of Saints Peter and Paul honors the great discoverer, as does a parade. At Aquatic Park a pageant in fifteenth century costumes re-enacts Columbus' momentous landing on the shóres of San Salvador.

In the fall, when truckloads of ripened grapes have been piled in cellars, North Beach waxes heady with the smell of fermenting wine. The owners of portable winepresses move from one cool basement to another, crushing grapes for the red *vino*. Besides beverages of domestic manufacture, North Beach merchants offer wines and liquors imported from Italy; and *vov* of Padua has converted many not of Latin blood to the colony's gastronomy and its casual way of life.

To industry, finance, sports, and politics the city's Italians have made distinguished contributions. The names of Amadeo Giannini, founder of the Bank of America, Armando Pedrini, and James A. Bacigalupi are known to the world's stock markets. (Until the 1929 stock market crash scarcely a North Beach Italian, from cook's helper to crab fisherman, did not own shares in Giannini's corporation.) Angelo J. Rossi was long the city's mayor (1931-1944) and another mayor, Joseph L. Alioto, was born in North Beach. Of National reputation in the world of sports were the Di Maggio brothers; Fred Apostoli, the boxer; Charlie Ferrara, golf champion; Vic Bottari and Angelo "Hank" Luisetti, football and basketball heroes.

Mostly immigrants from Italy's northern provinces, the robust inhabitants of North Beach maintain their attachment for the soil in spite of their urban mode of living. The Peninsula truck gardens owned by their compatriots supply the city's wholesale vegetable and flower markets. The colony's other roots, particularly for its Neapolitan and Sicilian elements, are in the fishing industry; and herein is revealed a communal strain that is in marked contrast to the individualism apparent in other Italian enterprises. Members of the Crab Fishermen's Protective Association own their boats and gear in common and share among themselves the profits of the catch they bring in to Fisherman's Wharf.

Ever since Juana Briones established her home here, Spanish-speaking people have lived in North Beach. Although most of them now live farther west near the base of Russian Hill, many still cling to their older habitat on the slopes of Telegraph Hill. Once an ill-concealed and profound antagonism existed between them and their Italian neighbors. They patronize small butcher shops and grocery stores owned by their own countrymen. At the base of the hill a barber shop finds it expedient to hire barbers of each nationality, with separate chairs, for its factional clientele. That the sins of the fathers may not be visited upon the coming generations, however, a third chair is provided, with a hobbyhorse mounted on its seat, which is shared by children of both nationalities.

The small colony of Spanish-speaking people in the vicinity of Powell Street and Broadway in time past may have envied or had some misgivings concerning the large amount of property owned by their Italian neighbors. The Mexicans and other Latin Americans maintain a separate life and a separate culture that clings to customs of their homelands. Although a common religion is their strongest bond with their immediate neighbors, Nuestra Señora de Guadalupe differs in aspect from the Italian church which overlooks Washington Square. Along the base of Russian Hill they have also their restaurants and social clubs, their *abarrotes* which offer Mexican candies, pastry, *huaraches,* and pottery; also a store with Spanish books, South American and Mexican periodicals.

Despite its Spanish origins, San Francisco had in 1940 only about 8,700 Mexicans, of whom approximately 7,000 were native born. Other scattered Spanish-speaking groups brought the total Latin American minority to about 14,000. Many old Spanish families still live in North Beach. However, about 80 percent of the Spanish speaking population—66,500 in 1968—are located in the outer Mission district, many having moved from the North Beach area. The Chinese having outgrown their confining Chinatown quarters are now spilling over into the shops and homes vacated in this section.

Along the Latin Quarter's southern boundary, Broadway, where it turns its face toward the rest of San Francisco, denizens of hill and beach—Italians and bohemians—meet and mingle with the rest of San Francisco. Gaily bedizened with glaring electric signs after dark, Broadway and its cross streets in the four blocks between Kearny and Powell Streets are bordered continuously with restaurants and night clubs whose food, wine, and entertainment draw nightly throngs: Vanessi's, Finocchio's, Fior d'Italia, New Joe's and Enrico's Coffee House. At the opposite end of North Beach near the waterfront with its wharves and warehouses, the lights of the Cannery and Ghirardelli Square dispel the gloom. And to the water front at Fisherman's Wharf, where the crabs brought in by the fishermen are cooked on the sidewalk in steaming caldrons, comes all of San Francisco for sea food at its many excellent restaurants, or open-front cafes.

The crest of the hill is another land. Around the park's patch of green, hemmed in by concrete walls, soaring modern apartment houses rear their blank stuccoed facades. Ragged eucalyptus trees shed their leaves on jumbled, varicolored roofs. From facades painted pink, green, blue, or yellow, expansive windows look out across the Bay. Behind heavy wooden doors, narrow brick-flagged passageways lead into courtyards sheltered from the cold blustering breezes off the ocean.

To those who love it best North Beach will remain the Latin Quarter: bohemia between the hills and neighbor to the sea, hospitable with the musical linguistics and the gracious folkways brought hither by *paisanos* from the hot countries. And the hill will still stand, with its crown of wind-swept eucalyptus, through the fog and the rain and the sun. And people will still come there at sunset to watch the long shadows creep upward from the trees of Washington Square and to feel in the stir of the gathering darkness the touch of George Sterling's "cool grey city of love."

POINTS OF INTEREST

Probably the best-known and best-loved bar in a city of countless bars was for many years ISADORE GOMEZ' CAFE, 848 Pacific St. Above its inconspicuous doorway a huge banner and a small lantern mark the entrance to a narrow flight of dirty wooden stairs. Upstairs is a long, smoke-filled room—a room (describes the *Almanac for Thirty-Niners*) ". . . dilapidated as in speak-easy days, retaining the broken plaster of the ceiling, the insecure chairs, the long pine bar . . ." Here from 1930 until his death in 1944 presided Izzy Gomez in his black fedora, greeting friends and strangers with tall, witty tales of life in his native Portugal, sometimes dancing Portuguese folk-dances with incredible grace despite his massive bulk. On occasion he expounded —punctuating with a ponderous forefinger—the three principles of his philosophy: "When you don't know what to say, say nothing"; "Life is a long road; take it easy"; "When you come to a pool of water on that long road, don't make it muddy; maybe you'll pass there again, and you'll be thirsty."

Helen K. Francis became manager upon Izzy's death and built a reputation for fine food as well as drink. Red chalk marks left by a spotter during Prohibition days were preserved as well as the famous mural back of the bar which recorded the faces of Izzy, of Joe and "Dad" and the more colorful characters who once gathered there. 1848 Pacific was demolished for a housing project that opened in 1961.

N. from Pacific St. on Powell St. to Broadway; E. on Broadway.

One of the churches in San Francisco whose services are conducted in the Spanish language is NUESTRA SENORA DE GUADALUPE, 908 Broadway, which derives its name from the shrine erected near Guadalupe, Mexico, in commemoration of the appearance before the peon, Juan Diego, of the Virgin Mary. One of its two stained-glass windows, softly lighting the rich interior, portrays Juan Diego kneeling before Bishop Sumaraga. The chastely simple Romanesque church building, its twin domes topped by gold crosses, was built in 1912. The first church in the United States to be constructed of reinforced concrete replaced the old frame structure (dating from 1875) destroyed by the 1906 fire. In April, 1939 Msgr. Antonio M. Santandreu had rounded out his fiftieth year as the church's pastor to become the oldest living priest on the Pacific Coast, totally blind and partially deaf, but serving with the assistance of younger men. He died in 1944.

In sharp contrast to the austere facade is the ornate interior, approached from stone steps. On the arched ceiling of the nave, supported by twelve pillars, is portrayed in fresco the Holy Sacrament and the Cor-

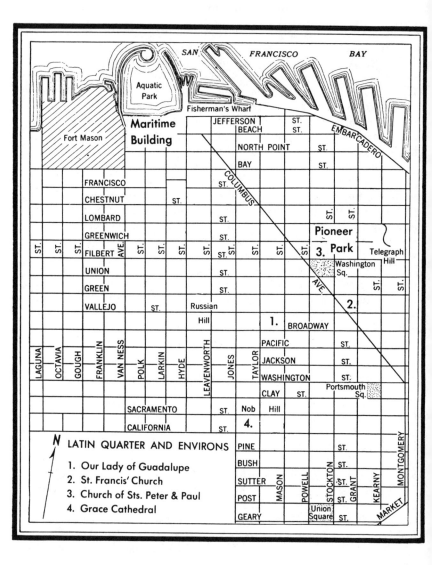

SAN FRANCISCO BAY

Aquatic Park

Fisherman's Wharf

Maritime Building

Fort Mason

JEFFERSON BEACH
ST. ST.
NORTH POINT
BAY
ST.
ST.

EMBARCADERO

FRANCISCO
CHESTNUT ST.
LOMBARD ST.
GREENWICH ST.
FILBERT AVE. ST.
UNION ST.
GREEN ST.
VALLEJO ST.

COLUMBUS ST.

Pioneer Park
3.
Washington Sq.
Telegraph Hill

Russian Hill

1.

2.

BROADWAY

LAGUNA
OCTAVIA
GOUGH
FRANKLIN
VAN NESS
POLK
LARKIN
HYDE
LEAVENWORTH
JONES
TAYLOR

PACIFIC ST.
JACKSON ST.
WASHINGTON ST.
CLAY ST.
Portsmouth Sq.

SACRAMENTO ST.
CALIFORNIA ST.

Nob Hill

4.

N

LATIN QUARTER AND ENVIRONS

1. Our Lady of Guadalupe
2. St. Francis' Church
3. Church of Sts. Peter & Paul
4. Grace Cathedral

PINE
BUSH
SUTTER
POST
GEARY

MASON
POWELL
STOCKTON
GRANT
KEARNY
MONTGOMERY

ST.
ST.
ST.
ST.
Union Square ST.

MARKET

onation of the Blessed Virgin. Behind the flood-lit white marble altar, standing at the end of the exquisitely tiled main aisle, is a mural depicting the Last Supper and the Multiplication of the Loaves and Fishes. By day, light streams through stained-glass windows portraying the miracle at Guadalupe and the Sermon on the Mount; by night, from massive and ornate candelabra. Every year during the nine days before Christmas, when Mexican families are commemorating the birth of Christ with the ceremonies of Las Posadas (the lodgings) in their homes, the church holds a novena with special singing and prayers.

N. from Broadway on Mason St. to Vallejo St.; E. from Mason on Vallejo.

122. First Roman Catholic parish church in San Francisco, ST. FRANCIS' CHURCH, 620 Vallejo St., owes its origin to the religious zeal of a group of the Gold Rush town's French residents, who persuaded a young officer of the United States Army to give them the use of a small room for services. Father Langlois, on his way from Oregon to eastern Canada by way of Cape Horn, was persuaded to remain as their pastor. In a new adobe chapel on the church's present site, on July 19, 1849, Father Langlois said Mass for the first time in the new building and administered the town's first Roman Catholic baptism. The French soon were joined by worshippers of so many other nationalities that in 1856 they withdrew to found a church of their own, Notre Dame des Victoires.

In the adobe chapel's schoolroom, on December 10, 1850, a reception was given for young Bishop Sadoc Alemany, just arrived to take charge of a diocese extending from the Rocky Mountains to the Pacific Ocean. Since St. Francis' congregation was still smarting from the indignity of having been embezzled by an impostor of funds, Father Langlois is said to have insisted on the Bishop's credentials. When it appeared that San Francisco, rather than Monterey, would be the chief city of the diocese, he returned as Archbishop Alemany, his formal translation to the Metropolitan See of San Francisco occurring July 23, 1853. Here he took up residence in a wooden shanty adjoining the church, which served as his cathedral until dedication of St. Mary's on Christmas, 1854.

Construction of a new St. Francis Church was begun five years later. Dedicated March 17, 1859, the fourteenth-century Gothic structure of cement-faced brick survived the 1906 fire with little enough damage to permit restoration. The interior is an aisled nave of seven bays with a shallow apse. In the apsidal arches above the ornate altar and reredos are a series of frescoes depicting events in the life of St.

Francis. Two larger frescoes over the side altars portray the death of St. Francis and the showing of the Stigmata.

N.W. from Vallejo St. on Columbus Ave.

In the heart of the teeming Italian section, WASHINGTON SQUARE, Columbus Ave., Union, Stockton, and Filbert Sts., a quadrangular oasis of lawn, is an out-of-doors refuge from the close-set flats of the locality. In the center of the square is a bronze Statue of BENJAMIN FRANKLIN, bequeathed by Henry D. Cogswell, philanthropist and temperance advocate, to: "Our boys and girls who will soon take our places and pass on." Inscriptions such as Vichy, Congress Water, and California Seltzer—proclaim the virtues of the drinking water that spouts from the fountain. On the east side of the park a granite marker carries the legend: "Astronomical and telegraph longitude, United States Coast and Geodetic Survey: Lat. 37.47', 57" N. Longitude 122.24', 37" W. Station Washington Square, 1869-1880." Facing Columbus Avenue is the VOLUNTEER FIREMEN'S MONUMENT (Haig Patigian, sculptor), a bronze group of three volunteer firemen—one holding a supine woman in his arms—dedicated to the Volunteer Fire Department of San Francisco, 1849-1866. It was erected in 1933 through a bequest of Lillie Hitchcock Coit. Washington Square, which served as a campground for homeless citizens after the 1906 holocaust, occupies land donated to the city January 3, 1850 by its first mayor, John W. Geary.

E. from Columbus Ave. on Filbert St.

The Roman Catholic CHURCH OF SS. PETER AND PAUL, 660 Filbert St., of concrete construction, lifts its two spires high above the Italian district it serves. Its cornerstone laid in 1922 by Archbishop Hanna, all but the exterior of the church was completed the following year. In 1939 and 1940 its facade again was shrouded in scaffolding in preparation for the long-planned embellishment of the exterior with mosaics on each side of the doorway, one of Dante at work on his *Paradiso* and another of Columbus landing in America. In the ornate interior seating 1,000, the Roman altar and many gilded images reflect the soft light filtering from the stained glass windows. Brought from Italy, the richly ornate altar, inlaid with mosaic and framed in white Carrara marble, bears a sculptured reproduction of Leonardo da Vinci's *The Last Supper*. The church's large statuary collection also includes a statue of patron saint John Bosco and a sixteenth-century carved wood figure of Jesus Christ.

Up Filbert St. steps to Telegraph Hill Blvd.; N. from Filbert on Telegraph Hill (by motor, N. from Filbert on Stockton St. to Lombard St.; E. from Stockton on Lombard to Telegraph Hill Blvd.; S. from Lombard on Telegraph Hill).

Crowning the brow of Telegraph Hill is PIONEER PARK, whose paved esplanade and parkway command a stirring panorama of the vast Bay and its shores and the city crowding to the edge of the Peninsula. Grown from loam-filled crevices on the bare rocky summit, its yellow broom, cypress trees, and stately eucalyptuses bank in greenery the base of COIT MEMORIAL TOWER (*elevator, 11-5 weekdays; 10:30-5:30, weekends*), a slim, fluted concrete column (Arthur Brown, Jr., architect) whose glass-enclosed observation gallery is 540 feet above the waters of the Bay. The tower is named for a life-long friend of San Francisco's firefighters, Lillie Hitchcock Coit, who in 1929 left funds to the city to be used for a memorial to the volunteer firemen of the 1850's and 1860's. As a girl of 15, she had been the mascot of the crack Knickerbocker Company No. 5. To the end of her life she wore the diamond-studded gold badge given her by the firemen, whether she attended a formal evening function or an early morning blaze. Where Coit Memorial Tower now rises stood, in the middle of the nineteenth century, the telegraph station for which the hill is named—"A place of much resort" in the fifties, reminisced Barry and Patten. ". . . it was good exercise to walk up there, and the view repaid the trouble. There were . . . refreshing milk-punches to be had in the room beneath the lookout on the roof, where privileged visitors could ascend and use the telescope."

A landmark in the history of government-subsidized art are the COIT TOWER MURALS, reflecting the contemporary scene in California city, factory and field in 1934, which were the result of the first work relief project for artists sponsored by the Federal government in the United States. Covering the walls of first and second floors and the stairway between them, they were executed by 20 members of San Francisco's art colony. On the main floor, above the entrance to the elevator room, a pair of Cyclopian eyes look down from Ray Boynton's mural symbolizing the mystic forces of nature, man in search of sustenance, and man in search of wealth. Other walls of the first floor graphically portray the characteristic activities of California life with their ten-foot figures by Malette Dean and Clifford Wight; industrial plants by Ralph Stackpole; a department store interior by Frede Vidar; a San Francisco street by Victor Arnautoff; and rich agricultural fields by Maxine Albro. A library cross-section by Bernard Zakheim shows readers scanning the headlines in contemporary newspapers. A mural by John Langley Howard depicts unemployed "snipers" panning gold and grim-faced workers massed in front of a smelter plant.

Facing the Golden Gate in a marble circle is the 12-ft., $50,000 bronze statue of Christopher Columbus. It was cast in Italy by sculptor Vittorio di Cobertaldo and shipped here for dedication on Columbus Day, 1957.

The MARCONI MEMORIAL, at the foot of the steps leading to Lombard Street, a modern, simply carved bench of Raymond California granite containing a bronze plaque (Raymond Puccinelli, sculptor) of Guglielmo Marconi, was erected to commemorate the inventor of the wireless in July, 1939. A Latin inscription reads: "Outstripping the lightning, the voice races through the empty sky."

N. on Telegraph Hill Blvd. to Lombard St.; W. from Telegraph Hill on Lombard to Columbus Ave.; NW. from Lombard on Columbus to Taylor St.; W. from Columbus on Taylor.

126. Twentieth-century commercialism and Old-World tradition go hand in hand at FISHERMAN'S WHARF, foot of Taylor St., where are moored in serried ranks the tiny, bright-painted gasoline boats of the crab fishermen and the tall-masted 70-foot Diesel-engined trawlers of the sardine fleet. The high-sterned junks with square sails of the Chinese shrimp fishermen who supplied the forty-niners with seafood have long since disappeared. The colorful craft of the Italians who supplanted them—rigged with triangular lateen sails like the fishing boats of the Gulf of Genoa or the Bay of Naples—have disappeared too, supplanted in turn by trim vessels powered with combustion engines. And the fish markets to which San Francisco housewives once drove in buggies have become neon-lit shops offering "curb service" to motorists. But the gulls still fight over morsels thrown into the lagoon; small boys still impale sardine bait on the troll lines; the oldsters of the crab fleet still sit cross-legged, mending their nets by hand with long wooden needles.

Heedless of onlookers, the sun-browned fishermen go about their work, tossing their fish from the holds to the wharves, where they are trundled off in hand trucks, hanging up their nets to dry in great brown festoons, painting and repairing their vessels, haggling with fish buyers. Sicilian in origin, many of the barrel-chested crab fishermen sport the tam-o-shanter, the knit jersey, and the heavy sea boots of their Mediterranean homeland.

The boats of the crabfishing fleet, like their larger sisters of the sardine fleet, are brightly painted, with blue and white the predominating hues. During the fishing season (November through August) the crab fleet usually leaves the wharf with the tide—between two and three o'clock in the morning—bound for fishing grounds between three and six miles outside the gate, where each boat anchors within hailing distance of its neighbor. In mid-afternoon they return, accompanied by screaming hordes of gulls. When not at sea, the crab boats are anchored at the inner harbor at Fisherman's Wharf, where the walks and planking are often plastered with nets drying in the sun.

Usually anchored outside the square lagoon of the crab fishermen are the sardine and bottom fish boats—large schooners and trawlers with deep after holds, their blue and yellow masts and booms towering above the smaller craft. In the sardine fleet, Norwegians and Slavonians predominate—excellent seamen, tanned by sun and wind, their faces wrinkled. Powered with 200- and 300-horsepower Diesel engines, the vessels venture northward as far as Alaskan waters and southward to Mexican shores. The dark of the moon between August and February is the best time for sardine fishing, because the sardine schools then are sighted most easily by the iridescent flash they create as they move through the water. The sardine fishermen use the net known as the purse seine, which is maneuvered in a circle by means of a skiff and then drawn together in much the same fashion as a tobacco pouch. The bottom fish vessels use the paranzella net, dragged between two boats, which revolutionized the industry when Pedro Costa introduced it in 1876. In these nets they trap sole, sand dab, rock cod, and flounder—which comprise 90 per cent of their catch—and occasionally starfish, octopi, and even sharks. The trawlers of the bottom fish fleet rank in size with those of the sardine fleet. It was the bottom fish fleet which first used steam-powered boats, also introduced by Costa—for which reason sole were first known around San Francisco Bay as "steamerfish." More than 2,000 men and 200 vessels are engaged in the fishing industry throughout the year; the annual catch totals nearly 300,000,000 pounds. Ranking first in size of catch is the sardine; second, the crab. The shore community at the wharf includes blacksmiths, boatbuilders, tackle menders and net repairers, and the dock includes a marine service station where the tanks of the gasoline-powered crab boats are filled. Fishing fleet boats are available for hire at an average cost of $15 per person.

Along the wharfside, the sidewalk is lined with huge iron cauldrons simmering over open fires of boxwood, where live crabs are boiled. Behind the kettles are piles of lobsters, trays of shrimp and prawns, shelves decked with rainbow-hued abalone shells, and little turtles with brightly painted designs on their backs for sale as souvenirs. Tourists walk the area eating seafood delicacies, while other diners sit by restaurant windows looking out over the masts of the boats moored in the lagoon.

Lords of the Hilltops

WHENEVER the builders of San Francisco could not go forward, they went up. In Currier and Ives' bird's-eye view, *The City of San Francisco—1878*, they already had leaped that crescent-shaped barrier of hills which swings from Telegraph Hill on the northeast to Twin Peaks in the middle of the Peninsula. Persistently the long files of houses climbed to the crests and down the other side. Where the heights defied scaling even by the cable car, the city's uphill progress was facilitated by steps.

No San Franciscan was amazed to behold even that doughty railroad builder, Collis P. Huntington, being towed uphill to his mansion by the California Street grip. The pinnacle to which a man's rise in riches might carry him had a name in those days—Nob Hill, inspired by those "nabobs" of commerce and finance who looked down from its crest. To Robert Louis Stevenson, the "great net of straight thoroughfares lying at right angles, east and west and north and south over the shoulders of Nob Hill, the hill of palaces, must certainly be counted the best part of San Francisco. It is there that the millionaires who gathered together, vying with each other in display, looked down upon the business wards of the city."

When Dr. Arthur Hayne, having made a comfortable fortune at his medical practice, desired to settle down with his bride, actress Julia Dean, he chose Nob Hill and, hacking a trail through the brush to the summit, built in 1856 a house of wood and clay on the future site of the Fairmont Hotel. A short time later, a merchant, William Walton, erected a more pretentious dwelling at Taylor and Washington Streets. Not until late in the 1860's, however, when the mass exodus of the elite from Rincon Hill began, was Nob Hill populated extensively.

Among the first men of wealth to settle there was Maurice Doré, banker William C. Ralston's confidante, who bought Walton's house. The first palatial homes built by millionaires—recalled Amelia Ransom Neville, chronicler of San Francisco's social elite—were Richard Tobin's, "distinguished by reason of having what might be termed a hand-picked library"; James Ben Ali Haggin's, "a large gray mansard with stables behind it where were all the most fastidious horses one could desire"; Lloyd Tevis', where "wonderful parties were given . . ." Later William T. Coleman built "a white Roman villa in a walled garden" and Senator George Hearst, "a long Spanish palace of white stucco."

The Hill's inducements as a residential site were greatly augmented by the advent of the cable car in the 1870's—that curious vehicle whose means of locomotion puzzled the visiting English noblewoman, Lady Duffus Hardy, almost as much as the "newly arrived Mongolian" whose remarks she quoted: " 'No pushee, no pullee, no horsee, no steamee; Melican man heap smart.' "

And from the summit of Nob Hill were rising, in the 1870's, those "really palatial residences, the homes of the railway and bonanza kings," of which Lady Hardy wrote. To advertise their new-found wealth, a half-dozen "get-rich-quick" millionaires—Leland Stanford, Mark Hopkins, and Charles Crocker of the Big Four; David Colton, who was known as the "½" of the "Big 4½"; James C. Flood of the Nevada Four; and E. J. ("Lucky") Baldwin—lavished their railroad and mining millions in unbridled display. Of wood treated to resemble stone they built their palaces, and stuffed them with *objets d'art* imported from Europe in shiploads. In their ostentation they were anything but discreet, as they must have realized when Dennis Kearny led an army of "sand-lotters" up the hill one autumn day in 1877 to shake angry fists at the mansions. For three decades the vainglorious display continued to dazzle all beholders—until one by one, the mansions burst into blaze as fire swept the hill in April, 1906.

Risen from the ashes, Nob Hill continues to justify its proud epithet, Hill of Palaces. Where the bonanza mansions stood, luxury hotels, aristocratic clubs, and towering apartment houses overlook the Bay. Fastidious old gentlemen still reach their homes on the heights by cable car. Nob Hill ladies out airing their dogs, doormen resplendent in uniform before gleaming entrances, shining limousines attended by liveried chauffeurs perpetuate the traditions of the hill's golden age. But the days of reckless ostentation passed with the fire; the Nob Hill of today breathes an air of subdued gentility.

Nob Hill was but one of the summits claimed and held by the rich. As the rest of the city began to swarm around, the vanguard of the Four Hundred moved northward to Russian Hill or westward to Pacific Heights, where they could dwell surrounded by gardens looking down upon the Golden Gate.

What part the Russians played in the naming of Russian Hill remains a mystery. According to one legend, a colony of Russian farmers raised vegetables on its slopes for the seal catchers of the Farallones; according to another, certain Russians of unknown identity were buried there; and according to still another, a Russian sailor of prodigious drinking habits fell into a well on the hill, where he drowned. The place made its earliest appearance in the city's annals as the site of a gibbet, where on December 10, 1852, one José Forni was hanged in the town's first official execution.

When Joseph H. Atkinson built his house in 1853 on the south side of Russian Hill, it stood alone. But Charles F. Homer, a government contractor, soon built next door; and next to Homer, W. H. Ranlett erected his House of Many Corners. William Squires Clark, who had constructed the town's first wharf, built the two-story house later purchased by William Penn Humphreys. And not far away were erected two of the city's eight octagonal houses.

One of the first panoramas of the city, drawn and lithographed from daguerreotypes made from the summit of the hill about 1862 by C. B. Gifford, shows a few straggling fences and a handful of isolated houses among unpaved streets on the hill's northern and southern slopes. From its summit rises the "observatory"—somewhat resembling an oil well derrick with a spiraling stairway—which Captain David Jobson erected in 1861. From the crow's nest atop this structure, known as Jobson's Folly, picnickers who had toiled uphill from Harbor View Park on the Bay could survey, for 25¢, the landscape and seascape through a telescope.

Almost from the beginning, Russian Hill was the haunt of the city's artists and writers. Of their number, however, Robert Louis Stevenson —whose "homes" are almost as numerous as the beds "in which George Washington slept"—was not one, although his widow came here to live after his death. Ambrose Bierce's cynicism found vent there. Joaquin Miller composed poetry there, as did Ina Coolbrith and George Sterling. Frederick O'Brien lived there when he wrote *White Shadows of the South Seas.* There Peter B. Kyne wrote many of his Cappy Ricks stories, and Stewart Edward White, his novels. Will and Wallace Irwin, in the days when Will was co-editor with Frank Norris and Gelett Burgess of *The Wave,* found refuge on the hill. It was because he lived there that Burgess conceived his "Ballad of the Hyde Street Grip":

> "Rush her at the crossings, catch her on the rise,
> Easy round the corners when the dust is in your eyes!"

Of the colony were John Dewey, before he acquired his fame in the East; Mary Austin and James Hopper, before they went to join the colony at Carmel; Kathleen and Charles Norris, before they deserted the city for the Peninsula. On the crest of the hill, Rose Wilder Lane found inspiration. And here Inez Haynes Irwin wrote *The Californians* and Charles Caldwell Dobie, *San Francisco: A Pageant.* Sculptors

Douglas Tilden and Haig Patigian have lived here, and the painter Maynard Dixon. In a walled cavern built from an old cistern, "Dad" Demarest, high priest of Russian Hill's bohemia for more than a half century from 1872 on, lived for two weeks after the fire in 1906—and he kept it fitted up as a den afterwards, "Just in case."

Tall apartment buildings began invading bohemia's province on the Hill long ago. Higher and higher the newcomers have lifted their steel-and-concrete shafts. But despite this invasion, Russian Hill is still a world removed, where steps climb and brick-flagged lanes twine up sheer heights between green hedges. Gracious homes and rambling studios perch among gardens spilling downhill on its slopes. Among the Tudor villas and the neo-French chateaux, chastely simple dwellings of plywood and glass brick, designed with corner windows and sun decks to admit sunlight, air, and the view, have begun to appear of late years.

POINTS OF INTEREST

From the verge of the hill, the 20-story MARK HOPKINS HOTEL, southeast corner California and Mason Sts., above a triangular plaza entered between pylons and enclosed by balustrades, lifts its beacon-tiped minarets 537 ft. above sea level. The hotel was opened December 4, 1926, on property purchased for $600,000 by the California Mason Realty Co. The fireproof, concrete and brick structure was constructed for this company by McDonald & Kahn at a cost of $2,500,000. The buildings' two basements were dynamited out of solid rock except for one section already excavated which was probably intended for a wine cellar in the home of Mark Hopkins. The Top of the Mark opened in 1939 with especially designed glass panels built to withstand 120-mile-an-hour winds. (Timothy Pfleuger, architect).

To guests of sybaritic tastes, the solid gold bathroom fixtures of several of the tower apartments may recall the overwhelming lavishness of the mansion that Mark Hopkins, railroad magnate, built on the site in the 1870's. Presented after Hopkins' death to the San Francisco Art Association, the mansion became the scene of extravagant annual Mardi Gras balls.

On the foundations laid by James G. ("Bonanza Jim") Fair for his Nob Hill mansion, the FAIRMONT HOTEL, California, Mason, Sacramento, and Powell Sts., rears its lordly pile of white granite. Only the granite walls enclosing the grounds had been built when domestic troubles interrupted Fair's plans. To commemorate her father, "Tessie" Fair Oelrichs undertook the erection of a de luxe hotel. The Fairmont stood complete but for its windows—and crates of sumptuous furnishings had been moved into the lobby—when the fire of 1906 demolished everything but the walls. Under the direction of Stanford White the hotel was repaired and refurnished, and on April 17, 1907—one day short of the anniversary of the fire—it was opened with a banquet for 500 guests. It at once became the resort of the elite, led by Ned Greenway, self-appointed social arbiter.

From a semicircular drive flanked by lawns and shrubs, a porte-cochère leads to the entrance, marked by six gray stone columns rising six stories to the roof. From the walls of the vast, white-columned lobby, splashed with vivid red furnishings, look down panelled Florentine mirrors mounted in carved frames inlaid with gold leaf, imported from the Castello di Vincigliata in Italy.

In 1961 the old hotel was topped by a 29-story, 252-room, Tower (Mario Gaidano, architect) featuring a glass enclosed skylift which climbs up the facade of the Tower in an open shaft. The crowning glory is the spectacular cocktail lounge called the Crown Room. The decorative symbol of the room is a huge 12-foot crown chandelier. Beneath it guests can relax in a slowly revolving seating arrangement, enabling all to see the panoramic view.

The PACIFIC UNION CLUB, northwest corner California and Masons Sts., occupies the only residence on the hill to survive the fire of 1906—the massive $1,500,000 Connecticut brownstone mansion built by James C. Flood after his return from a trip to New York, where he was impressed by the brownstone mansions. Flood's "$30,000 brass fence," recalled Amelia Ransome Neville, "flashed for the entire length of two blocks on the square . . . and it was the sole task of one retainer to keep it bright." The foundations of the Flood fortune were laid at the Auction Lunch provided by Flood and his partner, W. S. O'Brien, "where an especially fine fish stew drew patrons from the Stock Exchange nearby. Daily the proprietors heard talk of stocks and mining shares and together decided to invest. Results were overwhelming."

In Steve Whipple's saloon on Commercial Street was founded the Pacific Club, first "gentlemen's club" in San Francisco, of which Cutler McAllister, brother of New York's social arbiter, Ward, was a founder. It was amalgamated eventually with the rival Union Club, founded in 1854. Its memberships, restricted to 100, pass like inheritances from father to son.

Where nursemaids trundle streamlined prams along the shrubbery-bordered paths of HUNTINGTON PARK, California, Taylor, and Sacramento Sts., Collis P. Huntington used to stride up to his front door from the cable car stop on California Street. Huntington bought his mansion from the widow of his one-time friend, David D. Colton, legal counsel for the Big Four. After Colton's mysterious death in 1878, the Four brought pressure upon her for the return of securities on the grounds that Colton had embezzled funds from their properties. Mrs. Colton vindicated her husband's name by introducing at a subsequent trial the famous Colton Letters exposing the machinations by which the four partners had acquired their railroad properties. From his enemy in court, Huntington bought Colton's house. Unlike the mansions of most of his contemporaries, the railroad lawyer's was in good taste, copied (wrote Mrs. Neville) "from a famous white marble palace of Italy . . ." Its site was bequeathed by Huntington's widow to the city in 1915.

Like those Gothic churches of the Middle Ages under construction for generations, GRACE CATHEDRAL, California, Taylor, Sacramento, and Jones Sts., was still unfinished more than three decades after Bishop William Ford Nichols laid its cornerstone. In the 1940's its spire—from which its builders planned, when the remainder of the Cathedral should be completed, to raise an illuminated cross 230 feet above the hilltop—was still a gaunt skeleton of orange-painted girders. The dream which inspired its founders has been nurtured since September 1863, when the Right Reverend William Ingraham Kip, first Episcopal Bishop in California, placed his Episcopal Chair in Grace Church (founded 1850), thus establishing the first cathedral seat of the Protestant Episcopal Church in America.

The Grace Cathedral of Bishop Kip's day (California and Stockton Streets) was destroyed in the 1906 fire. On January 27, 1914, the Founders' Crypt of the new church was opened. The Chapel of Grace was completed December, 1930. The 2,000 seat Cathedral, up to and including the third bay, was completed in 1934. New construction was started in 1961, and the Cathedral was consecrated on November 20, 1964. The Diocesan House at 1055 Taylor was completed in 1935 and the Cathedral House, 1051 Taylor about 1912.

The cathedral is 340 ft long and 119 ft. wide across the main front. The towers rise 158 ft. from the street; the 87-foot-high nave extends 300 ft. The use of undisguised concrete for the exterior gives the massive, buttressed walls an air of enduring strength. In the Chapel of Grace are an altar from eleventh-century France, reredos of sixteenth century Flemish wood carving, and stained-glass windows by the artist Connick. The Chapel of the Nativity contains an altar and mural by John H. De Rosen. Supported by the north tower is a carillon of 44 bells—weighing from twelve pounds to six tons each—which were cast in Croydon, England.

The CABLE CAR MUSEUM, at Washington & Mason Sts., occupies a two-story brick building erected in 1887 for the Ferries & Cliff House Railroad. Severely damaged in 1906 it was rebuilt in 1907. The Public Utilities Commission refurbished the building in 1967 and set up a gallery that permits visitors to look down upon the engine room and the winding wheels that move the cables. *Open 8 a.m.-midnight.*

The OCTAGONAL HOUSE (*private*), 1067 Green St., is the

first of a number of such dwellings designed by Orson S. Fowler of New York in 1849 and constructed for George Kenny in 1857 or 1858. The house was extensively repaired and restored in 1957. Woodwork and doors in the two lower floors are redwood, and the main rooms have pierced plaster cornices and scrolled plaster chandelier bases and white marble mantelpieces.

Overlooking the Golden Gate from the end of a graveled walk between interlacing plane trees, half-way down the hill from the Lombard Street Reservoir, the GEORGE STERLING MEMORIAL, Hyde, Greenwich, and Lombard Sts., is a simple bench inlaid with warm-hued tiles, dedicated by the Spring Valley Water Company June 25, 1928, "To Remember George Sterling, 1869-1926." The bronze tablet is inscribed with a stanza from the "Song of Friendship," a musical composition whose lyrics were written by Sterling, and a quotation from the poet's "Ode to Shelley":

> O Singer, fled afar
> The erected darkness shall but isle the star
> That was your voice to man,
> Till morning come again
> And of the night that song alone remain.

The modern $6,000,000 white marble edifice at 1111 California St. is the CALIFORNIA MASONIC MEMORIAL TEMPLE, completed in 1958 (Albert E. Roller, architect). The temple features a 3,200 seat circular acoustically perfect auditorium and a 500-car garage. A large translucent mosaic window visible from the colonnaded marble entrance on California Street, represents pictures of fraternal symbols and Masonic activity in California. The window is 44 ft. high and 48 ft. wide. It cost $50,000 and was made by sandwiching plastic mosaic squares between sheets of glass designed by Emile Norman. The building also houses the executive officers of the California Masonic Grand Lodge and the Masonic Homes of California.

The SAN FRANCISCO ART INSTITUTE, 800 Chestnut St., an affiliate of the University of California, occupies a modified Italian Renaissance building constructed in 1926. It comprises a college, gallery, Art Bank of West Coast artists, and the Anne Bremer Memorial Library. The organization was founded in 1871 and was known as the Mark Hopkins Institute of Art when housed in the Hopkins mansion on Nob Hill after 1874. Later it was called the California School of Fine Arts. It is the oldest art school west of the Mississippi and enrolls up to 1,000 students annually. In the gallery a huge fresco by Diego Rivera illustrates the painting of a mural. After World War II the school introduced abstract expressionism to the West Coast and later was a center of figurative painting. Ansel Adams started the first course in photography as a fine art offered in any American college.

Embarcadero

". . . that harbor so remarkable and so spacious that in it may be established shipyards, docks, and anything that may be wished."

—FATHER PEDRO FONT (1776)

THE story of San Francisco is largely the story of its water front. As if it had grown up out of the sea, the original town clung so closely to the water's edge that one might almost have fancied its settlers—newly landed from shipboard, most of them—were reluctant to take to dry land. For years all the city's traffic passed up and down the long wooden wharves, sagging with business houses that ranged from saloons to banks. Many of the old ships lie buried now beneath dry land. Above the level of the tides that once lapped the pilings, streetcars thunder. Even old East Street, last of the water-front thoroughfares, has gone the way of the sailing vessels which once thrust proud figureheads above the wharves' wooden bulkheads. Around the Peninsula's edge, from Fisherman's Wharf to China Basin, sweeps the paved crescent of the 200-foot-wide Embarcadero, lined with immense concrete piers. Where the four-masters and square-riggers once disembarked, cargo-ships and luxury liners rest alongside vast warehouses, unloading their goods from all the corners of the earth.

By night the Embarcadero is a wide boulevard, dimly lighted and nearly deserted, often swathed in fog. Its silence is broken by the lonely howl of a fog siren, the raucous scream of a circling seagull, or the muffled rattle of a winch on a freighter loading under floodlights. The sudden blast of a departing steamer, the far-off screech of freight-cars being shunted onto a siding by a puffing Belt Line locomotive shake the nocturnal quiet. The smells of copra, of oakum, raw sugar, roasting coffee and rotting piles, and mud and salt water creep up the darkened streets.

Even before the eight o'clock wail of the Ferry Building siren, the Embarcadero comes violently to life. From side streets great trucks roll through the yawning doors of the piers. The longshoremen, clustered in groups before the pier gates, swarm up ladders and across gangplanks. The jitneys, small tractor-like conveyances, trailing long lines of flat trucks, wind in and out of traffic; the comical lumber carriers, like monsters with lumber strapped to their undersides, rattle along the street. Careening taxis, rumbling underslung vans and drays, and scurrying pedestrians suddenly transform the water front into a traffic-thronged artery.

A never-ending stream of vehicles brings the exports of the Bay area and the West and the imports of both the hemispheres. Although World War II interrupted the normal flow of imports, when peace came the Embarcadero's huge warehouses began to fill again with sacks of green coffee from Brazil; ripening bananas from Central America; copra and spices from the South Seas; tea, sugar, and chocolate; cotton and kapok; paint and oil; and all the thousand varieties of products offered by a world market. Here, awaiting transshipment, are wines from Portugal, Spain and France; English whiskey and Italian vermouth; burlap from Calcutta and glassware from Antwerp; beans from Mexico and linen from Northern Ireland.

At one time north of the Ferry Building docked the vessels of foreign lines. Here, too, were berths for many of the barges and river boats of the Sacramento and San Joaquin Rivers which brought to San Francisco the products of central California's great agricultural plains.

South of the Ferry Building were the docks from which transpacific passenger liners and around-the-world boats sailed until they were converted to wartime use in 1942. Four years later, revival of the gala festivities attendant on the sailings and docking of these big vessels were resumed for normal peacetime passenger travel. Here too was Man-o'-War Row, where United States Navy vessels of the Pacific fleet anchored.

Around China Basin and the long narrow channel extending inland from the Embarcadero's southern end are railway freight yards, warehouses, and oil and lumber piers. Of the bridges that span the channel, most important is the trunnion bascule lifting bridge at Third and Channel Streets, built in 1933. On the south side of the Channel entrance are the Santa Fe Railway Company's yards. Farther south is Mission Rock Terminal and the Army Street Terminal, largest pier on the West Coast.

Busiest section of the Embarcadero used to be the stretch between the Ferry Building and the Matson Line Docks. Opposite the great concrete piers was a string of water-front hotels, saloons, cafes, billiard parlors, barber shops, and clothing stores.

As on most American waterfronts, store windows are stuffed with dungarees, gloves, white caps, good luck charms, cargo hooks, and accordions. A tattoo artist decorates manly arms and chests with glamour girls, cupids, and crossed anchors. Gone today are the bumboat men, who once climbed aboard incoming ships from rowboats with articles to sell; the peddlers that patroled the Embarcadero, pushing carts with candy and fruits, mystic charms and shoestrings, lottery and sweepstakes tickets. At one time in many cafes or saloons longshoremen could cash his "brass," the small numbered metal token given him for presentation at the company pay windows. For cashing it, the charge was usually five cents on the dollar.

Scalers, seamen, longshoremen, warehousemen—all have their hiring and union headquarters in the Longshoremen's Memorial Building at Mason and Beach Streets. Here the men congregate between shifts and between jobs awaiting their turn for new jobs handed out through union dispatches. Their talk is interminably of union contracts, politics, jobs, lottery tickets, and horse racing. From the hiring hall the men are sent out, the longshoremen sometimes hurrying to docks and ports as far away as Crockett in Contra Costa County and the seamen packing their suitcases of working gear to the ships. All dispatching is done by rotation: this is the hiring hall system for which the men fought in the 1934 maritime strike.

The longshoremen with their white caps and felt hats, their black jackets and hickory shirts, their cargo hooks slung in hip pockets, outnumber the workers of any other craft in the maritime industry. As soon as a ship is tied up, they go aboard, and as the winches begin to rattle, unloading is under way. The jitney drivers pull up alongside with their trucks; checkers keep track of every piece of cargo. Meanwhile, ship scalers are aboard cleaning out empty holds, boiler tubes and fire boxes, painting sides and stacks, scraping decks, and doing the thousand jobs required to make a vessel shipshape.

Until 1962 the produce commission district was a stone's throw from the water front in the area bounded by Sacramento, Front, Pacific and Drumm Streets. It was a district of narrow streets lined with roofed sidewalks and low brick buildings, and was the receiving depot for the fresh produce that found its way into the kitchens, restaurants, and hotels of the city. Relocated in Islais Creek the district is now called the Golden Gateway.

"San Francisco is the only port in the United States," reports the United States Board of Engineers for Rivers and Harbors, "where the water front is owned and has been developed by the State, and where also, the public terminal developments have been connected with one another and with rail carriers by the Belt Line, owned and operated by the State." The Port has terminals and warehouses for special cargo; a shipside refrigeration and products terminal for handling and storing agricultural products and perishable commodities in transit; a grain terminal for cleaning, grading and loading grain for export; special facilities for the promotion and development of the fishing industry at Fisherman's Wharf; tanks and pipelines for handling Oriental vegetable oils and molasses; fumigating plants for cotton; lumber terminals. The entire waterfront and adjacent warehouses and industries are served by the State Belt Railroad, which has direct connection with all transcontinental and local railroads.

After 105 years of State control the port was returned to the city by popular vote in 1968. Today the citizens own a $350,000,000 shipping complex that stretches more than seven miles, including 42 active deep-water piers, a number of specialty terminals, and more than 650 acres of cargo handling area.

Before there was an Embarcadero the shoreline of a circling lagoon swept inward from Clark's Point at the base of Telegraph Hill and outward again to Rincon Point near the foot of Harrison Street. From August, 1775, when Lieutenant Juan Manuel de Ayala first sailed the *San Carlos* through the Golden Gate until September, 1848, when the brig *Belfast* docked at the water-front's first pile wharf, cargoes were lightered from vessel to shore. The favored landing place was Clark's Point, the small, rocky promontory sheltering Yerba Buena Cove on the north, first known as the Punta del Embarcadero (Point of the Landing Place). Here in September, 1847 William Squires Clark persuaded the Town Council to authorized construction of a public pier. Sufficient only to pay for the pier's foundations, the $1,000 appropriated was exhausted by the following January. In 1848 the Town Council agreed to appropriate $2,000 more for continuance of the work. This, when completed, was the first wharf built on piles on the Pacific Coast north of Panama.

"The crowd of shipping, two or three miles in length, stretched along the water . . ." wrote globe-trotter Bayard Taylor before the end of 1849. "There is probably not a more exciting and bustling scene of business activity in any part of the world, than can be witnessed on almost any day, Sunday excepted, at Broadway Street wharf, San Francisco, at a few minutes before 4 o'clock p.m. Men and women are hurrying to and fro; drays, carriages, express wagons and horsemen dash past. . . . Clark's Point is to San Francisco what Whitehall is to New York."

First wharf for deep-water shipping was Central or Long Wharf, built along the line of Commercial Street, which by the end of 1849 had been extended to a length of 800 feet. It was used by most of the immense fleet of vessels from all the world which anchored in the Bay in the winter of 1849-50. By October. 1850, an aggregate of 5,000 feet of new wharves had been constructed at an estimated outlay of $1,000,000. The wharf building was accomplished in haphazard fashion. Not until May 1851, when the State legislature passed the Second Water Lot Bill, was the city empowered to permit construction of wharves beyond the city line. No less than eight wharves, however, had been built by this time. Nearly one half of San Francisco rose on piles above water. The moment a new wharf was completed, up went frame shanties to house a gambling den, provision dealer, clothing house, or liquor salesman.

Soon, however, more substantial structures were being erected. Of these, perhaps the most famous was Meiggs' Wharf, built by Henry Meiggs in 1853. From the water line (then Francisco Street) at the foot of Mason Street, Meiggs' L-shaped pier, 42 feet wide, ran 1,600 feet north to the line of Jefferson Street and 360 feet east. Long after its builder had absconded to Peru (where he made a fortune building a railway through the Andes), following discovery of his embezzlement of $800,000 in city funds, the wharf was a terminal for ferryboats plying to Alcatraz and Sausalito. From the foot of Sansome Street, in the shadow of Telegraph Hill, ran the North Point Docks, built in 1853, where for many years landed most of the city's French and Italian immigrants.

The ten-year leases under which most of the important wharves operated expired in 1863—and in that year was appointed a State Board of Harbor Commissioners, which refused to grant renewals. Not until 1867, because of litigation with wharf-owners, was the board able to proceed with harbor development. A channel 60 feet wide was dredged 20 feet below low tide level, in which loads of rock dumped by scows and lighters were piled up in a ridge reaching the level of mean low tide. On top of the embankment were laid a foundation of concrete and, on top of the concrete, a wall of masonry. But the protracted litigation with water-front property owners, the decline in shipping caused by competition of the newly completed transcontinental railroad, and the grafting of private contractors who had undertaken to build the sea wall—all combined to hold up the work. Within two years after construction had been resumed in 1877, a thousand feet of the wall west of Kearny Street had been completed. From the scarred eastern flanks of Telegraph Hill, long lines of carts transported rock. In the course of construction, tons of rock were gouged from the hill's slopes, and tons more (more than 1,000,000) were ferried from Sheep Island, off Port Richmond. Not until 1913 was the sea wall finally completed.

The Belt Line Railroad was first debated in 1873, but not until 1890 was a mile-long line with a three-rail track built for both narrow- and standard-gauge cars. At first confined to the section north of Market Street, the road was extended southward in 1912 to link the entire commercial water front with rail connections to the south and thereafter westward through the tunnel under Fort Mason to the Presidio and southward to Islais Creek Channel.

Revolutionary as the port's physical changes have been in the past century, no less marked have been the differences wrought in the lives of the men who earn their livelihood on its ships and shores. During the years after '49, "the Front" gained the reputation of being one of the toughest spots in the world. In the last half of the century the shortage in sailors was so great that kidnapping or "shanghaiing" was practiced. The very expression "shanghaiing" originated in San Francisco in the days when voyages to Shanghai were so hazardous that a "Shanghai voyage" came to mean any long sea trip.

Notorious among the crimp joints of the 1860's was a saloon and boarding house conducted on Davis Street by a harridan named Miss Piggott. Here operated one Nikko, a Laplander whose specialty was the substitution of dummies and corpses for the drunken sailors the ships' captains thought they were hiring. Miss Piggott had a rival in Mother Bronson, who ran a place on Steuart Street. She would size up a likely customer, smack him over the head with a bung-starter, and drop him through a trap door to the cellar below where he awaited transfer to a ship.

Shanghai Kelly, a red-headed Irishman who ran a three-story saloon and lodging house at 33 Pacific Street, was probably the most notorious crimp ever to operate in San Francisco. The tide swished darkly beneath three trap doors built in front of his bar. Beneath the trap doors, boats lay in readiness. Kelly's most spectacular performance came in the middle 1870's. Three ships in the harbor needed crews. One was the notorious hell-ship *Reefer,* from New York. Kelly engaged to supply men. He chartered the paddle-wheel steamer *Goliath* and announced a picnic with free drinks to celebrate his "birthday." The entire Barbary Coast responded. Once in the harbor, Kelly fed his guests doped liquor, pulled alongside the *Reefer* and the other two ships, and delivered more than 90 men.

During the 1890's six policemen sent successively to arrest a Chilean, Calico Jim, were kidnapped in turn and put aboard outward bound boats. Ultimately, all six returned to San Francisco, swearing vengeance. The crimp had gone to South America. The policemen raised a fund and sent one of their number to Chile to wreak vengeance. Having found Calico Jim, he pumped six bullets into him, one for each policeman, and returned to duty.

The most famous runner for sailors' boardinghouses was Johnny Devine, the "Shanghai Chicken," who had lost his hand in some scrap and had replaced it with an iron hook. Devine was a burglar, footpad, sneak thief, pimp, and almost everything else disreputable. His favorite stunt was to highjack sailors from other runners.

Of all that lively collection of crimps, highjackers, burglars, pimps, and ordinary rascals, the least vicious—if not the least dangerous— seems to have been Michael Conner, proprietor of the Chain Locker at Main and Bryant Streets. Deeply religious, he boasted of never telling a lie. When ships' captains came seeking able seamen, Conner could swear that his clients had experience—for he had rigged up in his backyard a mast and spars whereon his "seasoned sailors" were put through the rudiments. On the floor of his saloon was a cow's horn, around which Conner would make the seamen walk several times so that he might truthfully say they had been "round the Horn."

The Embarcadero's reputation for toughness rapidly is being woven into legend, along with the doings of the pioneers. San Francisco's water front is no longer a shadowy haunt, full of unsuspected perils. Today, it occupies a place in the forefront of the city's industrial, commercial, and social life. The water-front men take an informed interest in civic affairs—and many of them own comfortable homes out on the avenues.

POINTS OF INTEREST

The MARINE EXCHANGE LOOKOUT STATION, Pier 45, Embarcadero and Chestnut St., whose glassed-in, hexagon-shaped cubicle, equipped with a powerful telescope, commands a sweeping view of the Golden Gate, has been called the eyes of the harbor. Once a familiar sight on the bay, the launch, the *Jerry Dailey,* used to carry its crew of old-timers through the Gate to meet incoming vessels whenever telephonic reports from the Marine Exchange's other lookout station at Point Lobos announced that a vessel had been sighted on the horizon. The lookout delivered mail and instructions for docking, received cargo statistics, running time, and other marine news. Returning to the station, he telephoned the information to the Marine Exchange, where news of the ship's arrival was listed on the blackboards.

Since its organization in 1851, the Marine Exchange has kept its day-and-night watch for inbound ships, at first with the aid of the lookout station erected by Messrs. Sweeney and Baugh in 1849 on Telegraph Hill, to which signals were relayed from the Point Lobos lookout.

The BALCLUTHA, the ship museum of the San Francisco Maritime Association, is berthed at Pier 43, foot of Powell St. The name is Gaelic for Dumbarton, a town on the Clyde River in Scotland. A steel, three-masted, full-rigged sailing vessel, it was built in Glasgow, Scotland in 1886 and has been a grain and nitrate carrier around Cape Horn, a lumber carrier in the Pacific, a freighter in the Alaska salmon trade, a showboat up and down the West Coast, and is now a museum ship (*open 10-10*).

The GOLDEN GATEWAY, the $85-million complex bounded by Battery, Broadway, the Embarcadero and Clay Sts., is the creation of a number of individuals, companies and government agencies. Ground was broken on August 30, 1962, for the five square 25-story tower apartment buildings; three larger, rectangular 22-story apartment buildings; the Alcoa office building; a public parking garage for 1,300 cars with two stories underground and one above; 106 two-story garden town houses; 75,000 square feet of shopping areas, and $1 million in recreation and community facilities including a one block park called the Sidney G.

Walton Square. (Wurster, Bernardi & Emmons and DeMars & Reay, Associated, architects)

The ROCKEFELLER CENTER WEST, largest private building venture in the West, is now being constructed at the foot of Market Street at a cost of $150 million. (John Portman, architect). The Center is designed to provide 2,000,000 sq. ft. of office space, 800 hotel rooms, a theater and recreation area. Plans include three office buildings, one of 25 stories, one of 45 stories, and one of 60. The Center will provide 9,000 man years in construction labor and will reap the City more than $3,000,000 in property taxes alone. The buildings have been placed to give pedestrians strolling on the Center's many plazas the benefit of a southern exposure.

The oldest maritime organization on the Pacific Coast has its headquarters at the BAR PILOTS STATION, Pier 7, Embarcadero and Broadway. Since 1850, the San Francisco Bar Pilots have been steering vessels over the San Francisco bar and through the Golden Gate to anchorage in the Bay. All master mariners, the pilots are former sea captains of long experience on the Pacific Coast. Each of the auxiliary schooners that serve them as pilot boats carries a crew including an engineer, a boat keeper, a cook, and sailors. Day and night one of these vessels stands by, about six miles off the Golden Gate, with sails spread to keep an even keel in high seas. During its five days at sea, the crew is on constant call. To the schooner at sea, the shore station reports ship movements by means of a wireless telephone system. Whenever an approaching vessel requires a pilot, the schooner is brought around to its lee. In a small boat the pilot is rowed over to the inbound ship. On the bridge of the vessel, he takes charge, steering a safe course into the harbor. Under the jurisdiction of the State Pilot Commission, the bar pilots are obliged to keep a 24-hour watch on the bar outside the harbor entrance and to provide pilotage service without undue delay to any ship requesting it.

The FERRY BUILDING, formerly more a symbol of San Francisco than any other landmark, is located at Market and the Embarcadero. Before the completion of the two bridges across the Bay, this was the gateway to San Francisco, its high clock tower the most conspicuous feature of the skyline to passengers on the lumbering ferries which churned the waters for nearly nine decades. In the years immediately preceding the opening of train service across the San Francisco-Oakland Bay Bridge, the long hallways of the historic structure echoed to the footsteps of as many as 50,000,000 passengers in a single year—a volume of traffic exceeded only by Charing Cross Station in London.

Erected by the State Board of Harbor Commissioners (1896-1903) on a foundation of piles beyond the edge of the original loose-rock sea wall, the Ferry Building was hailed at its opening in July, 1898, as the most solidly constructed edifice in California. It was built to replace the old Central Terminal Building erected in 1877, a wooden shed over the three ferry slips operated by the Central Pacific, Atlantic & Pacific, and South Pacific Coast railways, when the volume of traffic across the Bay dictated an improvement in terminal facilities.

Arthur Paige Brown, architect, designed a two-story building with an arcaded front extending along the water front for 661 feet. The clock tower, rising 235 ft., was modeled after the Giralda Tower of the Cathedral of Seville. Like the rest of the building, it was faced with gray Colusa sandstone until the 1906 earthquake shook off the stone blocks, after which they were replaced by concrete. When the tower clock was installed it was operated by a long cable wound on a drum, and a 14-foot pendulum; it has since been equipped to run by electricity. Each of the four 2,500 pound dials on the four sides of the tower measures 23½ ft. in diameter; each of the numerals, 2½ ft. in height. The hour hands are 7 and the minute hands 11 ft. long.

The famous 600-ft. relief map of California was displayed in the Ferry Building nave from 1924 to 1960. The map was built in Glendale, California, and took six railroad cars to move it to San Francisco, where 100,000 people viewed it the first day it was exhibited. The enormous map showing the topography of California at a scale of six inches to a mile was sold to Thomas Woods in 1960 for $1.00.

Opposite a huge mosaic of the Great Seal of California in the floor of the nave is the mezzanine stairway leading to the MINERAL MUSEUM of the California State Mining Bureau. The museum contains specimens of minerals from every part of the world, facsimiles of all of the important nuggets unearthed in California, and models of gold and diamond mines and ore crushers. The institution has been supported by the State and by individual contributors ever since its inception in 1897. *Open Mon.-Fri., 9-4.*

The WORLD TRADE CENTER, in the modernized north wing of the Ferry Building, was opened May 23, 1956. It contains offices of trade representatives from all parts of the world and has as its chief function the promotion of trade through the ports of San Francisco Bay. On the third floor are the rooms of the World Center Club, which has magnificent views of the Bay.

Alongside the two-story engine house of the Embarcadero Fire Department, Pier 22, Embarcadero between Folsom and Harrison Sts., is anchored the harbor's gleaming red and black, brass-trimmed fire boat, the PHOENIX. The boat is equipped with monitor batteries, more than 5,000 feet of hose, and water towers that can be raised 55 ft. above deck. It responds to emergency calls from all parts of the Bay and its islands.

Spanning the Embarcadero between Harrison and Bryant Sts. is the approach to the SAN FRANCISCO-OAKLAND BAY BRIDGE.

North side of the Ferry Building, between Ferry Building and Pier 1, is the HELIPORT, which provides helicopter service between the city and the San Francisco International Airport. The heliport opened for business February 28, 1950. Service was discontinued in 1964, but resumed in January, 1968.

South of Market

*". . . from all around, the hum of corporate life, of beaten bells,
and steam, and running carriages, goes cheerily abroad . . ."*
—ROBERT LOUIS STEVENSON

ISTORY has played fast and loose with that great segment of
the city which sprawls southward from Market Street to the
San Francisco-San Mateo County line. Athwart historic Rincon Hill, fashionable residential quarter of Gold Rush days, the streamlined approach to the San Francisco-Oakland Bay Bridge rises from an
area of factories, machine shops, railroad terminals, "skid-road" hotels,
and Greek restaurants. Westward from the water front—lined to
Hunter's Point with warehouses, stockyards, and shipbuilding plants—
the district spreads across Potrero Hill to the heights of Twin Peaks,
Buena Vista Park, Mount Olympus, and Mount Davidson. A broad
residential district whose most venerable landmark is Mission Dolores,
occupying a sheltered coastal plain and adjacent hillsides, "The Mission" is San Francisco's workshop, where live most of the city's work-
ing-class population. Here were the ranchos of Spanish dons, the
suburbs of the Argonauts; but today this is the city's most "American"
section, an area as socially homogeneous as an Iowa town.

POINTS OF INTEREST

ST. PATRICK'S CHURCH, Mission between Third and Fourth
Sts., is sometimes called "the most Irish church in all America." Considered a fine example of early Gothic ecclesiastical architecture, it was
rebuilt after 1906 from the charred shell of Old St. Patrick's (1868).
First mass was celebrated in 1851 by Father John Maginnis in a little
room on Fourth and Jessie Streets; from this chapel grew St. Patrick's
Parish, whose first church building was erected in 1854 on the present
site of the Palace Hotel.

To rebuild the gutted interior of the present church, Father John
Rogers, successor to its founder, brought from Ireland Caen stone and
green translucent marble of Connemara. Restored stained glass windows depict the visions of St. Patrick, the Four Apostles, and scenes
from Irish mythology. Irish artist Mia Cranwill designed the main
altar's metal crucifix inlaid with precious stones and the vestments of
cloth-of-gold, embroidered in ancient Gaelic patterns.

SOUTH PARK, 3rd between Bryant and Brannan Sts., survives largely as a memory of the first families whose dwellings once faced the little park. Machine shops and rooming houses now encircle the park, which the enterprising "Lord" Gordon laid out in the early 1850's after the plan of London's fashionable Berkeley Square. Factories and machine shops occupy the sites of the sedate Georgian houses which encircled the park. Here, among others, lived cattle king Henry Miller; the grandparents of Gertrude Atherton; Hall McAllister—until he lost his house in a poker game to a Captain Lyons; Senator and Mrs. William M. Gwin; and "Lord" Gordon's family. After the exodus of their fashionable tenants in the 1870's, the abandoned mansions fell into the hands of Japanese immigrants. Deterioration, the 1906 fire, and conversion to mundane uses have been the fate of this pioneer real estate development.

MISSION DOLORES, on Dolores, between Sixteenth and Seventeenth Sts., admirably preserved and extended from Spanish colonial times, is the oldest religious edifice in San Francisco. It was founded in 1776 by Father Junipero Serra, organizer of the great system of missions of California. The church was first named in honor of St. Francis of Assisi, but became generally known as Mission de los Dolores because of a near marsh called Laguna de Nuestra Senora de los Dolores (Lagoon of Our Lady of Sorrows). Padre Francisco Palou has told how the pioneer chapel of adobe was founded June 29, 1776, just five days before the signing of the Declaration of Independence. With the aid of sailors from the Spanish supply ship *San Carlos* "a building was completed which . . . was made of wood plastered over with clay and roofed with tules. To this was built of the same material . . . a church eighteen varas [or about fifty feet] long. Adjoining it was, in the rear of the altar, a small room which served as a vestry. The church was adorned in the best manner possible with various cloths, flags, bunting, and pendants from the transport ship." Dedicated on October 3, 1776, it was formally opened October 8. Here were performed the first marriage, the first baptisms of Spaniards and of Indians, and the first Christian burial on the San Francisco Peninsula.

On April 25, 1782, in the presence of Padre Jose de Murguia from Mission Santa Clara, Lieutenant Joaquin Moraga and officers from the Presidio, and an assemblage of priests and soldiers, Padre Palou laid the cornerstone of the present church. "Into the sepulcher of the first said stone," he wrote, "were placed the image of our Holy Father San Francisco, some relics from the bones of St. Pius and other holy martyrs, five medals of various saints, and a good portion of silver money to signify the Treasures of the Church."

Perhaps some of these sacred objects are still buried beneath the adobe walls, four feet thick, which support the old mission's low-pitched roof of brown tiles surmounted by a plain Franciscan cross. It has survived the years in remarkably good condition, marked neither by the decay nor the extensive restoration which have befallen some other California missions. The main entrance of the mission is flanked by pairs of engaged semi-Doric columns resting on massive stylobates, which support six pillars rising from the wooden balcony to the widely projecting eaves. Between the four middle columns, in niches cut in the wall, are hung with plaited rawhide the three bells brought from Mexico in 1780—Bret Harte's lyric "Bells of the Past" which once summoned from field and shop the Indian neophytes to midday meals. Measuring 22 feet in width and 114 feet in depth, the mission is a compact and well-proportioned structure in an architectural style whose eclectic Moorish and Classic features are conditioned by adaption to raw native materials and primitive craftsmanship. The joints of doors and windows throughout are secured with manzanita pegs; the struts and ridge-joints of the rafters are bound with thongs of rawhide.

Approached by a low flight of stone steps, its entrance is a wide Roman arch with double doors of panelled wood. The interior reveals Mexican churriguerresque design as interpreted by Indian craftsmen. As vivid as when painted by the neophytes a century and a half ago are the triangular designs of alternating red and white which cover the ceiling between its heavy beams. The beams and sanctuary arch bear chevrons of alternating red, yellow, gray, and white, painted—like the ceiling decoration—with vegetable pigments.

Hand-carved are the main and side altars brought with other furnishings from Mexico. In panels at the bases of the lavender-tinted side altars are bas-relief vases of roses which suggest the Italian influence in Mexican rococo art. In churriguerresque pattern is the large reredos behind the main altar, with its elaborate niches and lavender panels framed with ornamental gilt scrolls, garlands, and other conventional decoration. The door of the revolving tabernacle brought from Manila bears an old Italian-school painting of Christ, blessing the bread He holds before a table bearing a tall silver wine chalice. Over the tabernacle and the Crucifixion are two small paintings in oval frames, one depicting in faded hues a cross; the other, a cross and a soldier's bare arm and clenched hand upholding it. The monstrance is of French origin dating from 1757; Indian neophytes made the Pascal candle; the confessional doors came from Mexico. In their respective niches on the reredos are the original 13 statues of saints carved in wood, of which the St. Michael with staff and uplifted sword is the dominant figure. This soldier of the cross, between Franciscan and Dominican coats of arms, wears red drapery, gilded boots, and a green tunic with gilt flowers. A crowned figure of the Virgin stands to the right of the tabernacle; an exquisitely carved Mater Dolorosa, to the left. In brilliant costume over the right side altar stands St. Anthony, holding in one hand a sheaf of lilies and in the other an open volume on which rests a kneeling child. Side niches are occupied by kneeling figures of St. Francis Solano and San Juan Capistrano. On the opposite altar are represented St. Joseph, St. Bonaventure, and San Luis Rey.

When all this ecclesiastical furniture was installed is not known, but at the end of 1810 the *padres* reported to their superiors in Mexico the aquisition of the two side altars, the statue of St. Michael, several paintings on canvas in gold and silver frames, various silver vessels, a reliquary, and a pyxsis for sick calls. Although the records of the mission's construction are incomplete, it is believed to have been completed by 1800. The huge granary, built in 1794, adjoining a long low residential building of earlier construction which connected it with the church, appears in old prints and photographs to form a wing of the main building. The adjacent pasture and grain field were enclosed "to the distance of half a league" by a ditch. In 1795 twenty adobe homes for an equal number of neophyte families were erected. The closing decade of the eighteenth century also saw enclosed in the mission quadrangle a bathhouse, a tannery, and other structures.

For half a century, says, Fr. Zephrin Engelhardt's authoritative *San Francisco or Mission Dolores,* this "community formed a kind of co-operative association, a sort of Christian Communism, of which the missionaries were the unsalaried managers and the neophytes the beneficiaries." In return for giving up their liberty and such pagan customs as polygamy and accepting the daily routine of religious services, the converts were assured of a regular diet and decent homes as long as they faithfully performed their baptismal vows of labor and devotion. "They were informed that all the land they occupied with the herds belonged to themselves; that even to the missionaries nothing more was due of the property accumulated by the industry of the neophytes than the food and the clothing their guides needed; and that eventually, when they were capable of managing it, the property acquired by the community would be turned over to them exclusively, as was done in Mexico. . . . The priests would after that attend only to their spiritual wants."

Despite its somewhat unhealthy site near the marshes of Mission Creek, Mission Dolores remained fairly prosperous until its property was confiscated for the public domain by the Mexican government and promptly granted to private individuals. During the 57 years of its independent existence the Franciscan Fathers baptized 6,536 Indians and 448 Mexican children, married 2,043 Indians and 79 Mexicans, buried 5,187 Indian and 150 Mexican dead. "The community," declares Fr. Engelhardt, "at the end of the last general report, December 31, 1832, consisted of 204 Indians of all ages, which would mean about 50 families. The herds, on the same date, consisted of 5,000 cattle, 3,500 sheep, 1,000 horses, most of which were of no use, and 18 mules. Owing to the scarcity of able-bodied neophytes, the fields had yielded, in the year 1832, only 500 bushels of wheat, 400 bushels of barley, 50 bushels of corn, and 140 bushels of beans and peas. This harvest was about two-thirds of the usual product."

Twenty-two years later the *Annals of San Francisco* described the mission as a ruined relic of a bygone day: "The Mission has always been a favorite place of amusement to the citizens of San Francisco. Here, in the early days of the city, exhibitions of bull and bear fights frequently took place, which attracted great crowds; and here, also, were numerous duels fought, which drew nearly as many idlers to view them. At present (1854), there are two race-courses in the neighborhood, and a large number of drinking houses. . . . On fine days, especially on Sundays, the roads to the Mission show a continual succession, passing to and fro, of all manner of equestrians and pedestrians, and elegant open carriages filled with ladies and holiday folk." The mission's career as a "place of amusement" was a brief one, however, for in 1857 it was restored to the Roman Catholic archdiocese.

Enclosed by a white stuccoed adobe wall with red tiles, adjoining the mission, the old cemetery is a secluded little garden with clean-swept lawns whose headstones and monuments evoke memories of another era. Many of the graves are unmarked; others are overgrown with tangled ivy and myrtle.

Among the headstone inscriptions which revive for San Franciscans their city's Spanish days is one which reads: *"Aqui Yacen los Restos del Capitan Louis Antonio Arguello. Primer Governador Alta California Bajo el Governiero Mejicano. Nacio en San Francisco el 21 de Junio. 1784 y murio en el Mismo Lugar el 27 de Marzo. 1830"* (Here Lie the Remains of Captain Louis Antonio Arguello. First Governor of Alta California Under the Mexican Government. Born at San Francisco June 21, 1784 and Died At the Same Place March 27, 1830). "Sacred to the memory" of those victims of Vigilante justice, Charles Cora and James P. Casey, are other headstones. Casey's reads: "May God Forgive My Persecutors." Buried also in the cemetery is James ("Yankee") Sullivan, early-day champion pugilist, who while awaiting trial by the Vigilance Committee of 1856, hanged himself in Fort Gunnybags. A statue of Padre Junipero Serra by Arthur Putnam looks down upon the west end of the cemetery. In the center is a large rock shrine, the "Grotto of Lourdes," containing an old redwood cross— erected in 1920—which bears the inscription: "Dedicated to the Neglected and Forgotten Who Rest Here."

The "neglected and forgotten" include mostly the 5,515 Indians interred here and in the rear of the mission between 1777 and 1848. The Burial Register of the *padres* contains the short and simple annals of many a neophyte who died from smallpox, measles, and other epidemics whose periodic toll brought about the establishment of the "Hospital Mission" at San Rafael. Of the 196 white persons recorded in the old register, the most notable is Lieutenant Jose Joaquin Moraga, whose remains rest within the sanctuary of the mission besides those of the Very Reverend Richard Carroll, its pastor from 1853 to 1860. Beneath the paved courtyard behind the mission is buried Jose Noe, last Mexican *alcalde* of Yerba Buena, whose family headstone is set in the red tile floor within the mission entrance. Here too, is the resting place of William Leidesdorff, pioneer San Franciscan who was associated with Jacob Leese and Thomas Larkin during the Bear Flag revolt.

Mission Dolores is open daily May to October 31, 9-5; November to April 30, 10-4. Admission 25¢, including cemetery.

Big enough to accommodate the largest ships afloat are two of the six drydocks of the SAN FRANCISCO NAVAL SHIPYARD on Hunter's Point, foot of Evans Ave., one of the United States Navy's best-equipped repair bases. In the great cement-lined troughs, the rusting sides of a ship are exposed from deck to keel. Both docks are graving docks, equipped to permit scraping of the bottoms as well as the sides of vessels, and both are equipped with electric pumps and steam cranes. Graving Dock No. 2, built in 1901, is 750 feet long, has a depth at high water of 28 feet 6 inches; Graving Dock No. 3, built in 1919, is 1,020 feet long, has a depth at high water of 45 feet 6 inches. When filled, the larger dock holds 42,000,000 gallons of water, which its four 750-horsepower pumps can empty in nine and one-half hours. Besides its docks for large vessels, the base has three drydocks designed for overhauling of submarines and small craft, and vast facilities for repair.

The Hunter's Point base was acquired by the Navy from the Bethlehem Steel Company Shipbuilding Division in 1941. Under the Navy's management, four new drydocks were constructed, a hill was leveled and 250 acres of filled land created, and $75,000,000 worth of shops, piers and other structures were built. Here during World War II over 200 major and over 1,000 minor repairs on naval vessels were made by a working force which numbered 18,000 on V-J Day. After the end of the war, the yard built the Navy's largest crane, with a lifting capacity of more than 1,000,000 pounds, and other tools.

First drydock at Hunter's Point was built in 1868 by William C. Ralston, then a director of the California Steam Navigation Company, upon the suggestion of civil engineer Alexander Von Schmidt, whose newly invented process of drilling granite under water was employed in excavating the entrance. The cavity was carved almost entirely out of solid stone. From Puget Sound, Ralston imported immense timbers to line the excavation. For the keel blocks, California laurel was used. From the Rocklin quarries in the Sacramento Valley, ox teams pulled enough huge granite blocks to cover 13,000 yards. Cost of the dock, including mechanical equipment, was $1,200,000. Measuring 465 feet in length, 120 in width, and 22 in depth at high water, it was large enough to accommodate any ship afloat at the time except the *Great Western.* Before the stone dock had been completed, Ralston and his associates, who had formed the California Dry Dock Company with a capital of $1,000,000, already had begun construction of a floating dry-dock built of Oregon pine. The stone dock lasted until 1916, when it was removed and the present Graving Dock No. 3 built on its site.

From the foundries of the WEST COAST YARDS of the BETH-LEHEM STEEL COMPANY SHIPBUILDING DIVISION, Twentieth and Illinois Sts., have come ships, machinery, dredges, rail-road locomotives, and endless tons of steel equipment shipped to all parts of the world. Origin of the 30-acre establishment dates back to 1849, when Peter and James Donahue opened a blacksmith shop on Mission Street, which in 1862 became the Donahue Iron and Brass Company and a few years later—when H. J. Booth, Irving M. Scott, and George W. Prescott joined the firm—the Union Iron Works. The first steam loco-motive built on the Pacific Coast, for the old San Francisco-San Jose Railroad (1865), was constructed here. Between 1865 and 1870 thirteen railroad locomotives, including two 30-tonners, were built. The plant manufactured practically all the machinery and dredges used in California and Nevada gold fields and shipped tons of equipment to Alaska during the Yukon gold strike.

Following acquisition in the early 1880's of the present plant site, the Union Iron Works began a heavy program of shipbuilding. The *Olympic,* Admiral Dewey's flagship at Manila, and the *Oregon,* equally famous in the Spanish-American War, were built with a speed and thoroughness that amazed Eastern competitors and established San Francisco as a major shipbuilding base. Since the Spanish-American War period, cruisers, gunboats, destroyers, and submarines have been built in these yards, particularly for South American countries.

When the shipbuilding boom of World War I days collapsed, the plant (acquired by the Bethlehem Steel Company in 1906 but still known by its old name until 1917) lapsed into a semidormant state. Nevertheless, in the eleven years between 1919 and 1938 it constructed 142 vessels, including submarines, oil tankers, freighters, ferries, and passenger and freight ships. With the revival of interest in the mer-chant marine, the plant was modernized in 1938.

During World War II the yard not only repaired or converted over 2,500 vessels from the smallest tugs to 32,000-ton battleships, but also constructed 52 new ships, including cargo vessels, cruisers, destroyers, and destroyer escorts. Equipped with eight piers and four floating dry-docks, it was able by the war's end to berth more ships for repair or conversion than any other privately operated repair yard in the country.

Opening day April 12, 1960 found the San Francisco Giants, a National League Club, in their new $15 million home, windy CAN-DLESTICK PARK. The 1894 United States Coast & Geodetic Survey marked the area as "SE from and under Visitacion Knob, about 130 feet above high water and directly over 8 foot sharp pinnacle rock near highwater mark."

The stadium designed by John S. Bolles was the first stadium in major league baseball to be built entirely of reinforced concrete. It featured seats 20 to 22 inches wide; aisles from 6 feet to 7½ feet wide; and a radiant heating system in the 20,000 reserved seat sections. Center field fence is 420 feet from home plate; the backstop 60 feet behind home plate. The city purchased the land for the stadium for $66,000 an acre from the contractor, Charles L. Harney. Approximately 2.5 million cubic yards of earth had to be excavated from the eastern face of Bay View Hill for the stadium and was used to fill parking areas. The Municipal Railway runs special express buses between downtown points and the park before and after each game (fare—50¢).

Since 1971 Candlestick Park serves as home grounds for the San Francisco Giants and the San Francisco Fortyniners.

The 36-acre BUENA VISTA PARK on the peak of steep Buena Vista Heights, (569 ft.) was set aside in 1868 as a park in a master plan for the expanding city. As its name implies, it commands from its crest a superb view of the Coast Range of mountains from Mt. Hamilton on the south to Mt. Tamalpais on the north and Mt. Diablo on the east. It was officially designated as a park May 8, 1894 by the Board of Supervisors. Beneath the hill is the 4282 foot Sunset Tunnel which opened October 21, 1928.

In 1926 MOUNT OLYMPUS (570 ft.) was made a city park. According to legend, the hill received its name from a crippled milk peddler named Hanrahan, who familiarly was known as Old Limpus in the adjoining residential area in the 1860's. A partly ruined statue, *The Triumph of Light,* brought to this country in 1887 by Adolph Sutro, was mounted in the tiny hilltop square in the geographical center of the city; 12 ft. in height, it stood on a pedestal 30 ft high. In the Brussels original (by Antoine Wiertz) the standing woman holds a torch in her right hand and a sword in her left; in this copy the right arm was broken off at the elbow and the left was without a sword. Unsubstantiated was the popular story that both sword and arm were removed by irate seamen who declared the statue threw them off their course as they steered through the Golden Gate.

Today, if you look directly up Ashbury Street, you can still see the concrete pedestal, but the *Triumph of Light* is gone (removed in the 1950's) and the view has been impaired, partially cut off by buildings that skirt the summit on east, south, and west.

The white and gray concrete buildings of the MEDICAL CENTER of the UNIVERSITY OF CALIFORNIA occupy about 16 acres centering on Parnassus & Third Aves., backed against the dark eucalyptus forest of Mount Sutro and Parnassus Heights. The Center, formerly known as the Affiliated Colleges, began with the founding of the Toland Medical College on Stockton Street in 1865. Less than a decade later in 1873 it was deeded to the University of California and as the Medical Department became the University's first affiliate. In 1895 Mayor Adolph Sutro donated 26 acres of land to the University which provided the physical site on which the Medical Center now stands. In 1902 the properties were taken over by the University of California and support of the college was assumed by the university. As a result of the 1906 earthquake and fire, most of the private and public hospitals were destroyed. To accommodate victims of the disaster the first and second year classes of the Medical School were transferred to the Berkeley campus, and portions of the old Medical School Building were converted into a hospital. The University Hospital was completed in 1917 and the Clinics Building in 1934. Other buildings include the Langley Porter Neuropsychiatric Institute, the Herbert C. Moffitt Hospital, the Medical Sciences Building, and the Health Sciences Research and Instruction Building.

Clarendon Avenue passes through SUTRO FOREST, over a dark ridge of MOUNT SUTRO (918 ft.). Here Adolph Sutro in the late 1870's—after returning from the Comstock Lode a millionaire—purchased part of the old Rancho San Miguel. Sutro, who called his mountain Parnassus, planted trees here in 1887, after the legislature provided that property converted into forest land should be tax-exempt for five years. For years he employed a gardener who not only tended these trees, but those scattered over a 12,000-acre area which included Mount Davidson.

Today Sutro Forest is a rough wildwood in the heart of a modern residential district. The ground is covered by tangled undergrowth. Ivy clings to the trunks of the tall eucalyptus trees and sugar pines. Each spring it is brightly colored by wildflowers and blossoming brushwood.

Twin Peaks Boulevard encircles the TWIN PEAKS in a broad figure 8. The windy summits also are reached by trails and earthen steps that lead up steep, grassy slopes. To the east and south can be seen the bright-colored roofs and smoking chimneys of row upon row of apartment houses, laced together by a network of streets. Mount Davidson, topped by its giant white cross, forms a somber pile against the background of the western sky. Beyond is the long line of the Pacific. Distance lends a serene quality to the Marin hills and bays, darkly blue in the northwest. The long expanse of the East Bay shore rolls as far as the eye can reach.

Legends cloud the history of Twin Peaks. Once, said the Indians, the mountains were one: man and wife. But they quarreled long and bitterly and in time the Great Spirit heard them, and with thunder and lightning smote them in twain.

The Spaniards called the peaks Los Pechos de la Choca (*The Breasts of the Indian Girl*) in memory, so the story goes, of a beautiful maiden. She was softly beautiful, tall and slender. When one spoke to her she dropped her eyes in modesty. N. P. Vallejo, son of Mariano Vallejo, in describing her said, "Never have I seen a cultured maiden half so fair as this untaught, uninstructed daughter of the wilds."

The highest point in San Francisco is heavily-wooded MOUNT DAVIDSON (938 ft.), where on bright days the sunlight filtering through the treetops throws bright patches of light on the grassy leaf-covered ground. From its summit rises a great cross, illuminated during Easter week, which was dedicated March 24, 1934, at 7:30 p.m., when President Franklin D. Roosevelt pressed a golden key that sent electrical impulses across the nation to light the floodlights. The cross, 103 feet in height, is built of concrete and steel. Resting upon solid rock, its base contains a crypt in which are relics from the Holy Land, including a jug of water from the River Jordan. The concrete which seals the crypt itself was mixed with this water. The first of four crosses preceding the present one was erected atop the mountain in 1923, the year of San Francisco's first sunrise Easter service.

Once a part of the Rancho San Miguel, Mount Davidson formed part of the 12,000-acre estate of Adolph Sutro. When George Davidson of the U.S. Coast & Geodetic Survey surveyed it in 1852 he named it Blue Mountain. It remained a barren rocky peak until trees were planted on its slopes. In 1911 A. S. Baldwin purchased the mountain and spent $2,000 in building trails to its summit. In that year too it was named Mount Davidson in honor of its early surveyor.

When in 1926 the encroachment of real estate subdivision threatened it, Mrs. Edmund N. Brown, a member of the State Park Commission, secured the help of the Commodore Sloat Parent-Teachers' Association and other public agencies in a warm publicity campaign which persuaded the city to purchase 20 acres. The area was dedicated as a city park on December 20, 1929, the 83rd birthday of John McLaren (*see Golden Gate Park*).

Western Addition

". . . monotonous miles of narrow-chested, high-shouldered, jimber-jawed houses strongly reminiscent of the scroll-saw period of our creative artistry . . ."

—IRVIN S. COBB

LIKE the backyard of some imposing but superannuated mansion, the Western Addition is cluttered with the discarded furniture of the city's Gilded Age. It is a curious district whose claim to distinction is its disdain of all pretense. It is not beautiful, yet San Franciscans formerly referred to it affectionately as The Fillmore, the name of its busiest thoroughfare, and loved it, as Charles Caldwell Dobie says, "for its supreme grotesqueness."

Once it was what its name implies—the western addition to the old town—but now it lies in the very middle of the city. Its eastern boundary is the broad traffic-thronged artery of Van Ness Avenue, Automobile Row. Westward it spreads as far as Lone Mountain, once graveyards far out of town, in a sandy brush-grown wilderness. Northward it extends to the heights above the Marina, and southward almost to Market Street.

The preposterous old houses built here in the 1870's and 1880's when San Francisco was expanding westward, and spared by the flames of 1906, are monuments to the bonanza era. In them the *nouveau riche* of the Gilded Age attempted to outdo the fantastic wooden castles on Nob Hill. What the jigsaw and the lathe could not accomplish the builders supplied with Gothic arches and Corinthian pillars, with Norman turrets crowned by Byzantine domes, with mansard roofs, balconies, gables, and stained-glass windows. Interiors were resplendent with horsehair divans, marble-topped tables, and bronze statuary. Gaslight flickered in dim vestibules and up redwood staircases. No longer fashionable, the old mansions have been converted into boarding houses and housekeeping rooms.

In the days before the fire, while the Western Addition was still the abode of fashion, Fillmore Street was a suburban center of commerce. After 1906 it had a brief and sudden boom. Before the charred wreckage of Market Street could be cleared off and stores rebuilt, the flow of commerce ran into Fillmore Street—and its delighted merchants sought to keep it there. Arches supporting large street lamps were erected over each intersection from Sacramento to Fulton Street and festooned with electric lights. Through five or six years the great days lasted, but when Market Street reclaimed its commercial prestige after 1910, Fillmore Street was doomed. The ornate arches once incongruous reminders of its hour of greatness were removed during World War II and used for scrap metal. Fillmore Street, however, was more than a commercial thoroughfare. It represented a way of life, and was the stronghold of San Francisco's cosmopolitan tradition. Raffish, optimistic, blissfully vulgar, Fillmore Street kept alive that inimitable social spirit of which San Francisco is the larger expression.

From the Marina, north of the Western Addition, Fillmore Street climbs the precipitous slope of Pacific Heights, formerly scaled by two diminutive cable cars. Down the slope below Sacramento Street are stores, movie theaters, and restaurants, a scene of lively disorder. Chaste little antique shops stand next door to radio stores; hamburger joints thrive beside the austere facades of branch banks. Past the sidewalk vegetable stands stroll housewives, pinching grapefruits, tomatoes, and peaches with the fingers of connoisseurs. At convenient intervals are neighborly little bars offering the tired shopper a moment's refreshment. And day or night pass laughing Negroes, dapper Filipino boys, pious old Jews on their way to schule, sturdy-legged Japanese high school girls, husky young American longshoremen out for a quiet stroll with the wife and kids.

Near the southern end of Fillmore Street's lengthy market place, where noisy turbulence gave way to prosaic respectability at the foot of another hill clustered with turrets, bay windows, and mansard roofs, was the city's Jewish commercial center, the heart of the before-the-fire section, where bedizened old houses of the 1880's advertise housekeeping rooms on grimy signs. Yet, paradoxically, here was a gourmet's paradise; along adjacent blocks of Golden Gate Avenue and McAllister Street the atmosphere was spicy with the odors of delicatessen shops, bakeries, and restaurants. In a dozen strange tongues, bargaining went on along McAllister Street—San Francisco's "second-hand row"—for begrimed statuary, ancient stoves, Brussels carpets with faded floral patterns, chamber pots and perambulators, Dresden figurines and fishing tackle, gilt-framed oil landscapes and canary bird cages. Once gathered in this district were a large number of the city's Jews, most of them immigrants from eastern Europe. But Fillmore Street's Jewish quarter was scarcely representative of the city's Jewish citizenry as a whole. Not confined to any one district, profession, or mode of life, they have played a leading role in the city's development since the first of them came during the Gold Rush. Scattered throughout the Western Addition, as elsewhere in the city, are numerous synagogues, both orthodox and reformed, and their charitable institutions and fraternal organizations. Though the city's Jews have no native theater, they support a Yiddish Literary and Dramatic Society and numerous social clubs, musical societies, and schools.

Parks and Landmarks

JAPANESE TEA GARDEN, GOLDEN GATE PARK

CONSERVATORY, GOLDEN GATE PARK

WALK IN TEA GARDEN, GOLDEN GATE PARK

CANDLESTICK PARK

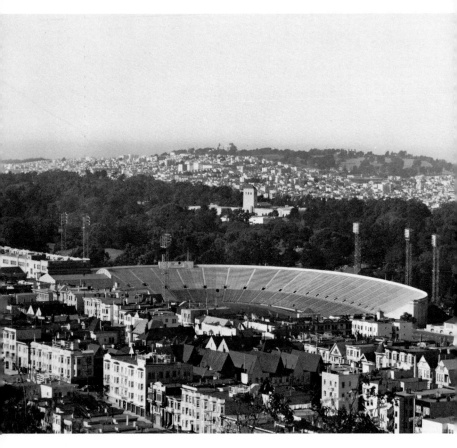

KEZAR STADIUM, GOLDEN GATE PARK

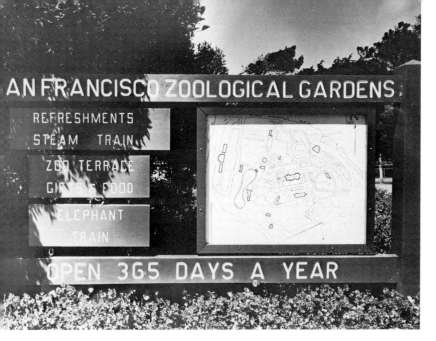

INVITATION TO ADVENTURE

POPULAR RESIDENT AT THE ZOO

THE CLIFF HOUSE FROM SUTRO HEIGHTS, 1907

THE CLIFF HOUSE TODAY

THE SKYLINE FROM ALCATRAZ

PRESIDIO OFFICERS CLUB

THE COIT TOWER ON TELEGRAPH HILL

East of Fillmore Street, north and south of Post Street, is Little Osaka, former home of the vast majority of the city's pre-war population of some 6,000 persons of Japanese ancestry. Evacuated under "wartime military necessity" orders, their former district was occupied by war workers.

War's dislocations have been many. Scores of organizations represented the local Japanese colony but with the evacuation and dismemberment of the old Little Osaka only one has survived. The Japanese American Citizens League with its local offices here has consistently maintained its program of the Americanism of the Japanese community. The legendary war performances of Japanese Americans in World War II have amply answered its critics. The Golden Gate Institute on Bush Street near Buchanan Street, formerly the second largest Japanese language school in the United States, and the Japanese branches of the YMCA and YWCA were converted to other uses during World War II. Following the return of many of the evacuees, service establishments and professional offices were reopened. Two Japanese newspapers are published.

In the local Japanese restaurants on Post Street and on Buchanan Street are served old country foods, such as *soba* and *udon* (noodles) ; roasted eel and rice; chicken soup, amber clear, with seaweed and abalone; and *tempura,* a fricasse of deep fried prawns, fish or vegetables. This distinctive cookery is noted in *Sukiyaki,* which is a table-hot preparation made with choice cuts of tender meat, green onions, *tofu,* gelatin strings, bamboo shoots, or other vegetables, eaten dipped in raw eggs.

Among the older generation reminiscences of pre-war customs are perpetuated. The Japanese New Year is celebrated on January 1 when the polite pay calls and partake of *sake* (rice wine) and foods especially prepared for the occasion. On March 3, the Doll Festival (*Hinamatsuri*) is observed with a ceremonial display of exquisite figures dressed in the costumes of old Japan and the colorful kimonos of Japanese ladies dressed in festival attire. Special foods known as *seki-han, sakura-mochi* (rice dumplings wrapped in cherry leaves) commemorate the occasion. While March 3 is Girls' Day, Boys' Day is set aside for May 5, and is intended to inspire young males to swim against the current of life with vigor and courage. This day is symbolized by the flying of colored paper carp fish and the display of colorfully garbed dolls.

Buddhist festivals, also observed by Buddhists of other races, include the Birthday of Buddha, celebrated on the Sunday nearest to April 8, and the Ura-Bon (Festivals of Souls), celebrated with religious dances on the Sunday evening nearest to the sacred day.

Throughout the former Japanese settlement is scattered a Filipino colony, smaller than the quarter on upper Kearny Street but distinguished by the same social features. Wherever these jaunty, small-statured people congregate at social functions, the *carinosa,* their national dance which resembles the tango, is danced to the orchestral accompaniment of *bandores,* twelve-stringed mandolins of native origin.

Their Community Center at 2090 California Street sponsors many social functions for the 25,000 Filipinos in San Francisco.

West of Fillmore Street and south of Sutter Street lived many Russians until they moved on into the Richmond District, or found a new home in the tight colony of Russians on Potrero Hill. Divided by opposing political loyalties, the city's Russians never have created a distinctive colony of their own. The older immigrants came to escape the Tsar, the newer to escape the Soviet regime. The ways of both are the ways of exiles who strive to keep alive the customs of their forebears among alien surroundings. In the Western Addition the Russian residents are chiefly *émigrés* from the Russian Revolution. The older generation is defiantly monarchist in politics and orthodox in religion. Through the 40's they kept up the courtly ceremonials of their former life, appearing in faded regimentals of the Imperial Army to pay each other elaborate respects over vodka, tea, and caviar. Annually they squandered the savings of a twelvemonth on a grand ball in honor of their Petrograd days. Easter is still celebrated as gaily as ever at the Russian Orthodox Church on Green Street at Van Ness Avenue.

The greater number of San Francisco's Negroes live in the neighborhood west of Fillmore between Geary and Pine Streets. Among them are representatives of every State in the Union, of Jamaica, Cuba, Panama, and South American countries. Of those from the South, many are Texans who arrived after World War I; these still celebrate "Juneteenth," Emancipation Day for the Texas Negroes, who did not learn of the Emancipation Proclamation until June 19, 1863. The colony's social life revolves around its handful of bars and restaurants, night clubs, its many churches of varying faiths, and the Booker T. Washington Community Center on Presidio Ave., where trained social workers guide educational and recreational activities for children and adults. Occasionally, in churches and clubs, are heard old Negro folk songs.

With its confusion of customs from half the world, the Western Addition is more entitled than any other section of the city to be called San Francisco's International Quarter. But the Western Addition abhors labels. It is just The Fillmore, and proud of it.

POINTS OF INTEREST

The six-story MASONIC TEMPLE, southwest corner Van Ness Ave. and Oak St., was dedicated on October 13, 1913. Of Romanesque design (William B. Faville, architect), the building is faced with Utah marble and adorned with sculptural decorations representing Biblical and allegorical figures by Adolph A. Weinman and Ralph Stackpole. A small rotunda leads into the main lobby of polished gray and white marble. In the large halls on the second and fourth floors are portraits of past grand masters, many by Duncan C. Blakiston. The great Commandery Hall on the third floor is surmounted with a dome rising 85 feet above the floor; two large murals on religious subjects are by Arthur F. Matthews.

SW. from Van Ness Ave. on Market St. to Haight St.; W. from Market on Haight.

A collection of frame and stucco structures, the five variously styled buildings of the UNIVERSITY OF CALIFORNIA EXTENSION CENTER, main entrance se corner Haight and Buchanan Sts., stand closely together surrounding a parking lot, on the two block hillside campus. Formerly located at Powell near Sutter St., the Extension Division moved into quarters vacated by San Francisco State College on March 29, 1958.

S. from Haight St. on Buchanan St. to Hermann St.; W. from Buchanan on Hermann.

The UNITED STATES MINT (*not open to public*), Hermann, Buchanan, and Webster Sts. and Duboce Ave. (Gilbert Stanley Underwood, architect), rears its fortress-like walls from the solid stone of steep Blue Mountain. Constructed of steel reinforced with granite and concrete, the building's severe facades are pierced by three sets of windows, the middle tier barred with iron. Above and between the middle sets are large bas-reliefs in concrete of United States coins of various denominations. On the first floor are a marble lobby and large storage vaults for gold, silver, copper, and nickel, with concrete walls two feet thick. Second and third floors hold offices, minting rooms, an assay laboratory, and a women's lunch room. On the fourth floor particles from the vapor given off by melting and refining furnaces is recovered in a series of tubes; the vapor is electrified with a 75,000-volt current which causes the metal particles to cling to the tubes' sides. A guards' pistol range occupies the fifth floor, and all approaches to the mint are covered by gun towers; the surrounding area can be illuminated by batteries of floodlights set in the walls. A network of pipes entering all key points of the building is designed to discharge a flood of tear gas at the sounding of an alarm. Both front and rear entrances are barred by electrically operated doors made of heavy double steel, only one of which can be opened at a time; the door guarding the main vault weighs 40 tons.

The landscaped terraces of 4-acre DUBOCE PARK, west end of Hermann St., rise gradually to the row of old-fashioned frame dwellings on its western side; once a mound-dotted wasteland on which tons of rock had been dumped, the park was opened in 1900.

In the city's western residential districts real estate prices shot skyward when SUNSET TUNNEL, E. Portal at S. side of Duboce Park, was opened October 21, 1928, with Mayor James Rolph at the controls of the first streetcar to make the tunnel trip. Piercing Buena Vista Hill, the tunnel is 4,232 feet long, 25 feet wide, and 23 feet high.

N. from Hermann St. on Steiner St.

In 1860, Charles P. (Dutch Charlie) Duane, undaunted by threats of the Vigilance Committee, fought for his squatter's rights to ALAMO SQUARE, Steiner, Fulton, Hayes and Scott Sts., 12 acres of smooth green lawn and rustling pine and cypress trees on the top of a hill. Wide cement steps ascend to a palm-fringed circular flower bed, and shrubbery-lined paths lead to an adjacent picnic grove and children's playground. Squatter Dutch Charlie, chief fire engineer from 1853 to 1857, gained the attention of the Vigilance Committee of 1851 for his shooting, two years earlier, of a theater manager. He was later exiled from the city under penalty of death by the Vigilance Committee of 1856 for the then greater crime of stuffing a ballot box. Returning in 1860, he waged an unsuccessful suit until 1877 for the property, which had been acquired by the city in 1853. Refugees from the fire of 1906 lived on the hill, and some of the victims, it is believed, were buried here.

The JACK TAR HOTEL, Van Ness, Franklin, Geary and Post Sts., is built upon land originally owned by Horace Hawes, a colorful early day politician, whose most noteworthy act was authorizing the bill that formed San Mateo County out of the southern portion of San Francisco County. Hawes gave the land to the Ladies Protection & Relief Society, which built a three story orphanage there in 1863. When the $14-million Jack Tar Hotel opened in April, 1960, it brought a futuristic look to Van Ness Ave. with its six story, 403-room hotel and adjoining nine-story office building. A motor lobby enables guests to register and check out by closed circuit television and parking facilities for 500 cars are provided.

N. from Hayes St. on Laguna St.

Five days after the 1906 fire the Board of Supervisors assembled in what was MOWRY'S OPERA HOUSE, southwest corner Grove and Laguna Sts., a three-story red-brick and frame building erected in 1879, on whose gaslit stage appeared "Gentleman Jim" Corbett to be acclaimed for his victory over John L. Sullivan. At subsequent secret sessions of the supervisors, during which Abe Ruef issued his instructions, detective William J. Burns gathered evidence leading to the graft prosecutions that destroyed the Ruef machine.

Since December, 1906, when it ceased to serve as a city hall, the sturdy old building, with its triangular wooden parapet decorated with a harp in bas-relief and its brick ground floor with huge double doors was occupied by various mercantile firms until it was destroyed by fire July 17, 1970.

JEFFERSON SQUARE, Golden Gate Ave., Laguna, Gough, and Eddy Sts., once was noted for the stormy character of its political meetings. On pleasant Sunday afternoons every shade of political and religious thought was expounded in open-air forums by old-age-pension advocates, single taxers, and fanatical champions of religious cults. In 1906 the park was used as a refugee camp. The park slopes downhill, its green sward broken by tall eucalyptuses, evergreens, and shrubs planted along graveled walks. In the playground, named for Margaret S. Hayward, for many years a city recreation commissioner, are tennis courts, volley and basketball courts, baseball diamonds and stands. In the center of the park is the low stucco building housing the San Francisco Fire Department's Central Alarm Station with its aerial and high-tension electric transformer towers. Situated in a congested area, the park is a favorite recreation center for youngsters of many national groups.

W. from Laguna St. on Golden Gate Ave. to Masonic Ave.; S. from Golden Gate on Masonic to Fulton St.; W. from Masonic on Fulton.

The UNIVERSITY OF SAN FRANCISCO, Fulton St., Parker and Golden Gate Aves., stands beside St. Ignatius Church on part of the site of the Masonic Cemetery, one of four former burial grounds encircling the base of Lone Mountain. Established as St. Ignatius Church and College in 1855, it was empowered by the State Legislature in 1859 to grant degrees and honors. The school won fame in 1874 when Father Joseph Neri, a professor, introduced San Francisco to the arc light with an exhibition on the roof of the school building; during the centennial celebration of American Independence in 1876, he strung three arc lamps of his own invention across Market Street. The university was renamed at the request of prominent San Franciscans in 1930. Conducted by the Jesuits, the university is open to students of all denominations and is now co-educational. On the broad 21-acre hillside campus stand the Colleges of Liberal Arts, Science, and Business Administration, and Schools of Law and Nursing. In 1965 the University initiated a $12,500,000 Master Development Program, which provided needed funds for additional faculty members and faculty chairs, for scholarships and grants for deserving students, for library volumes and operation, and for further campus expansion. The Special Collections in Gleeson Library include the internationally recognized St. Thomas More Collection which boasts all editions of the works of More, all important editions of works by and about contemporaries with whom More was personally involved, and representative editions of historical and critical works dealing in significant part with More. The best-known rarity in the collection is the first edition of More's *Utopia,* Louvain, 1516. In the 1971-72 year the university enrolled 6,559 students and had a faculty of 438.

Standing on Ignatius Heights, the buff-colored brick structure of SAINT IGNATIUS CHURCH, northeast corner of Fulton St. and

Parker Ave., with its campanile, twin towers, and golden dome glinting in the sun, is a San Francisco landmark. Dedicated in 1914, the church is seventeenth-century Renaissance in design (Charles Devlin, architect). Under the dome is the sanctuary, bordered by fluted pillars; above the white marble altar, flanked by filigreed gilt candelabra, is suspended an ornate gold sanctuary lamp. On the right are the altar of St. Joseph and the crucifix; on the left, the altar of the Blessed Mother and the pulpit. The altars, both of marble, stand against blue wall panels ornately filigreed with gold. The two murals of the altar, by Tito Ridolfi, are dedicated to St. Robert Bellarmine and depict the seventeenth-century Cardinal of Milan in two poses. Ridolfi also painted the series of murals in the frieze above the colonnades on either side, depicting the 14 stations of the cross, in which Christ is shown in mediaeval tradition wearing an under cloak of dull red and an outer cloak of dull blue. Above the frieze are round windows, to be replaced with stained-glass representations of Catholic scholar saints; the two installed depict St. Ives, patron of lawyers, and St. Augustine, doctor of theology. In the campanile is the old bell, now battered and rusty, that hung in the original church of 1855, obtained from a local volunteer fire company which had ordered it from England but was unable to pay for it.

Saint Ignatius Church was founded in 1855, when Father Anthony Maraschi dedicated a small wooden building in the waste land of what was then known as the Valley of St. Anne, south of Market Street between Fourth and Fifth Streets. The present buildings, both church and college, were begun in 1910 and completed in 1914.

N. from Fulton St. on Parker Ave.

From the top of Lone Mountain, the Spanish Gothic tower of the SAN FRANCISCO COLLEGE FOR WOMEN, Parker and Masonic Aves. and Turk St., lifts an iron cross 115 feet above the mountain's flattened crest. A curving road winds up from Turk Street, past neatly planted trees, shrubs and flower beds, to the flight of wide stone steps leading past terraced lawns to an ornamental arched doorway. The three-story building, Spanish-Gothic in design, has vaulted halls richly furnished with tapestries, paintings, statues, and wood carvings. In the east wing is the oak-beamed library; its 100,000 volumes, the majority donated by Monsignor Joseph M. Gleason, pastor of the St. Francis de Sales Church of Oakland, include rare manuscripts and first editions. Here are such rarities as the sermons of Pope St. Leo the Great; a set of wills and indentures covering the reigns of the English sovereigns from James I to George III; several papal bulls, one signed by nine cardinals who attended the Council of Trent in 1566, and the second by Pope Pius V, before the battle of Lepanto; a copy of the Nuremberg Chronicle;

and what is probably the most complete collection of bookplates in the United States. Americana include a newspaper published in the South on wallpaper during the Civil War, an unpublished and autographed poem by Henry Wadsworth Longfellow, and letters written by Ulysses S. Grant, Andrew Jackson, Andrew Johnson, and other notables.

Having purchased Lone Mountain in 1860, Bishop Joseph Sadoc Alemany, Roman Catholic Archbishop of San Francisco, had a giant wooden cross erected on the mountain top. When the city acquired all "outside lands" west of the former city boundary in 1869, Lone Mountain was reserved as a future park site; but Bishop Alemany, through the persuasive abilities of his secretary, John Spottiswoode, succeeded in regaining title to the property. The old cross was replaced by a new one in 1875, and in 1900 a storm blew the great cross down, for the boys of the neighborhood had tunnelled under its base to make a cave. Again restored, the cross remained on the mountain top until grading for the college began in 1930. When Archbishop Edward J. Hanna of San Francisco suggested in 1929 that a Roman Catholic women's college be opened in San Francisco, the Lone Mountain site was purchased by the Society of the Sacred Heart. When construction was completed in 1932, the present iron cross at the top of the tower replaced the cross erected in 1900.

W. from Parker Ave. on Anza St. to Lorraine Court; N. from Anza on Lorraine Court.

The SAN FRANCISCO MEMORIAL COLUMBARIUM, 1 Lorraine Court, was originally built in 1894 at the entrance of the Odd Fellows Cemetery at the base of Lone Mountain. It contains the cremated remains of 13,000 San Franciscans. Partially destroyed by the 1906 earthquake it was rebuilt in 1907. Following removal of the Odd Fellows Cemetery to San Mateo County the Columbarium fell into neglect and decay but was later remodeled and restored. Of modified Mediterranean design, the green-domed building of white concrete is noted for its stained glass windows. From the rotunda marble stairways wind upward. On its four floors are galleries of niches, each named for a stellar constellation.

Retrace on Lorraine Court; W. from Lorraine Court on Anza St. to Arguello Blvd.; N. from Anza on Arguello.

Dominating most of the city's western residential area, the massive orange-domed TEMPLE EMANU-EL, northwest corner of Lake St. and Arguello Blvd., is the religious and cultural center of Reformed Judaism in San Francisco. Of steel and concrete, faced with cream-colored stucco, the temple (Sylvain Schnaittaker and Bakewell & Brown, architects) is designed in the form of an L about an open court with low cloisters and fountain. The auditorium seats 1,700; besides assembly halls and Sunday school classrooms, the temple contains facilities for study groups and lectures, social halls, and a huge gymnasium.

Set in colored tile in the pavement before the main entrance is the familiar six-pointed star, the Seal of Solomon, surrounded by the seals of the Twelve Tribes of Israel. The vestibule of the auditorium is a low vaulted gallery finished in light blue to contrast with the ivory tones of the interior walls. In solitary splendor, contrary to custom, the Ark of the Covenant, a gilded bronze cabinet with cloisonné enamel inlay, stands out under its stone canopy against the undecorated walls and vaults around the altar. It contains two ornate scrolls of the Torah, one for regular services, the other for special occasions.

Like other reform congregations, Temple Emanu-El does not require observance of strict dietary laws, wearing of hats or skull caps by male members, and segregation of the sexes on opposite sides of the auditorium during services. Contrary to orthodox ritual, music accompanies worship here. An important part of the temple's program are its classes for boys and girls.

E. from Arguello Blvd. on Washington St.

Tucked away in a tree-shaded garden behind high walls overrun with climbing vines and rose bushes, the little tiled-brick ivy-bowered CHURCH OF THE NEW JERUSALEM (*services Sun. 11 a.m.*), northwest corner of Lyon and Washington St., is a reproduction of a village church near Verona, Italy. Surrounding a clear pool of water are trees from many lands. Completed in 1895, the church is a monument to its founder, the Reverend Joseph Worcester, who lived in close association with the artists of Russian Hill. Its heavy-timbered coffered roof is supported by great hewn madrone trees. The square-framed, tule-bottomed chairs on mats of rushes from the Suisun marshes, the open fireplace ablaze with pine knots, and the wax tapers in wrought iron sconces reinforce the outdoor atmosphere. On the windowless north wall four allegorical landscapes of seedtime and harvest by William Keith are set against plain dark-stained panels of pine. The two beautifully executed stained-glass windows are by Bruce Porter. Following the doctrines of Emanuel Swedenborg (1688-1772), the simple services are opened and closed with a biblical ritual.

S. from Washington St. on Lyon St. to California St.; W. from Lyon on California.

The JEWISH COMMUNITY CENTER, northwest corner of California St. and Presidio Ave., is headquarters for communal activities of Hebrew organizations. The two-story structure of smooth tan concrete with red tile roof was opened in 1933 and houses an art gallery, library and reading rooms, a little theater workshop, swimming pool and gymnasium, and classrooms and lounges. The multicolored mosaic of glazed household tiles decorating the fountain and pool in the patio is by Bernard Zakheim of the WPA Northern California Art Project.

Known to generations of San Franciscans, the site of LAUREL HILL CEMETERY, California St., Presidio and Parker Aves., a 54-acre area at the base of Lone Mountain, was preserved within the walls of Pioneer Memorial Park until 1946, when its conversion into residential property was begun. In 1854, San Franciscans established Laurel Hill Cemetery far out in the sand dunes so that it would not interfere with the city's growth. A long list of names important in the city's history once appeared on the head-stones: Fire Chief Dave Scannell; Mayor James Van Ness; smelting works founder Thomas Selby; barrister and bon-vivant Hall McAllister; Senator David C. Broderick, killed in a pistol duel with State Supreme Court Justice David S. Terry; and Bulletin editor James King of William whose murder by James Casey revived vigilante organization; William Sharon and James G. Fair of Comstock Lode fame. In 1912, when four cemeteries, Laurel Hill, Calvary, Odd Fellows, and Masonic, were grouped around the base of Lone Mountain, the Board of Supervisors, heeding the protests of the living, ordered the area vacated. All of the cemeteries save Laurel Hill were moved to San Mateo County. The controversy which ensued lasted for 28 years. In 1937 the people of San Francisco voted that the ground be cleared and emptied by the end of 1940. Coffins were transferred at the rate of more than 2,000 each month to Cypress Lawn Cemetery in San Mateo County. Contractor Charles L. Harney was paid 80 cents a ton to dump the walls, crypts and heavy markers in the bay as a breakwater, most of them placed along the east jetty at St. Francis Yacht Harbor.

FIREMAN'S FUND INSURANCE COMPANY, virtually wiped out by the 1906 disaster in the city the company was founded to protect, has its headquarters on a portion of the old cemetery, in a three level $4,500,000 structure of steel, concrete, glass, and brick (Edward P. Page, architect). The building located at 3333 California Street was dedicated July 9, 1957 and has a small museum containing the first fire engine built in California, Old Broderick, which is open to the public during working hours. A plaque bearing the following inscription was placed on the wall of the new building:

FORMER SITE OF THE LAUREL HiLL CEMETERY 1854-1946. THE BUILDERS OF THE WEST, CIVIC AND MILITARY LEADERS, JURISTS, INVENTORS, ARTISTS AND ELEVEN UNITED STATES SENATORS WERE BURIED HERE —THE MOST REVERED OF SAN FRANCISCO'S HILLS.

The IRWIN MEMORIAL BLOOD BANK, a subsidiary of the San Francisco Medical Society, was established in June, 1941, in the basement of the former William G. Irwin mansion at Washington and Laguna Streets. Today it is housed in a new many-windowed building at 270 Masonic Ave., a move made possible by the sale of the Irwin home at 2180 Washington St. The blood bank is one of the largest independent non-profit community blood banks in the country.

W. from Fillmore St. on Bush St.

The eight-spired Tudor Gothic tower of ST. DOMINIC'S CHURCH, northwest corner Bush and Steiner Sts., rises to a height of 175 feet, dominating the neighborhood. The present structure was completed in 1928 on the site of the original church destroyed in 1906. Stretched across the tallest of its interior vaulted arches is a rood screen bearing in its center the figures of a Crucifixion group. In the chief shrine along each side of the church is a figure of Christ, wearing a regal sceptre and robed in priestly garments. Woodwork of the altar rails and confessional doors is the work of the master carvers of Oberammergau, Bavaria, and of Bruges, Belgium.

N. from Bush St. on Steiner St.

ALTA PLAZA, Steiner, Scott, Clay, and Jackson Sts., was reclaimed by John McLaren when he filled a deserted rock quarry with rubbish, topped it with soil, planted lawns, and laid out walks and tennis courts. The stairway on the south side's steep terraced slope is a reproduction of the grand stairway in front of the gaming casino at Monte Carlo.

E. from Steiner St. on Jackson St.

The city's largest Protestant congregation worships in the CALVARY PRESBYTERIAN CHURCH, northwest corner Jackson and Fillmore Sts., founded in 1854 by the Reverend William Anderson Scott, who was hanged in effigy in 1861. A supporter of the original church, William C. Ralston, is reported to have scattered $20 gold pieces among its pews.

The cornerstone of the present classic structure with Corinthian features was laid July 4, 1901, to the accompaniment of fireworks and Protestant hymns. Offering its spacious facilities to other religious congregations and to the city government after the 1906 fire, Calvary had services conducted in its lecture room by the presiding Rabbi of Temple Emanu-El, concerts by the Loring Club in its auditorium, and sessions of the Superior Court in its gymnasium.

S. from Jackson St. on Webster St.

The PRESBYTERIAN MEDICAL CENTER, Webster, Buchanan, Clay and Sacramento Sts., is developing an extensive building program under the architectural direction of Skidmore, Owings & Merrill. The Center was organized May 1, 1960, when the Stanford University Medical School moved to its new quarters on the Stanford campus at Palo Alto. Dominating the older buildings is the five-story redbrick Lane Hospital, built in 1893, an outgrowth of the first medical college established on the Pacific Coast in 1858 by Dr. E. S. Cooper.

E. from Webster St. on California St.

TEMPLE SHERITH ISRAEL, northeast corner Webster and California Sts., is a pioneer stronghold of reformed Judaism which has played a role in the city's political history. Its stern main facade is distinguished by an entrance recessed behind a Roman arch which curves above a vast rose window. The interior auditorium is a huge square, surrounded by two tiers of galleries, from which a domed ceiling rises 80 feet above the floor. The present building was erected in 1904 for a congregation organized in 1850.

Serving as a temporary Hall of Justice immediately after the 1906 fire, the auditorium here was the courtroom in which Abraham Ruef was indicted on 65 counts of extortion by a grand jury. During a recess, a juryman named Haas, who had been exposed as an ex-convict, shot and wounded Francis J. Heney, chief prosecutor and leader of the graft investigations. Barely saved from lynching, Ruef was convicted and sentenced to 14 years in San Quentin. Asked by newspaper reporters how he liked exchanging his natty attire for a convict's striped gray uniform, the dethroned political boss of San Francisco replied: "The zebra is one of the most beautiful and graceful of animals. Why, therefore, should I cavil at my attire."

E. from Webster St. on California St. to Laguna St.; N. from California on Laguna.

Site of the first observatory in California, LAFAYETTE SQUARE, Washington, Gough, Sacramento and Laguna Sts., is a sloping green hill crisscrossed with hedges and graveled walks, topped with tennis courts and a small playground. Erected in 1879, the observatory was maintained privately for 20 years by George Davidson, geodesist and astronomer. The park was created in 1867, but the top of the hill was owned by Samuel W. Holladay, ex-Oregon stage driver and owner of the famous Overland Stage Line, whose glistening white home on "Holladay's Hill" was a mecca for literary and Gold Rush aristocracy. Repeated suits by the city failed to dislodge Holladay, and the old mansion, with weathered timbers that had come round the Horn, was not razed until 1936, when the site was incorporated into the park.

E. from Laguna St. on Sacramento St. to Octavia St.; S. from Sacramento on Octavia.

The JAPANESE CULTURAL AND TRADE CENTER, Laguna, Fillmore, Geary and Post Streets, a $15 million complex dedicated March 28, 1968, occupies a 5-acre portion of an urban renewal development launched by the San Francisco Redevelopment Agency for 108 acres of San Francisco's Western Addition. Located in the heart of the city's Japanese district, the Center is the product of an collaborative effort of the developer, architects, the Redevelopment Agency, and others in the Center's planning, financing, and construction.

The Center's overall design was conceived by Minoru Yamasaki in association with Van Bourg, Nakamura and Associates, of Berkeley. Major components of the center include: Three commercial buildings, two of which are linked by a wide, enclosed bridge of shops spanning over Webster Street. The Japanese Consulate General Building. The 14-story Miyako Hotel, featuring modified Japanese decor in the 172 rooms and including an extension floor of deluxe Japanese-styled suites atop the consulate building. Restaurants, meeting facilities, and an 800-car garage are other attractions. A central Peace Plaza paved with slate and landscaped with Japanese gardens and ponds surrounds the Peace Pagoda, designed by Professor Yoshiro Taniguchi. It is of white precast concrete, with 12 circular pillars supporting five roofs. The design was inspired by the round pagoda of eternal peace, built about 1,200 years ago for Empress Koken of Nara, ancient capital of Japan. Copper plating that will weather to a rich green patina has been used for the five tiers of the roof. These tiers decrease in diameter (46 to 34 feet) as they increase in height. Above the top roof is a Kurin, nine-ringed spire, a symbol of virtue. At the highest point is a hoshu, golden ball with a flaming head. A wide selection of Japanese products, such as automobiles, cameras, radios, art goods, textiles, apparel, optical goods, jewelry, and furniture are displayed in the Center's 106,000 sq. ft. of shopping space.

Directly north of the Japanese Cultural & Trade Center, in a 4-block, 10-acre, section of the second Western Addition renewal area is the NIHONMACHI. The plan for the Nihonmachi area proposes informal landscaped plazas and walkways through new and restored homes, small Japanese shops, and service buildings. While most of the commercial structures will be new, many of the homes will be rehabilitated to meet modern standards and their exteriors architecturally restored to be consistent with their historical origins and to preserve their intimate scale.

On the northern fringes of the Japanese quarter a hospital marks the site of the THOMAS BELL RESIDENCE, corner Octavia and Bush Sts., long known as the House of Mystery. The house itself was torn down about 1927 but a short row of eucalyptus trees that once hedged it remains. Here, during the heyday of the Comstock period, lived that formidable sorceress known to every San Franciscan as Mammy Pleasant. Ostensibly, the great mansion with its mansard roof, its inner courtyard, and its mirror-lined ballroom, which was never used for dancing, was the private residence of Thomas Bell, reputedly the power behind William C. Ralston's throne in the Bank of California. Mammy Pleasant was to all appearances his housekeeper. There was scarcely a man in public life who did not treat the scrawny little Negress with utmost deference.

The truth was, of course, that she was a procuress of unusual resources and connections, and a remarkable cook. On her arrival in San Francisco in 1848, she quickly attracted to her boarding house the leaders of the town. The entertainment she provided soon enabled her to open a whole chain of boarding houses. Obeying the injunction of her dead first husband she devoted part of her legacy received from him to the Abolitionist cause, traveling to Boston, where she presented John Brown with a draft for $30,000. When Brown was captured at Harper's Ferry, a note was found on him, signed with Mammy Pleasant's "M.P." It read: "The ax is laid at the foot of the tree. When the first blow is struck, there will be more money to help."

To ensure this, Mammy returned to San Francisco, and set up her *ménage* in the mansion. She squandered Thomas Bell's fortune on weird schemes, turned his wife against him, kept him virtually a prisoner, and starved his children. When he died of a fall into the courtyard from a third-story balcony, it was believed that his "housekeeper" had pushed him over. She carried on for years a bitter legal duel with members of his family. She died at the age of 92, penniless, asking only that her tombstone bear this epitaph: "She was a friend of John Brown."

E. from Octavia St. on Bush St.

First of its denomination on the Pacific Coast, TRINITY EPISCOPAL CHURCH, northeast corner Gough and Bush Sts., was founded in 1849. The present structure, built of rough-hewn Colusa sandstone, Norman in style, is flanked at either end of its main facade by bastions with conical turrets which contribute to the massive effect imposed by the square central belfry (A. Page Brown, architect). The interior nave of three bays contains lancet windows of stained glass portraying Biblical subjects, the work of Belgian craftsmen. Buried beneath the chancel is the Reverend Flavel Scott Mines, founded of the church, who died in 1852. Beside the altar stands a bronze angel with folded wings who bears aloft a flat brass scroll on which rests a large Bible. Until 1867 services were held in a private house. From that date until the erection of the present church in 1892, its congregation met in a large frame building at Post and Powell Streets.

S. from Bush St. on Gough St. to O'Farrell St.; E. from Gough on O'Farrell

Its peaked gray roof rising between a cone-topped turret and a square pyramid-roofed bell tower, ST. MARK'S EVANGELICAL LUTHERAN CHURCH (*services Sun. 8:30 and 11 a.m.*), O'Farrell St. between Gough and Franklin Sts., was the first Lutheran Church in California, founded in 1849. The red brick facade of the present structure, dedicated in 1895, is of Romanesque design. In 11 stained glass windows, which shed rich red, blue, and purple light on an interior decorated in French ivory and gold, are represented *The Pascal Lamb, The Holy Writ, The Sacred Chalice, The Cross, The Crown of Christ the King, The Ten Commandments,* and the name "Jehovah" in Hebrew. Behind the ornate altar rise the gilded pipes of the great organ, distinguished for its trumpet brass reed with clarion martial tone. One of the first pipe organs built in San Francisco, it was installed by Felix Schoenstein in 1886 in the church's former building on Geary Street. Until 1864, when orthodox members of its congregation withdrew to found the Church of St. Paulus, Masons and others belonging to secret orders were barred from membership. Following the 1906 disaster the slightly damaged church served as a refugee and hospital center. Until 1931 services were conducted in German.

ST. MARY'S CATHEDRAL OF THE ASSUMPTION, Gough, Ellis, Octavia and Geary Sts., is a new building in which Mass was celebrated for the first time Thursday, October 15, 1970. It cost $7,500,000 and takes the place of the original cathedral, which stood at O'Farrell St. and Van Ness Ave. and was the seat of the Roman Catholic Archbishopric of Northern California until destroyed by fire September 7, 1962.

The cornerstone of the old cathedral, a 500-pound granite block, serves the new cathedral. It was blessed in ceremonies held December 13, 1967, by th Most Rev. Luigi Raimondi, Apostolic delegate to the United States. The new cathedral has four massive concrete pylons supporting a 190-ft. tower, topped by a 50-ft. crucifix (McSweeney, Ryan & Lee, Pietro Belluschi & Pier Luigi Nervi, architects). Walls of diamond-shaped concrete coffers rise to the domed ceiling where stained glass windows, designed by Gyargy Kepes, form a cross. Temperature in the church must be kept at 65° so that the organ, built by Fratelli

Ruffatti of Padua, Italy, will not be thrown off pitch. The cathedral complex also includes a girls' school and faculty and priests' residences.

N. from O'Farrell St. on Van Ness Ave. to Geary St.; W. from Van Ness on Geary

The FIRST UNITARIAN CHURCH, southwest corner of Geary and Franklin Sts., an ivy-covered, gray stone edifice of modified Romanesque and Gothic design, with a square turret in place of the bell tower demolished by the earthquake of 1906, is reminiscent of the churches of the English countryside. In the little strip of churchyard is an oblong white marble sarcophagus bearing the simple inscription, "Thomas Starr King, born December 17, A. D. 1824—Died March 4, A. D. 1864"; here repose the remains of the militant pastor of the Civil War period with whom the church long has been identified. The church has a great circular rose window and perpendicular Gothic windows of stained glass. Bruce Porter's allegorical painting, *Lo At Length The True Light,* appears over the altar, which is flanked on either side by winged angels sculptured by Arthur Putnam. The marble baptismal font with rows of finely chiseled cherubs, under a spired Gothic canopy rising to the vaulted ceiling of the church, is the gift of the First Congregational Church of New York to the First Unitarian Church in San Francisco, made in 1864.

The city's first Unitarian religious service was preached on October 20, 1850, by the Reverend Charles A. Farley. A Unitarian society was soon formed and by 1852 was holding services in Armory Hall, then the largest auditorium in town. In a church of its own on Stockton Street the society began meeting in 1853. To this church in 1860 came a young Boston clergyman, Thomas Starr King. When the Civil War began a year later, he canvassed the State, helping to swing California to the side of the Union with his eloquence. Through King's efforts the cornerstone of a new church on Geary Street was laid in December, 1862. Only two months after its dedication January 10, 1864, King died of diphtheria. The Reverend Horatio Stebbins succeeded him and during the 35 years of his pastorate, many distinguished visitors spoke from the pulpit, among them Ralph Waldo Emerson, Julia Ward Howe, Edward Everett Hale, Charles Eliot, and David Starr Jordan. Since the dedication of the present church on February 10, 1889, its pastor and membership have carried on the tradition of Thomas Starr King, playing a leading role in movements for political, economic, and social reform.

N. from Geary St. on Franklin St. to Post St.; E. from Franklin on Post to Van Ness Ave.; N. from Post on Van Ness

The chaste white granite and limestone SCOTTISH RITE TEMPLE, northwest corner of Van Ness Ave. and Sutter St. (Carl Werner, architect), was dedicated in 1911 by the Masonic Order of Scottish Rite, first established in San Francisco in 1868. It has been used by clubs, political groups, and trade unions for grand annual balls, public forums, and convention headquarters. Beyond the lobby is the lodge room, seating 1,500, a vast two-storied chamber of English Tudor design, with high stained-glass windows lighting the dark walnut panels of the room. On the fourth and top floor is a library of 2,500 volumes, including a copy of Albert Magnus' *Sermons,* printed in 1479, bound in leather with covers of thin wood and the *History of St. Joan,* printed in 1722.

The HOLY TRINITY RUSSIAN EASTERN ORTHODOX CATHEDRAL, corner of Van Ness Ave. and Green St., where on Orthodox Sunday (first Sunday in Lent) deep-voiced Russian singers intone their laments for the godless, is the first Russian cathedral in the United States and the oldest Russian church in San Francisco. The present structure is authentically Byzantine in design, a buff-colored frame building, its green dome surmounted with a gold Greek cross. It faces east in the tradition of the Greek Orthodox Church. Within the belfry hang five bells, the largest of which, weighing two and one-half tons, was made expressly for the church in commemoration of the miraculous escape from death of the "little Father of all the Russias" in 1884. The church has two richly decorated auditoriums, one for daily services, the other for Sundays and holy days. Its murals depicting religious subjects are by Gleb Ilyn. The cathedral has no benches or pews, the congregation being obliged to stand or kneel on the bare floor while priests in colored vestments, thin and frayed from decades of use, intone the mass and vespers. Ikons are usually kept covered on a special table except during Easter, when they are placed on the altar for 40 days.

The first known services of the Russian Greek Orthodox Church held in San Francisco were conducted in 1863, when a priest from a Russian ship in the Bay baptized a Serbian infant in a private house. With the arrival of many Russian immigrants from Alaska, Father Ioann Metropolsky came in 1871 and organized the St. Alexander Russian Orthodox Church. In 1882-83 a cathedral was established on Powell Street; the memorial bells hung in the church were rescued during the fire and earthquake of 1906 and installed in the present structure after its dedication in 1909.

Of polyglot design the OLD TEMPLE of the VEDANTA SO-
CIETY OF NORTHERN CALIFORNIA, 2963 Webster St., was
designed by Swami Trigunatita. The first two stories were constructed
in 1905, and in 1908 the Temple was completed with the addition of
the third floor and towers. The Filbert Street entrance features a Mughal
type dome over a lobated arched doorway, the Webster Street entrance
has Doric columns in antis; overhanging bay windows in Colonial Revival style, lobated windows on the first floor, a lacey lobated arch colonnade on the third floor. There is a crenelated English turret on the southeast side, a double blubous dome on a cylinder at the corner, then an
octagonal bysanture melon dome, a cluster of pointed domes, Jain Temple
style, along with the Mughal type dome along the north side to give an
unbelievable building roof line. An auditorium for 112 and various offices
comprise the first floor; the second and third floors are occupied by the
Monastery of the Vedanta Society.

Rim of the Golden Gate

"*Thou seest the white seas fold their tent,
O Warden of two continents.
Thou drawest all things, small and great,
To thee, beside the Western Gate.*"
—BRET HARTE

FACING a little cove within the sheltering arm of Black Point, protected on the north and west by the semicircular sea wall that is Municipal Pier, is 34½-acre AQUATIC PARK, foot of Polk St. Reserved for service personnel during World War II, it was refurbished for public use when peace came. This $1,500,000 municipal recreation center was made possible by WPA funds, laborers, and artists. To create its quarter-mile stretch of clean sand and smooth surf, workmen excavated (1935-38) a large part of that area into which had been dumped in 1906 the debris from the ruins of Chinatown, uncovering jewelry and watches, pieces of jade, and coins from a dozen nations.

On this site in the 1870's were the Neptune Baths, from which William C. Ralston swam to his death in 1875, and industrial units of a woolen mill and smelting company.

In 1949 Mayor Elmer E. Robinson suggested the establishment of a community inspired maritime museum to "perpetuate forever the colorful romance of San Francisco's historic waterfront." Aquatic Park was selected as the site and on May 27, 1951, the new SAN FRANCISCO MARITIME MUSEUM opened. The museum is located at the foot of Polk Street in a triple-deck white concrete building designed to resemble a streamlined battleship riding at anchor (William Mooser, Sr., and William Mooser, Jr., architects). The main floor of the building is shared with a Senior Citizen's Recreation Center. On display are ship models, figureheads, anchors, and other relics of sailing ship days (*open daily 10-5*).

Popular with fishermen of all ages and Sunday promenaders is the 1,850-foot-long, white concrete MUNICIPAL PIER, foot of Van Ness Ave. The semicircular sea wall, constructed in 1929-34, swings northeastward to protect Aquatic Park's little harbor. From adjacent Transport Wharf Number 4, steamers once operated daily to and from Alcatraz and Angel Islands.

The HYDE STREET PIER is part of the San Francisco Maritime

State Historical Monument and encompasses the park bounded by Beach, Jefferson, North Beach and Hyde Streets. It was built by the Division of Beaches and Parks from tideland oil royalties.

The vessels displayed here are all important examples of a ship type developed, built and operated on the Pacific Coast for specific trades. The piers of San Francisco were their home and the words San Francisco painted on their sterns clearly indicated the port of registry—their home port. The ships are: The *Alma,* a scow schooner, capable of carrying bulky commodities in the Bay and rivers; the *C. A. Thayer,* a lumber schooner; the *Wapama,* a steam schooner; and the *Eureka,* the last paddle-wheel walking-beam engined ferry to operate on San Francisco Bay, her final trip was made in 1957 (*open daily 10-6 winter, spring & fall; 10-midnight summer; adults 50¢; children 25¢*).

GHIRARDELLI SQUARE, Polk, Larkin, North Point and Beach Sts., occupies the old red brick buildings where in 1897 Domingo Ghirardelli moved his chocolate factory to utilize the brick buildings abandoned by the Pioneer Columbia Woolen Mill and to be near the Belt Line Railroad. The buildings and corner clock tower always have been San Francisco landmarks and it is San Franciscans as well as tourists who have flocked to the square since its $10-million restoration in 1968 (Wurster, Bernardi & Emmons, architects).

The old Del Monte Fruit Cannery, now known as the CANNERY, occuping the eastern half of the block bordered by Jefferson, Leavenworth, Beach and Hyde Streets was saved from destruction in 1963 when purchased by Leonard V. Martin. The old building was sliced in two, exterior walls were preserved and the interior was transformed into attractive and unusual shops and restaurants (Joseph Esherick, architect).

S. on Polk St. to Bay St.; W. on Bay

Thrust northward into the Bay, its land boundaries Van Ness Ave., Bay and Laguna Sts. (main entrance Van Ness Ave. and Bay St.), is FORT MASON UNITED STATES MILITARY RESERVE (usually open 24 hrs.; subject to close without notice), whose 68½ acres enclose the site of Spanish fortifications built nearly 150 years ago. On April 4, 1797, Governor Diego de Borica instructed engineer Alberto de Cordoba to complete certain necessary repairs of Castillo de San Joaquin and to construct another battery where it would "further impede the anchorage of any hostile vessel in La Yerba Buena." Location chosen by De Cordoba for his Battery San Jose was Point Medanos (later called San Jose), today's Black Point, northernmost natural promontory of the reserve. Original defense for the little battery was five brass eightpounders; by 1798 it had achieved a sixth cannon; but by the turn of the century it was virtually abandoned. When General and Mrs. John C. Frémont in the 1850's moved to Black Point—said to have been so named because of its dense, somber laurel thickets—there was no trace of Battery San Jose.

The area was set aside for military purposes by President Millard Fillmore Nov. 6, 1850, but not until 1863 were troops quartered in the area. Meanwhile lawsuits had been waged over boundaries, water rights, and private claims which were to reduce the original 100-acre reserve to its present size.

Unsuccessful in their fight to gain possession of the area were Frémont and four friends who claimed it by squatters' rights. Colonel Richard Barnes Mason carried out the Presidential order to dispossess, thus incurring an enmity that culminated in a challenge by Frémont to a duel, which was never fought. In 1882 the reservation was named for Colonel Mason, California military governor 1847-49.

Former point of embarkation and arrival for troops stationed abroad were the ARMY TRANSPORT DOCKS in the northwestern corner of the reserve, foot of Laguna St. As headquarters for the Army Transportation Corps, Fort Mason was the center of operations of the San Francisco Port of Embarkation, which, during World War II, moved overseas, 1,644,243 soldiers and 23,589,000 ship tons of cargo. It was the largest Army port on the Pacific Coast and the second largest in the nation. In 1962, in an economy move, the Department of Defense moved the transport stops to Oakland, closing the piers, and in July 1963 ordered partition of the post, separating the residential and working areas and declaring most of the latter surplus. The action however did not affect the eastern half of Fort Mason, containing the historic buildings and the park-like areas which contribute so much to the scenic beauty and historical landmarks of San Francisco.

N. from Bay St. on Laguna St. to Marina Blvd.; NW. on Marina; or NW. from Bay St. and Van Ness Ave. on a Fort Mason road to Marina Blvd.; NW. on Marina

Comparatively new and fashionable is that residential district of stuccoed flats and broad-windowed apartment buildings known as The Marina, extending from Van Ness Avenue west to the Presidio and north from Lombard Street to Fort Mason and the Bay. The older part of the district was built up during the Panama-Pacific International Exposition of 1915; the newer, since 1922, on some 50 of the several hundred blocks on which the exposition was located.

Lying north of broad Marina Boulevard between Webster St. and Yacht Harbor, are the block-wide, level lawns of MARINA GREEN (*parking area; comfort stations*). Baseball and football players, picnickers, and kite and model airplane enthusiasts have replaced the local amateur aviators who made the park their unofficial landing field until 1925. In that year Marina residents objected so strenuously to the aerial menaces to their lives and property that the Park Commission decided to use the land for its originally intended recreational purposes.

On the Marina Green, near Fillmore Street, facing the Bay is a marble memorial to William C. Ralston, financier, builder of the old Palace Hotel and California Theater. It is 10 ft. high, 7 ft. long, and 5 ft. wide and was presented by Major Edward Bowes in 1941. Haig Patigian was the artist.

Berthed in municipally owned YACHT HARBOR and GAS HOUSE COVE, are nearly 700 craft ranging in size from the tiniest of catboats to large schooners. Sail and motor boats moored here dot the Bay on pleasant weekends and participate in regattas sponsored by the many local yacht clubs. A fueling float, including chandlery facilities, was opened in the East Basin on May 29, 1970.

On the 1,500-foot-long breakwater that shelters the harbor is the home of the ST. FRANCIS YACHT CLUB (*private*), a two-story cement-faced structure roofed with red and orange tile, all but obscured from the mainland by green pines. Spanish in both exterior and interior— with beamed ceilings looking down on rooms furnished in heavy dark wood and warmed by great open fires—the decorative motif is neverthe- less marine. A large glass-enclosed lounge affords an unusually fine view of the Bay and its shores. Among the clubrooms open to its 300 members are a dining room, a bar, steam and locker rooms, and courts for bad- minton, handball, and squash. Active in formation of the organization (1928) was Hiram Johnson, Jr. Non-profit and given to the promotion of frequent social events, the club's primary interest is yachting. Its annual open racing season (for craft of all classes) attracts sportsmen from the entire Bay region.

Beyond the club, at the eastern tip of the breakwater, stands a MINIATURE LIGHTHOUSE of stone and granite once publicized by Robert (Believe-It-or-Not) Ripley as the only municipally owned lighthouse in the world chartered by a national government. The granite in the 30- foot-high tower came from tombstones in an abandoned Lone Mountain Cemetery. A small park area guarded by reclining stone lions surrounds the litle building.

S. from Marina Blvd. on Baker St.

The PALACE OF FINE ARTS, one of the greatly admired struc- tures of the Panama Pacific International Exposition of 1915, once more stands forth as a memorial of that remarkable event. From the start this semicircular building with its Corinthian columns reflected in a lagoon was a favorite with the millions of visitors who thronged the exposition, and was chosen to remain in use after the other temporary buildings had been removed.

After the fair, in 1918, the Palace again housed an art collection—that of the San Francisco Art Commission; but after 1921, when the group moved its exhibit, the building was allowed to deteriorate. In 1927 the Federal Government deeded the 10-acre portion of the Presidio on which the Palace stood to the City of San Francisco, but not until 12 years later did San Francisco begin to expend the $500,000 necessary for its restoration.

On June 11, 1960, President Eisenhower signed into law a bill that cleared the way for the rehabilitation of the Palace, since the lagoon and certain surrounding roads were held by the Government. After Walter S. Johnson in 1959 donated a $2 million gift to the city for the project, the citizenry approved a $1.8 million bond issue. Reconstruction began in 1964 under the supervision of architect Hans U. Gerson, whose firm is the direct descendant of Maybeck & White, the original architects. The new Palace of Fine Arts was dedicated September 30, 1967.

The Palace has an outer circumference of 1,100 ft. and a width of 135 ft. In the center of the colonnade, opposite the main entrance, is an ornamental domed rotunda supported by eight pairs of columns flanking as many arches. The Palace's designer, Bernard Maybeck, is said to have designed the rotunda along lines suggested by Bocklin's painting, The Island of the Dead, and the peristyle after Gerome's Chariot Race.

In 1969 the Palace of Arts and Sciences Foundation was founded to sponsor the EXPLORATORIUM, a museum of science and technology designed to show how science relates to the humanities and the arts (*open 1-5 daily, except Monday & Tuesday*).

The 1,000-seat PALACE OF FINE ARTS THEATER, the permanent home of San Francisco's Annual International Film Festival, opened October 21, 1970.

W. from Baker St. on Lombard St., which leads into Lincoln Blvd.

THE PRESIDIO OF SAN FRANCISCO, UNITED STATES MILITARY RESERVATION (*usually open 24 hours; subject to close without notice; speed limit 20 m.p.h.; night parking prohibited*), main entrance at Lincoln Blvd. and Lombard St., is a wooded tract of 1,480 acres extending from West Pacific Avenue and Lobos Creek north to the rim of the Golden Gate. Largest military reservation within a city's limits in the United States, it embraces inside its boundaries not only the Post of Presidio of San Francisco proper, but also the post of Fort Winfield Scott (*see below*), Letterman General Hospital (*see below*), and Headquarters, Sixth Army. Within the reservation are barracks for enlisted men, officers' quarters, guard houses, recreation centers, hospitals, a cemetery, a parade ground, warehouses, machine shops, a hospital train unit and railway yards, commissaries and supply depots.

A fortified area since 1776—when it was chosen by Juan Bautista de Anza as military headquarters of the soldiers of Charles III of Spain —the Presidio has been occupied by Spanish garrisons, was host to Frémont's buckskin-clad followers, welcomed volunteers during the Spanish-American War, and trained doughboys for service in the first World War. In 1906 the Presidio became a tent city of refugees of the fire. In 1917-18 it played host in an even grimmer way, housing a concentration camp for enemy aliens. During World War II it was a large supply and service center and the headquarters of the Western Defense Command.

Associated with the Presidio are some of the most illustrious names of the United States Army. Stationed here were Generals William Tecumseh Sherman, P. H. Sheridan, E. V. Sumner, Winfield Scott, Irvin McDowell, and A. S. Johnson. Brigadier-General Fred Funston commanded the post during the reconstruction of the city in 1906 and General John J. Pershing was in command for a short time before leading the Punitive Expedition into Mexico.

On March 26, 1969, the facilities of LETTERMAN GENERAL HOSPITAL, the huge military institution at the eastern end of the Presidio, had its facilities augmented by the opening of a new 550-bed unit that cost $14.3 million. The new hospital provides a wide three-story base surmounted by a slender seven-story tower. Today, Letterman provides definitive medical, surgical and neuropsychiatric care to Armed Forces personnel, active and retired, and their dependents. Although not a sub-command of the Sixth U.S. Army, one of its primary missions is medical support of the Sixth Army. The hospital also receives patients from other areas of the United States and all overseas commands.

The institution was less pretentious when built in 1898 and named in honor of Jonathan Letterman, Medical Director of the Army of the Potomac. One of the finest medical officers of the Civil War, Letterman designed the pavilion type hospital used (with slight modification) by many countries.

Still in use is the old STATION HOSPITAL (near the Administration Building) constructed in 1854 of materials shipped around the Horn.

West of the hospital grounds, bordered on the north by Lincoln Blvd., is the MAIN PARADE GROUND, flanked by great red-brick barracks and their background of eucalyptus trees.

Nearby stands the OFFICERS' CLUB (*private*), only survival of the adobe buildings erected by the Spanish. In 1776 it was the headquarters of Lieutenant Jose Joaquin Moraga of the De Anza expedition (*see A Frontier To Conquer: The White Men Come*), who completed the garrison and dedicated the Presidio on September 17 of that year. Bronze cannons cast 250 years ago in Madrid, veterans of Pizarro's conquest of Peru, flank the club's entrance. A third, pointing at a marker honoring Lieutenant Moraga, bears on its breech the royal arms of Spain and the date 1679.

The NATIONAL MILITARY CEMETERY, Infantry Ter. and Lincoln Blvd., 25 acres of landscaped hillside overlooking the Golden Gate, is surrounded by groves of laurel, cypress, and eucalyptus trees. Among the remains of more than 16,000 men buried here are those of officers and enlisted men from abandoned cemeteries at Fort Klamath, Oregon; Fort Colville, Washington; the Modoc Lava Beds (scene of California's Modoc Indian Wars of 1872-73); and Old Camp Grand in Arizona. Headstones bear the well-known names of McDowell, Shafter, Funston, and Liggett. "Two Bits October 5 1873" is the inscription on a marble stone over the grave of an Indian interpreter from Fort Klamath. A huge heart-shaped plot with a granite monument, dedicated to the Unknown Soldier Dead, marks the burial place of 408 soldiers of World War I. Pauline C. Tyler—Union Spy, is engraved on the headstone of the grave of Pauline Cushman Tyler, young actress who was in the Union services during the Civil War and later received the honorary commission of brevet-major.

CRISSY FIELD, stretching along the Golden Gate between Marine Blvd. and Mason St., is now used mainly as a storage area, railway yard, and landing field for small planes. Named in honor of Major Dana H. Crissy, Air Service pilot who was killed in the Transcontinental Air Races of 1919, the field was used as an army aviation base from 1919 until supplanted in 1936 by Hamilton Field (*see North Bay Tour*).

N. from Lincoln Blvd. on Long Ave. to Marine Dr.; W. on Marine

FORT WINFIELD SCOTT, near the northern limits of the Presidio, was once headquarters of the chain of harbor defenses strung north and south of the Golden Gate, including Forts Barry and Baker (*see North Bay Tour*), Forts Miley and Funston. Within its area were the heavy gun units of the Coast Defense. In 1921 the fort was officially designated to return salutes of foreign vessels of war visiting the Port of San Francisco. Officers and enlisted men occupy the grey stucco buildings replacing the original structure named for General Scott.

FORT POINT, the promontory beyond Fort Winfield Scott, is the northern-most point of the San Francisco Peninsula. Constructed by the United States Army between 1854 and 1861 to guard the Golden Gate, it is the most massive brick fortification to be erected on the west coast of North America. Representative of pre-Civil War military technology, it never saw battle action and has long been obsolete. In 1961 the structure was relinquished by the Army on a lease basis to the custodianship of the Fort Point Museum Association. A bill to make Fort Point a national historic site won approval by the House Interior and Insular Affairs Committee on July 29, 1970, it authorized $5,250,000 to restore the fort. The fort was dedicated as the first National Park site in the San Francisco Bay Area on April 14, 1971, and ordered restored to its Civil War condition. Public facilities and a parking area for 400 cars are provided on the bluff to the east of the Golden Gate Bridge toll plaza. When opened, it is expected that 500,000 people a year will visit this reminder of the past.

Retrace on Marine Dr. to Lincoln Blvd.; W. (then S.) on Lincoln to Washington Blvd.; S. on Washington to Park Blvd.; S. on Park

Occupying 162 acres in the southern and central part of the reservation are the PRESIDIO GOLF LINKS, Washington and Park Blvds.

Adjoining the golf links on the west are the grounds of the six-story, yellow brick MARINE HOSPITAL, foot of Fourteenth Ave., with its surrounding staff quarters, laboratories, laundries, and greenhouses. Number 9 of 25 similar institutions operated by the Federal Public Health Service, its 500 beds are open to merchant sailors and all Federal employees injured in line of duty.

This hospital was built in 1932. The city's first Marine Hospital, a four-story brick building, had been erected 79 years earlier on Rincon Point. The first such institution in the country, said to be the oldest Government service, was founded at Norfolk, Virginia, in 1798, to combat cholera and yellow fever, and occupational diseases caused by unsanitary living conditions aboard early American merchant vessels. A merchant sailor's ticket of admission to these hospitals is a certificate from his ship's master and surgeon presented within six months of his discharge.

Just east of the hospital and within the Presidio is little MOUNTAIN LAKE, the first campsite of the Anza expedition that founded San Francisco in 1776. In 1939 the lake was reduced to half its former size when earth excavated in lowering the grade of the Funston Avenue approach to the Golden Gate Bridge was dumped into it.

Retrace on Park Blvd. to Lincoln Blvd.; S. on Lincoln, which leads into El Camino del Mar

Property of the War Department, but open to picnickers, bass fishermen, and sunbathers is BAKER'S BEACH, foot of Twenty-fifth Ave., a long sandy strip along the western edge of the Presidio (accessible by trails from the southwestern corner of the Presidio and from the foot of Twenty-fifth Ave.). The beach was named for Colonel Edward Dickinson Baker (for whom Fort Baker in Marin County; Baker, Oregon; and San Francisco's Baker Street also were named). An eloquent orator and lawyer, Baker came here in the 1850's and canvassed the State in the cause of the Union. After making himself unpopular by defending Charles Cora during the Vigilante trial of 1856, he moved to Oregon, where he became a United States Senator, but returned to command the first regiment of California volunteers in the Civil War. He was killed in battle in 1861. Near Sea Cliff, the impassible promontory at the southern end of the beach, is an old red-brick pumping station which long ago pumped water from Lobos Creek (southern boundary of the Presidio) through a tunnel at Fort Point to downtown San Francisco, but which now supplies only the reservation.

N. from El Camino del Mar on Twenty-seventh Ave. to Sea Cliff Ave.; W. on Sea Cliff, which leads into a footpath; N. on the footpath

Toward purchase of the short, irregular crescent of JAMES D. PHELAN MEMORIAL BEACH STATE PARK (*barbecue pits; comfort stations*), the man for whom the park is named left a bequest of $50,000. A five-year wrangle over the property by the city, the State, the Allen Company (Sea Cliff development group), and the newspapers culminated in its purchase in 1933 by State and city for $160,000. It still popularly is called China Beach, a name applied since Chinese fishermen camped on the protected inlet—their nightly bonfires giving rise to the legend that the cove was a rendezvous of pirates.

With the city behind it, and a spectacular panorama of the Marin shore, the Pacific Ocean and Golden Gate before it, it is a favored spot for picnicking and sunbathing.

Retrace on footpath to El Camino del Mar; W. on El Camino del Mar

In the extreme northwestern corner of city and peninsula are the 270 green-lawned acres of city-owned LINCOLN PARK, facing seaward on the north and west, bounded on the east by Thirty-third Ave. and on the south by Clement St. and Fort Miley Reserve. The terrain slopes gently to the south and east and drops abruptly to the sheer cliffs above the Golden Gate. El Camino del Mar winds the length of the park, at one point skirting high above the rugged rock-strewn shore. Across the Bay, beyond the Golden Gate Bridge, lie the soft Marin Hills and Point Bonita (*see North Bay Tour*); closer are Land's End and Phelan and Baker's Beaches.

Beneath Lincoln Park's smooth lawns lie the graves of thousands of San Franciscans who died during the latter half of the nineteenth century. Among the cemeteries here were the burial grounds of Chinese and Italians, and here was Potter's Field. The city has kept its promise made when it purchased the property in 1910, and has not disturbed the graves.

On the formally landscaped summit in the northern section of the park stands the city's largest art museum, the CALIFORNIA PALACE OF THE LEGION OF HONOR (*open daily 10-5; parking area; organ concerts Sat. and Sun. 3-4*), a memorial to California's dead in the first World War, the gift (1924) of Adolph B. and Alma de Bretteville Spreckels. The cream-colored palace, closely resembling the eighteenth-century classic Palais de la Légion d'Honneur (Paris, France), is approached through a Roman arch flanked by two porticoes with double rows of Ionic columns. The porticoes abut the two wings of the palace to form a rectangular court. The wings are flanked by peristyles, each with 22 columns, and the main facade is fronted by a portico with six Corinthian columns. One of the five original bronze casts of Auguste Rodin's *The Thinker* occupies the center of the court. The entire building is set off by a stone balustrade. Bronze equestrian statues (Anna Hyatt Huntington, sculptress), *El Cid,* and *Jeanne d'Arc,* flank the path leading to the entrance. A marble plaque beside the doorway, the gift of France, reads: *"Hommage de la France aux héros Californiens morts pour la défense du droit et la liberté"* (France's homage to the California heroes dead in defense of right and liberty).

Of the museum's 19 main-floor galleries, those to the left and rear of the central foyer contain the permanent collection, which includes a series of fine seventeenth-century Flemish tapestries, French tapestries of the seventeenth and eighteenth centuries—many from the Gobelin works, and a set of modern Gobelins presented by the French government. The paintings include a few of the early Italians, Vivarini, Beltraffio, and Fra Bartolemmeo; there are two fine Guardis, among them the *Rialto Bridge;* a Caneletto, and other eighteenth century Venetians. The Dutch school is represented by Rubens, Cuyp, David Teniers, de Vos, and Ruisdael; the Spanish, by Murillo, Velasquez and El Greco's *St. Peter.* The English eighteenth-century paintings number portraits by Raeburn, Lawrence, Reynolds, Hoppner, and Romney. There are two Constables and Turner's *Grand Canal at Venice.* The French eighteenth-century school, including Fragonard, de Troy, and Boucher, is well represented; the work is hung in galleries containing some fine pieces of French furniture of the same period. Among the works of sculpture are bronzes and marbles by Rodin and others influenced by him, including Arthur Putnam, and a bronze bust by Jacob Epstein.

The galleries to the right of the main foyer are used for loan exhibits. The lower floor houses a little theater and the Albert Bender collection of oriental painting, sculpture, and ceramics.

In the center of the diveway before the museum a 120-foot wooden flagpole marks the western terminus of the Lincoln Highway (US 40). A few yards east is *The Shades,* three nude male bronzes by Rodin, standing with heads bowed and arms outstretched. The group is a memorial to Raphael Weill, pioneer merchant and philanthropist. The semicircular stone balustrade at the edge of the parkway overlooks a curious obelisk of bronze, rising 24 feet from a 7-foot-square granite base bearing the information that it was "presented to the Ladies Seamen's Friend Society by Dr. Henry Cogswell. A landmark of the seamen's last earthly port and resting-place in which he waits the advent of the Great Pilot of his eternal destiny. . . ."

S. from the Palace of the Legion of Honor on an unnamed drive

Facing the driveway near one of the main entrances (Thirty-fourth Ave. and Clement St.), in the southeastern section of the park, is headquarters of the 18-hole LINCOLN PARK MUNICIPAL GOLF COURSE. LINCOLN PARK CLUBHOUSE (*lockers, restaurant*) is a large one-story white frame building which has the look of a comfortable country home. Near by is the CHILDREN'S PLAYGROUND (*play apparatus; handball courts*).

Retrace on unnamed drive to El Camino del Mar; NW. from El Camino del Mar on a footpath

A WPA-built trail, below El Camino del Mar just northeast of the Palace of the Legion of Honor, skirts the cliffside to LAND'S END, the wave-dashed headland forming the northwest rim of the city.

From the rocky shoal waters the hoarse siren of MILE ROCK LIGHTHOUSE (automatic since 1965) on the larger of the two Mile Rocks, echoes along the cliffs when fogs shroud the Bay; its light, atop a white cylindrical tower 78 feet above the water, is visible for 14 miles. Before the construction of the light (1903-06) the S. S. *Rio de Janeiro* foundered on Fort Point Reef (*see The Harbor and Its Islands*) in 1901, and sank with a loss of more than 100 lives and a reputed fortune in bullion and silk.

THE U.S.S. SAN FRANCISCO MEMORIAL is emplaced 200 ft. above the shore line of the Pacific Ocean on the edge of a natural esplanade on Land's End. The Memorial, latitude 37° 47′ North, and longitude 122° 30′ West, is oriented to the Great Circle course to Guadalcanal, 5,100 miles across the Pacific. It is easy of access being on the edge of the Observation Point parking area.

The Memorial is the actual bridge structure of the U.S.S. San Francisco, riddled with shells from the Japanese Naval Task Force during the night action at Guadalcanal, Nov. 12-13, 1942, together with the ship's mast upon which is mounted the ship's bell. The mast is set in a concrete pedestal to which are attached three bronze plaques—the citation for the action by Commander-in-Chief Franklin Delano Roosevelt, the list of those who gave their lives in the action, and the dedication.

Near the wreckage of the *Lyman K. Stewart,* a few stark, jutting beams compose the remaining FRAMEWORK OF PELTON'S TIDE MACHINE—formerly referred to as "Pelton's Folly"—a structure built on an isolated rock facing the sea. Here Alexander Pelton planned to harness the tides and thus develop electric power. An experimental plant costing $250,000 was three times swept out to sea. When his backer (said to be Adolph Sutro) would advance no further funds and his own were exhausted, Pelton abandoned the project.

Retrace on footpath to El Camino del Mar; W. on El Camino del Mar to Seal Rock Ave.; E. on Seal Rock

The UNITED STATES VETERANS' ADMINISTRATION FACILITY, Seal Rock and Forty-fifth Aves., is housed in a group of ultra-modern hospital buildings constructed of terra cotta and reinforced concrete, combining pyramidal motifs of Mayan Temple architecture with modern design. Built in 1933, the facility was opened as a diagnostic center to serve all veterans' hospitals west of the Mississippi River (and, by special arrangement, to treat also a limited number of Canadian veterans), one of 81 such institutions in the United States at that time. More than a hospital, it serves as a clearing house for veterans seeking compensation adjustments, physical examinations, and similar services. A consulting staff of many of the Pacific Coast's best-known physicians and surgeons augments the staff of doctors, dentists, nurses, ward attendants, and kitchen workers attached to the institution. Among the subsidiary buildings—in addition to the laboratories and the clinics—are quarters for nurses and married attendants, two duplex buildings for resident physicians, surgeons' homes, and a library, a recreation hall and a canteen.

During 1970 the hospital cared for 4,500 in-patients and treated 80,000 out-patients.

The facility is in the extreme southern section of FORT MILEY UNITED STATES MILITARY RESERVATION (*private*), whose 50 acres were set aside in 1900 and named in honor of Lieutenant Colonel John D. Miley, who had died at Manila the preceding year. A fortified reserve, it is surrounded by a strong wire fence and patrolled day and night by sentries. In 1911 Fort Miley was made a subpost of the Presidio.

Retrace on Seal Rock Ave. to El Camino del Mar; S. on El Camino del Mar to Point Lobos Ave.

SUTRO HEIGHTS (*open daily 9-5; no vehicles permitted*), Pt. Lobos and Forty-eighth Aves., once the home of Adolph Sutro, is now a public park. One of many enterprises of the Comstock millionaire who invested a fortune in the preservation of the city's natural beauty, the Heights are his most intimate memorial.

Sutro Heights commands a view of three miles of ocean beach below. Among the groves of trees in this neglected park are remains of broken statues. A white-painted wooden arch and gateway flanked by reclining stone lions marks the park's entrance. Directly within are an octagonal-shaped station house formerly used by a gatekeeper, and twin life-sized iron figures of guards in seventeenth-century cuirasses and helmets. A graveled central pathway, formerly a driveway, leads southward into the center of the garden under trees of a myriad variety, among them palms, firs, monkey trees, Monterey cypresses, and several from the islands of the South Pacific; a Norfolk Island pine, a Hawaiian *cazana,* and an *aurecara* of New Zealand. A smaller path, branching from the main pathway, leads to the top of the heights on the garden's western edge, a steeply descending cliff with terraced rock gardens planted in evergreens and perennials. A low granite wall on the edge of the terrace serves as a base for statues and urns placed alternately. Here also are two large muzzle-loading cannon, near each of which, as if in readiness, stand piles of huge iron shot. These ornaments originally decorated one of the city's earliest pleasure resorts, Woodward's Gardens.

A few paces back from the cliff's edge stood Adolph Sutro's home, built in the late 1870's and condemned and demolished in 1939. Only evidence today that a mansion once was here is a small stone strongroom, fitted with a heavy iron door and furnished with a safe bearing the imprint, "Adolph Sutro."

A native of Germany but a resident of California since 1850, Sutro had achieved wealth and prominence as a mining engineer. Visiting the property for the first time in the early 1880's, accompanied by his small daughter Emma, he was attracted by its possibilities, and forthwith purchased it from Samuel Tetlow, onetime proprietor of the Bella Union. He at once erected a new home on the site, acquired a stable of thoroughbred horses, imported statuary from Europe, and collected rare plants from many parts of the world. In the following years he spent more than $1,000,000 improving the estate, which at one time employed fifteen caretakers and three gardeners, in addition to a corps of house servants.

The Heights quickly became a fashionable gathering place, and its owner's hospitality a thing of renown. On one occasion a performance was given of Shakespeare's *As You Like It,* the cast of which included

Ada Rehan and John Drew, both of Augustin Daly's company. It proved eminently successful, although the footlights were only Japanese lanterns; the stage, one of the lawns in front of the mansion.

An uncommon foresight moved Sutro to acquire properties adjoining the Heights, and his estate eventually embraced much of the city which now skirts the sea-front. With Edward B. Pond, then mayor of San Francisco, he planned the magnificent system of boulevards from Thirty-third Avenue westward to the ocean, an area which included the sites of what is the present Lincoln Park and the Veterans' Facility, the Cliff House, and Sutro Heights. Sutro's public-spiritedness was perpetuated by his descendants. "Open house" was always maintained at Sutro Heights; a sign placed near the entrance gate for many years invited the public "to walk, ride, and drive therein." Sutro Heights in 1898 came into the possession of Sutro's daughter, Dr. Emma Sutro Merritt, who left it as a public park to the city on her death in 1938.

W. from El Camino del Mar on Point Lobos Ave.; N. from Point Lobos on Merrie Way to a footpath; W. on footpath

Westernmost tip of San Francisco is POINT LOBOS, called Punta de los Lobos Marinos (Point of the Sea Wolves) by the Spanish because of its proximity to the sea lions on Seal Rocks. Lieutenant Juan Manuel de Ayala, who had sailed past the point and through the Golden Gate in the *San Carlos* on the evening of August 5, 1775, had charted the promontory as Angel de la Guarde (Guardian Angel). Somewhere on the heights above, on December 4, 1774, Captain Fernando de Rivera y Moncado and Father Francisco Palou, with four soldiers from their exploring party climbed a summit from which they saw "a great bay . . . its waters were as quiet as those of a great lake." On a rocky headland, "which up to this time had never received the footprint of Spaniard or Christian," they set up a cross, supporting it by two rocks.

Seventy-nine years later enterprising Yankees were erecting a cross of a different nature on Point Lobos: that carrying the Pacific Coast's first telegraph wires to the Merchants' Exchange by way of Telegraph Hill. A lookout signalled news of the arrival of vessels.

Retrace to Point Lobos Ave.; W. on Point Lobos, which becomes Great Highway

SUTRO BATHS, a landmark of the last century vanished from the San Francisco scene in a spectacular fire on Sunday, June 26, 1966. Located at Point Lobos Ave. near Great Highway, it covered three acres of sloping beach in the lee of Point Lobos. Opened March 14, 1896, by Adolph Sutro it was long advertised as the world's largest six indoor pools; of both fresh and salt water, varying in size, depth, and temperature. It is said 25,000 persons visited Sutro's in one day. Wide-tiered galleries and promenades, bordered with palms, tropical plants, natural history specimens, and gay-colored tables and chairs accommodated 7,000 spectators. The water for the baths was supplied by an ingenious use of the ocean waves. A basin scooped out of solid rock received the water that dashed over the top, then it was conducted to a settling tank; by numerous small canals it made its way into the various swimming tanks, the largest containing the sea water in its natural state, the others being heated to different temperatures. If the tides were low, water was forced in at a rate of 6,000 gallons per minute by means of a large turbine pump placed at sea level, in a cave-like excavation hollowed out of the solid cliff and driven by means of a steam-engine, which was later replaced by a 35 horse power, 2-phase motor that could be controlled from the switchboard room and could be operated to suit the tides. The refuse water in the main outlet, into which all the tanks emptied, was piped hundreds of feet to the side of the headlands, where it passed into the tidal current away from the baths. The baths were protected from the sea by two enormous breakwaters aggregating 700 feet in length containing 750,000 cubic feet of rock.

After Sutro's death in 1898 his daughter Dr. Emma Merritt operated the baths until 1934 when Adolph G. Sutro took over. In 1937 one leg of the large L-shaped pool was turned into an ice rink. The baths closed September 1, 1952.

The CLIFF HOUSE Point Lobos Ave. at Great Highway, was last modernized in 1950. The restaurant was closed in 1969. Besides the restaurant, there was a bar, and gift shop. The cocktail lounge is finished in redwood and has a large brick fireplace in which open fires glow. From the lounge guests seated at the great plate glass windows on clear days look beyond Seal Rocks, for miles, across the Pacific.

The present Cliff House is the third to occupy the site. The first was built in 1863. Traffic to the cafe in the 1860's was by way of the Point Lobos Toll Road, built by James Phelan, William Herrick, John Buckley, and Salem Burdell. A horse-drawn omnibus made the trip from Portsmouth Square to the beach; the fare was 50¢. Second tenant was retired seaman Captain J. R. Foster, who managed the Cliff House for nearly two decades. When the Cliff House became less fashionable, Foster made it a rendezvous of politicians and "gaily dressed nymphs."

When Adolph Sutro purchased the property about 1879 it was known as the Cliff House ranch. Said Sutro: "I believe there was a dilapidated little farm house down on the beach." On the same beach in earlier years had been Seal Rock House (also confused by some historians with the Cliff House)—"a curious architectural conglomeration" formed by frequent additions to an original "nondescript building"—said to have been managed by Captain Foster.

The Cliff House's first mishap occurred in January, 1887, when the schooner *Parallel,* with her cargo of 80,000 pounds of dynamite, was driven into the bluff below; abandoned by captain and crew, the vessel was pounded against the rocks until the dynamite exploded and seriously damaged the building's foundations. On Christmas, 1894, the Cliff House burned to the ground. Reported the *Call:* "The fire was a hidden one between ceiling and walls . . . started from a defective flue. . . . Toward midnight hacks began to arrive from the city with those curious to view the destruction of one of the most noted resorts in the world. . . . Jets of flame followed it until the bold brow of the cliff shone out . . . It lit up the white forms of the plaster gods and goddesses on the parapet, and revealed the low house of the master and the ghastly figures under the trees [of Sutro's Heights]. . . . The hoarse bellowing of the frightened seals as they fled from the rocks to the depths was heard. . . . The corpulent king of the herd, Benjamin Harrison Cleveland, who succeeded Ben Butler, was first to seek refuge from the falling embers. . . ."

Adolph Sutro erected the second Cliff House two years later—a picturesque structure in the design of a chateau with spiralling towers. The dedication of what jokingly was called Sutro's gingerbread palace occasioned great celebration. With this auspicious start began another era of popularity for the resort. It was a favorite of James Flood, James Fair, John Mackay, and Claus Spreckels; played host to Presidents Hayes, Grant, McKinley, Roosevelt, and Taft; and was a rendezvous of such theatrical and literary lights as Sarah Bernhardt, Adelina Patti, Mark Twain, and Bret Harte. In 1901, E. D. Beylard of Burlingame (wrote Oscar Lewis and Carrol Hall) "inaugurated a tally-ho service for the benefit of the Palace [Hotel] guests. Beylard borrowed his idea from the East, where . . . smart hotels were offering daily rides on the tops of coaches driven by young men of social importance. The Beylard tally-ho . . . each afternoon . . . proceeded, via Golden Gate Park, to the Cliff House; there the four horses were changed and the return trip was made by a different route. Twelve passengers were carried and the charge was two dollars per person."

The Cliff House withstood the earthquake and fire of 1906, only to be destroyed by fire the following year. Immediately rebuilt by Sutro, its popularity continued until Prohibition. One attempt to operate it on a temperance basis was unsuccessful. In 1937 the abandoned Cliff House was purchased by concessionaires George K. and Leo C. Whitney, who modernized and reopened the famous old cafe.

The Cliff House was the scene of the first parachute jump in history according to the *Illinois Fact Book and Historical Almanac.* Thomas Scott Baldwin, a native of Quincy, Ill., and an aerialist, made the jump Jan. 30, 1887, after arranging with the carnival manager for a fee of $1 a foot. He dropped 1,000 ft. and thereafter performed successfully in major cities and in Europe.

Legal residents of the city and wards of the Park Commission since 1887, when their hauling ground was deeded by Congress to the City and County of San Francisco, are the sea lions on SEAL ROCKS, 400 feet offshore below the Cliff House. Known as Steller sea lions, they are closely related to the fur seal; both are of the eared seal family. Unlike the more modest leopard (or harbor) seal, also found along the California coast, they are polygamous, gregarious, and noisy—filling the air with their raucous roaring and barking. These Seal Rock lions breed during the latter half of June (the cow produces only one pup in a season) at their rookery on Ano Nuevo Island, about 25 miles south. Once slaughtered almost to extinction—both by fishermen, who believed that the animals interfered with their nets and depleted the fish supply, and by hunters, for their oil and hides—they are protected today by State and Federal laws. Hardly had they recovered from their alarm at the burning of the Cliff House in 1894 when the earthquake of 1906 provided a more serious disturbance—one so great that they retreated to the Farallones and did not return for several years.

Crowds have gathered on occasions to watch swimming races around the Seal Rocks. More thrilling were performances by tightrope walkers James Cooke and Rose Celeste, who balanced to the rocks and back on different occasions in the 1860's. A suspension bridge to the rocks constructed later was abandoned after it overturned with about 20 pedestrians, injuring several.

The OCEAN BEACH, between the Cliff House and Sloat Blvd., is thronged on pleasant days with picnickers, surf and sun bathers, equestrians, and sightseers. The pedestrian esplanade bordering the sea-wall affords a broad view of the Pacific. A vicious undertow is created by the sudden drop beyond the edge of the surf and annually takes its toll of the unwary.

At the northern end of the Ocean Beach is PLAYLAND AT THE BEACH, an amusement area consisting of various "rides," a score of games of chance and "skill," shooting galleries, fun houses, many eating places. In 1929 George and Leo Whitney, professional concessionaires, forced to return from operating Melbourne, Australia's Luna Park by the outbreak of the World War, were successful in taking over this entire area from its several owners. Born in Kansas about 1890, the Whitney brothers' careers began early with their perfection of a "quick-finishing" photographic process. Their first small photography shop was so successful that they began operating penny arcades; profits from these financed their concessions at the Alaska-Yukon Exposition of 1909, in Seattle, Washington.

One and one-half million dollars raised by bond issue in 1927 financed the two-year construction of the GREAT HIGHWAY AND ESPLANADE along Ocean Beach from the Cliff House to Sloat Boulevard, a distance of nearly three miles. Construction of the 4,298-foot-long Esplanade, extending from the highway's northern end to Lincoln Way, had begun as early as 1916, but was not completed until the new funds were acquired. Several methods of protecting the road along the ocean had failed until City Engineer Michael O'Shaughnessy designed the present tight cut-off wall of reinforced concrete interlocking sheet piling, which extends 12 feet below extreme low tide. Extending shoreward from the parapet wall, the Esplanade consists of flanking 20-foot sidewalks, 15 feet of lawn, and a paved highway between 150 and 200 feet in width. For a stretch of 3,000 feet, opposite Golden Gate Park, the Great Highway is the widest boulevard in the United States. Paralleling the road between Lincoln Way and Sloat Boulevard is a bridle path—a link in the continuous pathway from the Presidio to Fleishhacker's by way of Golden Gate Park.

Great Highway becomes Skyline Blvd.

Set in a little valley encircled by wooden hills are the 128 landscaped acres of FLEISHHACKER PLAYFIELD AND ZOOLOGICAL GARDENS, foot of Great Highway at Sloat and Skyline Blvds. This recreation center dates from 1922, when the city acquired from the Spring Valley Water Company 60 acres on which to construct a playground and pool. Only 37 acres at first were developed; opened in 1924, the park was named for Herbert Fleishhacker, then president of the Park Commission, who had donated the pool and the Mothers' House.

Said to be the world's largest outdoor plunge is the SWIMMING POOL, 1,000 feet long, 150 feet wide, with a graduated depth of from 3 to 14 feet. Several thousand persons can swim at one time in its 6,500,000 gallons of warmed salt water. Considered a noteworthy achievement is the system of heating the sea water. Nearby under windblown cypresses are plots for sunbathing.

The PLAYFIELD (*open daily 10-5, free*), in addition to an unusually large variety of play apparatus, boasts a merry-go-round, a miniature railway, and pony rides (*small fee*). Larger children and adults use the tennis courts, baseball diamond, and sporting greens. Facing the one-foot-deep wading pool for tots is the MOTHERS' HOUSE, a low, stuccoed, tile-roofed building providing a resting place for mothers and children; the gift of Fleishhacker, it is a memorial to his mother. Interior murals and mosaics are the work of WPA artists.

Adjoining the playground is the ZOO (*open 10-5:30; ages 16-64, 50¢; free on Tuesday*). Begun in 1929 with a few lion cubs and monkeys, gradually more animals were acquired (by purchase and donation), until the animal, bird, and reptile population reached 1,000. Noted is the fine collection of "cats," which includes lions, tigers, leopards, lynxes, and panthers.

In 1935 sixty-eight acres adjoining the zoo were purchased, and here WPA labor constructed the fine ZOOLOGICAL GARDENS (Lewis Hobart, architect), modeled after Germany's famous Hagenbeck Zoo. Here, among man-made streams, waterfalls, islands, cliffs, and caves, are simulated natural habitats of many animals—separated (where practical) from spectators only by moats and designed to give the animals the illusion of freedom. The concrete of the bear pits resembles natural rock. The aquatic bird building stands on the shores of a specially built lake; the "flight cage" is 220 feet long, with rocky refuges, nesting places, trees, shrubs, and a running stream. Also in the gardens are Monkey Island; the pachyderm house, with its separate enclosures and private swimming pools; lion dens; and a lake built for beavers and thoughtfully supplied with "chewy" logs. Construction of the gardens continued from the late 1930's into the next decade.

Adjoining Fleishhacker Playfield and Zoo on the south is FORT FUNSTON (*private*). Bordered on the east by Skyline Blvd., it stretches for about a mile and a half along the coast. Established as a military reservation during the Spanish-American War (1898), it was known as the Laguna Merced Military Reservation until 1917, when it was renamed in honor of Major-General Frederick Funston, commander of the Army troops who policed San Francisco after the 1906 disaster.

Historic LAGUNA DE NUESTRA SENORA DE LA MERCED (Sp., Lake of Our Lady of Mercy), Lake Merced and Skyline Blvds., is about five acres of fresh water surrounded by sand dunes and golf courses. The lake's original depth was lowered 30 feet on the night of November 22, 1852, by a mysterious disturbance surmised to be a temblor.

SAN FRANCISCO STATE COLLEGE, Holloway Ave. and 19th St., occupies a completely new plant built since 1945 on a gentle slope rolling toward Lake Merced. Originally devoted to teacher training, it has since added a program in liberal arts and sciences under the California State College System. A score of buildings on its 94-acre campus include a five-story Psychology-Air Science structure, a great Library with more than 315,000 vols., a School of Creative Arts complex, an eight-story Life Science Bldg., a College Commons with four dining halls, a three-level parking garage, and Cox Stadium, seating 6,500. In the 1971 school year the college enrolled 18,928 and had a faculty of 1,296.

During 1968 and 1969 San Francisco State received national attention when militant students demanded an autonomous Black Student Union and a black studies curriculum directed by black faculty and students. Two presidents resigned when they were unable to effect a compromise between the students and the board of trustes; an instructor and a leader were suspended and a faculty group voted to halt classes. Dr. Samuel I. Hayakawa took charge as acting president, ordered classes to be resumed and warned that faculty members who were absent five days would be considered resigned. When violence erupted he called the police to the campus and restored order. The college since has made some concessions to black studies and needs.

Retrace on Skyline Blvd. to Lake Merced Blvd.; SE. on Lake Merced

The PACIFIC ROD AND GUN CLUB (*private*), near Lake Merced Blvd. on the southwest shore of Lake Merced, is housed in three wooden buildings made of six schoolhouses purchased from the city. Waters of the south lake abound in black bass, blue gills, and other freshwater fish; these are replenished from the north lake breeding ground, which is closed to fishing and boating.

The site of the BRODERICK-TERRY DUEL can be viewed by following a path that leads from Lakeview Drive and El Portal Way, Daly City. Two granite shafts mark the positions of the contestants in the encounter which welded California's political factions on the eve of the Civil War. About 10 yards north a granite memorial bears the information that "United States Senator David C. Broderick and Judge David S. Terry fought a duel on this ground in the early morning of Tuesday, September 13, 1859. Senator Broderick received a wound from which he died three days later. The affair marked the end of dueling in California. . . ." Terry, Chief Justice of the California Supreme Court, had accused Senator Broderick of defeating his candidacy for reelection. Previously Broderick had befriended the fiery Southerner, who in 1856 had been imprisoned for stabbing an officer of the Vigilance Committee. On learning of Terry's arraignment of him before the 1859 State Convention of the Democratic Party, the "grand, gloomy and peculiar" Broderick remarked: "I have said that I considered him the only honest man on the supreme bench, but now I take it all back." Informed of this statement, Judge Terry demanded a retraction; and when this was refused, "the satisfaction usual among gentlemen. . . ."

Arriving at the appointed spot with their respective seconds in the raw foggy dawn, each contestant was provided with a Lafoucheux dueling pistol (these hair-trigger weapons had been chosen, according to custom, by the challenger). With his back to the rising sun, nervously fingering his weapon, Broderick fired at the count of "one," his bullet striking the ground midway between him and his adversary. Terry, with deliberate aim, shot Broderick through the right breast. Followed by a crowd of some 60 spectators, a carriage bearing the fatally wounded Senator drove the ten miles to Black Point where he died in the home of Leonidas Haskell.

A wooden plaque among rolling hills marks the northernmost camp site of the RIVERA Y MONCADA EXPEDITION, Lake Merced

Blvd. just north of the San Francisco-San Mateo County Line; here at eleven o'clock on the morning of December 4, 1774, headquarters were established by the third Spanish party sent to explore San Francisco Bay. It consisted of 16 soldiers, Father Francisco Palou, and a muleteer (with mules laden with provisions for 40 days), under the command of Captain Fernando Rivera y Moncada. An hour later Rivera, Palou, and four soldiers proceeded up the coast, where they planted a large wooden cross on Point Lobos. Returning to their hillside camp—which then overlooked a small stream running into Lake Merced—the whole party followed Portola's old route back to Monterey without having chosen a site for the projected Mission San Francisco de Asis—the selection of which had been one of the chief purposes of the expedition.

E. from Lake Merced Blvd. on Brotherhood Way to Junipero Serra Blvd.; S. on Junipero Serra

Organized in 1895, the SAN FRANCISCO GOLF CLUB, LTD. (*private*), Junipero Serra Blvd. and Brotherhood Way, occupies an 18-hole course of 184 acres bordered on the south by the city and county limits.

Retrace and Continue N. on Junipero Serra Blvd. to Nineteenth Ave.; NW. on Nineteenth to Sloat Blvd.; W. on Sloat

SIGMUND STERN MEMORIAL GROVE (*barbecue pits; picnic tables; sanitary facilities*), Sloat Blvd. between Nineteenth and Twenty-fifth Ave., occupies a natural amphitheater 100 feet below street level. The grass-carpeted glade is sheltered by eucalyptus trees planted nearly 70 years ago by homesteader George Greene, a New England horticulturist who came around the Horn in 1847. When it became known in the early 1850's that Congress was to pass an act giving title of this property to those holding land there, Greene and several other homesteaders erected a fort, and for weeks guarded their property day and night against encroachers. In 1892 Greene established the Trocadero Inn; boasting an open-air dance pavilion and trout lake, it was until 1916 a popular resort. The inn was used in 1907 as a hideout by ousted political boss Abe Ruef, and it was here that he was captured.

Mrs. Sigmund Stern purchased about 12 acres of the land and presented it to the city in 1931 as a memorial to her husband, with the provision that it be used only for recreational and cultural purposes. Enlarged later by the purchase of additional acreage by the Recreation Commission, and again in 1937 when another gift of Mrs. Stern made possible the acquisition of still more land, the park today covers more than 33 acres.

Golden Gate Park

"I'd go out into the country and walk along a stream until I came to a bonnie brook. Then I'd come back to the park and I'd reproduce what Nature had done."

—JOHN McLAREN

FEW demonstrations of man's mastery over nature have been more convincing than the creation of Golden Gate Park: that long stretch of evergreen outdoors—nine city blocks wide and four and a half miles long—cutting a swath from the heart of the city to the ocean's shore. Its grassy meadows and limpid lakes, its forested hills that alternate in the apparent confusion of a natural wilderness, interlaced with winding roadways, bridle paths, and foot trails—all are man's handiwork. When the city set out to create a park here in 1870, these 1,017 acres were a windswept desert. "Of all the elephants the city of San Francisco ever owned," said the Santa Rosa *Democrat* in 1873, "they now have the largest and heaviest in the shape of 'Golden Gate Park,' a dreary waste of shifting sand hills where a blade of grass cannot be raised without four posts to support it and keep it from blowing away." Three-quarters of a century later that "dreary waste" is a sylvan retreat in the midst of the city, where sheep graze placidly along rolling pastures, darting squirrels, scurrying rabbits, and chattering blackbirds fill the air with forest sounds, and haughty peacocks flaunt their plumage across velvet lawns. Thousands eat Sunday and holiday lunches on the shady slopes soft with leaf mold and sprawl in the sun on the wide lawns. The oldsters, conservatively dressed, listen to the afternoon band concerts, visit the museums, or gather around the checker boards at the eastern end of the park. The youngsters, clad in bright-colored sports clothes, play tennis, ride bicycles, crowd the children's playground or tumble after footballs.

Today as one walks among the innumerable flower beds and gardens, past lakes, brooks, and waterfalls, over rolling hills and pastoral meadows, he can hardly believe this magnificent evergreen playground entirely artificial. Buffalo, deer, and elk roam in paddocks landscaped to give an impression of fencelessness. So numerous are foxes and other small predatory animals that a hunter is required the year round to prevent destruction of other animal life. The dozen lakes of the park afford feeding and resting places for thousands of waterfowl.

Within the park's confines grow more than 5,000 kinds of plants. One may wander through groves of eucalyptus and conifers, through wild, brush-filled canyons or shaded glens luxuriant with ferns and blackberries, across hillsides riotous under a blanket of yellow chrysanthemums, violet wild radishes, brilliant orange poppies, snapdragons, and purple cestrum. One may find yellow daisies from South Africa or silverleafed ones from Teneriffe, fuchsias from Mexico and Peru, abelias from Mexico and the Himalayas, brooms from the Canaries and South Africa, cypress from Kashmir. Here grow the exotic crimson Waratah from New South Wales, blooming in the United States for the first time, and centuryplants, staggered in development so that at least one plant blooms every three years. The 109 varieties of eucalypti include the rare *alpina* from Australia, which rarely attains more than 12 feet in height. The acacias, as varied as the eucalypti, include a rare pink variety. More than 100 species of conifers are represented, including the Monterey pine and Monterey cypress, the Torrey pine, and the New Zealand kauri-pine. The native live oak is also prominent, as is the *Quercus ilex* from Italy. The principal shrubs are of the genus *Veronica* from New Zealand and the genus *Escalonia* from Chile. Of rhododendrons, which grow in unnumbered thousands throughout Golden Gate Park, there are more than 300 varieties— some from Thibet, India, Japan, Java, Portugal, Siberia, and Yunnan— and from 300 to 400 hybrids, many of which have been developed locally; the display is unrivaled except in Kew Gardens, which boasts more varieties but fewer specimens.

When public demand for a large recreation ground in San Francisco began to arise in the early 1860's, claimants to the area of the present park were asked to give up some of their land in exchange for an absolute title to the land which they retained. During the ensuing long battle over land titles in the courts and the legislature, Mayor Frank McCoppin, twice led delegations to the State Capitol to demand that the area be saved for a park. Finally, in 1868, $801,593 were paid for the desired 1,017 acres. In 1870 Governor Henry H. Haight appointed the first San Francisco Park Commission. The following year, when he had completed a preliminary survey of the proposed Golden Gate Park, William Hammond Hall was appointed Park Superintendent and authorized to proceed with the development.

To most people, the project of growing trees and grass on shifting sand was a foolish dream—and for years it appeared they were not mistaken. When in 1887 a new superintendent was appointed—a sandy-haired young Scottish landscape gardener, John McLaren—cultivation had been confined largely to the eastern end of the park. The Park Commission told McLaren: "We want you to make Golden Gate Park one of the beauty spots of the world. Can you do it?" He answered: "With your aid, gentlemen, and God be willing, that I shall do." And he kept his word.

With the treescape of the eastern part well established, the great task of improving the park proper remained. The two chief problems were to discover an economical and consistent source of fresh water and to fix in position the constantly moving sand dunes. The first was solved when subterranean streams were tapped south of Strawberry Hill. The second demanded infinite patience in experiment.

When native lupine and barley were found to be unable to hold the sand, McLaren resorted to the *Ammophila arenaria*, "sand-loving sand grass," a beach grass common to the coast of Northern Europe. Sending out a mass of roots well below the surface, this grass continues to grow as fast as the wind covers it over, refusing to be buried, until the dune has reached such a height that the wind velocity will no longer carry sand to the top. Second plant to be utilized in fixing the contours of the sand was the Australian tea-tree, a soil-holding shrub closely related to eucalyptus; third was the Australian acacia, a leguminous shrub, a soil-builder as well as holder. The few blue gums planted by settlers in the early 1850's and a few native live oaks were augmented by systematic planting of additional blue gums (eucalypti), manzanita, madrone, and laurel. Principal grasses to follow were Kentucky bluegrass, Australian ryegrass, fescue, and *Poa annua*.

The first years were hard for "Uncle John" McLaren. Time after time he awakened to find thousands of young trees covered with sand. Patiently he dug them out and nursed them back to life. Needing fertilizer, he asked for, and was given, the sweepings from the city streets. (When the automobile drove the horses from the streets, "Uncle John" was annoyed.) Allowed by tacit agreement with city officials to do his own hiring and firing, McLaren refused consistently to employ relatives or friends of the men in power. Neither would he tolerate interference in his plans. When he discovered the three young oaks planted in the parking area before the Park Police Station being dragged away with a steam roller, he replaced the trees. Later that day, when he found the oaks gone again and workmen paving the parking space, "Uncle John" had his own men shovel out the cement as fast as it was poured in. The Board of Public Works gave up its attempt to pave the area, and today three sturdy oaks hide the police station as McLaren had intended they should.

An attempt to retire McLaren when he reached 60 occasioned a minor uprising by the people of San Francisco; "Uncle John" stayed on. When he was 70 the people again came to his defense. In 1922 the Board of Supervisors adopted a resolution that not only exempted him from enforced retirement but raised his wages. He lived to celebrate his ninety-sixth birthday—still superintendent of the park—before his death early in 1943.

Despite its semi-miraculous development, Golden Gate Park was not easily to supplant Woodward's Gardens in the affection of the public. Woodward's in early years had been the established mecca for lovers of outdoor amusement. However, an elaborate children's playground (1886) and free municipal Sunday concerts in the "shell" built in the huge open-air tree-flanked Music Concourse added to the park's popularity. With the celebration of San Francisco's Midwinter Fair within its borders in 1894, Golden Gate Park came permanently into its own. Some of the special features of the Chicago World's Fair, including John Philip Sousa's band and Fritz Scheel's Vienna Orchestra, gave repeat performances at the Midwinter Fair. Thousands visited the conservatory to see the world's largest flower, a pond lily that came to be known as the *Victoria regina*. The famous Japanese Tea Garden, built for the fair, was so popular that it never was torn down.

Throughout the resplendent "gay nineties," the park became the rendezvous for the "horse-and-buggy" social set. Each Sunday they came dressed in the latest fashion. Some rode dog carts, some bicycles—built for one, two, three, or four—but most drove carriages. Trumpeting importantly for right of way, the tally-ho, with its complement of gaily caparisoned riders, cut across bicycles and dog-carts alike. Carriage occupants bowed politely to acquaintances, the men lifting their shining silk toppers. Less dignified were the bicyclists, one of whom inspired a columnist's rude comment, "ocean breezes reveal that—she pads." Tandem bicycles were eclipsed by four-passenger "bikes," seating two pairs of young men and women astride. A female "scorcher" arrested for speeding at the reckless rate of "ten miles an hour," also had committed the heinous crime of wearing the "new-fangled Bloomers." When the noisy horseless carriage first appeared, those seeking to heighten their social prestige by appearing in the park in these gasoline or electric "buggies" were chagrined when Golden Gate Park remained proscribed territory for vehicles mechanically self-propelled (the rule was enforced for several years).

Still observed is McLaren's early refusal to allow "Keep Off the Grass" signs. As in the days after the earthquake and fire of 1906, when the park provided haven for countless refugees, whole families still seek relief on its green swards whenever the city is engulfed by one of its rare heat waves.

And meanwhile, as the never-ending stream of visitors continues, the park grows in beauty. What today is a dry canyon tomorrow may be a sparkling brook. Up to the end of his life "Uncle John," assisted in the late 1930's by WPA labor, kept on shaping the park as he wanted it to be. He lived to be proud of his redwood forest, which he started growing from seeds when he was 80. People laughed. But today the trees are 30 feet high. In his half century as the park's creator, "Uncle John" had planted a million trees. Then he began planting his second-million and watching them grow.

PARK INFORMATION

Information Service: Information and maps at Park Lodge, near Stanyan and Fell Sts.

Streetcars and Buses: Municipal Ry. 1, 2, 5, or 38 coach or the N streetcar, and transfer to the No. 10 Monterey coach which goes through the Park.

Traffic Regulations: 15¾ miles of drives and roads, used by some 45,000 vehicles daily. No trucks, or delivery vehicles except on transverse drives, Ninth Ave. and Twenty-Fourth Ave. Speed limit 25 mph. Parking allowed, except where forbidden by signs. No double parking.

Accommodations: Drinking fountains and comfort stations throughout park. Tea and rice cakes at Oriental Tea Garden. Picknicking allowed on all lawns; barbecue pits near Horseshoe Courts; tables near Children's Playground, Pioneer Log Cabin, and in George Washington Bicentennial Grove. Emergency Hospital (always open) near Stanyan and Frederick Sts.

Art Collections and Museums: M. H. de Young Memorial Museum; lectures and study courses; classes in painting and modelling for children Sat. mornings, for adults Sat. afternoons. North American Hall, Stimson African Hall, Steinhart Aquarium.

Band Concerts: Music Concourse, Sun. and holidays 2-4:30.

Archery: Local, regional, and National tournaments in Golden Gate Park Stadium; participants provide own equipment.

Baseball: 9 diamonds between 5th and 7th Aves., near Lincoln Way; additional grounds in Recreation Field and near Golden Gate Park Stadium.

Basketball: Pavilion in front of Kezar Stadium.

Bowling: Golden Gate Green, Bowling Green Drive, daily 10-4.

Card Games, Chess, Checkers: Pavilion near Haight and Stanyan Sts.; tables accommodate 200 players.

Cycling: Bicycles rented outside park on Stanyan Street. Riding tri-park trail, 7½ m. Panhandle, Golden Gate Park, and Lake Merced.

Dog Training: Dog training classes by St. Francis Dog Training Club, Inc., Golden Gate Park Dog Training Area.

Fly Casting: Pools located near the polo field, west end.

Football: Recreation Field. Golden Gate Park Stadium.

Golf: Golden Gate nine-hole course, near west end of John F. Kennedy Drive.

Handball: Five outside, six inside near 7th Ave.; spectators' gallery.

Horseshoe Pitching: Horseshoe pits located on the North Ridge Drive.

Miniature Yachting: Spreckels Lake Clubhouse maintained by San Francisco Model Yacht Club, not open to the public.

Polo: Golden Gate Park Stadium.

Riding: 7½ miles of bridle paths. Mounts available at the Golden Gate Riding Academy in the park.

Tennis: 21 courts near Children's Playground. Free of charge weekdays. Holidays and weekends reservations must be made, charge of 50¢ per court hour when reservations are required.

POINTS OF INTEREST

At the entrance to the block-wide Panhandle, the cypress- and eucalyptus-shaded strip extending eight blocks eastward from the main area of the park, stands the McKINLEY MONUMENT (Robert Ingersoll Aitken, sculptor), Baker St. between Fell and Oak Sts., a bronze heroic female figure, emblematic of the Republic, towering 35 feet above a granite base. President Theodore Roosevelt broke ground for the memorial May 13, 1903.

W. from Panhandle park entrance on Kennedy Dr.

The sandstone, tile-roofed PARK LODGE, N. of Kennedy Dr. near Panhandle park entrance, stands on a slight elevation surrounded by wide lawns. Although only a few steps from hurrying city traffic, the lodge has the quiet appearance of a country estate. Built in 1896 at a cost of $25,000, it is occupied by Park Commission offices. Here too lived Park Superintendent "Uncle" John McLaren. A huge Monterey cyprus in front of the lodge has come to be known as "Uncle John's Christmas Tree."

The FUCHSIA GARDEN extends N. of Kennedy Dr. near the Panhandle entrance, between a double row of tall cypresses. The collection includes fuchsias of a great variety of sizes and colors.

N. from Kennedy Dr. on North Ridge Dr.

Steps made of old basalt paving blocks lead from North Ridge Dr. to the HORSESHOE COURTS, surrounded by trees and a stone retaining wall. The sixteen playing courts and the grounds were reconstructed in 1934 by the State Relief Administration. On the cliffs to east and south are giant bas-reliefs of a running horse and a man tossing a horseshoe, carved by "Vet" Anderson of the Horseshoe Club.

Retrace on North Ridge Dr.; W. from North Ridge Dr. on Kennedy Dr.

On a wide green against a background of oak and acacia stands the HALLECK MONUMENT, S. of Kennedy Dr., a tribute to the memory of Major-General Henry W. Halleck, General-in-chief of the Union Armies in 1862-64, "from his 'best friend'." It was erected in 1886 by Major General George W. Cullum. The granite pedestal supports a heroic-size granite figure of Halleck in full uniform, wrapped in his military cape (C. Conrads, sculptor).

THE BASEBALL PLAYER, S. of Kennedy Dr., an early bronze by Douglas Tilden depicting a mustachioed player of the eighties throwing a ball, cast in Paris in 1889, was erected in 1892 by W. E. Brown as tribute to Tilden's "energy, industry and ability."

In the shade of Monterey pines and cypresses the BOWLES RHODODENDRONS, N. of Kennedy Dr., border the approach to Conservatory Valley on the east. They were given by Mrs. Philip E. Bowles, as a memorial to her husband. Of the park's thousands of rhododendrons, some are always in bloom from February through June, although the largest number appear in full bloom in April.

The JAMES A. GARFIELD MONUMENT stands on a knoll N. of Kennedy Dr. On the steps of a granite base sits a mourning female figure holding a broken sword and a wreath. Above stands a heroic-size bronze statue of the martyred president. Modeled by Frank Happersberger and cast in Munich, the work was unveiled July 4, 1885.

N. of Kennedy Dr. from the broad lawns of shallow Conservatory Valley—where formal flower beds are gay with bloom the year round—a broad flight of steps leads to the CONSERVATORY (*open 8-4:50 daily*). This glass structure whose two wings flank a central octagonal rotunda and dome, modeled after the Royal Conservatories at Kew Gardens, is the successor to one constructed in 1878 of materials purchased in England by James Lick. Destroyed by fire in 1883, it was replaced with funds donated by Charles Crocker. A glassed-in vestibule leads into the rotunda, where rare palms from the Norfolk Islands, Central and South America, Sumatra and Java, China and Japan lift their green fronds above semitropical plants from Australia, New South Wales, and Lord Howe's Island. The center room of the east wing harbors a jungle-like growth of palms, vines, and ferns from Malacca, India, South Africa, Japan, Brazil, and Mexico. In the end room is a rockery green with ferns and other plants and a small pool stocked with gold fish. Plants from Peru, China, and South Africa grow in a hot and humid atmosphere. Floating on the waters of the pool here from July to January are the giant pads of the *Victoria regia,* a water lily native to the waters of the Amazon River, whose petals open in mid-afternoon and close in mid-morning when it blooms in September. In the center room of the west wing grow semitropical plants from Africa, China, India, Central and South America, and a small collection of orchids. The end room offers rotating seasonal exhibits of potted flowering plants. In the hothouse nurseries behind the Conservatory gardeners have developed a collection of orchids.

The LIBERTY TREE, a redwood planted by the Daughters of the American Revolution April 19, 1894, on the anniversary of the Battle of Lexington, stands in this area.

The McKINNON MONUMENT, S. side of Kennedy Dr. (J. McQuarrie, sculptor), depicting the uniformed figure of Father William D. McKinnon, chaplain of the First California Volunteers of the Spanish-American War, is set against a background of evergreen shrubs and cypresses.

The ROBERT BURNS MONUMENT (M. Earl Cummings, sculptor), S. of Kennedy Dr. near McKinnon Monument, a heroic bronze of the Scotch poet, stands on a sloping lawn against a background of cypresses and tall pittosporum. Here the birthday of "Bobby" Burns, January 25, is observed annually by enthusiastic Scots.

SE. from Kennedy Dr. on drive encircling Music Concourse

The MUSIC CONCOURSE (*band concerts Sun. and holidays 2-4:30*), S. of Kennedy Dr. near Eighth Ave. park entrance, a sunken, outdoor auditorium seating 20,000, is 12 feet below the surface of the surrounding roadway. It is bordered by clipped hedges and terraced lawns and roofed by formal rows of trees. In line with the central aisle are three circular fountains. Around the concourse were grouped the buildings of the California Mid-Winter International Exposition of 1894.

A memorial to the Unitarian minister who fought to keep California in the Union during the Civil War is the THOMAS STARR KING MONUMENT, Kennedy Dr. and Music Concourse Dr. (Daniel Chester French, sculptor). On the granite base bearing the bronze figure is inscribed: "In Him Eloquence Strength and Virtue were Devoted with Fearless Courage to Truth Country and His Fellow-Men. 1824-64."

The CERVANTES MONUMENT, NE. corner Music Concourse, a bronze head of Miguel de Cervantes (Jo Mora, sculptor), looks down gravely from a rugged pile of native rock upon the kneeling figures of Cervantes' fictional creations, Don Quixote and Sancho Panza.

Portrayed advancing with a tall cross, the *padre-presidente* of the California missions is memorialized by the JUNIPERO SERRA MONUMENT, opposite the Cervantes Monument. Dedicated November 17, 1907 by the Native Sons of the Golden West, the bronze is the work of Douglas Tilden.

The ULYSSES S. GRANT MEMORIAL, NE. corner Music Concourse, is a bronze bust of Grant (R. Schmid, sculptor). On the base are listed his principal battles.

On the NW. side of the Music Concourse, flanked by trim lawns and stately Irish yews, is the M. H. DE YOUNG MEMORIAL MUSEUM (*open daily 10-5*). Remodeled in 1950 it is no longer of sixteenth century Spanish design, but rather modern in appearance. Before the main entrance, lies the POOL OF ENCHANTMENT (M. Earl Cummings, sculptor), in which a sculptured Indian boy pipes to two listening mountain lions on a rocky island. At the building's southeast corner, a bronze SUN DIAL (M. Earl Cummings, sculptor) commemorates "the first Three Navigators to the California Coast: Fortuno Ximenes, 1534 —Juan de Cabrillo, 1542—Sir Francis Drake, 1579." In front of the west wing stands the VINTAGE, designed by Paul Gustave Doré, a massive three-ton bronze vase depicting in bas-relief the story of the grape. The symbolic sculptures above the main entrance to the museum are by Haig Patigian; other exterior sculptures, by Leo Lentelli.

The museum is a heritage of the California Mid-Winter International Exposition, whose guiding spirit, Michael de Young, publisher of the *Chronicle,* proposed that the $75,000 profits of the fair be used to house a permanent collection of art. In the fair's Egyptian-style Fine Arts Building the museum was opened March 25, 1895. A collection of 6,000 objects bought from the fair was the nucleus of the present collection of more than 1,000,000 items. Throughout Europe De Young searched for treasures, while pioneer-minded citizens sent grandfather's boots and grandmother's sunbonnets, until the museum was congested with "historical curiosities." The small, dark rooms were heaped to the rafters with Italian marbles, bric-a-brac, and *objets d'art* of the bonanza period. When the original Fine Arts Building became too crowded to hold anything else, construction was begun in 1917 on the first unit of the present building (Louis Mullgardt, architect)—erected with funds donated by M. H. de Young—to which a second wing was added in 1925, and a third (Frederick H. Meyer, architect) in 1931. Condemned as unsafe in 1926, the old building was torn down. All that remains as a reminder of the old structure are the two sphinxes and bronze lion to the east of the museum.

The museum's galleries, enclosing the sunken Great Court and extending through the wings on either side, are divided into four main sections: one devoted to loan exhibitions changing from month to month; one presenting the art traditions of Europe and America from the antique world through the nineteenth century; one showing art of the Orient and the Pacific Basin; and one of Californiana, which provides a graphic biography of San Francisco and its region. Collections of armor, musical instruments, ship models, historic documents, textiles, and American Colonial arts exist as additional interests.

The East Wing of loan exhibitions presents an ever-changing variety of shows, each lasting about a month—contemporary painting, sculpture, architecture, photography, decorative arts presented in exhibitions devoted to a special theme or illustrating a period or school of art. These are borrowed from other galleries and collections throughout the world to make available to San Francisco the most significant trends or achievements in art. Noteworthy past exhibitions have been the comprehensive exhibitions of the work of Vincent Van Gogh, gathered from Europe and America; "Seven Centuries of French Painting," borrowed chiefly from the Louvre Museum in Paris; "Meet the Artist," an exhibition of self-portraits by leading American cartoonists and painters.

The Central Wing, with 21 galleries surrounding the Great Court, is devoted to the arts of Europe and America. It contains examples of Egyptian, Greek, and Roman sculpture, ceramics, textiles, and jewelry; medieval and Renaissance stained-glass windows; French, German, and Flemish sculpture of the fourteenth and fifteenth centuries; Italian sculpture of later periods; furniture and furnishings characteristic of the highest qualities of each period; master paintings of the great periods of European culture; and American paintings of the nineteenth century. The master works in painting include such great examples as Paolo Veronese's *The Annunciation,* Rubens' *The Tribute Money,* and Lucas Cranach the Elder's *Virgin and Christ Child.* Each of the galleries is arranged to evoke the special quality of design and spirit of the period covered.

In the Northeast Wing the arts of the Orient and of the Pacific Basin are displayed in seven galleries: one large gallery of Chinese sculpture, ceramics, bronze vessels, and textiles; two galleries of Japanese art, including the reconstruction of a Japanese interior; and one gallery each for the arts and crafts of Indo-China and the Dutch Indies, the islands of the South Pacific, Pre-Columbian Central and South America, and North American Indians. Especially rare is the large collection of gold necklaces, bracelets, and other ornaments of the Incas of Peru. Each of the galleries presents the material as art rather than merely as work of ethnic interest.

San Francisco's colorful history is the theme of the West Wing. It is illustrated by paintings, prints and maps of the city and region from its earliest development; by four reconstructions of California living rooms of 1850, 1865, 1870, and 1885; and by a comprehensive costume collection which shows all items of apparel from the fashions of 1760 to those of yesterday. Portraits of early San Franciscans illustrating the fashions as actually worn complete the documentation of changing taste. There is also a gallery of paintings gathered in Europe, the selection and hanging of which typifies the taste of the wealthy American collector of the 1890's. This last contains such famous items of their day as Bouguereau's *The Broken Pitcher* and Makowski's *The Russian Bride's Attire.*

The Avery Brundage Collection of Asian Art is housed in a two-story wing of the De Young Museum that cost $3,000,000. It features comprehensive collections of ancient Chinese bronzes, ceramics, jade and paintings; Japanese lacquer, ceramics and paintings; Persian pottery and bronzes, and sculpture from China, India, Lamaist countries, Korea, Japan and Southeast Asia.

The museum's Education Department presents an opportunity for a knowledge and enjoyment of art beyond the scope of the regular collections and exhibitions. Frequent public lectures are given. Study courses on particular fields of art are scheduled throughout the year. Club groups, schools and professional societies may have lectures or courses designed for their special needs. Children's classes in painting and modeling are held each Saturday morning and practice classes for adults each Saturday afternoon. Educational exhibitions designed to further an understanding of art are frequently shown. The Art Reference Library and an extensive print collection are also available for research or for enjoyment.

The CIDER PRESS MONUMENT, northwest side Music Concourse, represents a nude male in heroic size operating a cider press; a child kneels at his feet holding an apple. Purchased from the French Commission, the statue (Thomas S. Clarke, sculptor) was presented to the park by the Executive Committee of the California Mid-Winter International Exposition in 1894.

In the $75,000 Italian Renaissance MUSIC PAVILION, southwest end Music Concourse, gift of sugar magnate Claus Spreckels in 1900, Sunday afternoon band concerts are presented. Built of gray Colusa sandstone, it has a high proscenium arch over the music platform flanked by balustraded colonnades.

Arching over the eastern entrance to the ORIENTAL TEA GAR-DEN (*open 8 a.m. to dusk*), west of Music Concourse, is a two-storied *ro-mon* (gate) carved of *hinoki* wood, used in Japan before temple entrances. Precipitous, bamboo-railed paths wander through the five-acre garden, over grassy slopes planted with camellias, magnolia trees, cryptomeria, and red-leafed Japanese maples. Between lichen-covered rocks, little streams crossed by small stone bridges descend to a chain of five small pools planted to water iris and stocked with goldfish. Over a still pool curves a "wishing bridge" whose reflection in the water completes a perfect circle. In spring, flowering quince, plum, and cherry trees burst into sprays of blossom. Here and there grow a hundred or more fantastically gnarled *bonsai,* misshapen conifers, some a century old but none more than three feet in height (to stunt their growth roots and branches are constantly pruned, and only a minimum of water is allowed).

In the thatched tea house near the eastern gate Chinese girls in native costume serve pale green tea and wafer-like cakes to guests sitting at tables made of tree trunks. Along one side of the pavilion, sunlight falls through a lattice arbor burdened with fragrant blossoms of white and lavender wistaria in season. Beyond the tea house is a two-story, four-room *zashiki* (house) with wooden walls, sliding panels, and window panes of rice paper. The interior is severely simple. The floors are covered with matting. There is a *tokonomo* (alcove) for the display of flower arrangements. A huge, red, black, and gold Buddha sits in serene contemplation at the foot of a slope on whose summit is a copper-roofed Shinto shrine. One of the chief attractions of the 1894 exposition, during which it was known as the Japanese Village, the garden is operated by the Park Commission.

The GIUSEPPE VERDI MONUMENT, southwest corner Music Concourse, was designed and executed in Milan (Orazio Grossoni, sculptor) and presented by the local Italian colony in 1914. On the granite base below the bronze bust of the composer a male figure holds an hour glass and a laurel wreath, and two children unfurl an Italian flag.

The BEETHOVEN MONUMENT, southeast side of the Music Concourse, a portrait bust in bronze, rests on a formal granite column at whose base stands Music, a draped female figure holding a lyre. The gift of the Beethoven Männerchor of New York, it was dedicated August 6, 1915.

The ROBERT EMMET MONUMENT, southeast side Music Concourse, a life-size bronze of the Irish patriot, bears in gold letters simply his name, in conformance with his last wish before he was executed: "When my country takes her place among the nations of the earth, then, and not till then, let my epitaph be written." The work of Jerome Connor, the statue was presented by Senator James D. Phelan in 1919. Here gather the United Irish Societies for yearly observances of Robert Emmet's birthday, which always includes a rendition of his "Speech Before the Dock."

Erected in 1887 with a $60,000 bequest of philanthropist James Lick, the FRANCIS SCOTT KEY MONUMENT, represents the author of "The Star Spangled Banner" sitting on a travertine pedestal inscribed with the words of his song under a canopy upheld by four Corinthian columns and crowned by bronze eagles, buffalo heads, and a heroic-sized bronze female figure of Liberty bearing a banner and a sword. The monument is temporarily in storage.

On the southeast side of the Music Concourse are the buildings of the CALIFORNIA ACADEMY OF SCIENCES, the oldest scientific institution in the West. Supported partly by endowments and bequests and partly by city funds, the institution maintains North American Hall, Steinhart Aquarium, Simson African Hall, Hall of Science, and Cowell Hall, buildings in harmonizing architecture whose white concrete walls enclose a paved quadrangle. (*Admittance, 12-18 years, 25¢, over 18, 50¢; free day 1st day of each month; hours: 10-5*)

The Academy's exhibits of flora and fauna are only one of its many activities. Its scientific expeditions have gone to Alaska, Panama, Asia, Africa, Australia, New Zealand, South America, and many of the Pacific Islands. It has furnished materials and facilities for original research in the biological and physical sciences, maintaining research departments in the fields of botany, entomology, herpetology, ichthyology, invertebrate zoology, ornithology, mammalogy, and paleontology. Its activities are primarily concerned with the natural history and geology of the lands bordering the Pacific Ocean and its islands.

On April 4, 1853, seven men interested in science met at Lewis W. Sloat's Montgomery Street office; on June 27, 1853, they incorporated as the California Academy of Natural Sciences. For many years their meetings were held in the office of Colonel Thomas J. Nevins, one of the seven founders and San Francisco's first Superintendent of Schools. The *Proceedings,* first published in a newspaper, began to appear in illustrated volumes. The library and museum grew and moved in 1874 to larger quarters in a church. In 1891 the Academy established itself on property at Fourth and Market Streets deeded to it by James Lick. Under the terms of Lick's will it became one of two residuary legatees, receiving one-half of whatever remained after all other bequests had been paid. With the $20,000 given by Charles Crocker in 1881 and additional funds from Leland Stanford, it created a large natural history exhibit. Other benefactors included John W. Hendrie and William Alvord. When the Market Street home of the Academy was demolished by the earthquake and fire of 1906, San Francisco citizens voted to re-establish it in Golden Gate Park.

On May 16, 1969, the city of San Francisco was presented with a $1,500,000 gift in the form of COWELL HALL (Milton T. Pflueger, architect), the latest addition to the world famous complex of buildings in Golden Gate Park, made possible by a single gift from the S. H. Cowell Foundation of San Francisco. Most imposing and important of the new exhibits is the dinosaur, an allosaur known scientifically as allosauris fiagelis. Its bony structure is some 30 feet in length and stands 13 feet tall. It dates back to 140 million years ago. The largest allosaur on display anywhere in the world it was taken from the Cleveland-Lloyd Quarry in Utah and reconstructed on the campus of the Univ. of Salt Lake, transported to the Academy and reassembled there. There are some 300 elements involved and it took 18 months of work to put it together.

The loggia and upper floor, devoted to administrative offices, adds an additional 20,000 feet of floor space to the already extensive Academy, which contains under a single roof a major aquarium, Steinhart; a planetarium, Morrison; and many other halls devoted to natural history and science.

NORTH AMERICAN HALL, the first unit of the California Academy of Sciences group opened September 16, 1916. Here are to be found 15 large habitat groups of North American mammals and six large groups of North American birds, constructed under the direction of John Rowley and Paul J. Fair, also 26 smaller habitat groups, the majority of which were constructed by Frank Tose.

STEINHART AQUARIUM. On September 21, 1916 at a luncheon at the Palace Hotel, Ignatz Steinhart made a public announcement of his intention to provide funds for an aquarium building amply equipped provided (1) that the aquarium be located in Golden Gate Park, (2) that it be under management and control of the California Academy of Sciences, and (3) that the City of San Francisco supply the funds for maintenance. Steinhart's death in 1917 delayed the construction of the building (Lewis Hobart, architect) and not until September 29, 1923, was the Steinhart Aquarium formally opened to the public.

In 1959 a $1,575,000 bond issue was approved by the citizenry for the much needed reconstruction of the Aquarium. The new Steinhart, with its 208 tanks ranging in size from 5 gallons to 62,000 gallons continues to present extraordinary displays of fish.

Among the new and unique exhibits is one in which polarized light makes the internal structure of glassfish visible; another, a tide pool filled with colorful sea anemones into which a wave crashes periodically; an eye-level tide pool tank with a conspicuous fluctuation of water level and accompanying sound effects; and a tank of archerfish which swim contentedly among mangrove roots and "shoot down" their food three times a day by spitting jets of water which knock it off a target.

The aquatic mammals usually seen at the Aquarium are, Pacific white-sided dolphins, harbor seals, a manatee (sea cow), and fresh water dolphins, all of which are particular favorites with visitors.

The swamp area of Steinhart Aquarium, consisting of 108 display tanks, houses one of the finest live collections of reptiles and amphibians in the world. Giant pythons, bizzare looking lizards, a wide variety of poisonous snakes and a colorful array of frogs and toads can be viewed the year around. Alligators and crocodiles live in the central swamp, bordered by countless tropical plants.

SIMSON AFRICAN HALL was dedicated December 14, 1934, and owes its existence to Mr. Leslie Simson, mining engineer and sportsman, of Berkeley, California. Realizing the educational value and importance of securing for posterity some visualization of the vanishing wild life of Africa, he proposed to the Trustees of the Academy that he would collect the necessary material at his own expense if the institution would properly construct and house habitat groups showing the animals as they appear in their native surroundings.

The MORRISON PLANETARIUM located in the $1,100,000 Hall of Science Building opened in November, 1952, and has presented over 16,000 showings to over 2,900,000 persons. The projector, itself weighing 8,000 pounds, was conceived, designed and built at the Academy and contains 141 separate projectors, 321 lenses, 304 ball bearings, 158 gears, 200 relay switches, and four miles of wire. The 65-foot dome of San Francisco's Theater of the Stars is a projection screen over which is spread the drama of the sky. Thousands of stars fill the make-believe firmament, and the sun, moon and planets march in orderly array as time rushes forward or backward. Dependent upon the subject of the show, you may see a meteor shower, an eclipse of the sun or moon, a comet with a streaming tail, or the eerie glow of the northern lights.

Also housed in the Hall of Science Building is the J. W. MAIL-LIARD, JR., LIBRARY which provides service to the Academy of Science staff and departments, Academy members, researching scholars, and other scientific and educational institutions.

The Academy endeavors to stimulate the youth of today to obtain a better appreciation and understanding of the natural sciences by means of their JUNIOR ACADEMY (*open to students ages 9-18*). Members meet in the department after school and on Saturday throughout the school year, with special courses being conducted during the summer.

In a bower of English laurel is the GOETHE-SCHILLER MONUMENT, east of Simson Hall, a pedestal of red Missouri granite supporting bronze figures of the two German poets. A reproduction of a monument in Weimar, Germany (Ernst Rietschel, sculptor), it was presented by citizens of German descent in 1901.

Facing the Music Concourse against a background of tall pines is the GENERAL PERSHING MONUMENT, northwest side Music Concourse, a bronze statue of General John J. Pershing (Haig Patigian, sculptor) in khaki field uniform with a crushed German helmet at his feet, presented by Dr. Morris Herzstein in 1922.

W. from drive encircling Music Concourse on Kennedy Dr.

A shaded road winds through HEROES GROVE, north of Kennedy Dr., a 15-acre tract of redwoods dedicated to San Francisco soldiers killed in World War I. Their names are inscribed on a large obelisk-shaped boulder.

The REDWOOD MEMORIAL GROVE, north of Kennedy Dr., was dedicated by the Native Sons and Daughters of the Golden West and the Gold Star Mothers of America to the San Francisco men and women who lost their lives in World War I. In the Grove of Memory, a section of the main grove, a redwood for each of the dead towers high above the DOUGHBOY MONUMENT, a bronze figure of a young soldier who stands, hatless and bare-armed, on a 20-ton rock base. Once part of the Panama-Pacific International Exposition, this statue (M. Earle Cummings, sculptor) was purchased by the 52 San Francisco parlors of the Native Sons and Daughters of the Golden West.

The PIONEER LOG CABIN, south of Kennedy Dr. on an un-named drive W. of Redwood Memorial Grove, was built in 1911 of logs floated down from Mendocino County. The structure, set in a redwood grove (*picnicking facilities*), is the property of the Association of Pioneer Women of California, who convene there monthly around the huge brick fireplace.

Composed of one tree for each of the Thirteen Original Colonies, a group of HISTORIC TREES, planted along a path leading south from the intersection of Kennedy Drive and the drive to the Pioneer Log Cabin, commemorates the surrender of Cornwallis at Yorktown in 1785. Notable are a cedar from Valley Forge and a tree from Thomas Jefferson's grave. The trees were planted in 1896 by the Sequoia Chapter, Daughters of the American Revolution.

The sandstone PRAYER BOOK CROSS, north of Kennedy Dr., modeled after an ancient Celtic Cross on the Scottish island of Iona, towers 57 feet above the edge of a bluff. It was erected in 1894 by the Northern California Episcopal diocese in commemoration of the first use of the Book of Common Prayer on the Pacific Coast by Francis Fletcher, Chaplain to Francis Drake, who conducted a service on the shore of Drake's Bay June 24, 1579.

On Sundays and holidays, tiny RAINBOW FALLS, north of Kennedy Dr., rush over a cliff at the base of Prayer Book Cross into a fern-bordered pool. Artificially fed from a reservoir atop Strawberry Hill, they were named when colored electric lights were strung along the cliff to make rainbows appear in the spray.

LLOYD LAKE, north of Kennedy Dr., fed by a tiny stream that ripples over a rocky ledge, is encircled by a graveled path.

The PORTALS OF THE PAST, six white marble Ionic Pillars reflected in the tranquil surface of Lloyd Lake, are all that remain of A. N. Towne's Nob Hill residence burned in the 1906 fire.

Nine-acre MARX MEADOWS, northwest of Lloyd Lake, were named for Mrs. Johannah Augusta Marx, who bequeathed $5,000 for beautification of the park in 1922.

BROOM POINT, S. of Kennedy Dr., since early days has been a landmark identified by the bright yellow blossoms of Scotch broom that grow there in profusion.

Within the confines of 25-acre LINDLEY MEADOW, south of Kennedy Dr., grazes a herd of sheep. Each December the meadow be-comes a living Christmas card, with shepherds in biblical costume herd-ing grazing sheep.

Homing ground for migratory game and domestic waterfowl, SPRECKELS LAKE, north of Kennedy Dr., supplies much of the water for the park irrigation system. Each Sunday from March to late Sep-tember the miniature sail and speed boats of the San Francisco Model

Yacht Club clip their trim way across its rippling waters, some attaining a speed of 40 miles an hour.

The MODEL YACHT CLUBHOUSE (*members only*), west of Spreckels Lake, a one-story structure of concrete and glass brick, is headquarters for miniature yacht enthusiasts. The Model Yacht Club members, in its fully equipped workshop, build tiny boats which duplicate in every detail their full-sized models.

The fences of the BUFFALO ENCLOSURE, north of Kennedy Dr., are so cleverly concealed in the surrounding forest that the herd of about 15 buffalo seem to be roaming at large.

Within the buffalo enclosure are the DEER PADDOCKS, occupied by small herds of Belgian deer and California elk.

The CHAIN OF LAKES, north and south of Kennedy Dr., is a series of artificial lakes bordered by wilder and more rugged vegetation than is found elsewhere in the park. North Lake, N. of Kennedy Dr., largest of the three, is dotted with several islands planted with birches, rhododendrons, and other shrubs. Waterfowl preen their plumage on the surface of the water and feed among the wild grasses in the shallows. Middle Lake, S. of Kennedy Dr., is framed by 800 camellia and Japanese cherry trees.

A 150-yard-long RECREATION FIELD, west of Kennedy Dr. facing the ocean, includes facilities for football, softball, soccer, and tennis players, and a dressing room with showers.

THE NORTH WINDMILL, east of Kennedy Drive, near NW. corner of park is an authentic copy of a Dutch windmill. It was constructed in 1902 to pump water for the park's irrigation system taking advantage of the prevailing westerly winds. Several attempts have been made to restore the mills. In 1967 The John McLaren Society took over the task with plans to restore the sails and let them be controlled by a governor to give the illusion of operating functionally. The Queen Wilhelmina tulip beds surround the mill.

At the west end of the John F. Kennedy Drive is the small nine hole (par 3) GOLDEN GATE GOLF COURSE. A small club house and snack bar are on the premises but no pro shop.

S. from Kennedy Dr. on Great Highway

The stumpy, schooner-rigged 47-ton sloop *GJOA,* east of Great Highway near NW. corner of park, only ship to negotiate the ice-bound Northwest Passage, rests in its rocky dry dock behind an iron-spiked fence overlooking the Pacific. The *Gjoa* was given to San Francisco in 1909 by her commander, Arctic explorer Roald Amundsen. The sloop was built at Hardanger Fjord, Norway, in 1872. After 29 years of active service as a herring boat and sealer, she was purchased by Amundsen. With her superstructure strengthened, her hull sheathed in hardwood, and iron strips bolted to her bow, she was equipped with a 13-horsepower motor. On June 16, 1903, the *Gjoa* set sail from Christiana (now Oslo), Norway, bound for the Arctic and that Northwest Passage, the existence of which for centuries had troubled the minds of the adventurous. Aboard were Amundsen, six companions, Eskimo dogs, scientific instruments, and enough stores for five years.

Disaster soon struck at the expedition. A fire broke out in the engine room. A mysterious malady killed many of the dogs. In the Northwest Passage the sloop was grounded on a reef and her false keel ripped off. Only after precious deck cargo had been tossed overboard was she refloated. At long last the *Gjoa* halted in King William Land, in a bay later named Gjoahaven.

For three years Amundsen remained in the Arctic, with the temperature often "60 degrees below." Completely cut off from civilization, the expedition nevertheless went busily about its work of gathering scientific data. In addition to discovering the Passage, they succeeded in fixing the location of the magnetic pole. Finally the *Gjoa* set sail once more, passing through the Bering Sea and thence into the Pacific Ocean and down the Coast to San Francisco. She dropped anchor off Point Bonita one October day in 1906. In the celebration that followed, American warships dipped their flags to the men who had at last sailed the near-legendary Northwest Passage.

The two-story BEACH CHALET (*private*), east of Great Highway, has a large glassed-in room overlooking the ocean and the Great Highway. The foyer is ornamented with murals and mosaics by WPA artists.

E. from Great Highway on South Dr.

The MURPHY WINDMILL (*not open to public*), north of South Dr. near SW. corner of park, the second of the park's two Dutch mills, is one of the largest sail-type structures in the world, having a wing spread of 114 feet. Erected in 1907 to supply water for irrigation, it was equipped with electric pumps in 1927.

In the EQUITATION FIELD, north of South Dr., a fenced, sandy area 25 by 75 yards, skilled equestrians urge their horses over practice hurdles. The adjacent Beach Stables house the horses used in the park.

NE. from South Dr. on unnamed drive

Not since early in the century has the three-quarter-mile track of GOLDEN GATE PARK STADIUM, north of South Dr., thundered to the hoofbeats of thoroughbreds. A bicycle track, a cinder path, a football field, and a polo field occupy the space within the hedge that borders the inner rim of the trotting track. At the end of the last century two driving clubs dominated equestrian activities in San Francisco: the Golden Gate Driving Club, composed of men of wealth, and the San Francisco Driving Club (the "Steam Beer Club") of members in more moderate circumstances. The organizations built the track by private subscription according to the designs of Park Superintendent John McLaren and Park Commissioner A. B. Spreckels. Chief use of the trotting track at present is for training purposes. The stables were replaced in 1939 by the WPA-built Polo Sheds, a group of four gray concrete tile-roofed buildings.

The stadium has been the site of many outdoor rallies, the most notable of which was the Family Rosary Rally, held October 7, 1961.

The angler finds an ideal practice pool in the cement-lined, WPA-built FLYCASTING POOL (*free*), west end of Golden Gate Park Stadium, hidden in a woodland setting with eucalyptus and evergreen trees mirrored in its placid surface. With an overall length of 450 feet and a width of 185 feet, the pool is divided into three sections, one of which is used for distance casting, one for accuracy, and the third, provided with graduated steps rising above the surface, for improving skill in difficult overhead shots. Overlooking the pool is Anglers' Lodge, a wooden building with hand-hewn window frames and wrought-iron fittings, headquarters of the Golden Gate Angling and Casting Club, which, as the San Francisco Fly Casting Club, functioned as early as 1890.

E. from unnamed drive on Middle Dr.

METSON LAKE, south of Middle Dr., part of the park irrigation system, with its grassy shores, large boulders, and background of conifers, has the appearance of a lake in a mountain meadow.

Retrace on Middle Dr. to unnamed drive; SE. from Middle Dr. on unnamed drive to South Dr.; E. from unnamed drive on South Dr.

Rock-rimmed MALLARD LAKE, south of South Dr., with its wooded islet and tiny falls, is a favored stopover for September's southbound duck traffic. Here thousands of transient mallard and canvas-back fraternize with their stay-at-home cousins, the drab little mud-hens. For years this was known as Hobo Lake, because transient workers on the roadways during the 1894 Mid-Winter Fair rested here between labors on the patches of seagrass.

Before the park animals were united in one area, ELK GLEN, north of South Dr., enclosed the elk, Scotch sheep, East Indian deer, and buffalo where they churned into dusty waves the brown earth around their miniature lake. The elk herd has grown from a pair of the animals given to the city by Alvinza Hayward in 1890. Although death-struggles between the bucks during mating time have occurred, the animals are gentle enough to nibble leaves from the hands of visitors.

The redwoods of the GEORGE WASHINGTON BICENTEN-NIAL GROVE, south of South Dr., were planted February 22, 1932, in honor of the bicentennial anniversary of Washington's birth.

The HERBERT HOOVER TREE, adjoining George Washington Grove, a redwood tree planted by the Daughters of the American Revolution in 1935, commemorates the ex-president's work in conservation.

Encircling the base of steep, wooded Strawberry Hill is STOW LAKE, north of South Dr., bordered by tree-lined walks and winding driveways. Central reservoir for the park's irrigation system, it is the largest of the park's artificial lakes. On the wooded islets that dot its surface nest waterfowl, both wild and domestic—brant, pelicans, black and white swans, and wild ducks, arriving in the autumn on their migration southward from as far north as the Arctic. Strawberry Hill, reached by two stone bridges across narrow parts of the lake, is the highest elevation in the park. The steep slopes are covered with cypress, eucalyptus, and long-leafed acacia. From the summit (428 alt.) are visible on clear days the Farallon Islands, gray dots on the horizon, 26 miles out in the Pacific.

HUNTINGTON FALLS once leaped 75 feet from the summit of Strawberry Hill down a bed of glistening, fern-lined rocks. It was named for Collis P. Huntington, railroad magnate, who contributed $25,000 for the beautification of the bleak sand dunes of the city's new park. The water for the falls was pumped to the top of the hill at the rate of 1,600,000 gallons a day.

Plants rare and useful from far-away places grow in the ARBO-RETUM (*open Mon.-Fri.*), S. of South Dr., a 40-acre plot of which a fourth is under cultivation. A bequest by Mrs. Helen Strybing has made possible plans which will include several acres of native California plants and a building housing a laboratory, library, and botanical collections. The new outlay also provides for classrooms where gardeners will be trained for their work in the park.

Plants are arranged in geographical groupings. Near the entrance, off South Dr., grow shrubs and trees from South Africa, including the aloe, which often reaches a height of 60 feet. South of this group is the Australian and New Zealand section, where grows the kauri, a primitive pine nearly extinct. West of the Australian group is the Mexican area with its Mexican or Montezuma cypress which is said to reach an age of 3,000 years. In the Chinese, Japanese, and Himalayan area, south of the Mexican section, are rare varieties of rhododendrons, including some brought from remote parts of Western China, Tibet, and the Himalayas. There are numerous trees and plants from South Africa. One area is given over to medicinal plants, including one from China from which recently was developed ephedrine. More commonly known are digitalis, from which the drug of the same name is derived; the recinus, or castor oil plant; the Arabian kath, whose leaves are made into a narcotic; and the white Chinese poppy, from which opium is made.

The $548,288 HALL OF FLOWERS, opened in 1960 (Appleton & Wolfard, architects). Facilities for meetings, demonstrations, and exhibits are provided garden and other civic groups.

NE. from South Dr. on Middle Dr.

A low, clipped hedge of myrtle fronts the GARDEN OF SHAKE-SPEARE'S FLOWERS, north of Middle Dr., wherein grow specimens of every flower, shrub, and tree mentioned in the writings of William Shakespeare. Flower beds bordering a lawn include pansies, marigolds, columbines, primroses, yellow crocuses and daffodils, and dainty bluebells. Trees shading the garden include the alder, apple, ash, cedar, chestnut, laurel, lemon, locust, orange, pine, pomegranate, walnut, and yew. There are beds of sweet briar, rue, and thyme. On either side of the plot facing the entrance, where an English holly stands, are marble benches backed by dense growths of box. In the ivy-covered brick wall along the east end of the garden is a glass-enclosed niche holding a bust of Shakespeare, a copy of the Gerard Jensen bust in the Stratford-upon-Avon church. The garden was established by the California Spring Blossom and Wildflower Association.

DE LAVEAGA DELL, south of Middle Dr., is a secluded glen, whose jungle foliage and fern-choked stream are the haunt of squirrels and birds. Giant tree ferns, some 20 feet high, grow among moss-covered rocks, mottled with shadows. Along each side of the twisting stream run footpaths carpeted with leaves and flanked by shrub-filled artificial gullies. At the dell's eastern end is one of the park's largest collections of rhododendrons and azaleas.

The LILY POND, north of Middle Dr., a long winding pool nestling at the foot of steep overhanging cliffs, was once a quarry. A walk bordered by huge rocks and tree ferns skirts the edge, and rushes and water grasses line the shores of the pond. Ducks paddle among the green pads of water lilies.

S. from Middle Drive on unnamed cross drive

From the 21 tree-protected, asphalt TENNIS COURTS, E. of cross drive, have been graduated such players as Maurice McLaughlin,

Bill Johnston, the Griffin brothers, and Alice Marble. It was here on some of the world's first asphalt courts, that McLaughlin developed the well-known "American twist" serve. The asphalt courts called for a much faster pace than clay and grass courts. Such pioneers as McLaughlin, after developing their games here, swept all before them in the East and Great Britain.

On quiet afternoons the BOWLING GREENS east and west of cross drive, first public bowling greens in the United States, present a picture of another era. White-clad men and women bowl on the well-kept turf, while spectators watch from benches on terraced slopes. A row of the rare Torrey pines protects the greens on the west.

E. from unnamed cross drive on South Dr.

The CHILDREN'S PLAYGROUND, north of South Dr., occupies a secluded valley sheltered by thickly planted trees and shrubbery. The first established in a public park in America, it was founded with $50,000 left by William Sharon in 1886. Its playground equipment, tiny farm and merry-go-round center about the Children's House, a two-story building of buff sandstone in Romanesque style.

When high, oval-shaped, municipal KEZAR STADIUM, south of South Dr., was opened with a track meet May 2, 1925, Paavo Nurmi, Finnish marathon champion, was a feature attraction. At first seating 22,000, it was enlarged in 1928 to a capacity of 60,000. Mary Kezar, for whom the stadium was named, gave $100,000 of its total cost of $450,000. It is of articulated reinforced concrete, with a deck of wood, covered by asbestos felt coated with sanded asphaltum.

Kezar Stadium is now used chiefly by football teams of San Francisco high schools.

The BASKETBALL PAVILION, east of Kezar Stadium facing Stanyan St., is a long, low, buff-colored cement building roofed with red tile. Its interior, lighted by great skylights, seats 5,500. During the basketball season high school teams play four afternoons weekly and college teams at irregular intervals at night.

The GAMES ENCLOSURE, north of South Dr. near Haight St. park entrance, a hedged retreat almost hidden by flowering shrubs, half of which is walled on three sides and roofed by glass, contains tables painted with chess and checkers markings and benches to accommodate about 200 players.

ALVORD LAKE, near Haight and Stanyan Sts. entrance, is a small lake sheltered from winds by tall cypresses and clumps of Coast live oak, the only tree native to the park area.

On April 4, 1970, the one hundredth birthday of Golden Gate Park was observed with a massive parade from the Polo Field to the Band

Street Scenes

CABLE CAR, SAN FRANCISCO'S MOST PRIZED UTILITY

CABLE CAR ON TURNTABLE, POWELL AND MARKET STREETS

CABLE CAR INFLUENCE: FLOWER STAND AT GEARY
AND STOCKTON STREETS

GRANT AVENUE, FORMERLY DUPONT STREET

HYDE STREET, SEEN FROM HYDE ST. PIER;

BRICK BUILDING AT LEFT IS THE CANNERY

HOW TO UTILIZE A STEEP HILL. LOMBARD STREET
DURING CONSTRUCTION OF ESCALATING ROAD, 1922

LOMBARD STREET TODAY

SUTRO'S BEFORE THE FIRE OF 1966

SAN FRANCISCO GAS LIGHT CO. BUILDING,
NOW MERRYVALE ANTIQUES

UNION SQUARE AND ST.
FRANCIS HOTEL, WHEN
TOWER WAS BEING BUILT

COVERING THE SKELETON
OF THE TRANS-AMERICA
PYRAMID, 1971

Concourse. The theme of the parade was historical, featuring antique cars and fire apparatus, the Wells Fargo Stage Coach, floats of historical significance and marching units in costumes of fashions of previous eras. The opening day of the centennial culminated in an hour long show presented by the playground children in the Band Shell. The Recreation Symphony Orchestra performed. Later, a massive balloon release was conducted, and, as the colorful balloons rose above the park the entire throng sang "Happy Birthday."

In 100 years Golden Gate Park has grown from an open space for San Franciscans to a great regional park attracting visitors from all countries of the world. The next century will no doubt confirm further the wisdom of those whose foresight and persuasiveness prevailed in the 1860's leaving us the heritage, "Golden Gate Park."

Part IV
Around the Bay

The Harbor and its Islands

FOR two centuries before discovery of the Golden Gate the navigators of Portugal, Spain, and England carefully avoided the sea approaches to the Port of San Francisco. The forbidding coastline and frequent fogs were not alone responsible for its prolonged obscurity: the outer islands indicated the danger of submerged rocks and shoals in the Gulf of the Farallones. Although soundings were taken by Sebastian Cermeno in 1595, not until 180 years later was any mariner bold enough to steer his ship through the Golden Gate. When the master of the *San Carlos* ventured through the strait in 1775, he sent a pilot boat ahead to chart the depth of the channel. Even within the Gate, Lieutenant Juan Manuel de Ayala's packet needed three attempts to enter.

Although modern aids to navigation long since have made San Francisco's harbor one of the safest in the world, incoming ships must begin exercising caution about six miles from shore. Outside the Gate is deposited the silt brought down from inland valleys and carried through the Bay by force of the current. Fanning from the entrance is an undersea delta whose rim, tilted upwards, forms a wide semicircle, the San Francisco Bar, lying only about 30 feet under the surface—on its north side, where it widens out in the Potato Patch, only 22 feet. During storms the waves break upon these rock-strewn shoals with disastrous force, and even in calm weather they are impassable to large vessels. Three channels cross the bar: the dredged Main Channel opposite the Golden Gate, kept open by dredges to a depth of approximately 50 feet, and the narrow North and South Channels, close to shore.

Since 1898 the entrance to the Main Channel was guarded by the San Francisco Lightship. Equipped with a foghorn and a transmitter for radio beacon signals this ship was maintained constantly by the United States Coast Guard. On April 26, 1971, a $350,000 automatic red saucer-like buoy replaced the lightship. In the area between the lightship and the bar, the pilot boats cruise, waiting for incoming vessels. When contact with a ship is made, a bar pilot puts out from their "home" at sea, the *California* or the *Golden Gate,* in a small yawl and makes his way to the incoming vessel. From the new automatic buoy the Main Channel is outlined with 14 buoys, 13 of them equipped with lights, five with bells, three with whistles, and one with an electric trumpet.

In strict nautical terms, the Golden Gate is the three-mile strait between the San Francisco and Marin Peninsulas. At its western end, lights and foghorns on the headlands and buoys in the North and South Channels (some equipped with lights and fog signals), make the entrance to the Bay more conspicuous in any weather than it was when mariners like Sir Francis Drake passed by without guessing the existence of an inland body of water. Radio beacon signals are flashed from the light on Point Bonita; between the cliffs stands Mile Rock Lighthouse. The Golden Gate itself is illuminated by two additional lighthouses, at Point Diablo and at Lime Point. And three life-saving surf stations are maintained along the strait, each with a staff of 9 to 22 men on duty 24 hours a day.

The efficiency of men and machinery in the modern life-saving service of San Francisco Bay is indicated roughly by comparing the casualties of two shipwrecks 39 years apart. The *Rio de Janeiro,* which sank in the Golden Gate during a fog in 1901, carried 128 people down with her. But when the *Pinto* was shattered on the "Potato Patch" in 1939—under circumstances that made rescue particularly difficult—not a life was lost. Even a ferryboat, the *Golden City,* has gone down in the harbor without loss of a single life. At Land's End may still be seen the rusty scraps of four hulks which testify to hazards of the Golden Gate, but no one drowned in any of these disasters.

The islands of San Francisco Bay, besides contributing to its natural charm, have played a notable part in its history. Yerba Buena, Alcatraz, the Farallones, and part of Angel Island were included in the huge Mexican grant claimed by Joseph L. Limantour, a Frenchman who swore that he received it in return for $4,000 he had advanced Governor Manuel Micheltorena in 1843. Besides the several islands the notorious Limantour Claim included about half the present area of San Francisco. Described by United States Attorney General Jeremiah S. Black, who prosecuted the case, as "the most stupendous fraud, the greatest in atrocity and magnitude the world has ever seen," the claim was finally denied in the 1850's after expenditure of $200,000 for litigation and the arrest of Limantour. Gradually, since their recovery by the Federal government, Alcatraz, Angel, and Yerba Buena Islands have been incorporated in the harbor defenses maintained by the Ninth Corps Area, United States Army.

Less prominent are the Bay's two other tiny islands, but they too have had their uses. Brooks Island, the larger of these, lies about half a mile off Point Potrero. Some 46 acres in area, rocky and very sparsely wooded, it is still uninhabited. Once known as Sheep Island, it was exploited years ago by a construction company operating a rock quarry there. Mission Rock, now called Mission Rock Terminal, is a vast shipping complex, once occupied only by a warehouse and a wharf, both partially destroyed by fire in 1936. According to water-front legend a Portuguese fisherman once stocked the rock with sheep; he rowed out to it once a year to harvest his crop with a shotgun, pulling the slaughtered sheep aboard with a boathook.

THE FARALLONES

Almost as remote as Guam or Samoa to most San Franciscans is that chain of islands known as The Farallones, which lie about 32 miles off Point Lobos. Despite their inclusion since 1872 in the City and County of San Francisco, their inaccessibility to the average citizen has invested them with the unfamiliarity of a foreign land. Even to sportsmen, for whose annual yacht races they are a hazardous goal, their history and conformation have little intimate significance.

The Farallones lie in two groups separated by seven and three-quarter miles of open sea. Seven isles constitute the southern group: Southeast Farallon Island, Sugar Loaf Isle, Aulone Isle, Seal Rock, Arch Rock, Finger Rock, and Sea Lion Islet. Of these, Southeast Farallon Island is the most important of the entire chain, and Sugar Loaf Isle (185 alt.) is the highest. Except for one island which rises to an altitude of 155 feet, the North Farallones are small and unimportant. Noonday Rock, marking the northern end of the chain, is a submerged peak so named for the clipper *Noonday* which struck it and sank in 1863. Midway between the two groups lies "lonely little Four Mile Rock." The Gulf of the Farallones, the stretch of water between the chain and the California coast, was called La Bahia de los Pinos (the bay of the pines) by the Cabrillo expedition in 1542 and Bahia de Puerto de San Francisco (bay of the port of San Francisco) by Vizcaino in 1603.

The Southeast, or South, Farallon, about 32 miles west of the Golden Gate, is about one mile long, half a mile wide, three and one-half miles in circumference. A rocky ridge runs its entire length, broken by gorges and a swift-running sea stream called "The Jordan" which separates the portion known as West End. The highest peaks of this island are Tower Hill (on which the lighthouse is built), and Main Top. In some places the slope from the ridge to the water's edge is too steep for a foothold; in others, there are ledges where sparse vegetation makes patches of green. The soil on these flats is a mixture of guano and granite sand. The forbidding coastline of the South Farallon is edged by grotesque rocky cliffs and caves. The contours of the island are suggested by some of the names given various parts: Indian Chief Cliff; Lost World Cave; Great Murre Cave; Giant's Bath, a natural swimming pool on Breaker Hill; Great West Arch, a natural arch with the sea swirling under it; and Breakers Bay, also called Franconia Bay for the *Franconia,* a wooden vessel of 1,462 tons which went ashore on West End June 4, 1881. Fisherman's or Tower Bay is the present anchorage.

Despite a popular belief to the contrary, the Farallon Islands support vegetation. Besides a group of Monterey cypresses growing in a sheltered spot and the small gardens cultivated by the lighthouse keepers, there are scattered growths of rock flowers, moss, and grass. The largest of several varieties of clinging weeds is the Farallon Weed, bearing a small yellow blossom, which grows in a mat formation, sometimes torn loose in sheets by the winds. It is used by the cormorants and other island birds in constructing their nests. Other weeds have been introduced through seeds contained in the hay shipped in for the solitary island mule.

Around the islands gather great hordes of Steller sea lions, the largest congregations being on Saddle Rock and Sugar Loaf. The California Harbor seal and Pribilof fur seal are seen occasionally. There are also numbers of hares, descendants of a few given by an English sea captain to a former lighthouse keeper. These animals increased so fast that they surpassed the supply of food (weeds) and at one time died of starvation in great numbers. During the last century, when tender service to the islands was less regular than now, the rabbits furnished the only supply of fresh meat for the keepers during periods of protracted storms.

The bird population of The Farallones includes California murres, Western gulls, cormorants, pigeons, guillemots, tufted puffins, Cassin's auklets, ashy petrels, and rock wrens. During the early 1850's, when fresh eggs were almost worth their weight in gold to San Franciscans, the pear-shaped eggs of the murres were gathered here and sold in San Francisco markets. The thick, tough shells of the eggs enabled their collectors to handle them with shovels and eliminated the necessity of packing, but gathering them was a dangerous occupation. So precipitous are the cliffs of these islands that the collectors, besides being liable to arrest as poachers, frequently fell off into the sea. The trade in murres' eggs continued until the late 1880's, when the supply had so decreased that the profits of collecting them no longer outweighed the risks involved.

According to some historians, the first white man to see the Farallon Islands was Bartolemeo Ferrola, who took command of Cabrillo's expedition after Cabrillo's death, although other authorities question the authenticity of the old Spanish chronicles which credit the discovery to him. However, Sir Francis Drake not only saw but landed on one of the Farallones on July 24, 1579—24 hours after leaving "Nova Albion" (Drake's Bay), where the expedition had been repairing their *Golden Hinde* since June 17. Drake named the islands the "Islands of St.

James" and described them as having "plentiful and great stores of seals and birds." Sebastian Cermeno and his companions apparently visited the Farallones in 1595 when they were proceeding down the coast from Drake's Bay in their launch, the *San Buena Ventura,* after their *San Augustin* had been wrecked.

According to Mildred Brooke Hoover, the islands had already been designated as The Farallones: "The name Los Farallones is derived from the Spanish nautical word meaning 'cliff or small, pointed island,' and was fixed on this particular group during the years when the Spanish galleons plied between the Philippines and Mexico." The implication that the islands were well known to mariners of the time is substantiated by the chronicle of Sebastian Vizcaino, who described them in 1603 as a mark for finding Punta de los Reyes and the harbor of Drake's Bay. The first to name individual islands of the group, he called the Southeast Farallon La Isla Hendido [*sic*] (the cleft isle) and the Northwest Farallon, Las Llagas (the wounds) to commemorate the stigmata of St. Francis.

First white inhabitants of The Farallones were fur-gatherers from the Russian colony at Bodega Bay. At a cost of much sickness and death due to improper food and water, they took 200,000 fur seals in three seasons. Although the supply of fur seals was seriously depleted at the end of that time, the Russians continued to keep hunters on the islands. In 1819 a new colony was planted there, including a number of Aleuts. They lived in huts made of stone, planks, canvas, and the sea lions' skins (some of the stone walls still stand). Lacking wood for fires, they used the fat of sea lions and seals. Only once did a Russian brig call at the island for their products. After several months most of the men, too weak to kill the seals, were barely subsisting on raw birds' eggs. By 1825 not one fur seal was left on the island and only one Russian family and 23 Kodiaks (northwest Indians) were living there.

Since 1855 the islands have been under the supervision of the United States Lighthouse Service and closed to the public. In 1909 bird lovers, aided by Admiral George Dewey, succeeded in having the islands declared a bird sanctuary.

Up to 1968 the Southeast Farallon was inhabited by about two dozen men of the Coast Guard, some with their families, manning the light, radio beacon, and fog signal. Still standing is Stone House, the structure put up during the 1850's when the first lighthouse was built. The original light has been replaced by a modern one, raised 358 feet above mean tidewater and visible for 26 miles. To reach the light, the keepers once climbed a zigzag path along steep bluffs. It is said that during winter gales they had to crawl on hands and knees along the unsheltered stretches of this path.

ALCATRAZ ISLAND

The history of Alcatraz Island begins with its discovery in 1775 by Lieutenant Juan Manuel de Ayala of the *San Carlos,* who named it Isla de los Alcatraces (Isle of the Pelicans) because of the great number of these birds he found nesting there. In 1846, Pio Pico, last Mexican Governor of California, sold the island to Julian Workman. In March, 1849 Alcatraz was resold to John Charles Fremont, who acted as representative of the United States Government. Before the $5,000 was paid for the property, however, Fremont disposed of the island to the banking firm of Palmer, Cook & Company which subsequently brought suit to recover possession of it. Because Fremont had acted as a Government agent, the suit was denied and the island was retained as Federal property.

When the United States began to fortify the harbor in 1854, a lighthouse and lantern were installed on Alcatraz. Temporary buildings were erected, a wharf was built, and construction of batteries was begun. Between 1854 and 1882 the Government appropriated $1,697,500 for fortifications on the island. Powder magazines were blasted from the rock and a citadel built on the crest. In 1859 the first Army detachment, Company H, Stewart's Third Artillery, arrived on Alcatraz, commanded by Captain Joseph Stewart.

The island in 1868 was designated a disciplinary barracks for prisoners having long sentences to serve. From the early 1870's on, troublesome Indians were sent to this post from time to time. A company of Indian scouts accused of mutiny at Cibicu Creek, Arizona Territory, was incarcerated here, as were five Indian chiefs who mutinied at San Carlos, Arizona Territory, in June, 1887, among them Kae-te-na, friend of Geronimo. Of the many prisoners who arrived from the Philippines in 1900 —one transport alone brought 126—most had deserted the United States forces and joined the Filipino insurgents. Civilians who commited crimes against the Army in China also were brought here. During the 1906 disaster, 176 prisoners removed from San Francisco jails were transferred to Alcatraz.

From 1895 to 1907 several Coast Artillery detachments were stationed here. In the latter year, when Alcatraz was designated the Pacific Branch of the United States Military Prison, the third and fourth companies, United States Military Prison Guard, were organized as its permanent garrison. It became a Federal prison for civilians in 1934.

Escapes from the island were seldom attempted and rarely successful. The most ingenious of these get-aways was engineered in 1903 by four prisoners, all trusties for good behavior, of whom one was a professional forger and another a printer by trade. Between them they succeeded in drawing up and printing a document recommending leniency in their cases, to which they forged the name of the commanding officer. Through a friend in the post office department they succeeded in having the document slipped into the outgoing mail. It made its way through all departments to the Department Commander, who then ordered the four released. They were given a military escort to the mainland. No sooner had they landed in San Francisco than they forged four checks to the sum of $125 on the quartermaster department, whereupon they repaired to a grog shop for liquid refreshments. Three of the men, fearing drunkenness, fled; but the fourth was picked up by police on a San Francisco street and promptly returned to the island. More successful were Roy Gardner, known as the gentleman bandit, who escaped alone from the island in the early 1920's, and two prisoners who made a sensational getaway in 1938 and never were found. In 1926 a plot for a mass exit was halted when the warden, learning of the plans, pointed to the Bay and told the rebels to "go ahead and swim." Again in 1946 a violent mutiny by prisoners who gained arms and put up a two-day battle was only quelled by a landing of the U.S. Marines.

Alcatraz' grim reputation caused San Francisco civic bodies to demand its abandonment; but though former United States Attorney General Frank Murphy in 1939 advised removal of its felons, it was not until the spring of 1963 that the prison was closed.

Following its closing Congress created a five member Commission to investigate and study future uses of the island. In April, 1964, the Commission met in San Francisco to review all proposals for the islands future use. After many months it unanimously agreed to support the proposal submitted by the San Francisco Chapter of the American Association for the United Nations, for a monument commemorating the June 26, 1946 founding of the United Nations in San Francisco.

On March 8, 1964, five warriors of the Sioux tribe disembarked on the island from a small boat and made formal land claims, saying they acted on an 1868 treaty with the Sioux nation that allowed Indians off the reservation to claim "unoccupied government land." They landed again on November 20, 1969, eighty-nine men, women, and children, prepared to make Alcatraz their home. Seventy-eight different tribes were represented including reservation and city Indians, full-bloods and mixed. They were governed by seven council members (three women and four men), elected to a ninety-day term of office by the general assembly. Five members were elected to act as negotiators with the Federal government, and their demands were set forth in the following manifesto:

Indians of All Tribes greet our brothers and sisters of all races and tongues upon our Earth Mother. We here on Indian Land, Alcatraz, represent many tribes of Indians.

We are still holding the Island of Alcatraz in the true names of Freedom, Justice and Equality, because our brothers and sisters of this earth have lent support to our just cause. We reach out our hands and hearts and send spirit messages to all Indians.

Our anger at the many injustices forced upon us since the first white men landed on these sacred shores has been transformed into a hope that we be allowed the long-suppressed right of all men to plan and to live their own lives in harmony and cooperation with all fellow creatures and with nature. We have learned that violence breeds only more violence and we therefore have carried on our occupation of Alcatraz in a peaceful manner, hoping that the government will act accordingly.

Be it known, however, that we are quite serious in our demand to be given ownership of this island in the name of Indians of All Tribes. We are here to stay; men, women, and children. We feel that this request is but little to ask from a government which has systematically stolen our lands, destroyed a once-beautiful landscape, killed off the creatures of nature, polluted air and water, ripped open the very bowels of our earth in senseless greed, and instituted a program to annihilate the many Indian Tribes of this land by theft, suppression, prejudice, termination, and so-called relocation and assimilation. We are a proud people! We are Indians! We have observed and rejected much of what so-called civilization offers. We are Indians! We will preserve our traditions and ways of life by educating our own chlidren. We are Indians! We will join hands in a unity never before put into practice. Our Earth Mother awaits our voices. We are Indians of All Tribes!!!

On June 1, 1970, the historic Alcatraz Island lighthouse—light inactive since May 28, 1970—and four other large buildings were destroyed by fire, the Indians refusing mainland fire-fighting aid. The first baby born on the Island was to an Indian couple on July 20, 1970.

It had become clear that the United States government expected the Indians to abandon Alcatraz during the bleak second winter, but the Indians said "they have come too far and through too much to start giving land back to the white man."

However, on June 11, 1971, the Federal Government, using a force of twenty armed marshals, three Coast Guard cutters and a helicopter, swept upon the island and forcibly, but peacefully, removed its fifteen remaining Indian residents, six men, four women and five children.

ANGEL ISLAND

Largest island in the Bay, mile-square Angel Island, roughly triangular in shape, rears its central peak (776' alt.) across Raccoon Strait from Point Tiburon. Once the site of a detention camp for hostile Indians captured during the Arizona campaign, it served after 1892 as San Francisco's Quarantine and Immigration Station, and during World War II served the Army as an internment camp for German and Italian prisoners of war. The grassy green of the island's slopes is broken by darker patches of trees and brush. In some places outcroppings of rock lend a fantastic color to the predominating gentleness of the landscape. The shoreline, nearly six miles in circumference, rough and steep in places, curves inward here and there to narrow strips of white sand. Above it a military road circles the island at elevations varying from eighty to three feet. A Federal game refuge, the island is stocked with deer, quail, and pheasant.

When the *San Carlos* dropped anchor in Raccoon Strait, Lieutenant Juan Manuel de Ayala named the adjacent island Nuestra Señora de los Angeles (Our Lady of the Angels). After a century and a half of consequent neglect, Angel Island was granted in 1839 to Antonio Mario Osio by Governor Juan B. Alvarado, who took this means to prevent its occupation by the Russians and other foreigners. Osio raised horses and cattle there, although he never lived on the island himself. However, his claim generally was recognized until California became American territory, whereupon Osio went to Mexico. When he returned in 1855 with a claim to the island, he found it had already been set aside in 1850 for military purposes by executive order of the United States Government. The island was occupied by Federal troops in 1863. By 1865 a battery of three guns had been established on the west slope of the island, commanding the approach through the Golden Gate, which was later increased to 18 pieces; and in 1867 a general depot for receiving and discharging recruits from the Atlantic Coast was established on the east shoreline.

Before the end of the 1850's, Angel Island had won local fame as the site of a celebrated duel, which grew out of a stormy conflict involving the slavery issue. One Charles A. Stovall had brought with him to San Francisco from Mississippi a Negro slave boy known simply as Archy. When Stovall decided to return home, Archy refused to go and escaped from a Sacramento river boat. His master had him arrested but the Sacramento police refused to hand him over, whereupon Stovall carried the matter to the State Supreme Court. Justice Peter H. Burnett ordered the Negro returned to him. Archy's case then was taken to United States Commissioner George Penn Johnson, who ruled on April 14, 1858 that he no longer was a slave. One of Johnson's closest friends, State Senator William I. Ferguson, a Southerner, challenged Johnson's decision. Feeling ran so high between the two that arrangements were made for a duel. On a tiny piece of level ground on the eastern side of Angel Island the principals met at five o'clock on the afternoon of August 21, 1858. Dueling pistols having been chosen, it was agreed the combatants would start firing at ten paces, this distance to be reduced to ten feet if the first fire ineffective. When neither contestant was hit on the first exchange, or on the second and third, Johnson demanded an apology or a fourth encounter. The latter course was chosen. Ferguson was hit in the right thigh and Johnson in the left wrist. Ferguson was taken to San Francisco, where he died on September 14 while his leg was being amputated.

Near Angel Island a prison brig had been anchored in 1852 with 35 convicts aboard, 17 of whom escaped at different times, overpowering or bribing the keepers. The island itself served as a prison camp during the 1870's for hostile Arizona Indians. A part of its eastern shore was set aside in 1900 as a detention and quarantine camp for soldiers returning from the Philippines. In 1900 the post was named Fort McDowell in honor of Major General Irvin McDowell, commander of the Union Army at the First Battle of Bull Run, and later of the Department of the Pacific. From December 1, 1901 to June 30, 1902 a total of 10,747 soldiers passed through the Angel Island station on their return from Manila.

By an act of Congress in 1888 the building of a permanent quarantine station on the island was authorized and an appropriation of $103,000 set aside for the purpose. Constructed on the shores of a sheltered indentation north of Fort McDowell, known as Hospital Cove, the quarantine station was opened May 1, 1892. In 1909 the Angel Island Immigration Station was established. Quarantine and immigration officers boarded ships from foreign ports for inspection. Individuals who did not pass inspection were taken to the Angel Island Station for further examination.

Angel Island is also the site of a Government-operated lighthouse, established on the southwest portion of the island, in 1886. The 640-acre island is now a State Park under the direction of the State Division of Beaches and Parks.

YERBA BUENA

Stepping stone for the bridge builders in spanning the Bay, cone-shaped Yerba Buena Island, rising between the eastern and western shores, is the anchorage for both the suspension and the cantilever spans of the San Francisco-Oakland Bay Bridge. Through a rock formation of the island passes a bore tunnel connecting the two. East of the tunnel, the first of the bridge's East Bay spans passes over the buildings of the island's naval reservation on a narrow tongue of land projecting into the bay, terminated by a barren low hill. Winding paved side roads lead to all parts of the island's landscaped and heavily wooded slopes, dotted by the neat dwellings of navy and lighthouse personnel.

Known to early navigators and whalers as Wood Island, Yerba Buena Island was indicated on old Spanish charts as Isla del Carmen. The English navigator, Frederick W. Beechey, gave it the present name in 1826, but it was known locally as Goat Island in the early 1830's when Gorham H. Nye pastured his goats on its slopes. Until after the 1850's, when the Land Commission denied the Limantour claim to the island and gave title to the Government, other early settlers raised goats there. Despite the subsequent disappearance of all goats from the island the colloquial name persisted, although various official documents referred to it as

Yerba Buena. (An 1858 map of California had called it Ghote [*sic*] Island.) In 1895 the U.S. Geographic Board adopted the local name.

Not until December 19, 1866 did the Government first take possession. First used as an infantry station, the island served in the early 70's as an artillery post, until fire destroyed the buildings, leaving as the only remaining Government service the lighthouse station established in 1875.

On April 12, 1898, President William McKinley signed an executive order setting aside a part of the island for a naval training station. At a cost of $74,400 barracks were erected to house 500 apprentices. The additional water supply necessary for the training station was piped under the bay from Contra Costa County. The island slopes were cleared and landscaped and a road built to its highest point. A fully rigged training ship, the *Boston,* was attached to the station for use in a six-months cruise of sea duty, following a like training period on shore. The old *USS Boston* of Commodore Dewey's fleet at Manila during the Spanish-American War, was stationed here up until the eve of World War I, when finally it was dismantled and sunk. Stocks of quail and pheasant turned loose on the island thrived until in 1916 an executive order set aside 141 acres as a National Game Preserve.

The campaign to change the name of the island, begun in 1916 by historian Nellie van der Grift Sanchez, succeeded in 1931 when the United States Geographic Board made the name Yerba Buena official. A newspaper account of the ceremonies held on the island in June, 1931 states: "The day's legend was that there was one remaining goat on the island, and he was to be thrown overboard to free Yerba Buena, like St. Patrick did Ireland. Jack Love, radio operator on the island, dressed up as a goat and was twice fed to the crocodiles."

Below the eastern entrance to the Bay Bridge tunnel, a road winds down around the island past a marine sentry post to the Naval Receiving Station on the southeastern shore. Commissary buildings, warehouses and a carpenter shop, a building marked General Court Martial and Brig, and the old barracks with its colonial portico stand below a span of the bridge.

Below the high bluff on the southwest shore are the buildings of the Coast Guard Depot, which services and supplies all aids to navigation along the California coast between Point Sal and the Oregon line. Three large buoy tenders, a smaller tender, and a work launch operate from the depot, placing buoys and servicing light stations. When not on station the Lightship *Relief,* with its white superstructure and its name painted in large white letters on its bright red hull, lies alongside the dock. This vessel relieves the San Francisco and Blunts Reef lightships during repair and drydocking periods.

Above the island's southwestern point, visible from the San Francisco span of the Bay Bridge, is the octagonal gray and white frame tower of Yerba Buena Light, erected in 1875. One of the smallest in the service, it is supplied by a 1,500-watt globe magnified to 12,000 candlepower by its prism shade, which operates at calculated intervals from sunrise to sunset. An astronomical clock regulates the light automatically to conform with changes in the daylight hours. The gray and white frame building with gabled red roof above the tower is occupied by the lighthouse keeper and his assistant.

TREASURE ISLAND

"It ought to be in the West, and have a tang of the Orient about it . . . at the last frontier of civilization's forward march, yet looking out upon the most ancient lands and the most exotic peoples." So was hailed—by Lewis Rex Miller in the *Christian Science Monitor*—the concept and construction of the Golden Gate International Exposition (1939-40) on Treasure Island. Today it is no longer a legendary city of towers and pavilions—like Kublai Khan's "stately pleasure dome" conjured up by scientific magic—that appears in the Bay beyond the filled-in causeway leading from Yerba Buena Island (*see Emporium of a New World: Engineering Enterprise*). Instead Treasure Island wears the brisked and ordered look of the United States Navy base which it became early in World War II.

The great exposition for which the island was created has left its mark, however, for some of its buildings remain. The architectural commission to whom goes much of the credit for the exposition's dominant features included such outstanding Western architects as Lewis P. Hobart, Ernest Weihe, Timothy Pflueger, William G. Merchant, and Arthur Brown, Jr. Until his death in 1937, George W. Kelham, supervising architect of the Panama-Pacific Exposition (1915), was chairman of the commission. Under its direction the goal which Kelham described as an attempt "to strike a golden medium between pageantry and structural beauty" was realized to a degree of perfection admired by millions of spectators. Working in close harmony with its designers of buildings, landscape architects such as Mark Daniels, Thomas D. Church, Butler S. Sturtevant, and the Misses Worn, under the supervision of John McLaren, chief landscape architect of the 1915 exposition and of Golden Gate Park, created floral designs and arranged for the planting of evergreens indigenous to the Pacific Coast. Besides rhododendrons and azaleas, native annuals, and perennials from all over the Far West, landscaping brought to this riot of color the exotic hues of flowers and plants imported from far countries of the Pacific area.

Midway down the Avenue of Palms rose two massive Mayan-Incan pyramids (Weihe) supporting huge stylized elephant figures—the exposition's main gateway to its great circular Court of Honor. Here the slim octagonal Tower of the Sun (Brown), pierced by airy embrazures and surmounted by a spire, rose 400 feet to dominate with a Renaissance gesture the conglomerate electicism of the surrounding architecture. Northward from the belvederes and statuary about its base stretched the immense oblong Court of the Seven Seas (Kelham). From the facades of the two pavilions which enclosed it protruded the rearing prows of galleys with carved figureheads, suggestive of travel and adventure. This *via triumphalis* set with standards and lanterns opened into the Court of Pacifica (Pflueger), across whose fountain and sculptures gazed Ralph Stackpole's amazonian statue, *Pacifica,* symbolic of peaceful co-operation between the Americas and their Pacific neighbors, stationed against a gleaming backdrop of tubes and metal stars designed to produce melodious sounds under certain climatic conditions. Eastward from the Tower of the Sun lay the long Court of Reflections with its serene sculptures and still pools, separated by a lofty arch (Hobart) from the adjoining Court of Flowers. Olof C. Malmquist's *The Rainbow* rose from the fountain dominating this enclosure, whose eastern entrance was guarded by twin Towers of the East (Merchant). The Court of the Moon and Stars (Kelham) adjoining the Court of Honor on the south presented a decorative vista of fountain, urns, and bas-reliefs. Beyond, in the direction of Yerba Buena Island, lay the sunken Enchanted Garden, where landscaping played unconfined about a huge fountain. Overlooking this verdant area, William Wurster's Yerba Buena Clubhouse achieved that gay and functional quality associated with this architect's rejection of ornament and fondness for modern materials.

Throughout the exposition's ensemble of almost a hundred buildings, as various in design as the purposes they served were many whose architecture was notable either for beautiful modernity or for features suggestive of cultures ranging from Alaska to Argentina, from Missouri to French Indo China.

The exposition proved a gigantic workshop for all but a few of the more renowned Bay region sculptors and mural painters. From Sargent Johnson's grotesque Inca Indians astride llamas beside the fountain in the Court of Pacifica and Adeline Kent's evanescent *Air and Water* above the arched west walls of the Court of Honor to Robert Howard's gamboling *Whales* in the fountain of the San Francisco Building and Herman Volz's gigantic mural, *The Conquest of the West,* on the facade of the Federal Building—the statuary and murals ran the gamut of the Bay region's artistic achievements. The academic tradition predominated in Olof C. Malmquist's *Fauna,* in Ettore Cadorin's *Moon and the Dawn,* in Haig Patigian's *Creation.* Purely decorative were Jacques Schnier's panel, *Dance of Life;* Raymond Puccinelli's restrained *Flora;* Ruth Cravath's fountain group, *North America.*

The conversion of Treasure Island into one of the Navy's key West Coast bases began when it was leased from the City and County of San Francisco on February 28, 1941. Exposition buildings were converted into barracks and galleys. A chapel, a hostess house, and a post office building were constructed; plumbing and drainage were improved and fire protection facilities installed. Throughout World War II the island served the Navy as a receiving ship, pre-embarkation and embarkation center, training center, and home base for many Pacific commands. It also became the first stop on the way back home for many naval and Marine veterans of the Pacific campaign. At the war's end, it continued functioning much as it had in the past, providing facilities for a variety of training programs. The Navy looked ahead to its continued operation as one of the most important of the far-flung network of bases which covers the Bay area.

East Bay: Cities and Back Country

IN SPANISH times the distant shoreline opposite the Golden Gate was *"la contra costa"* (the opposite coast), to the *conquistadores.* Today between the shimmering cables and steel girders of the San Francisco-Oakland Bay Bridge, the eastward traveler sees a continuous panorama of home and industry, extending north and south with hardly a break and almost to the crest of the wooded hills in the background. The "opposite coast" is now the East Bay, a heterogeneous urban area comprising many municipalities in two counties. The bridge is itself both a practical and a symbolical evidence of its close relationship to the other metropolitan areas on the western shore.

The hills seem to recede as the traveler speeds down the eastern half of the bridge: he sees a flat rectangular strip of land on which most of the industrial and business sections of the East Bay rest, as on a stage to which the residential hills are the backdrop. Ahead and to the right are the tall buildings of downtown Oakland, key city of the area, where the industrial district crowds down to the Outer Harbor in the foreground. Across the water to the far right a ferryboat dock— reminiscent of a vanishing era in Bay transportation—affords the only glimpse of Alameda, the island city. Far to the southeast, beyond the traveler's range of vision, are San Leandro and Hayward. Although the vast panorama of homes and business buildings shows no visible gaps, it is a jig-saw puzzle of independent communities closely fitted together—Piedmont, a residential community in the hills almost directly ahead; Emeryville, an industrial town crowding to the shore in the left foreground; Berkeley to the left, best identified by the white campanile and stadium on the university campus, spreading up the slopes beyond; El Cerrito, and Richmond, residential and industrial towns far to the left. With a combined population of over a 1,500,000, these municipalities form a continuous urban unit, yet maintain their political independence.

Its scenic attractions and garden climate—slightly more extreme in summer and winter than San Francisco's—make the East Bay the family homesite of more than 50,000 commuters, who ebb and flow daily across the bridge to business and professional offices. The panoramic setting of the entire Bay region is nowhere better seen than from the Grizzly Peak and Skyline Boulevards, which follow the crest of the hills above Berkeley and Oakland. With impressive authority, a noted traveler has cited this tour as "the third most beautiful drive in the

EAST BAY KEY MAP

SCALE IN MILES

0 1 2

world." It follows for a distance the boundary line between the two counties which share the east side of the Bay—Alameda and Contra Costa, the old Spanish name having adhered to the latter, although its meaning is generally lost on the monolinguistic inheritors of the ranchos.

Oakland

Air Services: Metropolitan Oakland International Airport, Port of Oakland, Doolittle Dr. and Airport Dr. Commuter Services to San Francisco. San Francisco-Oakland Helicopter Airlines, connecting with San Francisco International, San Francisco Heliport, Berkeley, Marin County, Palo Alto, San Jose-Sunnyvale. Oakland downtown heliport, 1220 Jackson St., Civic Center.

Buses: Greyhound Bus Lines, 2103 San Pablo Ave.; Peerless Stages, 2040 Castro,Continental Trailways, 2003 Telegraph Ave. Barrett Airport Limousine Service, 2003 Telegraph Ave.

Railroads: Southern Pacific, Passenger Terminal, 16th Western Pacific, Washington & 3rd Sts.

Streetcars and Buses: A.C. Transit, Transbay Service to San Francisco, East Bay City Express Service and Eastbay Local Service.

Bridge: San Francisco-Oakland Bay Bridge, toll 50¢ a car.

Traffic Regulations: Speed limit 25 mph in business and residential areas, 15 mph at intersections. Limited parking in business district.

Information: Oakland *Tribune,* 13th and Franklin Sts. Oakland Chamber of Commerce, 1320 Webster St. Oakland Travel Service Inc., MacArthur and Broadway. Radio Stations: KDIA, Bay Bridge Toll Plaza; KEWB, 77 Jack London Square; KSAY, Bay Bridge Toll Plaza.

Culture Centers: Oakland Museum, Oak Street between 10th and 11th Sts. Jack London Square, Foot of Broadway.

Parks: Lakeside Park, Bellevue and Grand Ave. Lake Merritt, center of downtown Oakland. Rancho Peralta, East 10th Street and 2nd Ave. Joaquin Miller Park, 33 Joaquin Miller Road. Redwood Regional Park, Redwood Road.

SPORTS

Archery: Peralta Park, 10th and Fallon Sts.

Baseball: Oakland-Alameda County Coliseum.

Boating: Lake Merritt.

Cricket: Golden Gate Playgrounds, 6142 San Pablo Ave.

Golf: Lake Chabot Municipal Golf Course, end of Golf Links Rd.

Lawn Bowling: Lakeside Park, N. shore Lake Merritt.

Riding: Bridle paths in hills.

Swimming: Diamond Park, Fruitvale Ave. and Lyman Rd. Lake Temescal, Broadway at Tunnel Road. Thomas J. Roberts Regional Park, Oakland Hills.

Tennis: Municipal courts.

Wrestling: Oakland Civic Auditorium.

Yachting: Oakland Yacht Harbor, foot of 19th Ave.

CHURCHES

Christian: First, 29th and Fairmount Sts. *Christian Science:* First Church of Christ, Scientist, 1701 Franklin St. *Mormon:* Church of Jesus Christ of Latter-day Saints, Oakland Temple, 4770 Lincoln Ave. *Congregational:* First, 2501 Harrison. *Episcopal:* St. Paul's, Grand & Montecito Ave. *Greek Orthodox:* Greek Orthodox Church of the Ascension, Lincoln Ave., south of Warren Freeway. *Hebrew Orthodox:* Temple Sinai, 28th & Webster Sts. *Lutheran:* St. Paul's, 1658 Excelsior. *Methodist:* First, 24th & Broadway. *Roman Catholic:* St. Francis de Sales Cathedral, 634-21st St. *Salvation Army:* 1601-6th Ave. *Seventh Day Adventist:* Oakland Central Church, 1811-11th Ave. *Unitarian:* First, 685-14th St.

OAKLAND (0-1900 alt., 361,561 pop. 1970; 367,548, 1960), seat of Alameda County, occupies roughly the central part of the East Bay metropolitan area. Berkeley and Emeryville to the north and Alameda, across the Estuary, limit its expansion, but to the east and southeast it sprawls without let or hindrance over hills and Bay-shore flats.

From the tall white City Hall in the heart of the city, streets, once country roads, radiate: San Pablo Avenue striking northwest to industrial Emeryville and West Berkeley; Telegraph Avenue and Broadway, north through the residential sections to the University of California; Fourteenth Street, west to the sprawling slums, and east and southeast from City Hall. Running zigzag past Lake Merritt are the small shops serving the higher income residents of East Oakland, Fruitvale, Melrose and Elmhurst.

Closely hemming the downtown section, where many new tall office buildings loom over squat business structures, are two- and three-story homes of the gingerbread era, slightly down-at-the-heel. Spreading north and east toward the hills from Lake Merritt in the heart of the city are thousands of wood and stucco houses, each with its shrubs and lawn. The one reminder of Oakland's Spanish heritage is the modern homes in the restricted districts—Rockridge, Broadway Terrace, and Claremont Pines —constructed in a modified Mediterranean style of architecture, tile-roofed and stuccoed, with wide arches, studio windows, and sunny patios. Semitropical trees—camphor, acacia, pepper, dracena, and palm— ornament city parks and sidewalks, and figs and citrus fruits ripen in the warm sunshine in many backyards.

Warmer in the summer than its metropolitan neighbor across the Bay, Oakland's climate is nevertheless tempered in summer by cooling winds and fogs from the ocean. This has attracted many San Francisco business men and office workers who, even before the building of the Bay Bridge, came here.

In the spring, the hills become green backgrounds for wildflower mosaics of scarlet and purple, blue and yellow. Besides the Coast live-oak for which the city is named, the Monterey pine and eucalyptus are abundant. The latter was introduced from Australia in 1856 and planted by the thousand in the hills to create a wooded watershed. Vivid with color during the spring months, the uplands are seared to silver-brown through summer and fall because of lack of rain.

Around the City Hall spread the 70 blocks of the retail shopping district. Oakland's department stores and speciality shops draw patronage from the entire East Bay region, but they also yield a certain percentage of such trade to the transbay metropolis, as San Francisco trade names on the doors of local shops indicate. Influenced by the close commercial tie-up between the two cities, Oakland's tempo of living varies with the time of day: by dawn commuters are on the move, feeder highways to the San Francisco-Oakland Bay Bridge are alive with speeding cars, and interurban buses travel the streets, crossing and re-crossing the great span. After the early morning rush, life in the downtown section settles into a somewhat more moderate pace. At the end of the day, as automobiles, and buses, carry thousands home from work, the main thoroughfares come to noisy life again.

South of the central business district, the section between Tenth Street and the shore of the Estuary, oldest quarter of the city, is now given over to bargain stores, second-hand shops, and workers' homes. On lower Broadway is a section of honky-tonk beer parlors and skid-road soup houses, where a burlesque show with lurid lobby portraiture is neighbor to a hole-in-the-wall pawnshop and an old-clothes emporium, where panhandlers linger on street corners and at entrances to penny arcades. Southward, interspersed with unpainted, grimy dwellings, are wholesale houses.

Along the Estuary itself, resounding to the grating squeak of winches and the staccato chug of wharf tractors are huge docks, a part of the Port of Oakland's Inner Harbor—one of the three on the city's 32-mile water front: Outer Harbor, between San Francisco-Oakland Bay Bridge approach and the Southern Pacific mole; Middle Harbor, bounded by the Southern Pacific and Western Pacific Railroads; and Inner Harbor, comprising the six miles of tidal estuary between Oakland and Alameda. Into the narrow Inner Harbor come freighters from the seven seas. Here are held crew races of the University of California, and here pleasure craft and fishing boats nose in and out.

West of downtown Oakland, extending from Market Street to the Bay and from the Estuary to Twentieth Street, is the West Oakland district. Crowding close about railroad yards and manufacturing plants are unsightly and dreary-looking dwellings. On some of the streets spacious old homes still maintain an air of shabby and aloof gentility, but many have been partitioned into crowded, rabbit-warren housekeeping rooms. Throughout the district are rows of ugly cottages with blistered paint and rickety stairs and porches, many of which are now being demolished to make way for new housing and business projects.

In West Oakland is the city's Harlem, home of the large black population once attracted by Oakland's position as the western terminus of two overland railway systems, which employed in great numbers waiters, cooks, and porters. West Seventh Street is the center of Negro life. Here are dance halls, restaurants, markets, barber shops, and motion picture theaters.

Although Oakland's population includes thousands of Portuguese, Italians, Mexicans, and Chinese, its various national groups are scattered throughout the city rather than settled in well-defined foreign quarters. Their customs and cuisine lend colorful variety to the city's life.

The Portuguese have been here for three generations, and yet they still hold to such national customs and festivals as the Feast of the Holy Ghost, celebrated annually. A large number of Portuguese-Americans in the environs are truck farmers and dairymen. The Italians, largest foreign language group, have influenced the culinary art of the community. Numerous Italian restaurants feature various *antipasti* with which to whet the appetite; *polenta,* a thick porridge of corn meal; and such delicacies as fried artichokes or squash blossoms dipped in batter and fried in deep olive oil. The Mexican population maintains a few restaurants which serve native Mexican foods—*enchiladas, tacos en tortillas,* and *chili rellena*—and an occasional hole-in-the-wall shop where strings of *chorizo* (Mexican sausage) hang from gray rafters and three-bushel jute bags of purple and crimson peppers stand in corners. Chinatown, with its dangling lanterns and picture word signs, houses its 3,000 Chinese in a loosely knit community centering in the wholesale district near Eighth and Franklin Streets. Up and down its sidewalks the soft-soled slippers of Old China shuffle along beside Young China's tapping occidental heels. On market pegs hang exotic fruits and vegetables, dried ducks and transparent octopuses.

Although the site of Oakland was first visited by white men in 1770, when Lieutenant Pedro Fages led an expedition here seeking a land route to Point Reyes, a half century passed before the land was first colonized. In 1820 Spain's last governor of Alta California, Pablo Vicente de Sola, granted to one Sergeant Luis Maria Peralta a tract of land in recognition of conspicuous military service in the Spanish Colonial Army. This grant became known as the Rancho San Antonio. Covering 48,000 acres, it included the area now occupied by Oakland, Berkeley, and Alameda. Threescore years of age at the time he received this prodigious grant, Don Luis never actually lived on it, preferring to remain at his home on a grant he had obtained in 1818, Portados la Rancheria del Chino, near the *pueblo* San Jose. He had four grown sons whom he placed in charge of Rancho San Antonio.

Not only was this the first, but it was also the most valuable, of the land grants on the east shore of San Francisco Bay. Lean years were few. The soil was rich, and herds multiplied rapidly; but agriculture was confined to the raising of a few staples grown in limited quantities.

In 1842 Don Luis, then past 80, divided his grant among his sons. To Jose Domingo he gave what is now Berkeley; to Vicente, the Encinal de Temescal (now central Oakland); to Antonio Maria, the portion to the south (East Central Oakland and Alameda); and to Ignacio, what is now Melrose and Elmhurst. Realizing the danger of future family altercations, he adjured them: "I command all my children, that they remain in peace, succoring each other in their necessities, eschewing all avaricious ambitions, without entering into foolish differences for one or two calves, for the cows bring them forth each year; and inasmuch as the land is narrow, it is indispensable that the cattle should become mixed up, for which reason I command my sons to be friendly and united."

To this sage advice his sons listened with respect. During the golden years of the Peraltas' reign over Rancho San Antonio, business was seldom allowed to interfere with pleasure. There were innumerable fiestas, and, on Antonio's share of the grant, bull fights were held. But while the Spaniards complacently watched their grazing herds of fat cattle "without entering into foolish differences for one or two calves," a new economic order was emerging. Gold had been discovered. Across the Bay the sleepy settlement of Yerba Buena had become a lusty brawling town crowded with men of all descriptions, including trigger-quick adventurers.

Shaken by the momentous events which were threatening the destinies of the Peralta clan, Don Luis called its members together—sons and grandsons—and spoke with grave earnestness, imparting final words of wisdom: "My sons," he said, "God has given this gold to the Americans. Had He desired us to have it, He would have given it to us ere now. Therefore, go not after it, but let others go. Plant your lands and reap; these be your best gold fields, for all must eat while they live."

In 1849 there arrived the first American settler in this region, a former sea captain, Moses Chase. Soon thereafter three newcomers, Robert, William, and Edward Patten, who had leased land from Antonio Peralta, added Chase to their group and became the first American farmers in this district, raising good crops of hay and grain.

With these tenants the Peraltas had come to terms, but a steady stream of new squatters also dotted their holdings. Unsuccessful in several attempts in 1850 and 1851 to eject the newcomers, they were forced at length to compromise by granting leases. Among these squatters was a man whose name was to be closely linked with the early history of Oakland—Horace W. Carpentier, who recently had been graduated from Columbia College in New York. Associated with him in the enterprises that were destined to make him many times a millionaire were A. J. Moon and Edson Adams. Having acquired with his partners a townsite where present downtown Oakland is situated, Carpentier in 1852 succeeded in having the town of Oakland incorporated, with himself seated securely in the mayor's chair. When the citizenry, who were seldom advised of what their mayor was doing, awoke, he held—among other concessions—a franchise for a ferry to San Francisco, the fare to be one dollar a trip.

Carpentier obtained absolute title to the entire water front in exchange for building a small frame schoolhouse and three tiny wharves. The water-front deal resulted in prolonged litigation, known as the "Battle of the Waterfront," by which the city tried to regain title to its doorstep. The fight was not ended until 1910, when assignees of Carpentier agreed to waive title to the water-front property in exchange for long-term leases.

The first combination rail and ferry service began operation to San Francisco in 1863, although ferry service alone had started as early as 1850. During the 1860's the "Big Four"—Stanford, Huntington, Crocker, and Hopkins—started building the Central Pacific Railroad, for which Oakland was the proposed western terminus. When in 1867 they asked the city for water-front rights, the city was unable to comply, having presented all such property to Horace Carpentier. However, the next year Carpentier founded a corporation known as the Oakland Waterfront Company. Associated with him in this enterprise, among others, was Leland Stanford, one of the "Big Four." Carpentier deeded to the corporation his water-front holdings and the corporation in turn conveyed to the railroad 500 acres of tideland. The railroad later appeared as the chief defendant, and loser, in the suit wherein Oakland regained these properties.

At one time the railroad officials had considered the Government-owned Yerba Buena Island as a western rail terminus. The citizens of San Francisco objected violently. It was feared "that the real intention was, by leveling the island and constructing causeways to Oakland, to rear up a rival city on the opposite shore that would be in substance owned . . . by the railroad company." The plan died when the Senate refused to approve the scheme. All obstacles finally surmounted, the first overland rail service began in 1869.

By 1870 there were two banks, three newspapers, and a city directory. Gas lamps illuminated lower Broadway. The first paving had been laid—at a cost of $3.40 per square foot. The University of California (later moved to Berkeley) was "spreading light and goodness," and a seminary for young ladies—now Mills College—was about to open.

The Central Pacific had entered the city, and the Oakland Railroad, already connecting with ferries to San Francisco, had been granted the right "to run horse-cars from the end of Broadway to Temescal Creek, and thence to the grounds of the College of California, for thirty years." Southeast of Lake Merritt the villages of Clinton, San Antonio, and Lynn had been consolidated into the town of Brooklyn—now East Oakland.

The social life of the town, also, had seen great change. No longer were posters seen such as the one which had announced in earlier days:

> "There will be a great bear fight in front of the American Hotel, Oakland, between the red bear Sampson and a big grizzly on Jan. 9th."

By 1870 this form of entertainment had been banned, and less sanguinary pleasures had taken its place: baseball instead of bullfights and typically Yankee "dime parties," socials, and church bazaars instead of Spanish fiestas.

In its growth as a suburb, it gained some distinction from the artists and writers who lived here. Jack London was developing from a water-front loiterer into an internationally known novelist. Joaquin Miller, the "Poet of the Sierras," was vaingloriously displaying his long hair and longer beard. Edwin Markham, while teaching in an Oakland school, awoke to find himself famous for "The Man With the Hoe." William Keith was painting the East Bay hills and trees. George Sterling, the lyric poet of whom London, his contemporary, said, "he looked like a Greek coin run over by a Roman chariot," lived in Oakland from 1890 to 1905, and Ina Coolbrith, who as librarian of the Oakland Public Library guided the early reading of Jack London, and who was a poetess in her own right, was here from 1873 until 1897.

Oakland's growth was greatly accelerated by the earthquake and fire that overwhelmed San Francisco in 1906. Although itself damaged by the earthquake, it escaped the fire which overwhelmed the neighboring city.

Up to 50,000 refugees fled to the East Bay region in one week. Not a few remained as permanent residents. This influx caused such a building boom that by the following year the population had jumped to 125,000. Industrial growth also was stimulated. During the World War, industry boomed as four large shipbuilding companies operated at peak capacity. By 1920 the population was 216,000.

The rapid growth of Oakland shortly after 1900 is credited largely to Francis Marion "Borax" Smith, of Death Valley fame. With the huge profits from his borax mines, Smith invested heavily in the future of Oakland. He tied together the numerous street railway systems of the East Bay and founded the Key Route Ferry System in opposition to the Southern Pacific; he acquired control of the East Bay Water Company, and in partnership with Frank C. Havens, pioneer capitalist, established the Realty Syndicate as a holding company for their many real estate properties. Land in every region of Alameda County was bought and developed, residential and industrial tracts were opened up, and interurban train service was extended into each new era. Smith came to own an estimated one-sixth of Alameda County.

In December, 1910 the $200,000,000 United Properties Company was formed by a merger of money and properties owned by Smith, William S. Tevis, and R. G. Hanford. This corporation, perhaps the largest in California history (excepting the Eastern-controlled Southern Pacific Railroad), was to absorb and develop the railways, ferry system, public utilities, and real estate of the East Bay. However, the company collapsed in 1913 because of unsound financial methods, carrying with it the fortunes of the three founders. Smith, the heaviest loser, saw $24,000,000 slip from his fingers almost overnight. But the company's loss was the city's gain, for its developments remained.

In the Bay region, Oakland's port ranks second to San Francisco in value of cargo handled, and third to Richmond and San Francisco in tonnage. Coordinated water-rail-truck facilities handle the 4,500,000 tons of cargo that pass over the water front annually. Principal exports are dried and canned fruits and vegetables, lumber, grain, salt, and petroleum. Imports include copra, coal and coke, paper, iron and steel, and fertilizer. Fir, pine, cedar, spruce, and redwood arrive from the Northwest and the interior of California to be made into finished lumber or wood products before distribution.

Oakland's water front is well-equipped not only to repair bay, river, and oceangoing vessels but also to lay down such craft and to launch and outfit them. Yachting, commercial fishing, towing, and general boat-building and repairing call for many smaller shipyards. Construction work on large yachts and other boats is facilitated by the proximity of large Diesel engine works.

Fortunate in having ample room for residential expansion, Oakland is still growing. On the outskirts, where garden space is available, files of newly built homes spread into the countryside. Thus Oakland, despite the encroachment of industry, retains its identity as a city of homes.

POINTS OF INTEREST

The ALBERS MILLING COMPANY PLANT, west end of Seventh St., is the base for Bay area operations of a huge cereal and feed milling combine with plants throughout the West, which manufactures food products and animal feeds.

The NAVAL SUPPLY DEPOT, end of Middle Harbor Road, was planned as the nation's largest when construction began on the eve of World War II with an outlay of $15,000,000. The Board of Port Commissioners and the City of Oakland donated approximately 400 of the 500 acres which the Center covers. The first piles were driven in August, 1940, and the Center was officially commissioned on December 15, 1941, eight days after Pearl Harbor.

The U.S. ARMY PORT OF EMBARKATION & GENERAL DEPOT, is the huge cargo center for the San Francisco Port of Embarkation, serving United States Armed Forces in the Pacific. Commissioned December 8, 1941, its facilities include, piers, warehouses, office buildings, shops of many kinds, barracks, mess halls and other Army camp accommodations.

The NATIONAL BISCUIT COMPANY, Fourteenth and Union Sts., ships much of its large output to countries around the Pacific. In the process of making shredded wheat, hard wheat is dry-cleaned, steam-cooked, and stored in steel tanks for ten hours. Shredded between grooved rollers under 1,700 pounds pressure, it emerges in 29 threadlike layers which are cut into biscuits and baked for 20 minutes.

Ground was broken for the OAKLAND MORMON TEMPLE (Harold W. Burton, architect) on May 26, 1962, and the cornerstone laid May 25, 1963. The exterior of the building is faced with Siera white granite, quarried in Raymond, California. The temple sits on the stylobate 210 feet from east to west and 190 feet from north to south. It faces two and one-half degrees west off true north. The central tower rises 170 feet from ground level to the tip of the finnial or spire. There are four 96-ft. spires directly over the four corner towers. The towers are perforated and are covered in a blue glass mosaic and gold leaf. Visiting hours begin at 9 a.m. There is no charge for admission or guide.

At ST. JOSEPH'S CHURCH, Seventh and Chestnut Sts., occurs the annual Portuguese Festival of the Holy Ghost, which originated in Portugal in the thirteenth century when Queen Saint Isabel had a vision of the Holy Ghost. To her he indicated a desire that a church be built in his honor. The ceremonial of the dedication of that church, with its procession, its crowning of a queen, and its placing of the crown on the Altar of the Third Person of the Blessed Trinity, has survived among the Portuguese to this day. The festival, centering around Pentecost Sunday, is celebrated with feasting on barbecued meats and dancing.

The OAKLAND PUBLIC LIBRARY, Fourteenth and Grove Sts., contains 750,201 volumes and a large collection of pictures and prints. Over the main stairway and on the walls of the second floor are murals by Marion Holden Pope and Arthur Matthews.

Oakland's CITY HALL, Washington St. between Fourteenth and Fifteenth Sts., is a 17-story building rising 360 feet, completed in 1914, and was designed by the New York firm of Palmer, Hornbostel, and Jones, winner in a national competition. Faced with white granite and terra cotta in mingled Doric and Corinthian design, it has three set-back sections, capped by a baroque cupola adorned with four clock faces. The clock was donated by Dr. Samuel Merritt, former mayor.

Opposite the City Hall, overlooked by towering downtown buildings, is the triangular MEMORIAL PLAZA, dedicated to American war heroes.

JACK LONDON SQUARE bounded by Broadway, Webster & First Sts., and the Oakland estuary, has been transformed from a decrepit waterfront section into a restaurant and convention center. The Square has been landscaped by the Oakland Park Department and offers spacious parking areas and docking facilities for pleasure boats. The Jack London Square Marina development includes 200 berths, a boat ramp, hoist, fueling station and office building. Other tenants include a motor lodge and boatel, gift shops, a television station, radio station, bank, ship chandlery, and U.S. Customs. The First and Last Chance Saloon, 50 Webster St., near the Oakland estuary, is a small, weathered, dilapidated structure, purchased in 1883 by Johnny Heinold. As a saloon it was a popular hangout, especially in the 1890's, for ready-fisted seafarers who crowded its bar and gambled at its card tables. Jack London, in his early teens, found a friend in the proprietor, through whose encouragement and financial assistance his genius flowered in adventure tales woven around the lives of South Sea traders, Arctic whalers, and Alaska sourdoughs. The scarred mahogany bar is still in service and the gambling tables on which young London often wrote are used for refreshments. On a wall, are letters and photographs, including a picture of Jack in knickerbockers pouring over Heinold's tattered old dictionary, and a letter written years later, inviting Heinold to the author's famous Glen Ellen home.

The POSEY TUBE, 4,436 long, passing under the 42-foot-deep channel of the Oakland Estuary between Harrison St. in Oakland and Webster St. in Alameda, when completed at a cost of $5,000,000 in 1928 was the world's largest under-water tube for vehicular traffic.

The 32-acre PERALTA PARK, facing Lake Merritt across Twelfth St., is dominated by the $1,000,000 steel and concrete, granite-finished MUNICIPAL AUDITORIUM, built in 1915. The building is in classical style, the main facade facing the lake ornamented by a series of bas-reliefs in terra cotta set in the alcoves above the entrance doors. Besides the arena, seating 10,000, which is used for conventions and sports events, it contains a large theater for dramatic and musical performances.

Across Tenth St. from the auditorium, in Peralta Park, is the EXPOSITION BUILDING, a one-story, concrete and steel structure used chiefly as an armory by the California National Guard, and for civic events. Within the park are a playfield, a militia drill ground, and the shooting ranges and lodge of the Oakland Archery Club, whose members meet and shoot every Sunday morning.

The ALAMEDA COUNTY COURTHOUSE, facing Lake Merritt on Fallon St. between Twelfth and Thirteenth Sts., is a steel and concrete structure of neoclassic design, built in 1936 at a cost of $2,500,000. Inside the main entrance, on opposite walls, are two murals designed by Marian Simpson and executed by the WPA Federal Art Project, which depict Alameda County in Spanish days and in Gold Rush times in more than 50 colors of marble.

LAKE MERRITT, a 155-acre body of tidal water extending northeast from Twelfth St., named for Dr. Samuel Merritt, ex-Mayor of Oakland who helped create it, occupies the once marshy, muddy lagoon adjacent to San Antonio Creek, dammed and dredged in 1909. Hydraulic gates control the water level. A boulevard, a macadam footpath, and a chain of lights encircle the lake. Directly north of the Oakland Public Museum is the large, concrete, brown-gabled BOATHOUSE, containing a dining room, crew quarters and meeting rooms. (*sightseeing launch operates daily during summer. 12 noon to 5:30 p.m., fare 25¢*)

The new OAKLAND MUSEUM, Oak Street between 10th & 11th Sts., (Kevin Roche, John Dinkeloo & Assoc., architects) was made possible by the passing of a $6.6 million bond issue in 1961. Three major galleries, Hall of California Ecology, Hall of California History, and the Gallery of California Art are on varying levels within a landscaped garden setting. There are also a theater, lecture hall and restaurant. *Tues.-Sun. 10-5; Fri. 10-10.*

The SNOW MUSEUM, 274 Nineteenth St., displays habitat groups of birds, animals, and other native life collected on various expeditions by the donor, Henry Adelbert Snow. In 1919-21, on one of these field trips, *Hunting Big Game in Africa,* the first wild-animal picture to be released by a major exchange, was filmed. The Cave Room displays miniature dioramas of prehistoric animal life showing dinosaurs, mammoths, mastodon, great long-horned bison, saber-toothed cats, and other beasts. *Open 10-5 weekdays, Sun. & holidays.*

Amid gardens of Old-World tranquillity, the COLLEGE OF THE HOLY NAMES, 2036 Webster St., stands in an eight-acre campus on Lake Merritt's western shore. This liberal arts Catholic coeducational college grew from a high school founded in 1868 by the Sisters of the Holy Names of Jesus and Mary, through the efforts of Reverend Michael King, pioneer Catholic priest, and received in 1880 a charter to award bachelor of arts degrees. Its scholastic department issued in 1872 the first high school diplomas granted in Oakland.

The 88-acre LAKESIDE PARK (*bowling greens, tennis courts, golf putting greens, boating*), Grand Ave. between Harrison St. and Lakeshore Ave., covers a blunt peninsula thrust between two arms of the lake. A granite boundary marker of the old Rancho San Antonio stands near the Bellevue and Perkins Sts. entrance. In a grassy amphitheater near the beach the Municipal Band gives concerts (*Sun. 2:30, July-Oct.*). A mounted torpedo porthole from the battleship *Maine* and a memorial tablet cast from metal recovered from the vessel stand about 200 yards northeast of the bandstand. The nine-foot McELROY FOUNTAIN of white Carrara marble on the south-central part of the esplanade walk was built in "Commemoration of the Public Services of John Edmund McElroy," Oakland attorney. Near the southern end of the peninsula is a brown-gabled canoehouse (*canoes for rent*) and landing, where privately owned sail boats of the Lake Merritt Sail Club are quartered.

East of the canoehouse and landing is the LAKE MERRITT WILD-FOWL SANCTUARY (*feeding hours Oct.-Mar., 10 and 3:30*). In 1869 the California Legislature designated Lake Merritt as a migratory water-fowl sanctuary, and in 1926 it became a banding station of the United States Biological Survey. From four to five thousand fowl are present during the winter months, and many nest on the small wooded island built in the lake by the city in 1923. Besides many species of ducks and geese, other visitors to the lake include the coot, egret, cormorant, grebe, gull, killdeer, loon, heron, swan, tern, plover, and snipe. Fowl tagged here have been shot as far afield as Siberia and Brazil.

From the site of EAST SHORE PARK at the easternmost tip of the lake, the Peraltas shipped hides and tallow. Their *embarcadero* is marked by concrete columns bordering a crescent-shaped brick wall, built in 1912.

The VETERANS MEMORIAL BUILDING, north side of Grand Ave., adjoining Lakeside Park, has an auditorium seating 700 and a collection of war trophies.

The FIRST PRESBYTERIAN CHURCH, Broadway at Twenty-sixth St., a fine modern adaptation of perpendicular Gothic architecture (William C. Hays, architect), has stained-glass windows designed by Stetson Crawford, a pupil of James McNeill Whistler.

A public recreation center, MOSSWOOD PARK (*8-8 daily*), Moss Ave. between Broadway and Webster St., contains playfields, tennis, roque, and croquet courts, horseshoe-pitching ranges, and a shrub-bordered garden theater. A little arroyo spanned by rustic bridges and bordered by flowering shrubs and ferns meanders beneath fine old oaks past the RESIDENCE OF JOHN MORA MOSS, built in the 1860's, which is now used as a clubhouse and tea room.

The MUNICIPAL ROSE GARDENS, in Linda Vista Park, Oakland and Olive Aves., eight acres in area, contain approximately 8,000 bushes.

KAISER CENTER, 300 Lakeside Drive (Welton Becket & Assoc., architects) was built in 1960 as the home office for Kaiser firms. It contains a shopping center, and a 3½ acre roof garden. *Open Monday through Friday 9-5.*

Founded in 1907, the CALIFORNIA COLLEGE OF ARTS AND CRAFTS, 5212 Broadway, which occupies several buildings on a four-acre campus, claims distinction as "the only art institution on the Pacific Coast authorized to grant college degrees" and as the only one in California "where, on a single campus, students may complete their work for state teaching credentials . . . [while] gaining their professional art training." As the former California School of Arts and Crafts, a nonprofit, coeducational institution, it served the West from 1907-37. In the Divisions of Fine Arts, of Applied Arts, and of Art Education are studios and exhibition halls. The campus with its flowers, shrubs, and trees, its native birds and small animals for art models is the setting for outdoor sketching and painting. The Aztec Indian pupil of Whistler, Xavier Martinez, born in 1873 in Guadalajara, Mexico, taught painting here. Dressing primitively in hand-woven materials, his black hair bound by a leather thong, "Marty" was unconventional as a teacher, bold and direct as a painter.

Entered through a massive stone gateway, MOUNTAIN VIEW CEMETERY, head of Piedmont Ave., on a beautifully landscaped hillside, has a fine view of San Francisco Bay. The pioneer Dr. John Marsh, Washington Bartlett, Governor Henry Haight, Joseph Le Conte, and Francis Marion "Borax" Smith are buried here.

In ST. MARY'S CEMETERY, Roman Catholic, head of Howe Street, are the graves of many Spanish pioneers, among them members of the Peralta family.

LAKE TEMESCAL REGIONAL PARK, Chabot and New Tunnel Rds., is an abandoned reservoir converted by WPA labor into a recreation center. From the brick boathouse (*open May-Sept.; 8:30-7; swimming free; canoes and boats 50¢ per hour*) juts a long float, equipped with springboards for swimmers. Another float has water targets for casting practice and tournaments.

The OAKLAND-ALAMEDA COUNTY COLISEUM, Nimitz Freeway & Hegenberger Rd., opened in November, 1966, and features a three deck stadium, convertible for football or baseball, seating 52,000. The glass-walled indoor arena seats 16,000 and is used as an exhibition and meeting hall for trade shows and conventions. It cost $25,000,000.

The OAKLAND YACHT CLUB, foot of Nineteenth Ave., established in 1913, has berths for about 100 yachts and motorboats. Each year its members contest for three trophies: the Wallace Trophy for sailboats, the Craven Trophy for "star"-type sailboats, and the Tin Cup Derby for motorboats (an engraved tin cup is the winner's award). At one time Jack London was an honorary member. For the club's annual midsummer party, "A Nite in Venice," to which the public is invited, the harbor is strung with colored lights.

DIMOND PARK (*horseshoe court, picnicking, tennis, swimming*), Fruitvale Ave. and Lyman Rd., lies in a canyon shut in at its northern end by precipitous slopes. The 12-acre tract, green with eucalyptus, oak and acacia, extending along Sausal Creek, was named for Hugh and Dennis Dimond, who became owners of this part of Rancho San Antonio. The 105-foot LIONS POOL (*bath house; sand beach*) is Oakland's principal outdoor plunge. In the park is the DIMOND COTTAGE, built in 1897 of adobe bricks from the original home of Antonio Maria Peralta, which stood at 2501 Thirty-fourth Avenue. The adobe, 16 by 28 feet, built by the Dimond brothers, is now the headquarters of a Boy Scout troop.

JOAQUIN MILLER PARK (THE HIGHTS), Joaquin Miller Rd. near Mountain Blvd. (*hiking trails; community kitchen; picnic areas*), is a 67-acre highland area purchased by Oakland as a memorial park in 1917. The 75,000 eucalyptus, pine, cypress, and acacia trees were planted by Miller—who resided here from 1886 to 1913—with the aid of friends and visitors. A native of Indiana, Cincinnatus Heine Miller (1839-1913), after a career of Indian-fighting and small-time politics—during which he took the first name of the bandit Joaquin Murietta—became California's white-haired "Poet of the Sierras." Participation in the Alaska gold rush and the Chinese war added more color to his last years. Eccentric in dress and demeanor, Miller was much beloved in England as a poet of the American frontier. He is best-known for his school-text poem, "Columbus," although he wrote prolifically. At The Hights (as he spelled the name of his estate), he provided homes for the poets, Yone Noguchi and Takeshi Kanno. George Sterling, Jack London, Harr Wagner, and Edwin Markham were among his frequent guests. Buried in the little cemetery here is Cali-Shasta, his daughter by a Pitt River Indian woman. Later in Oregon he married a young poet, who bore him three children before she divorced him. A daughter by a still later marriage to Abbie Leland resided at The Hights until her death in 1970, having reserved a life tenure in it when she sold the property to Oakland.

THE ABBEY, built in 1886, is a small, low gray frame building consisting of three one-room structures interconnected to form a single unit, each room roofed with a shingled peak. Miller said it was inspired by Newstead Abbey in England and spoke of it as a "little Abbey for little Abbie," his wife.

A loop tail beginning at the park's souvenir shop, which is flanked by Juanita's Sanctuary and Juanita's Wigwam, leads past the stone funeral pyre on which Miller wished to be cremated (but was not), the Pyramid to Moses, the Tower to Browning, and the Frémont Monument. Miller was his own mason in building these oddly asymmetrical monuments of native rock. In the center of the park are cypress trees planted in the shape of a cross.

The WOODMINSTER MEMORIAL AMPHITHEATER, constructed by WPA labor under the direction of the Oakland Board of Park Directors, is a memorial to California writers. A cascade beginning near the rear of the amphitheater flows through eight flower-bordered pools to an electric fountain illuminated by changing colors.

The 182 acres of SEQUOIA PARK, Joaquin Miller Rd. and Skyline Blvd. (*picnicking, outdoor grills, bridle paths*), are shaded by towering redwoods. Sequoia Point, within the park, a circular landscaped point, provides a panorama of the Bay to the south, bringing into view East Oakland, Alameda, San Leandro, San Leandro Bay, the Oakland Airport, and the Estuary.

Best-known women's college west of the Mississippi, MILLS COLLEGE, Seminary Ave. between Camden St. and Calaveras Ave., is also one of the oldest in the United States. The present residential, nonsectarian college began as the Young Ladies Seminary in 1852 in Benicia. In 1865 Dr. and Mrs. Cyrus Taggart Mills purchased the school and six years later removed it to the present beautifully wooded campus of 150 acres at the base of the San Leandro hills.

Mills was patterned after Mount Holyoke Seminary in Massachusetts. As a college of liberal arts, it has schools in fine arts, language and literature, social institutions, natural sciences, mathematics, and education, leading to the A.B. degree, and a school of graduate studies which gives an M.A. or M.Ed. degree. The faculty of 99 members, serving about 820 students, is large enough to permit small classes and individual attention. Visiting faculty members in the graphic arts have included Leon Kroll, Alexander Archipenko, Frederic Taubes, and the Bauhaus group; in music, Henry Cowell, Luther Marchant, and members of the Pro Arte Quartet; in dancing, Martha Graham, Hanya Holm, and Charles Weidman.

The campus buildings are notably successful adaptations in concrete of Spanish Colonial design. Through the Wetmore Gate on Seminary Ave. a winding road leads to EL CAMPANIL, a buttressed tower of tan-colored concrete, the gift of Francis M. "Borax" Smith, in whose pierced belfry is a chime of ten bells cast for the Chicago World's Fair of 1893. A number of residential halls in an informal style are grouped about beautifully landscaped courts and terraces. The MUSIC BUILDING, in the style of a Spanish Renaissance church, has a fine doorway with ornate carving and an auditorium with murals by Ray Boynton. Graceful triple arches lead to the foyer of LISSER HALL, whose auditorium seats 600. Before a lofty open arcade leading to the ART GALLERY (*open Wed., Fri., Sun. 2-5*) are two marble Dogs of Fu, Chinese carvings of the Ming dynasty in white marble. In addition to a permanent collection of oils, etchings, bronzes, textiles, and oriental *objets d'art,* the galleries have occasional loan exhibits. The 152,249 volumes in the LIBRARY (*open to visitors*), include the collection of about 5,000 rare books and manuscripts given by Albert M. Bender. The WOODLAND THEATER, a natural amphitheater in a eucalyptus grove, is the scene of outdoor plays. Bordering LAKE ALISO near the northern boundary of the campus is an outdoor stage used for dance programs.

CHABOT OBSERVATORY (*open Tues.-Sat. 7-9:30*), on Mountain Blvd., named for Anthony Chabot, pioneer, capitalist, and philanthropist, is one of the few California institutions of its kind serving the public schools. Lectures are given to classes from the Oakland schools and from Mills College, which assist jointly in maintenance of the observatory's large lecture hall, reading room, and astronomical library. Illustrated programs for adult astronomy students and meetings of the East Bay Astronomical Association are held here. The two-story stucco building, on the landscaped hillside, houses a spectroscope and 8- and 20-inch refracting telescopes. Connected with the institution is a meteorological station which collects data for Oakland weather reports.

KNOWLAND STATE ARBORETUM PARK AND ZOO, 98th Ave. and Mountain Blvd. *Open daily 9-4:30, Sat., Sun. & holidays to 5:30, admission 50¢ per car.* Formerly known as Durant Park and later as the Alameda County Zoological Gardens, the area covers 450 acres. The Zoo is a new concept in design, with a special gibbon cage, a primate apartment, and an elephant house. Picnic areas and hilltop miniature train, Skyline Daylight (25¢).

On the tidal flats of Bay Farm Island in San Leandro Bay is the OAKLAND INTERNATIONAL AIRPORT. There are 15 gate positions and 13 boarding rooms, as well as a customs facility. The 26-acre parking lot can accommodate more than 3,200 cars. Five hotels and motels are convenient to the airport and to the Coliseum complex, the center of Oakland's major sports activities.

Berkeley

Air Services: San Francisco-Oakland Helicopter Airlines, daily connections with Oakland and San Francisco airports.

Bus Lines: Greyhound Bus Lines and National Trailways, Shattuck Ave. and Addison St., and 2103 San Pablo Ave. Fares: 25¢ local, 55¢ transbay.

Railroad: Southern Pacific, University Ave. and 3rd St.

Highways: Interstate 80 combined with US 40, north-south along the Bay shore, crosses on Oakland Bay Bridge to San Francisco and junction with US 101, connecting with all north-south routes east of the Bay.

Traffic Regulations: 25 mph in residential and business sections; 15 mph at intersections; parking limit 1 to 2 hrs. in business districts.

Information and Accommodations: Berkeley Chamber of Commerce, 1834 University Ave. University of California administrative office, Sproul Hall on campus. Hotels and motels.

Concert Halls: Wheeler Hall, U. of C. Greek Theater. Berkeley City Club, 2315 Durant Ave. *Radio Stations:* KPAT, 601 Ashby Ave. KPFA, 2207 Shattuck Ave. *Amateur and Little Theaters:* Wheeler Hall, U. of C., for university productions. International House Auditorium, Piedmont Ave. and Bancroft Way. Berkeley Community Theater, Grove and Allston. Berkeley City Club Little Theater, 2315 Durant Ave.

SPORTS

Archery: Tilden Park.

Baseball: Diamonds at Berkeley High School, Grove St. and Bancroft Way, and many public playgrounds.

Boating: Berkeley Aquatic Park.

Football: U. of C. Stadium, foot of Bancroft Way. Berkeley High School, Grove St. and Bancroft Way.

Golf: Tilden Park Golf Course.

Ice Skating: Iceland Berkeley, Ward & Milvia.

Bowling: Berkeley Bowl, 2777 Shattuck Ave. International Lanes, 1631 San Pablo.

Softball: City Playground, 2828 Grove St. City Playground, Mavel and Oregon Sts., and many school playgrounds.

Swimming: Berkeley High School, Grove St. and Bancroft Way.

Tennis: U. of C. campus. Berkeley Tennis Club (private), Tunnel Rd. and Domingo Ave.

Recreational areas: City Hall, Allston Way and Grove St. Grove, 2828 Grove St. Codornices, 1201 Euclid Ave. James Kenney, 8th and Delaware Sts. Live Oak, Shattuck Ave. and Berryman St. San Pablo, Mavel and Oregon Sts.

CHURCHES

Churches (Only centrally located churches are listed): *Baptist.* First Evangelical Church, 2903 San Pablo Ave. *Christian.* University Christian Church of Berkeley, 2401 Le Conte Ave. *Christian Science.* First Church of Christ, Scientist, 2619 Dwight Way. *Mormon.* Church of Jesus Christ of Latter Day Saints, 2150 Vine Street. *Congregational.* First, 2345 Channing Way. *Episcopal.* St. Mark's, 2314 Bancroft Way. *Lutheran.* Church of the Cross, 1744 University Ave. *Methodist.* Trinity United Methodist, Durant and Dana Sts. *Presbyterian.* First, Dana St. and Channing Way. *Roman Catholic.* St. Joseph's, 1640 Addison St. *Seventh Day Adventist.* Berkeley Seventh Day Adventists, 2236 Parker St. *Other:* Vedanta Society, 2455 Bowditch St.

BERKELEY (0-1,000 alt., 116,716 pop. 1970; 111,268, 1960, inc. 4.9%) spreads across a great natural amphitheater opposite the Golden Gate, rising from the shore of the Bay eastward to the crest of the Berkeley hills. The name long has been synonymous with the educational achievements of the University of California, especially in nuclear science, and its position at the head of nine separate campus organizations enrolling nearly 100,000 students—actually, in the 1971-72 year, 99,786, with a faculty of 7,964. Beginning in 1964 Berkeley dominated the news reports as the site of student demonstrations for a variety of causes and defiance of college authority that set patterns for similar actions at other colleges in the United States. There were still battles with the police in 1968 and 1969. By 1970 the demonstrations had subsided; the authorities had conceded that students had grievances and made adjustments, providing for student councils and closer faculty relations.

While the university dominates the cultural life of the city, two-thirds of its people pursue normal mercantile and industrial activities or commute daily to San Francisco and the Peninsula over Interstate 80 and the San Francisco-Oakland Bay Bridge. Downtown Berkeley centers on Shattuck Ave., and although its extent is smaller than that normally found in a city of 100,000, it has a lively retail section supplemented by market centers farther out. For several miles along the Bay are light and heavy industrial plants with a fringe of workers' homes in detached houses and apartments. Private dwellings of members of the university are located among the hills on either side of the campus, where fraternity and sorority houses reflect affluence. Rambling terraced gardens are filled with shrubbery that almost hides houses clinging to the slopes.

The population has a preponderance of native-born whites, but the number of nonwhites has been increasing. Among them are the numerous foreign students at the university who lend a cosmopolitan area to the city. On their account an International House was established here by the Rockefeller Foundation.

Before the days of urban settlement the site of Berkeley was the great Rancho San Antonio of the Peralta family. When it was selected in 1866 as the new location of the College of California, Henry Durant, one of the trustees, gazing out over the Bay, quoted Bishop Berkeley's well-known line: "Westward the course of empire takes its way," and another trustee suggested that they name the new town for the prophetic English philosopher. The village that grew up around the campus was not incorporated until 1878, organization having been delayed by farmers who rejected the idea of imposing the expense of municipal government upon them. By 1900, however, streets had been paved, a reservoir built and pipes laid, residential tracts opened, and electric trains supplemented the noisy and smoky locomotives of the Southern Pacific.

The San Francisco fire brought so many new residents that the town by 1908 was large enough to make an effort to get the State capital away from Sacramento. At the same time many attractive homes were being built among scattered clumps of oaks on the rising ground north and south of the campus. In the fall of 1923 a grass fire, starting in the hills, destroyed a large part of North Berkeley. New homes and gardens have hidden the scars of the fire.

POINTS OF INTEREST

The BERKELEY AQUATIC PARK (*boating free with own craft; rowboats, sailboats, electric boats for hire*), East Shore Highway between University and Ashby Aves., is a mile-long, ninety-acre recreational waterfront development built by WPA labor, containing a long, narrow, tide-filled lagoon with a landscaped border. In the southern end of the lagoon, set aside for model-yacht racing, regattas in which the diminutive copies of yachts compete are held occasionally. A small grass-covered island midway along the western shoreline is reserved as a wild fowl sanctuary.

The BERKELEY MUNICIPAL FISHING PIER extends more than three miles over the mud flats to deep water.

The BERKELEY YACHT HARBOR, north of the Municipal Fishing Pier, developed in part with WPA funds, accommodates many small craft in waters protected by rock-faced earthen breakwaters.

The LAWN BOWLING GREEN, Allston Way west of Acton St., maintained by the city's Recreation Department, has been the scene of world championship tournaments.

MORTAR ROCK PARK, Indian Rock Ave. and San Diego Rd., once the site of Indian assemblages, is dominated by a huge irregular mass of rock, which commands a magnificent view of the surrounding territory. Here Indian women ground corn in the mortar-like rocks, whose smooth cylindrical holes still show the use to which they were put.

The seven-acre JOHN HINKEL PARK, Southampton Ave. and San Diego Rd., has an amphitheater seating 400, constructed in 1934 by the CWA, where plays are given by the Berkeley Community Players during the summer months.

CRAGMONT ROCK PARK, Regal Rd. at Hilldale Ave., covers four acres surrounding the freak rock formation for which the park was named. From the lookout station 800 feet above sea level is an excellent view of the Bay and its bridges. Easter sunrise services are held here.

CODORNICES (Sp., quail) PARK, Euclid Ave. at Bay View Pl., originally a steep, rocky, brush-grown gulch where quail were abundant, has been terraced by WPA workers as a rose garden, with tiers of roses of many varieties. The park has public tennis courts, a playground for children, and a clubhouse for community use.

The PACIFIC SCHOOL OF RELIGION (*open to visitors on application*), 1798 Scenic Ave., is a graduate theological seminary, interdenominational and coeducational, established in San Francisco in 1866 as the Pacific Theological Seminary. Moved the next year to Oakland, it was established here in 1925. Its present name was adopted in 1916 on its 50th anniversary. The school prepares students for all kinds of religious work. One department, known as the Palestine Institute, centers its activity in the Holy Land, where it is engaged in Biblical research.

The ADMINISTRATION BUILDING and the HOLBROOK MEMORIAL LIBRARY are of gray cut stone; the men's dormitory is of gray stucco. The library includes a Breeches Bible, printed in Geneva in 1560; a group of Babylonian cuneiform tablets; a collection of fourth-century Biblical inscriptions on papyrus; and a rubbing of the inscription on the Nestorian monument in China. An archeological exhibit in the same building consists of relics dating from 3500 B.C.

"Mother" C. A. Tusch's HANGAR, the famous little house at 2211 Union St., served as an aviation museum until it was razed for the expansion of the university in the late 1940's. During World War I, when a school of military aeronautics was established on the campus, "Mother" Tusch founded the University Mothers' Club to look after the boys away from their homes. Overseas flyers remembered the little white house and its motherly occupant, serving coffee and doughnuts, and sent her souvenirs from the battlefields. Among "Mother" Tusch's treasures was part of the fuselage of an Army plane, on which is carved with a penknife the last message of its pilots, Lieutenant Fred Waterhouse and Cecil H. Connolly, who were forced down on the Mexican border in 1919. One of the most unusual tributes came from a German ace—a pair of silver wings, inscribed: "To the Mother of us all, with love from Capt. Willie Mauss." She also had a black sealskin cap worn by Admiral Richard Byrd in Little America and a small Bible that Clyde Pangborn carried on his flight around the world. On the walls of the Hangar were the signatures of Capt. Eddie Rickenbacker, Col. Billy Mitchell, Sir Hubert Wilkins, Byrd, Pangborn, and other famous flyers. Only one woman's autograph was there—that of Amelia Earhart.

BARRINGTON HALL, 2415 Dwight Way, is the largest of five co-operative dormitories built on the university campus during the depression. The five are organized into the California Students' Cooperative Association, housing about 500 students.

The CALIFORNIA SCHOOL FOR THE DEAF, Warring and Parker Sts., at the foot of the Berkeley hills, is a residential school. The course of study embraces a 12-year period, three years of which is preparatory, enabling the child to reach the level of the first grade of the public school system. The entire course is intended not only to give the handicapped child a general education, but also to prepare him for a handicraft.

The CALIFORNIA SCHOOL FOR THE BLIND, 3001 Derby St., sharing the campus of the California School for the Deaf, serves visually handicapped children. Begun in San Francisco in 1860 it was moved to Berkeley in 1867.

The rambling, stuccoed CLAREMONT HOTEL, at the head of Russell St., erected in 1904, is surrounded by a large old-fashioned garden.

At the BERKELEY TENNIS CLUB (*tournaments May-June, Sept.-Oct.*), adjoining the Claremont Hotel, "Pop" Fuller developed two champion players, Helen Wills Moody and Helen Jacobs.

THE UNIVERSITY OF CALIFORNIA

Until the turn of the century the University of California occupied a heterogeneous assortment of buildings at the base of the Berkeley Hills on oak-studded slopes traversed by two branches of Strawberry Creek; but in 1896 Phoebe Apperson Hearst awarded a prize of $10,000 for a campus design to Emile Bénard of Paris, and his general layout, with modifications, has since guided the development of the grounds. In 1902 John Galen Howard, an American architect who had studied at the École des Beaux Arts and had worked with Bénard, came to the university, established a School of Architecture, and became supervising architect. The architecture of the campus strongly reflects his influence. He changed many details of the Bénard plan, but French academic influence is apparent everywhere both in the buildings and in their relation to each other.

The beginning of the university dates to the California constitutional convention of 1849, when a clause was adopted providing for the establishment of a university. A subsequent delay of nearly 20 years was due partly to a controversy between those who wished to establish a "complete university" and those who wanted only a college of agriculture and mechanics. Meanwhile Oakland's College of California was chartered in 1855 by two ministers, Henry Durant and Samuel Hopkins Willey. Absorbing the Contra Costa Academy, it had in 1860 a faculty of six and a freshman class of eight. In 1867 the founders and trustees offered to disincorporate and transfer to the State all their assets—the buildings at Oakland, the 160-acre building site at Berkeley, and a 10,000-volume library. The State accepted the offer on March 23, 1868, and on September 23, 1869 the new university opened in Oakland. In September, 1873 the buildings on the Berkeley campus were occupied by 40 students and a faculty of 10.

The university now has nine campuses and its largest segment, the UNIVERSITY OF CALIFORNIA at LOS ANGELES, enrolls practically the same number of students as Berkeley—27,000. It was established in 1919 and received equal rank with Berkeley in 1927. The Institution of Oceanography at La Jolla was merged with the university before the San Diego campus was begun. The Lick Observatory at Mount Hamilton is under the jurisdiction of the university. The nine campuses, their location, year of establishment, enrollment of students and number of faculty members for the 1971-72 school year were as follows: Berkeley (1868), 27,058, 1,900; Davis (1906), 12,250, 900; Irvine, (1965), 5,049, 300; Los Angeles (1919), 27,000, 1,800; Riverside (1907), 5,000, 500; San Diego (1912), 4,838, 450. San Francisco (1868), 2,184, 1,100; Santa Barbara (1891), 12,000, 1,000; Santa Cruz (1965), 3,097, 324.

In the value of its "practical" contributions, the University of California has a fine record. Its benefits to agriculture alone are estimated to save California farmers millions of dollars annually. In addition to experimental work in animal husbandry, horticulture, viticulture, and irrigation, the agricultural departments have developed and introduced to the farmer the spray plant, a device for spraying fruit trees and vegetation through underground pipes; the solar heater to prevent frost injury to orchard trees; the use of humified air for sterilizing dairy utensils; and a milk-cooling system. Boulder Dam, constructed under the direction of Dr. Elwood Mead, formerly of the university faculty, was built with a special low-heat cement developed in the Engineering Materials Testing Laboratory on the Berkeley campus. In the same laboratory test models of the San Francisco-Oakland Bay Bridge and the Golden Gate Bridge were made, while professors of geology were investigating the strata upon which the bridge foundations would rest. Materials used in many public works were first tested by the materials testing machine, capable of exerting a pressure of 4,000,000 pounds. The engineering department, cooperating with the U.S. Department of Defense compiles data obtained at the hydraulic tidal testing basin to aid in the maintenance of ship channels and the preservation of beaches. In its laboratories was developed an improved method of treating leprosy. Vitamin E and the growth- and sex-stimulating hormones of the pituitary glands were discovered by Dr. Herbert M. Evans of the Institute of Experimental Biology. Through experiments conducted in university laboratories, the canning industry overcame botulism, the sugar beet pest was conquered, and the mealy bug eliminated from citrus groves.

The major contribution of the University of California to scientific knowledge is the invention of the cyclotron or atom smasher by Dr. Ernest Orlando Lawrence, for whom the LAWRENCE RADIATION LABORATORY and the LAWRENCE HALL OF SCIENCE are named. For this achievement Dr. Lawrence was given the Nobel prize for physics in 1939. In the field of medico-therapy Dr. Lawrence and his staff have developed an x-ray apparatus capable of producing powerful rays for the treatment of tumorous growths. Dr. Lawrence was a member of the U.S. delegation at the Atoms for Peace Conference in Geneva when he died in 1958. During World War II he had been associated with the development of the atomic bomb. Another member of the staff, Dr. J. Robert Oppenheimer, directed the bomb laboratory at Los Alamos, N.M.

The complex of buildings devoted to nuclear research is located east of the main campus on Charter Hill. The Lawrence Hall of Science is above the Laboratory and overlooks San Francisco Bay. The Hall is a research center in scientific education and has programs for the instruction of teachers, daily lectures and demonstrations, and teaching exhibits. While the Hall of Science is a department of the Berkeley campus it is not supported by state taxes. The Hall was dedicated in May, 1968, as part of the university's centennial celebration. It has a Lawrence Memorial Room, and exhibit halls named for Edwin W. Pauley and William K. Holt; a 300-seat auditorium, a teaching amphitheater, a television studio, and classrooms. Visitors are invited to attend. *Open 10-4, Monday through Friday, 1-4 on Saturday; admission $1, students and senior citizens, 50¢; children under 12, 25¢.*

UNIVERSITY OF CALIFORNIA, BERKELEY

CENTRAL CAMPUS AREA

BUILDINGS ON THE CAMPUS

The visitor enters the campus from Bancroft Way and finds the Student Union opposite Telegraph Ave. In the lobby is the VISITORS' CENTER, where information is available about one-hour tours for individuals and groups. *Tours start at 1 p.m. Monday through Friday.* The office also provides a pamphlet, *A Tour of the Berkeley Campus,* which enables the individual to proceed at his own pace, inspecting galleries and museums as interest suggests. Buildings are open, but classrooms must not be entered when in use.

The STUDENT UNION was built in 1961 and contains lounges, meeting rooms, grill, fountain, bowling alley, bookstore and an underground garage. Nearby along Bancroft Way is ESHELMAN HALL, a seven-story structure with offices for student government, clubs, Intercollegiate Athletics. To the right, across the Plaza from the Union is ZELLERBACH HALL, which has an auditorium seating 2,000 and a theater seating 500. This leads to the DINING COMMONS, which has a cafeteria, snack bar, restaurant, and rooms for band and choral work. South of the Commons and west of Zellerbach is ALUMNI HOUSE, headquarters of the Alumni Assn.

A few steps upward lead to Sproul Plaza and SPROUL HALL, the administration building. It is named for Robert Gordon Sproul, first alumnus to serve as president. The Plaza and the Steps are used by student groups for their open meetings.

This area was the center of student demonstrations that erupted in the fall of 1964, which came about after followers of Senator Barry Goldwater had accused supporters of William Scranton, governor of Pennsylvania, of illegally recruiting student volunteers on campus during the pre-convention campaigning of Republican candidates. The university announced a policy of prohibiting political recruiting, fund raising for political use, and political and social action on campus. This stirred opposition of about 20 student organizations, some working for civil rights and others advocating civil disobedience. Rallies and sit-in acts resulted. The administration agreed to permit some political activity at certain designated areas, but ordered suspension of students who violated this rule. Agitators for various causes started the Free Speech movement, demanded reinstatement of suspended students and argued that only the courts could regulate political activity on the campus. The administration stood pat in the face of demonstrations by 3,000 to 4,000 students, including a sit-in in Sproul Hall that disrupted office work. On Nov. 30, 1964, the Regents of the university agreed to permit political activity at "carefully selected places" but refused to remove disciplinary actions against students engaged in unlawful acts. Radical activity continued for a number of years, and in 1968 and 1969 the Berkeley police were called in to disperse demonstrators and bring peace to the campus. The university made some concessions along the lines of studies of Negro history and student representation in university affairs.

In the center of the Plaza is Ludwig's Fountain, named for a German pointer dog that used to haunt the pool.

These buildings are located on ground once outside the campus, which was entered by SATHER GATE, built in 1909 by Jane K. Sather as a memorial to her husband. Assemblies of students not approved by the authorities used to "go outside the gate."

Beyond Sather Gate are several spacious classroom buildings. They include DWINELLE HALL, devoted to history, classics and foreign languages, WHEELER HALL, for the Department of English, named for Benjamin Ide Wheeler, president, 1899-1919. Beyond Wheeler is SOUTH HALL, the oldest surviving building, which with North Hall was there when the university opened September 25, 1873. North Hall was on a line with South Hall, but its site is now occupied by the Bancroft Library. Across the Drive from South Hall is MOSES HALL, which has the Institute of Governmental Studies, the Department of Philosophy, and offices of the College of Letters and Science.

STEPHENS HALL, next beyond Moses Hall, was built in 1921 as a memorial to Henry Morse Stephens, distinguished historian and member of the faculty. It was first used as the Student Union and alumni headquarters, but now contains the Hans Kelsen Graduate Social Science Library and several social science research centers.

Here SATHER TOWER dominates the area. It is usually known as the Campanile (*elevator 10-5, fee 10¢*), since it follows the design of the famous campanile of Venice. It was built in 1914 as a gift of Jane K. Sather and is made of California granite, 302 ft. tall, with four clock faces and an observation platform. It has a carillon of 12 bells, cast in England, and played manually three times daily.

To the right of the Tower are two physics buildings, LeCONTE HALL and BIRGE HALL, the latter erected in 1964. The trees in the Campanile Esplanade are London plane trees, which belong to the sycamore family and are a principal decoration of Paris boulevards. They were transplanted from the San Francisco Panama Pacific Exposition of 1916 and are pruned back every fall.

Across the way from the physics buildings is the huge mass of the libraries. The one in front is the BANCROFT LIBRARY, which has the university's rare books and the great collection of Western Americana, the nucleus of which was begun by the historian Hubert Howe Bancroft and acquired from him in 1905. There are now 164,000 books, 8,000,000 manuscripts, numerous documents and maps, and microfilms of newspapers. Here may be seen the "plate of brasse" that contains an inscription testifying that Sir Francis Drake placed it in California soil in

1579. It has been thoroughly studied and is believed to be authentic. It was found near a highway a few decades ago.

The DOE MEMORIAL LIBRARY is the great library of the Berkeley campus. With twenty departmental branches it has more than 4,000,000 bound volumes, and the number is continually growing. The reference room extends the full north width of the second floor. North of Doe Library on University Drive is the new MOFFITT LIBRARY, completed in 1970 for use by undergraduates; it is five stories tall and has two floors underground.

Farther north on the campus are a number of buildings devoted to science. EARTH SCIENCES BUILDING has the Departments of Geology, Geography, and Paleontology, and the University Seismographic Station. Here visitors may visit the Museum of Paleontology and inspect the seismometer and writing seismograph. Several halls nearby are part of the College of Engineering complex. DAVIS HALL, devoted to structural engineering, was added in 1969. CORY HALL has the Department of Electrical Engineering and Computer Sciences; EVANS HALL has the Departments of Mathematics and Statistics. The HEARST MEMORIAL MINING BUILDING, north of Mining Circle, was donated by Phoebe Apperson Hearst in 1907 as a memorial to her husband, Senator George Hearst. To the east of the Hearst Building is the DONNER LABORATORY, devoted to cancer research and medical use of nuclear products. East of the Mining Circle is the MOLECULAR BIOLOGY AND VIRUS LABORATORY, where the first crystallization of the polio virus was effected. The PHYSICAL SCIENCES LECTURE HALL is entirely circular, built in 1964. It has 550 seats, 16 hanging television sets, and a revolving stage with three separate experimental laboratories.

The GREEK THEATER, in a natural amphitheater half hidden in the eucalyptus grove above Gayley Road, seats 8,500. It is an adaptation of the ancient theater at Epidaurus. The enormous stage, 133 feet wide and 28 feet deep, is protected at back and sides by a 42-foot wall (the ancient *skene*), in front of which is a row of Doric columns. Half surrounded by tiers of concrete benches is the pit (the ancient orchestra), before the stage, where huge bonfires are built at student rallies. The theater, a gift of William Randolph Hearst, was first used at commencement in 1903, when Theodore Roosevelt delivered the address. The theater is used for university exercises and student rallies as well as dramatic and concert performances. In 1946 Hearst donated $400,000 for modernization of the theater.

The MEMORIAL STADIUM, at the mouth of Strawberry Canyon, seats 78,000. On the east side of the field, below the California rooting section, is the Andrew Latham Smith Memorial Bench, dedicated in 1927 in honor of the coach of the "wonder teams" of the early 1920's.

used for the most part except during the football season, the stadium is the scene of commencement exercises each spring.

The BOTANICAL GARDENS (*open 9-4*), in Strawberry Canyon east of the stadium, contain more than 50,000 plants of 7,500 species, including special collections of rhododendrons, roses, cacti, and succulents. Plants of rare beauty and value have been brought to the university from such remote places as the Tibetan Himalayas and the South American Andes. The collection includes the world's most complete series of species of Nicotiana. An OPEN-AIR THEATER, in a five-acre grove of pine and redwood trees, is a memorial to Stephen Mather, alumnus, who was first director of the National Park Service.

The LIFE SCIENCES BUILDING, Harmon Way between Axis Rd. and Campanile Way, is a massive concrete structure, completed in 1930. On the facade are panels and rosettes in which have been cast conventionalized representations of fish, reptiles, and mammals. Laboratories, classrooms, offices, and libraries of 13 life-science departments occupy the building, which also houses the Institute of Experimental Biology; the Museum of Vertebrate Zoology (*for students only*) with its specimens of mammals, birds, and reptiles; and the herbarium of the Department of Botany (*open 8:30-12, 1-5; Sat. 8:30-12*), containing plant specimens from all over the world.

The ART GALLERY (*open weekdays 12-4*), one block east of Sather Gate, is a former power house. The two large mosaics on the facade, symbolizing the seven arts, were designed and executed in Byzantine style by Helen Bruton and Florence Swift, assisted by workers of the WPA Federal Art Project. The gallery owns the Albert Bender collection of oriental art and a collection of Russian ikons.

The GYMNASIUM FOR MEN, Dana St. between Bancroft and Allston Ways, completed in 1933, has large gymnasium floors and swimming pool, special rooms for wrestling, boxing, and fencing and space for badminton and table tennis. Adjoining it are a baseball diamond and the George C. Edwards Memorial Stadium for track and field sports.

The PHOEBE A. HEARST GYMNASIUM FOR WOMEN, Bancroft Way and Bowditch St., provides women students with facilities for badminton, table tennis, and many other activities in its gymnasiums and swimming pools. On the spacious grounds outside, groups of students often engage in tennis, hockey, archery, and interpretive dancing.

INTERNATIONAL HOUSE, on Piedmont Ave. at the head of Bancroft Way, was donated by John D. Rockefeller Jr. in the interests of international understanding. Another is located at Stanford University.

Alameda

Highways: The Nimitz Freeway, US 17, in Oakland connects with the Posey tube, the Webster Ave. tube, and bridges over the Tidal Canal at Park St., Tilden Ave. and High St. State 61 in Alameda has similar junctions.

Airport: Naval Air Station, W. end of island.

Buses: Local and inter-city buses, fare 25¢; transbay, 55¢.

Traffic Regulations: Speed limit 25 mph in business and residential districts, 15 mph at intersections.

Information and Accommodations: Alameda Chamber of Commerce, 2437 Santa Clara Ave. City Hall, Oak St. and Santa Clara Ave. Motels.

Churches: Only centrally located churches are listed. *Baptist.* First, 1519 Santa Clara Ave. *Christian.* First, 2441 San Jose Ave. *Christian Science.* First Church of Christ Scientist, Central Ave. and Walnut St. *Congregational.* First, 1912 Central Ave. *Episcopal.* Christ Church, 1700 Santa Clara Ave. *Hebrew Orthodox.* Temple Israel, 2268 Alameda Ave. *Lutheran.* Immanuel, 1420 Lafayette. *Methodist.* First, Central Ave. and Oak St. *Presbyterian.* First, Santa Clara Ave. and Chestnut St. *Roman Catholic.* St. Joseph's, 1109 Chestnut St. *Seventh Day Adventist.* Alameda Seventh Day Adventists, 1515 Verdi St.

Theater: Alameda Little Theater, 1409 High St.

Sports: Boating. Aeolian Yacht Club, Bay Farm Island Bridge. Encinal Yacht Club, Pacific Marina, North Harbor. *Golf.* Municipal Golf Course, Bay Farm Island. *Yachting.* Aeolian Yacht Club, Bay Farm Island. Encinal Yacht Club, Pacific Marina, North Harbor.

ALAMEDA (sea level—25 alt., 70,968 pop. 1970; 63,855, 1960; inc. 11%) in Alameda County is located on an island shaped roughly like an elongated violin, lying parallel to East Oakland, with the neck pointing toward the Golden Gate. The island has an average width of about one mile, a total length of six and one-half miles. The two-mile neck and adjoining areas are chiefly occupied by an airport. The northeast shoreline, along the Estuary, is given over to industry and shipping, while the southwestern shoreline is a popular bathing area. Although only State Highway 61 passes through Alameda, five vehicular connections link it with the mainland. The five miles of the Estuary and two miles of artificially created tidal canal separating the island from the mainland serve as a deep-water harbor for both Oakland and Alameda. Three bridges cross the canal. Another connects with Bay Farm Island to the south. But the most frequently used entrance is the George A. Posey Tube under the Estuary.

Many residents do not know that the city proper was a peninsula until the tidal canal was dredged in 1902. More are unaware that its boundaries include a mainland agricultural district called Bay Farm Island, which now adjoins the filled-in Oakland International Airport. Government Island, once a shoal off the main part of the city, now lies across the main channel of the Estuary, approachable by bridge only from Oakland.

Alameda is one of the oldest East Bay cities, and the most modern. The contrast was found in schools and homes. Modern houses and apartments elbow ornate old buildings set in tranquil gardens on tree-shaded streets. Queer shrubs from foreign ports are common because the city is a well-known "port of retire" for old seamen, who settled here with souvenirs of travel.

All this flat expanse of fertile land, with its numerous sloughs and clumps of big drooping valley oaks, for generations gave shade and food and water to the Costanoan Indians. Included in the Peralta land grant of 1820, it was known as Encinal de San Antonio (the oak grove of St. Anthony) when Americans came here and found, grazing in the lush pasture land, many cattle branded with the Peralta initial. Waterfowl and small game attracted hunters, who found a ready market in San Francisco for their kill, and the thick stands of oaks brought in crews of charcoal burners, who likewise had no difficulty in marketing their product in the growing transbay city and in the Mother Lode's boom towns.

Among the early arrivals were Gideon Aughinbaugh, a Pennsylvania carpenter, and his partner, W. W. Chipman, a lawyer and school teacher from Ohio, who recognized the possibilities of the region. Through the flimsy walls of one of the kindling and cardboard shanties of early San Francisco, Chipman overheard H. S. Fitch, a San Francisco auctioneer, negotiating with Antonio Peralta for the purchase of the Encinal at a price of $7,000. Chipman immediately sought out Peralta and doubled the bid. By this bit of shrewdness the future city of Alameda passed into the hands of the partners, Chipman and Aughinbaugh. They needed money, however, and to obtain it offered Fitch a one-fourteenth interest for $3,000. Fitch accepted, and in partnership with William Sharon took possession of 160 acres.

Chipman and Aughinbaugh began to develop the land and to attract settlers. Grafted fruit trees were brought from the East (there are accounts of peaches in Aughinbaugh's orchard which sold for one dollar each). He obtained the use of a small steamer, the *Bonita,* which plied between Alameda and San Francisco. Sunday excursions, watermelon picnics, and gift lots to any one who would erect a $50 building were some of the devices used to further development. With more than 100 settlers by 1853, Chipman and Aughinbaugh took the initiative in founding a town in the vicinity of High Street.

The name, Alameda (poplar-shaded avenue), already in use by the recently organized county, was selected by popular vote. Two other towns also were laid out—one at the Point, named Woodstock, the other at the center of the peninsula, called Encinal.

With the increase of American population in California, the little hamlet, along with its neighbors, Oakland and San Leandro, got its share of new settlers, many of whom, returning unsuccessful from the mines, were looking for homes and land. In 1871 a bridge over the Estuary and a causeway across the marsh were constructed, establishing directed communication with Oakland. Incorporation took place in 1872. The city-manager form of government was adopted in 1917.

In the course of its history Alameda has counted among its residents Mark Twain, Jack London, and Harrison Fisher. The starting point for Robert Louis Stevenson's journeys to the South Seas, it figured prominently in his career. He first came here to visit the Orr family (Scots, like himself), who operated a copra oil mill. Because copra came from the South Sea islands, he grew interested in island lore and outfitted a ship, the *Casco,* to sail there under command of the New England skipper, Captain Albert Otis. Captain Otis, whose own declining years were spent in Alameda, was cast as Arty Nares in Stevenson's *The Wreckers*. The novelist later married a sister of Mrs. Orr, in Alameda.

Alameda was one of the first cities in the country to macadamize its streets. It had the first municipal power plant in California, established in 1890 at a cost of $40,000, which, during its first fifty years of operation earned profits of nearly $3,000,000, used in the construction of many public services and buildings.

One of the largest employers in the East Bay is the Alameda Naval Air Station, a permanent installation for aircraft maintenance and overhaul and a primary aviation supply center, which employs over 10,000 civilians.

Situated along the estuary are the cargo handling facilities of Encinal Terminals, as well as the ship repair facilities of the Todd Shipyards Corporation.

Within recent years, substantial new residential, commercial and industrial developments have been created along Alameda's south shore and on Bay Farm Island.

POINTS OF INTEREST

NIMITZ FIELD is the name given to the U.S. Naval Air Station, at the western tip of the island. It is one of the largest naval airports in the world, constructed during the early 1940's. Costing more than $75,000,000 and incorporating both the former Benton Field of the U.S. Army and the Municipal Airport, it has a total area of more than three and one-half square miles. Three piers accommodate the Navy's largest aircraft carriers. The base has nine land plane hangars with four main runways, five huge seaplane hangars facing the lagoon, administrative buildings and storehouses, and quarters for officers and enlisted men. Equipped with facilities for training and operation of two large carrier air groups, the Naval Air Station employed as many as 8,000 civilian workers during World War II. It was the United States terminal for the huge Mars flying boats. The first China Clipper flight began here November 22, 1935, when the airport was a base for the Pan American Airways System.

WASHINGTON PARK, Central Ave. and Eighth St., Alameda's largest municipal recreation center, is bounded on the Bay side by a public bathing beach (*lifeguard during summer months; no lockers*). Professional baseball was played here for the first time in California, and from this diamond have come some big names in baseball: Johnny Vergez, Dick Bartell, Lou Vezelick, and Al Browne.

West of Washington Park is the site of NEPTUNE BEACH, formerly a popular amusement park, now a residential subdivision. An outgrowth of Neptune Gardens and Croll's Gardens, it was the mecca for boxing and wrestling fans. John L. Sullivan, Bob Fitzsimmons, Jim Corbett, Kid McCoy, Billy Muldoon, and Farmer Burns all appeared here.

The ENCINAL YACHT CLUB, S. end of Grand St. founded in 1891, sponsors sailing events, and has anchorage for small yachts and other pleasure craft.

The members of the AEOLIAN YACHT CLUB, E. end of Calhoun St., take part in frequent class and handicap races and in cruises to Bay, river, and coast points. The Aeolian Juniors, made up of boys under 21, conduct races and regattas with their own fleet, under supervision of junior officers. Many of them have built their own boats.

The 18-hole ALAMEDA MUNICIPAL GOLF COURSE spreads its green lawns over Bay Farm Island directly across the bridge from Alameda.

INDIAN MOUND STONE MONUMENT, in Lincoln Park on High St. at E. end of Santa Clara Ave., commemorates the site of a former Indian shell mound that measured 150 by 400 feet. The mound was leveled in 1908 and the earth and mussel shells used on the roads of Bay Farm Island. The site, now under nearby homes and streets, is indistinguishable. The mound rose 14 feet above the level ground. From it were taken the remains of 450 Indians, all of whom had been buried facing the rising sun with knees drawn up to chins. Near the top was a brass counter bearing the image of George II and dated 1768, which possibly was brought here by Indians in contact with the Hudson's Bay Company.

The ALAMEDA PUBLIC LIBRARY, Santa Clara Ave. and Oak St., has a collection of about 342,827 volumes, including some valuable Californiana. Relics salvaged from the Indian shell mound, including shell ornaments, cooking implements and a brass counter, are on display.

The ALAMEDA BOAT CLUB, once located at the foot of Chestnut St., on the Estuary, was established in 1864 as a center for racing shells, the principal activity of its members being participation in motorboat races sponsored by other clubs.

The SHIP GRAVEYARDS on the Estuary, north end of Schiller St. and foot of a rutted, sandy road leading from end of St. Charles St., have been the final resting places for many ancient, worn-out vessels, including the long-idle *Unimak,* built in 1902 in Alameda, a 124-foot steam schooner that once pushed her way bravely through the ice of an early Alaska winter, homeward bound and loaded to the beams with the season's salmon pack; the *Kadiak,* a sturdy tug that once worked the Alaska waters; and the unnamed gray hulk called *No. 30,* once a water-carrier in the United States Navy. Here too, in contrast to these, rows of steel and wooden ships were maintained in a state of idle preparedness, awaiting the command to fire the boilers, prior to World War II.

The 100-acre GOVERNMENT ISLAND in the Estuary, reached by way of the Dennison Street Bridge from Oakland, is the base for a United States Coast Guard station with patrol boats and cutters on duty. Located here also are headquarters for various divisions of the Federal Government.

The island was created when the Estuary was dredged in 1916. In the Administration Building are frescoes by Beckford Young and John Haley depicting the history of road-building and activities of the Coast Guard and the Forestry Service, done under the WPA Art Project.

East Bay Tour 1

Oakland—El Cerrito—Richmond—Crockett—Martinez—Pittsburg—
Antioch; 50.5 *m*. US 80, State 4-24.

From the flat western sections of Oakland and Berkeley, this route
follows the contours of San Francisco Bay, San Pablo Bay, Carquinez
Strait, and Suisun Bay, passing residential, industrial, and "company"
towns in rapid succession—traversing a district whose petroleum-laden
atmosphere indicates immense oil storage tanks and great oil refineries—
and ends at the gateway to the rich garden region of the San Joaquin
delta.

The touring center of OAKLAND, 0 *m.*, is San Pablo Ave.,
Broadway, and Fourteenth Street.

North from San Pablo Ave., Broadway, and Fourteenth St. on Broadway to
MacArthur Blvd.; R. on Moss Ave.; L. on Oakland Ave. to PIEDMONT 1.8 *m*.
(800 alt., 10,917 pop.), contoured to glen and upland, a municipal island entirely surrounded by Oakland. Strictly residential, its stately mansions and
vine-clad cottages set in terraced gardens border streets that wind in a bewildering maze through canyons, across ridges, and around knolls. Like Oakland,
Piedmont was once a part of the 43,472-acre Rancho San Antonio (*see Oakland*).
Walter Blair, a New Englander, purchased the site for a ranch in 1852 at $1.25
an acre and in 1870 James Gamble divided it into town lots.

Thirteen-acre PIEDMONT PARK (*community hall, playground, tennis courts*),
in the approximate center of the city, is irrigated by a sulphur spring, around
which a health resort was built in 1876. Within the park are the largest collection of wild irises in the State and a one-acre sanctuary for Alameda County
wild flowers.

North from San Pablo Ave., Broadway, and Fourteenth St. in
Oakland, on San Pablo Ave., to EMERYVILLE, 2 *m*. (sea level-
60 alt., 2,681, pop. 1970; 2,686, 1960), a highly industrialized municipality in Alameda County dating from the middle 1870's when the
Oakland Trotting Track and the picnic grounds at Shellmound Park
"in the vicinity of Butchertown" were the chief attractions. In the park,
surmounting a large Indian shellmound, stood a dance pavilion. Frequent
fairs, circuses and exhibitions; National shooting tournaments; festivals
of the Swedish and Caledonian Societies with bagpipe and haggis; and
the Butchers' Annual Celebration all brought throngs to Golden Gate
Village, as the community was then known. In 1896 it became Emeryville, named for Joseph Stickney Emery, early resident and architect of
the San Francisco mint.

In that same year the California Jockey Club purchased the Oakland Trotting Track and changed it to a running track. There was grief in Emeryville when State legislative action abolished horse-racing in 1911; but this blow was a blessing in disguise. The race track properties brought handsome prices as these level acres near two transcontinental railroads attracted industry. By 1940 there were 120 industries, one for every 21 inhabitants.

BERKELEY, 3.2 m. (sea level-1,300 alt., 116,716 pop.) *See Berkeley.*

Right from Berkeley on Ashby Ave.—State 24—which becomes Tunnel Rd., to Broadway; L. on Broadway.

The twin bores of the BROADWAY LOW LEVEL TUNNEL (*see Emporium of a New World: Engineering Enterprise*), serve the opposing lines of traffic. Since completion of this tunnel in 1937, many people employed in the metropolitan area have chosen the sheltered slopes and valleys beyond it for home sites. From the tunnel's East Portal, State 24 descends the canyon of the west branch of San Pablo Creek through low hills.

At 7.5 m. is a junction with Moraga Road.

Right here, over a low pass into the orchard lands of Moraga Valley, is MORAGA, 4.5 m. (475 alt., 14,205 pop.), a village whose site was once part of the 13,316-acre Rancho Laguna de los Palos Colorados (Lagoon of the red trees), granted jointly to Joaquin Moraga and Jose Bernal in 1835.

The route continues L. from Moraga on a road to ST. MARY'S COLLEGE, 6 m., on a 500-acre campus in an arm of Moraga Valley, through which flows Las Trampas (the frauds) Creek. The $2,000,000 group of buildings designed in California mission style (John J. Donovan, architect) was dedicated in 1928. Springing from the little school opened by Reverend John T. Harrington in 1855 in the basement of old St. Mary's in San Francisco, the present St. Mary's College has grown to include a chain of State-wide preparatory schools and colleges, now administered by the Brothers of the Christian Schools, who assumed control of St. Mary's in 1868. Of the average student enrollment of 900, most major in arts and letters.

In the KEITH MEMORIAL GALLERY are hung thirty-three paintings, eight oil sketches and studies, and several drawings by William Keith, San Francisco artist who died in 1911 (*see Golden Era: Art and Artists*).

The CHAPEL OF OUR LADY OF MORAGA is surmounted by a 120-foot tower and a dome of many-colored tile. In the interior, modeled after a church at Monreale, Sicily, is an elaborately designed marble altar.

MADIGAN GYMNASIUM occupies one corner of a large athletic field, where the "Gaels" of football fame are trained. It is named for Coach "Slip" Madigan, under whose tutelage St. Mary's teams won renown.

Northeast of its junction with Moraga Road, State 24 climbs by an easy grade into the canyon of the Lafayette branch of Walnut Creek.

LAFAYETTE, 11.4 m. (200 alt., 20,484 pop. 1970) in Contra Costa County, incorporated in 1968 is principally a residential area. In 1848 Elam Brown, immigrant train captain, purchased the 3,500-acre Rancho Acalanes from Candelario Valencia, and sold a tenth of the rancho to Nathaniel Jones. The two erected frame buildings to begin the town.

State 24 cuts through the foothills of Lafayette Ridge across Reesley Valley to Walnut Creek 14.8 m. (147 alt., 39,844 pop. 1970; 9,903, 1960; inc. 302%), at the southern end of Ygnacio Valley. The business center parallels the creek; the residential section rises into low hills. Because of its location at crossroads the first American settlers gave the town the terse Yankee name of The Corners. Later the English equivalent of the earlier Spanish name, Arroyo de las Nueces (gully of the nuts), was restored because of the many native hard-shell California walnuts growing along Walnut Creek. Walnut culture, a thriving industry that centers here, began when pioneer growers first grafted the English walnut to hardy young native trees. Many kinds of fruit also are cultivated in the rich valley soil, and there are numerous poultry farms in the region.

South of Walnut Creek, State 21 follows narrow San Ramon Valley between the foothills of Mount Diablo (L) and Las Trampas Ridge (R).

In ALAMO, 18.4 m. (272 alt., 14,059 pop. including Danville, both unincorporated), giant maple trees shade the main street, although the village was named by Spaniards for the cottonwoods growing abundantly hereabout. The first adobe built here (about 1848) became in 1853 the only post office between Martinez and Mission San Jose; the mail was delivered by horse and cart twice a week.

Visible at 20.4 m. is the MILLER HOUSE, once home of playwright Eugene O'Neill. The white palatial residence stands on a hillside overlooking the road.

DANVILLE, 21 m. (365 alt.), a trading center, was named after Danville, Kentucky.

The side route continues L. from Danville on Mount Diablo Road, climbing out of the orchard lands of San Ramon Valley to the entrance of MOUNT DIABLO STATE PARK (automobile permit), 25.5 m. the road climbs along a confused mass of DEVIL'S SLIDE, 28 m., up Madrone Canyon past the grotesque, animal-like rock formations of the GARDEN OF THE JUNGLE GODS, 28.6 m.

Well-defined trails lead northwest from PARK HEADQUARTERS, 29.1 m., to the sandstone formation of ELEPHANT ROCK, SENTINEL ROCK, DEVIL'S STAIRWAY, PIGEON ROCK, and PENGUIN ROCK.

Rising majestically above broad plains, the conical summit of MOUNT DIABLO, 36.2 m. (3,849 alt.), often incorrectly said to be volcanic, is easily recognizable from great distances; it long has been a conspicuous landmark for both Indians and whites. To the east are the great San Joaquin and Sacramento Valleys and the long line of the Sierra from Mount Lassen to Mount Brewer; to the north, Mount St. Helena; to the west, Mount Tamalpais and the Pacific; to the south, Santa Clara Valley between parallel Coast ranges. Eighty thousand square miles of land and sea lie within the extreme limits of vision. All lands in California north of Kern and San Luis Obispo Counties, except the Humboldt region, are surveyed by reference to Mount Diablo (a meridian base).

Pedro Fages and his company in 1772 were the first white men to come near the mountain. Four years later Juan Bautista de Anza followed the trail blazed by Fages. General Mariano G. Vallejo reported that in 1806 a military expedition from San Francisco fought the Bolgone Indians, who were encamped on a foothill seven miles north of Kah Woo Koom (mighty mountain), as the Indians called Mount Diablo. During the battle "an unknown personage, decorated with the most extraordinary plumage and making divers movements, suddenly appeared. The Indians were victorious and the incognito, probably a medicine man impersonating the *puy* [evil spirit, or devil] . . . departed towards the mount. The defeated soldiers . . . named the mount 'Diablo' . . ."

In 1841 the first emigrant train to enter California by way of the Sierra Nevada, the Bidwell-Bartleson party, used Mount Diablo as a guide. Colonel Leander Ransom established Diablo as a base point for Government surveys in California in 1851. In 1862 the Whitney survey expedition climbed and measured the mountain. Before the days of automobiles it required a full day to ascend the steep and dusty road to the summit. A hotel on the mountainside, which cared for overnight visitors, was burned by settlers who objected to trespassers.

Crowning the summit are the heavily buttressed walls of MOUNT DIABLO MUSEUM, built of native miocene sandstone. The structure has a three-story octagonal tower flanked by an L-shaped wing. The main entrance opens into the ground floor of the tower, built around the base meridian marker. Against the walls is a series of dioramas and pictures relating to establishment of the mountain as a base meridian point and a triangulation base for the United States Geodetic Survey. In the adjoining wing are the Hall of Science, containing botanical, zoological, paleontological, and geological exhibits, and murals illustrating prehistoric animal life; and the Hall of History, with a series of dioramas and murals depicting Indian life and religious concepts, Spanish exploration and settlement in the Diablo region, early American settlements, and local industries, particularly the Mount Diablo coal mines. The second floor of the tower is an observation room. Above the windows are large photomurals showing the greatest distances in each direction which can be seen with the naked eye. The upper story of the tower is surmounted by a powerful revolving electric beacon.

In Alameda County's extreme northwest corner is ALBANY, 6.2 *m.* (sea level-300 alt., 14,674 pop.), with its many one-family homes of white stucco. The town site was part of the huge Rancho San Antonio granted to Luis Maria Peralta in 1820. The town was known as Ocean View until 1909, when the electorate renamed it in deference to Mayor Roberts, who came from Albany, New York.

GOLDEN GATE FIELDS, the former Golden Gate Turf Club, Fleming Point, was opened for horse racing on the eve of World War II. Taken over by the United States Navy, it served during the war years as a huge depot for landing barges. The race track is operated by the Pacific Turf Club, Inc., and can seat 14,000. The U.S. DEPARTMENT OF AGRICULTURE LABORATORY, 800 Buchanan St., conducts research on the industrial uses of fruits, vegetables and oil seeds.

EL CERRITO, 6.9 *m.* (sea level-500 alt., 25,190 pop. 1970; 25,437, 1960), occupies the southern portion of the old Rancho San Pablo, granted in 1823 to Francisco Maria Castro. Its incorporation dates from 1917.

The large white CASTRO ADOBE standing a few yards off San Pablo Ave. on Cerrito Creek, was built in the 1840's by Don Victor Castro, youngest son of the grantee of Rancho San Pablo. It has 34-inch outer walls and includes a private chapel. Bret Harte used the house as the locale of his play, *The Two Men of Sandy Bar.*

The heart of the war shipbuilding center of RICHMOND, 9.2 *m.* (sea level-100 alt., 79,043 pop. 1970; 71,854, 1960), lies in the direction pointed by an arrow-shaped electric sign above the highway. Though less than 40 years old, Richmond is Contra Costa County's largest city and the principal West Coast port for the transhipment of oil. It extends from the Contra Costa hills across three miles of low, level terrain to a steep headland from which two peninsulas—Point Richmond to the southeast and Point San Pablo to the northwest—jut into San Francisco Bay. Between Point San Pablo and San Pedro Point on the opposite Marin County shore is San Pablo Strait, joining San Francisco and San Pablo Bays. A six-mile water front fringed by an industrial belt and a series of modern home districts semicircling the business district comprise the 27 square miles of this scattered town.

Until 1900 this was farming and grazing land. The first settler, John Nicholl, had bought 200 acres of Rancho San Pablo in 1847. The hilly land from Point San Pablo to Point Richmond was acquired by

Jacob M. Tewksbury, surgeon and land-grabber. The greater part of the present waterfront and industrial belt was separated from the mainland by a slough and therefore would have been declared closed Federal land under the act of 1866 applying to all the islands in San Francisco Bay, had not Tewksbury built a small dam across the southern end of the slough which led to closing of the waterway by shoaling.

When the Santa Fe Railroad in 1899 selected the site as its western terminus, Richmond's development began. The Standard Oil Company built the first unit of its great refinery here in 1902. The dredging of the harbor began in 1912. By the eve of World War II, Richmond had become the home of more than 60 industries, including fish-reduction plants, chemical works, an asphalt products plant, and tile, brick, enamel, and pottery works. The four terminals along the waterfront were handling an annual cargo of more than 9,000,000 tons. Oil was by far the most important export.

The choice of Richmond by the Henry J. Kaiser Shipbuilding interests as the site of their San Francisco Bay yards led to Richmond's transformation, almost overnight, from small town to big city. The first of the Kaiser yards, built in the swampy land fronting the Inner Harbor, was opened in 1941 to build cargo vessels for the British Government. In rapid succession, three others were built. Richmond's population increased nearly five-fold as shipbuilders flocked here from all over the country. At peak employment more than 90,000 were at work. By the fall of 1945 they had built 747 ships. Yards I and II built 489 Liberty cargo vessels—more than any other shipyard in the nation—including the *Robert E. Peary,* built in 4½ days, a world record.

The KAISER SHIPYARD, end of Point Potrero, built in 1942, was constructed for permanent rather than temporary use, unlike the other three Kaiser yards. It has five basins carved out of rock.

The STANDARD OIL REFINERY (*adm. by pass*), Standard Ave., occupies a tract of 1,800 acres. It has a daily capacity of more than 100,000 barrels of crude oil.

The FORD MOTOR COMPANY ASSEMBLY PLANT, 1414 S. Tenth St., which covered a stretch of 58 acres along the Inner Harbor, closed in 1955 and the building now serves as a storage center for the University of California.

NICHOLL PARK (*tennis, handball, baseball, bowling*), Twenty-ninth St. and McDonald Ave., is Richmond's largest recreation center. The eight-room JOHN NICHOLL HOUSE, 2800 McDonald Ave., built in 1857 of redwood, is shaded by great eucalyptus trees.

Toll plaza of the RICHMOND-SAN RAFAEL BRIDGE is located at the Richmond end of the bridge (toll-65¢). The 5.45 mile long bridge opened Sept. 1, 1956. The bridge has two cantilevered main spans which rise 185 feet and 135 feet over two shipping channels.

Western Drive continues to WINEHAVEN, 8.7 *m.,* sheltered by Molate Point

(L), where formerly a large winery occupied the extensive buildings facing San Pablo Bay. It is now a ghost town, its plant and warehouses empty of machinery, its company-owned hotel and rows of cottages, which once housed 150 workers and their families, decaying in peaceful loneliness. So favorable for the aging and blending of wines were climatic conditions in this sheltered Bayside spot that $1,500,000 were invested in this property in 1906. The plant was abandoned in 1921 after a brief attempt at making grape juice for a dry nation. But to it clings the memory of the fine California wines it processed—wines that competed for world favor with the best of other lands.

SAN PABLO, 11.4 *m*. (28 alt., 21,461 pop. 1970; 19,687, 1960), was named for Rancho San Pablo, a four-league tract which Francisco Maria Castro, Spanish artillery corporal, acquired in 1823. Castro died a few years later, leaving 12 children, one of whom, Martina, married Juan B. Alvarado, Mexican governor (1836-42) who later came into possession of the greater part of this rancho.

Its rear wall facing the highway, the ALVARADO ADOBE, US 40 and Church Lane, 90 feet long with broad porches and overhanging gables, has served as the storeroom of a grocery. It was built in 1838 by Antonio, eldest son of Francisco Castro. After the American occupation, Governor Alvarado made it his home until his death in 1882.

Left from San Pablo on a hard-surfaced road 12 *m*. to a junction with a driveway leading to the GUTIERREZ ADOBE (*private*), visible from the road. Two frame wings have been added to the original 24- by 48-foot building whose thick walls, sheathed in wood and resting on a stone foundation, are well preserved. This adobe, built about 1845, was the home of Candido Gutierrez and his wife Jovita. Under one of the wings is the grave of Maria Emma Gutierrez, who died at the age of six. Her tombstone, inscribed with a Spanish verse, almost touches a floor beam.

At 12.4 *m*. on US 80 is a junction with a hard-surfaced road.

Left on this road, at the northern tip of Pinole Point, was the company town of GIANT, 2 *m*. (10 alt.), plant-site of the Atlas Powder Company. Although it had homes for about 30 families, a majority of the workmen lived elsewhere. Formerly called Nitro, the place dates from 1867, when the Giant Powder Company, first company in California to manufacture dynamite, built a plant here.

US 80 veers northeast, still following the contour of the Bay. The Contra Costa hills decline into rolling ridges which flatten out as they approach the water. This region was known as the Sobrante district during late Mexican and early American days, the tract being *sobrante* (unclaimed or left-over portion) between Ranchos San Pablo and El Pinole. Sheep and cattle trails wind through occasional groves of eucalyptus and willow.

At the foot of hills commanding views of Bay and mountains, PINOLE, 16.4 *m*. (32 alt., 15,850 pop. 1970; 6,064, 1960, inc. 161%), through which runs Pinole Creek, is chiefly a residential community for employees of plants along the Contra Costa shore. The town is named for Rancho El Pinole, claimed in 1823 by Lieutenant Ignacio Martinez, who named it in commemoration of the rescue of a party of Spanish soldiers, lost in this district, by a band of friendly Indians, who fed them

North and South of the Golden Gate

THE GOLDEN GATE BRIDGE. VIEW TOWARD THE MARIN SHORE

FORT POINT, PRESIDIO OF SAN FRANCISCO

FORT POINT, INTERIOR

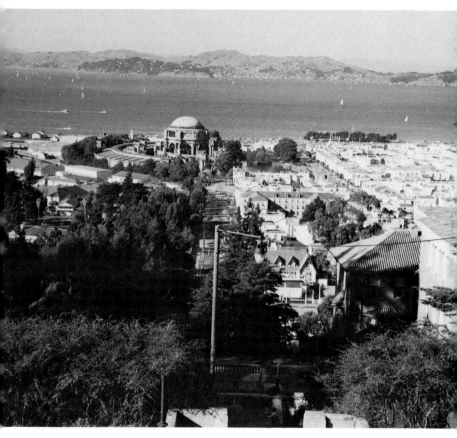

THE MARINA DISTRICT AND THE PALACE OF FINE ARTS,
FROM THE TOP OF LYON ST.

CALIFORNIA PALACE OF THE LEGION OF HONOR

TRANSBAY TRANSIT TERMINAL

OAKLAND BAY BRIDGE DURING CONSTRUCTION

GOLDEN GATE BRIDGE DURING CONSTRUCTION

FERRY BUILDING FROM THE LAND SIDE. FERRIES RUNNING, OAKLAND BRIDGE UNBUILT

FERRY BUILDING FROM THE BAY SIDE

YACHT HARBOR AT MARINE GREENS

FLEISHACKER POOL DRAINED FOR MOPPING UP

AERIAL VIEW TOWARD OAKLAND BAY BRIDGE
ACROSS DOWNTOWN

a coarse gruel made from acorns, which they called *pinole*. The canyon, farther east, where they first lost their bearings, came to be known as the Cañada del Hambre (valley of hunger) later corrupted to Alhambra.

In 1849 a young Englishman, Dr. Samuel J. Tennant, once physician to the King of the Sandwich Islands, stopped here on one of his trips to the gold regions, met Rafaela, daughter of Don Ignacio, and later married her. On that part of the rancho inherited by him and his wife, he founded the town of Pinole.

At 16.6 *m.* is a junction with a hard-surfaced road.

Left on this road is the company town of HERCULES, 0.7 *m.* (8 alt., 252 pop.), where the Hercules Powder Company established its plant in 1869 to provide powder for the mining industry. The residential district borders the road which winds along the tree-covered ridge fronting San Pablo Bay. As a measure of safety, powder and acid houses are built in separate pockets. Underground storage magazines are scattered throughout the flat lands to the east.

At 17.4 *m.* is a junction with State 4.

Right on State 4 up Franklin Canyon, the fertile valley of Rodeo Creek, still partly covered with live oaks. The cleared land is planted to apricots, walnuts, and tomatoes.

At 9.2 *m.* is a junction with a paved road—State 4; L. here 0.1 *m.* to the RANCHO LAS JUNTAS ADOBE (*private*), a well-preserved white house built in the 1840's, facing away from the road under old locust trees.

On State 4 at 2 *m.* is Martinez.

On State 4 at 9.4 *m.* the large, old-fashioned, cupolaed JOHN STRENTZEL HOUSE (L) overlooks rolling orchard land. Here the great naturalist, John Muir (1838-1914), who originated the first plans for a system of National parks, spent the latter part of his life. The estate was originally part of Rancho Las Juntas.

At 9.7 *m.* is a junction with hard-surfaced Alhambra Road; R. here to the JOHN MUIR HOUSE (L), 1.1 *m.* (*private*), the original part of which was built in 1853 by Dr. John Strentzel, who gave it to his daughter and Muir after their marriage in 1880. The Muirs lived here for ten years (1880-90), moving to the Strentzel House shortly after Dr. Strentzel's death. Many of the books, pieces of furniture, and other possessions used by Muir are here. Near a large eucalyptus tree visible from the road Muir and his wife are buried. An annual pilgrimage to the graves is made on the Sunday nearest April 21, anniversary of his birthday.

Also on Alhambra Road is the JOHN SWETT HOUSE (*private*), 1.6 *m.*, on the banks of a tree-shaded stream on Hill Girt Ranch. John Swett (1830-1913), State Superintendent of Public Instruction from 1863 to 1867, co-founder of the first State normal college and intimate friend of John Muir, lived here. Nearby is a well-preserved adobe, built in the 1850's, when this was part of Rancho Las Juntas.

From its junction with Alhambra Road, State 4 continues east to a junction with State 21, 12.7 *m.*

Right on State 21 to the LOUCKS HOUSE (*private*), 0.4 *m.*, built by G. L. Walwrath in 1853 on a hill (L). The timbers, cut from Moraga redwoods, are covered with sheathing that was brought round Cape Horn. George P. Loucks bought the house in 1856.

PACHECO, 0.8 *m.* (21 alt.), a sleepy inland village, stands beside Walnut Creek, a stream that served as the boundary line for two ranchos—Las Juntas and Monte del Diablo. Grayson Creek, which also flows through Pacheco, joins Walnut Creek north of town to form Pacheco Creek. Within a few months after the town site was laid out in 1860, the village burned to the ground. A devastating flood in 1862, two more fires in 1867 and 1871, and an earthquake in 1868 were no boost to the town's growth.

Left from Pacheco 1.8 m. is CONCORD (65 alt., 85,164 pop. 1970; 36,000, 1960, inc. 136%), a pleasant tree-shaded town, busy shipping point for the produce of Diablo Valley. The young village laid out in 1876 around the plaza was called Todos Santos (All Saints) by the Spanish and Drunken Indian by the Americans. Early hopes for the district were outlined in the *Contra Costa Gazette* of February 13, 1886: "Contra Costa County is destined to become a paradise of vineyards and orchards, of which Ygnacio and Diablo Valleys will be the central portion." The prediction has in a measure been realized. Strawberries and vegetables are also grown in large quantities.

At Concord and Salvio Aves. stands the PACHECO HOUSE, a sturdy adobe with balconies and shuttered windows, set among pepper trees. Now encased in wood and well preserved, the century-old house was the home of Salvio Pacheco, grantee of Rancho Monte del Diablo, embracing 17,921 acres of the surrounding fertile valley.

State 21 continues south from Pacheco to a junction with State 24, 3.4 m.

The main side route follows State 4 from its junction with State 21 to a junction with State 24, 1.6 m., with which it unites as State 4-24, and continues L. to a junction with former State 4, 19.7 m. (*see below*).

US 80 crosses a low range of hills into the valley of Rodeo Creek.

At the mouth of the creek on San Pablo Bay is RODEO, 19.3 m. (an unincorporated town of 5,356 pop. 1970). During Spanish and early American days great rodeos were held yearly up the canyon. There is still some cattle-raising in the back country. The Bay is in view as US 80 continues across the rolling terrain, with great oil tanks on the hillsides—a portion of the 900 in this district.

The smell of petroleum near OLEUM, 20.2 m. (76 alt.), comes from the Union Oil Company Refinery. The plant refines thousands of barrels of oil daily. The "cracking" towers which tower above the highway are gigantic stills in which crude oil is heated to 700° Fahrenheit. The volatility of the component parts of the oil determines at which level of the tower they will be sucked out by the condensers and deposited in other tanks. The high octane aviation gasoline is drawn off at the top of the tower, ordinary gasoline and kerosene at a lower level and the heavier motor and fuel oils near the bottom.

TORMEY, 20.8 m., a station on the Southern Pacific line, was named for John and Patrick Tormey, whose 7,000-acre cattle ranch with a three-mile frontage on San Pablo Bay was before 1861 a part of Rancho El Pinole.

At 21 m. is a junction with a paved road.

Left on this road is the company town of SELBY, 0.2 m. (0-100 alt.), named for Prentiss Selby, who established the plant in 1884. A 605-foot-high smokestack marks the location of the American Smelting & Refining Company plant. Ore vessels unload at company docks; chief products are gold, silver, lead, and antimony.

Ascending a hill, US 80 climbs to a wide parking space, 21.5 m., cut in the hillside directly above San Pablo Bay, which affords a view of Carquinez Strait, Carquinez Bridge, and the north Bay hills and valleys. The broad expanse of San Pablo Bay narrows into six-mile-long and one-mile-wide CARQUINEZ STRAIT. The town of Vallejo and the Mare Island Navy Yard lie opposite. A long breakwater protects the deep channel to the Navy Yard; towering steel masts mark a powerful Naval radio station.

John Sutter, in command of three small vessels, looked out upon these shores en route to empire and riches in 1839; and this was the water route for men and supplies during the Gold Rush. Today ocean-going vessels buck the swift currents on their way to the deep-water port of Stockton, while flat-bottomed river boats push to and from the great central valleys. In season hundreds of tiny craft bob on the swells, as fishermen pit their skill and patience against the wariness of the gamey striped bass.

At 22.3 m. is a junction with a paved road, on which the route branches R. from US 80.

Left here on US 80, across CARQUINEZ BRIDGE (35¢ per car), is VALLEJO, 3.5 m. (see North Bay Tour).

The route continues R. on the paved road to CROCKETT, 22.7 m. (25 alt., 3,698 pop.), which rises from the narrow strip of land fronting Carquinez Strait up the steep adjoining hills. The original owner of the town site, Thomas Edwards, Welsh by birth and a former mate on Mississippi River steamboats, drove his own covered wagon to California in 1849-50. Securing 1,800 acres along the Strait, he went into the cattle business. With the coming of the Central Pacific in 1877, the Edwards ranch became the site of Valona Station. In 1881, when a foundry selected the site as a new home, Edwards laid out the present town. He named it for J. B. Crockett, a former member of the California Supreme Court, whom he had known in St. Louis as a young lawyer.

In 1897 the California Beet Sugar Refining Company erected a small refinery on the shore, the nucleus of the present CALIFORNIA HAWAIIAN SUGAR REFINING CORPORATION PLANT (visiting hours 10-1). The corporation has its own ships which bring tons of raw sugar from the Hawaiian Islands to its docks.

East of Crockett the route parallels Carquinez Strait. Now at sea level, now on the hillsides, the road winds around points and dives into canyons.

In PORT COSTA, 25.2 m. (11 alt., 271 pop.), an elm-shaded lane leads down to a cove which was formerly an important harbor. When grain was California's principal crop, sailing vessels of many nations loaded wheat at this port. Until 1930, when the Southern Pacific built a bridge across the strait (see below), the main line trains were ferried from here to Benicia. One of the boats, the Contra Costa, with a capacity of 36 freight cars and two locomotives, was the largest railroad ferry in the world.

MARTINEZ, 31 *m.* (12 alt., 16,506 pop. 1970; 9,604, 1960, inc. 71%), sits on a crescent-shaped cove on Carquinez Strait, where the hills turn south to form the narrow Alhambra Valley into which the town is growing. Martinez was laid out in 1849 by Colonel William M. Smith on lands of Rancho El Pinole, to which in 1850 was added, east of Del Hambre Creek, a part of Rancho Las Juntas (the junction points), granted in 1852 to William Welch, a Scot. When Contra Costa County was organized in 1850, Martinez became the county seat. River boats docked here, and a ferry crossed to Benicia. In 1878 the Central Pacific built a branch line from Port Costa to Martinez and later another line south into the San Ramon Valley. The Mountain Copper Company began manufacturing fertilizers and various copper derivatives here in 1905. The town grew slowly, however, until 1914, when the Shell Oil Company with its refinery became the chief industry. Martinez also ships wine, acids, alcohol, furniture, fish oil and meal, spring water, redwood panels, and electric fixtures.

1. Right from Martinez on State 21 to a junction with State 4, 4.3 *m.* (*see above*).

The main route goes east on Escobar Street through the Shell Oil Refinery property and past the SOUTHERN PACIFIC RAILROAD BRIDGE, which spans the eastern end of Carquinez Strait between Suisun Point and Army Point. The bridge was completed in 1930 at a cost of $12,000,000.

Site of one of World War II's worst home-front disasters is PORT CHICAGO, 37.8 *m.* (18 alt.), formerly called Bay Point, which looks out toward the low-lying islands of Suisun Bay. Hundreds of lives were lost when two Liberty vessels exploded at the Navy's ammunition loading docks with a blast that shook the countryside for miles around. Port Chicago grew up with the C. A. Smith Lumber Company which came here in 1907 and flourished during World War I when the Pacific Coast Shipbuilding Company maintained yards here, but later declined in population when these companies moved away. In 1955 the U.S. Navy decided Port Chicago was in peril if another disaster occured during loading of Vietnam-bound explosives. After a bitter 13-year fight the Navy received congressional authorization and $19,500,000 to purchase all land within a 2½-mile safety zone.

East of Nichols, Suisun Bay narows to a deep channel into which pour the Sacramento and San Joaquin Rivers after draining the great central valleys.

At SHELL POINT, 42.9 *m.,* are a chemical plant and experimental laboratories of the Shell Oil Company.

PITTSBURG, 46.2 *m.* (21 alt., 20,651 pop. 1970; 19,062, 1960), faces the deep waters of New York Slough, near the confluence of the

Sacramento and San Joaquin Rivers. Although it is a highly industrialized town, it has clean, well-paved streets, and many of its residents own their own homes.

The founder of the first settlement here was Jonathan B. Stevenson, ex-colonel of New York Militia, who led a regiment of New York Volunteers to California to help restore order in 1847. Stevenson turned to real estate with the idea of founding a "New York of the Pacific." In 1849 he purchased a part of Rancho Los Meganos (sand dunes), including the site of Pittsburg, engaged an obscure young engineer, one William Tecumseh Sherman—destined to become well-known in the State of Georgia—to lay out this Pacific Coast Manhattan, and tried to infuse Californians with his own "big-town" enthusiasm. Those who thought the city would become a "second New York" were doomed to disappointment, for the citizens sat up nights waiting for the boom and fighting off the hordes of mosquitoes infesting adjacent swamps. By 1865 they had become resigned to the waiting and the mosquitoes—and to the town's name of "New York Landing," which had been substituted for the colonel's grandiloquent "New York of the Pacific." When in the 1880's coal was discovered on the slope of Mount Diablo, the town was renamed Black Diamond. In 1910, after the Columbia Steel Company had built a modern mill, it received its present name.

The mills, foundries, and shops of the COLUMBIA STEEL CORPORATION PLANT (*visitors admitted by special permission*), where rolled steel products are manufactured, cover 387 acres. This plant is the principal subsidiary on the Pacific Coast of the United States Steel Corporation.

ANTIOCH, 50.5 *m.* (42 alt., 28,060 pop. 1970; 17,305, 1960, inc. 62%), lies on the south bank of the San Joaquin River. The town is the gateway to the rich San Joaquin delta, which produces the bulk of the Nation's asparagus. Along its water front pass ships and barges to Stockton, one of the country's leading inland ports. The founders of Antioch, J. H. and W. W. Smith, ministers by profession and carpenters by trade, arrived in San Francisco from Boston on July 6, 1849. The brothers took up jointly two quarter-sections of land where Antioch now stands. On December 24, 1849, they set up tents and broke ground, working the land just enough to hold it, while carrying on their carpenter work. On February 5, 1850 the Reverend W. W. Smith died, but his brother remained at Smith's Landing. Learning that a shipload of settlers from Maine had arrived in San Francisco planning to found a colony in California, he hurried to the city and offered each a lot for a home. They brought with them the traditions of a sturdy, God-fearing race and selected the Biblical name of Antioch for their new home. Antioch prospered during the Gold Rush, when ships with men and supplies made it a port of call and farmers began to cultivate the surrounding rich agricultural lands.

Today one of Antioch's largest industries is the Fibreboard Products Company, which spreads over a 30-acre tract producing boxboard, paper boxes, packing cases, and wallboard. Other industries include a ship-building plant and several fruit and vegetable canneries.

The substantial GEORGE W. KIMBALL HOUSE, Third St., erected in 1851, was one of the first structures in the State to be built of Douglas fir—the Oregon pine of lumbermen.

⟨⟨◆

East Bay Tour 2

Oakland—San Leandro—Union City—Fremont—Milpitas—San Jose; 41.7 m. State 17.

This route follows the rich agricultural lands on the east side of San Francisco Bay, country occupied by Franciscan missionaries and Spanish *rancheros* long before the coming of Americans.

South from Fourteenth St. and Broadway in OAKLAND, 0 *m.,* on Broadway; L. on Eighth St. (State 17), which curves into E. Twelfth St.

SAN LEANDRO, 8.7 *m.* (50 alt. 68,698 pop. 1970; 65,962, 1960), is an industrial and residential center on a narrow strip of exceptionally fertile land between San Francisco Bay and low foothills. A green wedge-like plaza and old-fashioned frame buildings soften the business district's otherwise typical Main-Street atmosphere. Both the old frame houses and the new stucco-finished bungalows are fronted by well-kept gardens. The more pretentious old wooden homes have an air of faded grandeur.

For almost a century, San Leandro was primarily agricultural. Potatoes and barley were grown commercially on the Estudillo and Peralta ranchos, and these were prosperous crops for several generations. When it was decided tomatoes were an edible fruit, San Leandro proved to be a fertile spot for them. Most successful crop of all, however, was the plump, juicy, bright-red cherry—a fruit that proved to be the backbone of local economy for 40 years.

Cherries, potatoes, barley and tomatoes are now grown on a comparatively small scale, for residential and industrial districts have taken over agricultural areas, but San Leandro's pleasant sunshine and rich soil still contributes to city commerce. Flowers bring in excess of $6,000,000 in trade each year, with local nurseries including more than two million rose bushes and facilities for growing large amounts of gardenias, carnations, delphiniums, dahlias and even orchids. Each day these nurseries ship large quantities of cut flowers throughout the world.

Today industry forms the basis of the city's economy, with more than 265 plants in operation.

The city's site was formerly part of Rancho San Leandro, granted Don Jose Joaquin Estudillo in 1842. Before the United States Government could confirm the title, however, many settlers had staked out claims. In early days San Leandro was an important stagecoach stop between Oakland and San Jose. Of all the stage drivers who made the run, the most hell-roaring was Charley Parkhurst, a swaggering bully with one eye covered by a black patch, lips and chin habitually stained by tobacco juice, who wore a buffalo-skin cap and turned up the cuffs of his blue jeans to show off elegant boots. Not until "his" death was Charley discovered to be a woman, Charlotte Parkhurst, who had come to California at the age of 20 in 1848. Unsuspected, she registered as a voter 50 years before woman's suffrage, her name (in its masculine form) appearing on the Santa Cruz register for 1866.

San Leandro has a large Portuguese settlement, founders of the colony (originally from the Azore and Madeira) came here from Sandwich Island sugar plantations where, because of a labor shortage, they had been held in virtual peonage. In the 1870's many Portuguese sailors, picked up at the Azores by New Bedford whaling vessels, rounded Cape Horn, jumped ship in San Francisco, and came here with little more than the small gold earrings which the majority of them wore. By their industry and thrift these patient, liberty-loving people were able to send passage money to other Azorean countrymen eager to take up life in the New World. The Portuguese celebrates with church services, banners, street parades, and fireworks, the Feast of the Holy Ghost.

San Leandro has its own unified school district and recreation department. The San Leandro Community Library Center (Francis J. McCarthy, architect) opened in 1961 and covers over $3\frac{1}{2}$ acres.

In ROOT PARK, E. Fourteenth St. and San Leandro Creek, a historical marker indicates the boundary between Rancho San Antonio and Rancho San Leandro.

The ESTUDILLO HOUSE (*private*), 1291 Carpentier St., erected 1850 or 1851, is the city's oldest residence. It was badly damaged in the 1868 earthquake. The balcony extending along two sides of the 14-room house, which still has its original clapboard sheathing and window sashes, is supported by wooden-covered brick pillars. On the lower floor were originally the kitchen, dining room, wine cellar, and quarters for Indian servants; on the upper floor were living quarters for the family. Behind the mansion is a fig tree over 90 years old, while nearby stands an almost equally venerable pear tree. Two large gnarled stumps in the front yard are remains of Alameda County's first pepper trees.

The Alta Mira Club, Leo & Lafayette Sts., is housed in the old IGNACIO PERALTA HOUSE. Sergeant Luis Maria Peralta, grantee of Rancho San Antonio, divided his holdings among his four sons in 1842, and Ignacio, coming into the southern portion, built this home in 1860. The house, a one-story, rectangular structure, is of brick, the first in the county built of that material. Extensively repaired and remodeled, it is painted a light tan. The front porch, extending the width of the house, is shaded by two large magnolias.

South of San Leandro, where blue mountains appear across the Bay, once orchards, hayfields, and truck gardens covered the flat land. Diminutive Japanese women wearing large sunbonnets and legginged overalls worked in berry fields and truck gardens, and tilled fields on hillsides created a patchwork quilt.

SAN LORENZO, 12 *m.* (31 alt., 24,633 pop. 1970; 23,773, 1960), formerly a commercial center for surrounding farms and orchards, was once known as Squatterville. Here on the banks of San Lorenzo Creek Americans began in 1851 to overrun Don Jose Joaquin Estudillo's Rancho San Leandro. Some of the squatters expressed their pioneer disrespect for property rights by shooting Estudillo's horses and cattle and fencing watering places away from his stock. Following a court decision favorable to Estudillo in 1854, they began to take leases and eventually bought the land.

The former SAN LORENZO HOTEL, now a tavern and private dwelling, is a two-story building beneath whose casing of brown shingles is the original siding. Built in 1854 by Charles Crane, it was a stage station on the Mission Road between San Jose and Oakland.

MOUNT EDEN (25 alt.), is now a subdivision of Hayward. The name is misleading, for the town site is flat. Established in 1850, it was known in the early days both as Eden's Landing and Johnson's Landing. John Johnson, first American to extract salt commercially along San Francisco Bay, shipped his product to pioneer settlements of California from a crude landing near here.

1. Right from Mount Eden on a paved road 1.8 *m.* to the LESLIE SALT WORKS, extending over flat land, where water from the Bay, confined in square shallow areas enclosed by banked-up earth, is reduced to crude salt by evaporation. Windmills, squat copies of the Dutch type, pump water from one area to another. Huge piles of white salt stand like cones of snow. Long before the white man came Indians gathered crude salt from natural basins along the nearby shore line.

In San Mateo, 13.1 *m.* is the junction with US 101 Bypass (*see Peninsula Tour*).

At 3 *m.* is the east approach to the new high-level SAN MATEO-HAYWARD BRIDGE (toll 70¢). The 12-mile long structure, completed in 1968, has doubled the original width of the bridge.

Left from Mount Eden on a paved road is HAYWARD (115 alt., 93,058 pop. 1970; 72,700, 1960; inc. 28%), a trading center for a rapidly growing residential and industrial area. It connects with State 17, Interstate 580, and US 50. Incorporated March 11, 1876, it only recently, March 7, 1956, became a chartered city. In 1940 it had only 8,243 pop. There is a wide variety of business carried on in the city; the major industries are food processing, steel fabrication, truck assembly, construction materials, paper boxes, machinery and furniture.

The town, which occupies a portion of the Rancho San Lorenzo, granted to Guillermo Castro in 1841, derived its name from William Hayward, who in 1851 mistakenly pitched his tent in Palomares Canyon on Castro's land with the intention of homesteading. Later Hayward purchased a plot on the rancho from Castro. Since roads leading to the gold fields passed through Hayward's property, his rude habitation soon became a trading place for miners. The shrewd Yankee established a combined stagecoach inn and general store. Soon the fame of "Haywards" was such that San Francisco people made the trip by boat and stagecoach to spend vacations there.

DUBLIN, 11.1 m. (367 alt., 13,641 pop. 1970) an unincorporated town, once called Amador, was a portion of Rancho San Ramon, granted in 1833 to Jose Maria Amador, a hard-boiled soldier, onetime major-domo of mission San Jose. Centered here was his 16,517-acre rancho, stocked with great herds of cattle, sheep, and horses. In 1846, when Captain John Charles Frémont, ostensibly making "surveys," rode through the property and confiscated 57 of Amador's horses, a quarrel arose; but Frémont, at the head of his column of campaign-toughened fighters, presented a formidable argument to which Amador was forced to yield. The enterprising Amador was perhaps the first industrialist in the region now comprising Alameda County. Using Indian and Mexican labor, he early manufactured soap, leather goods, blankets, wagons, and other commodities. After 1852, when James Witt Dougherty purchased most of the Amador grant, the settlement was known as "Dougherty's Station." Because the area became settled largely by the Irish, the little town ultimately became known as Dublin. Surrounded by very fertile land, it is noted for fine Hereford stock, and dairy and farm products.

Little white frame ST. RAYMOND'S CHURCH, built in 1859 by Tom Donlan, was the first place of worship in the valley. A hawthorne-lined driveway leads behind the church to the cemetery in which have been interred the pioneers of the region. Jig-saw scrolls ornament the overhanging eaves of the two-story AMADOR HOTEL, on the west side of US 50, built in 1860 by James W. Dougherty with redwood lumber brought from Redwood City. In 1870, John Scarlett, a local bartender, purchased the hotel. A modern front has been added to the first story.

Straight ahead (south) on State 21 from Dublin, along the western edge of Amador Valley and the eastern base of Pleasanton Ridge, 1 m. to the remodeled JEREMIAH FALLON HOUSE (L), built in 1850 of redwood timbers hewn from the San Antonio forest east of Oakland. The house was moved here from a previous location when the highway was rerouted.

A giant oak shades the ALVISO ADOBE (L), 3.4 m., built in 1846. The one-story house, with a storehouse in an abutting wing, overlooks vast green alfalfa fields extending to Pleasanton (see below).

The white-plastered AUGUSTIN BERNAL ADOBE (R), 5.8 m. (private), dates from 1850. The roof extending over the long front porch is supported by heavy square posts. The gable windows are later additions. The present ranch is a small part of the vast 48,000-acre Rancho El Valle de San Jose, which included a large part of the Livermore and Sunol Valleys. It was granted in 1839 jointly to Augustin Bernal, his brother Juan Pablo, Antonio Maria Pico, and Antonio Maria Sunol (see below).

At 6.2 m. on State 21 is the junction with an improved road; R. here 0.3 m. to the former PHOEBE APPERSON HEARST RESIDENCE, a white, Spanish-styled, two-story building topped by two towers and roofed with red tile. Here the wife of Senator George Hearst frequently—and lavishly—entertained students from the University of California. Centered in the patio is a marble well-head of Veronese sculpture from which the estate took its name, Hacienda del Pozo de Verona (estate of the Veronese well). Inside the mansion are 40 rooms. The surrounding 500 acres, lying on the low foothills of Pleasanton Ridge and wooded with many fine varieties of conifers, white oaks, and cork elms, were bought by Senator Hearst in 1890 and converted into a blooded horse-breeding farm. For several years after Mrs. Hearst's death a golf course and country club occupied the estate. It was destroyed by fire in August 1969.

At 6.3 m. on State 21 is the junction with the Pleasanton-Sunol road (see below).

West from Dublin the main side route follows US 50 across the level stretches of the fertile Livermore Valley to SANTA RITA, 14.8 *m.* (346 alt.), originally part of Rancho Santa Rita issued in 1839 to Jose Dolores Pacheco.

Right from Santa Rita on a paved road is Pleasanton, 2.8 *m.* (*see below*).

The ROBERT LIVERMORE MONUMENT, 20.2 *m.*, built of native rock in 1935, commemorates the first English-speaking settler in this region. Livermore, who had served in the British navy, entered the merchant marine service only to jump his ship, the *Colonel Young*, at Monterey Bay in 1822. Quickly learning Spanish, he became a favorite among the Mexicans. After marrying Senorita Josefa Higuera, whose father owned the Rancho Agua Caliente. Livermore came with his wife and José Noriega into this valley in 1835, settled on the 8,800-acre Rancho Las Positas (the little water holes), and planted the first orchard and vineyard in the valley. Livermore died in 1858 and was buried at Mission San Jose de Guadalupe (*see below*).

At 20.6 *m.*, is the junction with a paved road, on which the route goes R.

LIVERMORE, 21.3 *m.* (487 alt., 37,703 pop. 1970; 16,058, 1960; inc. 134%), located partly on what was once Robert Livermore's Rancho Las Positas, was a cattle and agricultural community where "ten-gallon" hats and jingling spurs, mingle with more conservative attire. During the annual Livermore Rodeo in June, residents don "Western" hats, high-heeled boots and chaps, and proceed to take the town apart.

Alfonso Ladd named the town site Laddsville as early as 1850. In following years many settlers drifted into Livermore Valley where they harvested bumper crops of wheat, barley, and oats. But not until the advent of the Central Pacific Railroad in 1869 did the town burgeon into importance. The introduction of the wine industry assured it of a prosperous development.

Livermore Valley has been called the Sauterne capital of America. James Concannon, the Wente Brothers, and others, discovering here chalky soils similar to those of the Sauterne areas in southwestern France, sent to France for cuttings in the early 1880's. The yield of grapes, one and one-quarter tons per acre, is small, but the varieties are of the highest quality. Vintages from the imported cuttings have won gold medals in competition with wines from grapes of the parent stock.

Right (south) from Livermore on L Street, which crosses the Arroyo Mocho and becomes a paved county road, 4.2 *m.* to the UNITED STATES VETERANS' HOSPITAL. In the white stucco buildings with red tile roofs, about 300 tubercular veterans are treated.

The main side route continues from Livermore on West First Street to the junction with a paved road, 27.1 *m.*, and L. here across the Arroyo del Valle.

PLEASANTON, 27.3 *m.* (361 alt., 18,328 pop. 1970; 4,203, 1960; inc. 336%), is the center of an area devoted to agriculture, dairying, grape culture and wine-making. The local wineries sponsor an annual festival called "La Fiesta del Vino." The town's name honors General Pleasanton, a cavalry officer who served under John Charles Frémont in the Missouri campaign of the Civil War. Though sedate and quiet today, Pleasanton was once melodramatically "Western," with fire-spitting guns, swinging saloon doors, and spangled dancehall girls. Pleasanton's old-fashioned houses and white wooden church appeared in the motion picture *Rebecca of Sunnybrook Farm,* which, with Mary Pickford appearing in the title role, was filmed here in 1917–18.

Laid out in the early seventies, the PLEASANTON RACETRACK became famous throughout the country for its harness races and trotting exhibitions. The track west of town is still in use as a trial ground for promising horses; the stables and adjacent grounds are also used as a resting place for racing stock from Tanforan, Santa Anita, and other tracks.

The ROSE HOTEL, 540 Main St., a shabby three-story building built in 1874, formerly was much patronized by owners of thoroughbreds and racetrack followers.

Founded in 1902, the LORETTO WINERY (*open to visitors*), 124 St. John

St., makes both dry and sweet wines and brandy. It has two oaken casks whose heads are examples of fine wood carving.

The JUAN P. BERNAL ADOBE, on the north bank of Arroyo del Valle, was built in 1852. A soldier of the San Francisco and San Jose presidios, Bernal here became a large landowner. His daughter married an Austrian, John W. Kottinger, first storekeeper in Pleasanton, who erected an adobe on the opposite bank of the arroyo.

South of Pleasanton, the valley narrows into the Arroyo de la Laguna. At 29.2 *m.* is the junction with State 21 (*see above*), on which the route continues through the arroyo to the junction with Niles Canyon Road, 31.5 *m.*

Straight ahead through a grilled iron gate 0.5 *m.* to the SUNOL WATER TEMPLE and a shaded picnic ground (*open 7-7*). The Water Temple (Willis Polk, architect), inspired by the ancient Temple of Vesta at Tivoli, consists of a circular arcade of ten Corinthian columns supporting a dome. Immediately below the dome is a deep circular enclosure through which flows a torrent of water from the Sierra Nevada, which having been filtered here, flows on to San Francisco via Crystal Springs Lake (*see PENINSULA TOUR*).

The main side route goes R. on Niles Canyon Road across the Arroyo de la Laguna to SUNOL, 33.1 *m.* (250 alt.), an agricultural center at the northern end of Sunol Valley, which is drained by Alameda Creek. The town was named after Antonio Sunol, who prior to settling here served in the French navy. Sunol and others were granted the Rancho El Valle de San Jose in 1839. The region's chief products are apricots, tomatoes, walnuts, grapes, grain, and hay.

West of Sunol, Alameda Creek winds through steep, narrow Niles Canyon. The creek is crossed and recrossed as the road winds and twists into the canyon, with it buckeyes and wide-spreading sycamores. In the shade are many spots for picnicking, camping, and swimming.

A stone aqueduct, paralleling the road south from 38 *m.*, once carried water to Vallejo's Mill, whose ruins still stand in Niles (*see below*).

NILES (*see Fremont*), 39.4 *m.* (77 alt.), was the center of an intensive flower-fruit- and vegetable-growing area. The town stands on part of what was Rancho Arroyo de la Alameda, 17,705 acres granted in 1842 to Jose de Jesus Vallejo, an older brother of General Mariano Vallejo. Its name honors Judge Addison C. Niles, who in 1871 was elected to the California Supreme Court. In the nickel-odeon era, when movies were in their silent but lusty infancy, the now defunct Essanay Studios, in which Charles Chaplin, Ben Turpin, and Wallace Beery began their movie careers, were located here.

UNION CITY (11 alt., 14,724 pop. 1970; 6,618, 1960; inc. 125%), includes the communities of Decoto and Alvarado and was incorporated in January 1959. The city's industrial growth in recent years has occurred in the Alvarado district and the Central Bay and Union City industrial parks developed by the Western Pacific and Southern Pacific Railroad Companies respectively.

In the early 1850's three rival towns were laid out here: Union City, New Haven, and finally Alvarado. On March 15, 1853, Henry C. Smith, founder of New Haven, introduced into the State legislature a bill to create Alameda County, "designating New Haven as the county seat and Alvarado as seat of justice." The new county officials met in the upper story of Smith's store in New Haven, but their first minutes are dated "Alvarado, April 11, 1853," indicating that the name Alvarado had been accepted for the entire community as well as the county seat.

Firms which have located operations in Union City during the past five years include American Distilling Company; American Forge Co., Division of Pacific States Steel; Campbell Chain, Division of Unitek Industries; Associated Food Stores; and White Front Stores.

Right to the DUMBARTON TOLL BRIDGE, 6.9 *m.* (*toll, 70¢*). At 10.7 *m.* is the junction with US 101 Bypass (*see Peninsula Tour*).

FREMONT (50 alt., 100,869 pop. 1970; 43,760, 1960; inc. 130%), formerly Centerville, was originally known as Hardscrabble, a town consisting of a small store on the old Mission Road to San Jose. One of the first schools in the State was organized here in 1852. Centerville grew slowly and uneventfully until the earthquake of 1906 started a fire which all but destroyed the village. In January 1956, five communities (Centerville, Irvington, Mission San Jose, Niles and Warm Springs) and adjacent agricultural lands incorporated to form the city of Fremont. Although each of the five communities has retained its own distinct district within the city, with shopping areas, schools, and community organizations, the Fremont city government furnishes planning, public facilities, public safety, and other services to meet overall city needs. Encompassing 96 square miles Fremont is the third largest city in area in California. Orchards and truck farms occupying approximately 10 percent of the city's area are gradually being replaced by subdivision and industrial development.

Right from Fremont on a paved road is NEWARK (21 alt., 27,153 pop. 1970; 9,884, 1960; inc. 174%). First known as Mayhew's Landing it was founded about 1875 by James G. Fair, one of the Nevada silver millionaires, and A. E. Davis, who later renamed it for his birthplace in New Jersey. Newark was incorporated in 1955 and covers an area approximately eight square miles. Salt processing by evaporation from San Francisco Bay, established in the area in 1852, is Newark's oldest and largest industry. Both Leslie and Morton Salt Companies have major plants in the city, along with more than 25 other industrial firms.

At 7 *m.* is the Dumbarton Bridge (*see above*).

IRVINGTON, now a subdivision of FREMONT, was first known as Washington Corners, an important pioneer trading post. It took the name of Irvington in 1884.

Left from Washington Blvd. on a paved road 1.2 *m.* to a cement-walled INDIAN CEMETERY, where a plain granite monument explains that "here sleep 4,000 of the Olhone Tribe, who helped the padres build this Mission San Jose de Guadalupe" (*see below*). MISSION PEAK (2,508 alt.), a landmark in the mission days, rises directly ahead.

MISSION SAN JOSE, 2.1 *m.* (300 alt.), formerly known as Mission Town, was once the scene of numerous fiestas. When Mexican *rancheros* assembled here with hundreds of their retainers for sports and amusements, the town's single thoroughfare was temporarily enclosed and sufficient seats for the population of the entire countryside were erected. The festivities included feats of horsemanship, bull and bear fights, barbecues, and gay dances.

Languishing after the decline of the mission era, the village again awoke after discovery of gold. Miners on their way to the gold fields, fur traders, trappers and desperadoes stopped here. The dining room of the Red Hotel served as a dance hall. The wife of the hotel manager asserted her individuality by adorning herself with five-dollar gold pieces in place of buttons. As late as 1859 the last bull fight was staged.

Fourteenth of the 21 California missions, MISSION SAN JOSE DE GUADALUPE (*adm. 25¢*), founded by Padre Fermin Francisco Lasuen on Trinity Sunday, 1797, originally was known as La Mision del Gloriosisimo Patriarca Señor San Jose (The Mission of the Most Glorious Patriarch, St. Joseph). According to legend, disagreement about the selection of a site among the members of an exploration party was settled by prayer and the law of gravitation. A huge stone, after being blessed, was rolled down a steep hillside. Where it came to rest the mission was built.

The mission founders knew privation, struggle, and opposition. To Christianize the Indians, who sometimes fought against preemption of their land, it was sometimes necessary to use the sword and the whip. The natives often rebelled against the hard, monotonous work forced upon them. During church services guards equipped with long goads moved among the congregation, prodding natives who assumed other than a kneeling position. For outstanding work, however, the Indians were rewarded with beads and gaudy trinkets. It is recorded that friction developed even between the *padres* and the military when soldiers refused to serve as *vaqueros* or to do other non-military work.

Despite all these obstacles the mission grew to become one of the most prosperous of the mission establishment, being fourth in wealth and second in the number of converts.

Under the guidance of capable padres many converts were taught trades and crafts. Indeed, Padre Duran, beloved mission prefect, developed a stringed orchestra of more than 20 musicians who were in constant demand at social functions. Padre Duran also made good wines and better brandies. The old leather bound "guest book" of the mission, now among the chief treasures of St. Mary's of San Francisco, contains the signatures of men of science, travelers from many countries, as well as trappers, woodsmen, and outlaws who were early mission visitors.

After secularization, Mission San Jose fell into such a state of deterioration that in 1846 it was sold for only a fraction of its former value. After California entered the Union the Land Commission restored the property to the Church. It is now under the custody of the Sisters of St. Dominic. The first mission building, constructed of heavy timber and covered with a grass roof, later was replaced by a more elaborate structure of adobe which was destroyed by earthquake in 1868. All that remains of the original cluster of buildings is a large common room, whose thick walls are weatherworn and cracked. The dark interior is festooned with cobwebs. The present place of worship, built of wood, stands on the foundation of one of the original structures. In 1884 a fire destroyed several nearby buildings; water was scarce, but the chapel was saved by barrels of wine which vintners from the surrounding countryside had stored in an old mission cellar. Among old relics at Mission San Jose are some vestments worn by mission founders, candlesticks, a baptismal font surmounted by a wrought-iron cross, and two old mission bells cast in 1815 and 1826.

On the hillside behind the mission building is the QUEEN OF THE HOLY ROSARY COLLEGE, a training school for sisters of the Dominican order. In the modern concrete building about a hundred nuns prepare for teaching. The old red-brick building adjoining is the convent, established in 1890. The school's site was part of the mission property. Many of the old olive trees along the lane leading to the convent and cemetery were planted by the *padres*.

The SANTA INEZ LODGE, the summer home of the Sisters of the Holy Names, was formerly a resort hotel, near six warm springs, flowing at the rate of 60,000 gallons per day. First white man to see the springs, Juan Bautista de Anza, named them Agua Caliente in 1776. Fulgencia Higuera in 1836 obtained a land grant to this property, which he named Rancho del Agua Caliente. He sold the rancho in 1850 to Clement Columbet, who made it a fashionable spa. After the 1868 earthquake partially destroyed his hotel, A. A. Cohen and William Ralston bought and remodeled it. In 1870 they sold out to Leland Stanford, who set out a fine vineyard and in 1887 built a red-brick winery, still standing west of the hotel. The property passed in 1920 into the hands of Frank Kelly, who tore down some of the old buildings, built new ones, and laid out gardens. Stanford's vineyard was dug up and the winery converted into stables for Kelly's race horses. In 1927 Kelly sold the ranch to the Sisters of the Holy Names. Today the Stanford Winery is operated by the Weibel Vineyards (*visitors Mon.-Fri. 10-12, 1-4, Sat. & Sun. 1-4*).

WARM SPRINGS (65 alt.) now a subdivision of FREMONT, was an agricultural hamlet receiving its name and its past fame from the springs of the nearby SANTA INEZ LODGE.

MILPITAS (little maize fields) (13 alt. 27,149 pop. 1970; 6,572, 1960; inc. 313%) in Santa Clara County, once part of a vast land grant, is now an agricultural and industrial settlement. First called Penitencia, for the creek that runs through it, it was renamed because of the usual mispronunciation by Yankees, for Nicolas Berryessa's Rancho Milpitas. In earlier years Milpitas served somewhat as a political barometer: "As goes Milpitas so goes the State." The reports of voting here many times have indicated State-wide election results before complete returns were in.

Left from Milpitas on paved Calaveras Road 2 m. to the junction with Piedmont Road, where stands (R) the neat, white ALVISO ADOBE (*private*), built here on Arroyo de los Coches about 1841 by Jose Maria Alviso, who succeeded Berryessa as owner of Rancho Milpitas. The second story, of frame, was built some time later.

Calaveras Road continues east and then north through the rugged mountains to CALAVERAS RESERVOIR, 12 m., an auxiliary source of water for San Francisco. As far back as 1875 there were plans for municipal development of this site, but the Spring Valley Water Company, which was already supplying the city, purchased these lands and water rights also. After the company was purchased by the city, Calaveras Valley was converted into a 32,000,000,000-gallon reservoir in 1925 when an earth and rock fill dam was completed at the lower end of the valley. A dam on Alameda Creek, about three miles east of the reservoir, diverts water to Calaveras by way of a 9,709-foot tunnel. From the reservoir a 44-inch pipe line carries water to the Hetch Hetchy aqueduct that empties into Crystal Springs Lake by gravity (*see Peninsula Tour*).

On the bluff above the Coyote River, crossed by State 17 at 38.3 m., on the grounds of the Clark Nursery, is the largest eucalyptus in California, planted in 1868. Its trunk is nine feet in diameter.

SAN JOSE, 41.7 m. (100 alt., 445,779 pop.) *see San Jose.*

North Bay Tour

The North Bay area is a land of contrasts. Gray fog swirls over its high mountain tops and down steep slopes forested with giant redwoods; highways wind through its flatlands past sleepy towns that doze in the sun; quiet creeks drain its valleys and clear streams rush down its dark canyons to Bay and ocean. Paved highways have replaced dusty roads; tiny vineyards of early winemakers have expanded to cover whole slopes and wide flatlands; orchards and gardens and modern chicken hatcheries spread over the valley floors. The Russian River, the sandy beaches and sheltered coves are popular vacation spots, and the mountain slopes are terraced in rows of modern homes inhabited by men and women who work in San Francisco. The rugged Pacific shore and the Bay's indentations are favored by fishermen, and yachtsmen sail their craft around the headlands and between the islands.

San Francisco—Sausalito—San Rafael—Vallejo—Benicia; 52.7 *m*. US 101, State 37, County roads.

Paved roadbed throughout.
Greyhound interurban busses serve Marin County.

This route follows US 101 across the Golden Gate and cuts north through low hills bordering San Francisco and Richardson Bays. It swings east on State 37, following the contour of San Pablo Bay to the mouth of Suisun Bay, where inland waters of the Sacramento and San Joaquin Rivers pour through Carquinez Strait. Its course is through vacation communities, yachting centers, little towns overlooking the Bay, houseboat colonies, wide dairy acres, and flat marshlands.

North from Van Ness Ave. and Fulton St. in SAN FRANCISCO, 0 *m*., on Van Ness Ave. to Lombard St.; L. on Lombard; R. on Richardson Ave. to the main approach of Golden Gate Bridge.

The bridge approach rises gradually on concrete piers across the northern edge of the Presidio. At 4.7 *m*. is the toll plaza (*automobiles, 50¢; pedestrians, 10¢*) of GOLDEN GATE BRIDGE. For 1.2 miles the route follows the second longest and highest single-span suspension bridge in the world, an integral link in the great highway between Canada and Mexico.

At 6.6 *m*. is the junction with a paved road.

Right on this road through a part of FORT BAKER UNITED STATES MILITARY RESERVATION, 0.5 *m*.

SAUSALITO, 2.4 *m*. (8,600 alt., 6,158 pop. 1970; 5,331, 1960; inc. 15%), faces San Francisco from the steep flanks of the Marin hills. Its one business street is built on a narrow shelf beside the Bay, where pleasure craft, fishing boats, and Coast Guard cutters lie at anchor. All have one thing in common—a view of the Bay.

The first white man to come here was Spanish navigator Captain Juan Manuel de Ayala, who named the cove Ensenada del Carmelito (Bay of Little Mount Carmel). The Spaniards who followed named the spot Saucelito (from *salcedo*—willow) for its many small willow thickets.

The cabin of the young Irishman, John Read, who settled here in 1826, was the first permanent home of a white man in Marin County. When Read died from the excessive bleeding practised by the physicians of the day, his widow married the bandit, "Three-fingered Jack" Garcia, friend of Joaquin Murrieta.

In 1838 an Englishman, Captain William Antonio Richardson, was granted the 19,000-acre Rancho Saucelito. He was a harbor pilot, operated a transbay ferry, raised cattle, traded with Yankee ships, and sold water from Sausalito's springs to Yerba Buena.

Sausalito once was known as a town where gambling dens and saloons rid the unwary of his money quickly and efficiently; and its elections were stormy battles. But since 1907 it has been a haven of graceful living. Fishing and the building of small craft were its only important industries until the Marinship yards were built here during World War II to construct cargo vessels and tankers.

Sausalito contains some of the most imaginative and expensive residential development in the United States, and the city is often compared with towns on the Italian Riviera. Taking advantage of its Mediterranean character, Sausalito has developed a commercial area of small unique shops and fine restaurants which draw heavily from the entire Bay Area.

The DANIEL O'CONNELL MONUMENT, Bulkley and Harrison Aves., a granite bench shaded by pepper trees, is a memorial to the Irish poet and political refugee.

On the slope below the monument the thick, bastion-like WALLS OF SEA POINT, a former home of William Randolph Hearst, face the Bay above Bridgeway Blvd. Hearst razed it after a quarrel with local residents.

At 4.6 m. is the junction with US 101 (see below).

On US 101 at 7.1 m. is the junction with a private road.

Left on this road 6 m. to FORT BARRY UNITED STATES MILITARY RESERVATION, whose fortresses overlook San Francisco Bay. Once part of Fort Baker Reserve, the 893-acre area was set aside in 1904 and named in honor of Civil War veteran General William F. Barry.

Marking the northern entrance to the Golden Gate is POINT BONITA, 7 m. Atop the white tower of POINT BONITA LIGHTHOUSE (built in 1855 and reconstructed in 1877), 124 feet above the water, is a 40,000-candlepower light visible for 17 miles. A cannon brought here in 1850 thundered the first fog warnings in the vicinity.

US 101 continues northward into the hills above Sausalito, passes through deep cuts and a long tunnel, and drops down to RICHARD-SON BAY, named for William A. Richardson.

At 10.2 m. is the junction with State 1.

Right on State 1, across the Marin Peninsula hills and down Green Gulch to the junction with a gravel road, 6 m.; L. here 0.7 m. across an arm of Big Lagoon to MUIR BEACH (swimming, fishing).

State 1 skirts the ocean shore northward to STINSON BEACH, 12.5 m. (boats, tackle and bait for surf fishing), a small resort town at the southern end of Bolinas Lagoon.

At 16.8 m. is the junction with a paved road, on which the route turns L. along the western edge of BOLINAS LAGOON, named for Francisco Bolanos, pilot of the Sebastian Vizcaino expedition of 1603.

A few rotting piles at 17.2 m. mark the site of the BOLINAS LIGHTER WHARF (L), where oxen in the 1850's hauled lumber from inland mills in crude wagons whose wheels were solid sections of redwood logs.

Facing Bolinas Lagoon is the AUDUBON CANYON RANCH. It is comprised of 569 acres of rolling grasslands, chaparral, woodlands, and two canyons forested by redwood and Douglas fir. Adjoining the ranch, 368 acres of the water and tidelands of Bolinas Lagoon are under lease from the Bolinas Harbor District for a wildlife refuge. About 55 species of water birds are likely to be seen at the Ranch during the year, and 90 species of land birds. The ranch is open March 1 through July 4, 10-4 p.m.

US 101 continues north over a half-mile-long bridge across the upper reaches of Richardson Bay and on through rolling foothill country bright with wild flowers in spring.

At 12.1 m. is the junction with a paved road.

At 3.2 m. is the junction with a paved road; R. here across a causeway to BELVEDERE, 4.3 m. (350 alt., 2,599 pop. 1970; 2,148, 1960), at the southern end of Belvedere Island in Richardson Bay. A quiet suburban town with fine homes and terraced gardens, it looks out from its steep slopes toward Sausalito and Angel Island.

Belvedere's SAN FRANCISCO YACHT CLUB, on Beach Rd., was organized in 1869, the first yacht club in California.

L. from Belvedere across another causeway to TIBURON, 4.7 *m.* (10 alt., 6,209 pop. 1970), on Point Tiburon, southwestern tip of Tiburon Peninsula. Many homes at the water's edge boast small private piers for swimming and boating. To the southeast, across Racoon Strait, lies the green bulk of Angel Island.

East from Tiburon, then northwest around Tiburon Peninsula to CALIFORNIA CITY, 7.4 *m.*, training base for the CALIFORNIA NAUTICAL SCHOOL (*visitors Sat. and Sun. 1-5*), established in 1929 to train young men for service as officers in the merchant marine. When the training ship *California State* docks after an extended cruise, the 125 cadets live aboard the modern ship and study ashore. The ship is kept in repair by the Navy, by which it is owned; all other expenses are defrayed by the State.

PARADISE COVE, 8.6 *m.*, a sheltered picnicking and camping place, is frequented by the owners of small sailing craft.

At 13.2 *m.* is the junction with US 101 (*see below*).

2. Left on this road is MILL VALLEY, 2.1 *m.* (57 alt., 12,942 pop. 1970; 10,411, 1960; inc. 24%), a residential town built in the narrow canyons and on the steep wooded slopes along two small streams. Originally part of Rancho Corte Madera del Presidio (*see below*), the town slumbered for two generations, but after the building of an electric railroad from Sausalito it became the home of business men and of artists, musicians, and writers.

OLD MILL PARK, on Throckmorton Ave., is the site of the region's first sawmill, built by John Read about 1834. Read, an Irish sailor, who had acquired Rancho Corte Madera del Presidio, whipsawed timber here for his house in Sausalito and afterwards supplied lumber for San Francisco. Down the small stream draining Mount Tamalpais' southern slopes he floated the logs to the twin wheels of his water mill, whose frame still stands. Read's adobe, one-half mile northeast, was occupied after his death by the desperado, Bernardino "Three-fingered Jack" Garcia, who married Read's widow.

In Mill Valley the side route turns L. from Throckmorton Avenue on Old Mill Dr.; L. on Cascade Dr.; R. on Molino Ave.; sharply R. on Birch St.; R. on Edgewood Ave.; L. on Sequoia Valley Rd. up a ridge to a junction at the summit with Panoramic Highway, 4.6 *m.*

Left on Sequoia Valley Road 1.6 *m.* to MUIR WOODS NATIONAL MONUMENT (*picnicking, hiking, riding; no fires permitted*), a 424-acre park of virgin redwoods in a mountain ravine. The taller trees are from 200 to 250 feet in height, and from 12 to 17 feet in diameter. The woods, deeply scarred by fire 175 years ago, are noted for their abnormal growths of burls, albino shoots, natural grafts and strange formations. REDWOOD CREEK, where salmon and steelhead spawn, flows through the park at the base of such redwood giants as the Gifford Pinchot Redwood Cathedral Grove, Bridge Tree, William Kent Fir, and Albino Redwood. With the redwoods are dense growths of Douglas fir, oak, and laurel, with azaleas, wild huckleberry, and other plants.

Senator William Kent bought this grove for $45,000 and deeded it to the Nation in 1908 as a monument to John Muir, the naturalist who so loved the California mountains. In the condemnation proceedings necessary to acquire the land, Theodore Roosevelt and Gifford Pinchot gave valuable aid.

The main route follows Panoramic Highway from its junction with Sequoia Valley Road along the northern edge of 960-acre MOUNT TAMALPAIS STATE PARK (*camp sites, hiking trails*). A wooden trestle, 6.4 *m.*, spans the roadbed of the abandoned Mill Valley and Mount Tamalpais Scenic Railway, laid out with a hand level by the promoters. Built at a cost of $147,000 in 1896, the eight-mile track, known as the "Crookedest Railroad in the World," had 281 curves. At one difficult place a "double bow-knot" paralleled itself five times within 2,000 feet, thereby achieving a rise of 100 feet. Oil-burning logging engines drew trains to the summit.

At Rock Springs, 11.1 *m.*, is the junction with Ridgecrest Boulevard on which the side route turns R. to the MOUNTAIN THEATER (R), 11.3 *m.* (*admission to performances, $1.25*), a natural amphitheater on the flank of Mount Tamalpais from which the audience can look beyond the stage across 70 miles of Bay, plain, and mountain. On stone seats rising in circular tiers, from three to seven thousand people gather annually on the third Sunday in May to watch a dramatic production.

Ridgecrest Boulevard curves uphill within a few hundred yards of the summit of MOUNT TAMALPAIS. There are three crests in the Tamalpais Range, West Peak (2,560 alt.), Middle Peak (2,470 alt.), and East Peak (2,571 alt.). From the summit a third of northern California is visible on clear days. The whole of San Francisco Bay spreads out below, spanned by its two bridges, bordered by cities and orchard lands. A white cluster of buildings is San Jose at the southern end. Beyond the Mount Hamilton and Mount Diablo ranges, the flat San Joaquin Valley stretches east to the blue Sierras. Westward, out to sea, the Farallon Islands seem near and ships appear on the horizon. To the north are the multiple Coast Ranges dividing inland valleys.

The first man to climb the peak was Jacob Leese, Marin County pioneer, who made the ascent to refute the Lacatuit Indian legend that evil spirits haunted the mountain. On the summit, Leese set up a cross of tree limbs. Marin, the Indian chief, to prove his valor, climbed up and hung his blanket from the cross, thereby gaining much prestige with his tribe.

On US 101 at 13.8 *m.* is the junction with a paved road.

Left on this road is CORTE MADERA (Sp., wood-cutting place), 0.5 *m.* (56 alt., 8,464 pop. 1970; 5,962, 1960; inc. 42%), a sung community of homes. Its name came from logging operations in surrounding hills where Luis Antonio Arguello cut timbers to repair and enlarge San Francisco's Presidio buildings. Corte Madera's BALTIMORE PARK GROVE, on Madrone Avenue, is a small grove of redwoods extending up a narrow canyon.

The hilly suburban town of LARKSPUR, 1.6 *m.* (18 alt., 10,487 pop.), looks out over green marshes and meadows from the base of the hills.

The famous Larkspur Bowl, a huge open-air dance floor, accommodating 2,000 closed in 1963. The pavilion was managed by the Larkspur volunteer fire department, funds from which maintained the fire department without drawing on the town's treasury.

One of the chain of quiet residential towns in Ross Valley is KENTFIELD, 3.1 *m.* (100 alt.), settled early by men of wealth. In Mexican days the spot where the highway now croses Corte Madera Creek was known as the Embarcadero and later as Ross Landing for James Ross, who owned the surrounding Rancho Punta de Quentin (Point Quentin). The settlement was next called Tamalpais and finally Kentfield, for Senator William Kent's father, Albert Emmet Kent, who had come here in search of health.

ROSS, 3.6 *m.* (26 alt., 2,742 pop. 1970; 2,551, 1960), once known as Sunnyside, is a community of homes, many with extensive grounds set in back of tall trees and hedges. It was once part of the vast and much-sought Rancho Punta de Quentin, purchased from Benjamin R. Buckelew by James Ross in 1859. The latter, a Scot, who brought a wife from Tasmania, had become a successful wine merchant in San Francisco. When Ross moved into Buckelew's home, leg-irons used on the convicts who built the house were found in the basement.

Founded in 1875, SAN ANSELMO, 4.6 *m.* (52 alt., 13,031 pop. 1970; 11,584, 1960; inc. 12%), is a town of hillside houses and gardens along winding shaded streets. According to a local tale, it was started by a quarrel between two Irish families who lived at Ross Landing (*see above*). One day, while their husbands were at work on the North Pacific Coast Railroad, the two wives quarreled more seriously than usual; one threw the other into a well and sat on the lid. When rescued by her raging husband, the wife in the well was found clinging to the bucket rope, uninjured and eager for the free-for-all that followed. The railroad company grew alarmed at the ensuing feud for fear it would lose a prized foreman. Hence, one day a section crew heaved one family's shack onto a handcar and pushed it two miles up the tracks. It was unloaded, and there was San Anselmo.

The route goes L. from San Anselmo around the base of RED HILL, where sunrise services are held on Easter.

From the edges of FAIRFAX, 6.6 *m.* (108 alt., 7,661 pop. 1970; 5,813, 1960), rise brush-covered mountains that have the look of velvet from a distance. The 6,000-acre Rancho Canada de Herrera (valley of the blacksmith's wife), once embracing its site, was granted in 1839 to Pedro V. Sais, a soldier and civil officer in San Francisco. When in 1849 a visitor from Virginia, Dr. A. W. Taliaferro, expressed a wish to buy 40 acres, Sais, with characteristic early California generosity, gave him the land, saying that it was worth that to have a good neighbor. To the large house which Dr. Taliaferro built, came as a visitor in 1856 a direct descendant of the English baron famous in Virginia history, Charles "Lord" Fairfax. Remaining as a permanent guest, he inherited the estate when the doctor died without heirs. After Fairfax's death, the home was for years the restaurant of Madame Adele Pastori, Italian opera singer, who served meals in the garden under the trees.

Northwest from Fairfax, the route curves over Whites Hill and descends through rolling oak-covered foothill country into San Geronimo Valley.

SAN GERONIMO, 12.1 *m.* (286 alt.), was the home of Lieutenant Warren Revere, grandson of Paul Revere. While hunting elk, Revere, who had been sent by the Government to conduct a survey of timber, found this attractive valley. Buying the two-league Rancho San Geronimo, he settled down to lead the life of a Spanish *ranchero.* The once powerful Nicasio Indians caused him some trouble by running off his horses for food. When he captured an Indian, he forced him to make adobe bricks in payment for the lost horses.

Right from San Geronimo on a paved road over low hills 3.8 *m.* to a junction with a county road; (1) R. here 2 *m.* up Lucas Valley to the LUCAS VALLEY REDWOODS (*picnicking, camping*), named for John Lucas, a nephew of Timoteo Murphy (*see below*), from whom he inherited Rancho Santa Margarita. At 10.6 *m.* is the junction with US 101 (*see below*). (2) Left here is NICASIO, 4.5 *m.* (177 alt.), a tree-shaded hamlet with an old wooden church and school house and a few dwellings in need of paint, dating from the 1850's and 1860's. After disease and drink had decreased the local tribe of Nicasio Indians, Chief Jose Calistro bought 30 acres two miles east of Nicasio and settled his people upon it. The large stand of prime redwood in the region began to fall in 1862 when James Ross built the first mill one and one-half miles east of town. At 13.3 *m.* is the junction with State 1 (*see below*).

The main side route continues west from San Geronimo to the summer resort center of LAGUNITAS, 14.1 *m.* (219 alt.), and plunges into cool Lagunitas Creek canyon between high redwoods and firs, past mountain cabins perched on hillsides and flats along the stream. Fishing is forbidden to protect the salmon that spawn in the shallow, gravelly reaches.

Once known as Taylorville, CAMP TAYLOR (*camping*), 17 *m.* (138 alt.), in a grove of virgin redwoods on a flat next to the stream, is the site where in 1856 Samuel Penfield Taylor built the first paper mill on the Pacific Coast and employed Chinese to collect rags for raw material. Among old-timers, Lagunitas Creek, whose pure water was particularly adapted to paper making, is still known as Paper Mill Creek.

TOCALOMA, 20.8 *m.* (66 alt.), is a hamlet in a secluded glen on the creek banks.

OLEMA, 22.7 *m.* (68 alt.), with its white-steepled church and tree-shaded houses, has the look of a New England village. Alemaloke was the name of a former Indian village near here. The place was headquarters in 1837 of the great Rancho Tomales y Bolinas. In the 1860's a 12-passenger stage rumbled between here and San Rafael, an old wagon cradled on thick leather straps and covered with tarpaulin. The earthquake of 1906 stirred the old town considerably. According to report, a cow on the nearby Shafter ranch fell head first into a yawning chasm which closed together, trapping the unfortunate animal with rump and tail still visible above ground. When the milkers at Skinner's dairy rushed out of the barn (according to Oscar Lewis and Carroll Hall in *Bonanza Inn*), they saw that "the cypress trees and the rose garden had moved away from the front of the house and now stood in front of the barn. The clump of raspberry bushes had slid down from the north and occupied the space vacated by the roses. The eucalyptus trees had marched to a position opposite the barn and in the process one had shifted from the foot of the line to the head. The piles of manure before the barn had each moved some sixteen feet south of the window to which it belonged."

At Olema is the junction with State 1, which the route follows R. up Olema Creek to the junction with a paved road, 24.4 *m.*, where it turns L.; R. here on State 1 is POINT REYES STATION, 0.3 *m.* (31 alt.), center of a dairy region, surrounded by rolling pastures, which ships butter to San Francisco. State 1 continues north along the eastern shore of TOMALES BAY, a narrow, finger-like inlet first sighted in 1775 by Lieutenant Juan Francisco de Bodega y Cuadra, who believed he had found a passage connecting with San Pablo Bay. Looping inland, State 1 passes through the sleepy farming communities of TOMALES, 18.2 *m.* (75 alt.), VALLEY FORD, 25 *m.* (45 alt.), and BODEGA, 31.1 *m.* (40 alt.). Right from Bodega 1 *m.* to the SITE OF KUSKOF SETTLEMENT, marked by a flagpole, where Russian colonists raised cattle and grain and converted the Indians to Christianity 130 years ago and (adjoining) the ruins of CAPTAIN STEPHEN SMITH'S ADOBE MANSION, built in 1843, headquarters of the owner of 30,000-acre Rancho Bodega. West of Bodega, State 1 returns to the coast at shallow, marsh-edged BODEGA BAY, named for its discoverer (1775). It skirts the coast northward through thinly settled country, treeless except for occasional clumps of Douglas fir and Bishop pine. At 47.2 *m.*, on the north side of a bridge across the Russian River, is the junction with State 12 (*see below*).

West from its northern junction with State 1 the main side route goes L. to INVERNESS, 28.2 *m.* (10 alt.), a summer resort and boating center on Tomales Bay at the foot of wooded hills. The town took its name from the birth place of James Black, a Scottish sailor who arrived in California in 1832 and later took up cattle ranching on a part of Rancho Nicasio facing the east side of Tomales Bay.

The road curves west and south from Inverness over Inverness Ridge.

At 34.2 *m.* is the RCA RADIO STATION (R), where short-wave antennas, spread over 1,500 acres, catch transpacific signals.

The road continues south along a rocky, windy promontory where many ships have been wrecked.

At 39.9 *m.* is the junction with a dirt road; R. here 0.7 *m.* to the UNITED STATES RADIO COMPASS STATION, from which ships at sea take bearings to fix their positions.

At 42.9 *m.* on the main side road is the junction with a dirt road; L. here 1.3 *m.* to the UNITED STATES COAST GUARD LIFE-SAVING STATION above the white cliffs facing DRAKE'S BAY. In this sheltered cove Sir Francis Drake beached the *Golden Hinde* on June 17, 1579 (Julian Calendar) and claimed the region for Queen Elizabeth. He remained for several weeks, revictualing and repairing his ship. In the garden of the life-saving station is a marker commemorating his landing. On the cliffs overlooking the cove stands a white wooden cross, erected by Bishop William Ford Nichols, commemorating the first use of the English language and of the Book of Common Prayer on the California coast. An annual pilgrimage and service on or about St. John Baptist's Day, June 24, is held here.

This coast is the locale of Bret Harte's "The Legend of Devil's Point," according to which Drake chose "this spot to conceal quantities of ill-gotten booty taken from neutral bottoms, and had protected his hiding place by the orthodox means of hellish incantation and diabolical agencies. On moonlight nights a shadowy ship was sometimes seen when fogs encompassed sea and shore . . . the creaking of a windlass, or the monotonous chant of sailors, came faint and far, and full of magic suggestions." Whatever factual basis supports the legend, "a more weird and desolate-looking spot could not have been selected for [its] theatre. High hills . . . enfiladed with dark *cañadas,* cast their gaunt shadows on the tide . . . sea fog [comes] with soft step in noiseless marches down the hillside, tenderly soothing the wind-buffetted face of the cliff until sea and sky [are] hid together."

At Laguna Ranch, on the east side of Drake's Bay, a chauffeur in 1933 discovered a plate of solid brass which he subsequently discarded near Point San Quentin. Another motorist, halted by a flat tire, rediscovered the plate and offered it to the University of California for inspection. Revealed beneath the blackened surface was this inscription:

BEE IT KNOWNE VNTO ALL MEN BY THESE PRESENTS
IVNE 17 1579
BY THE GRACE OF GOD AND IN THE NAME OF HERR
MAIESTY QVEEN ELIZABETH OF ENGLAND AND HERR
SVCCESSORS FOREVER I TAKE POSSESSON OF THIS
KINGDOME WHOSE KING AND PEOPLE FREELY RESIGNE
THEIR RIGHT AND TITLE IN THE WHOLE LAND VNTO
HERR MAIESTIES KEEPEING NOW NAMED BY ME AN TO
BEE KNOWNE VNTO ALL MEN AS NOVA ALBION
FRANCIS DRAKE

The plate has been thoroughly studied by scientists and scholars and the consensus is that it is genuine.

The main side road continues to the remote tip of the headland, where the white 16-sided pyramidal tower of POINT REYES LIGHTHOUSE, 44.3 *m.,* shines its light 294 feet above the sea. Its 120,000-candlepower light, whose three-ton lens was ground in France and installed at Point Reyes in 1870, is visible in clear weather for 24 miles. But even this beam and the blast of the fog signal have failed to prevent many ships and even one air liner from piling up on the saw-toothed shore.

Across rolling foothill country runs US 101, rising to hilltops and dipping through valleys, with the Bay seldom out of view.

At the tidal mouth of Corte Madera Creek is GREENBRAE, 15.1 *m.* (32 alt.), once a colony of house boats.

Right from Greenbrae on a paved road which winds along the hills that rise above the West Gate (for official use only) of San Quentin Prison (*see below*), 1 *m.,* where armed guards are stationed in yellow octagonal towers. The route goes around and above the prison grounds with their neat guard cottages and high wire fences to the junction with a paved road, 2 *m.,* where it turns R. to the San Quentin Wharf, once terminus of the Richmond-San Rafael Ferry, now the western anchorage of the Richmond-San Rafael Bridge (*toll 75¢*). Visible from the Richmond-San Rafael Bridge is RED ROCK, three miles offshore, a two-acre uninhabited island whose color is due to the presence of iron oxides, and where legend has placed buried gold and jewels. Boundary corners of three counties meet on the little island.

In the small village of SAN QUENTIN, 3 *m.* (12 alt.), prison guards and employees live with their families.

The side route ends at 3.1 *m.,* at the main gate of SAN QUENTIN PRISON, operated by the State Department of Corrections. The prison is the largest correctional institution in California and has capacity for approximately 4,500 inmates.

The snouts of machine guns protrude from nearby towers. Visible beyond the gates are the grey walls and the stocky unornamented cell blocks of the prison, pierced by barred windows. Behind these walls 5,200 men are "doing time." Women, once kept here, now are sent to Tehachapi; recidivists—"two time losers"—are sent to Folsom Prison.

New prisoners usually are put to work in the jute mill making burlap and other rough fabrics; later they are placed in work more suited to their individual abilities. Prison farms and dairies offer some of the men outdoor work. Others are employed in furniture shops, printing plants, machine and plumbing shops, bakeries, and kitchens.

The most famous prisoner here for two decades was Thomas J. Mooney, accused of planting a bomb and killing several persons during a parade in San Francisco in 1916. He was pardoned in 1939 by Governor Culbert L. Olson. Also confined here were Matthew Schmidt and J. B. McNamara, convicted in the Los Angeles *Times* explosion case of October, 1910.

Convicts built the first prison cells here in the early 1850's to house other convicts then chained in the black holds of prison boats. The first ten years of the prison's existence were stormy with escapes and uprisings. The most desperate break occurred July 22, 1862, when 400 convicts rushed the front gate, and, using Lieutenant-Governor John F. Chellis as a shield, stormed and carried the gun post near the steamer landing. The convicts released Chellis three miles from the prison and headed for the hills, where they were blocked by a citizens' posse. Thirty-three escaped, three were killed, and the others captured.

North of Greenbrae, US 101 cuts across tidal lands reclaimed from the marshes. In 1866 this road, built three feet above the marsh lands, was a toll road whose surfacing material had been taken from Indian shell mounds. Tolls ranged from two and one-half cents each for sheep and hogs to one dollar, which admitted three yoke of oxen and a loaded wagon. Today's highway is lined by gas stations, "hot dog" stands, and stores.

Seat of Marin County and suburban trading center is SAN RAFAEL, 17.5 *m.* (10 alt., 38,977 pop. 1970; 26,460, 1960; inc. 90%). Bisected by San Rafael Creek, the city extends north to steep, round-headed San Rafael Hill. Its business streets are lined with old-fashioned brick buildings; many of its homes are set back of green lawns and tall shade trees.

Father Vicente Sarria founded here, on December 14, 1817, the twentieth of California's missions as an *asisténcia* (auxiliary) to Mission Dolores, whose Indian converts were rapidly dying off from the effects of measles and other diseases contracted from white men. By 1834 the new mission boasted 1,250 converts, but in that year it was secularized and its converts scattered. In 1844 Governor Manuel Micheltorena granted a considerable part of the present town site to Don Timoteo Murphy, administrator of the secularized mission.

In the 1850's the little town became a busy but dirty center for the surrounding ranches. Streets bottomless with dust in summer, with mud in winter, were crowded with dogs, children, and Mexicans, and the few plank sidewalks tripped the unwary. Here the daily Petaluma stage and the thrice-a-week "mud wagon" from Olema and Bolinas connected with the San Quentin stages that met the San Francisco ferries, stopping, "with popping of whips and panting of horses . . . in front of the hotel. Now all is bustle, the men in long dusters, the women swathed in 'veils.' A crowd follows the mail-bag, the women retire to apartments upstairs, and the men line up at the bar . . ."

The seat of county government is the MARIN COUNTY CIVIC CENTER located about three miles north of San Rafael. In 1956 the Marin County Board of Supervisors authorized an expenditure of $511,000 for the purchase of a 140 acre site for development of a civic center complex and county fairgrounds. Frank Lloyd Wright was engaged to prepare a master plan for this concept. The master plan connected gently sloping hills with graceful horizontal buildings springing in great arches over entrance roadways between the hills. Rising from these arches the various levels of the building seem to float from hill to hill. From without, the buildings form a tranquil line in harmony with the surrounding landscape. A central mall covered by a plastic skylight extending the full length of the building affords natural light into otherwise darkened areas. The Administration Building dedicated in October, 1962, at a cost of $5,152,000, represents the first of the four proposed stages of construction. Next stages will house the Hall of Justice in a building that will span the next lower knoll and terminate in the third higher hill and will have an architectural grammar similar to that in the already completed building.

In addition to the administration building, the civic center complex now includes a branch post office, also designed by Frank Lloyd Wright, and a National Guard Armory and Marine Corps training center. The adjacent fairgrounds have been partially developed and include a 12-acre lagoon.

Of MISSION SAN RAFAEL ARCANGEL little remains but a few fragments of tile. The building was demolished for its timber in 1860; nine years later a new church was built on the site, but this in turn was destroyed by fire in 1917. The present ST. RAPHAEL'S CHURCH, Fifth Ave. and A St., occupies the site of the old mission, which is depicted in a bas-relief above the central door. A statue of Saint Raphael stands in the main tower.

A bank at 1304 Fourth St. marks the site of the MURPHY ADOBE built in 1844 by Don Timoteo Murphy, who as *alcalde* held here many a *baile* and reception. In 1853, after Timothy Murphy's death, the county court was moved from a leaky room in the old mission to this adobe, which a progressive citizen had bought for $1,000 and sold to the county for $5,000. The old road leading from Murphy's to the freight landing of the 1850's is now C Street.

The first local building of the DOMINICAN COLLEGE, Grand

Ave. between Locust and Acacia Sts., was dedicated in 1889 on land given by Don Timoteo Murphy and William Tell Coleman. The dormitories occupy three handsome old residences, but the educational buildings are modern. In addition to grammar and high school departments, the institution offers a full college course. Since its founding in Monterey in 1850 the college has given much attention to music; many distinguished musicians have taught and lectured here. The music library has some valuable illuminated missals and a number of rare books on music. The campus covers 35 acres planted to pine and eucalyptus by Coleman, who tried to reforest the region. Forest Meadows, a part of the campus, is the setting for the WOODLAND THEATER, an outdoor auditorium built in 1934 and used for the annual concerts.

SAN RAFAEL HILL (717 alt.), rising steeply from the north end of B St., is a municipal recreation area, the gift of Captain Robert Dollar. On the summit, which offers an unusual view, Easter sunrise services are held.

Right from San Rafael on Third St., which becomes San Pedro Road, running along San Rafael Creek between the hills and marshes. The MARIN YACHT CLUB, 1.3 m., participates in all San Francisco Bay regattas. The green marshes end in the Bay waters. Offshore about one mile are the two small MARIN ISLANDS, on one of which the Lacatuit Indian chief Marin sought refuge from the Spanish. Captured, he was baptized at San Rafael. Later his name was given to the county.

At 3.9 m. once stood the three tall kiln stacks of the McNear Brick Works, where haydite, a light concrete aggregate was manufactured. Today the area has been developed with single family residences and apartment units called Marin Bay.

At 5 m. is the junction with an improved road; R. here 0.5 m. to McNEAR'S BEACH (picnic grounds; boats for hire), once McNear's Landing, which offers good bass and rock cod fishing. The beach is sheltered by the tip of San Pedro Point, westermost of two promontories marking the entrance to San Pablo Bay.

The Main side route continues north across low hills to bluffs above San Pablo Bay. In a small cove is CHINA CAMP, 6 m., where a rickety pier extends over the water (boats for hire). The Chinese settled here in the 1880's when the Chinese Exclusion Act and boycotts forced 10,000 Orientals to migrate to Marin. They eked out a livelihood by fishing for sturgeon, clamming and netting shrimp from brightly colored Chinese junks.

At 11.4 m. is the junction with US 101 (see below).

Stretches of US 101 north of San Rafael are lined with rows of eucalyptus trees, planted in the 1880's and 1890's as windbreaks.

ST. VINCENT'S SCHOOL FOR BOYS (visitors welcome), 22.4 m. (R), occupies a group of Spanish Renaissance buildings. A Catholic orphanage, it was opened in 1855 on land deeded by Don Timoteo Murphy. The 1,800 acres of ground produce all the dairy and farm products used by the school.

The highway winds smoothly up a range of hills and down into a broad valley to the gates (R) of HAMILTON FIELD (open only to visitors on official business), 23.7 m. is headquarters for the 28th Air Division and the 28 NORAD Region and in addition is the home of the 78th Fighter Wing. The base was named for Lt. Lloyd Andrews Hamilton of the 17th Aero Squadron, shot down in France, August, 1918.

The airport, begun in 1932, covers 928 acres of drained marshland sloping imperceptibly to the Bay.

IGNACIO, 24.7 *m.* (10 alt.), was named for Don Ignacio Pacheco, much-married *alcalde* of San Rafael, who owned a large ranch here. His horses were so admired by John C. Frémont that the American explorer is said to have kidnapped him and demanded a ransom in horses.

At 25.3 *m.* is the junction of State 37 with US 101. The route goes R. on State 37.

Left on US 101, in little Novato Valley, where dikes thrown up against the incursion of tides have formed green meadows planted to alfalfa and grain, is NOVATO, 2.5 *m.* (17 alt., 31,006 pop. 1970; 17,881, 1960; inc. 73%), below the hills bordering San Pablo Bay. The town stands on the former Rancho Novato, granted to Don Fernando Feliz in 1839.

In one of the farm buildings (L) of RANCHO BURDELL (private), 5.7 *m.,* is an adobe wall once part of the home of Camillo Ynitia, last chief of the Olompali Indians. Soon after he sold the Olompali Rancho for $5,200, Ynitia was murdered by his brother, who believed he had hidden the gold in the nearby hills. Jacob Leese, Marin County's first English-speaking settler, once owned the rancho, as did Bezaar Simmons, who built a wooden house here in 1850, and James Black, who gave his daughter the property when she married Dr. Galen Burdell.

The rich earth of PETALUMA VALLEY, 9.6 *m.,* supports cattle ranches, fruit groves, dairies, and chicken farms.

Claiming the title of the World's Egg Basket, PETALUMA, 13.5 *m.* (15 alt., 24,570 pop.), which lies at the head of navigation on Petaluma Creek, is the center of a region whose millions of hens lay the utmost modern methods can produce.

In 1834 Petaluma was a sleepy Mexican village within the boundaries of the Rancho Petaluma, which took its name from an early Miwok Indian village. After 1840 the fertile valley experienced a general invasion of settlers. By 1852, Yankees dominated the village. They continued to raise grain, built a flour mill, and shipped their produce down the creek to San Francisco. For nearly a half-century wheat, lumber, wool, bricks, and basalt blocks were carried by a fleet of thirty odd schooners.

The poultry industry, long Petaluma's foremost, began in 1878 when a young Canadian, Lyman C. Byce, coming here in search of health, saw that this region with its even climate, sandy soil, and marketing facilities was admirably suited for chicken-raising. An inventive genius, Byce began manufacturing incubators and brooders, which are today widely used. Petaluma, while more closely associated with poultrying, is the largest manufacturing center in Sonoma County. According to the Petaluma Chamber of Commerce, the city has the world's largest chick hatchery, largest manufacturer of fishing lines and largest manufacturer of oil-burning furnaces, plus the largest cooperative creamery in the United States, the biggest pile-casting yards, the largest egg candling plant in the world, and the largest concentration of the mixed feed and grain industry in the western states.

The Petaluma Livestock and Poultry Pathology Laboratory which is of major importance to the many poultry and livestock producers in Sonoma and neighboring counties, is located in Petaluma. Operated by the State Dept. of Agriculture's Division of Animal Industry, the laboratory aids practicing veterinarians and poultry and livestock growers in the diagnosis and prevention of infectious and contagious disease of livestock and poultry.

Right from Petaluma on Washington Street 2.8 *m.* to a junction with a paved road; R. here to what was General Mariano Vallejo's CASA GRANDE, 4.4 *m.,* built in 1833-34. When Vallejo stood on the broad second-story balcony, his eyes could see no land that was not his own, for the great house was headquarters for his 75,000-acre Rancho Petaluma. The white plaster on the adobe walls is cracked and crumbling in spots, and a shingled roof has replaced the original tiles; but the massive walls are the same that Vallejo's Kanaka workmen put together, and the original beams of hand-hewn redwood support ceilings and balconies. The rear wing has been destroyed. In the inner courtyard formed by the four great walls, Vallejo's two thousand Indians gathered to hear his orders.

On US 101 at 21.5 *m.* is COTATI (113 alt., 1,368 pop. 1970), founded on land once part of 17,000-acre Rancho Cotati, whose owner, Captain Juan Castaneda, gave up his claim in 1849 to the district's American sheriff, Dr. Thomas S. Page. The sheriff's son, Wilfred Page, laid out the town around a hexagonal plaza, from which the streets radiate in a spider-web pattern. When asked why he had not used simple squares and straight lines in the great expanse of land, Page replied, "Any fool can plant that and come out right, but it takes brains to start on angles and have your plans click."

SANTA ROSA, 29.9 *m.* (160 alt., 50,006 pop. 1970; 31,027, 1960; inc. 61%), seat of Sonoma County, is an attractive, prosperous city in Sonoma County, at the base of the Sonoma Mountains on the eastern edge of a rich alluvial valley. In 1829 Father Juan Amores, on a missionary expedition from San Rafael, named the valley and creek for Saint Rose of Lima but the Indians prevented him from establishing a mission. In 1833, Mariano Vallejo tried to begin a settlement here, but abandoned it in favor of Sonoma. The town was not founded until several years after the discovery of gold, when the Argonauts turned to farming. Almost immediately the enterprising community asked to be made county seat (then Sonoma) ; they received the honor in 1854.

The earthquake of 1906 wrecked Santa Rosa's entire business district with a loss of forty lives, but the town was rebuilt and has continued to keep pace with the subdivision of the surrounding agricultural lands. Local industries include fruit processing, large-scale manufacturing of ice for refrigerator cars, egg-packing, and the manufacture of shoes.

On the track which for fifty years was an experimental farm of Luther Burbank (1849-1926), who arrived in Santa Rosa in 1875, are the one-and-one-half-acre BURBANK MEMORIAL GARDENS, Santa Rosa Ave. and Tupper St. Property of the Santa Rosa Junior College botany department, the gardens contain a great variety of plants, including many Burbank discoveries. Under an enormous cedar of Lebanon grown from a seed sent from the Holy Land, Burbank is buried.

While a young man, Burbank accidentally discovered the potato named for him on his Massachusetts truck-farm. With the $150 he received for his discovery and ten of the new Burbank potatoes, he followed his brothers to California. Soon he began the experiments with plants destined to add hundreds of new varieties of vegetables, flowers, and fruits to nursery and seed catalogues. He believed in the inheritance of acquired characteristics, and that these acquired characteristics could be fixed, or be made permanent. Among his best-known hybrids are the spineless cactus; Burbank potato; Gold, Wickson, American, and Climax plums; Splendor and Sugar prunes; and many improved varieties of quinces, berries, and vegetables. His Shasta and Alaska daisies; "crimson flame" and softly colored single and double California poppies; roses; callas; gladioli; dahlias; and many improved flowering shrubs have added color and fragrance to gardens all over the world.

The slim-spired white FIRST BAPTIST CHURCH, B St. between Fifth and Sixth Sts., was built in 1873 of lumber cut from a single redwood tree. Sufficient lumber remained of the same tree to build a five-room residence.

The side route continues L. from Santa Rosa on Sebastopol Avenue (State 12).

In the heart of a countryside which flowers with acres of fruit blossoms in spring is SEBASTOPOL, 37.8 *m.* (68 alt. 3,993 pop. 1970; 2,694, 1960; inc. 36%), center of Gravenstein apple and cherry orchards. J. H. P. Morris named the town Pine Grove when he founded it in 1853 on the site of the adobe house of Joaquin

Carillo's Rancho Llano de Santa Rose (Plain of St. Rose). Two years later a local feud ended in a street battle in which one participant barricaded himself in a store. Enthusiastic spectators, recalling the Crimean city of Sebastopol, then in a state of siege, immediately adopted its name, first for the store, then for the town.

Left from Sebastopol on Gravenstein Highway 0.6 *m.* to the SONOMA BUDDHIST TEMPLE, ENMAN-JI, which was shipped from Japan for exhibit in the South Manchurian Railway display at the Chicago World's Fair in 1933 and afterwards dismantled and erected here. In authentic Kamakura style, the building has a green pagoda roof, bell-shaped windows, and stucco walls.

North of Sebastopol State 12 runs through orchard lands and vineyards, skirting the western edge of a rich hop-growing region, to the shores of the RUSSIAN RIVER, 51.8 *m.* a vacation area for as many as one hundred and fifty thousand persons annually. Rising in Mendocino County, the stream cuts directly across the Coast Range. In this part of its course the river's meanderings have created a string of beaches covered with yellow sand. The Russians named the river Slavianka (Slavic) when they penetrated the fertile region in 1812 and began trapping for furs along the stream. The Americans, who followed, logged the area, built lumber mills, and farmed the cleared land.

The population of GUERNEVILLE, 52 *m.* (52 alt.), swells in the summer to seven thousand, filling resort cottages, cabins, and camp-grounds. The town occupies a wide river meadow encircled by mountains, edged by firs and redwoods. The business street is lined with one-story, false-front buildings and old wooden sidewalks. The town took its name from George C. Guerne, who with Harmon G. Heald erected the region's first sawmill in 1865.

Right from Guerneville on a paved road 2.8 *m.* to 400-acre ARMSTRONG WOODS STATE PARK (*camping and picnicking*). Here, deep among a fine stand of redwoods, is the ARMSTRONG FOREST THEATRE, whose redwood log benches seat 1,800.

State 12 continues to the junction with a paved road 57 *m.*; L. here across the river is MONTE RIO, 0.2 *m.* (41 alt.), at the foot of steep hills whose slopes are covered with summer homes and resort hotels. The side route goes L. from Monte Rio to BOHEMIAN GROVE (*visits by special permission*), 1.1 *m.*, the 2,437-acre redwood grove of San Francisco's Bohemian Club. Here, in an outdoor theater whose log seats accommodate 1,200, the club since 1878 has held its annual stag Hi Jinks, staging its Grove Play against a natural background of great trees. During a two-week encampment, some six hundred men "rough it" in tents or cabins, eat in the open air, tell tall tales around a campfire, and attend a music-drama written and played by fellow members.

The main side route follows State 12 west from Guerneville along the north bank of the Russian River to a junction with State 1, 65.6 *m.*

BLACK POINT, 28.4 *m.* (8 alt.), formerly a railroad shipping point for dairy products, lies in a corner where the hills come down to the marshes. The dark appearance of the wooded point projecting into San Pablo Bay suggested the name.

Hills and meadows are left behind as State 37 enters a region of strong winds and wide horizons. Tules are the chief growth in these sloughs, creeks, and tidal lagoons where wild ducks are abundant in the late autumn.

At 32.9 *m.* is the junction with Sears Point Road, on which the route goes R.

Left on State 37, which leaves green sloughs where red-winged blackbirds wheel and follows the base of low foothills on which sheep and cattle graze.

The *embarcadero* (landing place) on Sonoma Creek at the site of SHELL-VILLE, 7.4 *m.* (10 alt.), once piled high with merchandise bound to and from

Sonoma, was first named Saint Louis by early Missouri settlers. It was renamed for Theodor Schell, one of the promoters of the Sonoma Valley Prismoidal Railway in 1875, who bought 1,400 acres here in 1860.

The route goes L. from Shellville on State 12 toward the Sonoma Mountains, past the wide orchards and old ranch houses of Sonoma Valley.

At 9.2 m. is a junction with the surfaced Petaluma Road; L. here 1.3 m. to a junction with a dirt road; R. here to the entrance of the Coblentz Ranch (*private*), 2.2 m. About a half-mile from the road, almost hidden by masses of venerable trees (L), are the stone walls and blue-green roof of TEMELEC HALL, built by Bear Flag revolutionist Captain Granville Perry Swift, once the finest private house north of San Francisco. The south wing is said to have been built as early as 1849 by General Persifor Frazer Smith, military governor of California, who sold the 12,000-acre ranch to Swift, a newly rich miner. First and second floors of the 20-room house are surrounded on three sides by colonnaded balconies and the roof is topped by a small gazebo. The massive stone wall in the rear, which once continued around the house and joined the reservoir on the north, was an excellent defense against marauding Indians or bandits. Just south of it were adobe quarters for 40 Indian servants,. At each side of the formal gardens of the front terrace—where cypress, acacia, and lemon verbena, planted by Swift, still flourish—is a tiny ornate stone summer house with high, pointed roof. The two-story stone stable, topped by a tall pigeon cote, once had an inclined driveway for carriages.

Northward from the junction with Petaluma Road through orchards and vineyards State 12 follows the wide road laid out by Mariano Vallejo.

On the east side of the valley at the base of low hills is SONOMA, 11 m. (97 alt., 4,112 pop. 1970; 3,023, 1960; inc. 36%), which has never quite lost its leisurely Mexican air. It owes its existence to Franciscan priest Jose Altimira and soldier Mariano Gaudalupe Vallejo. When Governor Argnello urged Altimira in 1823 to consolidate Missions San Francisco de Asis and San Rafael and move them farther north, ostensibly for the health of the Indian neophytes, but also to check Russian colonization, the young priest came into the Sonoma Valley. Here he dedicated the "New San Francisco" before a willow altar.

The Franciscan authorities, annoyed at the young priest's temerity and impulsiveness, insisted that Missions San Rafael and San Francisco de Asis should remain where they were founded. Altimira fought back in long letters until finally he was permitted to have a mission here—the last founded and most northerly of the California missions—which was named San Francisco de Solano. Neophytes from San Jose, San Rafael, and San Francisco built a few mud-plastered wooden buildings below the billowing hills. In a few years permanent buildings of adobe were finished. Stockaded gardens and vineyards surrounded the mission and small herds of cattle, sheep, and horses roamed the valley. When a chief of the local Chocuy-on Indians was baptised "Sonoma," the pleasant name was adopted for the valley and the town that grew up around the mission.

In 1835, the missions having been secularized, Governor Jose Figueroa appointed young Lieutenant Mariano Vallejo as *comisionado* of the Sonoma mission lands and stock and sent him to found a fortified *pueblo* at Sonoma. Without equipment other than his pocket compass, Vallejo laid out the town in large squares about a plaza. He fortified the hills behind the mission with a few small cannons. With the aid of Indians he built barracks surrounded with a loop-holed wall and adjoining them a *palacio* with a two-story castle-like tower which was regarded as one of the most pretentious residences in California. Around the dusty plaza where Vallejo put his perspiring Indian soldiers through their paces were built the homes of relatives and friends to whom were granted the broad reaches of the present valleys of Sonoma, Petaluma, Santa Rosa, and Napa.

After a few sharp skirmishes with neighboring Indians, Vallejo was able to make an alliance with Sem Yeto (the mighty arm), over-lord of many tribes, who persuaded his people to submit to the Spanish. Sem Yeto was baptized at the mission and christened Francisco Solano. (The first constitutional convention in Monterey, at Vallejo's suggestion, gave Solano's name to the county east of Napa; a statue has been erected to him in Fairfield.) Under Vallejo's paternal rule the Indians lived in a mild form of peonage.

By the middle 1840's Sonoma already had some American residents. The Spanish eyed uneasily the newer American immigrants—and with good reason, as it appeared in 1846. The *pueblo's* fortifications were no handicap to 33 Yankees led by Ezekiel Merritt, who on the morning of June 14 surprised the garrison's 18 men and "captured" the defenseless commander. Under the crude banner painted with a bear and a star which they hoisted in the plaza, the rebels proclaimed the California Republic. It lasted less than a month, for on July 9, 1846, when Lieutenant Joseph Warren Revere of the U. S. Army took command, the Bear Flag was replaced by the Stars and Stripes. "At last the rag of that dirty rabble had been supplanted by the glorious flag of the United States," wrote Senora Vallejo to the general in the *calaboza* at Sutter's Fort.

When Lilburn W. Boggs, former Governor of Missouri, was appointed *alcalde* of Sonoma by General Stephen W. Kearny, the appointment was contested by John H. Nash, Bear Flag revolutionist who had grabbed for himself the post of *alcalde*. Nash refused to turn over the city records. Only after Governor Richard B. Mason had dispatched Lieutenant William Tecumseh Sherman to seize and carry off Nash did Boggs become head of the community. After a few months Vallejo, who promised not to bear arms against the Americans, returned to Sonoma and settled down to master the difficult language of his new country and act as Indian agent for the district. Garrisoned by the Army, Sonoma quieted down.

Sonoma always has centered around its PLAZA, bounded by Napa and Spain Sts., First St. W. and First St. E. In its northeast corner is the BEAR FLAG MONUMENT, a bronze statue of a pioneer (John MacQuarrie, sculptor) holding the new flag, mounted on a 40-ton boulder of volcanic rock. In the center of the Plaza is the buff stone COURTHOUSE AND CITY HALL, which replaced in 1908 an old adobe courthouse that once housed the county seat, although a grand jury had condemned it as "not fit for a cattle shed." When a special election in 1854 decided in favor of the lusty young town of Santa Rosa as county seat, two jubilant new officials drove a team of mules from Santa Rosa one dark night and rifled the courthouse. The county clerk is said to have prodded the mules home with his wooden leg.

The oldest building in Sonoma, the MISSION SAN FRANCISCO DE SOLANO, built in 1824, is an L-shaped adobe roofed with red tile and surmounted by a plain Latin cross. Hanging from an ivy-covered framework in front is a bell cast in Peru in 1829. After the secularization of the missions in 1835, the mission church became the parish church, but when a new church was built in 1880, it was sold. The old buildings then served as a hay-barn and a wine cellar; the patio, as a butcher's slaughter yard. A small wooden saloon crowded against the front wall of the church. For years small boys threw rocks through the crumbling walls. After long neglect the mission was purchased in 1903 by public-spirited citizens who presented it to the State. It is now a State landmark and museum.

The MISSION MUSEUM (*open 10-4*) contains early California papers, portraits of pioneers, part of the Sonoma flagstaff, timbers and millstone from Sonoma's first gristmill, Indian baskets shownig beaded and feathered work of the Pomo, long handwrought iron hinges from Fort Ross, and timbers from the ship *Ocean Hero,* which was towed to Lakeville and there sunk to serve as an *embarcadero.*

The BLUE WING HOTEL, 217 E. Spain St., is an adobe building 100 feet long whose second-story balcony extending over the sidewalk, similar to one in the rear, is supported by octagonal redwood posts rising to the roof. The original 12-light windows, open beams and wooden ceiling, and handmade doors with ogee mouldings are well preserved. The museum, formerly the hotel bar, contains a gold scale once used in a store across the street, a music box that tinkles "Linger Longer Lou," a small red altar from the local Chinese joss house, and a long quartermaster's account with John C. Fremont covering the disbursement of $1,242 in small sums. Sonoma's man-power fire engine is flanked by an automobile bought by Luther Burbank in 1915. The collection also includes General Persifer Smith's medicine cabinet and the walnut desk used by Frank Soule while writing *The Annals of San Francisco*.

Its wide verandah facing the Plaza, the old MEXICAN BARRACKS, Spain St. and First St. E., which cost Vallejo $9,000 of his private funds, is a two-story structure built in 1836 of adobe and hand-hewn redwood timbers hauled to the site by oxteam. Used as headquarters for Vallejo's Mexican soldiers and as a munition depot, it was later garrisoned by the Bear Flag rebels and finally by United States officers.

The EL DORADO HOTEL, 145 First St. W. (now a restaurant), erected in 1846 by General Vallejo's brother, Captain Salvador Vallejo, became a famous California hostelry. The original building is hidden by ugly modern additions except on the north side, where appear the old 42-inch-thick adobe walls.

The SALVADOR VALLEJO ADOBE (*private*), adjoining the El Dorado Hotel on the south, is a two-story adobe of nice proportions. A row of tall posts rises from the sidewalk to the second-floor roof, which extends over a shallow balcony reached from inside through French doors. Although he had ranchos, vineyards, horses, and cattle, Salvador Vallejo became so financially involved that in 1853 all his personal belongings were attached: even the gold epaulets from his Mexican uniform and such trifles as brandied peaches and feather fans.

The FITCH HOUSE (*private*), 347 First St. W., a two-story adobe with a cantilevered balcony extending over the sidewalk. Built in 1836 by Jacob Leese for Henry D. Fitch, Vallejo's brother-in-law, it boasted the first fireplace in the county. General Persifer Smith made his headquarters here. In the 1850's, St. Mary's Hall, an Episcopalian boarding school for young ladies, occupied the building.

The two-story RAY HOUSE (*private*), E. Spain St. and Second St. E., is a long rectangular adobe and frame structure, the small wooden portion of which was built in 1846 and supplemented four years later with a large adobe addition. The two sides facing the streets are surrounded by rows of redwood posts supporting an open-raftered, low-pitched roof extending eight feet beyond the walls. American Army officers were quartered here in the 1840's and 1850's. Later the building housed the first Masonic organization in the county.

In the northwestern part of town, at the end of a tree-shaded lane opening off W. Spain St., is the VALLEJO HISTORICAL STATE MONUMENT, Vallejo's $150,000 estate, Lachryma Montis (Lat., tear of the mountain), established in 1851. The family home, a two-story yellow house in "American Gothic" style, has a high pitched roof with many gables decorated with elaborate jig-saw tracery. Vallejo's 13th child, Señora Luisa Vallejo Emparan, the last of his immediate family, has a life tenancy of her old home. The whip-sawed house timbers were hauled here by oxteam.

The SWISS CHALET (*open 10-4*), now a museum, is a two-story half-timbered house with the second floor overhanging. The original frame and bracing timbers were shipped around the Horn from Switzerland, numbered for assembly. The enclosing walls are of a soft rose-colored brick. In a recent restoration many of the original oak timbers were replaced with red-wood and the whole building set upon a foundation of concrete. The building was used as a store house and as Indian servants' quarters. On the long dining table used by Vallejo and his family of 16 children stand two globes made in 1823, one of the world and one of the skies. In the cases are the sword and uniform the General wore when Mexican *Comandante-General;* his elaborately embroidered christening robe; the silk-lined, enameled jewel case which, with a set of jewelry, was a wedding present to Señora Vallejo; and a charming daguerreotype of the side-whiskered general surrounded by six pretty ringletted, hoop-skirted daughters and granddaughters.

In SONOMA CEMETERY, at the northern end of W. First St., is the grave of General Vallejo (1808-90) and his wife, Francisca Benicia Carrillo de Vallejo (1816-91), marked by a black granite monument.

State 12 goes west from Sonoma on West Napa Street to the junction with a paved road, 12 m., where it turns R.

BOYES SPRINGS, 13.7 m. (150 alt.), long a vacation center, was settled in 1883 by Captain Henry Ernest Boyes, who had come to California from England. Boyes and his wife heard stories of the old hot mineral springs used by the Indians and investigated—the captain digging and Mrs. Boyes hoisting the bucket. Located here are BOYES HOT SPRINGS (*mineral water plunge; picnic grounds*).

The SONOMA MISSION INN (*tennis courts, saddle horses, swimming pool*) occupies a large white concrete building with the twin towers, rounded arches, and tiled roofs typical of the California missions.

FETTER'S SPRINGS, 14.1 m., were developed about 1907 on the 100-acre ranch of Mr. and Mrs. George Fetter, who built a hotel there. This resort and AGUA CALIENTE, 14.6 m. (75 alt.), are open throughout the year.

HOOKER'S MONUMENT (L), 15.2 m., a boulder bearing a bronze tablet dedicated to Colonel "Fighting Joe" Hooker of Civil War fame, stands on the edge of the 550 acres which he acquired in 1851, during a two-year leave from the Army, with the thought of becoming a "Southern planter of California." In a clump of oaks 350 yards west is the snug little four-room clapboard HOOKER HOUSE, the timbers of which were cut in Norway and shipped 'round the Horn.

Adjoining is the GEORGE WATRESS HOUSE, a two-story stone and timber building built in 1853 by Hooker's successor on the ranch. Watress, former proprietor of the Astor House in New York, arrived in San Francisco in 1851 and became proprietor of a hotel before moving to Sonoma Valley.

State 12 winds through low, chaparral-covered foothills drained by Calabazas (pumpkin) Creek.

At 18.3 m. is the junction with a paved road, on which the route goes L. to GLEN ELLEN, 19.3 m. (227 alt.), shaded by tall trees that grow along Sonoma Creek, once a railroad terminal and a fashionable summer resort. It has long been famous for its wine grapes. The JACK LONDON MEMORIAL LIBRARY AND COMMUNITY CENTER (L) was built by the Glen Ellen Women's Club and other admirers of the novelist.

The JACK LONDON HISTORICAL STATE PARK, established in 1959 by the State Park Commission, provides a memorial of splendid scenic value to a California writer of world renown. About 40 acres of the author's famous Beauty Ranch comprise the park, which includes the House of Happy Walls, the Wolf House and Jack London's grave.

The House of Happy Walls was built in 1919 by Charmian London, three years after her husband's death. In the home of rough native stone are the London collection of South Pacific art objects, some of the massive Wolf House furniture, the furnishings of the writer's original study and numerous mementos of his vigorous, richly varied life, activities and interests. The Wolf House, reached by trail about one-half mile from the parking area, was completed by London in 1913. The unique massive structure was destroyed by fire before the London's had moved in. Jack London's grave is near the Wolf House. On this wooded knoll the writer's ashes were placed in accordance with his expressed wish, under a boulder near the graves of two pioneer children, who were buried nearly a century ago. The ashes of Charmian London, who died January 13, 1955, are also on the site (*open daily to the public from 10-5 p.m., 25¢*).

The route goes east on Sears Point Road, a lonely stretch of highway, across marshlands, past sloughs and lagoons to the junction with a paved county road, 42.7 *m.,* on which it goes R.

At 43.7 *m.,* on the outskirts of Vallejo (*see below*), is the junction with Tennessee Street.

Right here over a causeway 0.9 *m.* to MARE ISLAND NAVAL SHIPYARD (*usually open, subject to special restrictions*), headquarters of the San Francisco Naval Base, at the southern end of a narrow peninsula flanked by the Bay on the west and the Napa River on the east. The largest shipbuilding and repairing facility of its kind in the world, capable of designing and manufacturing most articles used in ships. The shipyard was the first west coast facility to build atomic submarines. The U.S. Naval Schools Command has more than 1,300 military personnel in the Guided Missile School, Naval Tactical Data System School, and Cryptographic Record School.

By the end of World War II the yard had launched a total of nearly 400 new vessels—destroyers, submarines, landing craft, destroyer escorts, submarine tenders, and others—besides overhauling a vast number of damaged Navy craft. Its machine shop is the largest west of the Mississippi. It has a mobile power plant, capable of generating enough power for the whole yard—one of two in the nation's Navy yards. Its submarine base is one of two in the country which regularly build and repair submarines. At the peninsula's southern end is a Naval ammunition depot, where war vessels load or discharge explosives.

The ADMINISTRATION BUILDING incorporates the original structure built in 1870 along with later additions. ST. PETER'S CHAPEL is the oldest building on Navy property erected solely for worship. The NAVAL HOSPITAL, its 30 buildings covering 47 acres, was a rehabilitation center for amputees.

Mare Island was established as a Navy yard in 1854 with Admiral David G. Farragut as its first commander. The site had been discovered in 1775 by the crew of the *San Carlos.* It is believed that it was first called La Isla de la Yegua (the island of the mare) because General Mariano G. Vallejo, who once claimed ownership, found grazing there a prized mare lost when a ferry overturned with a load of livestock in Carquinez Strait. Purchased by the Government for $83,410 soon after California became a State, it was quickly pressed into service as a repair base when a floating drydock built in New York and shipped around the Horn was anchored here. The first stone drydock, 507 feet long, was constructed in the 1870's at about the same period when the first new vessel was launched, the U. S. S. *Saginaw,* a wooden frigate; a second drydock, 740 feet long and large enough to hold any Navy ship afloat, was completed in 1919. Here during World War I, 50 vessels were completed, including the U. S. S. *Ward,* launched 16 days after keel laying, and the U. S. S. *California,* then the nation's deepest draft battleship.

VALLEJO, 42.5 *m.* (10 alt., 66,733 pop. 1970; 60,877, 1960), a hilly city of treeless residential streets and old-fashioned business blocks, is located at the confluence of the Napa River and San Pablo Bay. The first mention of the town reveals that in 1817 a group of Spanish soldiers led by Lieutenant Jose Sanchez engaged a band of Suisun Indians headed by Chief Malica near Vallejo's site. Sanchez emerged victorious after a short skirmish but the chief retired to his wickiup. When the invaders approached he set fire to it, burning himself to death.

In April, 1850, General Mariano Vallejo donated 166 acres of land for a town site and promised $370,000 for the construction of a State Capitol. Two years later the capital was transferred here from San Jose. The State legislature met in a hastily erected building but, dissatisfied with their accommodations, abandoned it within a week.

Three brothers, Levi, John, and Eleazer Frisbie, played important roles in the history of Vallejo. Levi and John laid out the city in 1851. John, builder of the California Pacific Railroad and manager of Vallejo's great estate, had left the Army in 1848. Levi married Doña Adela Vallejo, said to have been the most beautiful of the General's daughters. Eleazer was appointed first postmaster of Vallejo and later Associate Justice of the California Supreme Court.

Captain Frank Marryat described Vallejo in the 1850's as "a few scrubby-looking hills that bordered on the bay . . ." A store-ship laden with corrugated iron plates for the construction of houses had sunk at her Vallejo moorings. When Marryat raised her and found the cargo unfit for sale in San Francisco, he used the tide to clean the cargo stacked on the beach and soon was able to erect "a very handsome hotel" out of the salvage. When the legislature returned to Vallejo, only to abandon it a second time, Marryat reported that "the city made to order was then pulled down and sold for old materials . . ."

Having twice lost the capital, the city played for smaller stakes in 1873 when it attempted to take the county seat from Fairfield. Vallejo won in a special election, but Fairfield brought a special suit enjoining the action. After a bill was introduced into the legislature whose passage would divide Solano County so that Vallejo should be separated from it—making her a county seat with no county outside her own confines—Vallejo immediately capitulated and Fairfield retained the county seat.

The industries of Vallejo, located along the water front and on the outskirts of the city, include a brick and tile factory, oil and sugar refineries, a smelter, a die-casting company, and a flour mill. Much of its patronage and not a few of its residents come from Mare Island (*see above*).

The site of the SECOND STATE CAPITOL BUILDING, Santa Clara and York Sts., is marked by a bronze plaque.

On Sacramento St. near York St. is the RICHARDS RESIDENCE, a two-story structure built of redwood in the early 1850's by C. B. Richards, first harness maker in Vallejo. Its lower and upper verandahs are supported by columns of redwood, and the original green shutters still hang at the windows.

Facing Mare Island at the foot of Carolina St. is the VALLEJO YACHT CLUB, a two-story structure topped by a square lookout tower. Often docked here is the three-masted schooner, *California,* once representative of the club in the San Francisco-Honolulu race. This clubhouse for more than 35 years has been the goal for yacht races from parts of the Bay region.

Left from Vallejo on State 29, between the Napa River and the Sulphur Springs Mountains, to the entrance (R) to NAPA STATE HOSPITAL for insane persons and alcoholics (*visiting hours: relatives daily, 9-11, 2-4; public Mon., Wed., Fri., 9-11*), 12.1 *m.* At the end of a wide driveway, flanked by dormitories (L) and cottages (R) and bordered by large magnolia trees, is the main building, built in 1873, a four-story stone building in Gothic style. Its red roof, tweaked up into dormers over attic windows, breaks into a square central tower and round conical towers on each corner. The Gothic idea is so omnipresent that the tortoise, a Gothic emblem, is carved on beams within the building. The gray granite entrance portico is adorned with niches in which are white marble statutes symbolic of various virtues. Opened in 1875 with a capacity of 500, the asylum was full by the end of the year. A program of enlargement was undertaken. Today the institution has 5,113 beds and currently cares for approximately 4,800 patients. Since World War II the State has expended $18,053,000 for expansion and modernization of facilities.

North on State 29, the well-preserved one-story JUAREZ ADOBE, 13.6 *m.*, built in 1845, was the second of the Juarez adobes on Rancho Tulucay. About 90 feet long, it has walls between two and three feet thick, with deep window embrasures, built of adobe bricks covered with plaster. An earlier adobe in the rear built in 1840 is in ruins. Bricks have tumbled from the walls, revealing the chopped straw used as a binder for the mud. Most of the roof has vanished, but some of the hand-split redwood shakes rest on the huge beams.

NAPA, 14.6 *m.* (24 alt., 35,978 pop. 1970; 22,170, 1960; inc. 31%), covers the flat lands around the head of navigation on Napa River and the low hills to the east. It is a substantial residential community and commercial industrial, and governmental center and the largest city in Napa County. Manufacturing in the area is diversified and products include leather and leather goods, wearing apparel, steel pipe, building materials, and electronic components. A civic center was started by the city in 1952 and the city hall, main fire station, and police station have been completed.

The Indians called the place Nappo. That they had long lived here was shown when street graders at Franklin and Laurel Streets cut into a burial ground where almost a hundred skeletons, with mortars, pestles, and other artifacts, were found. When settlers came into the valley, the Indians moved their brush shelters to the hills or to the edges of ranches where they could find work. John Bidwell's diary of 1842 says: "Wheat, Corn, and Potatoes are seldom surrounded by a fence, they grow out on the plains and are guarded from the cattle and horses by the Indians, who are stationed in their huts near the fields. You can employ any number of Indians by giving them a lump of Beef every week and paying them about one dollar for same." In 1856, when Napa was a sizeable town, one historian said that the Indians "made the night ring with their revelry . . . and when they could secure the means got dead drunk."

In 1836 Nicolas Higuera, one-time soldier at the San Francisco Presidio, received Rancho Entre Napa to the southwest of the present town. Near the river, he built a house of wicker plastered with mud and thatched with tule grass. Cayento Juarez, who brought in stock the next year, received in 1840 Rancho Tulucay, a two-square-league section east of the river on which he built an adobe (*see above*). Salvador Vallejo, brother of the General, received Rancho Napa, some 3,000 acres northwest of the town, in 1838 and stocked it with cattle.

First commerce in this country was conducted by "Boston" launches which visited ranchos around the Bay to trade for hides and tallow. In 1841, young John Rose and John C. Davis launched a schooner about the size of a whale boat near the present First Street. John A. Sutter sailed the little *Sacramento* up the river in 1844, loaded with settlers bound for the fertile valley lands. One of them, Bartlett Vines, later married a daughter of George C. Yount and became the father of Napa County's first American baby. Sutter's return cargo was lime, which he bought from Higuera.

When Higuera gave Nathan Coombs 80 acres in payment for work on the former's new adobe house in 1848, Coombs had a surveyor stake out a town-site. Harrison Pierce bought a load of lumber from Bale and Kilburn's mill on Napa

River and began work on a small building, which he intended for a saloon. When Coombs and Higuera came to look it over, they found it right in the middle of the proposed Third Street. Deciding that Mr. Pierce must have been sampling his own wares too generously, they insisted that he move the building out of the street on to his lot. Pierce barely got the roof on his building when gold was discovered. He spent the summer at the mines, but when snow fell in the mountains he came back and opened the Empire Saloon, where he served square meals of beef, hard bread, and coffee for $1.00. A man named Thompson built a store that year, and General Vallejo and General Frisbie opened a second in 1849. After 1850 steamboats churned the water between Napa and San Francisco. First of these was the little *Dolphin,* fitted with a locomotive boiler. It was said that she had to be "trimmed" by shifting the passengers and that her tall captain, F. G. Baxter, was always sighted long before the stack. The second steamer was the *Jack Hayes,* brought around the Horn in pieces and assembled at Benicia. Soon boats were carrying not only passengers but the lumber, cattle, and wheat of the surrounding ranches.

The 1850's were roistering days for Napa, for miners found it a good town to winter in. Coin of the realm included gold dust, foreign coins, and the five- to fifty-dollar gold slugs made in San Francisco. By 1854, 400 people lived here. A subscription was taken up in 1855 and the first public school in the valley opened. A small newspaper, the *Napa County Reporter,* appeared on the streets on the Fourth of July, 1856; it was known as a tri-weekly, because after it appeared one week, the publisher spent all of the second week trying to get out the next issue, which would then appear the third week. A new City Hall was built in 1856. A silver boom in the mountains around the valley emptied the town in 1859; one man said, "If they can find silver in Washoe, why not in Napa." Promoters hastily issued and sold stock, but the bubble burst when assays proved the ore to be low in value, and hotel and saloon keepers emptied bulky specimens into the streets "making quite a contribution of paving material to the streets of Napa." These streets were quagmires of muck where bundles of straw were thrown to make paths, and woe "to the unlucky wight who had too much 'tangle-foot' aboard, for a single misstep would send him in mud to his waist." In summer, when the dirt was ground into deep ruts by wagons, they were "canopied with intolerable clouds of dust through which people floundered over a strange mosaic of rubbish, cast-off clothing, empty bottles and sardine cans."

But in the 1860's the first shacks of adobe and split wood were being replaced by more substantial buildings, the citizens trod on wooden plank sidewalks, and bridges spanned the river so that it was not necessary to go to the ford north of town or to take the ferry to get to the other side. In 1865 Napa celebrated the completion of a railroad to Suscol; free rides were given to anyone who "wanted to embrace the opportunity." "Pony," the diminutive, wood-burning engine, was succeeded by the magnificent $9,000 "Napa City," with a four and one-half foot drive wheel. In 1868 the road was continued to Calistoga, where Samuel Brannan feasted the first train load of passengers.

The town's later growth, based on the productiveness of the surrounding country, has been steady though not spectacular. Its products include gloves, athletic equipment, shirts and pants, and basalt paving and building materials.

Surrounded by green lawns and tall elms, the NAPA COUNTY COURTHOUSE, Second, Third, Coombs, and Brown Sts., was built in 1878, replacing a courthouse erected in 1856. The gray, cement-covered brick building has a tower of the most unexpected contours. George Dyer observes that it "might have been brought from the Kremlin, Moorish windows, turnip top and all."

The NAPA HOTEL, First and Main Sts., oldest building in town, a three-story crenellated structure, has been extensively remodeled since it was built in 1851 by James Harbin.

TULUCAY CEMETERY, on the hills east of Napa on Third St., was opened on land given by Cayetano Juarez in 1858. Many plots are outlined in native stone and names of early families are commemorated in handsome large mausoleums of warm-colored stone. Huge eucalyptus trees shadow the graves and coveys of grey quail mince along the paths.

The route continues east from Vallejo on Georgia Street, which becomes Benicia Road.

SOUTHAMPTON BAY, 50.9 *m.*, on Carquinez Strait, is remembered as the site of the Corbett-Choynski prizefight; here on the grain barge *Excell* the celebrated bloody ring battle was fought June 6, 1889. The fight began at seven in the morning and lasted an hour and forty minutes—until a swig of brandy failed to revive Choynski in the 27th round. Corbett wore three-ounce gloves; Choynski, driving gloves. A sports writer described the opening of the fifth round: "Choynski came up in a rollicking way and did some good work but the professor quickly scored a flush hit with a left on his nose . . ."

Where the western end of Suisun Bay narrows to form Carquinez Strait lies BENICIA, 52.7 *m.* (10 alt., 8,783 pop. 1970; 6,070, 1960, inc. 44%), whose past was of greater interest than its present until expansion of ordnance production at its United States Army Arsenal during World War II turned it into a boom town. Benicia's founder was Dr. Robert Semple, a lean, hardy Missourian six feet, eight inches tall, who gave the impression of even greater size in his coonskin cap and loosely-fitting buckskin hunting jacket. (According to local legend, he wore his spurs on the calves of his legs when horseback riding and waded Carquinez Strait when the ferry was late.) Semple came to the Bay region from Monterey, where in 1846 he had established California's first newspaper, the *Californian* (*see Social Heritage: Gentlemen of the Press*). He had been a member of the group, who, after the Bear Flag rebellion, had taken General Mariano Vallejo as a prisoner to Sutter's Fort. Quick to note the advantages Benicia's site offered for a thriving metropolis, he had persuaded Vallejo to deed him five square miles of the Suscol Rancho.

Thomas O. Larkin, the American Consul in California, became a partner with Vallejo and Semple when the transfer of the land was concluded in the autumn of 1846. The town laid out the following year was called Francisca, in honor of Vallejo's wife; because of its similarity with the name San Francisco, Señora Vallejo's middle name, Benicia, later was adopted.

The fickle legislature, which had been dividing its attention among San Jose, Sacramento, and Vallejo, made Benicia the State capital in February, 1853. Unfortunately for the town's elaborate civic plans, the legislators abandoned it for Sacramento a year later. A visitor of that forlorn time wrote of Benicia: ". . . instead of raising an imposing front in evidence of man's progress, it hides its diminutive head among the few huts that stand in commemoration of its failure."

Between 1853 and 1868 a steamer ferry, the *Ione,* owned by Semple, operated between Benicia and Martinez, across the strait. Each of her two engines controlled a paddle-wheel, and since the two frequently became asynchronized, the little boat would reel around in drunken circles. At such moments the swift current would add considerably to the skipper's navigating problems.

The largest wooden dry dock ever constructed on the Pacific Coast was built in the shipyard of Captain Matthew Turner in 1895 for a San Francisco company. Today Benicia's chief industry is the canning of meat, fish, and vegetables. Also located here is a large factory that manufactures gold dredges.

The PACIFIC MAIL DOCKS, east of the Benicia-Martinez Ferry Slip, were built when the Pacific Mail Steamship Company established its California headquarters in Benicia. By 1853 they had constructed great wharves, foundries, and machine shops. The company's great early steamers *California, Oregon,* and *Panama* berthed in Benicia between trips for repairs and refueling. After 1881 the company could no longer compete with overland railroad transportation, and the property was sold.

At the lower end of First St. a marker indicates the site of JACK LONDON'S HANGOUT (Jorgenson's Saloon), where the future novelist spent much of his time during the adventurous days of 1892-93 when he was an officer on the fish patrol. London lived on a water-front barge; to his seafaring intimates he was "Curley-headed Jack." His Benicia experiences are recalled in his novel, *John Barleycorn.*

The old STATE CAPITOL BUILDING, on the north side of G St., now the City Hall, library, and museum, a two-story brick building with a Doric portico, was built to house the State legislature, which held its second Benicia session here 1853-54. Later the building became the county courthouse and schoolhouse. The first-floor museum (*open daily 9-5*) houses a collection of pioneer items relating to Benicia: old lithographs of buildings and of the ships that slipped from local ways, ancient guns, a Wells Fargo safe with a secret keyhole; and the inevitable old music box that still plays lively tunes.

In the State's first MASONIC HALL, J St. west of First St., a two-story redwood buiding erected in August, 1851, the legislature met in February, 1853.

ST. PAUL'S EPISCOPAL CHURCH, First and J Sts., a large wooden Gothic structure topped by a slender spire, had cathedral status when Benicia was the see for the Diocese of Northern California. The house of the diocesan, Bishop John H. D. Wingfield, and the entrance gate to the campus are all that remain of the College of St. Augustine, which was the successor to a school founded in 1847.

In 1851 the two-story SOLANO HOUSE, First and E Sts., was built of redwood. Long the leading hotel in the region, it was host to such notable guests as Generals U. S. Grant and William T. Sherman; California Governors Bennett Riley and Frederick F. Low; John Sutter; and Colonel Silas Casey, the famous Indian fighter.

On I St. west of First St. is the marked site of BENICIA SEMINARY. One of the first Protestant girls' schools in California, the seminary was established in 1852 for several denominations by the Reverend Sylvester Woodbridge and others. Its first teachers were sent here by Governor E. Fairbanks of Vermont. The Reverend Cyrus T. Mills, who purchased the school in 1865, was the founder of the present Mills College (*see OAKLAND*).

In BENICIA CITY PARK, First between K and L Sts., is the site of the FIRST PROTESTANT CHURCH IN CALIFORNIA, established April 15, 1849, by the Reverend Sylvester Woodbridge, a Presbyterian minister. The church declined and was finally closed in 1871 after controversy over adherence to the Union.

A portion of the adobe CALIFORNIA HOUSE still stands on the south side of H St., west of First St. Built by William Tustin in 1847, it became one of California's first hotels. Ex-Governor L. W. Boggs of Missouri performed Benicia's first wedding ceremony here when Frances Cooper became the wife of Dr. Robert Semple. In 1854 the building was sold to John Rueger, who turned it into a brewery.

Doña Maria Concepcion Arguello (Sister Dominica), in the years following her tragic love affair with Count Nikolai Rezanov (later romanticized by Bret Harte and Gertrude Atherton), found religious refuge in ST. CATHERINE'S CONVENT, West L St. between First and Second Sts. The original cream-colored brick building with its old dormer windows still stands. The school has expanded into modern buildings of the mission style.

A private residence on the north side of H St. between Second and Third Sts. was once the PEABODY HOSPITAL, established in 1849. Here returning gold miners were treated by Dr. W. F. Peabody, later Mayor of Benicia.

Brought around the Horn in sections in 1849, the CAPTAIN JOHN WALSH HOUSE, 117 East L St., still stands, well preserved. Walsh settled in Benicia in 1849 and became deputy collector of the then important port.

Still used by the United States Army is the BENICIA ARSENAL, northeast edge of town, established in 1851. A large stone building, in its day it was the most pretentious structure in Benicia and a social as well as a military center. The Benicia Barracks was established here in 1849. During World War II the Army's vast ordnance-producing program, carried on in modern machine shops with the most up-to-date facilities, attracted so many workers that Benicia's population tripled.

North from Benicia on First St. 1 *m.* to the ROMAN CATHOLIC CEME-TERY, where a simple cross marks the grave of Dona Maria Conception Arguello.

Down the Peninsula

The wedge-shaped strip of territory known to all San Franciscans as "the Peninsula," broad at its base in the south and pinched to a tip by ocean and Bay at its northern end, is a multicolored land. It embraces tall mountains darkly forested, white sandy beaches enclosed on three sides by steep rocky cliffs, peaceful farms with chaste white buildings, broad walled estates with stately old mansions, and busy towns bright with red and green roofs of modern stucco homes. Spanish explorers and Catholic mission builders, trudging north from established Monterey, were the first white men to look on its hills and water and plain.

Crude ox teams and speeding mounted couriers packed the earth hard on the Peninsula's first trail, a trail that became a road and was named El Camino Real—the King's Highway. As San Francisco grew and spread across the Peninsula's northern tip the city's wealthy built palatial homes on the eastern slopes of the Coast mountains, near to the King's Highway, and drove thundering coachloads of famous guests to the lavish banquets they staged in mansions filled with *objets d'art*.

Today thousands of San Franciscans live on the Peninsula and drive to work or ride the commute trains playing never-ending games of bridge on tables held on knees between coach seats. On Sundays and holidays the many roads and highways that climb along mountain ridges, trace the ocean's shore, and skirt the southern regions of the Bay are black with the cars of picnickers and sightseers who flock to man-made lakes, crowd the barbecue stands, and drink beer in the cafes of tiny towns nestling in the shade against the mountain slopes.

Beyond the base of the Peninsula, sweeping away from the southern end of the Bay, lies the Santa Clara Valley, in springtime a red, pink, and white confusion of blossoms, for its broad rolling acres are an almost endless orchard of apricot and prune trees. And up the slopes that climb gradually toward the forested mountains to the west spread green vineyards. The valley is walled on east and west by mountains. The eastern hills are dotted with live-oak and laurel, and their slopes are green with thick-growing grass as winter changes to spring. Above the foothills rises Mount Hamilton, highest peak of the eastern range, whose crest in winter is sometimes whitened by snow. Redwoods, fir, maple, laurel, and madrone darken the western mountains, where twisting roads emerge at intervals from the thick forest upon sweeping views of deep canyons and distant blue ridges.

At the valley's southern end, some of the richest quicksilver mines in the world once operated, but the buildings are rotting now and the long shafts and tunnels, their length and depth increased by legend, are caving. The valley is rich in legends—and often the legends are substantiated by the crumbling adobe walls of a home built in the days of the ranchos or a weed-grown dirt road, leading down into some narrow canyon.

❖❖❖❖❖❖❖❖❖❖❖❖❖❖❖❖❖❖❖❖❖❖❖❖❖❖❖❖❖❖❖

Peninsula Tour

San Francisco—Burlingame—San Mateo—Redwood City—Palo Alto —Santa Clara—San Jose; 101.9 *m*. US 101.

Paved four-lane road throughout.
Southern Pacific R. R. parallels route; Greyhound Bus Line follows it.

US 101 follows "down the Peninsula" part of the most famous of all California roads, El Camino Real (The King's Highway), which from the eighteenth century has linked together the long line of missions and *pueblos*. Once little more than a trail, it has seen an ever-growing number of travelers until today, as a four-way arterial, it retains little more of the past than the musical names of its towns and cities.

South from Van Ness Ave. and Fulton St. in SAN FRANCISCO, 0 *m.*, on Van Ness Ave. to Mission St.; R. on Mission (US 101).

DALY CITY, 6.7 *m*. (190 alt., 66,922 pop. 1970; 44,791, 1960, up 49.4%) in San Mateo County, is located on hills from which the land drops to Lake Merced and the ocean. San Bruno Mountain (1,375 alt.) rises steeply in the east. The site was originally part of Rancho Laguna de la Merced. The earliest American settlers, homesteaders engaged in growing vegetables, were involved for several years in lawsuits growing out of attempts by speculators to drive them off their land. Until the 1906 earthquake the northern part of the town site was a dairy ranch owned by John Daly. Many refugees from the Great San Francisco Fire, given small portable two-room houses, moved here, forming the nucleus of the thriving town. In 1950 the city of 10,650 people, began a period of phenomenal growth. By 1965 the population reached 60,500. It is expected to profit from the complete development of the Serramonte area.

COLMA, 8 *m*. formerly a separate town, is now a district of Daly City.

At LAWNDALE, 8.4 m. (113 alt.), the quick are greatly outnumbered by the dead. Cemeteries extend into the hills from both sides of the highway. The beautifully landscaped acres, through which streams descend into Colma Creek, provide burial places for members of many nationalities and religious faiths. In GREEK ORTHODOX MEMORIAL PARK many of the tombstones bear photographs of the deceased developed in enamel and set into the stones. The JAPANESE CEMETERY has many graves marked according to Japanese custom by square wooden posts with pyramidal tops. Some of the vaults in the ITALIAN CEMETERY may be opened and the remains seen behind glass. In the SERBIAN CEMETERY many of the tombstones are in the form of the patriarchal cross common in the iconography of the Greek Orthodox Church. CYPRESS LAWN, largest and oldest of the interdenominational cemeteries, with beautifully kept lawns and clumps of pines and other trees, extends up sloping ground for nearly a mile. In HOLY CROSS, a large Roman Catholic cemetery, is an ornate stone chapel. At the entrance to the CHINESE CEMETERY, occupying a grassy slope overlooking the Bay, stands a shrine with two fireplaces in which the strips of paper carried in funeral processions still are burned.

In the willows along Baden Creek near the former BADEN, 11.7 m., now a part of South San Francisco, a tall Alsatian named Charles Lux met in 1857 an ambitious young German, Henry Kreicer. The latter had come to California on a non-transferable ticket belonging to a friend named Miller, whose name he adopted. With Lux he built up a cattle business which soon reached far beyond this part of Rancho Buri Buri. By 1880 Miller and Lux holdings spread over nineteen counties in California, chiefly in the Coast Ranges and the west side of the San Joaquin Valley, and San Francisco's meat business was under their control.

At the BADEN KENNEL CLUB, greyhounds once were raced. Since betting on races was illegal in California, the Greyhound Exchange resorted to the ingenious devise of selling "options" on the competing dogs. Before crowds of enthusiastic spectators, the dogs followed a realistic mechanical rabbit around a quarter-mile track. In 1939 the State Attorney General ordered all dog tracks closed.

TANFORAN RACE TRACK, destroyed by fire, July 30, 1964, was built in the 1880's. It attracted San Francisco horse-racing enthusiasts until the Legislature in 1912 made betting on races illegal. When the pari-mutuel system was legalized in 1933 the track reopened. In 1913 the first flying in California was done here by Jean Poulhan. Crowds gasped in wonder at seeing him go several hundred feet aloft in his little plane.

South of Tanforan the highway is bordered by tall eucalyptus trees set out in the seventies and eighties by large landowners. They once extended in an almost unbroken line from here 20 miles south to Palo Alto.

SAN BRUNO, 14.1 *m.* (20 alt., 36,254 pop. 1970, up from 29,063, 1960), a residential city, borders in part on the San Francisco International Airport. A small settlement was here before the American occupation, on part of the Sanchez family's Buri Buri Rancho, which extended some nine miles along the Bay shore and between two and three miles into the hills.

When California passed into American hands the members of the Sanchez family were among the few to make a heoric last stand. With a little band of compatriots they captured and held prisoners for several weeks Yerba Buena's alcalde, Washington Bartlett, and several other Americans. Uncle Tom's Cabin, a restaurant formerly known as the Fourteen Mile House, was located at the southern outskirts of San Bruno. Its barroom occupied one of the earliest hostelries on the Mission Road, a small cabin erected in 1849.

Left from San Bruno on a paved road 0.8 *m.* to the junction with US 101 Bypass; R. (south) here 0.6 *m.* to the SAN FRANCISCO INTERNATIONAL AIRPORT, one of the largest air terminals in the West, providing intrastate, interstate, and global air service. Its construction was begun on 1,376 acres purchased from the Mills estate in 1927, later expanded to 3,722 acres.

The main side route continues north on US 101 Bypass to SOUTH SAN FRANCISCO, 2.8 *m.* (11 alt., 46,646 pop. 1970; 39,418, 1960, up 18%), at the southern base of San Bruno Mountain. The site of "South City" occupies part of the home ranch of Miller & Lux. Stockmen and meatpackers, among them Henry C. Crocker, P. D. Armour, G. P. Swift, and Henry Miller, invested here in 1889; later came steel mills, foundries, and manufacturing plants. The town has an attractive residential section with a view of the Bay.

MILLBRAE, 15.9 *m.* (8 alt., 20,781 pop. 1970; 15,873, 1960, up 30%), was until 1849 part of the Buri Buri Rancho. In that year Darius Ogden Mills, a Sacramento merchant and banker, acquired about 1,500 acres from Jose de la Cruz Sanchez, descendant of the original grantee, for $10,000. He built a three-story, 42-room, mansion which was a landmark until destroyed by fire June 23, 1954. During World War II the mansion served as the United Seaman's Service Rest Home. With the great increase in the demand for suburban homes after 1906, most of the large estates have gradually been subdivided.

BURLINGAME, 17 *m.* (30 alt., 27,320 pop. 1970; 24,036, 1960, up 13%), extending from the Bay shore to Buri Buri Ridge, is almost entirely a suburban residential community. The well-kept residential streets, the modern homes with trim lawns and gardens, a library and fine school buildings reflect a prosperous middle class. The town includes the northern part of Rancho San Mateo, granted to Cayento Arenas by Governor Pio Pico. In 1846 the land was sold for $25,000 to W. D. M. Howard. Emulating the Spanish predecessors, Howard built up a hide and tallow business, but unlike them, he grew wealthy with the growth of San Francisco. Burlingame's moderate climate and oak-covered hills early attracted a number of prosperous San Franciscans looking for country home sites, notably A. L. Easton, who in 1860 acquired property and settled in what is now North Burlingame. Easton and Howard were not the first to recognize the natural beauty of the land. Captain George Vancouver on his visit in 1792 had observed that ". . . it could only be compared to a park, which had been originally planted with the true old English oak . . . The soil was covered with luxuriant herbage and beautifullly diversified with pleasing eminences and valley; which with the range of lofty rugged mountains that bounded the prospect, required only to be adorned with the neat habitations of an industrious people . . ."

The community bears the name of Anson Burlingame. Son of a humble Methodist lay preacher, Burlingame had risen rapidly to become a Congressman from Massachusetts, and in 1861 Lincoln appointed him minister to China. His Burlingame Treaty made him an international figure, and his unfortunate plan for importation of coolie labor won him considerable prestige in California. In 1866, while enroute to China, he purchased 1,043 acres of land adjoining the Easton property. Though Burlingame died four years later, and had visited the place only once, when Burlingame Country Club was organized in 1893 it was named for him, as was the Burlingame Post Office a year later. "Blingum" was for years synonymous with wealth and fashion; but after the division of the Easton property in 1905, the population increased and the town took on its present suburban characteristics.

The SOUTHERN PACIFIC RAILWAY STATION, Burlingame Ave. and California Dr., in California mission style, is roofed with the old hand-made tiles from the mission hospice used by the Franciscans and early travelers as a stopping place halfway between Mission Dolores and Santa Clara.

Standing near a wide driveway, with a magnificent view of open country, semi-forested, rolling hills, and the distant Bay, is the MERCY HIGH SCHOOL, Adeline Dr. When it was the home of C. Frederick Kohl it was known as The Oaks. In Tudor style, it is of dark red brick trimmed with brown stone (Howard and White, architects). *Little Lord Fauntleroy,* starring Mary Pickford, was filmed here.

Between 18.4 *m.* and 18.6 *m.,* El Camino Real is the eastern boundary of HILLSBOROUGH (40-700 alt., 8,753 pop. 1970; 7,554, 1960, up 15%), which occupies an irregular, wedge-shaped area between Burlingame and San Mateo. It was separately incorporated in 1910 to keep out all business establishments. The town has no sidewalks; its homes, most of them set in grounds a half-acre or more in extent, are surrounded by high hedges. Along the winding roads are fine old shade trees.

The BURLINGAME COUNTRY CLUB (*private*), Floribunda Ave. in northern Hillsborough, was organized in 1893, the first country club in California and one of the first places in the United States where polo was played. Golf, too, was popular here at a time when but few Americans played the game.

The informal Italian gardens of NEW PLACE (*private*), Stonehedge Rd., residence of the late W. H. Crocker, were laid out by Bruce Porter; the Italian villa was designed by Lewis P. Hobart. Crocker amassed an art collection including notable paintings by Monet, Millet and Rousseau; some fine work by the Venetians: Bellini, Canaletto, and Guardi; and exquisite bronzes.

SAN MATEO, 19.8 *m.* (22 alt., 78,991 pop. 1970; 69,870, 1960; up 18%), is another example of an area devoted to country estates that has become a bustling city in its own right. In 1863, when the San Francisco-San Jose railroad was completed, streets were laid out east of the highway, but settlement was slow and by 1890 it had only about 1,000.

Here on the banks of San Mateo Creek, where it emerges from a brushy canyon into the oak-covered plain, the Franciscan fathers built of adobe a small chapel and a hospice, for many years the only accommodation for the traveler between Santa Clara and Mission Dolores. As a part of Rancho San Mateo, the land became the property of W. D. M. Howard, who after the earthquake of 1868 saved the roofing tiles of the adobes later used for the Burlingame railway station. Two pioneer merchants and bankers of San Francisco, Frederick Macondray and John Parrott, built country homes here in the 1850's.

Set back of trees and lawns are ST. MATTHEW'S EPISCOPAL CHURCH and BAYLARD HOUSE, El Camino Real and Baldurn Ave. The setting of the buildings resembles that of an English village church. In the church is the tomb of the Howard family.

The new SAN MATEO CITY HALL is built upon the property formerly the home of the San Mateo-Burlingame Polo Club. At one time the club had two seasons of polo, spring, March and April, and fall, August to Christmas.

The BAY MEADOWS RACETRACK (*general adm. $2.50*), on San Mateo's southern outskirts, has spring and fall meets. The plant, built in 1934 by a syndicate headed by one-time newsboy, William P. Kyne, accommodates about 25,000 spectators.

Left from San Mateo on East Third Avenue 3.7 *m.* to the SAN MATEO-HAYWARD Toll Bridge (Toll 35¢). Beyond the eastern end of the bridge is a junction with State 17 at Mount Eden, 13.6 *m.* (*see East Bay Tour 2*).

Right from San Mateo on West Third Avenue, which becomes Crystal Springs Road, to a junction with Sawyer Camp Road, 2.8 *m.*; R. here to a junction with State 35 (Skyline Boulevard), 3.7 *m.*, on which the route goes L. over

SKYLINE DAM, built across the deep canyon of San Mateo Creek to impound the water of CRYSTAL SPRINGS LAKE, a reservoir for San Francisco's water supply. The lake extends south for five miles, its lower end covering the site of the house of Domingo Feliz, grantee of the Rancho Feliz. Beneath the water is the site of Crystal Springs, around which grew the vineyards of Colonel Agaston Haraszthy, Hungarian nobleman, who had set out six varieties of wine grapes here by 1852.

At 5.3 *m.* is the junction with a paved road; L. here to the junction with Cañada Road, 1.2 *m.;* R. here to the WATER TEMPLE, 3.6 *m.,* a circular structure inscribed: "I give waters in the wilderness and rivers in the desert to my people." This is the west end of the Hetch Hetchy pipe line. Cañada Road continues south through oak-covered hills to Woodside, 9.3 *m.* (*see below*).

The main side route goes R. on State 35 onto an earthen causeway across Crystal Springs Lake and climbs wooded slopes to the crest of Cahil Ridge at the junction with the Half Moon Bay Road, 8.3 *m.,* where the main side route goes R. (straight ahead); L. here on State 35 over thickly forested hills to the junction with Kings Mountain Road, 7 *m.* (*see below*).

The main side route continues west from the junction with State 35 on the Half Moon Bay Road, twisting down Pilarcitos Creek Canyon to HALF MOON BAY, 13.6 *m.* (10 alt. 4,023 pop.), a town at the junction with State 1, center of the artichoke-growing Pilarcitos Valley. The original settlement, known as Spanish-town, grew around the adobes of Candelario Miramontes and Tiburcio Vasquez, grantees, respectively, of the local Rancho Miranmontes and Rancho Corral de Tierra (enclosure of earth). Half Moon Bay was known during Prohibition for its conflicts between rum-runners and Coast Guard. A submerged reef extending south for two miles from nearby Pillar Point forms a breakwater for the harbor and protects the arc-shaped white sandy beach.

The nation's commercial production of globe artichokes is confined largely to the coastal strip between Half Moon Bay and Monterey Bay, where the cool foggy summers and mild wet winters make growing conditions ideal. Though widely used in France and Italy, artichokes are not a staple article of food in the United States outside California. They are on the San Francisco market almost all seasons, but the greater part of the crop is cut from January to April. Canning (first done in 1917) provides an outlet for the less marketable small-sized artichokes, the canned product consisting only of hearts.

South of Half Moon Bay the route skirts the coast on State 1 to PURISIMA (immaculate), 18.1 *m.* (46 alt.), a bleak and decaying old town on a hill above Purisima Creek, which served as the northern boundary of Rancho Cañada de Verde y Arroyo de la Purisima (valley of verdure and creek of the immaculate one), granted to Jose Maria Alviso in 1838.

Once a lumbering town, SAN GREGORIO, 26 *m.* (100 alt.), lies beside San Gregorio Creek, which drains the vast acreage of the former Rancho San Gregorio, granted to Antonio Buelna. Reaching here on October 24, 1769, Portola camped two days to rest his men, all of them weary and many ill of scurvy. The frame SAN GREGORIO HOUSE, painted a rusty red and half-hidden by tall maples, was once a popular resort.

PESCADERO (fishmonger), 33.4 *m.* (56 alt.), standing in the flat valley about three miles from the ocean, is within the boundaries of Rancho El Pesca-dero, granted in 1833 to soldier Juan Jose Gonzales, whose adobe stood on the north bank of Pescadero Creek. Father Crespi, the historian of Portola's party, proposed the founding of a mission near the beach, where an Indian village stood. Pescadero was known as Spotless Town for many years after the ship *Colombia* ran ashore here and was battered to pieces, for the residents—nearly all of whom were New Englanders—salvaged the cargo of white lead and painted their houses gleaming white.

At Pescadero is the junction with Blooms Mill Creek Road (*see below*).

At LAKE LUCERNE, 38.6 *m.*, sometimes known as Bean Hollow Lagoon, a salt-water lake lying at the mouth of the Arroyo de los Frijoles (Bean Hollow), is the junction with Pebble Beach Road; R. here along the shoreline past Pescadero Point, 2.6 *m.*, to mile-long PEBBLE BEACH (*surf fishing*). The deposit of pebbles here includes agates and chalcedony, from amygdaloid rocks, made popular by San Francisco jewelers in the eighties. Here stand the ruins of COBURN'S FOLLY, the large three-story hotel erected by Loren Coburn in 1892. He spent money lavishly, expecting to have a popular and profitable resort upon the arrival of the proposed Ocean Shore Railroad from San Francisco. The railroad's failure to build this far south left Coburn possessor of a vacant and useless building. He closed the road to the beach, thus bringing on a long series of quarrels with the citizens of nearby Pescadero (*see above*). Barriers which he built across the road were destroyed again and again. Lawsuits followed, and Coburn, who was eventually awarded damages against his fellow citizens for $1,000, became a hated and ostracised old man.

PIGEON POINT, 41.3 *m.*, was named for the clipper ship (*Carrier Pigeon*), wrecked here May 6, 1853. A Portuguese whaling station once was here, and from the pier, lumber and dairy products were shipped. The high cliff is topped by the white conical tower of PIGEON POINT LIGHTHOUSE, 148 feet above water level, built in 1872. Its 900,000-candlepower beam is visible for eighteen miles.

Whitehouse Creek, 10.3 *m.*, is named for ISAAC GRAHAM'S HOUSE (*private*), a lone white, two-story frame dwelling brought around the Horn, for many years a landmark for mariners but now almost hidden by a grove of eucalyptus trees. FRANKLIN POINT, a mile west, commemorates a sea disaster in 1865 when eleven were lost in the wreck of the *Sir John Franklin*.

LA PUNTA DEL AÑO NUEVO (New Year's Point), 49 *m.*, sighted and named by Sebastian Vizcaino on January 3, 1603, is crowned by the white tower of NEW YEAR'S POINT LIGHTHOUSE. Along the shore here the shifting sand frequently reveals evidence of former Indian occupation in the form of arrowheads, skeletons, and shells. The vast and fertile Rancho Punta del Año Nuevo once covered 17,753 acres north from the point. From grantee Simeon Castro the rancho passed into the hands of Loren Coburn, who leased the land to dairy farmers (*see above*).

South of San Mateo the highway climbs the lower slopes of rounded, oak-covered hills—once on Rancho Las Pulgas—which hem in the little valley originally called Cañada del Diablo.

BELMONT, 24.2 *m.* (32 alt., 23,667 pop. 1970; 15,996, 1960, up 48%), is a town of suburban residences, schools and sanitariums. In the early 1850's, when it was for a short time the county seat, a hotel here was a stopping place for stages.

The former rambling white mansion of William C. Ralston is now one of the buildnigs of NOTRE DAME COLLEGE, Ralston Ave. In 1854 Count Leonetto Cipriani, an Italian political refugee, acquired the site, Cañada del Diablo (Devil's Valley), and built a small villa, which in 1866 he sold to Ralston. The financier began transforming it into an extravagant show place, adorned with parquetry floors, mirror-panelled walls, and chandeliers. He built greenhouses, a gymnasium with a Turkish bath, stables panelled in carved mahogany, a gas-works to provide gas for illumination and a dam and reservoir to provide water. After Ralston's death in 1875 the big house was successively a private school and a hospital. In 1923 it was occupied by the Sisters of Notre Dame, who removed their convent and college here from San Jose. The mansion is now called Berchman's Hall, honoring one of the founding sisters. Ralston's famous ballroom is the school chapel.

US 101 continues south through country largely devoted to flower growing. Chrysanthemums are the most important crop. The growers are usually Chinese or Italians. From here each year on All Saints' Day, New Orleans gets thousands of white chrysanthemums for its graves.

SAN CARLOS, 25.1 m. (21 alt., 25,924 pop. 1970; 21,390, 1960, up 21%), occupies a site within the former boundaries of Rancho Las Pulgas (the fleas), which got its unhappy name from the innumerable fleas infesting the Indian village that stood here. Today it is a pleasant residential town without any remains of the past either in the form of insects or old buildings.

REDWOOD CITY, 27.1 m. (10 alt., 55,686 pop. 1970; 46,290, 1960, inc. 20.3%), seat of San Mateo County, was known in Spanish-American days as the Embarcadero because of the slough which was navigable up to what is now the center of the business district. Other names given it were Cachinetac and Mezesville, for S. M. Mezes, who laid out the town in 1854. Shortly after the Gold Rush the fine stands of redwoods nearby attracted lumbermen, who shipped the timber down Redwood Slough. A number of schooners built here carried lumber, hay, and grain to San Francisco. The town has grown rapidly since 1920, but many old frame houses of the fifties and sixties are still standing. A cement works and two tanneries are the largest industrial plants.

Facing Broadway at Hamilton St. is the SAN MATEO COUNTY COURTHOUSE, a resolutely modern building built in 1939, which stood forth in incongruous contrast to the former courthouse, an old domed building of Colusa sandstone. The PUBLIC LIBRARY and CITY HALL, Jefferson Ave. and Middlefield Rd., are a well-proportioned group of buildings employing concrete with red-tiled roofs in a severe modern style.

The two-story, square, stuccoed MORGAN HOUSE was moved to Chestnut and Spring Sts. from the tidal lands of the Bay, where it had served as a residence, anchored on piles, for Captain John Stillwell Morgan, promoter of oyster culture in San Francisco Bay.

1. Left from Redwood City on a paved road 3.1 m. to the PORT OF RED-WOOD CITY, completed in 1937. The channel has been dredged to accommodate ocean-going vessels. Large shipments are made of fresh and canned fruit and vegetables. Lumber, once the chief export, is now the chief import.
The PACIFIC PORTLAND CEMENT PLANT, 3.2 m., utilizes the oyster shells that bed the bottom of the shallow mud flats; dredged from the Bay, pulverized, and calcined, they are converted into lime.
2. Right from Redwood City on Jefferson Ave. 2.1 m. to EMERALD LAKE AND BOWL, in a nine-acre park. A natural bowl seats 12,000 at Christmas and Easter celebrations.

3. Right from the southern end of Redwood City at Five Points on paved Woodside Road is WOODSIDE, 3.9 *m.* (486 alt., 4,731 pop. 1970; 3,592, 1960; up 31%), at the southern end of San Raymundo Valley, first settled in the 1830's by William (Bill the Sawyer) Smith and his partner James Pease, deserter from a British ship, who made carts and farming implements for the *padres* at Santa Clara. Woodside now represents the combined old settlements of Greersburg and Whiskey Hill, where flourished three saloons.

Left from Woodside on Portola Road, past large country houses set well back of hedges and gardens, to the junction with a paved road, 2.1 *m.;* R. here 0.2 *m.* to the junction with a dirt road; R. here to the HOOPER ADOBE (*private*), 0.3 *m.,* built by Charles Brown, an American who deserted a whaling vessel in 1833, acquired part of Rancho Cañada de Raymundo, and settled here. Later Colonel "Jack" Hays used the building as a lodging house for lumbermen. Other owners have been E. W. Burr and John A. Hooper, president of the San Francisco National Bank. Two tall eucalyptus trees and a trim hedge frame the one-story house with its tiled roof extending over the veranda. An enormous Banksia rosebush climbs to the ridge of the roof.

On Portola Road at 2.3 *m.* is SEARSVILLE LAKE (*swimming, boating*). Near here in the fifties was Searsville, with 2,000 inhabitants, a busy center for redwood lumbering and convenient stopping place for mule- and ox-team drivers crossing the ridge. Only reminder of its lusty days are the rows of trees which shaded its main street. In 1890, when the supply of timber was exhausted, the Spring Valley Water Company removed the buildings and built a dam which forms the present lake. It is now a reservoir whose waters irrigate the greenery of the Stanford University campus (*see below*).

The main side route goes west from Woodside on La Honda Road.

At the junction with Kings Mountain Road, 4.7 *m.,* under a large oak, is the JOHN COPPINGER STOREHOUSE, now used as a residence, built in 1854 of hand-hewn timbers by Coppinger, grantee of 12,545-acre Rancho Cañada de Raymundo. The two curious dormer windows of its upper story are slightly awry. Coppinger, who married Maria Luisa Soto, member of an influential Spanish family, built an adobe house here in 1840 which stood until destroyed by the 1906 earthquake.

The route turns R. on Kings Mountain Road to the WOODSIDE STORE, 5.2 *m.,* a two-story shingled structure shaded by a large live oak. Built in 1854 by R. O. Tripp, a dentist, the store (now a library) was the trading center for fifteen sawmills. More than a thousand lumberjacks got their mail, food, and liquor here. Hand-hewn, octagonal posts support the porch roof; the joists also are hand-hewn. "Old Doc" Tripp at ninety-three still presided behind his counter.

At 5.8 *m.* Kings Mountain Road enters wooded HUDDART PARK, a 973-acre undeveloped recreational area bequeathed to San Francisco by James M. Huddart in 1931. The sharply winding road climbs into the wooded canyon to a junction with State 35 (Skyline Boulevard), 9.2 *m.* (*see above*), at the summit of Cahil Ridge, also known as Kings Mountain for a Mrs. Honoria King who formerly kept a tavern accommodating travelers by stage over the toll road from Woodside. The route goes L. on State 35.

At 11 *m.* is OBSERVATION POINT, a stone-buttressed parking lot area offering a superb view of the Peninsula towns, San Francisco Bay, and the East Bay shore. Mount Tamalpais, Mount Hamilton, and Mount Diablo are clearly visible.

Near the summit of Sierra Morena (2,400 alt.) at 11.6 *m.* is the SKYLINE METHUSELAH REDWOOD (L), an ancient lone redwood with storm-shattered top, fifty-five feet in circumference.

State 35 drops by well-engineered grades to a junction, at 14.2 *m.,* with La Honda Road, on which the route goes R.; L. here on State 35 to Saratoga Gap, at the junction with State 9, 13.9 *m.* (*see below*).

The route goes R. on La Honda Road through dense firs and redwoods into the deep canyon of La Honda Creek. LA HONDA (the deep), 20 *m.* (403 alt.) (*hotel, cabins, campgrounds*), was founded in 1861 by John L. Sears of Searsville.

The LA HONDA STORE was built for Sears by Jim and Bob Younger, who a littler later were arrested as members of the Jesse James gang.

At LA HONDA PARK (*campgrounds, swimming*), 20.5 *m.*, a summer resort, is a junction with a paved road; the route turns L. here on Alpine Creek Road into a densely wooded canyon to the junction with Blooms Mill Road, 22 *m.*; R. on Blooms Mill Road to SAN MATEO COUNTY MEMORIAL PARK (*camping $1; special weekly rates*), 26.5 *m.*, a 310-acre grove of redwoods dedicated to the memory of San Mateo County men who died in war.

Blooms Mill Road winds down Pescadero Creek to PESCADERO, 34.5 *m.* (56 alt.), at the junction with State 1 (*see above*).

South of Redwood City the Bay narrows and the level land between the highway and the mountains widens. The country originally had great natural beauty, but the section facing the highway has been so defaced by real estate offices, sandwich stands, and billboards that Bay region drivers have petulantly echoed Ogden Nash's couplet:

"I think that I shall never see a billboard lovely as a tree;
Perhaps, unless the billboard fall, I shall not see a tree at all."

ATHERTON, 29.1 *m.* (52 alt., 8,085 pop. 1970; 7,717, 1960; up 4%), bears the name of Faxon D. Atherton, a pioneer settler, whose daughter-in-law, Gertrude Atherton, in her autobiography, *Adventures of a Novelist,* recounts much interesting gossip of fashionable life here in the 1880's. Atherton has remained a residential community, its roads winding in and out among tree-lined estates. The MENLO CIRCUS CLUB, Isabella Ave., occupies part of the site of Valparaiso Park, the estate of Faxon Atherton. At the club's annual (August) horse show fine horses from many parts of the country compete for prizes.

MENLO PARK, 30.1 *m.* (63 alt., 26,734 pop. 1970; 26,957, 1960), was named in 1851 for Ireland's Menlo Park by Dennis J. Oliver and D. C. McGlyn, who had purchased 1,700 acres of the Rancho Las Pulgas. The town grew up after the opening of the San Francisco-San Jose railroad in 1863, attracting many people of wealth. More recently families of moderate means have settled here, but except for nurseries and local retail shops Menlo Park has no commercial activities.

1. Left from Menlo Park on Ravenswood Ave. 0.2 *m.* to the PACIFIC COAST MILITARY ACADEMY, occupying a large old-fashioned house surrounded by oak trees. This was formerly the home of Edgar Mills, brother of Darious Ogden Mills.

The square-towered TIMOTHY HOPKINS HOUSE, 0.3 *m.*, stands a quarter-mile south of the road in a grove of fine oaks. In the fifties, this property belonged to E. W. Barron of quicksilver fame. It later passed to Senator Milton S. Latham, but the home built by Barron burned before Latham and his bride could move into it. Latham built the present house, which he named "Sherwood Hall." From him it passed to Mary Hopkins, widow of Mark Hopkins, and from her to Timothy Hopkins, one of the original trustees of Stanford University.

At 0.6 *m.* is a junction with Middlefield Road; the route goes R. here.

In 1898 ST. PATRICK'S SEMINARY, 0.9 *m.*, an institution of collegiate rank, was founded by the late Archbishop Thomas Riordan to train men for the Roman Catholic priesthood. The instructors are members of the Order of

St. Sulpice; resident seminarians number more than one hundred. The buildings stand well back from the road in a setting of green lawns, great oaks, palms and rose gardens.

At 1.3 *m.* is the junction with Willow Road; L. on Willow Road.

The VETERANS' ADMINISTRATION HOSPITAL, 2.1 *m.*, is a diagnostic center with 900 patients. The buildings stand on attractive wooded grounds.

On Willow Road at 2.4 *m.* is the junction with US 101 Bypass; straight ahead on Willow Rd. to DUMBARTON BRIDGE (*35¢ per car*), 4.7 *m.*

Visible south of Dumbarton Bridge is the BAY CROSSING OF THE HETCH-HETCHY AQUEDUCTS. Underneath the navigable channel on the east side of the Bay, the steel cylinder and reinforced concrete pipes are entrenched twenty-five feet down in the mud, seventy feet beneath the surface of the water. On the shallower western side of the Bay, the submerged pipes enter a concrete caisson and from there are carried to the San Mateo County shore over a steel bridge resting on concrete piers (*see Emporium of a New World: Engineering Enterprise*).

At 13.4 *m.* is the junction with State 17 (*see East Bay Tour 2*).

2. Right from Menlo Park on Cambridge Avenue 0.7 *m.* to the ALLIED ARTS GUILD (*open weekdays 9-5:30*), an institution organized in 1930 to help finance the Stanford Convalescent Home for Children in Palo Alto. The guild maintains a tea room and a group of studios which display weaving, ceramics, metal- and wood-craft, and block printing. These are housed in a group of buildings admirably designed in seventeenth-century Spanish Colonial style by Gardiner Bailey on land owned originally by John and Margaret Murray, who came here in 1854. The estate's great charm is enhanced by the beautifully appropriate landscaping of the gardens.

Where US 101 crosses San Francisquito Creek, 31.3 *m.*, appears a few hundred feet west, near its bank, the solitary redwood, PALO ALTO (tall tree), a landmark for explorers and travelers since the Gaspar de Portola expedition first saw it in 1769. It was not a tree of remarkable height among redwoods, but standing far removed from any others, it towered above its neighboring oaks, visible for many leagues. It appears in early prints and on the seal of Stanford University as a double-trunked tree; one section has fallen.

US 101 divides Stanford University from the city of PALO ALTO, 31.9 *m.* (63 alt., 55,966 pop. 1970; 52,287, 1960, up 7%), itself bisected by its chief thoroughfare, University Avenue. When the university came into being in 1891, the greater part of what is now Palo Alto was but a great wheat field dotted with oak trees and a few scattered houses and stores; early students and instructors went to Menlo Park for their mail and food supplies. But by 1894 Palo Alto was large enough to incorporate. Mayfield, now a Palo Alto suburb, once was a separate unregenerate town where Stanford students could drink beer.

There are 1,052 acres in the city limits zoned for light industry, 704 acres comprise the Stanford Industrial Park adjacent to Stanford University where nationally known firms are located in a restricted cultural environment for select electronics, research and development, and publishing operations.

Examples of an intelligent adaption of the Spanish Colonial style to modern use are the POST OFFICE, Waverly St. and Hamilton Ave.; and the PALO ALTO HIGH SCHOOL, El Camino Real and Embarcadero Rd.

Palo Alto's attractive COMMUNITY CENTER and MITCH-ELL PARK have diversified recreational activities for everyone. The Community Center's Spanish buildings are set amid flower gardens and broad lawns. The children have their own theater and Junior Museum with craft workshops, science exhibits and laboratories. Adjacent to the Community Center are the new CITY HALL and MAIN LIBRARY. A municipal golf course is located on Embarcadero Road near the Palo Alto Municipal Airport and the Yacht Harbor.

The junction of US 101 with University Avenue and Palm Drive marks the entrance (R) to the campus of STANFORD UNIVER-SITY, founded by Senator and Mrs. Leland Stanford as a memorial to their only child, Leland Stanford, Jr., who died at the age of sixteen. The cornerstone of the first building was laid in 1887; the university was opened in the autumn of 1891. Stanford began not only with a great endowment and a fine group of buildings, but with distinguished faculty members, including Vernon L. Kellogg, Theodore Hoover, Henry R. Fairclough, Robert Eckles Swain, Melville Best Anderson, and Lewis M. Terman. Among its early alumni are Charles K. "Cheerio" Field, Whitelaw Reed, Dane Coolidge, Herbert Hoover, H. L. Davis, Will and Wallace Irwin, Holbrook Blinn, Homer Lea, and Ray Lyman Wilbur. It always has been coeducational. Until 1933 women students were limited to 500; afterward, to approximately 40 percent of the total enrollment. By 1970 it enrolled 11,193 students and had a faculty of 1,283.

The heavy sandstone piers flanking the entrance have taken the place of the low Romanesque towers, pierced by heavy round-headed arches with open pier arcades on each side, which were destroyed in the 1906 earthquake. The great memorial arch, beyond which rose the fine central tower of the Memorial Church—both pivotal features of the unified architectual scheme—also was destroyed.

Right from US 101 on Palm Drive, bordered by shrubs and trees from many parts of the world in a 600-acre arboretum, 0.1 *m.* to the junction with a paved road; R. here to STANFORD MEDICAL CENTER (1959). It comprises the School of Medicine and Stanford University Hospital (436 beds). Included in the School are research laboratories, outpatient clinics, and the Lane Library of medical books. Part of the Hospital is the Herbert Hoover Pavilion, off Palm Dr. near El Camino Real. *Tours daily, 3 p.m.*

On Palm Drive at 0.6 *m.* is the junction with Campus Drive.

Right here 0.1 *m.* to the STANFORD MAUSOLEUM, built of white granite in the form of a Greek temple. The entrance is flanked by marble sphinxes; polished Ionic columns support the architrave. Nearby (R) is the TOMB OF HENRY J. LATHROP, Mrs. Stanford's brother, surmounted by a white marble figure called the *Angel of Grief*. The route follows a winding drive (L) from the mausoleum, past the CACTUS GARDEN, which contains a great variety of desert plants.

Left on Campus Drive 0.3 *m.* to the junction with Galvez Street; L. here past the campus tennis courts, football and baseball fields, and track oval 0.3 *m.* to the STADIUM, seating 89,000, where the Stanford-California football game —northern California's "Big Game"—takes place on alternate years.

Campus Drive continues past ENCINA GYMNASIUM, men's athletic center, to the junction with Galvez, 0.4 *m.;* R. here past ENCINA HALL, TOYON HALL and BRANNER HALL, both in simple Spanish Colonial style. Encina Hall, formerly a dormitory, contains many administrative offices.

The main side route follows Palm Drive south from its junction with Campus Drive to the junction with a paved road, 0.7 *m.;* R. here 0.1 *m.* to the LELAND STANFORD JUNIOR MUSEUM (*open daily 1-5 p.m.*), a large neoclassic structure built of yellow sandstone. At the entrance doors are four tall Ionic columns; on each side the facade is ornamented with large mosaics. Nucleus of the museum is the collection made by Leland Stanford, Jr., between 1880 and 1884, including Egyptian bronzes, Tanagra figurines, Greek and Roman glass, armor, mosaics, Sèvres and Dresden ware. In Stanford Memorial Room are collections of personal belongings of the founders of the University, views of its buildings in construction, and details of the mosaics used in the Memorial Church. Another room contains the "Governor Stanford," the first locomotive used on the Central Pacific Railroad (1863), and cases of items related to early California history—among them practically all the implements extant of San Francisco's Mission Dolores.

Also housed in the museum are the Di Cesnola collection of Greek and Roman pottery and glass from the island of Cyprus; Indian mound relics and artifacts; rare art materials from the Orient (the Ikeda Chinese and Japanese Collection); and Chinese and Japanese *objets d'art,* including the well-known De Long Collection of Japanese rarities. Among the rare objects in the Egyptian Room is a collection of Babylonian tablets. *Open Monday-Friday, 10-5, Sat.-Sun. 1-5.*

Palm Drive continues south to the junction with a paved road; L. here 0.1 *m.* to the LAURENCE FROST AMPHITHEATRE, a sunken oval seating 8,000, presented by Mr. and Mrs. Howard Frost as a memorial to their son. The approach is through a tree-lined walk. The tiers of seats are placed along terraces of turf, closely cut and beautifully green. Commencement exercises are held here.

Adjoining on the south is the center of Stanford's dramatic activities, MEMORIAL HALL, completed in 1937 at a cost of $600,000. The main theater seats 1,700; the rehearsal theater, 197.

Around a large oval planted to lawn and shrubs, dividing Palm Drive into two roadways, the route curves to the junction with Serra Street, 0.9 *m.,* at the foot of Palm Drive, beyond which extends the Outer Quadrangle (*see below*); R. on Serra Street 0.2 *m.* to SEQUOIA HALL, oldest of the men's dormitories.

Heart of the campus is the group of buildings known as the OUTER QUADRANGLE (length 894 feet, width 760 feet). A passage leads to the INNER QUADRANGLE, formed by twelve one-story buildings and the Memorial Church all connected by a continuous arcade. The red tile roof, the open arches, the long colonnades resembling cloister walks are reminiscent of the California missions, but the work in its essential features is Romanesque, the architect—Charles Allerton Coolidge of Boston—having been a disciple of Richardson. The buff sandstone of rough-faced ashlar used in these, the first buildings to be erected, came from a quarry twelve miles south of San Jose. Both architecturally and academically the two quads are the heart of the university.

The STANFORD MEMORIAL CHURCH (*open daily; services Sun. 11 and 4, also 7:30 p.m. during summer quarter; organ recitals precede services*), faces the cloistered inner quadrangle from the south. Set in the pavement before the entrance are a series of brass tablets, a new one being added for each graduating class. Built by Mrs. Leland Stanford as a memorial to her husband, the church was almost completely ruined by the 1906 earthquake. Rebuilt without its former central tower, the present structure is less graceful than the original. The mosaics of the facade, like those destroyed, were made in Venice; they follow largely the original design. In the spandrils above the triple doorways with their Romanesque piers and carved arches, the mosaics represent figures symbolic of the theological virtues. A large round-headed window fills the central space above the doorways; at each side are three smaller windows. The space above and between this fenestration up to the apex of the roof is filled with a huge mosaic, *The Sermon on the Mount,* against a background of gold.

The mosaic decoration in the vestibule consists of colored medallions in the form of the Chi Rho and the Alpha and Omega against a gold background. The same buff sandstone used for the exterior has been used for the interior walls and piers. The interior is a nave of four bays with narrow aisles, each with a single large round-headed window. The clerestory has two small windows to each bay. The transepts have apsidal endings and balconies, each with a semicircular carved balustrade supported by heavy Romanesque piers. From the crossing, with its four massive arches, seven white marble steps rise the entire width to a shallow choir. The sanctuary rail is of marble. The apse is semicircular with fourteen small recessed arches faced with gold mosaic and three large windows in the upper story. Above the marble altar is a reproduction in mosaic of Cosimo Rosselli's *The Last Supper*. The mosaics which cover the upper walls of the entire interior depict Biblical scenes and individual figures of prophets, patriarchs, and saints. The work lost in the earthquake was replaced from the studios of Antonio Salvati in Venice, where the original designs had fortunately been preserved.

The route goes L. on Serra Street from the foot of Palm Drive to the junction with Lasuen Street, 1 *m.*, and R. on Lasuen Street.

The Romanesque THOMAS WELTON STANFORD ART GALLERY (L), built in 1917, gift of a brother of Senator Stanford, has a small permanent collection of the work of nineteenth-century American artists. Like the buildings adjoining on the south (*see below*), it is a unit in a projected new guadrangle, one of two planned to flank the present Outer Quadrangle (*see above*), on the east and west.

The facade of the LIBRARY (L), 1.1 *m.*, built in 1919, is adorned with stone figures carved by Edgar Walter. Its volumes include the Hopkins Railway Library presented by Timothy Hopkins in 1892, the 5,000-volume Hilderbrand Library of Germanic philology and literature, the Jarboe collection of literature of the French Revolution and Napoleonic era, the Thomas Welton Stanford Australasian Library of early travels and voyages, and the Flugel collection including works of writers of the 15th, 16th, and 17th centuries.

Surmounted by a fourteen-floor, 280-foot tower, the adjoining HOOVER LIBRARY FOR WAR, PEACE, AND REVOLUTION, a concrete and steel structure built in 1940 (Bakewell, Weihe, and Brown, architects), houses Herbert Hoover's collection of 150,000 printed and manuscript items dealing with the first World War and its aftermath, including collections on communism, facism, Nazi and socialist revolutions. Atop the Tower is a carillon of 35 bells donated by the Belgian-American Educational Foundation. Adjoining is the LOU HENRY HOOVER BUILDING, opened in 1967 to provide more space for the collections. *Mon.-Sat. 8-5, Sun. 12-5.*

WHITE MEMORIAL PLAZA has a 16-ft. fountain by Aristides Demetrios of San Francisco. At the end of the Plaza is the TRESIDDER MEMORIAL UNION a community center with cafeteria, services, lounging rooms and art exhibition rooms. Facing the Union is the MUSIC BUILDING of the Dept. of Music, which has an auditorium seating 728. The OLD UNION now has offices of the Dean of Students, Registrar and Admissions.

PHYSICS LECTURE HALL (1957) is a circular hall financed by royalties on the Klystron tube, invented by Stanford physicists, one of whom is honored in the RUSSELL H. VARIAN LABORATORY OF PHYSICS. The JACK A. McCULLOUGH BUILDING (1965) is a center for materials research. The WILLIAM F. DURAND BUILDING FOR SPACE ENGINEERING AND SCIENCE and the HIGH ENERGY PHYSICS LABORATORY are also in this area.

The LOU HENRY HOOVER HOUSE, the former campus home of the Hoovers, was given to the university by Hoover and is now the residence of the university's president.

At the STANFORD STABLES Leland Stanford established his stock farm in 1876. On the base of a monument to a famous trotter are inscribed a list of names and records of Stanford's best horses. A tablet commemorates the pre-Edison motion picture experiment conducted here in 1878 in connection with horse racing. By means of a battery of cameras fitted with electric shutters, men and animals were portrayed in motion.

STANFORD UNIVERSITY

AND VICINITY

SCALE IN FEET

0   500   1000   2000   3000

At 33.2 *m.* on US 101 is the junction with Stanford Avenue.

Right on Stanford Avenue 0.5 *m.* to the PETER COUTTS COTTAGE (L), standing beside a plain two-story brick library and office building. Both structures were built in the seventies by Paulin Caperon, political fugitive from France who reached America on the passport of Peter Coutts, his cousin. Caperon bought the Matadero Ranch (later purchased by Governor Stanford), and here he developed orchards and vineyards, tunneling the hillside for a water supply. A racetrack for his thoroughbreds was laid out near the present corner of Stanford Avenue and US 101. Caperon and his family returned to Europe in 1880. Young Dr. David Starr Jordan occupied the cottage in 1891.

The STANFORD LINEAR ACCELERATOR CENTER, built under contract with the U.S. Atomic Energy Commission, houses a two-mile accelerator on a 500-acre site near Sand Hill Road. Cost of the Center was $114,000,000. The accelerator extends from the foothills to the university campus and is housed in a concrete box, 10,000 ft. long, 10 by 11 ft. in cross section, placed under 25 ft. of soil to absorb radiation.

South of Palo Alto, US 101 enters the great orchard region of the Santa Clara Valley, where around 87,000 acres are planted to deciduous fruits. Early in the mission period the Franciscans found that both the vine and fruit trees did well in California, but no extensive planting of fruit trees was made until about 1856, when Louis Pellier brought from southwestern France a number of prune scions. To him and to nursery men goes the credit for the beginning of a great industry. By the 1940's

STANFORD UNIVERSITY AND VICINITY

1. Arboretum
2. Palo Alto Hospital
4. Cactus Garden
5. Troutmere Guernsey Farm
6. Leland Stanford Junior Museum
7. Administration Building
8. Jordan Hall
9. Inner Quadrangle
10. Stanford Memorial Church
11. Sequoia Hall
12. U. S. Department of Agriculture Experimental Station
13. Roble Hall
14. Lagunita Court
15. Women's Gymnasium
16. Stanford Union
17. Cubberley Building
18. Library
19. Art Gallery
20. Memorial Hall
21. Laurence Frost Amphitheater
22. Encina Gymnasium
23. Athletic Field
24. Stanford Bowl
25. Encina Hall
26. Toyon Hall
27. Branner Hall
28. Lagunita
29. Gold Course
30. Stanford Stables

there were more than seventy thousand acres in prunes alone. Second in importance of the valley's products is the apricot; about twenty thousand acres have been planted in belts relatively free from frost. The variety most grown is the Moor Park. Pears are planted to more than six thousand acres.

Early American settlers in the valley discovered an artesian zone north and west of San Jose which provided ample water for irrigation. Since 1915 the increased pumping draft and the decrease in average rainfall have lowered the ground water level nearly one hundred feet. Some one hundred thousand acres affected by this gradual depletion today are under irrigation.

At 36.7 *m.* is a junction with San Antonio Ave. Right on San Antonio Avenue is LOS ALTOS, 2.8 *m.* (200 alt., 24,956 pop. 1970; 19,696, 1960, up 26%), a town of fine houses and gardens on land once a part of Rancho San Antonio.

Surrounded by orchards and truck gardens is MOUNTAIN VIEW, 37.7 *m.* (67 alt., 51,092 pop. 1970; 30,889, 1960, inc. 65.4%). Here are canneries, planing mills, and a plant for pre-cooling berries and fruits before shipment to Eastern markets. Mountain View's Pacific Press Publishing Association, one of the largest presses in the West, is operated by the Seventh-Day Adventist Church.

The site of old Mountain View lies nearly a mile south. Before the building of the railroad, a large hotel here was a stopping place for the daily San Francisco-San Jose stage and a meeting place for settlers from scattered grain and stock ranches. A few old-timers remember with regret the fine quail, pigeon, and duck shooting they enjoyed before the land was planted to orchards.

At 38.5 *m.* is a junction with paved Alviso Road.

Left on Alviso Road 2.3 *m.* to the junction with US 101 Bypass. Stretching northeastern are the 1,000 acres of MOFFETT FIELD, a Navy airbase. The great hangar, a landmark for miles around, is 1,133 feet long, 308 feet wide, and its height of 193 feet is that of an eighteen-story building. It was the home of the dirigibles *Akron* and *Macon,* both of which met with tragic accidents. Constructed here in the early 1940's was the $10,000,000 AERONAUTICAL RESEARCH LABORATORY, under the authority of the National Advisory Committee for Aeronautics, to serve as a sister station to one at Langley Field, Virginia, conducting research on unsolved aeronautical problems.

Alviso Road continues east to ALVISO, 7 *m.* (8 alt.), at the head of a navigable slough at the southern end of San Francisco Bay, a small town of treeless streets and weatherbeaten houses. Originally the port for Mission Santa Clara and nearby ranches, it enjoyed a great boom with the Gold Rush. Produce from the valley went from here to San Francisco and up the Sacramento and San Joaquin Rivers in stern-wheelers. Of these old boats the best-known was the *Jenny Lind,* whose energetic captain forced her boilers and caused an explosion that cost 35 lives. With the completion in 1864 of the railroad from San Francisco, Alviso's decline began, though freight continued to be shipped by steamer for some years. Prosperity may return to Alviso if the City of San Jose carries out its plans for the creation of a deep-water port on adjoining land.

Left from Alviso 4 *m.* to a junction with States 17 at Milpitas.

The main side route continues south (R) from Alviso. At 9 *m.* is AGNEW (20 alt.). The fine grounds and buildings of AGNEW STATE HOSPITAL border the highway. The mentally deranged, alcoholics, and women narcotic addicts are treated here. The original buildings, erected when the hospital was established in 1888, were destroyed by the 1906 earthquake.

At 12 *m.* is the junction with US 101 at Santa Clara (*see below*).

SUNNYVALE, 41 *m.* on US 101 (95 alt., 95,408 pop. 1970; 52,-898, 1960, inc. 80.4%), is located in the northwest portion of Santa Clara County. The town site is a part of Rancho Pastoria de la Borregas (the lambs' pasture), which was divided soon after the period of American occupation between Mariano Castro and Martin Murphy, Jr. Sunnyvale's population doubled during World War II when its Joshua Hendy Iron Works gave jobs to a huge labor force building ship engines. Initially the city's development was tied closely to the agriculturally-oriented economy of Santa Clara County; however, in recent years the city's economic base has become increasingly diversified as a broad cross-section of new industrial facilities have located in the city's several planned industrial parks.

Right from Sunnyvale on State 9 is CUPERTINO, 3 *m.* (215 alt., 18,216 pop. 1970; 3,664, 1960, inc. 397.2%) a retail trading center which serves the surrounding orchard and vineyard country.

Right from Cupertino on Stevens Creek Road to a junction with Permanente Road, 1.5 *m.;* R. on Permanente Road to the PERMANENTE CORPORATION CEMENT PLANT, 2 *m.* The plant includes a laboratory building, precipitator, mills, 500,000-barrel storage silos, and the tall stack—all built in 1939. The company contracted (1940) to supply 5,800,000 barrels of low-heat cement for the Central Valley's Shasta Dam project. Its kilns were the largest in the world, 12 feet in diameter and 450 feet long when built. Their capacity was sufficient to give the Permanente plant, at the time of their installation, the rank of the world's largest cement manufacturing plant. An important department is that which manufactures fifty tons per hour of sugar rock (carbonate of lime) for beet-sugar refineries.

The main side route continues south from Cupertino on State 9 to SARATOGA, 7.4 *m.* (500 alt., 27,110 pop. 1970; 14,861, 1960, inc. 82.4%), in the midst of orchards and vineyards on the rolling hills above Campbell Creek. The town was founded by one Martin McCarthy as a convenient starting point for a toll road leading to the fine timber up Campbell Creek. Its early name, McCarthyville, was replaced in 1863 by its present one because, like its New York namesake, it was near several medical springs. Saratoga's later prosperity has come from the surrounding orchards and vineyards. Each spring, when the orchards are at the height of their bloom, the town has its Blossom Festival, a pageant which originated as a service of thanksgiving for the recovery of the orchards from the drought of 1898-99.

1. Left from Saratoga on Saratoga Road to VILLA MONTALVO, 0.5 *m.,* formerly the home of James D. Phelan, at the end of a winding driveway, the entrance gates surmounted by carved griffins. The house of light grey sandstone in the style of an Italian villa is surrounded by broad lawns and formal gardens with rows of tall Italian cypresses leading up to fountains, Etruscan vases, and marble statuary groups. Large Irish yews are a distinctive landscaping feature. A bronze plaque commemorates the fifteenth-century Spanish writer for whom the estate was named, Ordanez de Montalvo, in whose *Las Sergas de Esplandian* (The Exploits of Esplandian), the name "California" first appeared. As a United States Senator, Phelan, who had been mayor of San Francisco, entertained here not only politicians but also writers, painters, and actors. "A Day in the Hills" was an annual event honoring Cali-

fornia authors. Phelan bequeathed the estate to the San Francisco Art Association for use as a center where composers, authors, and painters might live while doing creative work. It was opened as such in the summer of 1939.

Saratoga Road continues to LOS GATOS, 4 *m.* (412 alt., 23,735 pop. 1970; 9,036, 1960, inc. 162.7%), at the junction with State 17 (*see below*).

2. Right from Saratoga on Oak Street, which becomes Bollman Road, 2.8 *m.* to JOHN BROWN'S LODGE, the home from 1881 to her death in 1884 of Mary Brown, the widow of John Brown of Harper's Ferry. It is said that a substantial part of the $1,850 paid by Mrs. Brown for the ranch was donated by the Negro population in and around San Jose.

The main side route goes R. from Saratoga on State 9 up Campbell Creek.

At 8.7 *m.* is the junction with Pierce Road; R. here 0.1 *m.* to the junction with a one-way dirt road; L. here to the PAUL MASSON CHAMPAGNE WINERY (*admission by appointment only*), 1.6 *m.*, a stone structure replacing one destroyed in the 1906 earthquake, where champagne was first produced in California. Coming to California from France in 1852, Charles le Franc found here on the rolling slopes the peculiar combination of soil and climate needed for the aristocratic champagne grapes, Pinot Chardonnay and Pinot Noir. Later Paul Masson married Le Franc's daughter and subsequently inherited the winery.

State 9 continues to CONGRESS SPRINGS, 9.4 *m.*, where D. O. MILLS and Alvinza Hayward in the 1860's financed a fashionable spa with a large, much verandaed hotel. The hotel was burned in 1903, but the springs are still frequented by picknickers.

West of Congress Springs the route follows State 9 up a wooded canyon to Saratoga Gap at the junction with State 5, 14.8 *m.* (*see above*).

State 9 descends gradually through a heavy growth of redwood, madrone, live oak, laurel, and buckeye to BIG BASIN REDWOODS STATE PARK, 26.4 *m.*, occupying a bowl-shaped depression on East Waddell Creek, called Big Basin by early lumbermen. This is part of a dense redwood forest which before lumbering operations began extended a hundred miles from the Pajaro River north almost to San Francisco. About 1885 Ralph S. Smith of Redwood City first attempted to save some of the Coast redwoods from lumbermen. Others, including the Sempervirens Club of San Jose, at length were successful in getting an appropriation from the State Legislature sufficient to purchase the 3,800 acres of Big Basin. By subsequent gifts and purchases, the park was increased to 11,886 acres. Principal tree here is the *Sequoia sempervirens.* Campsites and picnic areas, a campfire center, natural history museum and postoffice are year-round features. In summer a supply store is open and a naturalist is on duty.

On US 101 at 43 *m.* is the site of the BATTLE OF SANTA CLARA, the Battle of the Mustard Stalks, fought January 2, 1847 on a field covered with tall mustard stalks, when Californians under Francisco Sanchez revolting against plundering Americans were defeated by a small force led by Captain Ward Marston.

Neither the old-fashioned houses on the tree-shaded streets of SANTA CLARA, 47.6 *m.* (72 alt., 87,717 pop. 1970; 58,880, 1960, inc. 49%), nor the typically American business blocks dating from the seventies and eighties suggest the town's origin as a settlement surrounding the mission dedicated in 1777 to St. Clare, superior of the first Franciscan nunnery.

The first buildings put up by Father Tomas de la Pena and his colleagues were flooded. The Franciscans rebuilt in 1781, but their second structures, damaged by a severe earthquake in 1812, were destroyed completely by another earthquake six years later. A third adobe church and its surrounding secular buildings were dedicated in 1822 on the site of the University of Santa Clara (*see below*).

So many Americans settled here early in the 1850's that the Spanish-speaking population became a small minority. The town's recent growth has been slow but substantial. Fruit-packing house, a tannery, a pottery, and a cement works are its principal industrial establishments.

The SANTA CLARA WOMEN'S CLUB, 1067 Grant St., occupies an adobe built in 1782 as one of the buildings of Mission Santa Clara, the oldest structure in the Santa Clara Valley.

Behind a high rose-colored wall in a park with fine old trees is the CARMELITE MONASTERY, Lincoln St. opposite Franklin St., one of the few houses in the United States of this cloistered order whose members, giving all their time to prayer and contemplation, never leave the monastery.

CITY PARK, Lexington and Main Sts., was the plaza when Santa Clara was a Mexican *pueblo*.

The second site of SANTA CLARA MISSION is marked by a cross and monument at Campbell and Franklin Sts. In the rear of the Bray House (*private*), Scott Lane, an old-fashioned frame dwelling, stands a low one-story adobe with a tiled roof, a lonely relic marking the site of the SANTA CLARA MISSION INDIAN VILLAGE.

The FERNANDEZ ADOBE (*private*), 401 Jefferson St., a grey-white plastered adobe dating from the 1840's, is shaded by an olive tree and a grapevine of unusual age and size.

The UNIVERSITY OF SANTA CLARA, Franklin and Grant Sts., occupying a fifteen-acre campus, owes its creation to Archbishop Joseph Sadoc Alemany of San Francisco. Hoping to save Santa Clara Mission from complete deterioration after its secularization, he invited the Jesuit Order to Santa Clara to build a college. In 1851 the Reverend John Nobili adapted what was left of the old adobe buildings to the needs of a school. Although chartered as a university in 1855, it was actually a college of arts and sciences until the establishment of colleges of law and engineering in 1912. A school of business administration was added in 1924. The enrollment totals over 5,600 and there is a faculty of 281. Santa Clara was the first institution in California to bestow an academic degree; first alumnus was Thomas I. Bergin, A.B., who became a successful attorney.

Among widely known faculty members have been John J. Montgomery, who made a successful flight in a glider as early as 1883; the late Father Jerome Ricard, the "Padre of the Rains," who by a system of co-ordinating the Government forecasts with his own observations based on the sun spots and their relation to atmospheric conditions, hoped to make accurate long-time weather forecasts; and Father Bernard Hubbard, Alaskan explorer and present head of the geology department.

The university buildings in Spanish Colonial style are all comparatively new with the exception of the theater, which dates from 1870. The *Mission Play of Santa Clara* has been produced here several times.

The MISSION SANTA CLARA, reconstructed in 1927 from old drawings of the adobe mission church of 1822, is the university chapel. An earlier restoration was destroyed by fire in 1926. Students and faculty were able to save some articles dating from the Spanish period which have been incorporated in the new building; among these are a large crucifix, the holy-water fonts, the wooden statues of saints at the side altars, and the reredos over the high altar. Three bells dating from the late eighteenth century and destroyed in the fire were replaced by a gift from King Alphonso XIII. The large redwood cross in front of the mission is the one which Spanish soldiers and Indians put up in 1777 on the first site of the mission, and was moved each time the mission was moved.

VARSI LIBRARY, named for the Reverend Aloysius Varsi, S.J., president of Santa Clara from 1868 to 1876, contains more than 100,000 volumes, among them some rare Spanish works on general science, medicine, and agriculture of the seventeenth and eighteenth centuries.

US 101 south of Santa Clara follows The Alameda, a tree-lined avenue following the old road that linked Mission Santa Clara with the *pueblo* of San Jose de Guadalupe. In 1799 Father Magin Catala planted a double lane of willows on each side of El Camino Real, and in the years that followed they gave a grateful shade to all those traveling between mission and *pueblo:* the bride and groom in lumbering *carreta,* the mounted fast-riding *vaquero* and *ranchero,* and the solemn marchers to the cemetery.

SAN JOSE, 50.8 *m.* (92 alt., 445,779 pop.) (*see San Jose*).

1. Right from San Jose on First Street to San Carlos Street; R. on San Carlos Street, which becomes Stevens Creek Road, to the junction with Bascom Avenue, 2.9 *m.* on which the main side route turns L.; R. (straight ahead) on Stevens Creek Road 1 *m.* to the junction with paved Los Gatos Road; L. here to the WINCHESTER MYSTERY HOUSE (*adm. $1.75*), 1.3 *m.* This fantastic structure with its strange assortments of roofs, spires, and cupolas contains 143 rooms extending over six acres. It was the creation of Sarah Winchester, widow of Oliver F. Winchester, millionaire manufacturer of firearms, who purchased upon her arrival here in the 1880's the seventeen-room house, then under construction on the site, from which all the rest has evolved. Obsessed with the idea that if building were to stop, she would die, Mrs. Winchester kept a crew of workmen constantly busy for thirty-six years until her death in 1922. The result was a structural nightmare; stairways leading to blank walls, bathrooms with gold-plated fixtures and glass doors, fireplaces without flues, small rooms built inside larger rooms like Chinese puzzle boxes, and her private chamber, in which walls, ceiling, and even the floors were covered with white satin.

The route follows State 17 L. from the junction with Stevens Creek Road on Bascom Avenue to the junction with paved Campbell Avenue, 5.4 *m.;* R. here is CAMPBELL, 0.7 *m.* (195 alt., 24,770 pop. 1970; 11,863, 1960; inc. 108.8%), known as The Orchard City. Here along Los Gatos Creek, Benjamin Campbell, a Kentuckian, sold lots for the town in 1887, with the proviso that the land should be forfeit to him or his heirs if liquor were sold upon it. The town's fruit-canning plants produce annually about 7,500,000 cans; its packing plants ship about 150 carloads of dried fruit.

State 17 continues to LOS GATOS, 11.2 *m.* (412 alt., 23,735 pop. 1970; 9,036, 1960, inc. 162.7%) which lies at the point where Los Gatos Creek flows out of its narrow canyon into the broad fertile valley. Curving about the town are two mountain ridges, El Sereno (the night watchman) and El Sombroso (the shadowing one). San Thomas Aquinas Creek, a mile to the east was the boundary of Rancho Rinconada de los Gatos (little corner of the cats), which Jose Hernandez got by grant from the Mexican government in 1840 and named for two wildcats that he saw battling in the neighborhood. The first building on the townsite was a flour mill built in 1850 by James Alexander Forbes, a Scot who had been in California since 1832, and who had served as British vice-consul at Monterey since 1843. For lack of water, the mill prospered little. The village that grew up around it was slow to develop until the extension of the railroad from San Jose in 1877. Fruit ranches dominated the hills through the 1920's and 1930's; the community was definitely rural. The Los Altos community didn't begin its phenomenal growth until the 1940's when World War II speeded the urbanization of the Bay Area.

The FORBES FLOUR MILL, now a sub-station of the Pacific Gas & Electric Company, on the bottom land of Los Gatos Creek, is most easily reached by crossing a foot bridge in the rear of the Los Gatos Grammar School, University Ave. between Main St. and Mullen Ave. The walls, of a hard sandstone, are heavily buttressed, and the lintels are braced with redwood timbers. The mill-wheel was turned by water brought through a wooden flume from a dam further upstream. Only a portion of the original four-story building survived a fire in 1872.

Bordering Los Gatos Creek, MEMORIAL PARK, Main and Park Sts., has a swimming pool, horseshoe courts, and picnic grounds shaded by large plane trees.

The mission-style buildings of the NOVITIATE OF THE SACRED HEART, Prospect Ave. above College Ave., overlook the town from a hill. Founded in 1868, the novitiate is a training school for the Jesuit Order. After four years of training here the novices go to St. Michael's, Spokane, for three years, spend two or three years more in teaching, and finally four years at the theologate branch at Alma in the near-by mountains. The garden has a replica of the famous well of Lourdes. The novitiate owns a vineyard of 485 acres, from whose grapes it makes sweet and dry wines.

2. Right from San Jose on First Street to Alma Avenue, R. on Alma Avenue to the junction with paved Almaden Road, 2.1 *m.;* L. on Almaden Road across the Guadalupe River and up Alamitos Valley.

ALMADEN, 13.8 *m.* (473 alt.), drowses in a pocket in the hills. Its two streets, following the line of Alamitos Creek, are lined with trees, chiefly the smooth-barked sycamore (*Platanus racemosa*). Behind the narrow brick sidewalks and trim hedges are rows of small adobe and frame houses set in old-fashioned gardens.

The quicksilver mines, for which this region is famous, have (with the exception of the mines of Spain) produced more quicksilver than any other field in the world. They were known to the Indians, who used the cinnabar for coloring their faces and bodies. In 1824 Antonia Maria Suñol, a Spaniard who had been in the French navy and who was then a shop keeper in San Jose, with Luis Chabolla developed the mine in a small way, thinking it contained silver.

Not until 1845 did a Mexican officer, Andres Castillero, discover quicksilver. He realized that if there were extensive deposits his fortune was made, for quicksilver was scarce in Mexico. He filed his claim and, forming a partnership with *Padre* Real of Mission Santa Clara and with some members of the Robles family who had earlier explored the region, he engaged an American named Chard to begin reducing the ore. Chard's equipment was primitive: six whaler's try-pots, three inverted over the other three, to form a furnace.

Two years later Castillero sold some shares to Barron, Forbes and Company of Tepic, Mexico, whose agent, James Alexander Forbes, introduced improved methods. By 1850 the mines had an annual yield worth $750,000. The California gold mines kept up a steady demand for the metal, which was put in iron flasks and taken by oxcart to tidewater at Alviso. The Comstock boom added to the demand. In 1865, the year of greatest output, the mine produced 47,000 flasks of mercury with a value of $2,160,000. That such production had its effect on the world market was shown when Lionel, Baron de Rothschild, lessee of the great Spanish mines, came here as a visitor in the sixties.

Throughout the 1870's the mine continued to be highly profitable. As many as 1,000 men were employed, and the population rose to 6,000. As it became necessary to go deeper for deposits of cinnabar, however, the cost of operation rose. Moreover, quicksilver dropped in price. During the World War, the need for mercury in making fulminate caps created a new boom, and in 1940 the mines again were active.

CLUB ALMADEN, the former Casa Grande, at the northern end of the town, is a large two-story white house built of bricks brought around the Horn from Glasgow. It was erected in 1850 as a hotel. When J. E. Randol became mine owner in 1870, he made it his private residence, in which he entertained lavishly. The drawing room fireplace has an ornately carved ebony mantel with small medallions of mother-of-pearl and painted glass. Back of the house is a swimming pool (*open weekdays 9-3*).

The OLD STORE at the southern end of the town, an adobe structure with brick corbie-steps at the gable ends, has been used continuously since its erection about 1850. The main roof, supported by hand-hewn posts, extends over the narrow sidewalk.

South of the old store is the half-ruined MINE OFFICE, an adobe and brick building with a wooden porte-cochere. It contains a brick vault where flasks of mercury were stored.

A trail leads south 300 yards to the smelters and furnaces, from which rise brick towers 150 feet high built against the steep slope of the canyon. The cinnabar, after being pounded into pieces about the size of an egg, was placed in the ore bed. When the fuel was fired, mercury, highly volatile, rose with the smoke into the towers and passed through a series of apertures to be cooled in a condensing chamber. By the time the smoke reached the chimney, the greater part of the mercury had been released and collected.

3. Left from San Jose on Santa Clara Street, which becomes paved, tree-lined Alum Rock Road, to the junction with Mount Hamilton Road, 6 *m.*, on which the main side route turns R.

Left on Alum Rock Road into the wooded, rocky gorge of Penitencia Creek, named for the "house of penance," a small adobe which once stood on the banks, where priests came to hear confessions.

The 643-acre ALUM ROCK PARK, 2.1 *m.* (520 alt.), owned by the city of San Jose, was named for a 200-foot cliff (L) with a surface residuum of alum dust, standing in the lower part of the canyon. Once part of the pueblo lands of San Jose, the park has become a playground landscaped so as to enhance the natural beauty of the surroundings. Before the arrival of the Spaniards, the Indians held their rituals here twice a year, bathed in and drank the health-giving waters. At the lower picnic grounds, there are a swimming pool, zoo, and hot sulphur baths. Six beautifully arched, native rock bridges lead to the various points of interest above the auto parking area. The park's twenty-two mineral springs are housed in rock grottos, reached by trails extending up the canyon from the end of the road. Here also are a deer paddock, a song-bird aviary, and a serpentorium.

From the lower picnic grounds Penitencia Creek Trail ascends the canyon 0.2 *m.* to the junction with a trail; L. here 0.3 *m.* to the JOAQUIN MURRIETA HIDEOUT, a natural cavern thirty feet long and four feet wide,

On San Francisco Bay

SAN FRANCISCO AS SEEN FROM THE AIR

TREASURE ISLAND AS SEEN FROM YERBA BUENA ISLAND

LAND'S END AND SEACLIFF DISTRICT FROM THE PRESIDIO

UNITED STATES NAVAL VESSELS LEAVING THE BAY, 1935

CLEANING UP OIL SLICK ON BEACH NEAR CLIFF HOUSE, 1971

SAN FRANCISCO MARITIME MUSEUM

VIEW ACROSS CITY AND BAY FROM LOOKOUT POINT

CROSS ON SUMMIT OF
MOUNT DAVIDSON WHERE
EASTER SERVICES ARE
HELD

LOOKING SOUTH FROM
THE SUMMIT OF TWIN
PEAKS

AIR VIEW OF THE CAMPUS, UNIVERSITY OF CALIFORNIA
AT BERKELEY

STOCKTON STREET TUNNEL, SACRAMENTO SIDE

CALIFORNIA ACADEMY OF SCIENCES

UNITED STATES MINT

another of the countless places in California where the bandit who has become the subject of a thousand tales is said to have concealed himself. The Penitencia Creek Trail follows up the wooded canyon to the junction with the North Fork Trail, 1 *m.;* L. here 0.6 *m.* to EAST WATER FALLS (1,200 alt.), where the waters of the creek drop sixty feet over a rocky ledge. The North Fork Trail continues to INSPIRATION POINT, 0.9 *m.* (1,500 alt.), which affords a wide view of the park and Santa Clara Valley. The main trail goes R. up South Falls Trail to SOUTH FALLS, 2.3 *m.*

The main side route turns R. on Mount Hamilton Road from the junction with Alum Rock Road and climbs rugged oak-dotted slopes to the crest of MOUNT HAMILTON (*no accommodations*), 26.4 *m.*, crowned by silver-domed LICK OBSERVATORY (*open Mon.-Fri. 1-5*). The observatory was a gift to the people of California from James Lick, a Pennsylvania piano maker who had followed his trade successfully in South America. Arriving in San Francisco in 1847 with a stake of $30,000, Lick became a millionaire through land investments and miserly practices. Though he was unkempt in appearance and his clothes were often ragged, he was capable, occasionally, of lavish spending, as when he built near Alviso a flour mill finished in mahogany and other expensive woods. At his death in 1876 he left an estate of $3,000,000. With the exception of a small gift to an illegitimate son, all this fortune was devoted to public benefactions.

Lick's deed of trust charged the trustees to expend the sum of $700,000 "for the purpose of purchasing land . . . and putting up on such land . . . a powerful telescope, superior to and more powerful than any telescope yet made . . . and also a suitable observatory connected therewith . . . The said telescope observatory are to be known as the Lick Astronomical Department of the University of California." On June 1, 1888, the telescope and buildings were completed and a scientific staff from the University of California began its work. Lick's body was removed from Lone Mountain Cemetery in San Francisco and buried in a crypt beneath the great 36-inch equatorial refractor.

Mount Hamilton, named in honor of the Reverend Laurentine Hamilton, pioneer missionary preacher of San Jose and first white man to climb the mountain, is a ridge running east and west and rising to three peaks. Before December, 1876, when the county completed the road to the summit, as specified in Lick's deed of trust, it took five days to get supplies and materials from San Jose. (Even the completed road, climbing 2,000 feet, makes 365 turns in the last five miles of its ascent.)

On the western peak is the silver-domed main building of the observatory, housing a 36-inch and a 12-inch equatorial refractor. The 36-inch instrument has a magnifying power which can be varied from 270 to 3,000 times that of the naked eye. The main building contains also the offices and computing rooms and a technical library of 20,000 items. The movable floor, permitting a rise and fall of 16½ feet, was the first of the kind to be constructed. Detached buildings house a 36½-inch reflecting telescope, a 6½-inch meridian circle instrument, a 6½-inch comet-seeker, a photographic telescope and a three-prism spectrograph. To enable the staff at Mount Hamilton to extend observations in the Southern Hemisphere, an observatory with a 37¼-inch Cassegrain reflector is maintained in Chile.

The scientists who use the mighty telescopes to penetrate the mysteries of distant space, recording minute and seemingly unrelated flares of ancient light in their effort to plot the courses of remote stars, work with facts that are but fantasies. Often graphs and calculi which have taken years to work out are required to account for a single flash of light. During the Australian eclipse in 1922, the Lick Observatory, with fifteen-foot twin cameras, photographed images of the stars. When the photographs were compared with plates made of these stars by the same cameras four months previously, a measured deflection of 1.72″ was shown: the gravitational attraction of the sun had bent the light. Thus a startling theory in physics had been proved in part. In September, 1892, the big 36-inch refractor found the fifth satellite of Jupiter, the first discovered since Galileo turned his glass to that planet. In 1904, 1905, and 1914, three more were discovered and photographed with the Crossley Reflector. The observatory has discovered thirty-three comets, 4,800 double stars, several score spectroscopic binary stars, and many hundred new nebulae. The first great success in photographing comets and the Milky Way was achieved here.

San Jose

Air Services: San Jose-Sunnyvale Airport. Intrastate and commuter air carrier. San Francisco-Oakland Helicopter Airlines.

Buses: Greyhound Lines, 70 Almaden Ave. Peerless States, 70 Almaden Ave. San Jose Lines, 860 W. San Carlos. Sightseeing buses: Smith's Charter Bus Service, 45675 Warm Springs Blvd., Fremont.

Railroad: Southern Pacific, 65 Cahill.

Highways: US 101 north to San Francisco, 44 *m.;* State 17 up east side of Bay to Oakland, Berkeley; Interstate 680, bypasses Oakland, connects with Interstate 80 to Sacramento, 119 *m.*

Information: San Jose Chamber of Commerce, Civic Auditorium, 145 W. San Carlos. California State Automobile Association, 80 Saratoga Ave., Santa Clara. Convention & Tourist Bureau, Civic Auditorium, 145 W. San Carlos.

Museums: New Almaden, 21570 Almaden Rd., New Almaden. Triton Museum of Art, 1505 Warburton Ave., Santa Clara. Oriental Museum, Naglee and Park Aves.

Concert Halls: San Jose Civic Auditorium, 145 W. San Carlos. Santa Clara Fairgrounds, 344 Tully Road.

Amateur and Little Theaters: Montgomery Theater, 145 W. San Carlos.

Baseball: South 10th & Alma.

Basketball: Civic Auditorium, 145 W. San Carlos.

Football: San Jose State Spartan Field, S. 7th and E. Humboldt Sts.

Golf: Parmaker Fairgrounds, 57th & Tully Rd. Pleasant Hills Golf & Country Club, 400 Bailey Ave.

Swimming: Almaden Golf & Country Club, 6663 Hampton Dr. Alpine Park and Lodge, 2300 Canoas Garden Ave.

Tennis: San Jose Tennis Courts (lighted), 57th & E. Humboldt St.

Parks: Alum Rock Park, Alum Rock Ave. has 716 acres, swimming pool, museum, trails, mineral springs. Happy Hollow Children's Park, Keyes & Senter Rd. Parks Field Office, South 6th & East Empire.

SAN JOSE (92 alt., 445,779 pop. 1970; 204,196, 1960, inc. 118%) seat of Santa Clara County, is located at the southern extremity of San

Francisco Bay, at the center of one of California's most rapidly developing industrial areas. Of the 1970 population only 1,829 could be designated as living in a rural area. Although San Jose is one of the oldest cities in the State, it today is a leading example of progressive community planning and development. The downtown area is perhaps the most representative of the changes taking place as a very large renewal project is well under way.

One of the major reasons for the industrial and residential expansion of Metropolitan San Jose is the efficiency of its transporatation system. Modern freeways, two major railroads, and a newly expanded airport provide ready access to the local, national, and international market while also providing excellent individual commuting facilities.

In 1777 Lieutenant Jose Moraga, acting under orders from Don Felipe de Neve, selected nine soldiers "of known agricultural skill" from the presidios of San Francisco and Monterey and five *pobladores* (settlers); these men and their families—66 persons—he took to the site chosen for the *pueblo* San Jose de Guadalupe—about a mile and a quarter north of the present center of San Jose. To each man were given a homesite and a small piece of ground to till. Although the soil was excellent, it was flooded each winter by the Guadalupe River. In 1797 the *pobladores* moved to a new location centering at the corner of what is now South Market and West San Fernando Streets. There is little recorded of the happenings in the *pueblo* during the occupancy of its original site, although in 1784 "some of the settlers were imprisoned and put in irons for refusing to work on a house for the town council," and "two boys drowned an Indian to amuse themselves, but in consideration of their tender years were dismissed with twenty-five lashes administered in the presence of the natives."

In the 1820's the *pobladores* received their first English-speaking settler, Robert Livermore, who moved north after a few years into the valley which now bears his name. Other Englishmen and Americans had arrived before 1835, but by marrying into the Higuera, Galindo, Saiz, and other influential families they became identified with the native Californians. Within another ten years, however, the Americans had so increased that with the reorganization of the *pueblo* after the American occupation of California in 1846, six out of twelve committee men were Americans, as was the new *alcalde*.

With an eye to the *pueblo's* future, the citizens met in September, 1849 and offered to the Constitutional Convention assembled in Monterey some 21 acres "for the sole purpose of erecting State buildings thereon." The offer was accepted. In December of that year the Legislature met in an adobe building at San Antonio and Market Streets. Among the official acts at that first session was the incorporation, March 27, 1850, of the capital city, which thus became the first incorporated community in California (San Francisco's charter was granted three weeks later).

The capital was moved to Vallejo in 1852, thence to Benicia, and finally to Sacramento. The citizens of San Jose strove earnestly but unsuccessfully for its repossession. Victory hove in sight when the Supreme Court decided on an appeal in 1854 that San Jose was the legal capital, but soon afterward it reversed its decision.

As early as 1851 there had been talk of a railroad to San Francisco, for the fare by stage was $16 and the cost of shipping lumber from Alviso, $15 per thousand. The railroad finally came in 1864—"a proof," in the opinion of the San Jose *Mercury,* "of American enterprise, foresight and determination." Cattle and grain were still the chief products, the country south of Gilroy being an almost unbroken wheat field, but the number of orchards was increasing, and some vineyards were already known, particularly that of Colonel Naglee, who had set out (in what is now the northwestern part of town) more than 100 varieties of grapes. Within the city, which by 1870 had a population of about 13,000, were carriage and wagon shops, foundries, breweries, tanneries, and woolen and flour mills run by water from the abundant artesian wells. In this same year the State Normal School was established. With the building of many new homes, San Jose began to call itself the "Garden City."

The subdivision of the great wheat ranches and the planting of orchards continued. San Jose was shipping more and more dried prunes to the Eastern markets. The nascent art of advertising was being used to attract people with money to Santa Clara County. In a ten-acre park the big wooden Hotel Vendome with its fat bay windows was ready in 1889, "with electric lights and hot water."

In 1894 San Jose's Dr. Charles D. Herrold transmitted a distance of 60 feet California's first wireless message. By 1909 he had perfected the first successful "radio telephone station" in America, and by 1913 he was communicating with the Fairmont Hotel in San Francisco. (Except during the World War this station, now KQW, has broadcast without interruption.) Continuing San Jose's reputation for "firsts," Dr. August Greth in 1903 built America's first dirigible, the 85-foot *Spirit of California,* which Captain Thomas S. Baldwin flew over San Francisco. In the same year an ambitious young producer named Sid Grauman (who was later to build Hollywood's Egyptian and Chinese Theaters) opened on Santa Clara Street a vaudeville house which, in deference to the gentility of San Jose, displayed the sign, "No liquor or cigars will be allowed, and no tickets sold to persons not fit to be with women and children." Here Al Jolson made his debut and Roscoe "Fatty" Arbuckle was chore boy and ticket seller.

San Jose's then foremost industry, the shipping of fresh, dried, and canned fruit, meanwhile was growing enormously. A little woodshed in 1871 housed Santa Clara County's first commercial cannery when J. M. Dawson and his wife packed 300 cases of peaches, pears, cherries, and apricots. Today the county is still one of the nation's major food processing centers, however the agricultural sector of manufacturing has lessened in relative importance. While the trend toward greater manufacturing activity began in the early 1940's, the year 1950 marked the beginning of the major influx of large manufacturing firms and expansions, which continues today.

POINTS OF INTEREST

ST. JOSEPH'S CHURCH, 90 S. Market St., occupies the site of the original adobe church built in 1803 and dedicated to San Jose de Guadalupe. The larger adobe which replaced this in 1835 was so badly damaged in 1868 that it was torn down and the present church—an attempt at the neoclassic in wood, brick, and plaster—erected in its place.

On the site around which grew the original pueblo is CIVIC PLAZA, an oval plaza dividing S. Market St. between W. San Fernando and W. San Carlos Sts. into two wide parkways. In the plaza a plaque marks the site of the FIRST STATE CAPITOL, NE. cor. W. San Antonio and S. Market Sts. The adobe capitol building was 60 feet long and 40 feet wide, "protected by a veranda all round."

SAN JOSE STATE COLLEGE, the oldest public educational institution in the State of California, began as the State Normal School in San Francisco in 1862. It moved to the present site in San Jose in 1870. The college was destroyed by fire in 1880, rebuilt and again demolished, this time by the earthquake of 1906. Today it represents an investment of more than $50,000,000. The college offers a wide variety of undergraduate and graduate level courses with more than 1,400 educators on the faculty. Student enrollment in 1970 reached 23,478.

Now used as the infirmary of the San Jose State College, the EDWIN MARKHAM HOUSE, 430 S. Eighth St., is an old-fashioned residence faced with clapboard. Here the poet lived in the early 1870's when a student at the normal school, and here his mother continued to live in later years.

The distinguishing feature of ST. JAMES PARK, N. First, N. Third, St. John, and E. St. James Sts., is a bronze MONUMENT OF WILLIAM McKINLEY erected in 1902. In this park in 1933 occurred the lynching of two men accused of the kidnaping and murder of a wealthy merchant's son. An infuriated mob broke into the jail across the street and brought their victims to the park. The nation rang with reverberations over the incident, heightened when Governor James Rolph, Jr., announced his approval of the mob's action.

The NEW CIVIC CENTER, First & Mission Streets, is situated on a 66-acre site. The City Hall (Donald F. Haines & Assoc., architects), was built in 1956 with bright-colored curtain walls of porcelain-covered steel panels and glass.

The PERALTA ADOBE, in the rear of 184 San Augustin St., was built about 1840. Formerly a residence, later a barn and hay loft, it is now a storeroom. The adobe walls are partly faced with boards.

ROSICRUCIAN HEADQUARTERS, Naglee Ave. from Chapman St. to Park Ave., is the center for North and South America of the "Ancient and Mystical Order of the Rosy Cross" (AMORC). Claiming great antiquity, the order gives the names of Pythagoras, St. Francis, Dante, and Professor Albert Einstein as members. The buildings, which include an auditorium, a lecture hall and laboratories, and an oriental museum, are of concrete in a variety of oriental styles.

The Moorish arches and buff-colored concrete walls of the EGYPTIAN TEMPLE AND ORIENTAL MUSEUM (*open Sat. Sun. Mon. 12-5; Tues.-Fri. 9-5*) are finished to simulate stuccoed walls in the process of peeling. Here the Rosicrucian order has a miscellaneous collection of old books and tapestries; Egyptian pottery, tomb images, and scarabs; and reproductions of an Assyrian gateway and an Egyptian temple. Visitors are given free pamphlets soliciting membership, one of which has an introduction signed, "Profundis XIII."

The PLANETARIUM BUILDING, called The Theater of the Skies, is devoted to the Rosicrucian explanation of the roles of the planets and stars.

In the MUNICIPAL ROSE GARDEN, Naglee and Dana Aves., whose 5½ acres of formal planting are intersected by long aisles of grass, flourish many varieties once popular but now seldom grown. The garden is pervaded by the old-time perfume of the Centifolia, the dusky sweetness of the Damask (Rose of Lancaster), the acid freshness of China roses, the pungency of the moss rose, the scent of winter apples in the foliage of the sweet briar. Standard and hybrid teas much grown 50 years ago, Safrano, Duchess de Brabant, La France, and Captain Christy, are well represented, as are the many newer and more striking hybrids. Against the brick walls grow many varieties of climbing roses.

INTERNATIONAL BUSINESS MACHINES CORPORATION (IBM) located at Monterey & Cottle Roads on a 356-acre site, is the scene of research, education, systems development, and testing and manufacturing. There are 17 buildings with over 1,000,000 sq. ft. of space.

The CALIFORNIA CANNING & PACKING COMPANY, West end of W. San Carlos St., is the largest canning-packing plant in San Jose. The huge canning and packing units each occupy a modern red-brick building roofed with dark tin. Salad fruits and vegetables are canned the year around; asparagus from April to June; string beans, from June to November; spinach from January to April. The peak season for apricots, peaches, plums, pears, and tomatoes comes in July, August, and September.

The two-story STOCKTON HOUSE, Spring and Newhall Sts., built in 1850, is one of a number of houses cut to size and brought around the Horn by Commodore Robert F. Stockton. It has a wide veranda and, rising from the central gable, a square balustraded turret.

The 640-acre site north of San Jose of the LOCKHEED MISSILES & SPACE COMPANY employs approximately 23,400 persons. Basically a missile and satellite manufacturing facility, the Lockheed complex also represents a diversity of research and production facilities.

PART V
Appendices

A Chronology of the San Francisco Bay Region

1542   Nov. 16 (O. S.)   Portuguese explorer Juan Rodrigues Cabrillo enters gulf outside Golden Gate and discovers Farallon Islands.

1579   June 17. (Julian Calendar).   English navigator Francis Drake lands in present Marin County (Drake's Bay), and claims land as New Albion for Queen Elizabeth.

1595   Nov. 6.   Sebastian Rodrigues Cermeno enters Drake's Bay and names it La Bahia de San Francisco for Saint Francis of Assisi.

1603   Jan. 5.   Sebastian Vizcaino sights extreme southwest point of present San Mateo County and names it Punta del Año Nuevo (New Year's Point).

1769   Oct. 18.   Gaspar de Portola expedition arrives in sight of Santa Cruz.

       Nov. 1-3.   Portola's chief scout, Sergt. Jose Ortega, discovers present San Francisco Bay.

       Nov. 7-10.   Exploring party sent out by Portola expedition traverses country east of Bay, probably to San Pablo Bay.

1772   Mar. 27-28.   Golden Gate first sighted from present sites of Oakland and Berkeley by Capt. Pedro Fages expedition on way north from Mission San Carlos Borromeo by way of Santa Clara Valley.

1775   Aug. 5.   The *San Carlos,* first ship to enter Bay, is piloted through Golden Gate under command of Lt. Juan Manuel de Ayala.

1776   Mar. 28.   Juan Bautista de Anza, arriving at site of San Francisco with colonists from Mexico, selects site for presidio.

       Mar. 29.   Anza selects site for Mission San Francisco de Asis (Mission Dolores).

       Sept. 17.   Presidio founded by Lt. Jose Joaquin Moraga.

       Oct. 8.   Padre Francisco Palou dedicates Mission San Francisco de Asis.

1777   Jan. 12.   Mission Santa Clara founded.

       Nov. 29.   *Pueblo* of San Jose de Guadalupe (San Jose), first in California, is founded.

1791   Aug. 28.   Mission Santa Cruz founded.

1792   Nov. 14.   Capt. George Vancouver arrives in *H.M.S. Discovery,* first foreign vessel to enter Bay.

1797   June 11.   Mission San Jose de Guadalupe is dedicated.

1803   Aug. 12.   First American vessel, *Eliza,* Capt. James Rowan, enters harbor.

1806   Apr. 8.   Count Nikolai Rezanov arrives to buy supplies for starving Russian colony at Sitka.

1812   Sept. 10.   Fort Ross, Russian trading post, is dedicated.

1816 Oct. 2. Russian commander Otto Von Kotzebue and crew arrive in *Rurik* to gather information on Spanish settlements.

1817 Dec. 14. Mission San Rafael Arcangel, "hospital mission" for sick converts of Mission San Francisco de Asis, is founded.

1820 June 20. Luis Maria Peralta receives grant (Rancho San Antonio) to vast East Bay area.

1821 Feb. 21. Spanish rule overthrown in Mexico City by Agustin Iturbide.

1823 July 4. Mission San Francisco Solano (Sonoma) dedicated.

1825 Mar. 26. California formally declared province of Republic of Mexico.

Apr. 24. Oath of allegiance to Republic of Mexico administered at San Francisco presidio.

1826 Nov. 6. Capt. Frederick William Beechey, of *H.M.S. Blossom,* arrives to make survey of Bay.

1827 Jan. 27. French trading ship *Le Heros,* Capt. Auguste Duhaut-Cilly, arrives in Bay.

1829 May 5. Spaniards subdue rebellious Cosumnes Indians in battle near San Jose.

1833 Aug. 17. Mexican Congress decrees secularization of missions.

1834 Aug. 24. Mission Santa Cruz secularized.

1834 Aug. 24. Mission Santa Cruz secularized.

Sept. Missions San Francisco de Asis and San Rafael secularized.

Dec. 7. First *ayuntamiento* (council) organized in San Francisco district and Francisco de Haro chosen first *alcalde* (mayor) of *pueblo* Yerba Buena.

1835 June 24. *Pueblo* of Sonoma founded.

June 25. William A. Richardson, first harbormaster, erects first dwelling in Yerba Buena.

1836 July 1. Jacob Primer Leese arrives at Yerba Buena and establishes first retail firm.

1837 Dec. Los Meganos Rancho near Mount Diablo granted to Dr. John Marsh.

Mission San Jose secularized.

1838 Feb. 11. Rancho Saucelito (Marin County) granted to William A. Richardson.

1839 Apr. 15. Russian government orders Fort Ross abandoned.

1841 Dec. 30. Hudson's Bay Company establishes agency at Yerba Buena.

Oct. 19. Lt. Charles Wilkes, U. S. N., visits Bay on hydrographic survey of Pacific Coast.

Nov. 4. First overland immigrants reach ranch of Dr. John Marsh.

1844 Mar. 8. Capt. John Charles Frémont and survey party arrive from overland journey at Sutter's Fort.

1845 July 10. Mexican decree forbids further American immigration.

1846 June 14. American settlers seize Sonoma and raise Bear Flag of California Republic.

June 24. First battle of Bear Flag Revolt fought near Petaluma.

July 7. Commodore John D. Sloat raises American flag at Monterey and proclaims California annexed to United States.

July 9. American flag hoisted at Yerba Buena and Sonoma.

1847 Jan. 2. Battle of Santa Clara concludes Yankee conquest of northern California.

Jan. 9. First issue of San Francisco's first (and California's second) newspaper, *The California Star,* appears.

Jan. 30. Yerba Buena renamed San Francisco.

1848 Jan. 24. Gold discovered by James Marshall at John A. Sutter's sawmill on American River.

Feb. 2. Treaty of Guadalupe Hidalgo ends war with Mexico and cedes California to United States.

Apr. 3. First American public school opened in San Francisco.

1849 Jan. 9. First commercial bank established in San Francisco.

Feb. 28. *California,* first Gold Rush steamer, arrives.

Apr. 1. Steamship *Oregon* inaugurates mail service to East.

Apr. 30. U.S. Army post established at Benicia.

June 22. Stephen Massett gives first public entertainment in San Francisco.

Oct. 25. Democratic Party of California organized.

Nov. Moses Chase, Oakland's first settler, arrives in East Bay.

Nov. 13. San Jose becomes capital of California.

Dec. 15. First American territorial legislature at San Jose.

Dec. 24. First of six great fires causes $1,250,000 loss in San Francisco.

1850 Population: San Francisco, 34,776.

Feb. 18. Legislature creates Bay region counties: San Francisco, Contra Costa, Marin, Santa Clara, Sonoma, Solano, and Napa.

Mar. 27. City of San Jose incorporated.

Apr. 1. San Francisco County government established.

Apr. 15. City of San Francisco incorporated.

June 24. San Francisco Typographical Society, city's first trade union, is organized.

Sept. 9. California admitted to Union.

Kangaroo ferry inaugurates San Francisco-East Bay service.

1851 Mar. 19. Santa Clara College established (chartered 1855).

May 3. San Francisco's fifth and most disastrous fire destroys 22 blocks, causing $12,000,000 loss.

June 9. First Committee of Vigilance organized.

Aug. 31. Clipper ship *Flying Cloud* slashes time from New York from 159 days to 89 days, 21½ hours.

1852 Jan. 5. State Legislature opens its third session in Vallejo.

May 4. City of Oakland incorporated.

1853   Mar. 25.   County of Alameda created.

1854   Feb. 25.   State capital established permanently at Sacramento.
        Sept. 16.   Admiral David Farragut establishes Mare Island Navy Yard.

1855   College of California (University of California) incorporated.
        Feb. 23.   Black Friday, initiates California's first panic.
        Apr. 19.   San Mateo County created.

1856   May 15.   Second Vigilance Committee organized.

1857   Sept. 7.   First Mechanics Fair is held by Mechanics Institute, in San Francisco.

1859   Apr. 30.   College of St. Ignatius (University of San Francisco) incorporated.
        Sept. 13.   Broderick-Terry duel helps crystallize anti-slavery sentiment in San Francisco.

1860   Population: San Francisco, 56,802; San Jose, 4,579; Oakland, 1,543; Alameda, 460.
        Apr. 14.   First Pony Express rider arrives from St. Joseph, Missouri, in San Francisco.
        Oct. 8.   Telegraph line opened between San Francisco and Los Angeles.

1861   Feb. 15.   Fort Point, San Francisco Presidio, occupied by U. S. troops.
        June 28.   Central Pacific Railway Company incorporated.
        Oct. 24.   Overland Telegraph Company establishes communication between San Francisco and New York.

1863   Mar. 15.   Schooner *J. M. Chapman,* Confederate privateer, is seized in Bay.

1864   Jan. 16.   San Francisco-San Jose Railroad completed.
        July 5.   William C. Ralston and associates found Bank of California.

1868   Mar. 23.   Legislature charters University of California.

1869   May 10.   Tracks of Central Pacific and Union Pacific joined.
        Sept. 6.   First transcontinental train arrives in Alameda.

1870   Population: San Francisco, 149,473; Oakland, 10,500; San Jose, 9,089; Alameda, 1,557.
        Mar. 11.   San Jose Teachers' College, California's first normal school, permanently established at San Jose.
        Mar. 18.   Golden Gate Park established.

1871   Mills Seminary (now Mills College) established in Oakland.

1872   Mar. 7.   City of Alameda incorporated.

1873   June 2.   Ground is broken for world's first cable street railway in San Francisco.

1875   Aug. 26.   Bank of California failure causes local panic, followed next day by drowning in Bay of president W. C. Ralston.

1876   July 4.   San Francisco's first public exhibition of electric light.
        Sept. 5.   Rail connection with Los Angeles established.

1877 July 23. Anti-Chinese sentiment results in first of San Francisco's "Sand-lot riots," prompting organization of Committee of Safety under William T. Coleman.

Oct. 5. Workingmen's Party of California organized.

1878 Apr. 1. City of Berkeley incorporated.

1880 Population: San Francisco 233,959; Oakland, 34,555; San Jose, 12,567; Alameda, 5,708.

July 23. Construction of Lick Observatory begins.

1882 May 6. President Chester Arthur signs Chinese Exclusion Act.

1883 Oct. 29. Merchants' and Manufacturers' Association, pioneer employers' council in San Francisco, established.

1885 Dec. 5. Luther Burbank founds experimental farm near Sebastopol.

1890 Population: San Francisco, 298,997; Oakland, 48,682; San Jose, 18,060; Alameda, 11,165; Berkeley, 5,101.

1891 Oct. 1. Stanford University opens to students.

1892 Mar. 19. First "Big Game" between University of California and Stanford.

Jan. 1. California Midwinter International Exposition opens.

1894 Dec. 25. First East-West football game (Stanford vs. University of Chicago) is played in San Francisco.

1898 May 26. San Francisco electorate accepts new city charter, authorizing municipal acquisition and ownership of public utilities (put into effect Jan. 1, 1900).

1900 Population: San Francisco, 342,782; Oakland, 66,960; San Jose, 21,500; Alameda, 16,464; Berkeley, 13,214.

1901 Jan. 7-9. Initial step taken to organize State Federation of Labor.

July 30. Teamsters' Union strike starts sympathy walkout.

Dec. 16. State Building Trades Council formed.

1902 Dec. 14. S.S. Silvertown begins laying cable to Honolulu.

1904 Oct. 17. Bank of Italy (Bank of America) established by A. P. Giannini with capital of $150,000.

1906 Apr. 18. Earthquake starts great fire destroying most of San Francisco with loss of $300,000,000.

1907 July 8. Mayor Eugene Schmitz sentenced to five years in San Quentin Prison for corruption in office.

1908 Dec. 7. Abe Ruef, political boss, sentenced to fourteen years in San Quentin.

July 9. Muir Woods, Marin County, becomes Muir Woods National Monument.

1909 Oct. 18. Portola Festival celebrates San Francisco's recovery from earthquake and fire.

1910 Population: San Francisco, 416,912; Oakland, 150,174; Berkeley, 40,434; San Jose, 28,946; Alameda, 23,383.

1913 Dec. 19. Ratification of Raker Act permits development of Hetch-Hetchy power system by San Francisco.

1914 Feb. 16. Silas Christofferson makes first airplane flight from San Francisco to San Diego.

1915 Feb. 20. Panama-Pacific International Exposition opens.

1916 July 22. Preparedness Day bomb explosion occurs in San Francisco, resulting in life prison terms for Thomas Mooney and Warren K. Billings (Mooney pardoned Jan. 7, 1939; Billing's sentence commuted to time served Oct. 16, 1939).

1917 July 14. Twin Peaks Tunnel dedicated in San Francisco.

1919 Nov. 3. Crissey Field, San Francisco airport, dedicated.

1920 Population: San Francisco, 506,676; Oakland, 216,261; Berkeley, 56,036; San Jose, 39,642; Alameda, 28,806.

1920 July 29. First transcontinental airmail flight from New York completed at San Francisco.
Sept. 8. Regular airmail service established between Mineola, N. Y., and San Francisco.

1922 Oct. 1. Philo T. Farnsworth establishes laboratory in San Francisco where principles of television were first perfected in 1927.

1927 Jan. 17. Dumbarton Bridge is completed.
May 7. San Francisco Municipal Airport (Mills Field) dedicated.
May 21. Carquinez Bridge opens.

1928 Oct. 27. Posey Tube, under Estuary, connects Alameda and Oakland.

1929 Mar. 3. San Mateo Bay Bridge opens.

1930 Population: San Francisco, 634,394; Oakland, 284,063; Berkeley, 82,109; San Jose; 57,651; Alameda, 35,033.

1931 Apr. 3. Mount Diablo is made part of State park system.
June 9. Construction of U. S. Naval Air Station at Moffett Field (Sunnyvale) begins (transferred to Army Air Corps, 1935).

1932 Jan. 8. San Francisco's present charter is ratified.

1933 Oct. 12. U. S. Department of Justice takes over Alcatraz Island as Federal penitentiary.

1934 May 9. Walkout of maritime workers leads to general strike, first in Bay region's history.

1935 Jan. 12. Amelia Earhart Putnam lands at Oakland Airport on first solo flight from Hawaii.
Nov. 22. *China Clipper* leaves Alameda on first airmail flight to Manila.

1936 Nov. 12. San Francisco-Oakland Bay Bridge opens.

1937 May 27. Golden Gate Bridge opened.
Dec. 5. Broadway Low Level Tunnel in Alameda County opens.

1939 Jan. 14. Ferries to East Bay close.
Bay Bridge train service opens following day.
Feb. 18. Golden Gate International Exposition opens on Treasure Island.

1940 Apr. 21. Funston Avenue approach to Golden Gate Bridge opens.
May 25. Golden Gate International Exposition re-opens.

1945 Apr. 25-June 26. International conference meets to draft the Charter of the United Nations.

1946   May 2-4.   Prisoners revolt at Alcatraz Island Prison, three prisoners, two guards killed.

1947   Apr. 10.   Treasure Island fire.

1948   May 25.   Station W6XJD transmits first San Francisco telecast, from Hotel St. Francis.

1949   Jan. 22.   Chinatown telephone exchange closes.

1951   Feb. 16.   City hall dome fire.

       May 27.   Maritime Museum, foot of Polk Street, opens.

1952   Feb. 8.   Mission Dolores designated first minor basilica in West.

       Aug. 26.   Fluoridation of city's water begins.

       Dec. 21.   Broadway tunnel opens.

1953   Dec. 1.   U.S. House Committee on Un-American activities opens hearings.

1955   Aug. 3.   Chinatown police squad disbanded.

1956   May 23.   World Trade Center in Ferry Building dedicated.

       Aug. 20.   Republican Convention opens in Cow Palace.

1958   May 8.   Demolition of Crystal Plunge Pool begins.

       July 29.   S.P. Bay ferries discontinued.

1959   July 25.   Storyland at Fleishhacker Zoo opens.

       Aug. 1.   Crystal Palace Market, Market at 8th St., closes.

       Nov. 11.   Demolition of Seals Stadium begins.

1960   March 1.   Civic Center Garage opens.

1961   Aug. 1.   New Hall of Justice opens.

       Oct. 7.   Family Rosary Rally in Golden Gate Stadium.

1962   Aug. 30.   Ground broken for Golden Gateway project.

       Sept. 7.   Fire destroys St. Mary's Cathedral on Van Ness Ave.

1962   Feb. 28.   Fox Theater demolition begins.

1963   March 22.   Alcatraz Island prison closes.

       June 25.   San Francisco has a new day—Flower Day.

       Sept. 27.   Dedication of new Produce Terminal at Islais Creek.

       Oct. 5.   Hyde Street Pier reopened as a State Historical Park.

1964   June 19.   Republican Convention opens in Cow Palace, nominates Barry Goldwater.

       Oct. 1.   Cable cars declared a National Landmark.

       Oct. 5.   Fire Dept. Museum, Presidio Ave. & Euclid, opens.

1965   Jan. 27.   Alcoa Building dedicated.

       April 20.   Paramount Theater closes.

       Aug. 19.   Mile Rock Lighthouse prepared for automation.

1966   June 26.   Sutro Baths destroyed by fire.

1967   Jan. 19.   Autos banned from band concourse area in Golden Gate Park.

       Aug. 28.   Col. Stewart Evans swims from Farallon Islands to San Francisco.

1968   March 27.   Japanese Trade and Cultural Center opens.

       April 18.   Old Hall of Justice demolished.

1969   June 19.   Bike route, Lake Merced through Golden Gate Park dedicated.

       Nov. 20.   Indians occupy Alcatraz Island.

1970   March 26.   Golden Gate Park Conservatory made a landmark.
June 1.   Five buildings on Alcatraz Island destroyed by fire.
Aug. 6.   Judge Harold J. Haley and two convicts shot and killed in San Rafael Courthouse.
Oct. 15.   First mass is said in the new St. Mary's Cathedral.

1971   Jan. 19.   Standard Oil freighters collide beneath Golden Gate Bridge and release oil into Bay.
April 14.   Fort Point dedicated as first National Park site in San Francisco Bay Area.
April 26.   Lightship San Francisco replaced by automatic buoy.
June 11.   United States marshals recapture Alcatraz Island from Indians.
Aug. 21.   San Quentin prison revolt; three guards, three convicts die.

A Selected Reading List

Adams, Ben. *San Francisco: An Informal Guide.* New York, 1968.
Aitken, Frank W. *A History of the Earthquake and Fire in San Francisco.* San Francisco, 1906.
Asbury, Herbert. *The Barbary Coast.* New York, 1933.
Bancroft, Hubert H. *History of California.* 7 vols. San Francisco, 1884-1890.
Barry, T. A., and B. A. Patten. *Men and Memories of San Francisco.* San Francisco, 1873.
Benet, James W. *A Guide to San Francisco and the Bay Region.* New York, 1963.
Block, Eugene B. *Immortal San Franciscans: For Whom the Streets Were Named.* San Francisco, 1971.
Bloomfield, Arthur J. *The San Francisco Opera 1923-1961.* New York, 1961.
Bronson, William. *The Earth Shook, The Sky Burned.* Garden City, 1959.
Brown, Allen. *Golden Gate. Biography of a Bridge.* New York, 1965.
Brown, John Henry. *Reminiscences and Incidents of Early Days of San Francisco (1845-50).* San Francisco, 1886.
Caen, Herb. *Baghdad-By-The-Bay.* New York, 1949.
———. *Don't Call it Frisco.* New York, 1953.
Caen, Herb and Dong Kingman. *San Francisco, City on Golden Hills.* New York, 1967.
Chapin, William. *The Suburbs of San Francisco.* San Francisco, 1969.
Clarke, Dwight L. *William Tecumseh Sherman: Gold Rush Banker.* San Francisco, 1969.
Coblentz, Stanton A. *Villains and Vigilantes.* New York, 1936.
Cowan, Robert E. *Forgotten Characters of Old San Francisco.* Los Angeles, 1964.
Cross, Ira B. *Financing an Empire.* 5 vols. Chicago, 1927.
Dana, Julian. *The Man who Built San Francisco.* New York, 1936.
Davis, William Heath. *Seventy-five Years in California.* San Francisco, 1929.
Dickson, Samuel. *Tales of San Francisco.* Stanford, Calif., 1965.
Dillon, Richard. *Embarcadero.* New York, 1959.
———. *The Hatchet-men: The Story of the Tong Wars in San Francisco.* New York, 1962.
Dobie, Charles Caldwell. *San Francisco, A Pageant.* New York, 1933.
———. *San Francisco's Chinatown.* New York, 1936.

469

Doss, Margot Patterson. *The Bay Area at Your Feet*. San Francisco, 1970.

———. *Golden Gate Park at Your Feet*. San Francisco, 1970.

———. *San Francisco at Your Feet*. New York, 1964.

Eldredge, Zoeth Skinner. *The Beginnings of San Francisco*. 2 vols. New York, 1912.

Englehardt, Fr. Zephyrin. *Mission Dolores*. Chicago, 1924.

Fages, Pedro. *Expedition to San Francisco Bay in 1770*. Berkeley, 1911.

Federal Writers' Project. *California: A Guide to the Golden State*. New York, 1939. Revised edition, 1967.

Ferrier, William Warren. *Ninety Years of Education in California. 1846-1936*. Berkeley, 1937.

Font, Fr. Pedro. *Font's Complete Diary. A Chronicle of the Foundation of San Francisco*. Translated and edited by Herbert Eugene Bolton. Berkeley, 1933.

Gagey, Edmond M. *San Francisco Stage: A History*. New York, 1950.

Genthe, Arnold. *As I Remember*. New York, 1936.

Gentry, Curt. *The Dolphin Guide to San Francisco*. New York, 1969.

———. *The Madams of San Francisco: An Irreverent History of the City by the Golden Gate*. New York, 1964.

———. *Frame Up; The Incredible Case of Tom Mooney & Warren Billings*. New York, 1961.

Gilliam, Harold. *The Natural World of San Francisco*. New York, 1967.

———. *San Francisco Bay*. New York, 1957.

Glasscock, C. B. *Lucky Baldwin*. Indianapolis, 1933.

Godwin, John. *Alcatraz: 1868-1963*. New York, 1963.

Harlan, George H. *San Francisco Bay Ferryboats*. Berkeley, Calif., 1967.

Hart, Jerome. *In Our Second Century*. San Francisco, 1931.

Hittell, John S. *A History of the City of San Francisco*. San Francisco, 1878.

Hittell, Theodore H. *History of California*. 4 vols. San Francisco, 1885-1897.

Holdredge, Helen. *Firebelle Lillie*. New York, 1967.

———. *Mammy Pleasant*. New York, 1953.

Iacopi, Robert. *Earthquake Country*. Menlo Park, Calif., 1964.

Irwin, William Henry. *Pictures of Old Chinatown*. New York, 1908.

———. *The City That Was*. New York, 1906.

Johnson, Kenneth M. *The Life and Times of Edward Robeson Taylor*. San Francisco, 1968.

Jordan, David Starr, ed. *The California Earthquake of 1906*. San Francisco, 1907.

Judnich, Martin W. *San Francisco Government. A Summary of the San Francisco City and County Charter, The Laws & Ordinances, & The Works of the Various Depts*. San Francisco, 1967.

Junior League of San Francisco. *Here Today: San Francisco's Architectural Heritage*. San Francisco, 1968.

Kemble, John H. *San Francisco Bay*. Cambridge, Maryland, 1957.

Kennedy, John C. *The Great Earthquake & Fire*. New York, 1963.

Kinnaird, Lawrence. *History of the Greater San Francisco Bay Region.* New York, 1966.

Lavender, David S. *The Great Persuader.* New York, 1970.

Lewis, Oscar. *Bay Window Bohemia.* New York, 1956.

———. *Big Four.* New York, 1938.

———. *San Francisco Mission to Metropolis.* Berkeley, Calif., 1966.

Lewis, Oscar, and Carroll D. Hall. *Bonanza Inn.* New York, 1939.

Lick, Rosemary. *The Generous Miser.* Los Angeles, 1967.

Lloyd, Benjamin E. *Lights and Shades in San Francisco.* San Francisco, 1876.

Longstreet, Stephen. *The Wilder Shore.* New York, 1968.

Lyman, George D. *Ralston's Ring.* New York, 1937.

McGloin, John B. *California's First Archbishop; The Life of Joseph S. Alemany, 1814-1888.* New York, 1966.

Melendy, Howard B. *The Governors of California.* Georgetown, Calif., 1965.

Morphy, Edward. *The Port of San Francisco.* Sacramento, 1923.

Muscatine, Doris. *A Cook's Tour of San Francisco.* New York, 1969.

Myers, John M. *San Francisco's Reign of Terror.* New York, 1966.

Neville, Amelia Ransome. *The Fantastic City.* Boston, 1932.

Newhall, Ruth W. *San Francisco's Enchanted Palace.* Berkeley, Calif., 1967.

O'Brien, Robert. *This is San Francisco.* New York, 1948.

Older, Cora M. *San Francisco; Magic City.* New York, 1961.

Older, Fremont. *My Own Story.* San Francisco, 1926.

Pennell, Joseph. *San Francisco, The City of the Golden Gate.* Boston, 1913.

Peterson, Joyce. *The San Francisco I Love.* New York, 1970.

Phillips, Catherine C. *Portsmouth Plaza.* San Francisco, 1932.

Potter, Elizabeth Gray. *The San Francisco Skyline.* New York, 1939.

Prieto, Guillermo. *San Francisco in the Seventies.* San Francisco, 1938.

Sackett, Georgia. *San Francisco Firehouse Favorites.* New York, 1965.

San Francisco Chronicle. *Hills of San Francisco.* San Francisco, 1959.

Scherer, James A.B. *The Lion of the Vigilantes.* Indianapolis, 1939.

Scott, Mel. *The Future of San Francisco Bay.* Berkeley, Calif., 1963.

Soule, Frank, John H. Gihon, and James Nisbet. *The Annals of San Francisco.* New York, 1855.

Stewart, George R. *Committee of Vigilance: Revolution in San Francisco, 1851.* Boston, 1964.

Taylor, Bayard. *Eldorado: or Adventures in the Path of Empire.* New York, 1882.

Thomas, Lately. *A Debonair Scoundrel.* New York, 1962.

Todd, Frank Morton. *The Story of the Exposition (Panama-Pacific International).* 5 vols. New York, 1921.

Vail, Wesley D. *Victorians: An Account of Domestic Architecture in Victorian San Francisco 1870-1890.* San Francisco, 1964.

Walker, Franklin. *San Francisco's Literary Frontier.* Seattle, 1969.

Watkins, Tom H. *San Francisco in Color.* New York, 1968.

Williams, David A. *David C. Broderick, A Political Portrait.* San Marino, 1969.

Williams, Mary Floyd. *History of the San Francisco Committee of Vigilance of 1851.* Berkeley, 1921.

Wilson, Katherine. *Golden Gate Park. The Park of a Thousand Vistas.* Caldwell, Idaho, 1947.

Wilson, Neill C. *Here is the Golden Gate.* New York, 1962.

Woon, Basil. *San Francisco and the Golden Empire.* New York, 1935.

Young, John P. *San Francisco: A History of the Pacific Coast Metropolis.* 2 vols. Chicago, 1912.

Index